The Renaissance and Reformation Movements

The Renaissance and Reformation Movements

Lewis W. Spitz
Stanford University

Rand McNally & Company · Chicago

RAND M^{c}NALLY HISTORY SERIES

Fred Harvey Harrington, *Advisory Editor*

TO
David M. Potter

184

Preface

CONTEMPORARY MAN is suffering from amnesia. He is drifting along in a state of mind that Sören Kierkegaard once referred to as "a kind of world historical forgetfulness." The French savant André Malraux intones somberly: "Western civilization has begun to doubt its own credentials." This condition is part of the price paid for modern man's pathetic attempt to live entirely in the "specious present," seeking relevance only in those fleeting moments that glide so quickly into the past. The loss of history means the loss of identity. The knowledge of history gives man "divine perspective." "Who I am," says the existential philosopher Karl Jaspers, "and where I belong, I first learned to know from the mirror of history."

The Renaissance and the Reformation were clearly high points of Western history. The Renaissance was an age of supreme cultural achievement and the Reformation was a time of most profound spiritual revolution. We have fallen heir to a golden age, but as St. Bernard once observed in his *De diligendo Deo,* "To possess what one knows nothing about, what glory can there be in that?" Certain implicit assumptions of this history merit explicit expression. This study emphasizes the thought, literature, art, morals, faith, and spirit of man, the culture and religion of the age, without neglecting its socioeconomic developments or political events. Highly personal ideas are as effective springboards for action as impersonal historical forces. It is not popular to cite Thomas Carlyle these days, but occasionally his observations still apply with epigrammatic force, as when he wrote in his *Essays:* "What is all knowledge, too, but recorded experience, and a product of history; of which, therefore, reasoning and belief, no less than action and passion, are essential materials?"

The age of the Renaissance and Reformation was not a static unified period within which time and history stood still. It was above all an age of movement, a time of accelerated transition. From Dante and Petrarch to Erasmus and Rabelais, from Giotto and Fra Angelico to Michelangelo and Pontormo, from Savonarola to Loyola, from Philip the Fair to Henry IV, from the Hundred Years' War to the Thirty Years' War, Europe was in motion. This critical period of history as a movement was felt in all aspects of life. In *The Future of Man*, Teilhard du Chardin accurately assigns to history its role in human knowledge:

> It is clear in the first place that the world in its present state is the outcome of movement. Whether we consider the rocky layers enveloping the earth, the arrangement of the forms of life that inhabit it, the variety of civilizations to which it has given birth, or the structure of languages spoken upon it, we are forced to the same conclusion: that everything is the sum of the past and that nothing is comprehensible except through its history.[1]

One problem with many textbooks is that no one lives longer than a few lines. It is much like dividing up the beautiful Pacific coast and assigning two inches of it to each citizen of California. A better understanding of the past can be gained by focusing most of our attention on the major protagonists, allowing the leading actors in the drama of history to speak their pieces. Nor should the men of that day, any more than those of our own, escape all moral judgment. The great Catholic historian Lord Acton criticized Bishop Creighton, author of *The History of the Papacy During the Period of the Reformation*, for going "through scenes of raging controversy and passion with divided judgment, a hung jury, and a pair of white gloves." The real tragedy would be for the author to get in the way of the story itself or to trivialize the universality of the human experience in those exciting centuries. "There is only one way to make love," quipped Dorothy Sayers, "but there are a thousand ways to commit a murder." If this book kills the subject or deadens its impact, it would have been better left unwritten.

For a single historian to give an account of three centuries (1300–1600) of European history requires greater temerity than anyone should possess. Perhaps only a fool would make such a bold attempt. And yet in his *Praise of Folly* Erasmus observed: "There are two main obstacles to the knowledge of things, modesty that casts a mist before the understanding, and fear that, having fancied a danger, dissuades us from the attempt." A general work such as this, after all, rests upon the research of hundreds and even thousands of specialists in the field. This book might well say with Tennyson's *Ulysses,* "I am a part of all that I have met." I am indebted to the work of many more scholars of various nations than could possibly be acknowledged in the notes. But I owe a special debt to certain colleagues, students, and friends.

For my general approach to Renaissance and Reformation history I am indebted to my loyal friend and genial graduate school mentor, Dr. Myron P. Gil-

---

[1] Pierre Teilhard du Chardin, *The Future of Man* (New York, 1964), p. 12.

more, who now serves as director of the Villa I Tatti in Florence. Dr. Gene Brucker, chairman of the history department of the University of California at Berkeley, a noted authority on Florentine social history, read the portion on the Renaissance and gave me the benefit of a detailed critique, for which I am most grateful. My able colleague Dr. Paul Seaver read and improved upon the chapters concerned with English history. My energetic assistant Mr. Mark Edwards chose the illustrations and selected the maps for this volume. My heartfelt thanks to them and to my editor, Mrs. Barbara H. Salazar, who has refined the manuscript and prepared the index with skill, grace, and literary talent. I wish to express my appreciation also to Mrs. Wilbert Rosin and to Mrs. Linda Edwards, who did the typescript. My wife, Dr. Edna Spitz, aided in many ways and at all times during the years this book was under way.

I owe an equally genuine if less immediately obvious debt to my students. The undergraduates, with their ingenuous, intelligent, critical candor, have ways uniquely their own of keeping a professor reasonably honest and humble. The graduate students have contributed not only historical knowledge but human insights and new methodology of the greatest value. Among these young scholars, many already holding important teaching and research positions across the land, I wish to mention especially the following: of the ladies, Ruth Arnon, Cissie Bonini, Patricia Covey, Virginia DeMarce, Sue Diamondstone, Lynn Hunt, Sharon Kettering, Margaret King, Arlene Miller, Anne J. Schutte, Kay Solon, Linda Taber, and Sister Marian Leona Tobriner; of the gentlemen, Darrel Ashcraft, Michael Baylor, John Biddle, Jules Bouret, Noel Brann, John Bray, James Bullard, David Bycina, Michael Carter, Theodore Casteel, Abraham Friesen, James Hinz, Larkin Kirkman, James Kittelson, William Klaustermeyer, Robert Lear, David McNeil, Steven Ozment, William Painter, Louis Reith, Charles Stinger, and Hugh West. "The young, too," said Luther, "must soon stand up and speak out after us."

I dedicate this book to my distinguished colleague David M. Potter, who has this year been honored by the entire profession, becoming at the same time the president of the Organization of American Historians and of the American Historical Association. His tremendous learning is equaled by his great strength of character and his capacity for true friendship.

Lewis W. Spitz

October 1970
Stanford University

Contents

PREFACE   *vii*

CHAPTER 1 : *The Age of the Renaissance*   *1*

CHAPTER 2 : *The Church in Crisis*   *20*

CHAPTER 3 : *The State in Transformation*   *62*

CHAPTER 4 : *Italy: Home of the Renaissance*   *90*

CHAPTER 5 : *The Rise of Capitalism*   *118*

CHAPTER 6 : *Renaissance Humanism*   *139*

CHAPTER 7 : *Renaissance Philosophy, Literature, and Science*   *171*

CHAPTER 8 : *The Fine Arts*   *192*

CHAPTER 9 : *The Dwarfing of Italy*   *233*

CHAPTER 10 : *Renaissance and Reconnaissance*   *250*

CHAPTER 11 : *Humanism Beyond Italy*   *274*

CHAPTER 12 : *The Age of the Reformation*   *301*

CHAPTER 13 : *Luther's Evangelical Thrust*   *328*

CHAPTER 14 : *The Empire in Crisis*   *357*

CHAPTER 15 : *Zwingli and the Radicals*   *381*

CHAPTER 16 : *Calvin and Calvinism*   *411*

CHAPTER 17 : *The Reformation in England and Scotland*   *441*

CHAPTER 18 : *The Catholic Reformation* 469

CHAPTER 19 : *Civil War in France and the Spanish Preponderance* 496

CHAPTER 20 : *England Under Elizabeth* 523

CHAPTER 21 : *The Impact of the Renaissance and the Reformation on Society and Culture* 547

INDEX 593

Illustrations

GIOTTO. The Death of St. Francis   *194*
Alinari

MASACCIO. The Rendering of the Tribute Money   *201*
Alinari

BOTTICELLI. Primavera   *203*
Alinari

BRUNELLESCHI. Florence Cathedral   *211*
Alinari

LEONARDO DA VINCI. The Virgin of the Rocks   *215*
Reproduced by courtesy of the Trustees, The National Gallery, London

RAPHAEL. The School of Athens   *218*
Alinari

MICHELANGELO. The Last Judgment   *222*
Alinari

GIOVANNI BELLINI. The Feast of the Gods   *226*
National Gallery of Art, Washington, D.C., Widener Collection

DUTCH ENGRAVING OF THE SEVENTEENTH CENTURY. The Candlestick:
The Light of the Gospel Was Rekindled by All the Reformers   *302*
Prentenkabinet, Rijksmuseum, Amsterdam

BROSAMER. The Seven Heads of Martin Luther   *307*
From F. W. H. Hollstein, *German Engravings, Etchings, and Woodcuts*
(Amsterdam, n.d.), vol. 4, p. 248

HANS SACHS. Woodcuts showing various sixteenth-century occupations   *320*
From F. W. H. Hollstein, *German Engravings, Etchings, and Woodcuts*
(Amsterdam, n.d.), vol. 2, p. 47

ALBRECHT DÜRER. Knight, Death, and the Devil   *324*
   Courtesy of Fogg Art Museum, Harvard University, Grey Collection

BREU THE ELDER. Proclamation of the Indulgence   *336*
   From F. W. H. Hollstein, *German Engravings, Etchings, and Woodcuts*
   (Amsterdam, n.d.), vol. 4, p. 179

CRANACH THE YOUNGER. The Last Supper of the Lutherans and the
   Fall to Hell of the Catholics; in the Center Luther Preaching   *339*
   From F. W. H. Hollstein, *German Engravings, Etchings, and Woodcuts*
   (Amsterdam, n.d.), vol. 6, p. 127

PETRARCA-MEISTER. Von Adeligem Ursprung   *345*
   From Walter Scheidig, *Holzschnitte des Petrarca-meisters* (Berlin,
   1955), p. 60

CATHOLIC SATIRE. Luther and His Wife Carrying and Wheeling
   Home the Expelled Protestant Preachers   *351*
   From *Encyclopedia of World Art* (New York: McGraw-Hill Book Co.,
   1966), vol. 11, plate 447

THE COUNCIL OF TRENT   *487*
   Courtesy of the Trustees of the British Museum, London

ALBRECHT DÜRER. Perspective   *575*
   From K. A. Knappe, *Dürer: The Complete Engravings, Etchings, and
   Woodcuts* (New York: Abrams, 1965), p. 371

FLÖTNER. Light Reflections   *585*
   From Heinrich Röttinger, *Die Holzschnitte zur Architektur und zum
   Vitruvius Teutsch des Walther Rivus* (Strassburg, 1914)

Maps

European Civilization During the Renaissance   114

The Operations of the Medicis and Fuggers   126

The Hanse Towns   129

Italy in the Late Fifteenth Century   234

The Age of Discovery   264

Europe in the Middle of the Fifteenth Century   310

The Empire of Charles V   358

Religious Divisions About 1550   377

Division of the Netherlands, 1579   513

Established Churches and Religious Minorities About 1600   550

The maps entitled "European Civilization During the Renaissance," "The Operations of the Medicis and Fuggers," and "The Age of Discovery" are from *Atlas of World History,* ed. R. R. Palmer (Chicago: Rand McNally & Company, 1965). All others are from Bryce Lyon, Herbert H. Rowen, and Theodore S. Hamerow, *A History of the Western World,* cartography by Willis R. Heath (Chicago: Rand McNally, 1969).

CHAPTER 1

The Age
of the
Renaissance

When the great Swiss historian Jacob Burckhardt enrolled at the University of Berlin to study history in 1839, he was astonished by the first lectures he heard from Leopold von Ranke, Gustav Droysen, and August Boeckh, for he realized that the same thing was happening to him that had happened to Don Quixote. He had loved historical science when it was only hearsay to him, and suddenly here it was appearing before him in such splendid proportions that he had to lower his eyes. The student of history who first approaches the Renaissance is apt to feel a bit overwhelmed, for even the skeptical Voltaire described it as one of the four golden ages in European culture (together with the age of Pericles in Athens, the age of Augustus in Rome, and Voltaire's own age in Bourbon France). It was a time of outsized men, a culture studded with geniuses: Leonardo da Vinci, Alberti, Michelangelo. Italy emerged as a major intellectual and artistic force and assumed its proper place among the peoples of Europe. There was movement, excitement, joy and sorrow, vibrant life and sudden death. It was as though centuries of compressed action had been released in a few decades.

Even in the interest of scholarly blandness it would be wrong to minimize the achievements of these Renaissance men or to trivialize the universality of their life experience. Although our bourgeois mentality may prefer gradualism and feel uncomfortable in the presence of outstanding creativity and singular greatness, we must recognize the special dynamism of the Renaissance and its unparalleled accomplishments in many areas of social life and higher culture. Of course, in any exploration of the historical landscape, one cannot merely leap from peak to peak, but must descend into valleys, mount foothills, and then scale new heights. But by any criteria upon which most men of cultural experience can agree, the Renaissance towers above most other regions in history's topography. Just as some men achieve more than others, so some generations overshadow others. Such an exquisite moment in the millennia of man's past was the Italian Renaissance.

The Problem of the Renaissance

THE HISTORIAN necessarily defines periods of history as a conceptual framework upon which to construct his narrative. Whether his limits and divisions merely follow verbal conventions, whether they arbitrarily tear the "seamless web" of history, or whether they reflect history as past actuality are crucial questions. The Renaissance as an extremely complex sociopolitical and cultural phenomenon has defied easy categorization and remains a difficult and hotly debated concept. The standard division of all Western history into ancient, medieval, and modern came into being during the Renaissance itself, and entered historical literature toward the end of the seventeenth century when Cellarius (Keller), a Lutheran who had enjoyed a classical education, introduced the term *medium aevum* to cover the period between ancient and modern times. Subsequently European historians who saw great unity from the fifteenth to the eighteenth centuries and saw the French Revolution as the decisive break with the past have referred to the years after 1789 as *histoire contemporaine*. To the communists, of course, the October Revolution of 1917 constituted the decisive breakthrough of a new era. Some contemporaries believe that the full impact of industrialization, mass population, and the electronic revolution in communications is only now being felt, and choose to speak of the present time as "postmodern."

The idea that the Renaissance and the Reformation constituted twin sources of modernity goes back to the humanists and reformers. Theodore Beza, Calvin's understudy and successor as the Protestant leader in Geneva, ascribed the revival of learning to the flight of the Greek scholars to the West after the fall of Constantinople in 1453. The date remained fixed in Western tradition as a most critical one, which conveniently divided medieval and modern times. The year is late, however, for after all Francesco Petrarch, who has been called the father of Renaissance humanism, lived and died in the fourteenth century (1304–1374). Boccaccio, Salutati, Poggio, Leonardo Bruni, and a host of lesser men had come and gone before 1453, and Greek scholars had traveled to the West seeking aid and imparting knowledge before the Turks captured their capital in the East. Absolute beginnings elude us, since in any era few events are not related in some way to some preceding event. Polyphony and polarity existed during the Renaissance, for innovative forces did not follow after the traditional ones, but rose up alongside them. The age had its share of the "already here" and the "lingering on." One cannot therefore paint a still life of any one moment in time. It is necessary rather to catch the trend and to see the direction in which the midpoint of contrary pressures is moving. If this is done intelligently, the modern element in the Renaissance will emerge as that which is no longer characteristically medieval, and the Renaissance itself will be seen not as a static epoch, but as movement.

Consciousness of Change

WHAT MEN BELIEVE to be true of themselves and of their times is often as great a force in moving history forward as are the more sober facts of the case. Fiction has a force of its own, and the "fortunate error" has been an important factor in history everywhere. Intellectuals during the Renaissance believed that their age had a natural coherence that set it off from the dark ages preceding it, that it marked a rebirth, a renewal, a restoration of classical antiquity, and the dawn of a new era.

The term Renaissance was itself not a novelty. Throughout the medieval period "renaissance" (in Latin, *renovatio*) was often used in the New Testament sense of a spiritual rebirth. (Jesus said to Nicodemus: "Verily, verily, I say unto thee, Except a man be born again, he cannot see the kingdom of God" [John 3:3].) The idea of Rome as the capital of the world and center of classical culture persisted throughout the Middle Ages. Roman law, which came into renewed prominence from the twelfth century on, used the term *restitutio,* or restoration. Moreover, the Italian Renaissance did not fall like a meteor from black skies. Although many humanists considered the Middle Ages as "a thousand years without a bath," in reality a series of educational and cultural flowerings had prepared the way for their own renaissance. Historians now speak of an Iro-Celtic renaissance by the monastic carriers of classical culture who preserved Latin and even some Greek learning after the barbarian invasions. Given the chaos that marked the demise of the Roman Empire and the primitive state of Germanic culture, one could argue with some plausibility that Europe never made such noticeable progress as between the fifth and eighth centuries. The appreciation of the classics at the court of Charlemagne and the achievements of Alcuin, Lupus of Ferrières, and other cultural heroes merit the name Carolingian renaissance. The Ottonian renaissance at the court of Otto the Great (crowned 962) was less impressive, but still a reality. Under Emperor Otto III (980–1002) there was talk of a "renewal of the empire" and a "renewal of the church." The twelfth-century renaissance was of quite a different order. Cathedral schools at Chartres and elsewhere broadened the educational base and produced men of impressive classical learning, such as John of Salisbury. But the twelfth-century renaissance was still very much a clerical phenomenon, sponsored by the church and cultivated in the shadow of Gothic cathedrals. At least one medievalist speaks of a series of renaissances between the twelfth-century renaissance and the Italian Renaissance.

While it is now possible to see the steps ascending toward the heights of the Renaissance, it seemed to Renaissance men themselves that their age had emerged suddenly from a great darkness. This view seemed legitimate to the humanists because there was an actual cultural lag between Italy and the higher culture of medieval France. Moreover, on an absolute scale, the achievements of the Italian Renaissance in letters, art, music, history, rhetoric, and classical learning, including Greek literature, far outstripped all preceding renaissances. Moreover, the Italian Renaissance was not limited to court circles or to the clergy. There was substantial lay participation. While it is useful to remember that the style and quality of life of the broad masses of the population were virtually untouched by the achievements of the Renaissance, it must also be acknowledged that Italian Renaissance culture affected a larger lay clientele of aristocrats and bourgeoisie than had any of the earlier cultural revivals.

As the Italian humanists conceived of the Renaissance, it involved two basic notions, the rebirth of culture in general and the rebirth of classical culture in particular. Petrarch set the style in viewing the centuries preceding as shrouded in the darkness of night. He distinguished the ancient times (*antiqua*) from modern times (*nova*), by which he meant the dark ages in which he still lived and from which culture had to be freed. Giovanni Boccaccio (1313–1375) asserted in his *Life of Dante* that the great poet was the first since the Romans to open the door to the Muses. The Florentine Giovanni Villani, who was inspired to write his chronicle by gazing on the ruins of Rome, made no division between the Middle Ages and the Renaissance. His Florentine chronicle ran from the creation of the world to 1348 and was continued by his brother Matteo. Matteo's son, Filippo Villani (1325–1405), added a final section. Writing around 1400, Filippo was already aware of a revival of culture. He saw the renewal of the plastic arts not so much as a reversion to antiquity as a reversion to nature, from which the artists "had strayed away in childish fashion through the ignorance of the painters."

For Leonardo da Vinci the mathematical precision and naturalism of his generation of artists constituted a reaffirmation of classical standards. Modern style (*maniera moderna*) equaled the good ancient style (*buona maniera antica*), in contrast to the old style (*maniera vecchia*) now being transcended. Palladio's Villa Rotonda (1552) was more like the Roman Pantheon than like the Gothic cathedrals of Milan or Orvieto. In his *Lives of the Most Eminent Painters, Sculptors, and Architects* (1550), the sixteenth-century painter, architect, and art historian Giorgio Vasari held up the period from Giotto (*c.* 1276–1337), who revived "the noble art of painting, which had fallen on evil days," to Michelangelo (1475–1564) as a new age. He used the word *rinascita* to describe the rebirth of art.

In letters too the period from Petrarch to Erasmus was held to mark a new day. Leonardo Bruni, the Florentine chancellor, held up Dante, Petrarch, and Boccaccio as three great moderns rivaling the ancients in stature. Paolo Giovio in his *Eulogies of Famous Men of Letters* applied the word *rinascita* to the rebirth of literature. In his famous description of Italy, *Italia illustrata* (1448–1453), Flavio Biondo praised Petrarch as the pioneer of the new style in literature. Few scholars would challenge the designation of the Renaissance as a new period in art and literature, one no longer medieval.

If the Italians sneered at Gothic as the German style (*maniera tedesca*), the Germans for their part paid the Italians the flattery of imitation. Albrecht Dürer, who more than any other artist introduced Italian Renaissance style to the north, referred to the Renaissance as a *Wiedererwachung,* or reawakening. The young German knight Ulrich von Hutten exclaimed: "What a century! What genius! It is sheer joy to be alive, even though not yet in tranquillity. Learning flourishes, men are spiritually quickened. O Barbarism, take a rope and prepare for extinction!" Guillaume Budé, the leading French humanist, exulted: "The best part I think we have in our hands saved from the deluge of more than a thousand years; for a deluge indeed, calamitous to life, had so drained and absorbed literature itself and the kindred arts worthy of the name, and kept them so dismantled and buried in barbarian mud, that it was a wonder they could still exist."[1] The sixteenth-century Frenchman Pierre Belon was among the first to use the French term *renaissance,* which has been more commonly used than the Italian *rinascimento.* The prince of the humanists, Desiderius Erasmus, wrote in a letter to Wolfgang Capito in 1517: "I anticipate the near approach of a golden age." There can be no doubt that the chief protagonists of Renaissance culture were convinced that they lived in a new age, an "age of light," as Rabelais called it.

Renaissance as an Operative Concept

THE SWISS HISTORIAN Jacob Burckhardt spoke of his book on *The Civilization of the Renaissance in Italy* (1860) as a "child of sorrow," which he had to write out

---

[1] Guillaume Budé, *De studio literatum* (1527); see Charles Sears Baldwin, *Renaissance Literary Theory and Practice* (New York, 1939), p. 4.

of "inner necessity." It was written, as Nietzsche said all books should be written, with blood. He was attracted so powerfully to the period because he believed that it was, like his own, an age of transition, in which the old was going and the new was not yet formed. Any bright young social scientist with insight into the problems of change and continuity in history can assert with aplomb that every period in history is an age of transition. But the Renaissance was not like every other period, for it was an age when transition was accelerated. The stream of history flows steadily toward the sea of infinity. It is always in motion, but it does not always flow at the same speed, any more than does the life of the individual. There are points along its course where various tributaries join to push it ahead through narrow channels and down angry cataracts. Action generates action, vital minds stimulate others, events crowd in on one another, history is made more speedily, things are set in motion. The Renaissance was such an age.

In all areas of life, aesthetic, moral, social, political, and religious, there was a renewed and very intense interest in man's achievements. Nor was the age secular in the sense of being irreligious. The Platonism that constituted a very important strand of Renaissance thought really tended to divinize the world itself. The formal piety of the elite and the great reservoir of popular religious fervor that fed the Savonarola incident and overflowed into the Catholic Reformation prove that Italy was anything but secular in a radical sense. It is possible, in fact, to speak of an increase of religious concern in northern Europe during the century and a half leading up to the Reformation. There was, however, a subtle shift toward interest in and anxiety about man in the here and now, as well as in the hereafter. The contemplative ideal gave ground to the active and studious life. One can with justice speak of greater intellectual freedom, fewer inhibitions, and a more pronounced individualism during the Renaissance than during the centuries preceding it. In his autobiography Albert Schweitzer used the term *Weltanschauung,* or world view, for the fundamental springboard of ideas propelling a man into action. The change in *Weltanschauung* during this period may be described as a move away from official other-worldliness to an interest in man in this world—sometimes a very religious interest, in fact. There was a change of course in man's mental evolution from the medieval to the modern world, for life was no longer merely a period of probation for the life beyond. One must be cautious, however, in assuming that this shift was experienced by all levels of society, for the articulate witnesses are drawn from the upper classes, not from among the mute masses. Nor were the new ideas expressed by the leading humanists and philosophers understood by lesser minds among the educated as their authors had intended them. What the nature of the accelerated transition in social and political life was, and what the actual content of the Renaissance mentality proved to be, can be learned only from a study of the age itself.

The Renaissance World

THE YOUNG German humanist Ulrich von Hutten (1488–1523) once wrote that all the world's a stage and all the men and women merely players, a thought he derived from the classics, well before Shakespeare. It will perhaps be useful to look briefly at the stage setting upon which the dramatic action of the Renaissance took place.

The historical savant Arnold J. Toynbee has observed that around the year 1300 all societies in the world were structurally very much alike. They were all agrarian, and in all of them the land was owned by a relatively few men. The vast majority of the people lived as peasants, at or near subsistence level. One of the most astonishing developments in world history is the disintegration of Europe's agrarian economy and life style from the thirteenth through the nineteenth centuries, and the development of urbanization, capitalism, commerce, and industrialization. The age of the Renaissance saw the decline of the manorial economy and of feudal political institutions, both replaced with surprising speed by new economic and political forces.

The ethnographic map of Europe was practically the same in 1300 as it is today, except for the subsequent intrusion of the Turks into the Balkans and far up the Danube. The linguistic borders have shifted very little, a matter of a few kilometers here and there between the German and French areas of Switzerland, for example. The economic and political developments, however, tended to cover all of Europe, and were not exclusively the work of one or another ethnic or linguistic group.

MANORIAL AND FEUDAL DISINTEGRATION

At the beginning of the thirteenth century the economy of Europe still had a predominantly agrarian base. The manor was the smallest economic unit, and each manor strove for self-sufficiency in foodstuffs and clothing. The lord or seigneur who provided protection held the best portion of the land as his domain or demesne. The peasants worked his land and he was entitled to the manor's surplus products, if any. Concepts of ownership hardly applied; it was rather a matter of the right to the use of the land. Both free and unfree tenures existed, but always on the condition of some fees, payments, or rents owed to the lord. Agricultural methods were still primitive and productivity was low. In western and central Europe a somewhat heavier plow with an iron share was now in general use, made feasible by the earlier invention of the horse collar. But in eastern Europe, though the German colonists introduced the new plow east of the Elbe, the light hook plow was still in general use, with poor results.

Most manors in western and central Europe had by this time changed from a two-field system, which meant leaving half the land lie fallow each year, to a three-field system, which naturally increased production. Families of peasants by custom had the right to cultivate their strips in the two or three big fields adjoining the village, and each had a section of the vineyards or orchards. From the eleventh to the thirteenth centuries the agrarian economy expanded slowly but steadily, by internal colonization, the cutting back of forests, the clearing of swamps, and the cultivation of marginal land. The emigration east of the Elbe River relieved population pressure somewhat, but in the fourteenth and fifteenth centuries the agricultural economy and the rural population experienced a time of troubles.

With the stability achieved during the eleventh century, a century sometimes called the foundation of the Middle Ages, a general revival took place. The period from 1050 to 1250 was one of dramatic growth and creativity, notable for its political stability and demographic expansion. Greater localization and specialization of production developed together with increased exchange by trade and larger town markets. As a money economy evolved, the upper classes were under great pressure to keep up the appearances of their position by the conspicuous consumption of luxuries. The response of the nobles to their need for money took various forms. The lord could move to town and rent the land to tenants on a lease calling for payment in cash. Or he could convert the land to the production of a single crop, which would then be sold for a cash income. In England this development came early and continued beyond our period, with the conversion of land to enclosed pasture for the production of wool. The same trend was occurring in Castile. The lord could choose to stay on the land, but commute the dues of the peasants from payment in kind and in services to payment in cash. Some lords insisted upon the right of arbitrarily taxing their peasants. The enclosure system created a floating landless population by eviction, and a great many other peasants discovered that by emigrating to the colonial areas east of the Elbe or to newly cleared or drained lands they could improve their lot. Others found that by moving to town they could sometimes earn more as simple artisans plying a trade than they could accumulate by hard work on the land. Many towns served as safety valves for excess or expendable rural population, although some towns refused to allow the country folk to establish themselves within their walls.

As the political counterpart of the manorial socioeconomic system, feudalism evolved in tandem with it. Originally a system of military defense, it became less important for that function. During the fourteenth and fifteenth centuries, when the peasants suffered economically, the lesser nobility suffered with them. With the loss of real social utility the knights fell into increasingly desperate straits, and sometimes turned to highway robbery. They preyed upon the merchants moving from town to town, and some free cities kept their own militia to patrol the roads.

Noblemen who adapted to the new money economy cultivated a chivalric code that frequently was more a matter of posturing than of any social reality.

Despite the fact that the countryside of Europe suffered from many difficulties, particularly between 1350 and 1450 and especially where wheat was the main product, the manorial system survived as the foundation stone of its economy, though it underwent many changes. East of the Elbe it became entrenched, whereas west of the Elbe it lost strength and importance, for there towns and cities and a capitalistic economy made greater inroads. But the manorial system lingered on.

GROWTH OF TOWNS AND TRADE

In the agrarian society of the high Middle Ages the social classes corresponded basically to Plato's *oratores* (clergy), *bellatores* (nobility), and *laboratores* (serfs). With the growth of the towns a fourth class came into being, townsmen or burghers. Trade had never totally died out, not even during the Dark Ages, as numismatic evidences prove. But as the situation stabilized, trade increased and towns grew, especially in the twelfth century and after. Constantinople remained the only really large city in Europe, and the towns in the early fourteenth century had for the most part from two to three thousand residents. The Flemish cities of Ghent, Bruges, and Ypres had around 50,000 inhabitants, London about 25,000, Venice and Florence between 75,000 and 100,000. Town growth was more rapid in Italy, in the Netherlands, and along rivers such as the Rhine, Rhône, Thames, Seine, and Danube, which carried trade and supplied the hinterland. Roads were very poor, canals were nonexistent, and while the rivers were not controlled by regulated channels, they remained the most efficient means of transporting goods. The medieval towns grew for various reasons, including protection, but there can be no doubt that their importance as centers for trade was the main reason for their growth. The growth of towns and a money economy disturbed the traditional agrarian economy and gradually undermined feudal society.

The medieval city was both a juridical and an administrative entity, for by the twelfth century the city council wielded vast powers, which included tight control over commercial practices, so that it virtually regulated the city's whole economic life. As the protector of seller and buyer alike, it set what it considered just prices on commodities. The very heart of the medieval commune was the pledge of mutual assistance that was the idealistic basis of the laws and governmental administration. The merchants and craftsmen, who were gaining industrial skill in their specialized crafts, wielded power roughly commensurate with their wealth through a patriarchal guild system. But in the late fourteenth and in the fifteenth centuries, as individual capitalists amassed huge fortunes, as foreign trade over great distances increased, as monopolies and cartels grew powerful, the guild system broke down. Some of the more tradition-bound city trade centers, such as Bruges and Ghent, were outstripped by Antwerp and other new centers of trade, cities less hampered by the old regulations and traditional privileges for the few. Cartels even managed the financial policy of the state, when they could, in order to ensure the value of their holdings.

Maritime trade grew between west and east in northern Europe, and between Italy and the eastern Mediterranean ports. The more highly developed products, such as Flemish textiles, were exchanged for furs, amber, lumber, and other raw materials in Russia and the Baltic area. The Italian cities of Venice, Genoa, and to a lesser extent Pisa exploited the eastern Mediterranean virtually as an economic colony. Venice had played the role of villain in the devastation of Constantinople by the Latin army of the Fourth Crusade in 1204, and it benefited most from the difficulties of Byzantium, now under constantly recurring pressure from the Turks. Venice built trading posts and forts to protect them at strategic points throughout the East. Eventually it even eliminated Genoa, its only serious rival. The end of the imperial control exercised over the cities of northern Italy by the Hohenstaufens in 1250 allowed a new freedom for the communes. Prosperity and relative plenty were in evidence not only in Italy, but throughout the greater part of Europe. The period from the eleventh century to the end of the thirteenth saw the gradual improvement of economic conditions, but there followed then a century of disasters and economic setbacks of a most discouraging kind. Famine, the plague, war, and peasant revolts swept the continent like the four horsemen of the apocalypse.

A TRAUMATIC CENTURY: FAMINE, PESTILENCE, WAR, REVOLT

Famine.   Until very recently in man's history, hunger and famine stalked him like a beast of prey. In the medieval economic system there was a maldistribution of properties and income, and as a result people were tempted to consume and not to invest. Families could barely subsist on one, two, or three hectares of land. By the fourteenth century the exploitation of arable land had been pushed about as far as it could go. The marginal lands provided a less certain return, and formerly fertile lands were becoming eroded or impoverished for lack of fertilizers, by disregard of fallow periods, or because of inadequate rotation of crops. It was not possible to wrest new tillage from the forests, for those that remained were needed by the poor and were being exploited for metallurgical "factories" in industrial areas. There was as yet no scientific seed production or any radical technological breakthrough that would make for a higher yield on a limited acreage. It is possible also that a new climatic cycle began about this time, with colder winters and wetter summers inducing rust and rot in the wheat crop. Potatoes, with their high yield per square foot of land, were, of course, not yet known.

Moreover, just as in modern China and India, local famines were an inevitable result of poor transportation. Bad seasons increased after 1300, and starting in northern Europe terrible famines fell upon various countries from 1309 to 1315. A chronicler in Alsace reported that starving people cut corpses down from the gibbet and ate them. It is impossible to calculate how many victims hunger claimed in the remote rural areas. But in the big famine of 1315 to 1317 in the Lowlands, the leading Flemish textile and trading centers such as Ypres and Bruges lost from 5 to 10 percent of their populations, and the survivors were weakened by the ordeal. From the early fourteenth century until about 1450 there was a decline in the European population, which reached its lowest point shortly after 1400. This demographic retreat was not uniform, for some countries and places escaped it. But the evidence of deserted tenancies and villages, statistics showing the fall in city populations, reports on the hearth tax, and parish records all incontestably show a major decline in the population of Europe. Not until the sixteenth century did history usher in the era of population expansion which has lasted down to the present.

Pestilence. Death hovered over rich and poor alike. The food shortage that reduced so many people to the subsistence level weakened them and made them readily susceptible to disease. The crowded cities enclosed by heavy walls, with sewage poured into the streets and primitive conceptions of hygiene, were ripe for epidemics. The doctors were quick to flee when symptoms of contagion appeared, or worse yet, stayed and administered remedies that all too often further weakened the victims of disease. The year 1348 was the *annus horribilis* in which the Black Death struck Europe. The term Black Death refers specifically to bubonic plague, but pneumonic plague, a different though equally virulent form of the disease, seems to have been present at the same time. The plague germ (*Pasteurella pestis*) was carried by fleas on rats that were brought by ship from the Near East to Mediterranean ports in southern Europe. The plague spread from Italy, France, and Spain northward, scourging England and the Germanies the following year. It moved on then to Scotland and the Baltic area in 1350, spreading panic and terror, for it seemed to be like an invisible angel of death passing over the land, as during the slaying of the firstborn of Egypt during Israel's captivity.

The years that followed the Great Plague were perhaps the most gloomy in the history of Europe. At no other time in all the centuries of the Middle Ages was so much written about the miseries of human life. A profound pessimism and a renunciation of life pervaded the writings of the period and were reflected in its art. The dance of death became a common theme in etchings, woodcuts, and manuscript illuminations. No age was more acutely aware of the brevity of life and the certainty of death. In northern cathedrals there appeared sculptures of damsels that were beautiful to behold from the front, but which from the rear were seen to be hollowed by rot and decay, filled with lizards and tokens of vice and death. In Italy preachers such as Jacopo Passavanti drove home the lesson of the transiency of life to weeping crowds. In the predella below the madonna by Giovanni del Biondo in the Vatican there is a representation that has no precedent in Tuscan art. A bearded old hermit points in warning to a decaying corpse consumed by snakes and toads, while a man and his dog recoil in horror. "Remember that you must die!" is the message of mural and altarpiece. In the great fresco in the *campo santo* in Pisa, done around 1350, Francesco Tranini showed the sick and dying, the horror of rotting flesh, and the sudden, unpredictable coming of death.[2]

The plague often claimed as victims the very old, children, and adults with low resistance due to malnutrition, although it also struck down men in their prime. It caused fever, a swelling of the lymph nodes, and discoloration, and sometimes induced pneumonia. Modern historians agree with the chronicler Froissart that the Great Plague swept away a third of the population of Europe. During the summer months of 1348 more than half the inhabitants of Florence and Siena fell victim to the plague. In the *Decameron* Boccaccio wrote that Florence became a huge sepulcher, and described how the bodies were stacked up in trenches for burial like merchandise loaded in a ship. In little Givry in Burgundy the normal annual mortality ran from 14 to 43, but in the year of the Great Plague, deaths listed in the parish register leaped to 649. The weakened condition of the populace had the further result of reducing reproduction, and in some areas recorded births sank to a mere 60 percent of normal.

Italy suffered several major epidemics in the century and a half that followed the introduction of the Black Death. They declined in frequency and severity in the years following 1348, but recurred into the seventeenth century. It has been suggested that a species of brown rats killed off the black rats that carried the disease, that people built up immunities, or that the bacillus mutated into a less virulent form. But by then enormous damage had been done to mankind in body and spirit.

War.   The ravages of war were added to the losses of the plague as the English and French monarchs embarked upon a duel for England's continental possessions. The so-called Hundred Years' War dominated the history of England and France from 1337 to 1453, the closing act of a drama that began with the Norman conquest of England in 1066. From the time of William the Conqueror, the English kings had possessed large fiefs in France as the vassals of the French kings. Beginning with the reign of Louis VI, the French undertook the recovery of those territories, until early in the fourteenth century the English held only Gascony. But a series of incompetent French monarchs squandered their obvious military advantages, and in the fifteenth century the Burgundian rival to the east arose, so that the English were encouraged to attempt to regain their holdings on the continent.

---

2 Millard Meiss, *Painting in Florence and Siena after the Black Death* (New York, 1964), p. 74.

Although the French suffered disaster in the early years of the war and occasionally thereafter, they had the advantage of being on the continent, while the English troops had to cross the channel. The English kings pressed on, and the armies of both sides, which were becoming increasingly made up of mercenary troops, wreaked havoc on the countryside. Even in the intervals between major campaigns, hostilities were continued by roving bands of freebooters. Mercenary troops led by professional guerrilla fighters made sweeping raids into the Lowlands and northern Italy, seeking spoil and plunder. English forces gutted the French countryside, and the French even applied a scorched-earth policy to their own land to starve out the English. Order broke down in the countryside as robber knights and highwaymen made the roads unsafe for commerce and travelers. The inefficiency and corruption revealed in the French and English governments alike further disillusioned the common people.

Revolt. There was an acute shortage of bullion in the fourteenth and early fifteenth centuries. Governments, burdened with war debts, indulged in monetary manipulation, devaluation of currency, and debasement of coinage. Taxes became increasingly more oppressive to finance the wars. The nobles proved unable to protect the peasants from marauders. The feudal system was discredited and the oppressive monarchs were hated. As is usually the case, the cost in blood and money eventually had to be borne by the lower classes.

Conflicting forces were at work on the peasantry. On the one hand, the decimation of the population by famine, plague, and war produced such a shortage of agricultural laborers that those who survived were in an advantageous position. Vast areas of land were going uncultivated and the free peasants purchased it at low prices. Bondsmen could either demand freedom as the price of staying with their lords or secure more favorable terms as tenants. On the other hand, the peasants were nevertheless restless, for much of the cost of the wars had fallen on them, and when the lords tried to retain their bondsmen by force or to impose seignorial obligations upon the free peasants, they rebelled. Liberty and serfdom do not make good bedfellows. Peasant revolts swept across Europe during the fourteenth, fifteenth, and early sixteenth centuries, yet another scourge for the embattled continent.

The peasant revolt in Flanders between 1323 and 1328 was the first major uprising and one of the bloodiest. The free Flemish peasants were furious at the subservience of the count and nobles to the French kings, resented seignorial taxation, refused to pay the tithe and other dues to the gentry, and resisted efforts to encroach upon the freedom and gains they had already won. In a reign of terror the Flemish peasants hacked and slaughtered the seigneurs, and even held the count of Flanders captive for a time. Encouraged and abetted by disgruntled members of the lesser guilds in the textile manufacturing and trading towns, the peasants had amazing durability. They resisted the gentry, defied a pacification attempt in 1326, and finally were defeated and crushed only when a French royal army joined the count of Flanders against them in the Battle of Cassel on August 23, 1328.

The revolt in Flanders poses a familiar question: Did the revolution come because of the peasants' desperation at the miserable conditions under which they lived or did it come after their position had been considerably improved? The census of those peasants who were killed at Cassel and whose property was confiscated provides fairly clear insight into the situation. In editing the lists, the great Belgian medievalist Henri Pirenne discovered that nearly all of those free peasants owned two or two and a half measures of land, a house, a barn, cattle, and other possessions. Only a few were without property. There is only one conclusion we can reach: that the peasants had in earlier decades improved their condition and that revolt followed only upon the attempts of the upper classes to reimpose old duties and former conditions of servitude.

In the area surrounding Paris a revolt known as the Jacquerie broke out in May 1358 in protest against the plundering of the countryside by troops quartered in and around the city. Artisans joined the peasants in their furious assault on the nobility, who had been unable and seemingly unwilling to protect the peasants from the soldiers. Castles were leveled and nobles killed. But the nobles quickly rallied, and by the end of June the rebellion was suppressed. It is estimated that twenty thousand peasants lost their lives in the fighting and by execution.

In England the peasants in the counties around London rose up in the Great Revolt of 1381, which spread also into Kent and Essex. There was a profound feeling of unhappiness about legislation, specifically the Statute of Laborers, which attempted to freeze wages and prices, to keep the peasants tied to the land, and to impose new taxes, including a poll tax (1380) on everyone over fifteen. Wat Tyler led a march on London in June 1381. The rebels, joined by sympathizers in the city, administered their version of justice to certain officials and frightened the government into acceding to nearly all their demands. At the meeting Tyler was killed. Soon after the peasants had scattered, the government of Richard II canceled all its concessions. Just as in the Flemish revolt, certain egalitarian and agrarian communist sentiments were expressed by the revolutionaries. John Ball, who claimed clerical status, expressed anticlerical and egalitarian sentiments in a verse that became widely popular:

> When Adam delved and Eve span,
> Who was then the gentleman?

The revolts spread throughout Europe; there were others in central and eastern Europe, and there were at least a dozen smaller peasant revolts in the Germanies before the great conflagration of 1525. And Machiavelli in the early sixteenth century warned the state solemnly against putting arms into the hands of the unreliable peasantry.

When the whole situation is surveyed, several features stand out. The first is that the revolts tended to be associated with a rising level of expectation. The plagues, famines, and wars had reduced the manpower available and put the common peasants and laborers in a good bargaining position, which they used to gain privileges and to improve their lot. The revolutionary battles were fought by men who had made gains, not by the despairing and downtrodden. The peasants were impatient with the rate of improvement in their status and feared a forced return to their previous condition. The fact that the most important uprisings took place near urban centers suggests that the safety-valve aspect of city growth and the relative freedom of the artisans raised the hopes of the peasants in the surrounding countryside. The revolutionary ideology, with its admixture of anticlericalism fed by the heretical tenets of Lollard and sectarian preachers, was a straw in the wind indicating that the following centuries would see a proliferation of sects and heresies.

Although these bloody revolts were shocking and dramatic, and their repression cruel and merciless, they had little effect on general economic trends. Serfdom was doomed by economic forces that ran deeper and were more inexorable than lords or peasants realized. The manorial system proved to be less productive than a freer system under which tenants paid rent and participated in the benefits of increased production, no longer living as serfs. The logic of this lesson was learned very slowly, and the emancipation of the serfs spread eastward so gradually that it took an act of state by Tsar Alexander II in 1861 to free the serfs in Russia.

THE QUATTROCENTO

As a whole, Europe made a gradual comeback in general stability and prosperity during the 1400s, especially during the second half of the century. Recovery may have begun sooner and progressed more rapidly in Italy than in the north, although some demographers believe that the statistics of population loss in Italian towns at the time of the plague do not allow for those who escaped to the country, and that therefore the recovery of normal populations in the cities may be attributed at least in part to the return of people who had been away only temporarily.

A *guerre de savants* is still being waged as to whether the fifteenth century in Italy reached the levels of prosperity attained at the close of the thirteenth century and the early decades of the fourteenth, when such families as the Bardis, Peruzzis, Frescobaldis, and Acciaiuolis accumulated enormous wealth in Florence. Some argue that the miracle of the Renaissance is that even in hard times people invested heavily in culture. There is some evidence, however (greater silk production, for example), of an increase in wealth over that of the depressed late fourteenth century. Then came foreign invasion (1494), wars for the control of Italy, and the denouement of the Renaissance.

CHURCH AND STATE

The two great medieval institutions, the Holy Roman Catholic Church and the Holy Roman Empire, lost universality and power during the late Middle Ages and the Renaissance. The proud boasts of preeminence in the *Unam sanctam* (1302) of Boniface VIII sounded quite hollow during the sequence of disasters that befell the papacy in the centuries that followed. The nearly seventy years of the church's "Babylonian Captivity," during which the French king dominated the papacy, were followed by the papal schism, which more than any single event weakened the authority of the pope and brought into question the line of succession and the validity of sacerdotal acts. Conciliarism, which sought constitutional change and made one final effort to reform and revitalize the church, succumbed at last to the monarchical episcopate of the papacy. In the second half of the fifteenth century and down into the Protestant Reformation itself the church degenerated under the disastrous rule of Renaissance popes who transported their princely privileges and proclivities into the Vatican.

The religious situation during the fifteenth century offered a seemingly contradictory spectacle. For just as the Italians could combine with a fear of death the enjoyment of a naïve vitality, so in some ways they displayed sloth and indifference to religious values and in others a will to reform and a great formal piety. The faithful, looking for miracles, could easily be caught up in saints' cults, witchcraft, and inquisitional persecutions. A bureaucratic, juridical, sophisticated hierarchy presided over people who were often zealous, emotional, even pagan in some folk superstitions. Together they built the beautiful temples of the Renaissance.

On the political scene, movement from the universal to the particular was the order of the day. The theoretical grand unity of the empire gave way to a plurality of states as the rising dynastic kingdoms asserted their independence from both the empire and the papacy above and from dependence on the feudal dukedoms below. Feudal monarchy, especially in France and England, made positive political advances, achieving a wider loyalty to the crown, especially among the burghers, adding to the royal domain, and developing a more effective bureaucracy and military organization. During the fifteenth century the Habsburg emperors lost control to an elite group of territorial princes in the diet. Burgundy virtually sheared off the Netherlands from the empire and the Swiss achieved de facto independence, although neither fact was formally acknowledged until the Treaty of Westphalia in 1648.

Between the empire and France the duchies of Savoy, Burgundy, and Lorraine served as buffers, but also as prizes to be fought for. The Habsburg-Spanish alliance against France in 1495 set the stage for the Habsburg-Valois wars, which put Europe on the rack during the first half of the sixteenth century. An actual balance of power was achieved as the states consolidated and shifted into defensive formations.

Italy followed its own peculiar course. As the homeland of the papacy and with the Papal States stretching across the leg of the peninsula like a garter, Italy related to the church differently than did the other European states. The city-states thwarted the growth of a national state and the patriotism of the burghers was local, not attached to a monarch or emperor. The cities suppressed and absorbed the feudal nobility and bishops in the countryside surrounding them. The city-states combined against each other and carried on internecine warfare. The Mediterranean Sea served as a highway for Italy's merchants, but it also brought foreign raiders and hostile fleets.

The skills of international diplomacy developed by the Italian city-states during the course of the *Quattrocento* were imitated and widely adopted by the states outside of Italy. Even the Turkish sultan, successor to the Byzantine Palaeologi after 1453, respected and adopted certain Renaissance diplomatic usages. The revival of Roman law aided the princes in the consolidation of their territories and the establishment of more efficient rule over them.

The age of the Renaissance was an age of contrasts and contradictions. It was an age of powerful personalities, cruel military men, clever and ruthless statesmen, but also of exquisite artists, gentle poets, and dedicated scholars. There were men of enormous wealth, but multitudes who suffered abject poverty. It was a time when nights were consumed in debauchery, but also devoted to vigils and prayer. It was a time for display and pomp, but a time also for preachers of penitence, humility, and withdrawal to a solitary life. It was a day for progress coupled with retrogression. It boasted of the dignity of man but bewailed his misery. It could be humanistic and yet act totally inhumane. It coupled a pronounced interest in man with a weariness with life and a longing for a celestial home. The Renaissance was colored in many hues, changing sometimes subtly, sometimes sharply, often swiftly. Contrasts and contradictions are basic to human nature and present in nearly every man; what brings them so clearly into focus in the Renaissance is the fact that history was in rapid movement and Italy was in a state of accelerated transition.

Such, then, was the Renaissance world, the stage on which the action took place. But from the spectator's seat the stage is of little interest until the actors appear and, quite without previous rehearsal, bring their story to life. David Hume, a respectable philosopher and a historian not completely without merit, once exclaimed:

To see all [the] human race, from the beginning of time, pass, as it were, in review before us, appearing in their true colors, without any of those disguises which, during their lifetime, so much perplexed the judgment of the beholders—what spectacle can be imagined so magnificent, so various, so interesting?[3]

Bibliography

General histories, texts, and handbooks:

ASTON, MARGARET. *The Fifteenth Century: The Prospect of Europe.* New York, 1968.

BARBAGALLO, C. *L'Età della Rinascenza e della Riforma, 1454–1556.* Turin, 1936.

BURCKHARDT, JACOB. *The Civilization of the Renaissance in Italy.* London, 1892, and many other eds.; original German ed., Basel, 1860.

CHEYNEY, E. P. *The Dawn of a New Era, 1250–1453.* New York, 1936.

ERGANG, ROBERT. *The Renaissance.* Princeton, 1967.

FERGUSON, WALLACE K. *Europe in Transition, 1300–1520.* Boston, 1962.

GILMORE, MYRON P. *The World of Humanism, 1453–1517.* New York, 1952.

GOETZ, WALTER, et al. *Das Zeitalter der Gotik und Renaissance, 1250–1500.* Berlin, 1932.

GREEN, VIVIAN H. H. *Renaissance and Reformation: A Survey of European History Between 1450 and 1660,* 2nd ed. London, 1965.

HASSINGER, ERICH. *Das Werden des neuzeitlichen Europa, 1300–1600.* Brunswick, 1959.

HAUSER, HENRI, and RENAUDET, AUGUSTIN. *Les débuts de l'âge moderne,* 3rd ed. Paris, 1946.

HAY, DENYS. *The Italian Renaissance in Its Historical Background.* Cambridge, 1961.

———. *Europe in the Fourteenth and Fifteenth Centuries.* New York, 1966.

LUCAS, HENRY S. *The Renaissance and the Reformation,* 2nd ed. New York, 1960.

LUCKI, EMIL. *History of the Renaissance, 1350–1550,* 5 vols. Salt Lake City, 1963–1965.

PIRENNE, HENRI, et al. *La fin du moyen âge,* vol. 1, pp. 1285–1453; vol. 2, pp. 1453–92. Paris, 1931.

PLUMB, JOHN H. *The Horizon Book of the Renaissance.* New York, 1961.

POTTER, G. R. *The Renaissance, 1493–1520,* vol. 1 of *The New Cambridge Modern History,* ed. G. N. Clark et al. Cambridge, 1957.

SYMONDS, JOHN ADDINGTON. *Renaissance in Italy,* 7 vols. London, 1875–1886.

THOMSON, S. HARRISON. *Europe in Renaissance and Reformation.* New York, 1963.

TRIMBORN, HERMANN, et al. *Weltkulturen: Renaissance in Europa,* vol. 6 of *Propyläen-Weltgeschichte: Eine Universalgeschichte,* ed. Golo Mann and August Nitsche. Frankfurt and Berlin, 1964.

The concept of the Renaissance:

CHABOD, FEDERICO. "The Concept of the Renaissance," in *Machiavelli and the Renaissance,* pp. 149–200. New York, 1965.

DANNENFELDT, KARL H. *The Renaissance: Medieval or Modern?* Boston, 1959.

---

[3] David Hume, "Of the Study of History," in *Essays Moral, Political, and Literary,* vol. 2 (London, 1889), pp. 389–90.

DURAND, DANA B., and BARON, HANS. "Tradition and Innovation in Fifteenth-Century Italy." *Journal of the History of Ideas,* 4 (1943): 1–49.

FERGUSON, WALLACE K. *The Renaissance in Historical Thought: Five Centuries of Interpretation.* Boston, 1948.

———. *Renaissance Studies.* London, Ont., 1963.

HALE, JOHN, ed. *Europe in the Late Middle Ages.* Evanston, Ill., 1965.

HAY, DENYS. *The Renaissance Debate.* New York, 1965.

HELTON, TINSLEY, ed. *The Renaissance: A Reconsideration of the Theories and Interpretations of the Age.* Madison, Wis., 1961.

JACOB, ERNEST F., ed. *Italian Renaissance Studies.* London, 1960.

LEWIS, ARCHIBALD, ed. *Aspects of the Renaissance.* Austin, Tex., 1967.

PANOFSKY, ERWIN. "Renaissance and Renaissances." *Kenyon Review,* 6 (1944): 201–36.

"Il Rinascimento: Significato e limiti." *Atti del III convegno internazionale sul Rinascimento.* Florence, 1953.

SELLERY, G. C. *The Renaissance, Its Nature and Origins.* Madison, Wis., 1950.

WERKMEISTER, WILLIAM H., ed. *Facets of the Renaissance.* Los Angeles, 1959.

CHAPTER 2

The Church
in Crisis

When Catherine of Siena (1347–1380) was presented together
with her interpreter, Raimondo Capuano, O.P., to Pope Gregory XI, she bowed
low to the supreme pontiff. Then she slowly raised her head and said, "To the
honor of Almighty God I am not afraid to say that I smelled the stench of the
sins committed in the Roman See more strongly in my native town than do the
people in this very place who commit them here daily." The pope remained silent.

Catherine was a mystic and reformer whose ignorance of Latin did not keep
her from writing, perhaps through an amanuensis, to dukes, kings, and popes.
Her most urgent cause was bringing the papacy home to Rome, back from its
Babylonian Captivity in Avignon. The calls to reform in the late Middle Ages
were shrill, strident, desperate. The situation was deteriorating rapidly. Typical of
the criticism were the *Speculum aureum de titulis beneficiorum,* a "golden mirror"
revealing the abuses of the system of benefices, and the *Squalores curiae romanae,*
on the "filthiness" of the Roman curia.

One crisis after another racked the church: the exile of the papacy in Avignon
(1309–1377), the Great Schism (1378–1415), conciliarism, the more than half century of Renaissance popes, and then the Protestant Reformation. When the historian considers the frailty of the church, the force of the hostile waves beating
against her, and the tremendous assaults she has endured, he can only marvel at

[20]

her power of survival. The basic problem, as most medieval reformers saw it, was the involvement of the institutional church in the world. The role of the pope as ruler over the Papal States, originating in the supposed transfer of the keys of the city of Rome to the bishop of Rome when the emperor moved the capital to the east, involved the popes in all the political intrigues of the Italians. The estates of the church banded the Italian boot at mid-calf, where they were both strategically important and vulnerable. But there were deeper socioeconomic causes for the troubles of the church not readily apparent to the moralistic critics of the time. The church had become so involved in feudal society and the feudal economy that it had enormous difficulty in adjusting to the money economy and capitalist society. The papacy's administrative machinery and financial resources were not equal to the demands made upon them. With the best will in the world the most pious of pontiffs could hardly have coped with these tremendous difficulties, stemming from such deep underlying causes.

The Concept of Christendom

MEDIEVAL MEN thought of Christendom (*corpus christianum*) as a religious-meta-physical entity encompassing the spiritual and secular authorities. As the spiritual head of the church, the pope held the power of the keys and wielded the spiritual sword. As Thomas More put it in the sixteenth century, the Roman Catholic Church is universal, visible, and organic (not just mystical). The emperor was the titular head of the Holy Roman Empire and the chief political authority. In the year 494 Pope Gelasius I had defined the independent powers of church and state as spiritual and secular swords. "There are," Gelasius wrote in a letter to the By-zantine emperor Anastasius I, "two powers by which this world is chiefly ruled: the sacred authority of the priesthood and the power of kings. Of these the impor-tance of the priestly power is much greater, as even for kings of men it will have to give an account in the divine judgment." The spiritual sword, then, in having responsibility for the welfare of the secular ruler's soul, was held to have pre-eminence over the secular sword.

How much reality the concept of Christendom had in the minds of medieval men is difficult to determine. Dante in the fourteenth century and the Anglican theologian Thomas Hooker in the sixteenth century spoke of the *corpus chris-tianum,* or the "common body of Christendom." It was a community of belief on a number of levels and a common structure of institutions with variations in local communities. While many men were doubtless not conscious of holding such a concept, others did articulate it. It is evident in late medieval maps, which show Christendom as distinct from other areas of the Roman world. During the Renaissance the humanists and imperial political theorists began using the term "Europa" instead of "Christendom." The name was derived from the Greek myth about a Phoenicean princess whom Zeus loved. Disguised as a white bull, he carried her off to Crete. As Christendom evolved into modern secular Europe, the church entered a period of crisis that many pessimists mistook for death throes, signs of the last times.

The Institutional Crisis

DURING THE FOURTH CENTURY the Christian church, intermittently and ineffectively persecuted by the state since the days of the apostles, not only was granted toleration by Emperor Galerius, but was even given official status by Emperor Theodosius I, who proscribed paganism. The popular identification of the Christian church with the Christian state was a development of momentous historical importance. It brought new prestige to the church, but at tremendous cost to its spiritual integrity.

The reversal of the historical situation inverted the prevailing theories of the relationship between church and state. St. Augustine had justified the state as a check on evildoers and as a promoter of relative justice in human society, with its authority rooted in natural law. The Augustinians of the Carolingian period, however, understood the term "justice" (*iustitia*) as righteousness in the theological or religious sense, rather than as the impartial administration of merited rewards and punishments, and came to the congenial conclusion that the state is duty-bound to support the cause of the church. During the Merovingian and Carolingian periods of Frankish history the rulers exercised virtually complete control over the church in their domains. On the local level, too, the processes of economic and political decentralization led to the feudalization of the church. There was general acceptance of the proprietary church as a legal construction under which the lord virtually dominated the church within his territory, controlling appointments to ecclesiastical offices and finances in the parish or diocese within his power.

From the time of Pope Gregory VII's struggle for "the right order of things in the world" in the eleventh century, the church became increasingly a clerical institution marked by ever greater centralization in the papacy. An unwholesome gap developed between clergy and laity, between the secular and the regular clergy, and between the upper clergy, drawn largely from noble families and on occasion from enterprising bourgeois families, and the lower clergy, drawn from the lower classes and given minimal education. Major historical movements tend to build up greater force than necessary to achieve limited and attainable objectives. Thus, to overcome the evils resulting from the control of the church on the local level by lay lords, under the proprietary arrangements typical of the early and high Middle

Ages, the papacy succeeded in establishing the claim, and some of the substance, of absolute rule over the church.

The theoretical basis of this claim was the assertion by some papal canonists that the pope possessed a "fullness of power," by which they meant power to rule not only over the church but at least indirectly over the entire world. Pope Innocent III took the title of "true emperor" seriously and accepted great kingdoms, including Naples and England, as vassalages subject to his feudal overlordship. In a letter to the archbishop of Ravenna, Innocent wrote: "Never is ecclesiastical liberty better provided for than when the Roman church possesses the plenitude of power in both temporal and spiritual things." When Innocent presided with hierocratic splendor over the great Fourth Lateran Council in 1215, pontifical preeminence reached its apex. But at that very council Pope Innocent charged the fathers with effecting reform within the church. During the thirteenth century, however, the church further centralized its administration, and although this was not at all a bad thing in itself, it did open the way for abuses. Innocent's pronouncement that "all churches and all things ecclesiastical are in the power of the pope" was given a practical application by Clement IV's famous decretal of 1265, which added the principle of provision (the right of the pope to name appointments to church posts not yet vacant) to the principle of general reservation (his right to fill vacant posts as he wished). Later popes could easily use this principle to reserve more and more patronage appointments for themselves.

Not quite a full century after Innocent III, Pope Boniface VIII gave the strongest expression to papal claims to preeminence in his bull *Unam sanctam* (1302), in which he asserted the effective possession by the church of both the spiritual and the secular swords, since the princes were to wield the secular sword on the instruction of the priestly power. He boldly declared that "it is altogether necessary to salvation for every human creature to be subject to the Roman pontiff." Boniface was a canon lawyer and may well not have intended the document to be so rigidly controlling as it sounded. At the most he claimed an indirect power of directing the secular powers to a "spiritual end," and not the day-by-day direction of affairs in the secular kingdoms. Egidius Romanus, a tutor of Philip the Fair of France, wrote a treatise entitled *On Ecclesiastical Power,* in which he developed the theory of papal dominion: All dominion must be held by those who are in proper communion with the church. Later other writers applied this argument to property, holding that Christians alone had the right to be property holders or that property holders should be Christians—a dangerous proposition should churchmen prove to be unworthy or unchristian! The reaction of the rising secular powers against papal pretension was signaled by the humiliation of Boniface VIII himself by Philip the Fair. Boniface's imprisonment by Philip's man Guillaume de Nogaret in 1303 marks the end of an era that began in 1077 with Emperor Henry IV standing barefoot in the snow at Canossa in repentance before Pope Gregory VII.

The Babylonian Captivity of the church, during the course of which the papal see was located in Avignon, where Pope Clement V, a Frenchman, moved it in 1309, was in itself detrimental to the prestige of the papacy and weakened the loyalty of the English, who were engaged in their century-long struggle with France. The period of the Avignonese papacy did great harm to the church. It was not merely the absence of the papacy from Rome that proved harmful, for popes had been away from Rome before this. Between 1100 and 1304, a period of 204 years, the popes had spent 122 years away from Rome, only 82 in Rome. They had a palace in Viterbo, where the climate was better, where the plague was less threatening, and where they could escape the disputes of the rival Orsini and Colonna factions. But certain developments during the pontifical residence in the grand palace above the bridge in Avignon brought the church ever nearer to the brink of disaster.

During this period the papacy further centralized the administration of the church. The extension of papal supervision and actual jurisdiction was justified on the grounds of the need to combat the evils still remaining in the proprietary churches. Establishing the "right order of authority" meant intervention from above to prevent local political control of the church by the appointment to church offices of the younger sons of the nobility. Bold hypothesizers have scored verbal triumphs with catchy formulas such as "No Innocent III, no Louis XIV!" The truth is that the monarchs of kingdoms such as France were in many respects ahead of the church in creating bureaucracies and professional armies. The Avignonese papacy, with worldwide obligations to administer justice in church courts, to manage its vast landholdings, to supervise benefices, and to exercise control over appointments, felt the same need for administrative expansion and evolved in the same way as the new dynastic states. If the monarch could tax his subjects, however, the pope had to tax his ingenuity to discover new sources of revenue to pay for his governmental structure. The *camera,* or office of finance, extended taxation and raised fees. Canon law became a concrete expression of the church's universal jurisdiction.

The distribution of benefices, church posts endowed with property or funds, provided one major source of income. By the thirteenth century there was canonical provision for direct papal disposition of benefices in certain cases. If an official died in Rome or Avignon—a cardinal, for example—then the papacy could dispose of his benefice. This papal privilege of reservation, the right to nominate to a vacant benefice, was extended during the fourteenth century, and churchmen even paid the equivalent of the first year's income, or annates, from a see in anticipation of appointment in case of the resignation or death of the incumbent. A charge that appears frequently in the literature of the period is that "everything is for sale in Avignon." The latest studies suggest, however, that the amount of annual income that the Avignonese papacy derived from taxation and various other financial devices has been wildly exaggerated. Europe experienced acute financial problems in the second half of the fourteenth century, exacerbated by plagues, wars, and famines. The returns to the papacy were very small compared with the income of the rising national states, or even of a city-state like Venice. Moreover, the Italian bankers who handled papal finances understood well how to use them to their own enrichment. The city of Rome was in constant turmoil, and half-independent *signori* took over control in almost every city in the Papal States. The loss of revenue from the Papal States forced the papacy to seek new sources of income from the church at large, which increased the general resentment against it.

The papacy was much weaker than outward appearances would suggest. During the late Middle Ages and especially during the decades of the Renaissance popes, the papacy was simply unable to assert effective control over the church outside of Italy. The popes could have done something by way of lofty precept or good example, but even if they had wanted to institute a thorough reform in all parts of the church, it is doubtful that they had the power to do so. The moralistic reformers in the late Middle Ages, however, looked at the outward show of pomp and the worldliness of the court and flayed the papacy. What people believe to be true is often historically a more powerful force than the actual facts, and people were beginning to think the worst of the papacy. They feared that the very dangers of ecclesiastical centralization, bureaucracy, and fiscalism, against which St. Bernard had warned in the twelfth century, were now coming to pass.

The way in which the fourteenth-century exile in Avignon ended, however, was more damaging than the absence from Rome itself. When the papal residence was returned from Avignon to Rome and a small group of dissident cardinals elected an antipope, they precipitated the Great Schism, destroyed the juridical unity of the church, and harmed its credibility and spirituality. A contemporary, Nicholas de Clemanges, wrote a treatise *On the Ruin of the Church*. The trouble started when Pope Gregory XI, who had returned to Rome in 1377, died soon after arriving. In 1378 the College of Cardinals met for the election of a new pope under tremendous pressure from the local populace, which rioted and screamed for the election of an Italian pontiff. The cardinals agreed on one candidate, pretended to be electing another, and finally voted for Pope Urban VI, who favored Rome. Urban VI very quickly managed to offend some of the cardinals, and a rump faction elected a French pope, who chose the name Clement VII.

The schism was not simply an expression of nationalistic opposition of French cardinals to the Italian pope. The basic cause for the rift was the development of the idea of a transfer to the College of Cardinals of some of the power centered in the papacy. Urban VI had been elected as a mediocre stopgap; Clement was chosen by the disaffected cardinals in part as an expression of their dissatisfaction with Urban's rule. Although the king of France was not responsible for the schism, he did help to perpetuate it. Generally France and to some extent Spain supported Avignon, while Germany and England supported the Roman line. In subsequent centuries the church officially concluded the question of the legitimacy of the succession in favor of the Roman line and against the two schismatic powers of Avignon, Clement VII (1378–1394) and Benedict XIII (1394–1424). The schism lasted nearly four decades, dividing the loyalties of all Europe, eroding the prestige of the papacy, and worst of all, rendering doubtful the validity of the sacraments by obscuring the authentic line of sacerdotal succession, a withering blight on piety and spirituality.

Critics and Conciliarists

FACED WITH this institutional crisis, concerned churchmen recognized that there were four ways of healing the schism: the relinquishment of the papacy by one pope or the other, a compromise between them, withdrawal of obedience to both of them, and a general council willing to take responsibility for breaking the impasse. During the early period of the schism, from 1381 on, they worked for the resignation of one pope or the other and for compromise, possibly by the resignation of both in favor of a third. But neither pope was willing to yield. Between 1398 and 1403 special efforts were made to secure the withdrawal of obedience to the popes by national synods and kingdoms, but by 1407 it was clear that this way was hopeless. The fourth and final way was a church council, as advocated by the conciliarists, on the theory that councils were higher in authority than the popes.

The strong desire for church unity was the main driving force behind the conciliar movement. Such a universal concern was sure to produce a host of programs for reform. Some of the proposals involved changes in the constitutional structure of the church itself. Some of the more radical conciliarists opposed the whole system of centralized papal authority, since the monarchical episcopate was so obviously vulnerable, as the schism itself was demonstrating. The church had to act as an effectively united organism even when it lacked a single head to maintain the powers of the entire church. A council representing the will of the church universal was to be the agency by which a single competent pope could be chosen; but this solution denied the unique competency of the pope through the very procedure by which it was to be reestablished. The conciliar theory stressed the corporate association of the members of the church as the true principle of ecclesiastical unity, which was to be exercised through the council when the single effective head failed to act or was rendered incapable of action because of a schism.

In a general move to broaden the base of the central authority, particularly the role of the College of Cardinals, churchmen in the papal curia took an active part in initiating the constitutional reform movement. In 1378, in fact, three Italian cardinals proposed the idea of calling a general council with this reform program in mind. But the university men were more articulate than the cardinals in expressing conciliar theory, and in the course of the councils assumed an increasingly important role in leadership.

There had been many demands for reform during the thirteenth and early fourteenth centuries, many of them associated with ideas for the constitutional reform of the church. One of the most radical of these writings was the *Defensor pacis* (1324), in which Marsiglio of Padua (*c*. 1275–1348) portrayed the church in a way scarcely related to the existing, visible, historical church. Thinking possibly of the model of the bourgeoisie in an Italian city-state such as Padua, Marsiglio spoke of the "company of citizens" as the sovereign body responsible for law and for the election of the ruler. By analogy he ascribed similar sovereign rights to the "totality of believers" in the church, represented by a general council consisting of clergy and laity. Marsiglio coupled this line of thought with an attack upon the scriptural and historical foundations of the papacy in a really radical assault upon the traditional structure of the church. The church should devote itself to spiritual functions and should be without wealth, provided for by the secular government. In view of Marsiglio's sharp attack on the hierarchical structure of the church, it is not at all surprising that Pope John XXII declared parts of his work to be heretical and excommunicated him.

William of Occam (*c*. 1270–1349), who came under the influence of Marsiglio, joined the Franciscans and protested in favor of "evangelical poverty." He was a severe critic of the worldliness and wealth of Pope John XXII. Occam saw service—first to Christ, then to his followers—as a basic function of the church, with the power of law. The external church, whose societal structure involves it in the sphere of worldly power, must constantly be pressed to conform to the "true church" of service. He advocated principles that proved to be significant for conciliarism. The key to many of his writings was his attempt to define precisely and to delimit papal prerogatives. He was really more revolutionary than Marsiglio, though more difficult and less direct. Occam recognized the principle of representation: the emperor, he pointed out, was chosen by the electors, who in theory represented all the people in the empire and acted for their benefit. Similarly the acclamation *viva voce* of the pope and bishops in an earlier period was an example of election by the people. In appointing the prince, the people invested him with their own rights and yet retained as much liberty as considerations for the common good permitted. This conception of representation, while certainly not to be understood as democratic in the modern sense, was obviously important for the conciliar movement.

Another fourteenth-century radical, John Wycliffe (*c*. 1328–1384), studied at Balliol College, Oxford, where he earned his M.A. degree and a doctorate in theology. He considered himself a disciple of Marsiglio of Padua and William of Occam, and was very sympathetic to the Franciscan ideal of apostolic poverty.

He entered the service of the English crown, somewhat embittered by his failure to receive a lucrative position promised him by Pope Gregory XI. King Edward III presented him with the parish of Lutterworth, which supported him the rest of his life. He encountered papal financial manipulators when he was sent to Bruges to negotiate for England in a dispute about the tribute that England had owed to the papacy ever since King John became a feudal vassal of the pope. By the time Wycliffe entered public service in 1374 he had developed his concept of lordship, which logically justified the confiscation by the state of ecclesiastical property under certain conditions. In two treatises based on his Oxford lectures, *On Divine Lordship* (1375) and *On Civil Lordship* (1376), he developed his ideas more fully.

Wycliffe argued that "divine lordship is the basis of any lordship of the creature." Man has been given dominion over all things below him in creation. Divine lordship is not diminished when God extends some dominion to man, for man serves as a steward who holds his power in trust from God. Only so long as a man is in the state of grace can he be said to hold his possessions righteously. Therefore a pauper in the state of grace has a stronger moral right to dominion than an emperor or a pope who is in a state of mortal sin. Since only the righteous are justified in holding possessions, ecclesiastical lords are lords only when they are truly servants of others and not their masters. Therefore, when churchmen manifest by the wickedness of their lives that they are not in a state of grace, the secular authority should deprive them of their property. Wycliffe believed that wealth and temporal power were the ruination of the church. He urged the king to expropriate the property of the "Caesarean" clergy, disendow the "delinquent" church, and re-establish a priesthood of grace.

He had an Augustinian view of the church as the body of predestined believers and described the state of the church as the church militant here on earth, the church triumphant in heaven, and the sleeping church of those in purgatory. In a treatise *On the Power of the Pope* (1379) he flatly denied the divine origin of the papal office as it was constituted and argued that the bishop of Rome held only a spiritual office. He identified the pope as the Antichrist and his followers as the "twelve daughters of the diabolical leech." When he died he was busy training poor priests to preach the gospel in the language of the people. Wycliffe based his reform upon the supreme authority of the Scriptures, which he described as "the standard of faith" for every Christian and "of all human perfection." This emphasis on the Scriptures and the work of his poor preachers, nicknamed Lollards for their restrained style of preaching (their detractors, accustomed to priestly declamation, derided them for "lolling," or muttering), linked Wycliffe to the Reformation of the sixteenth century.

The papal schism itself served as the great catalyst for conciliar thinking. Two German professors at the University of Paris, Henry of Langenstein and Conrad of Gelnhausen, were early conciliar theorists. In his *Letter on Behalf of a Council of Peace,* Henry of Langenstein (d. 1397) wrote of the great corruption in the church and the responsibility of those who exercised royal authority to seek to bring about a reformation with the help of a council. He emphasized the representative nature and the responsibility of the council, but he was by no means clear as to precisely who should summon the council or how it was to be organized. He referred to the secular princes in a general way, but did not indicate how the initiative was to be exercised. Conrad of Gelnhausen, in a number of works, including his *Letter of Concord,* analyzed the constitution of the church theoretically, trying to skirt the need of the pope to summon a council. Christ is the head of the church, and when his vicar fails to act, others can act in his name. "It is impossible," he wrote, "for the general council to be held or celebrated without the authority of the pope." He defined the church as "the congregation of the faithful in the unity of the sacraments."

The great French theologian Pierre d'Ailly and his student Jean Gerson dominated the period of the councils of Pisa (1409) and Constance (1414–1418). D'Ailly reminded Christendom that the church was built upon Christ and not upon the papacy, and observed that even the pope may become guilty of heresy. Neither a pope nor a council is strictly infallible, but only the church universal. Since the council represented the church universal, all of the faithful, including the pope, had to submit to its decisions. D'Ailly formulated concrete suggestions as to the structure of the council, applying to the church constitutional doctrines that political philosophers applied to the state. While he supported the claim of an ecumenical council to superiority over the pope, he nevertheless respected the dignity of the papacy itself. D'Ailly was not a flaming radical either in his program of reform or in his doctrine of the church; he was really a staunch advocate of the established theology of his day. The canonist Francesco Zabarella supported his contention that, since schism produced heresy, the cardinals had the privilege of calling a council to deal with it.

Jean Gerson, who succeeded D'Ailly as chancellor of the University of Paris, in 1409 wrote the treatise *On Unity,* which virtually represented the program of the Council of Pisa. Gerson was not a radical attacking the papacy, but a devoted scholar and patriot. He was a member of the leading theological faculty and a churchman with a high regard for the see of St. Peter. He argued that equity must supersede legalism in order to reestablish the indispensable unity of the church. The pope was subject to the general council and might even be imprisoned, if it should come to that, for the good of the church. The cardinals should elect no pope who would not be assured of being universally acknowledged. Although a general council could not abolish the papacy, it did have control over the method of electing the pope. Since popes change while the office remains permanent, a council could remove an undeserving incumbent and replace him with another.

Two German churchmen, Dietrich of Niem and Nicholas Cusanus, represented respectively the most radical assaults on papal centralization and the most comprehensive statement of conciliar theories. Dietrich of Niem, who had served as an official in the papal court itself, argued in his treatise *On Ways of Uniting and Reforming the Church in Universal Council* that merely healing the schism would not cure the ills of the church, for the real cause of all the troubles would remain: the centralization of power in papal hands and the attendant corruption in the church. The usurped powers of the pope must be either limited or abolished, if private interests and greed were to be eliminated from the heart of the universal church.

Nicholas Cusanus (d. 1464), at first a conciliarist, then from 1437 on a member of the papal party, bishop of Brixen, and cardinal, wrote the finest and most comprehensive statement of the conciliar position in his work *On Catholic Harmony*. Cusanus enthusiastically supported the elective principle in the church as well as in the empire. He favored the naming of delegates by small homogeneous units, so that the whole church might be well represented. He sought to demonstrate that the church was a united and comprehensive body, willing to accept and comprehend those who differed, for in the totality of the church all differences were harmonized.

These were the conciliar theories, but the course of the conciliar movement in history is even more instructive.

The Councils

WHEN THE FIFTEENTH CENTURY opened, the church was still torn by schism, with a French and a Roman pope. The Avignonese pope, Benedict XIII, was a skilled canonist who had many good qualities and won the respect of his contemporaries. He was supported by the French king and the French national synod of 1398. His opponent was the Neapolitan Boniface IX (1389–1404), a clever diplomat and strong ruler, who restored the Castel Sant' Angelo and fortified the Vatican for defense. It was well that he did, for in January 1400 he had to fight off an attempted coup d'état by the powerful Colonna family. He also had to oppose the duke of Milan, Gian Galeazzo Visconti. After Gian Galeazzo's unexpected death, Boniface gained Bologna and Perugia for the Papal States. Not only did he do nothing to heal the schism, adamantly insisting that his rival resign, but he further scandalized the church by authorizing massive sales of indulgences. His successor, Innocent VII (1404–1406), was equally set against concessions.

Pressure against both popes was now building up, as concerned churchmen grew impatient with their callous obstinance. Innocent's successor, Gregory XII

(1406–1415), was at the outset willing to compromise and even to resign in order to restore unity, but he was urged by various rulers, including the rulers of Hungary and Bohemia, Naples, and the Venetian Republic, not to make any concessions that would strengthen French influence. He thereupon did an about-face and forbade his cardinals to attend the negotiations with the Avignonese curia scheduled for May 1408. Most of them went anyway and made an appeal to a general council against their own pope. Meanwhile, Benedict XIII was losing the nearly solid backing he had enjoyed among the French. When the French king himself declared France's neutrality in the dispute, Benedict withdrew to Perpignan in his native Aragon, for he now enjoyed the support only of Spain and Scotland. Cardinals of both obediences joined in summoning a general council to Pisa on March 25, 1409.

The Council of Pisa was an impressive assembly, which for a time numbered over five hundred, including four patriarchs, twenty-four cardinals, eighty bishops, and a host of abbots, canon lawyers, and theologians. The day after the council opened, proceedings against the two popes were begun. Thirty-seven articles were read aloud accusing them of heresy, of misgovernment, and even of practicing sorcery. It was necessary to charge heresy in order to facilitate the deposition. On June 5, 1409, both popes were condemned as heretics and *ipso facto* deposed. The French faction at the council was very strong, and the conclave elected the French archbishop of Milan pope as Alexander V (1409–1410). The council did little more about reform than to present a list of desiderata to the new pope. Since the proposed reforms encroached upon papal prerogatives, Alexander V dissolved the council on August 7, 1409. Because the other two popes did not acknowledge the legitimacy of the council and still had adherents, Christendom was now stuck with three heads instead of one.

Kindly Pope Alexander V was succeeded by a crafty Neapolitan, John XXIII (1410–1415), a worldly militarist and simoniac who had no conscience about reform. Now the emperor felt it necessary to intervene in behalf of the church. In the days of the ancient church Emperor Constantine had sanctioned the conciliar theory, and the great ecumenical councils, preeminently the Council of Nicea in 325, had enabled the church to achieve confessional unity and organizational strength. In this grave crisis a millennium later, the Holy Roman emperor as a Christian authority looked to a general council to save Christendom from schism. Emperor Sigismund (1410–1437), as protector of the church, had Pope John XXIII convoke a council to convene on November 1, 1414. It actually did meet in Constance on November 5 and lasted nearly four years. Sigismund invited Byzantine Emperor Manuel II Palaeologus (1391–1425) to Constance, for Byzantium was now hard-pressed by the Turks, and the need for East-West unity was increasingly urgent.

The need for restoring unity at any cost was so desperate that even conciliarists such as D'Ailly, cardinal bishop of Cambrai, who had been active at Pisa, recognized the need for a completely fresh start. John XXIII, who had come to Constance expecting to see his rivals deposed, sensed that he himself might be cut off. He escaped in disguise with the connivance of Duke Frederick of Austria, who kept him in his fortress of Schaffhausen. Sigismund declared war on the duke, and on May 29, 1415, the council deposed Pope John XXIII. The Roman pontiff, Gregory XII, saw the handwriting on the wall and resigned "voluntarily." Deposing the resourceful Benedict XIII proved to be a complicated matter, but finally on November 4, 1416, the council began proceedings against him and deposed him as a schismatic and notorious heretic. On November 11, 1417, the fifty-three conclavists assembled and elected Oddo Colonna as Pope Martin V (1417–1431). Martin proved to be a wily statesman who concluded a series of favorable concordats with various secular rulers in order to assure himself of continued continent-wide approval. The schism was ended and unity was restored.

The council passed two startling decrees, the *Sacrosancta* (1415) and the *Frequens* (1417). The *Sacrosancta* boldly asserted that a general council derived its authority directly from Christ, the true head of the church, and therefore the whole universal church was bound by its decisions. Pope Martin V and his successor accepted this decree, it is interesting to note. The *Frequens* called for regular council meetings, the first to take place after five years, the second after seven, and decennially thereafter. The specific reform measures were much disputed and the council finally instructed the pope to negotiate the specifics of reform with each nation. On this weak note the council adjourned on April 22, 1418.

Eugenius IV succeeded Martin V in 1431, and after a bitter battle with the Colonna clan, which had come to take a proprietary view of the throne of St. Peter, was able to turn his attention to the problems of the church universal. He opened the Council of Basel on July 23, 1431, but by December it adjourned. Two years later he agreed to reconvene it, but now a duel developed between the conciliarists of Basel, who proclaimed the superiority of the council over the pope, and Eugenius, who insisted on his own prerogatives. Finally, on September 18, 1437, the pope dissolved the council and set Ferrara as the location for future meetings.

Eugenius IV was much concerned about the welfare of the eastern "Roman Empire" and church, for the Turks were tightening their grip on Byzantium. He convened a papal council in Ferrara on January 8, 1438, to discuss reform and to explore the possibility of reunion with the Eastern church. A year later, because of the plague, the council was moved to Florence. Finally in June, after long debate, Eastern churchmen agreed with reservations to acknowledge the supremacy of the pope and to yield on other disputed points. On July 6, 1439, the bull *Laetentur coeli,* "Let the heavens rejoice," proclaimed the reunion of the Roman and Greek churches, separated for so many centuries. The *Te Deum* rose upward in the Florentine cathedral, where a golden plaque celebrating the reunion of

Christendom is still to be seen. Some Greek churchmen, such as Bessarion, remained in the West rather than face hostility to their concessions at home. Some enraged Greek Orthodox zealots even declared that they would prefer the Turks to the pope, and they very shortly got what they wanted with the fall of Constantinople in 1453.

Meanwhile, back in Basel, the antipapal conciliarists triumphed. Still holding to the premise that councils are superior to popes, they annulled the papal decree of dissolution and deposed Eugenius IV on June 25, 1439. They then elected as pope Duke Amadeo VIII of Savoy, who took the name of Felix V. He was acknowledged, however, only in Savoy, Switzerland, southeast Germany, and Denmark. The Holy Roman emperor Frederick III recognized Eugenius IV as the rightful pope. With the death of Felix V in 1449, Christendom saw the last of the rival popes. Eugenius IV had died two years earlier. His successor, Nicholas V, is usually called the first of the Renaissance popes.

Although we now rehearse the succession of popes and councils in a prosaic way, it would be a mistake to think that these events were of no special importance to the people of the period. The fervor and fears, faith and despair, hope and hate of millions were invested in the outcomes of these struggles. In 1460 Pope Pius II issued the bull *Execrabilis,* designed once and for all to end appeals to a council over the head of the pope. Pius declared an appeal to a council to be a detestable thing that made one automatically a schismatic and heretic. Yet he realized that terrible storms were brewing which would rock the ark of the church. "Dangerous times are before us," he warned. "Storms threaten everywhere. . . . The waves of Basel have not subsided. . . . We won through force, they say, and not by convincing arguments." A priest may also be a prophet.

The Hussite Revolt

PIUS II had once written a history of Bohemia, including accounts of the Hussite wars, and firsthand knowledge of that unhappy land may have contributed to his pessimistic outlook, for Bohemia was still filled with a fierce hostility to the Roman see. The Council of Constance declared the teaching of John Wycliffe to be heretical and had the poor man's bones exhumed and burned. Even less fortunate were Jerome of Prague and Jan Hus, who were summoned to Constance and, in spite of safe-conducts issued by Emperor Sigismund, were burned at the stake in 1415. They were victims of the casuistry that safe-conducts do not hold for heretics.

It was once held that Jan Hus (1374–1415) was little more than an echo of John Wycliffe. After Wycliffe's death, Lollardy continued to be popular in England, quietly tolerated by King Richard II (1377–1399). Despite their condemnation by ecclesiastical courts, the Lollards even dared in 1395 to petition the parliament for help in "reforming religion according to the precepts of Scripture." King Henry IV (1399–1413), however, needed the support of the hierarchy, and he put the secular sword into the service of the church. In 1401 the statute *De haeretico comburendo* was directed against the Lollards and serious efforts were made to destroy them. But the movement continued underground, and Lollardy was still a significant element in the sixteenth-century Reformation. There was a dynastic tie between England and Bohemia, for Richard II had married Anne, a daughter of King Wenceslas of Bohemia. The political connection increased traffic and facilitated the transfer of ideas between the two lands. This consideration, plus the affinity of several of the ideas of Hus and Wycliffe, very naturally led to the traditional assumption that Hus was merely a pale version of Wycliffe.

The fact is that there was an independent Czech reform movement before the public emergence of Hus, with Matthew of Janov as its leading protagonist. Hus became the spokesman for this native reform movement, particularly after 1402, when he was appointed preacher in Bethlehem Chapel, near the university in the heart of Prague. Jan Hus was born into a poor family, studied at the Charles University in Prague, and became a lecturer there in 1398. Deeply pious and concerned about the moral impact of his preaching, he quickly gained a reputation as a popular lecturer and powerful preacher. Jerome of Prague was actually the man who introduced Wycliffe's works into Bohemia. In 1403 there was a flurry of excitement over Wycliffism. Two older leaders of the reform movement were cited to Rome and subsequently experienced a change of heart.

At this juncture Hus moved to the fore as leader of reform. He debated with Johann Hübner on simony and obedience to the pope. Preaching in Czech, Hus rapidly became a national hero. Fearing his popularity and the implications of his teachings, the local clergy urged Archbishop Zbynek of Prague to proceed against him, and the curia condemned Hus's teachings. The controversy tore the university apart, and in 1409 the German students and masters, alienated by the fierce Czech nationalism, left Prague to found the University of Leipzig. When Hus was forbidden to preach in Bethlehem Chapel, he persisted, declaring that "in the things pertaining to salvation God is to be obeyed rather than man." In March 1411 the ban was again pronounced against Hus as a disobedient son of the church. Shortly thereafter the whole city was put under the interdict for harboring a heretic.

The situation now reached a new critical phase. In May 1412 a papal emissary arrived in Prague to proclaim papal bulls authorizing the sale of indulgences remitting the canonical penances and purgatorial punishment due for sins. The proceeds were to be used to finance a papal war against the excommunicated King Ladislas of Naples. Hus denounced the sale, declaring that an indulgence can never be sold without simony and should not be granted by the church except when the recipient is truly contrite and repentant.

It would be difficult to imagine a greater contrast than the rascally John XXIII and the pious Jan Hus. The bulls were paraded through the streets of Prague in a popular demonstration and burned. At this juncture King Wenceslas intervened in the interest of public order, and three young men were sentenced to death for declaring the indulgences unlawful after all had been enjoined to silence. At the insistence of the king, Hus withdrew to the estates of sympathetic Czech nobles outside of Prague. He used this period of a year and a half in relative seclusion to write expositions on the faith, the Decalogue, the Lord's Prayer, simony, and, most important of all, *On the Church*. He proposed a highly spiritual conception of a church of believers under the headship of Christ, which reflected several of Wycliffe's key ideas. "O Christ," Hus exclaimed, "it will take a long time before the proud priests will become so humble as to subject themselves to the church for sin, as thou, being innocent, hast subjected thyself!"

The Council of Constance now summoned Hus, for the problem of Bohemia was at the top of the agenda. Hus had a presentiment of death and put his private affairs in order before starting out for Constance on October 14, 1414. Emperor Sigismund provided a safe-conduct promising his safe return to Bohemia no matter what decision the council reached on his teachings. Hus was confined by the bishop of Constance and his case finally was heard on June 5, 1415. The charges against him wcrc for the most part based upon his *On the Church*. When he tried to speak in his own defense he was shouted down, and finally he concluded quietly, "In such a council as this I had expected to find more propriety, piety, and order."

Pierre d'Ailly, the Parisian conciliarist, presented the final resolution of the council: (1) Hus should humbly confess that he had erred in all the articles cited against him; (2) he should under oath promise not to hold or ever teach them again; and (3) he should make a public recantation. Hus refused, and for four weeks withstood enormous pressure to change his position. He wrote to his supporters in Prague: "I write this in prison and in chains, expecting tomorrow to receive sentence of death, full of hope in God that I shall not swerve from the truth, nor abjure errors imputed to me by false witnesses."

On July 6 the council condemned him to death in the presence of Emperor Sigismund and committed his soul to the devil. Hus, a pale, thin wisp of a man, stood with uplifted eyes commending his soul to Christ. He was then delivered to the "secular arm," led to the place of execution, tied to a stake, and burned. When the faggots were piled around him he was called upon once again to recant, but he answered, "God is my witness that I have never taught or preached that which false witnesses have testified against me. He knows that the great object of all my preaching and writing was to convert men from sin. In the truth of that gospel which hitherto I have written, taught, and preached, I now joyfully die." As the flames licked at his body, huge blisters formed under his skin. Before the smoke choked out his voice he was heard to pray, *"Kyrie eleison"*—Lord, have mercy!

The Hussite movement in Bohemia took a revolutionary turn as soon as news of Hus's death reached Prague. The outrage felt at the execution of the Czech hero and at the emperor's treachery was enormous. Nobles favorable to reform sent to the council a *Protestatio bohemorum* angrily condemning the execution. Sigismund made matters worse by writing the Czechs that he would very soon "drown all Wycliffites and Hussites!" In some parishes the people drove out their Roman priests, and rebellion was under way.

The Hussites very soon divided into two major parties, the moderate Utraquists or Calixtines and the radical Taborites. The name Utraquist was derived from the Latin words *sub utraque specie,* "under both kinds," and refers to the bread and wine of the Eucharist. The Utraquists believed that communicants should receive both bread and wine, not merely the bread, as the church had decreed. The name Calixtine was derived from *calix,* cup, and also indicates a demand that communicants share in the drinking of Christ's blood. The Taborites took their name from the city of Tabor, which became the main center of their activities. They recognized only two of the traditional seven sacraments, baptism and communion, and were opposed to elaborate church ceremonies. Both parties of Hussites spread through the countryside and roused the people for war against Sigismund, who was urging King Wenceslas, his brother, to suppress them.

Great forces in history are often released by relatively trifling incidents. On July 30, 1419, when a priest led a Hussite procession through the streets of Prague, rocks were hurled at them from the windows of the city hall. The hot-tempered John Zizka (1376–1424) stormed the building and threw the mayor and several city councilmen out the window. They survived the fall but were murdered by the mob below. King Wenceslas had a seizure when he was told of the incident, and he died a few days later. Riots broke out all over Bohemia and a fierce battle between royal mercenaries and Hussites gutted Prague. Zizka and his followers withdrew from Prague to Pilsen and from there to Tabor, where they established the capital of their new democratic government. As one of four elected captains of the people, Zizka organized a formidable and well-disciplined army.

On March 17, 1420, Pope Martin V proclaimed a crusade against the "Wycliffites, Hussites, and all other heretics in Bohemia." Sigismund, various German princes, and a rabble of freebooters descended on Prague and laid siege to the city. Sigismund rejected the Articles of Prague, in which the Hussites laid down their basic tenets. He was fought to a standstill and had to withdraw. In August 1421 Sigismund launched another invasion, largely with German troops, but on January 6, 1422, Zizka won a decisive victory at Nemecky Brod.

Then a civil war developed between the Utraquists, with Prague as their capital, and the Taborites, led by Zizka, with Zizka once more victorious. A papal call for another crusade failed. In 1424 Zizka died, but the Hussites fought on, repelling foreign invasions in 1426 and 1427. In 1434 the Utraquists thoroughly defeated the Taborites in the Battle of Lipan. Since they now had control, they formulated a more moderate position, and the Council of Basel granted the Utraquists an official status within the church. They remained the established church of Bohemia until after the Battle of the White Mountain in 1620, at the outset of the Thirty Years' War. The Habsburg victory over Bohemia led to the proscription of all churches other than the Roman Catholic. The Bohemian Brethren, however, and some other groups later identified with Protestantism have managed to maintain themselves in Bohemia and Moravia to the present time. Jan Hus was truly prophetic when he declared: "You may burn this goose [*hus* in Czech], but the swan will come which you will not be able to burn." During the sixteenth-century Reformation, the evangelicals identified the swan of which Hus spoke with Luther.

Crisis in Spirit

A MEDIEVAL PREACHER would immediately have recognized these lines as coming from the book of Proverbs (18:14): "The spirit of a man will sustain his infirmity; but a wounded spirit who can bear?" The institutional crisis of the medieval church took an enormous toll in spirituality. If some of the very churchmen who should have served as models of deportment and provided inspiration were patently worldly and cynical, their influence on lesser churchmen and the laity was sure to be negative. Even the strong defender of papal power Álvarez Pelayos warned: "Those who rule in the church are wolves: they feed themselves with blood, every soul is burdened with blood." Pope Pius II could speak of the struggle for the golden fleece in this way: "It is not about the pasture of the sheep, but about their wool." The fact that the church survived the traumatic experiences of the fourteenth and fifteenth centuries prompts one to ask what resources of intellect and heart made survival and even an increase in religious fervor possible.

There was, of course, much health left in the body of the church, the "seven thousand in Israel, all the knees which have not bowed unto Baal, and every mouth which hath not kissed him." There were not only reformer types in the upper ranks, but thousands of parish priests and monks who were pious and faithful shepherds. And there were other spiritual forces stirring within the church. The most powerful of these was a spiritual phenomenon usually given the imprecise name of mysticism. There was, moreover, more life in late scholasticism than the humanists, reformers, and most modern scholars have been willing to concede. Christian humanism of the Renaissance, with its renewed stress on moral philosophy, patristic writings, and the Scriptures, contributed a religious dimension that offset somewhat the pagan influence of classical antiquity. Finally, popular religious impulses welled up from the depths and stirred the masses.

MYSTICISM

Because of its highly personal, protean, and evanescent quality, mysticism is difficult to define in a general way. It has to do with the intuitive and emotive appeal of spiritual reality. Goethe once referred to it as "the dialectic of feeling." Mysticism is based on the assumption that the ultimate nature of reality or the divine essence may be known by the mystic through immediate apprehension, insight, or intuition. The mode of perception differs from all ordinary sensation and ratiocination, for the mystic experiences union or intercourse with the divine being in vision, in trance, or by absorption. Since the experience is unattainable by the natural intellect, it cannot be communicated or analyzed by ordinary linguistic tools, and a sense of its nature can best be suggested by symbols. Within the Western Christian tradition all mystics agree that true beatitude consists of union with God and that this union is attained through ecstatic contemplation. The nature of this contemplation is love, and this love is made possible by a life of discipline and order regulated to that end.

Certain general concepts important for later mysticism developed during the early Middle Ages, especially among those thinkers who were under the influence of St. Augustine. The first of these was the body-soul dichotomy. This was not a metaphysical dualism, for the body was believed to be necessary to the nature of man. The mystics held that man should never be identified merely with his soul, for man is a composite substance. The second concept was perfectionism, for they considered anything short of perfection to be sin. The life of monastic renunciation in flight from the world was the most promising way to attain perfection. Many mystics belonged to the regular clergy. The third concept was that of love, seen as a ground of reference above reason. Since the religious experience transcends reason and ordinary vocabulary used in propositional statements, the need to resort to symbolism was early recognized. John Scotus Erigena in the ninth century offered a good explanation of the problem when he stated that a divine revelation that needs symbolic interpretation does not imply that the universe is irrational, but that there is much more to it than the rational. The use of symbol is the first step toward the realization of the complexity of the universe.

Certain fundamental ideas appear in various expressions of medieval mystical experience. One of these is that the mystical experience is achieved only as a result of a long, difficult, and even arduous effort. The word "ascent" is often used, and the motive force is overwhelming love of God. A second idea is that the mystic way requires an astringent ascetic preparation in order to drive out the baser elements, a *vita purgativa*. A third idea is that the course of mystical ascent draws one away from the senses and into meditation and contemplation. This contemplation is of varying modalities, some mystics stressing intellectual effort, others a willful gazing with the "inner eye of the soul."

In his "Essay on Immortality" the philosopher Alfred North Whitehead comments that every philosophy must find a basis in experience. For the mystic, his personal experience offered proof of the existence of God and the truth of Christian doctrine. Many of the most important high medieval mystics were influenced by St. Augustine: Bernard of Clairvaux in the twelfth century, the Victorine mystics Hugh, Richard, and Walter, and St. Bonaventure in the thirteenth century. Many Franciscans were in the mystical tradition, and many leading nominalists—scholastics who stressed the priority of the individual to the universal—were Franciscans. The mystics of the fourteenth and fifteenth centuries described their mystical experiences in increasingly concrete terms.

The thirteenth century saw the greatest triumph of scholastic philosophy in the incomparable summary of theology (*Summa theologica*) of St. Thomas Aquinas (*c.* 1225–1274). Thomas devoted his encyclopedic learning to reconciling Aristotelianism and Christian dogma, harmonizing reason and revelation, so far as this was possible. The fourteenth century witnessed a great resurgence of mysticism side by side with a continuance of scholasticism. A general revival of Augustinianism in theology and of Platonism in philosophy provided a broad setting for the new developments in mystic thought, but the mystical experience is a highly personal thing, so that only the individual mystic can speak with authority on this dimension of spiritual experience.

The unrivaled master of "cerebral mysticism" was the Dominican Johannes Eckhart (1260–1327). In view of what has been said about mysticism, the Franciscans, and the nominalists, it is fascinating to note how much the Dominicans too contributed to the flowering of fourteenth-century mysticism, along with their Thomistic theology. Their mystical piety, which was cultivated in the Dominican monasteries along the Rhine, especially in Cologne and Strassburg, was spread by their writings and sermons to their sister convents and to lay groups in the cities. Mechthild of Magdeburg (d. 1277), a Cistercian nun in a convent near Eisleben, had already written mystical treatises in German, and several German theologians at the turn of the century had written speculative mystical treatises, but Meister Eckhart towers so far above them that they have been all but forgotten.

Of a noble family near Gotha, Meister Eckhart became a Dominican and received his master's degree at Paris in 1302. From 1303 to 1311 he served as provincial head of the order in Saxony. He returned to teach in Paris in 1311, spent some time in Strassburg, and rounded out his career as lecturer in Cologne. He wrote a large scholastic theological work, German tracts, and sermons he had preached in a Dominican convent, expressing his mystical theology in nontechnical language for the ladies, most of whom were of course considered too weak-minded to follow a technical discourse, and in any case had received little education. Because of his notion of the divine spark in man, which unites with the divinity in the mystical experience, he was accused of pantheistic tendencies. He died while his heresy trial was under way, and when it was concluded two years later, the inquisitors condemned twenty-eight of his sentences.

Eckhart was influenced by Bernard of Clairvaux, the Arabic philosophers Avicenna and Averroës, the Jewish Aristotelian Moses Maimonides, and most of all St. Thomas. His work was largely concerned with traditional church dogma, and the trend of his thought was toward a Neoplatonic interpretation of St. Thomas. He believed God to be absolute being (*Esse est deus*). The central religious experience is the mysterious occurrence of the birth of God in the soul. Through this birth the downward flood of the divine reaches its goal and proceeds in that same instant to flow again toward its center in the heart of God. The mystical way begins with negation, a mental purgative, an emptying of the soul of every created thing, of all images. In this state of emptiness one is overwhelmed by a feeling of despair —the dark night of the soul, as the Spanish mystic St. John of the Cross was later to call it. At that moment, when one feels that one is farthest from God, there occurs the birth of God in the soul. The divine spark (*scintilla*) in man leaps across the chasm and experiences momentary union with God. The traditional dogmas of sin, grace, the incarnation in Christ fade into the background in this context, and pantheistic tendencies are truly in evidence.

Two passages from Eckhart's sermons will serve to illustrate not only his central theme, but also the way in which he endeavored to make his mystical theology religiously effective.

> God is foolishly in love with us; it seems that He has forgotten heaven and earth and happiness and deity; His entire business seems to be with me alone, to give me everything to comfort me; He gives it to me suddenly, He gives it to me wholly, He gives it to me perfect, He gives it all the time, and He gives it to all creatures [Sermon XCI].
>
> Know then that God is bound to act, to pour Himself out [into thee] as soon as ever He shall find thee ready. . . . Finding thee ready, He is obliged to act, to overflow into thee. . . . God cannot leave anything void and unfilled. . . . It is one flash the being ready and the pouring in: the instant spirit is ready, God enters without hesitation or delay. Thou needest not seek Him here or there, He is no further off than the door of thy heart; there He stands lingering, awaiting whoever is ready to open and let him in. He waits more patiently than thou for thee to open to Him. He longs for thee a thousandfold more urgently than thou for Him: one point, the opening and the entering [Sermon IV].

Eckhart's influence upon later intellectual history was very great, one religious line running through the Reformation to Pietism, another philosophical line running to Nicholas Cusanus, Jakob Böhme, Immanuel Kant, and German idealism. But his most immediately powerful influence was upon younger German mystics.

Johann Tauler (*c.* 1300–1361), a famous preacher in Strassburg in the best Dominican tradition, was strongly under the influence of Eckhart. He stressed the inwardness of religious experience, sought to avoid the pantheistic implications of

Eckhart's theology, and stressed the practical good to be derived from the mystical experience when the believer returns from union with God to perform works of love toward his neighbor. He had an important influence upon the fifteenth-century Rhenish mystic-reformer Wessel Gansfort, who died in Groningen in 1489. Tauler also made a great impression upon Luther in his formative years.

Henry Suso (1295–1366), a Dominican of a noble Swabian family, lived most of his life in Constance and Ulm. A delicate, poetic, gentle soul who lived a strenuously ascetic life, he wrote a sweet life of *The Blessed Henry Suso Himself,* which reveals his inward experiences. His *Book of Eternal Wisdom* was a beautiful expression of mystical experience.

The leading mystic in the Netherlands was Johannes van Ruysbroeck (1293–1381), a priest and later a canon near Brussels. Nicknamed the *doctor ecstaticus,* this Augustinian mystic stressed the simplicity of the Christian life and the participation of the laity in religious life.

Groups of devout folk joined together in loose associations during these years to share and encourage each other in their efforts toward mystical experience. The Friends of God, like other groups of the kind, included both lay members (Ruleman Merswin, a Strassburg merchant, was one) and religious (Henry Suso's spiritual friend Elsbeth Stagel, a nun in Winterthur, was another). It is difficult at times to distinguish associations of this kind from the heretical sects that sprang up in the Rhineland during these centuries of the waning Middle Ages.

Mysticism was not exclusively a German phenomenon by any means. England produced the *Book of the Nine Rocks.* Catherine of Siena was, of course, Italian. Two of the greatest mystics of all time, St. Teresa and St. John of the Cross, lived in Spain's golden age in the sixteenth century. A militant young girl who heard the voices of saints, Joan of Arc, was the heroine of the French. And the most influential movement of the time, the Brethren of the Common Life, was Dutch in origin and inspiration.

In Gerard Groote (1340–1384) the Netherlands produced a most remarkable man. Born in Deventer, he studied first in Aachen and then took up medicine, theology, and canon law at the Sorbonne in Paris, returning home when scarcely eighteen years old. He taught in the cathedral school in Deventer and at the University of Cologne, well supported by prebends. A former fellow student at the Sorbonne warned him so earnestly of the vanity of his life that Groote underwent a conversion experience and retired to an ascetic life of devotion. An encounter with the mystic Johannes van Ruysbroeck further deepened his mystical impulses, and he spent three years in repentance and prayer. He received a license to preach and attracted a devoted following. His best student, Florentius Radewyns, once put to him this question: "Master, why do we not pool our efforts and earnings, why do we not work and pray together under the guidance of our common Father?" And so the Brethren of the Common Life came into being, a free religious organization of clerics and laity living a life monastic in style but without an official vow. Groote dreamed of organizing the various communities at Zwolle, Deventer, and Windesheim into a brotherhood of canons regular, but he died of the plague while caring for the sick and further organization was left to Radewyns.

Groote was a successful practical mystic. Whereas for Eckhart and other cerebral mystics speculative reason played an important part in the preliminary stages of the mystical experience, the love of God so moved the "voluntaristic mystics" to love their neighbors that they were impelled to apply in everyday life the religious inspiration derived from the mystical experience. This practical emphasis explains the activist philosophy of the Brethren. It was possibly one more manifestation of the shift during the Renaissance away from the contemplative life as the highest good in itself to an appreciation of the active life as the expression of the inner spirit of man.

The Brethren of the Common Life, or *Devotio moderna,* attempted to live like the primitive Christian communities described in Acts 4. Laymen were in a majority, and each community was likely to select a layman as rector. Thomas a Kempis (*c.* 1380–1471) became the virtual embodiment of the Brethren's ideals of piety. His life spanned ninety-one years and he lived through most of the vigorous first century of the association's growth. The son of a peasant, Thomas was educated at Deventer in mystical theology and practical benevolence. He was a withdrawn, scholarly man, and on the counseling of Florentius Radewyns he entered the Augustinian convent of Mount St. Agnes in Zwolle. The order of Augustinian or Austin canons had a certain affinity with the Brethren in theology and way of life, and contributed much to religious reform in the Netherlands and the Germanies. Thomas labored as a copyist, wrote biographies of Groote, Radewyns, and other Brethren, composed tracts on the monastic life, and was the author or compiler of one of the most influential books the world has ever seen, *The Imitation of Christ,* which exists in hundreds of editions and has been translated into more languages than any other book with the exception of the Bible itself. The *Imitation* taught a practical piety, offered useful admonitions, and recommended a devout way of life in imitation of the Master. There is nothing of a highly rationalized theology, but rather, as in the fourth book on the Sacrament, a communication of the religion of the heart filled with celestial love.

The brothers worked as artisans in shops, instructed the poor, taught in their own schools, supported homes for poor students near cathedral schools and in university towns, copied classical and Christian manuscripts, and operated printing presses for devotional and even some scholarly material. In the schools they used the texts of the "safe classics"—that is, the moral philosophy of Seneca and Cicero, the clean poets, and pedagogically sound rhetoricians. They have, in fact, been described with some truth as one source of the northern Renaissance. Their spiritualist emphasis and Stoic ethic inadvertently tended to minimize the importance of the sacerdotal apparatus for the salvation of the individual.

From Deventer, Zwolle, and Windesheim the Brethren spread through the

Netherlands, along the Rhine through Westphalia, Hesse, and Württemberg, as well as eastward along the North and Baltic Seas into Saxony and as far as Kulm. Many of the most famous men of the fifteenth and sixteenth centuries were educated or supported by the Brethren, including Cusanus, Agricola, Celtis, Mutian, Erasmus, and Luther. Only one of the Brethren's communities joined the Protestant Reformation as a group, for they represented essentially an efflorescence of late medieval piety. They declined rapidly in the second half of the sixteenth century, and by the middle of the seventeenth century all the houses had passed out of existence.

When we look back upon this great efflorescence of mysticism in these centuries, it is hard to resist speculating on why it occurred when and where it did. It was a time of turmoil and crisis, of course, and one could easily conclude that such times drive people to an internal migration. But other periods of crisis failed to produce such a movement, and the Spanish mystics emerged at a time when their land was flourishing. Perhaps with the desiccation of theology by the later scholastics, religious impulses found natural expression in mysticism. But the absolute contrast once made between scholasticism and mysticism seems no longer tenable, for some scholastics had a mystical component to their thought, and at least some mystics, such as Eckhart, were schooled in scholasticism. Nor can mysticism be considered a form of rebellion against institutional religion, for most of the mystics were obedient and devoted sons of the church. The implications of the mystics' direct encounter with God were nonsacerdotal and could be nonsacramental. But mysticism cannot be communicated to the masses, so it must be considered more a personal reaction than a general form of rebellion.

Another fascinating theory is that there is a pendular movement in intellectual history from the rational to the nonrational, or from rationalism to romanticism. The Augustinian Platonic period in the early Middle Ages was followed by the first stage in the development of scholastic theology in the eleventh century. There followed then the twelfth-century Renaissance of humanism and mysticism. The high period of scholastic thought in the thirteenth century and the first half of the fourteenth century was then superseded by humanism in Italy and mysticism in the North during the fourteenth and fifteenth centuries.

There is some small element of truth in each of these explanations. But the more immediate source of mysticism was the intensification of religious feeling in the fourteenth and fifteenth centuries, a direct product of the crisis in spirit that accompanied the medieval institutional breakdown and the accelerated pace of historical change.

SCHOLASTICISM

In the medieval vision of reality the whole universe belonged to an objective and cosmic system. Everything had its place in a static hierarchy of complexity and value. This order was ideal and could be grasped by the human mind. This general optimistic confidence in man's intellectual capacity was a necessary precondition for the philosophical and theological enterprise of the scholastic doctors, for they believed that theology as well as philosophy was well ordered and could be treated systematically, even by logical syllogisms.

A scholarly controversy still rages around the question of the decadence or vitality of scholasticism in its third and final phase at the end of the Middle Ages. The older view, still widely held, was that the thirteenth century saw the grand synthesis in the Dominican St. Thomas' *Summa theologica* and *Summa contra gentiles,* and that the fourteenth century was dominated by the Franciscan nominalists, who precipitated the disintegration of scholastic philosophy. Late scholasticism was a decadent form of school learning, not only lacking in creativity and originality, but given to an antirational voluntarism, semi-Pelagianism, and epistemological skepticism.

This view of late scholasticism as a school subject cultivated by Johnny-come-latelies derived from the very days of the Renaissance, when humanists and reformers poured scorn upon the scholastic doctors as pedants and bores. Erasmus wrote them off with phrases such as this: "A scab of a fellow, theology incarnate!" His friend Sir Thomas More sneered: "A man might as soon obtain bodily nourishment by milking a he-goat into a sieve as spiritual nourishment by reading the schoolmen." The futility of refined scholastic distinctions became a fixed idea in literature. The French playwright Molière has a famous satirical passage in which the scholastic student recites by rote the profundity that opium makes one sleep because it is possessed of a dormitive virtue. In referring to the famous scholastic argument from the purpose of created things, Francis Bacon made the wicked thrust: "Teleology is like a virgin consecrated to God, it is noble but produces no offspring." Given a press like that, it is little short of miraculous that late scholasticism should find apologists and a revisionist school to defend it.

The founder of the *via moderna* in scholastic thought was William of Occam, the critic of the church discussed previously, who wrote during the first half of the fourteenth century. An English Franciscan and pupil of the *doctor subtilis* Duns Scotus, Occam taught as a professor in Paris. In 1328 he fled to the protection of Ludwig of Bavaria, who as secular ruler was defying the pope, and died in Munich. The modernists celebrated Occam as their "venerable teacher," and he was highly regarded in this theological tradition as late as the time of Luther, who spoke of "Occam, my dear master." Occam wrote no complete summa as such, and yet from the great bulk of his writings a fairly consistent point of view and unified system emerge.

The position he took on the question of universals is perhaps the most widely known feature of his thought, important for the problem of knowledge in philosophy as well as for its theological implications. On the question of whether universals exist prior to the particular (*universalia ante rem:* high realism), whether they exist in the particular (*universalia in rem:* moderate realism), or whether they are terms derived from the particular (*universalia post rem:* terminism), Occam most nearly approached the third position. This epistemological assumption that universals are terms (*termini*) or symbols, which have no reality outside the mind of man, came to be known from the fifteenth century on as nominalism, a term derived from *nomen,* name, since the universal was merely a convenient name for a collection of particulars. Occam was accused of fostering skepticism, and certain later nominalists were flatly accused of being skeptics, since it was readily seen that a consistent nominalism made certain theological concepts, such as the Trinity and transubstantiation in the Eucharist, very difficult to hold. The revisionist view on Occam, however, while granting his importance for symbolic logic, denies that he was an extreme empiricist or an extreme skeptic. For Occam the mind works actively on an object, and therefore a high degree of empirical knowledge is possible. Nor were his followers thorough skeptics either in philosophy or in theology.

On the question of faith and reason, Occam was said to hold that faith and knowledge are far from each other and that it is impossible to base faith upon reason. This position contributed to a double theory of truth, it has been asserted: that some things are true in philosophy that are not true in theology and vice versa. Occam argued that religious truth had to be accepted upon the authority of the church. Like Thomas Aquinas, Occam believed that some things are known by reason and some by revelation. He did lower the line between the two realms, putting a larger number of religious truths within the scope of revelation. Occam resorted to the Bible and to the authority of the church as the basis of religious truth. Two characteristic statements read:

> Therefore the Christian is not by the necessity of salvation bound to believe; nor is he to believe what is neither contained in the Bible, nor can be inferred by necessary and manifest consequence alone from the things contained in the Bible.
>
> This is my faith, since it is the Catholic faith; for whatever the Roman church believes, this alone and not anything else do I believe either explicitly or implicitly.

It is interesting to note that Occam was never officially condemned by the church for his teachings, any more than was St. Thomas when certain of his propositions were called into question.

A central question in theology was the doctrine of justification: how man, a sinner, is made righteous and acceptable to God. Occam stressed the omnipotence of God and the force of his will so strongly that the idea that God quite arbitrarily predestines some men to salvation and some to condemnation seemed to be a natural corollary. At the same time, Occam seemed to emphasize man's freedom of will and his ability to do good works, and thus to contribute to his own salvation. A closer study of Occam, however, shows that he stressed the difference between divine omnipotence as an absolute power (*potentia absoluta*), by which God can do anything he chooses to do, and a regulated power (*potentia ordinata*), by which God actually does only those things he has chosen to do. God has set limits to his own actions, so that they are not arbitrary, but regulated. The terms of salvation that he has laid down for man in revelation and in church teaching allow for a substantial contribution by man to his own salvation. Occam and his followers were consistently semi-Pelagian on the question of justification. The idea that man, while dependent for salvation upon God's forgiving grace, can and must, on his own initiative, take steps to accept or reject God's help in overcoming original sin harmonized nicely with church teachings and popular religious practices in those centuries.

Erasmus professed to be badly bewildered by the many schools of thought and the refined differences among the scholastics. "One might sooner," he sighed, "find one's way about a labyrinth than through the intellectual mazes of the Realists, Nominalists, Thomists, Albertists, Occamists, Scotists." Although Erasmus habitually put the worst construction on things, he was justified in professing confusion in this instance, for the picture of two fairly well-defined scholastic systems at war with each other is much oversimplified. The renowned "battle of the *viae*" in the universities, with the *via antiqua* of Thomas engaged in a struggle to the death with the *via moderna* of Occam, was really less a pitched battle between well-ordered forces than a running skirmish and confused guerrilla warfare. Many philosophers and theologians were trained in both *viae,* and the humanists, followed by the reformers, were variously educated in one or the other of them.

The mendicant orders were in decline during these last two centuries, with rival groups within both the Dominican and Franciscan orders. Moreover, the universities, which were still important centers of intellectual life in the fourteenth century, lost their preeminence in intellectual life to academies and court circles during the fifteenth century. The newer universities in the empire, founded for the most part by princes and city councils, showed greater vitality, but did not reach the level of eminence Oxford or Paris had held. Universities became a major force again in the sixteenth century with the founding of new Lutheran and Calvinist universities and the revitalization of some older Catholic centers.

The overall picture that emerges from the newer studies of late scholasticism is not one of complete decadence. Nominalism was not uniformly skeptical or subversive of theology. If many minor figures and pedantic teachers of logic killed the subject with nice but unimportant distinctions, there were other men, such as Marsilius of Inghen and Gabriel Biel, still capable of thinking through the problems posed by Thomas and Occam. Their writings reveal deep pastoral concern and cover a broad range of theological subjects. But if one asks whether the late scholastics were truly creative in the sense of innovation and insight beyond the achievements of the great schoolmen, the response must be in the negative. Perhaps their theology, to say nothing of their philosophy, had run its course. The humanists and reformers certainly overstated their case against the schoolmen and misled even modern scholars with their vilifications; but the alternatives they offered had more appeal to their contemporaries, and so history moved from medieval thought into the Renaissance and Reformation.

POPULAR RELIGION

The gap that always exists between the highly educated intellectual elite and the great mass of the people was an enormous chasm in the fourteenth and fifteenth centuries. An apt parallel could perhaps be drawn between the scholastic theologians and superstitious masses then and today's handful of high-energy physicists, who really understand what can be known of the secrets of the atom, and the great bulk of the population, which enjoys only some faint glimmer of what science has to teach. There were then far fewer educational and technological devices for the dissemination of learning than today, so that to find the masses given not only to a primitive piety but often to abject superstition is not at all surprising.

During the somber fourteenth century an apocalyptic mood settled over Europe and it lasted into the sixteenth century, with some relief in Renaissance Italy in the *Quattrocento*. The Great Plague in the middle of the fourteenth century and the continued recurrence of this pestilence brought home to everyone the transiency of life. The shadow of the crescent across Christendom, as the Turks made their seemingly irresistible advance up the Danube and repeatedly landed in Italy, contributed to the feeling of despair. At the end of the fifteenth century a new scourge in the form of syphilis, against which Europeans had virtually no immunity or resistance, swept across the continent. On all levels of society, rich and poor, powerful and powerless, men feared an early and miserable death. In the fourteenth-century tapestries in the Cathedral of Angers, the woodcuts of the depressed Albrecht Dürer, the paintings of the great flood to come by Leonardo da Vinci— everywhere brooded death and impending catastrophe.

The masses were swept up into feverish religious activity. Old religious practices were revived and embraced with new fervor. New forms of religious expression were devised with astonishing ingenuity. Prayers at the fourteen stations of the cross along the *via dolorosa* were introduced. The use of the rosary became common. Mary became the gentle intermediary between the sinner and Christ, the stern judge who will preside at the last day. As a corollary to the idea of the Immaculate Conception of Mary, a Scotist idea that the Franciscans championed against Dominican resistance, the cult of St. Anne, the mother of Mary, spread across Europe from Spain to Poland. New saints came into vogue: St. Christopher for travelers and St. Rochus, a special protector against the plague. New relics, massive sales of indulgences, and new shrines for pilgrims appeared everywhere. Tens of thousands of pilgrims clogged the roads to the shrine of Loreto near Ancona, to St. James of Compostela in Spain, to St. Michael's in Normandy, to

Jerusalem, and to the graves of the apostles in Rome. With the invention of printing, travel guides and city directories to local shrines were published. Artisans and
merchants, men and women alike, joined in sodalities or brotherhoods, in order to
combine their prayers, good works, and spiritual efforts to build up a treasury of
merit for their mutual insurance.

This religious fervor affected all classes: kings, princes, burghers, countrymen.
The mighty men of earthly kingdoms, and some wise humanists, donned monkish
garb to die and were buried in monastic churches. In the age of the Renaissance
people of wealth added an individualistic innovation: rather than involving themselves with the whole community in the construction of cathedrals, as in the
Middle Ages, they built small but impressive private chapels. One thinks almost immediately of the Pazzi Chapel, begun in 1429, the Brancacci Chapel at the Church
of the Carmine in Florence, the Medici Chapel, the Fugger Chapel in Augsburg,
and the many new oratories. The city of Cologne, with nineteen parish churches,
had at this time more than a hundred chapels, many of them privately built and
endowed.

Inside the cathedrals the aristocratic and wealthy bourgeois families endowed
their own altars, side-aisle chapels, stained-glass windows, liturgical ornaments and
vestments. Anxious patrons subsidized altar paintings and murals. Enrico Scrovegni, eager to atone for the evil done by his father, a notorious usurer whom Dante
relegated to the seventh circle of hell (*Inferno,* Canto 17, lines 64–66), endowed the
fresco cycle in the Arena Chapel in Padua, Giotto's most wonderful surviving
monument. The paintings of the time took up new religious themes, with a special
predilection for the passive, as if to encourage the viewer to contemplate the sufferings of Christ and the saints. In the fourteenth century the theme of Mary weeping
for her dead son lying across her lap was transposed from poetry to art and appeared in the sculptured *Pietà*. Christ, formerly seen as remote and passionless, was
now frequently represented as a man of sorrow and acquainted with grief. A new
technique was employed for achieving a central perspective in altar paintings. But
despite all the innovations and additions, the high altar dominated all the rest as
mother church remained for the time being intact.

It is a striking fact that when the printing press began the large-scale production of books, devotional tracts and prayerbooks by far outnumbered titles of any
other kind. It is necessary to bear this religious fervor in mind, for one cannot
otherwise understand the impact of Savonarola's preaching, the sweetness of
Raphael's Madonnas, or the very existence of Ludovico il Moro's beautiful black
vellum prayerbook.

In such a garden of religious flowers, the devil was sure to plant his seeds of
superstition, deceit, black magic, and witchcraft. The ignorance and credulity of
the age provided fertile soil for some of the most heinous outgrowths ever to afflict
the earth. Popular religion consisted of a fascinating mixture of Christian and old
pagan elements. The world was still full of demons and things that go bump in

the night. The fear of the incubus and succubus, male and female evil spirits that lay in intercourse upon mortals, was a real terror to many simple folk. Incantations and magic formulas offered some sort of control over the mysterious forces of nature and the supernatural. The declining Middle Ages saw the greatest flourishing of the art of alchemy. With the spread of the Neoplatonic cosmology, with its light metaphysic and theory of the sympathetic bonds that held all parts of the universe together and related a man to the stars, belief in astrology actually increased during the star-crossed Renaissance. It appealed not only to the simple, but to men in high stations. Kings and scholars consulted their horoscopes.

Emotional religious groups of flagellants—the Beghards, Beguines, Humiliati, Brethren of the Free Spirit, and others—were not simply drawn from the urban proletariat or from the illiterate peasantry. Attractive though the theory may be that these were assemblies of the dispossessed, early victims of a heartless industrial society, the truth is that their membership was not drawn solely from the textile workers or uprooted peasants. Members included people of all walks of life, and their literature is replete with admonitions to put away luxuries, warnings the desperately poor hardly needed.

Even though the church had worked for centuries at rooting out pagan idolatries and superstitions, in these decades churchmen did unspeakable damage by lending credence and support to a most vicious form of demonology. In 1484 Pope Innocent VIII authorized two Dominicans, Heinrich Krämer and Jakob Sprenger, talented inquisitors, to root out witchcraft in the diocese of Constance. The papal bull *Summis desiderantes affectibus* graphically described the evil deeds of witches and even prescribed ecclesiastical punishment against anyone who protested against the prosecution of witches. The two experienced "hounds of the Lord" then published in 1487 a book entitled *Malleus maleficarum (The Hammer of Evildoers)*, which codified the many devices of witches and told how they could be recognized. This book had appeared in over thirty editions by the middle of the seventeenth century. The craze lasted well into the seventeenth century (there was an isolated case of the execution of a witch in Mexico as late as the nineteenth century) and claimed the lives of hundreds of thousands of poor wretches, many burned alive. Not until the twentieth century did man's inhumanity to man equal these horrors. Innocent VIII, it must be remembered, was not a prelate of the Dark Ages, but a famous Renaissance pope of good family.

The Renaissance Popes

A THOUSAND YEARS had passed into history since St. Ambrose wrote to St. Augustine, "If you are at Rome, live in the Roman style; if you are elsewhere, live as they live elsewhere." A good moralist could hardly recommend living in the Roman style to a saint in the *Quattrocento;* quite the opposite. An embittered realist, the historian-statesman Francesco Guicciardini, wrote, "So much evil cannot be said of the Roman curia that more does not deserve to be said of it, for it is an infamy, an example of all the shame and wickedness of the world." Bemoaning the ills of one's own age is a pastime not without value and certainly not without precedent. At the height of Roman civilization the poet Horace wailed, "We are the degenerate descendants of fathers who in their turn were degenerate from their forebears." But the decades of the Renaissance popes marked the nadir in the long history of the papacy.

It is ironic that just when Pius II marked the triumph of the monarchical episcopate over councils with his bull *Execrabilis* (1460) and the popes were in a position to reassert verbally their claims to fullness of power, they were reduced to the status of Italian princes. The papacy, largely because it possessed the Papal States, became the plaything of powerful Italian and Spanish families. Both Sixtus IV and Alexander VI seriously contemplated secularizing the papal territories into a family principality.

The tone of the whole curia was exceedingly worldly. The cardinals, analogous to the old Roman senate under the emperor, thought it their duty to live as princes of the church, with courts of their own. These lofty wearers of the red hat in conclave elected new popes, counseled the pontiff on financial, diplomatic, and legal questions, facilitated appointments to office, served as secretaries, legates, and nuncios, and acted in many other important capacities. The Renaissance popes were free with appointments and greatly enlarged the college. Pope Sixtus IV created thirty-four cardinals and Alexander VI and Leo X each created forty-three. From the close of the year 1471 to May 1527 there were 183 cardinals, about 90 percent of whom resided in Rome and served as part of the curia. Since many were elderly at the time of their appointment, an average of twenty-five or thirty were members of the curia at any given time.

Many came from princely families or rich bourgeois Italian banking families, and lived in Roman *palazzi* in the style to which they were accustomed. Cardinal Pietro Barbo's palace and the Riario palace rivaled the papal palace itself in size and grandeur. In 1509 the average cardinal's household had 154 servants, with many additional attendants. The cardinals served as official hosts to visiting royalty and high ecclesiasts, and so needed a high income. Erasmus wrote in 1535 that no one with an income of less than three thousand ducats a year could become a cardinal. In reality a few cardinals had incomes well over twelve thousand ducats a year. They drew their incomes from curial sources (fees for services and so on), revenues from benefices, pensions, and private fortunes; for some owned mines, and others, like the Farneses, had rich family estates.[1] These grandees, given to

---

[1] D. S. Chambers, "The Economic Predicament of Renaissance Cardinals," in *Studies in Medieval and Renaissance History*, ed. William M. Bowsky, 5 vols. (Lincoln, Nebr., 1963–1968), vol. 3, pp. 289–371. See also P. Partner, "The Budget of the Roman Church in the Renaissance Period," in *Italian Renaissance Studies*, ed. E. F. Jacob (London, 1960), pp. 256–78.

splendid living and enjoying great power, were not likely to be very reform-minded or to welcome a pontiff who would be a radical renovator.

The Renaissance pope, successor to St. Peter, the lowly fisherman, was in a difficult position. He was the head of a worldwide institution and prince of an Italian state, but at the same time he was the spiritual leader looked to for inspiration by all Christendom. Moreover, in such a brilliant age the lure of beauty was apt to cast a powerful spell. "The beautiful," a fifth-century Christian had declared, "wherever it may be, is the property of the truth." This thought may well have served as the motto, or the rationalization, for the popes of the Renaissance.

NICHOLAS V

The first of the Renaissance popes, Nicholas V, elected in 1447, still had the task of facing down Felix V, the Council of Basel's counterpope. He was taken with two big ideas, internal reform and external crusade. He envisioned a spiritual renewal in Christendom and encouraged John of Capistrano in his preaching mission in Italy, the empire, and Poland. He entrusted to Cardinal Nicholas Cusanus the reform of abuses among the secular and regular clergy of the empire, but Cusanus' ability to accomplish much in this direction should have been called into question by his failure as bishop of Brixen, where he had been besieged by the archduke of Austria and nearly killed. The pope entrusted to Cardinal William d'Estouteville the reform of schools and colleges in France. He himself undertook the overhaul of government in Rome and the Papal States.

Nicholas V was a great patron of men of art and letters. The humanist Poggio Bracciolini served as one of his secretaries. He founded anew the Vatican library and developed grandiose schemes for rebuilding Rome. He repaired the walls of the city, refurbished its churches, began the rebuilding of St. Peter's, and offhandedly tore down the basilica of Constantine to make room for a new building in the Renaissance style. The famous Trevi Fountain was built during his pontificate. In 1450 he presided over a grand jubilee, which drew great throngs of people to Rome, but the plague struck with disastrous fury.

Shaken by the message that the Turks had taken Constantinople, he planned a crusade to free the city, a futile gesture. That very year a young nobleman was caught in a plot to assassinate him. So well intentioned and yet so often frustrated, Pope Nicholas died in March 1455, it is said of grief and sorrow.

CALIXTUS III

The election of the Spanish cardinal Alfonso Borgia as Pope Calixtus III was ominous, for it was a sign that Spain's shadow was lengthening over Italy. Notorious for nepotism, he brought to Rome his nephew Rodrigo Borgia, the future

Alexander VI. His love of his nephew was equaled only by his hatred for the Turks. He swore that he would shed his own blood to liberate Constantinople. He called the princes to a crusade and sold many of his own belongings to build a papal fleet. In the Magyar noble János Hunyadi he found his man. Mohammed II planned to take the rich plains of Hungary and needed to capture Belgrade as the key to the central Danube valley. Hunyadi fortified Belgrade and on July 14, 1456, his flotilla annihilated the Turkish fleet. A week later he captured the Turks' camps and forced the sultan to withdraw to Constantinople. Hunyadi died of the plague only three weeks after his great victory, and although Belgrade itself remained in the hands of the Hungarians, internal dissention in Hungary enabled the Turks to bring all the rest of Serbia under their control within three years. The Turks then turned their attention southward; and on the very day that Corinth fell, Pope Calixtus III died.

PIUS II

In his *Memoirs* the humanist Aeneas Silvius Piccolomini left to posterity a beautiful document providing exciting insights into his mind and view of life. He wrote descriptions of Bohemia and praised German culture, which flourished under the aegis of the Roman church. He was a papal ambassador at the court of the Holy Roman Empire in Vienna. He wrote a novel, *Eurialus et Lucretia,* in which he portrayed the primitive passions of a love affair between a German knight and a Sienese lady. He also wrote a comedy entitled *Chrysis.* But once he was elected pope in 1458, Aeneas abandoned his secular literary pursuits and became a serious churchman. Taking the name Pius, he urged everyone to *"Aeneam reiicite, Pium recipite"* (reject Aeneas, accept Pius).

As pope he had to struggle against the exuberance of his times. His former fellow humanists were disappointed that he showed them fewer favors than they had hoped to receive. In a visit to Florence he was received like a Renaissance prince. The city staged a great spectacle by turning loose in the Piazza della Signoria a swarm of lions, dogs, deer, and other beasts for a general melee. But the lions lay down lazily and refused to attack, to the general disappointment of the crowd.

Pius II was most serious about a crusade against the Turks, who were now making punitive raids on Italy itself, and announced that he would personally lead a crusade against them. But other business detained him, and by the time the fleet of twelve galleys that he had summoned from Venice arrived at Ancona, on the Adriatic coast, on August 12, 1464, his other forces had dwindled away. Pius had been waiting for the ships at Ancona for some time. Though he knew a crusade was impossible now, he blessed the ships, and three days later he died—of a broken heart, it was said. "A good death," Pius declared, "atones for an evil life."

PAUL II

The conclave chose next a luxury-loving Venetian, Paul II, who reigned from 1464 to 1471. The new pope loved beauty, collected antiquities, and was a friend of learning. He was much maligned as illiterate by the humanists, because he suppressed as pagan the Roman Academy, headed by Pomponius Laetus. The academy drew many of its members from the College of Abbreviators in the papal chancery. They affected ancient Roman styles, celebrated Plato's birthday, and made a convincing show of reviving the pagan past. A man of courage, Paul II deposed George of Podiebrad, king of Bohemia, for his heretical "Hussite" beliefs.

SIXTUS IV

Paul's successor, Francesco della Rovere, the first of the three evil geniuses of the Renaissance papacy, had been general of the Franciscan order, and seemed determined by his lavish spending to reduce the whole church to the poverty of the mendicants. An unabashed nepotist, he sought to carve out of the Papal States a principality for his nephew Girolamo Riario. He almost certainly knew of Riario's involvement in the plot that resulted in the assassination of Giovanni de' Medici and the wounding of Lorenzo the Magnificent in the Florence Cathedral in 1478.

Although he lived a simple and fairly austere life himself, he was a veritable Maecenas, giving away papal money as long as he had any to give. He favored the mendicants, of course, and built a foundling hospital. He built the Sistine Chapel and patronized Domenico Ghirlandaio, the famous fresco painter, as well as the splendid artists Botticelli and Perugino.

INNOCENT VIII

The most notorious of the bad popes was quite literally *pappa*. The sire of sixteen children, he acknowledged his bastards openly and celebrated their nuptials in the Vatican. Cynicism and corruption corroded the moral fiber of the whole curia. The pope's vice-chamberlain was quoted as saying, "The Lord desireth not the death of a sinner, but that he live and pay." A ring of cardinals made a huge sum of money by forging bulls for sale. The pope had to pawn his triple tiara in 1484 for 100,000 ducats. It is not surprising, then, to see him accepting 40,000 ducats annually from the Turkish sultan Bayazid II to keep as his prisoner Djem, the sultan's brother and rival for the throne, who had fled for protection to the Knights of St. John. As though to choke off criticism by a show of force, the pope encouraged Torquemada and the Inquisition, issued a bull calling for the extermination of the Waldensians, an ascetic evangelical sect that had been persecuted for centuries, and sponsored a sale of indulgences to finance another drive against them.

ALEXANDER VI

Rodrigo Borgia, the nephew of Calixtus III, virtually bought the papacy. With most of Spain united by the marriage of Isabella of Castile and crafty Ferdinand of Aragon, Spanish fortunes were in the ascendancy. When Innocent VIII died in 1492, the same year that the reconquest of Spain from the Moors was completed, Rodrigo Borgia was in a splendid financial condition to bribe enough cardinals to assure himself of the two-thirds of the votes necessary to elect him to the papacy. As Alexander VI he was a good manager of papal finances, but his aim was subversive, for he sought to carve out of the Papal States a principality for his family.

His favorite son, Giovanni, was murdered by another of his sons, Cesare, many believed, and his body dumped into the Tiber. His daughter Lucretia was in charge of the papal palace. Notoriously immoral as a young woman, she seems after her marriage and with added years to have become a respectable matron. But Cesare Borgia became legendary as an unscrupulous murderer and assassin, thanks largely to the attention that Machiavelli paid to his methods of statecraft. Until his repudiation of the offices in 1498, Cesare was archbishop of Valencia and a cardinal. He fought fierce and bloody battles against the Roman nobility and feudal lords. The sudden death of Alexander VI in 1503 and Cesare's near-fatal illness, presumably caused by poison intended for a cardinal, ruined the Borgias. Cesare fled to Spain, where he died in 1507 in the service of the king of Navarre. The ultimate degradation, Friedrich Nietzsche once sneered, would have been Cesare Borgia as pope.

Alexander VI played the role of an earthly potentate in international relations. The Turk Djem was his personal friend and companion. The pope even sided with the sultan against the most Christian king of France. He excommunicated and engineered the burning of the reformer Girolamo Savonarola in Florence. It was Alexander VI who issued the bulls dividing up the newly discovered Western Hemisphere between Spain and Portugal.

Alexander VI was also a distinguished patron of the arts. He renewed the section of the city around the Vatican called the Borgo. He rebuilt and enlarged the Borgian apartments in the Vatican. He had Pinturicchio ornament them with their famous frescoes, one of which shows Alexander kneeling devoutly as he views the miracle of the resurrection.

JULIUS II

After the very brief interlude of Pius III in 1503, Alexander VI was succeeded in the same year by the nephew of Sixtus IV, Giuliano della Rovere, who became pope as Julius II. His countenance is familiar to us from the portraits of Bramante and Michelangelo, but above all from Raphael's painting showing him in armor astride a steed—not the prince of peace, but the victorious leader of the church militant. Guicciardini said of Julius II:

> He would have been a pope worthy of the highest renown, if he had been a secular prince or if the care and diligence he showed in glorifying the church in the temporal sphere and through the art of war had been used to glorify it in the spiritual sphere through the arts of peace; yet he was worthier than any of his predecessors to be honored and held in illustrious remembrance.

Julius II continued the wars of Cesare Borgia in order to secure actual control over the Papal States. He wished to build up the estate of the church, not of his own family. Julius battling for Mirandola, laying siege in the cold winter, with frost glistening on his white beard, makes a curious picture. Observers spoke of his *terribilità,* his fierce and restless energy. He took Perugia and Bologna, and then, in alliance with the French, pressed on against Venice. Then he joined with Venice and Spain to organize the Holy League in order to drive out the king of France. He even called upon Henry VIII of England to occupy France. Louis XII of France reaffirmed the pragmatic sanction giving the Gallican church great independence, and in 1511 he summoned a council to Pisa to act against Julius II. But the Milanese and Swiss, friendly to Julius, sabotaged the council, and the French army had to withdraw north of the Alps. Thereupon Julius put the Council of Pisa under the interdict and convoked the Fifth Lateran Council as a counterthrust (1512-1517). In 1513 Pope Julius II enjoyed a triumphal entry into Rome worthy of a conquering caesar.

Julius spent lavishly not only on war, but on works of art, for he wished to make Rome a capital without equal. Already as a cardinal he had the architect Giuliano da San Gallo build for him a splendid *palazzo.* Now he had the renowned architect Bramante tear down the basilica of St. Peter and begin the construction of the greatest edifice in Christendom, St. Peter's Cathedral. Designed in the shape of a Greek cross and crowned by a mighty dome, it was to be the capitol of the Roman Catholic Church. Construction began on April 18, 1506. Bramante built additional structures north of the Vatican to extend this complex. Julius employed Perugino and Sodoma to redecorate with new frescoes the rooms above the Borgian apartments. From 1508 till his death in 1520, the incomparable Raphael executed the frescoes in the Julian apartments, which critics revere as perhaps the most beautiful of the entire Renaissance. With his taste for classical art, Julius had the Greek sculpture of Laocoön, unearthed in 1506 near the Baths of Titus, placed in the Belvedere Palace of the Vatican. No less an artistic giant than Michelangelo was commissioned to do a magnificent tomb for Julius, celebrating his military triumphs over the various principalities he had conquered. From 1508 to 1512 Michelangelo painted the frescoes on the ceiling of the Sistine Chapel, portraying the creation and the fall of man.

A peculiar combination of worldling and supernaturalist, Julius in 1507 sanctioned as a shrine the holy house of Loreto, which was commonly believed to have been the Lord's boyhood home, miraculously transported by angels from Nazareth. But even such gestures of piety or credulity were not enough to assuage the anger and disgust of religious men who believed that Christ's kingdom was truly not of this world. One of Julius' most devastating critics was the Christian humanist Erasmus. Erasmus had witnessed Julius II riding triumphantly into Bologna. Julius was, as a matter of fact, so proud of his victory that he commissioned Michelangelo to create a giant statue of himself, which he then placed over the entrance to the Church of San Petronio in Bologna. The Bolognese so hated Julius that at their first opportunity they tore it down and, since it was made of copper, melted it down and used it to make a cannon. Erasmus caught the grim irony and futility of the triumph of Pope Julius II, successor to St. Peter. In his *Praise of Folly* (1511) he wrote:

> Although in the Gospel the Apostle Peter says to his divine Master: We have left all and followed Thee, yet the popes call His patrimony lands, cities, tribute, principalities; for which, being enflamed with the love of Christ, they contend with fire and sword, and not without loss of much Christian blood, and boast that they have then most apostolically defended the Church, the spouse of Christ, when the enemy, as they call them, are valiantly routed. . . . Here you'll see decrepit old fellows acting the parts of young men, neither troubled at their enormous cost nor wearied with the labor involved . . . becoming, in short, the scourges of the human race.

Erasmus was so shocked that he could not let go of the subject. In his treatise *The Complaint of Peace* (1517) he still had Julius II in mind when he wrote, "What have the helmet and miter in common? What connection is there between the Holy Gospel and the buckler? How, O bishop standing in the room of the Apostles, dare you teach the people the things that pertain to war?"

Erasmus was so notorious as a scourge of Pope Julius that when an anonymous tract appeared in France attacking Julius, it was almost immediately attributed to Erasmus, although he seems to have been truthful in disclaiming authorship. This dialogue, entitled *Julius exclusus,* has the pope appearing at last before the pearly gates:

> *Julius:* Open the door quick. If you had done your duty, you would have met me with the full ceremonies of heaven.
> *St. Peter:* You seem to like giving orders. Tell me who you are.
> *Julius:* You recognize me, of course.
> *St. Peter:* Do I? I've never seen you before, and at the moment I find the sight extraordinary.
> *Julius:* You must be blind. Surely you recognize this silver key. . . . Look at my triple crown and my jeweled pall.

St. Peter: I see a silver key. But it looks nothing like the keys which Christ, true
pastor of the Church, gave me. . . .[2]

Forbidden to enter, Julius threatens that when more of his troops arrive, he will
batter down the gates of heaven.

A tidal wave of moral indignation was sweeping across Europe on the very
eve of the Reformation.

LEO X

When Giovanni de' Medici, the unspiritual, art-loving, libertine son of Lorenzo
the Magnificent, entered the city of Rome as Pope Leo X in 1513, he came as
though celebrating a Roman triumph disguised as a Corpus Christi procession. The
cardinals and their families appeared in gorgeous attire. Then came the pope himself in ceremonial robes, riding under triumphal arches and flanked by columns
mounted with naked statues. One bold inscription read: "Once Venus ruled, then
Mars, but now Pallas Athena." The reference was obviously to Alexander VI,
Julius II, and Leo X.

Less warlike than Julius II, Leo X was an even more lavish spender. Already
in 1513 his debts amounted to more than 125,000 ducats. He loved luxury, pageantry, and entertainment, the more decadent the better. He loved to go hunting on
his estates, following the chase in a sedan chair carried by servants. He was entertained in the papal palace by three court jesters, two renegade monks, and a legless
cripple. Balthasar Castiglione, author of *The Courtier,* related in a letter to the
marquis of Mantua how Leo X had attended a revue at a carnival in 1521.
The pope particularly applauded the last tableau, which portrayed a group of
handsome young men, in the garb of monks, sleeping. Cupids entered and danced,
awakening the young men with their arrows. The monks stirred, joined in the
dance, and flung their frocks into the fire with joyful abandon.

King Manuel of Portugal understood the pope's mentality very well. He delighted Leo with the gift of a rhinoceros and an elephant. Leo rode through Rome
atop the elephant.

Leo X was no warrior, but a wily diplomat. He skillfully managed the Fifth
Lateran Council (1512–1517), which offered the last chance for conciliar reform before the great Protestant rebellion. In the opening address Aegidius (Giles) of
Viterbo had called for reform and offered a Christian humanist program for achieving it. But the council consisted mostly of reliable Italian churchmen, so that Leo X
had not too much to fear from them.

There was a general consensus at the council that the Turks were a terrible

---

[2] Owen Chadwick, *The Reformation* (Grand Rapids, 1965), p. 17.

threat, and on March 11, 1513, Leo X organized the Brotherhood of the Holy Crusade. The council decreed that heresy and schism should be suppressed; that the immortality of the soul must be held as the orthodox position against the Averroist denial; that the mobs must be restrained from looting the *palazzi* of cardinals when a pope died; and that unauthorized preachers must be forbidden to teach and the publication of bad books must be stopped. The council took a position against episcopalism, a condemnation that Leo X trumpeted in his bull *Pastor aeternus* (1516). And much to Leo's satisfaction, as a final act the council reaffirmed the claims of the bull *Unam sanctam* (1302), which had helped to bring such great misery down upon the church under Boniface VIII. It almost seemed as though the churchmen in the council assembled had indeed learned nothing and forgotten nothing, even after the passage of two disastrous centuries.

As a Medici, Leo X enjoyed all the advantages and suffered all the handicaps of coming of age in an urbane, sophisticated, and somewhat overrefined social situation. When as a mere boy he was made a member of the College of Cardinals, his worldly-wise father admonished him to be virtuous and added a warning: "I well know that as you are now to reside at Rome, that sink of all iniquity, the difficulty of conducting yourself by these admonitions will be increased. . . . You will probably meet with those who will particularly endeavor to corrupt and incite you to vice."[3] Leo X had a smooth and somewhat unctuous manner. He was affable rather than cordial, always controlled and poised, whether granting an official audience or peering at a masquerade through his jeweled opera glasses. He loved the company of men of letters such as Cardinal Pietro Bembo and Cardinal Jacopo Sadoleto. He was a patron of humanists and artists in the very best Medici tradition.

The years of Leo's pontificate are commonly referred to as the Leonine Age, for the special stamp that Leo impressed upon Renaissance art. A man of exquisite taste, he appreciated the genius of Raphael, and like his predecessor Julius II he commissioned Raphael to do many frescoes in the Vatican. One of the best known of these was in the room called Heliodorus, showing Leo I as the savior of Rome confronting Attila and the Huns. Raphael used the face of the tenth Leo to portray the first. Bramante had built a loggia on the Vatican's third story, and Raphael ornamented it with a fascinating combination of classical and Christian subjects. Bramante continued as chief architect for St. Peter's until he died in 1514, and then Leo appointed Raphael as his successor. Leo recognized the great genius of Michelangelo as well. He had him plan the façade for the Church of San Lorenzo in Florence, though nothing came of this, and commissioned him to do the massive tombs of the Medicis in the Church of San Lorenzo, a monument that will remain for all times a great triumph of Western art.

---

3 William Roscoe, *The Life of Lorenzo de' Medici,* 10th ed. (London, 1851), pp. 285–86.

Periodization in history is always open to discussion. Some scholars prefer to end the line of the Renaissance popes with Leo, for his death in 1521 coincided with the emergence of Luther upon the world scene at the Diet of Worms, ushering in the age of the Reformation. Others consider that the year 1527, when Rome was sacked by the troops of Charles V, more appropriately marks the close of the high Renaissance. Still others see the reign of earnest Adrian VI (1522–1523) as a mere interlude, and the pontificate of the second Medici pope, Clement VII (1523–1534), as still an integral part of the Renaissance. The somber Paul III (1534–1549) was the first pope of the Catholic Reformation. With Adrian, a Dutchman, and the pontificate of Clement, however, events in northern Europe became the critical determinants of the course of church history. Leo X was the last pope who in every way belonged to the age of the Italian Renaissance.

The Renaissance popes were really as much victims of their circumstances as they were the villains that historians have chosen to make them. They represented, even Alexander VI, a peculiar mixture of worldliness and formal personal piety, cynicism and credulity, evil design and good intentions. They managed to build up an enormous reservoir of distrust and hate and did the church untold harm; but the presence of unworthy men in ecclesiastical office did not in itself destroy the efficacy of the church. The judgment of Ludwig Pastor, the great nineteenth-century Catholic historian of the papacy, merits a sympathetic hearing:

> An imperfect setting does not affect the intrinsic worth of the jewel, nor does the golden coin lose its value when it passes through impure hands. In so far as the priest is a public officer of a holy Church, a blameless life is expected from him, both because he is by his office the model of virtue to whom the laity look up, and because his life, when virtuous, inspires in onlookers respect for the society of which he is an ornament. But the treasures of the Church, her Divine character, her holiness, Divine revelation, the grace of God, spiritual authority, it is well known, are not dependent on the moral character of the agents and officers of the Church. The foremost of her priests cannot diminish by an iota the intrinsic value of the spiritual treasures confided to him.[4]

Bibliography

ANGELERI, CARLO. *Il Problema religioso del Rinascimento.* Florence, 1952.
AUBENAS, R., and RICARD, R. *L'Église et la Renaissance, 1449–1517,* vol. 15 of *L'Histoire de l'Église,* ed. A. Fliche and V. Martin. Paris, 1951.
BARRACLOUGH, GEOFFREY. *Papal Provisions.* Oxford, 1935.

---

[4] Ludwig Pastor, *Geschichte der Päpste seit dem Ausgang des Mittelalters,* vol. 3 (Freiburg, 1895), p. 475, cited in "Alexander VI," in *The Catholic Encyclopedia* (New York, 1907), vol. 1, p. 293.

BROOKE, Z. N. *The English Church and the Papacy.* Cambridge, 1931.

CHAMBERS, D. S. *Cardinal Bainbridge in the Court of Rome, 1509–1514.* London, 1965.

CLARK, J. M. *The Great German Mystics: Eckhardt, Tauler, and Suso.* Oxford, 1949.

CREIGHTON, M. *A History of the Papacy During the Period of the Reformation,* 6 vols. London, 1887–1894.

DANNENFELDT, KARL H. *The Church of the Renaissance and Reformation.* St. Louis, 1970.

FERGUSON, WALLACE K. "The Church in a Changing World." *American Historical Review,* 59 (1953): 1–18.

FLICK, A. C. *The Decline of the Medieval Church,* 2 vols. London, 1930.

GILL, JOSEPH, S. J. *The Council of Florence.* New York, 1959.

———. *Eugenius IV: Pope of Christian Union.* Westminster, Md., 1961.

GUILLEMAIN, B. *La cour pontificale d'Avignon (1309–1376): Étude d'une société.* Paris, 1963.

HALLER, JOHANNES. *Das Papsttum: Idee und Wirklichkeit,* 5 vols. Stuttgart, 1934–1950.

HEYMANN, FREDERICK G. *John Zizka and the Hussite Revolution.* Princeton, 1955.

HUGHES, PHILIP. *A History of the Church,* vol. 3. London, 1947.

JACOB, ERNEST F. *Essays in the Conciliar Epoch,* rev. ed. South Bend, Ind., 1963.

KAMINSKY, HOWARD. *A History of the Hussite Revolution.* Berkeley, 1967.

KNOLES, DOM DAVIS. *The Religious Order in England,* vols. 1 and 2. New York, 1955.

LORTZ, JOSEPH. *Geschichte der Kirche in ideengeschichtlicher Betrachtung,* 2 vols., 23rd ed. Münster, 1962.

LUNT, W. E. *Papal Revenues in the Middle Ages,* 2 vols. New York, 1934.

McDONALD, E. W. *The Beguines and Beghards in Medieval Culture.* New Brunswick, N.J., 1954.

MACEK, JOSEF. *The Hussite Movement in Bohemia.* Prague, 1958.

MOLLAT, G. *Les papes d'Avignon, 1305–1378,* 9th ed. Paris, 1949; London and New York, 1963.

MONTICELLI, G. *Chiesa e Italia durante il pontificato avignonese.* Milan, 1937.

MORRALL, J. B. *Gerson and the Great Schism.* Manchester, 1960.

OAKLEY, FRANCIS. *The Political Thought of Pierre d'Ailly: The Voluntarist Tradition.* New Haven, 1964.

OBERMAN, HEIKO A. *The Harvest of Medieval Theology: Gabriel Biel and Late Medieval Nominalism.* Cambridge, Mass., 1963.

———. *Forerunners of the Reformation: The Shape of Late Medieval Thought.* New York, 1966.

ODLOŽOLIK, O. *Wycliffe and Bohemia.* Prague, 1937.

O'MALLEY, JOHN W. *Giles of Viterbo on Church and Reform.* Leiden, 1968.

PARKER, G. H. W. *The Morning Star: Wycliffe and the Dawn of the Reformation.* Exeter, 1965.

PARTNER, P. *The Papal State Under Martin V.* London, 1958.

PASTOR, LUDWIG VON. *The History of the Popes,* 40 vols., 3rd ed., vols. 1–16. St. Louis, 1891–1953.

RANKE, LEOPOLD VON. *History of the Popes: Their Church and State,* 3 vols. New York, 1901.

RENOUARD, Y. *Les relations des papes d'Avignon et des compagnies commerciales et bancaires de 1316 à 1378.* Paris, 1941.

SEPPELT, FRANZ X. *Das Papsttum im Spätmittelalter und in der Zeit der Renaissance.* Leipzig, 1941.

SPINKA, MATTHEW. *John Hus and the Czech Reform.* Chicago, 1941.

———. *John Hus' Concept of the Church.* Princeton, 1966.

———, ed. *Advocates of Reform from Wyclif to Erasmus.* London, 1953.

TIERNEY, BRIAN. *Foundations of the Conciliar Theory.* New York, 1955.

ULLMANN, WALTER. *The Origins of the Great Schism.* London, 1948.

———. *The Growth of Papal Government in the Middle Ages.* New York, 1955.

CHAPTER 3

The State
in
Transformation

"States are great engines moving slowly," Francis Bacon observed in his *Advancement of Learning*. The nation-states of modern Europe did evolve slowly through the centuries, but the rate of transformation seems to have quickened during the era of the Renaissance and Reformation movements. While the Holy Roman Empire was losing all semblance of universality and was being denied its claims to Italy and to Rome itself, the new monarchies in France, England, and Spain were developing the dynastic strength and political cohesion that enabled them to enter the modern world as well-defined nation-states. Those political developments were of critical importance for the rise of modern Europe.

Shakespeare's Richard II saw in history little more than "sad stories of the death of kings." But however sad their endings, the kings of Europe were transforming their feudal suzerainties into more centralized and effective monarchies at the expense of feudal lords, urban communes, and the church.

Political and economic developments were intimately related and mutually reinforcing. During the early and high Middle Ages economic life was largely agrarian and was very much restricted to the local scene. Where towns flourished, trade was for the most part limited to dealings with the people of the surrounding countryside. But as a money economy developed, trade expanded, and larger territories and political jurisdictions proved to be more favorable for its development than the local feudal institutions. The kings and territorial princes were able to exploit the new money economy in order to build up their governmental bureaucracies and military forces. The new capitalists and burghers, in turn, favored the central government over local feudal lords. The landholding nobles were involved in economic difficulties, for just as they were commuting payments in kind to money payments, currencies were often subjected to devaluation. Moreover, the price of most items they had to purchase rose. With the increasing use of mercenaries by kings and princes, the nobility was losing utility as a military factor. This situation and other troubles, such as the problem of the peasants, especially during the second half of the fourteenth century, worked great hardship on the feudal nobles and left them poorer and weaker than before. Monarchies and territorial states, kings and princes came out ahead.

These developments varied in different parts of Europe. In the Holy Roman Empire the emperor was prevented by unique political circumstances from capitalizing upon the social and economic tendencies favorable to the development of a strong central government. Since the position of emperor was elective, not hereditary, and the emperor actually ruled only in his own hereditary domain, the emperors were unable to build up a strong centralized government. The territorial princes pursued their own interests and exploited the economic trends to build up the virtual sovereignty of their principalities. In the Germanies and in Italy, where the small city-states failed to coalesce, national unification was not achieved until late in the nineteenth century.

In France, England, and Spain, however, the royal monarchs were able to build kingdoms stronger and more unified than those over which their medieval predecessors had reigned. France, which had been the most completely feudalized country of Europe, developed a strong centralized monarchy. The law of primogeniture (or succession by the eldest son), the unbroken line of Capetian kings, lasting nearly three and a half centuries, and the long reigns of some of its strongest kings enabled the monarchy to build up the royal domain until it embraced a large part of central France. The French kings built up the machinery of government, the sources of revenue, and the military establishment essential to a truly national monarchy. Dynastic monarchy prepared the way for eventual national unity.

England not only was smaller and more compact than France, but also had a much smaller population. The Norman conquest in 1066 and the subsequent imposition of a feudal organization from above gave to English society a somewhat different structure than that in France. The English king and his feudal barons had their landholdings distributed over the whole land and not just in one central royal domain or in more or less independent feudal duchies out in the provinces, as in France. This fact gave to the central government a distinct advantage, since its jurisdiction followed its holdings throughout most of the kingdom. During the Lancastrian period the parliament and other representative institutions made progress. The trials of the century—long war with France and the acute internal crisis of the baronial wars in the fifteenth century—did not prevent the development of a national monarchy analogous to those of France and Spain.

Spain developed political unity much later than did France. The Iberian peninsula was inhabited by many races and a large part was occupied for a long time by Moslem invaders. The kingdom of Aragon was itself made up of three major constituent parts. It was oriented toward Mediterranean trade and culture. The kingdom of Castile stretched from north to south across mountains and arid highlands. Its major rivers flowed parallel to each other to the west, providing no natural center for the country. The kingdom of Portugal had not only an independent political history, but even a different language. In the south the kingdom of Granada had absorbed much Islamic art and culture. None of these disparate kingdoms were effectively joined together until 1479, when the crown of Aragon was inherited by Prince Ferdinand, who ten years earlier had married Isabella, daughter of the king of Castile. Isabella had meanwhile inherited the Castilian crown; thus when Ferdinand became king of Aragon, their kingdoms were joined. From then on there was steady and reasonably rapid progress toward centralization and consolidation, although Portugal was added only in the next century and the road to unity was rocky.

Despite the general tendency toward greater cohesion and centralization in western and, to a lesser extent, in central Europe, there was no inexorable natural law in operation, drawing nations together under unifying monarchies. A case in point is the situation in Scandinavia, where a promising coalition of states, which might have led to national unity, disintegrated. The diets of Denmark and Norway had in 1387 elected Margaret, daughter of King Waldemar IV, queen of both countries. In 1388 the diet of Sweden followed suit, so that Margaret in her own person embodied the union of Scandinavia. All three kingdoms sent representatives to Kalmar, a seaport town on the Baltic coast, where they signed a formal document establishing the Union of Kalmar (1397). The three kingdoms were to retain their individual identities, but were to have but a single ruler and were to work for their mutual interest.

In view of their close ethnic relationship, common background, and many mutual interests in war and peace, every prospect favored the continued organic growth of a great Scandinavian nation. But Margaret made blunders that subverted the strength of the union. For one thing, she appointed a disproportionate number of Danes to office. A rebellion broke out in 1434 against her successor, Eric, and in 1439 he was deposed in Denmark and Sweden. After a protracted struggle the Swedes established their marshal Karl Knutsson as King Charles VIII. The rivalry of the Danes, Norwegians, and Swedes proved to be stronger than any forces working toward unity. People, not impersonal laws, make history.

The Holy Roman Empire

LORD BRYCE, in his classic history of the Holy Roman Empire, comments that if someone had learned in August 1806 of the resignation of Emperor Francis II, he might have known that the oldest political institution in the world had come to an end. The miracle of the Holy Roman Empire is that it could remain on its feet so long after it had actually turned moribund. During the late medieval and Renaissance period the empire continued to lose significance as a political institution. The territorial principalities within its borders grew in strength and achieved virtual sovereignty. The national monarchies outside its borders increased in power, and France began to whittle away at the western territories.

The empire was undermined when, during the investiture controversy between the papacy and the empire in the eleventh and twelfth centuries, the princes were freed of their obligations of loyalty to the emperors. When Emperor Frederick II (d. 1250) transferred his headquarters to southern Italy in the thirteenth century and lost interest in the Germanies, the princes took advantage of the situation, and the pope made an all-out attack on the last of the Hohenstaufen family. There followed an interregnum from 1254 to 1273, during which a virtual state of anarchy ruined what remained of central government or imperial unity. The electors finally chose as emperor a minor Swabian prince, Rudolf of Habsburg, whom they considered strong enough to restore order but not so strong as to pose a threat to the princes themselves. The emperors were almost entirely dependent upon the goodwill of the princes, for they could not raise troops or levy taxes outside their own family territories. It is no wonder that most of the emperors concentrated on enlarging their hereditary estates through conquest or marriage rather than attempting to unify or strengthen the empire as such.

HENRY VII AND DANTE

The electors' calculated policy of building weakness into the imperial setup had the desired result. Since Rudolf of Habsburg, who was handsome, strong, and energetic, proved to be effective, they next chose Adolf of Nassau. He was deposed soon thereafter, and Albrecht, another Habsburg, was elected. A nephew and a band of hired assassins murdered him. The electors felt uneasy about the ability and aggressiveness of the Habsburgs, so they turned next to a small and seemingly innocuous prince, Henry of Luxemburg, whom they elected in 1308, initiating nearly a century of Luxemburg emperors. This Henry VII literally bought the election, and his own brother, as archbishop of Trier, was one of the electors. As Ovid once observed of ancient Rome, "Truly now is the golden age; the highest honor comes by means of gold!" Although Luxemburg was part of the empire, Henry's education had been French, and he was oriented more toward France and Italy than toward eastern Europe. He gave Bohemia to his son John, and in order to win French support he gave Burgundy as a fief to the son of King Philip the Fair. Then with a small army he went to Italy in the fall of 1301 to be crowned emperor.

The exiled Florentine poet Dante Alighieri (1265–1321) hailed Henry VII as the hero who would free Florence and Italy of Guelph oppression and raise the empire to its ancient glory. During the second half of the thirteenth century Florence had become predominantly Guelph (on the side of the papacy) and anti-Ghibelline (against the empire). Now the city was torn by Black and White Guelph factions. The Blacks favored Pope Boniface VIII and Charles of France, his ally. At the very close of the thirteenth century, before Henry VII's invasion, the Blacks suppressed the Whites. They exiled Dante and even condemned him to death by burning should he return. Dante bombarded Henry VII with letters and tracts urging him to come to Italy. When Henry came, Dante traveled to Milan to persuade him to attack Florence. He wrote a letter to Florence announcing that the time of judgment was at hand.

This political situation explains the thrust of Dante's treatise *De monarchia*. Dante argued that a universal monarchy is necessary for the peace and stability of human society. He believed that Christ's birth within the jurisdiction of the Roman Empire indicated divine sanction for it. He asserted that the emperor received the imperial monarchy directly from God and not merely indirectly, through the papacy. Dante did not argue for a single autocratic ruler governing all of Christendom. He favored rather a hierarchy: the individual, the city, the province, the kingdom, the empire. The first four levels were consistent with the scheme of Aristotle, and in the final chapter Dante drew on Aristotle to describe the natural end of man. But Dante went beyond this to argue that an overall empire is necessary because of man's sinful condition. Each member of this hierarchy is supreme within the limits of his sphere. The emperor is therefore not supreme or absolute, but rather the highest authority in rank. Dante's political theory was backward-looking, running counter to the tendencies of the times. Lord Bryce dubbed his *De monarchia* "an epitaph rather than a prophecy."

In hoping for an imperial victory in Italy, Dante was indulging in wishful thinking, for the cities of Lombardy and Tuscany joined the pope in opposing Henry VII. There was a symbolic confrontation between the old and the new, for Emperor Henry paid his troops with gold coins transported in a wagon while Florence paid its soldiers with letters of credit. When Henry VII made his way to Rome, it was more as a suppliant than as a conquering hero. On June 29, 1312, three cardinals crowned him emperor in the Church of St. John Lateran. Much of Italy rose up against him and the world witnessed the spectacle of the Holy Roman emperor, following the will-o'-the-wisp medieval concept of empire, entrapped in the quicksands of Italian politics. His death of disease in a convent near Siena in 1313 was perhaps the easiest way out of a hopeless situation.

LUXEMBURG AND HABSBURG REIGNS

There followed a brief interlude in which Ludwig the Bavarian charged head-long into a first-class imbroglio with Pope John XXII. Ludwig gained the support of Milan, Verona, Mantua, and Lucca, and moved into Rome in January 1328, forcing King Robert of Naples to withdraw. The pope put Rome under an inter-dict, but Ludwig retaliated by deposing the pope for *lèse majesté* and heresy. He called the pope a veritable Antichrist and had a counterpope elected in Rome. In August 1338 the diet in Frankfort declared that the power of the emperor was derived directly from God and not indirectly through the pope. Ludwig gave sanctuary to such antipapal writers as Marsiglio of Padua and William of Occam. In October 1347 Ludwig died unexpectedly while on a hunt.

With the election of Charles IV (1347–1378) the imperial crown returned to the house of Luxemburg. Charles proved to be in nearly every respect a remark-able ruler. He made of Prague a beautiful capital city, and in 1348 founded there the first university in German lands. He learned a great deal from the France of Philip the Fair, and introduced into Bohemia methods of centralized government, establishing more precise fiscal control, the use of Roman law, and a territorial law codified as the *Majestas carolina*. At the diets of Nuremberg, 1355, and of Metz, 1356, he gave the empire the beginnings of a written constitution.

The Golden Bull of 1356 regularized in law the imperial electoral college, which had grown up by custom and long usage. Three ecclesiastical princes (the archbishops of Mainz, Trier, and Cologne) and four secular princes (the king of Bohemia, the margrave of Brandenburg, the duke of Saxony, and the count pala-tine of the Rhine) were to serve as the seven electors. The territories of the electors were declared to be indivisible and the four secular principalities were to be in-herited by the law of primogeniture. Charles's aim had been to regularize election proceedings and thus to stabilize the political situation in the empire. The effect of the Golden Bull was to elevate the most powerful princes to a state of virtual sovereignty and to acknowledge legally their authority in the empire, to the dis-advantage of the emperor.

Under Wenceslas (1378–1410), the son of Charles IV, the empire quickly got out of hand, for Wenceslas was a playboy. The Rhenish electors deposed him, gave the crown to Rupert of the Palatinate, and finally turned to a younger son of Charles IV, Sigismund. Sigismund (1410–1437), the last of the Luxemburg em-perors, had been married to the daughter of King Louis of Hungary and Poland. When Louis died it seemed that Sigismund would rule over a mighty kingdom embracing Poland, Bohemia, and Hungary, but the Poles broke away and elected as their king Prince Jagiello of Lithuania. Sigismund took possession of Hungary, but that triumph brought him face to face with the terrible Turk. The Turks defeated the Serbs in 1389 and at Nicopolis in 1396 they slaughtered the Hungarians and came close to capturing Sigismund himself. Luckily for Sigismund, the Turks then turned their attention to Greece and Byzantium, giving the West a brief respite. The highlight of his career was the role he played as a "new Constantine," leading in the reform of the church at the Council of Constance. But the burning of Jan Hus precipitated the Hussite revolt in his own Bohemia. Sigismund died without a male heir.

With the election of Sigismund's son-in-law Albrecht II (1438–1439) the Habsburgs once again assumed the imperial title. During the long reign of his lethargic successor, Frederick III (1440–1493), the Habsburgs suffered tremendous losses. Not only did the emperor lose Bohemia and Hungary, but he even evacuated Vienna and ruled from Linz out of fear of King Matthew Corvinus of Hungary. The independent Swiss confederation encroached further on Habsburg holdings and various lands were disbursed among members of the Habsburg family. On the other hand, Frederick III lost none of the Habsburg talent for arranging profitable marriages for his family. He married his son Maximilian to Mary, daughter of Duke Charles the Bold of Burgundy, thereby bringing under Habsburg control France-Comté, Luxemburg, and various prosperous industrial provinces in the Netherlands.

On Frederick's death his son Maximilian (1493–1519) aroused high hopes for a restoration of vigorous imperial leadership. He was an athletic type, renowned as a bear hunter and mountain climber, gallant and chivalrous, every inch a knight. He was the darling of the nationalistic German humanists for his patronage of artists and authors and for the promise he offered of the restoration of German greatness. The imperial eagle would at last soar far above the Gallic cock and the Venetian lion! But in both domestic and foreign policy Maximilian proved to be impractical and ineffective. Yet once again Habsburg fortunes rose, for they gained before the altar what they failed to win by the sword.

Philip, the son of Maximilian and Mary, was married in 1496 to Joanna, daughter of King Ferdinand and Queen Isabella of Spain. When in October Philip arrived to claim his bride, he was eighteen and she sixteen. The two young people fell madly in love at first sight. Overwhelmed by passion, they could not wait for a formal church wedding. The court chaplain married them that evening and they slept together that very night. But alas, Philip's ardor soon cooled, and a chronicler relates that while Joanna "loved her husband with a great passion, he did not respond to her feelings in a like manner." Hell has no fury like a woman scorned, as a number of people have had occasion to remark, and Joanna attacked Philip with a pair of scissors. She was declared to be quite mad. But for all their personal difficulties, the laws of dynastic inheritance were still operative. Through Joanna

Philip came into possession of Castile. Furthermore, Joanna bore him a son, Prince Charles, who was to inherit an empire in Europe and in faraway lands discovered by an Italian adventurer whose voyages had been sponsored by his grandmother.

Charles, born in 1500, inherited from Philip the Burgundian lands and Castile when he was only six years old. In 1516, on the death of his grandfather, King Ferdinand, he fell heir also to Aragon, Sicily, Naples, Sardinia, and Hispanic America. When Maximilian died in 1519, Charles received in addition the Austrian lands from Tyrol to Styria. In that same year the electors chose him emperor of the Holy Roman Empire. Charles ruled over half of Europe as Charles I of Spain and Charles V of the empire. The clever turn of phrase applied in later centuries to the Austrian branch of the family was no less true of the early Habsburgs: "Others make war, but you, fortunate Austria, marry!"

TERRITORIAL PRINCIPALITIES

Within the empire the power of the princes steadily increased from the fourteenth to the sixteenth centuries. The emperors themselves were for the most part dependent upon the revenues and manpower of their family territories. In effect, they were princes who bore also the title of emperor. The electors and other princes of the empire, great and small, long persisted in treating their lands as feudal possessions, but they gradually learned to administer their territories as integral states. The territories developed diets (*Landtage*) analogous to the imperial diets. The princes employed learned chancellors, built up bureaucracies and standing armies, developed fiscal systems, and introduced Roman law, just like the national monarchs to the west. Württemberg, Bavaria, Hesse, Brandenburg, the Palatinate, and Saxony were already powerful states at the start of this period. They never ceased to aggrandize themselves further at the expense of the church, their smaller neighbors, the emperor, and the cities.

The cities were gradually losing their freedom and initiative. The Hanse cities in the north were in decline and the free cities in the west and south were tiny enclaves embedded in territorial principalities, hemmed in and unable to expand. Within the walls the city councils exercised great control over the hospitals, endowments, chapels, and churches.

The territorial princes assumed astonishing prerogatives in governing the church within their own domains. They were in many cases virtually lay bishops over the proprietary church, for they nominated clergy for appointments, controlled finances, cared for church buildings, and even, like sacramental kings, decided matters of a spiritual nature. The duke of Cleves, for example, declared himself to be "pope in his own land." Rudolf IV of Austria in the fourteenth century announced, "On my soil I intend to be pope, archbishop, bishop, archdeacon, and deacon." Even when one makes allowances for rhetoric, it is obvious that the princes were in the ascendancy. The empire as a political power was in decline and the church was experiencing increasing difficulties.

The New Monarchies

IN CONTRAST to the empire, the kingdoms of France, England, and Spain developed national monarchies and eventually became nation-states. Certain lawyers of the period, in order to explain the obvious discrepancy between the theoretical subordination of a king to the emperor and the actual independence of the monarchs in the west, coined the phrase "A king is emperor in his own kingdom."

FRANCE

France enjoyed a more advantageous geographic location than the empire, which had no natural frontiers. With the sea on three sides, France was almost inevitably impelled toward the Rhine, its natural boundary on the east. France was also fortunate in the amazing continuity of its royal lineage. From Hugh Capet in 987 to Louis Philippe in 1848, all its kings were princes of the Capetian line. Many of its rulers were strong and able, such as Philip II Augustus in the twelfth century, Philip IV (the Fair) at the end of the thirteenth century and the beginning of the fourteenth, and the dynamic Louis XI near the end of the fifteenth century.

The French monarchy succeeded in developing a centralized bureaucracy designed for the efficient mobilization of societal resources, in contrast to the feudal self-regulating society, which distributed social functions according to status groupings that were defined by custom and inheritance. During the second half of the thirteenth century the council of the king (*curia regis*) began differentiating its functions more clearly. There developed the *parlement* for justice, the *chambre de comptes* for finance, and the *grand conseil* to serve the king. During the fifteenth century this council divided into a large council and a smaller secret or privy council, which during the following century came to be known as the *conseil des affaires*. Royal authority was represented locally by agents called the *prévôts*, who served as judges and financial officers. The central government learned early to appoint deputies (called *baillis* in the north and *sénéchaux* in the south) to represent it in specific divisions of the royal domain, which by the end of the fifteenth century included most of the realm.

During the thirteenth and fourteenth centuries the French monarchs were still relatively weak and had to turn to the provincial estates for financial support, beyond the revenue drawn from their own domain. The estates general evolved as a "national institution," although for a long time the representatives of the north and of the south (Languedoc) met separately. The feudal duties of vassals to provide aid (*auxilium*) and advice (*consilium*) were reflected in the deliberation of the estates general, which could articulate grievances only after having first voted funds for the ruler. These taxes were significantly known as *aides*. As the French monarchs gained in strength, they found that they could manage well without convening the estates general, which became increasingly insignificant as the fourteenth and fifteenth centuries wore on, and in reality did not represent the whole realm.

The French monarchy developed a royal army that was not dependent upon the feudal obligations of vassals. The Great Ordinance of 1439 forbade powerful feudal lords to retain private troops and reserved to the king the power of appointing captains. The century-long war with England greatly accelerated the changes in the bureaucracy, the fiscal system, and the military organization as France underwent its metamorphosis from a feudal state to a more unified monarchy.

The Hundred Years' War. As France and England developed a stronger sense of national identity, they were drawn into conflict. For the English king held the duchy of Guienne, in southwestern France, as a fief under the French crown, and therefore was required to do homage to the French king as his vassal. The English crown enjoyed valuable revenue from the export-import duties on Bordeaux wine from Guienne, but resented holding it as a dependency and wished to assert a full sovereign claim to it. Another conflict of interest involved Flanders, an industrial area that was a rich fief highly coveted by the French, but which was also of great economic importance to the English. Four-fifths of England's raw-wool exports went to Flanders in exchange for finished textiles, and the English king profited from duties on the trade. The English therefore supported the counts of Flanders in their efforts to retain independence, and when Flanders was overrun by the French, the English encouraged the cities of Flanders to resist them.

The first serious clash came in 1294 in a trial of strength between the dynamic French king Philip the Fair (1285–1314) and one of England's greatest monarchs, Edward I (1272–1307). But both were distracted by other problems and made peace in 1303. In 1337 Edward III (1327–1377), grandson of Edward I, initiated a war with the French which was to drag on for over a century. The English were angry with the French for supporting their ancient foes the Scots. Moreover, the French king Philip VI (1328–1350) seemed to be unusually vulnerable, for he was a dreamer who cultivated a fanciful court life and schemed to acquire the imperial crown, to win new lands in Italy, and even to retake the Holy Land. Edward III managed his finances cleverly, licensing wool exports, forbidding wasteful tourneys, raising taxes against the hated French, and repudiating debts to Italian bankers. He had the English well organized militarily, with two musters a year, increased use of foot soldiers, who were less expensive than cavalry, and companies of longbowmen. His strategy was to raid at will, ravaging the countryside throughout western France and thus weakening his rival. In this long first phase of the war the English won three particularly important victories, one by sea and two on land. In the sea battle at Sluis, the port for Bruges, a combined English and Flemish fleet destroyed the French flotilla. In 1346 at Crécy, near the Somme River, the English won a pitched battle against the French army. From an elevated position above a valley, thousands of English longbowmen rained death on the French below. The longbow could be shot much more rapidly than the crossbow, which needed to be rewound after each shot. Though the English were greatly outnumbered, their superior weapons and mobility proved devastating to the French in their cumbersome armor. The French king's own brother fell, and Philip VI himself had two horses killed under him. The English went on to attack Calais and took it after a siege lasting nearly a year. Calais was an important port and bridgehead for troop landings. The French were glad to accept an armistice in 1347. Both sides were so ravaged by the Black Death in the two or three years that followed that they felt no great urge to kill each other.

The reign of Philip VI's son and successor, John II (1350–1364), was disastrous for France. The English thought the time ripe to strike again. Edward III's heir, Edward the Black Prince, who was a brilliant field commander, landed troops at Bordeaux in 1355 and led them southward almost to the Mediterranean. The next year he won the second great land battle in the first phase of the war, the battle of Poitiers. The French had learned nothing from Crécy, fought ten years before, and sent succeeding waves of heavily armored knights straight into a hail of arrows. The English cavalry rode around behind the French and took King John II himself captive. The French gladly accepted the Treaty of Bretigny in 1360, which assured the English of sovereignty over Calais and their territory in the southwest.

With the king in a London prison, France nearly disintegrated. The estates general, led by a wealthy merchant, Étienne Marcel, turned on the dauphin, Charles, executed some of his courtiers, and forced him to accept some reforms. The peasants, enraged by taxes and the failure of the king and feudal lords to protect them from marauding bands of mercenaries, unleashed a terrifying revolt, called the Jacquerie (the gentry, who could hardly be expected to concern themselves with peasants' names, called them all Jacques). Marcel allied himself with the peasants, but in a street uprising in the city he was killed, and the dauphin reentered Paris. When King John II died in London, the dauphin ascended what was left of the throne as Charles V.

Charles V (1364–1380) earned the sobriquet "the Wise" by introducing a new style of government. He placed the fiscal system on a firmer basis by requiring regular and continuous taxation. He reorganized the royal army, and sent able captains such as the wily Bertrand du Guesclin into the field when he renewed the war in 1369. Constable Guesclin avoided pitched battles, but harassed the English until he wore them down. The French retook all the English territories except Calais, Bordeaux, Bayonne, and some minor fortified places. In 1375 Pope Gregory XI managed to arrange an armistice, just in time for a change in the cast of characters. The Black Prince died in 1376, Edward III died in 1377, and Charles V died in 1380. There followed about thirty-five years of relative quiet, for both countries were beset by internal difficulties. Under its next two kings France fell into nearly complete chaos.

Royal power reached its nadir under Charles VI (1380–1422), known in the chronicles as "the Mad." He was only twelve when fate lifted him to the throne. The Flemish burghers took advantage of his minority to revolt and the feudal lords seized the opportunity to regain their former independence. On an expedition in 1382 to Brittany, which the French had long sought to unite with their realm, the first unmistakable signs of the king's mental disorder appeared. The next year several people were burned to death at a ball, and at the sight of this horror the king went completely out of his mind.

Then civil war broke out, for the houses of Orléans and Burgundy saw an opportunity to move into the power vacuum. Duke Louis of Orléans, the king's brother, opposed the ascendancy of the house of Burgundy. In 1407 Duke John of Burgundy had the duke of Orléans assassinated in a Paris street. His son, Charles of Orléans, and his supporters, called the Armagnacs after his tough father-in-law, who came from Armagnac in southwestern France, took up arms against John of Burgundy. The butchers and artisans of Paris rose up, organized a commune, declared in favor of Burgundy, and seized the Bastille, while the mad king donned the white cap of the Parisians. But the Armagnacs triumphed, suppressed the revolt, made war on the duke of Burgundy, and kept the king under control.

To the English the moment seemed right to strike again. In 1415 they renewed the war, closing the second phase of relative quiescence and initiating the third and final phase, which began with victories for the English and ended with their defeat. The bellicose young King Henry V (1413–1422), urged on by the English nobility, saw a chance for glory. Henry V not only claimed the territories once taken by Edward III, but declared himself to be the rightful heir to the French throne and demanded the daughter of Charles VI for his queen. His claim was not wholly fanciful. Edward III, Henry's great-grandfather, had actually been more closely related to Charles IV of France than Philip VI, who inherited Charles's throne. Philip was the son of Charles's uncle; Edward was the son of Charles's sister, who had married Edward II of England. Philip claimed the throne of France under Salic law, which barred females from the line of succession, but the English had ever since claimed that the French throne should have gone to Edward, and after him to his heirs.

Henry V landed at Calais and in the legendary battle of Agincourt he inflicted a near total defeat upon the French. The French confronted him there with a feudal army, largely made up of the Armagnacs, and repeated the blunders of Poitiers and Crécy. The crossbowmen were placed in the rear, where they were ineffective. The knights dismounted and sloshed forward in heavy armor until, weary and mired down in inches of mud, they were virtually immobilized. Those who escaped the rain of arrows were cut down where they stood by English foot soldiers. The flower of French chivalry lay dead on the field at the close of the day, including Charles of Orléans and the duke of Bourbon.

Even with the hated English on its soil, France was torn apart by civil war. The Burgundians acknowledged Henry V as king of France, entered Paris, and slaughtered the Armagnacs. In 1419 the Armagnacs treacherously murdered Duke John the Fearless of Burgundy to avenge the assassination of the duke of Orléans twelve years before. The new duke of Burgundy, Philip the Good (1419–1467), joined England's Henry V, who had been systematically conquering Normandy, in an offensive against the dauphin, Charles. By the Treaty of Troyes, 1420, Henry V was made heir to the French throne. He married Catherine, the daughter of Charles VI, and entered Paris with Charles. The estates general accepted the treaty and the dauphin retreated south of the Loire. At this critical juncture Henry V died. Then occurred one of the strangest episodes in all of French history.

Henry VI (1422–1461) was a ten-month-old infant when he was proclaimed in Paris to be the king of England and France. During his minority his two uncles, the duke of Gloucester and the duke of Bedford, governed for him in England and France respectively. North of the Loire River only Orléans held out against the English, and in 1428 Bedford undertook to bring it to submission. The French claimant to the throne, Charles VII, was a weakling, dubbed the king of Bourges for his provisional capital, who had neither the will nor the ability to save Orléans. In this major crisis France was saved by a peasant girl and the will of an aroused people, who hated the foreigners on French soil.

At Domrémy in Champagne, Joan of Arc heard the voices of saints urging her to free France and to bring Charles VII to Rheims for his royal coronation. Born in 1412, Joan was the youngest child in a family of five. She could neither read nor write, but she was a pious, serious girl who learned to spin and sew like other peasant girls. When only thirteen Joan first became aware of voices speaking to her, sometimes accompanied by a blaze of light—the voices of St. Michael, St. Margaret, and St. Catherine, and the voices of angels. By May 1428 she was certain of her mission to save France, and a few weeks later she presented herself to the commander of Charles VII's troops in the nearby town of Vancouleurs. The commander told the cousin who had come with her to "take her home to her father and give her a sound thrashing."

The voices were insistent: "It is God who commands it." In January 1429 Joan appeared again before the skeptical officer and impressed him by announcing the

French defeat near Orléans days before the news arrived. On March 8 she was permitted to travel in male attire to Chinon to see Charles VII. He disguised himself among his attendants to test her, but she spotted him immediately and spoke to him of her mission. A commission of bishops and theologians found nothing heretical in her views. She then ordered the English to leave France and led an attack against them. On April 30 she entered Orléans. On May 7 she was wounded by an arrow in the breast, but the next day the last English stronghold outside the city fell.

The king's fearful counselors hesitated to follow up the victory with a quick campaign against the English, but they opened up the road to Rheims. There, with all the ancient pomp and ceremony, Charles VII was crowned on July 17, 1429. Joan stood by, bearing her standard, for, she said, "since it had shared in the labor, it was only fair that it should share also in the victory." An attempt to take Paris late in August failed, and Joan, wounded in the thigh by a bolt from a crossbow, was out of action for the winter.

On May 24, 1430, she led the French troops into Compiègne at sunrise to prevent its occupation by the Burgundians. Toward evening she was captured on a sortie outside the walls. The Burgundians sold Joan to the English for a handsome price. Charles VII, to his shame, did nothing to rescue her. Imprisoned in Rouen, at first in an iron cage with her neck, hands, and feet in chains, she was tried for heresy before the unscrupulous bishop of Beauvais, a tool of the Burgundians. On May 30, 1431, she was executed. Tied to the stake, she asked for a cross, and someone brought her one. As the flames and smoke rose up around her she gazed at the cross, called upon Jesus, and until the last "declared that her voices came from God and had not deceived her." Her ashes were scattered into the Seine.

Charles VII, tagged "the Well Served," had good counselors. He introduced regular and systematic tax levies not dependent on the approval of the estates general. He took advantage of a truce with the English to reorganize his troops into twenty "ordinance companies" under professional captains. Each company consisted of a hundred lances, each lance made up of six cavalrymen and accompanied by bowmen and artillery. In 1449 the French renewed the offensive, liberated Normandy, and seized Bordeaux and Bayonne. In 1453 the French repulsed a new invasion attempt at Castillon and the long war was over. The English retained a toehold on the continent, however, by keeping Calais until 1558.

The Emergence of Strong Monarchy. During the century that followed the end of the Hundred Years' War four French kings of unusual ability graced the throne. All of them were able to build upon the administrative, fiscal, and military reforms of Charles VII. The first of these was Charles VII's son Louis XI (1461–1483), who won a place in history as one of France's great monarchs. A man of feverish impatience, he worked with restless energy to make his centralized government more efficient. Philippe de Commynes, a famous chronicler, who went over to the king from Burgundy, analyzed his tactic of finding support with the burghers and common people against the feudal forces. He improved the economy by introducing new textile industries in the north, a silk industry in Lyon, and an improved system of government inspection and quality control. He was ostentatiously pious in order to hold the loyalty of the clergy.

He needed all the strength he could muster, for the forces of feudalism in alliance with the land of Burgundy now made one last effort to challenge the king and the consolidation of a national dynasty. Charles the Bold (1467–1477) of Burgundy had visions of building an independent state in the old Lotharingian territories by adding Alsace and Lorraine to Burgundy and Flanders. He even envisioned winning the French crown or the imperial crown. Luckily for Louis XI, Charles was killed outside the walls of Nancy in 1477 and the threat subsided. Louis XI succeeded in gaining only a small portion of Burgundy for France, however, for Mary, the heiress of Burgundy, married Maximilian of Austria in 1477. When she died in 1482, Maximilian and Louis XI concluded the Treaty of Arras, by which Maximilian yielded a sizable part of French-speaking Burgundy to Louis XI.

Charles VIII (1483–1498) was a boy of thirteen at the time of his father's death. He grew up to be a man of action like his father, but he lacked judiciousness. He foiled the Habsburgs' scheme to acquire Brittany by their usual method, marriage. They arranged for Princess Margaret of Austria to wed Charles VIII, while Maximilian was to marry Anne of Brittany. But in a sudden reversal, Charles VIII marched into Brittany and compelled Anne to marry him.

Although it might appear that Charles was showing concern for rounding out the natural frontier of France by securing the great peninsula reaching out into the sea, he proved very shortly that he was still thinking dynastically rather than nationally. For in 1494–1495 he embarked upon an ill-fated Italian expedition to assert French claims upon Naples. Only a fool or a madman would have done it, Commynes observed, for he risked much with but little to gain. But it was a spectacle that long excited the imagination of patriotic Frenchmen. When those foot soldiers of Charles VIII padded down into the plains of Lombardy, the historian Jules Michelet burbled, "The Alps were lowered forever!" Charles VIII withdrew within a year, for his troops were decimated by disease and he feared that his long communication line might be cut. But that unhappy adventure initiated a series of invasions and decades of dominance over Italy by the great states of the north and west.

Louis XII (1498–1515) of the house of Orléans married Charles VIII's widow, Anne of Brittany. He devoted himself to further strengthening the central government and to subduing feudal vassals. It was fortunate for France that he succeeded so well, for as a result of further adventures in northern Italy involving claims to Milan, he became embroiled in a struggle with the Habsburgs. His successor, Francis I (1515–1547) of the house of Angoulême, had to fight out four wars with Emperor Charles V, whose lands encircled France on nearly all sides. Under Francis I Renaissance culture flowered in France.

Even this necessarily abbreviated account of French history from the fourteenth to the sixteenth centuries makes quite clear how the vicissitudes of war, the accidents of life and death, the will of the people when the king lacked one, the most bizarre and unforeseeable events all made the formation of the French national monarchy and state anything but a foregone conclusion. The tendencies toward political centralization and the development of a capitalist economy were active as historical forces, but the will and ability of men aided or frustrated by seemingly chance events determined the actual course of French history.

BURGUNDY

Strange as such a judgment may seem against the somber account of the Hundred Years' War, the most serious threat to the French state may have been posed by Burgundy. The dukes of Burgundy came very close to establishing a rich and powerful "middle kingdom" that would have shut France off from eastward expansion and left it in a relatively weak position. The dukes of Burgundy, as a French line, succeeded in winning the loyalty of many French-speaking areas and were deeply involved in the struggle against the dukes of Orléans and the French kings themselves. Ironically, a French monarch quite inadvertently gave to Burgundy its opportunity for a century of greatness.

When the Burgundian ducal family died out after 330 years, King John II of France bestowed Burgundy upon his youngest son, Philip the Bold (1364–1404), as a feudal appanage, and Philip began the process of territorial aggrandizement that eventually made of Burgundy a major power. When he married Margaret, heiress of Flanders and Artois, he combined agricultural Burgundy with industrial Flanders, a potentially dynamic union. In subsequent decades the dukes of Burgundy added Picardy, Brabant, Hennegau, Zeeland, Holland, Luxemburg, and Gelders. John the Fearless (1404–1419) contributed less to the rise of Burgundy, but Philip the Good (1419–1467) and Charles the Bold (1467–1477) worked toward a centralized administration for Burgundy, although the only tie with Flanders and their other territories remained dynastic and personal rather than constitutional and public.

The final confrontation of France and Burgundy came during the reigns of King Louis XI and Duke Charles the Bold. Charles the Bold was consumed with the ambition of building a kingdom between France and the empire which would correspond to ancient Lotharingia. His territory would run from Switzerland to the North Sea, and he would no longer be duke, but king, under the suzerainty of the Holy Roman emperor. During his last years Charles seemed increasingly to lose his grip on reality and to undertake rash and ill-advised adventures. At last, on January 5, 1477, while besieging Nancy, Charles the Bold was killed by the duke of Lorraine. Half his army betrayed him and the other half was slaughtered in flight. Charles's body was found two days later, surrounded by the bodies of Burgundian nobles. His head was split from the crown to the jaw and his face had been gnawed away by wolves.

Burgundy was an anomaly, for even while the duke was centralizing its administration and introducing ordinance companies into its military on the French pattern, court life and manners remained chivalric. In society and custom it was the classic example of the waning of the Middle Ages. In 1430 Philip the Good created the Order of the Golden Fleece, an exclusive fraternity of aristocrats limited at first to twenty-four and then to thirty gentlemen. Olivier de la Marche recounted how in 1454, after the fall of Constantinople, the court held a great banquet in order to rally the men of good blood for a crusade. The decorations included such elaborate ornaments as a cake with twenty-four musicians inside playing their instruments. At the climactic moment the noble knights arose, took a vow to go on a crusade to free the Christian East from the Turks, and then went home again. In the decadence of fifteenth-century Burgundy, the substitution of symbol for action seemed perfectly reasonable.

In retrospect it is easy to see some of the weaknesses inherent in the Burgundian position that made the dreams of Charles the Bold impossible. Unlike France, which had a geographical center and a nucleus in the royal domain on which to build, Burgundy stretched along the Rhine from Switzerland to the North Sea, with its nuclei of power strung out in a wavering line. Theoretically the economy was diversified and complementary: Burgundy was agricultural and Flanders was industrial, which should have made for cohesion and strength. But the trade lines were set in other directions—Flanders engaged in trade with England, for example—and rationalizing the economy on a major scale was beyond the conception of the dukes and surely beyond their ability. Moreover, the dukes were at a political disadvantage, for the French monarch enjoyed the aura of divinity that hedges round a king, while the duke of Burgundy never acquired the status of royalty. He was duke of Burgundy, duke of Brabant, but count of Flanders, with no single title for all his domains. In the seventeen provinces of the Netherlands he had to deal with the estates in terms of local law and custom. A century did not provide sufficient time for Burgundy to coalesce into a unified power.

ENGLAND

The fourteenth and fifteenth centuries were of critical importance for the development of the English state, for they witnessed the decline of medieval institutions and the transition to a new style of monarchy. The king had enjoyed nearly unrestrained powers in a relatively narrow sphere. Now the conception of a primarily tenurial relationship with lines running down through the feudal hierarchy gave way to a broader vision of the king as leader of all the people of the realm, concerned with the common welfare. People in turn were conceived of less in relation to their positions in the feudal hierarchy than as members of estates or orders within society. The king came to consult these estates, represented in parliament, rather than merely his feudal tenants in chief as part of his council. The estates gradually came to appreciate the fact that those who had the power to grant the requests of the king also had the power to refuse them, and thus the formal political instrument for restraining the king and his bureaucracy came into being. The bureaucracy itself established procedures, created precedents, and developed traditions that made the workings of government less personal and served as a restraint upon the will of the king. A feeling of identity as a people and of identification with the king, an incipient form of nationalism, developed as a corollary to the new relation of the monarchy to the people. The old schism between Norman overlords and Anglo-Saxon underlings gave way to a common feeling of Englishness that was to help sustain the realm against foes on the island and across the channel.

King and Parliament. The fourteenth century opened with one of England's greatest monarchs on the throne, Edward I (1272–1307) of the Plantagenet line. A tall and handsome man, he had a passion for military exercises and tournaments. The general effect of his reign, however, was to move England away from feudalism toward a new phase in political life. As a strong ruler he kept the barons under control. He broadened the sources of royal revenue to include property taxes and customs duties. He appointed councilors who served as efficient bureaucrats in carrying out the ordinary duties of government and in preparing legislation for parliament to act on. During the first two decades of his reign, which were relatively peaceful, a large body of legislation was enacted into law which codified as statutes the precedents of common law in both civil and criminal matters. Finding himself in great difficulty as a result of a rebellion in Wales, Scottish resistance, and trouble with France, he summoned the "Model Parliament" in 1295, representing all three estates, clergy, nobility, and commons. The magnates and representatives of the shires and towns approved the grants of money that the king needed for his governmental and military operations. In his summons to the parliament, Edward I expressed the idea that the parliament represented the nation: "What touches all should be approved of all, and it is also clear that common dangers should be met by measures agreed upon in common."

Parliament grew out of the Great Council of the king's ecclesiastical and lay vassals. From the outset Edward I summoned it frequently, and in 1295 he called together a parliament made up of the lords temporal and spiritual, two or more knights elected from each shire by the freeholders at the shire court, and two or more burgesses from every city, borough, and important town. He wished to gain the support of the propertied classes for his policies and to strengthen the ties between the central and local governments. Subsidies for the crown voted by the barons and the representatives of shires and towns assembled in parliament constituted a legal impost upon the whole realm. Voting taxes upon oneself was considered a dubious privilege. The clergy remained aloof and met in its own convocations in Canterbury and York to vote subsidies. Many representatives of the commons were reluctant to vote taxes, were shy about sitting with the great magnates, and were discouraged by their fellows from collecting their expense money of two shillings a day, and so they absented themselves whenever they could. Ironically, it was due to the fact that the king was strong enough to make them attend parliamentary sessions that parliament developed as the most important institution in English political life. It was not at first thought of as a check by the people upon the arbitrary use of royal power.

The fact that parliament was summoned always to a specific place, Westminster, instead of to various towns about the country, gave it a more permanent character than it would otherwise have had. Parliament developed important judicial functions as a high court to hear petitions and order the redress of grievances, handling cases not within the competence of the common law courts. A fixed place of meeting also encouraged the development of parliament as a court of appeal.

The reign of Edward II (1307–1327), a weak and ineffective king, was fairly disastrous at home and abroad. He was dominated by his queen, Isabelle of France, imprisoned, and finally murdered by his custodians. In his one great military adventure his army was soundly beaten at Bannockburn by Robert Bruce and the Scots in 1314. His very ineffectiveness, however, enabled parliament to insist upon the right to approve the king's councilors and to punish them for abuse of their authority. The parliament finally even deposed the king and declared the succession of his son.

The long reign of Edward III (1327–1377) was of tremendous importance for the political evolution of England, for the king's war with the Scots and his deep involvement in the Hundred Years' War meant that he had to make great concessions to parliament at home. The king's need for the goodwill and support of the populace led to constitutional developments important not only for England but for the whole Western democratic tradition. The question of whether officials were responsible to the king as his servants, as Edward III held, or to the entire realm represented in parliament was crucial. During Edward's preoccupation with the French war parliament pressed for the principle of impeachment, the Lords bringing officials to trial at the request of the Commons.

Parliament itself went through a critical development during this period as it assumed what was to be its permanent shape. Up to this time the lower clergy had deliberated separately, while the knights and burgesses, recognizing their common social and economic interests, began to sit together. By the mid-fourteenth century parliament had separated into two houses, Lords and Commons, with somewhat specialized functions. Edward III summoned to the Great Council, metamorphosing into the House of Lords, men whose fathers had belonged to the Great Council, thus developing a parliamentary peerage. The ecclesiastical component of the Lords was reduced, but remained numerically preponderant. But perhaps even more significant was the formalization of the House of Commons, made up of the knights of the shire and the representatives of the towns. The principle of representative government, which already had a long tradition in the local courts, was thus transferred to the national central institution. The House of Commons met separately in the chapter house of the abbot of Westminster. It still had an inferior position to the House of Lords, to which it presented petitions for action. If these were passed and accepted by the king they became official statutes. Gradually the Commons established the custom that all financial legislation had to be initiated by them. The purse strings thus came more and more into the hands of the Commons, and if the Commons could grant money, they soon learned also how to refuse it.

In the early fourteenth century statutes were not framed by the judges and entered on the statute rolls until parliament had been discharged from attendance. Significant discrepancies began to appear between the intent of parliament and the final form of statutes. It was not until early in the fifteenth century that legislation by bill and statute was regularized so that the will of parliament was no longer expressed merely by petitions subject to change by the king's ministers. Who could tell that the future belonged to parliament and the people, not to king or queen?

Royal Government. The development of the royal government was one of the most striking political facts of the fourteenth century. Members of the king's *curia regis,* officials who were part of his personal entourage, became more specialized in function as a court of exchequer, a court of common pleas, and, under Edward I, a court of king's bench, which evolved in response to the need for expertise in handling fiscal and legal matters. The House of Lords became well established as the supreme court of the land. Since the king was to administer justice, but was otherwise occupied, the chancellor assumed this duty, and from this developed a new court of the chancellor.

Further noteworthy developments took place in the judiciary as concomitants of the development of local government. The establishment of justices of the peace was a most portentous innovation, for the JPs became very important instruments for implementing the will of the royal government on the local level. The king appointed these justices, usually from among the landed gentry and lesser land-holders. They took over many of the duties once exercised by the sheriffs and took charge of police-court jurisdiction, licensing of alehouses, and setting of wages for laborers, when the central government undertook by statute to regulate prices and wages. The Statute of Laborers of 1351, for example, was designed to force laborers to accept job offers at the same pay scale as prevailed before the labor supply was reduced by the Great Plague of 1349, and the JPs were expected to enforce it locally. They were quite ineffective, however. In 1388 the quarterly sessions were estab-lished, requiring the JPs to meet four times annually to hear cases and to admin-ister certain legislation collectively. Thus, paradoxical as it may seem, the reign of a king whose preoccupation was so predominantly with foreign policy and war proved to be of tremendous importance for England's internal development. The war, in fact, forced Edward III to delegate authority in the interests of fiscal, bureaucratic, and military efficiency. By accentuating his dependence upon the propertied people with land or capital, it furthered the cause of parliamentary government.

During the last quarter of the fourteenth century England went through a severe governmental crisis. If there was something naïvely heroic about Edward III, the career of his successor, Richard II (1377–1400), evokes pity. He was a boy of ten when he inherited the crown, and a council ruled the kingdom during the first difficult years. Shortly after his accession an ill-considered poll tax and other problems precipitated the great peasant revolt of 1381. As the king began to assert his personal control over the government, his weaknesses became apparent, for he was a spendthrift, had a bad temper, and catered to favorites. His idyllic marriage with Anne of Bohemia, daughter of Emperor Charles IV, ended in sorrow with her death in 1394. Richard struck down a traitor, Thomas of Gloucester, who opposed peace with France, and undertook to exercise absolute power, pronounc-ing laws from the throne and levying taxes arbitrarily. While the king was off in Ireland, Henry of Lancaster led a baronial revolt against him. The king surren-dered and in the Tower of London signed his abdication. Parliament deposed Richard II and declared Henry of Lancaster king as Henry IV.

Crises and New Direction.   For England the fifteenth century was one long series of crises. During the first half of the century it scored a triumph in the Hundred Years' War with France and then went down to final defeat. During the second half of the century England was torn apart by baronial warfare until the triumph of the first Tudor king, Henry VII.

In Shakespeare's play *Henry IV* the king declaims, "Uneasy lies the head that wears a crown." Henry IV was beset with trouble on all sides: a revolt in Wales, Scottish resistance, French attacks on the coast, and a rebellion of the earl of Northumberland. Henry beheaded the archbishop of York, who had supported the earl. Executing a man of the church brought great odium upon him, and the populace ascribed Henry's lingering illness to the wrath of God.

His son Henry V (1413–1422) sought to establish peace in the realm by a kind of consensus politics. He gave Richard II an honorable reburial and recalled sworn enemies to court. He reestablished unity in the English church by adopting a hard line against the Lollards and effectively drove their movement underground. With peace and order achieved in church and state, Henry V was free to concentrate on foreign affairs. In that sphere he enjoyed brilliant success, triumphing on the battlefields of France and very nearly winning for himself and his heirs the crown of France. But he left behind an infant son, Henry VI (1422–1571), who was never too bright and at the age of thirty went out of his mind. His rule was chaotic and England suffered losses abroad and disorder at home.

It was in the final year of the Hundred Years' War that the king became mentally deranged. Richard, duke of York, became protector and ruled England until Queen Margaret drove him from power and out of England. Richard returned with an army and launched the first of a series of civil wars known as the Wars of the Roses. The red rose was the badge of Lancaster, the white rose the symbol of York. After a bloody struggle Edward of York emerged as King Edward IV (1461–1483). He devoted his last years to consolidating his power by reducing to impotence the feudal families that opposed him. When he died he left behind two young sons and several daughters. His brother, Richard of Gloucester, became protector of the realm and apparently began to prepare for the coronation of his nephew. But quite precipitously parliament pronounced the two sons of Edward IV to have been illegitimate. Duke Richard assumed the crown at Westminster as Richard III (1483–1485).

Richard III had the two princes imprisoned in the Tower of London and presumably had them killed and buried there. The rumors that the king had murdered his nephews were widely believed throughout England. The *Chronicles of London* relate that for this "cause Richard lost the hearts of the people." When the rumor spread that he was about to marry his niece, Elizabeth of York, popular feeling shifted even more strongly in favor of his rival, Henry Tudor of the house of Lancaster. Richard was not the monster that Tudor historians have made him out to be, but he clearly did not enjoy a good press or a very savory reputation even in his own day.

Henry introduced the great age of the Tudors, which witnessed the birth of English humanism, the Reformation, and the Elizabethan age, by winning with the help of French troops a sensational battle at Bosworth on August 22, 1485. Richard III died fighting fiercely, betrayed by many of his own men, and Henry Tudor became king as Henry VII. He wisely honored the promise he had made to his Yorkist supporters and married Elizabeth, the oldest daughter of Edward IV and the sister of the two princes who had died in the Tower. The white and the red roses were united and all occasion for further fighting was removed, although Henry VII did subsequently have to contend with some annoying Yorkist plots. The Wars of the Roses had been largely confined to the nobility, who fought with their bands of retainers (bastard feudalism) for mastery. They involved no great constitutional principle and no class conflict, and the great mass of the people were not directly concerned. Nevertheless, the unruly barons caused considerable damage, and the constant insecurity and lack of stability were so costly that the townsmen and the gentry alike were thoroughly sick of the whole thing. They were ready now to support a strong king who would check anarchy and establish peace and order. That man was Henry VII.

In spite of the historical legend derived in part from Francis Bacon's history of his reign, Henry VII was not in actual fact a great innovator. He did not inaugurate a "new monarchy," but actually did very little that had not already been begun by the Yorkist kings. In his nearly quarter of a century as king he summoned parliament only three times. His council acted as the court of the Star Chamber, named after the room in which it met, which helped to consolidate his power and restrain insurrection. He was very conservative in his expenditures and husbanded his resources so carefully that in his last years he acquired the reputation of a miser. The security he established encouraged trade and commerce. The people were very grateful and responded with a show of genuine patriotism. An aura of success and pride in the English nation prevailed.

In order to assure the continuity and greatness of his house, Henry VII arranged for the marriage of his oldest son, Arthur, to Catherine, the daughter of Ferdinand and Isabella of Spain. Catherine came to England and married Arthur in St. Paul's Cathedral in 1501. The young prince was only fifteen at the time and their cohabitation was delayed until he should further mature, but maturity never came to him: the following year he died. The king married his daughter Margaret to James IV of Scotland in a move designed to pacify that troublesome neighbor to the north. This marriage had important results in later times, when the Stuarts came to succeed the Tudors on the throne of England. Another daughter, Mary, became the wife of Louis XII of France. Henry VII's second son, Henry, was married to his brother Arthur's widow, Catherine of Aragon. In 1509 he succeeded to his father's throne as King Henry VIII.

SPAIN

A casual glance at the map would suggest that if any state in Europe has natural boundaries set by geography and should have achieved unity with relatively little struggle, that state is Spain. The Iberian peninsula is not only bounded on all sides by the seas, but is marked off by the Pyrenees along its land attachment to neighboring France. Moreover, the national consciousness of Catholic

Spain in subsequent centuries would seem to imply that there was something almost inevitable about the unification of Iberia under Spanish rule.

But in reality centrifugal forces were so powerful that, upon closer examination, the unification of Spain strikes one as having been almost fortuitous. The Iberian peninsula was populated with peoples of a variety of backgrounds and languages. The Basques were different in ethnic background and language from the Castilians. The Navarrese were oriented toward France. The Aragonese spoke a Castilian dialect, but the Catalonians and Valencians, as well as the inhabitants of the Balearic Islands, spoke Limosé, a southern French dialect. The Galicians spoke a language of their own, quite different from the Andalusians'. Moreover, the political history of the constituent parts varied greatly. Castile was plagued with a succession of minor and incompetent kings. Aragon was for centuries oriented toward a Mediterranean policy, and Portugal, which was not united with Spain until 1580, and then only temporarily, had a language, tradition, and foreign policy of its own. The national unification of Spain was anything but assured. In fact, Spain's two most prominent constituent states, Castile and Aragon, maintained separate political institutions and tariff barriers beyond the sixteenth century.

Like the territories of the Holy Roman Empire, both Castile and Aragon increased the centralization of their separate political institutions, but this very fact made their coalescence into a unified Spain more difficult. The king in each country had a great amount of power that could be used despotically. The cortes, or parliament, was not a national institution, for even though Castile and León had a common cortes after 1301, Aragon, Catalonia, and Valencia each had a cortes of its own, and these were never united. Moreover, the basis for representation in the cortes differed in each state. Although the townsmen gained representation as the third estate in every cortes, there was no systematic representational principle. In Castile and León some eighteen leading towns finally preempted the right of representation for the third estate. But no formal constitution defined the rights of the cortes, and the legislative power of the assembly was very limited. How much influence it exercised over the country depended entirely upon the strength or weakness of the monarch. Royal power vacillated wildly, especially in Castile.

The union of Castile and Aragon was achieved in the marriage bed. With the marriage in 1469 of Isabella of Castile (1474–1504) and Ferdinand of Aragon (1479–1516), the two kingdoms were united in the persons of their rulers. The two Catholic monarchs were proclaimed king and queen of Castile together, although Isabella never conceded any of her sovereign power to Ferdinand.

The Spanish Inquisition became an important instrument for the unification of Spain, for it was for a long time the one institution common to all parts of the kingdom. It was authorized by Pope Sixtus IV in 1478, and the three chief inquisitors functioned as a department of the government. Spain still glowed with crusading fervor from the long, hard drive against the Moors. The Inquisition now undertook to complete the Catholicization of the land, forcing the converted Jews (*Marranos*) and Moslems (*Moriscos*) to give up their former religious practices or suffer the consequences. In 1492 the Jews who resisted conversion were expelled from Spain. The cost to Spain in able tradesmen and intellectuals was enormous, as many of its most energetic and enterprising citizens fled to other parts of Europe.

Between 1481 and 1492 Ferdinand and Isabella completed the final subjugation of Granada, the last independent Moslem state on the Iberian peninsula. In a series of measures culminating in their final exile in 1502, the Moslems were driven out. With the homeland secure, Spain's monarchs were now free to promote the exploration of new routes to the Far East. Their support of Columbus' first voyage in 1492 proved to be one of the best investments ever made.

Ferdinand manipulated his foreign policy very cleverly. In exchange for a promise to remain neutral while the French king Charles VIII embarked upon his expedition to Naples in 1494, Ferdinand won the return of Roussillon to Spain. In 1497 Ferdinand intervened in Italy himself and began a duel with France for the domination of Italy that continued in the Habsburg-Valois wars in the sixteenth century. He managed his family marriages in such a way as to make maximum gains for his dynasty, principally directing them as diplomatic weapons against France. He married his daughter Catherine of Aragon, it will be recalled, to Prince Arthur, the oldest son of Henry VII of England, and then to Arthur's brother, Henry. Ferdinand's daughter Joanna married Philip, the son of Emperor Maximilian. By this alliance, however, Spain was drawn into the Habsburg political nexus and the affairs of central Europe, instead of remaining free to pursue its own rather obvious national interests of expansion into Portugal and North Africa. But on the surface it seemed like a brilliant match.

Ferdinand's domestic rule was for a decade ably administered by the brilliant Cardinal Ximénez, archbishop of Toledo. When, therefore, Ferdinand's grandson became King Charles I of Spain, he inherited a powerful kingdom that had made great strides toward world leadership. Small wonder that Machiavelli, who so prided himself on his political realism, held Ferdinand in great esteem as an admirable and successful prince.

IN RETROSPECT

The rise of the modern states of Europe was a long, slow process. But the engines of state were in motion, no matter how slow, uncertain, and unpredictable their movement. The general trend in the political development of western Europe was clearly toward centralization. The economic change in the direction of a capitalistic or money economy reinforced this political tendency by subverting the old feudal institutions and supporting monarchs and territorial princes. In turn the rising centralized states, with their more efficient bureaucracies, stronger fiscal policies, and more effective armies, provided an environment more congenial to the new economic forces. As it turned out, France and England developed the strongest national monarchies of all. The overall tendency in France was toward a strong, not to say absolutist, monarchy. The limitations imposed upon the English king by law and parliament contrasted significantly with the French monarchy by the end of the fifteenth century. The century-long war between France and England increased national patriotism in both countries. Unification and centralization came later to Spain, but eventually they came with force. What happened on a national scale in western Europe took place on the level of territorial principalities within the empire, sealing the doom of that venerable universal medieval institution through the triumph of particularism.

At the beginning of the fourteenth century Dante could call upon the Holy Roman emperor Henry VII to save Florence and restore the empire. But at the end of the fifteenth century Savonarola summoned a national monarch, Charles VIII of France, to save Florence and restore Italian liberty. Italy retained its system of small, independent city-states throughout the period. In the end it was overshadowed and overpowered by the great states to the north and west. It became, in fact, the battlefield where the giants fought, with Italy itself as the prize to be won.

Bibliography

General:
HALE, J. R.; HIGHFIELD, J. R. L.; and SMALLEY, B., eds. *Europe in the Late Middle Ages.* London, 1965.
WAUGH, W. T. *A History of Europe, 1378–1494,* 3rd ed. London, 1949.

Holy Roman Empire:
ANDREAS, WILLI. *Deutschland vor der Reformation,* 5th ed. Stuttgart, 1948.
BACHMANN, ADOLF. *Deutsche Reichsgeschichte im Zeitalter Friedrich III und Maximilian I,* 2 vols. Leipzig, 1884–1894.
BARRACLOUGH, G. *The Origins of Modern Germany.* Oxford, 1946.
BELOW, GEORG VON. *Der deutsche Staat des Mittelalters,* 2nd ed. Leipzig, 1925.
KRAUS, V. VON, and KASER, K. *Deutsche Geschichte am Ausgang des Mittelalters,* 2 vols. Stuttgart, 1905–1912.

RODES, JOHN E. *Germany: A History,* chaps. 4 and 5. New York, 1964.
ULMANN, HEINRICH. *Kaiser Maximilian I,* 2 vols. Stuttgart, 1884–1891.
WAAS, GLENN. *The Legendary Character of Kaiser Maximilian.* New York, 1941.

France:
BEAUCOURT, GASTON DU FRESNE. *Histoire de Charles VII.* Paris, 1881–1891.
BRIDGE, J. S. C. *A History of France from the Death of Louis XI.* 5 vols. Oxford, 1921–1936.
CHERRIER, CLAUDE DE. *Histoire de Charles VIII, roi de France,* 2 vols., 2nd ed. Paris, 1870.
DUPONT-FERRIER, GUSTAVE. *La Formation de l'état français et l'unité française,* 2nd ed. Paris, 1934.
GANDILHON, R. *Politique économique de Louis XI.* Paris, 1941.
GROSJEAN, G. *Le sentiment national dans la Guerre des Cent Ans.* Paris, 1927.
LAVISSE, ERNEST. *Histoire de France, depuis les origines jusqu' à la révolution,* 9 vols., vols. 3–5. Paris, 1900–1911.
MAJOR, J. RUSSELL. *Representative Institutions in Renaissance France.* Madison, Wis., 1960.
MAULDE, LA CLAVIÈRE, RENÉ DE. *Histoire de Louis XII,* 6 vols. Paris, 1889–1893.
PERROY, É. *The Hundred Years' War.* New York, 1951.

Burgundy and the Low Countries:
CALMETTE, J. *The Golden Age of Burgundy.* London, 1962.
CARTELLIERI, O. *The Court of Burgundy.* London, 1929.
DUMONT, GEORGES. *Histoire des Belges,* 3 vols. Brussels, 1954–1956.
HUIZINGA, JOHAN. *The Waning of the Middle Ages.* London, 1924.
PIRENNE, HENRI. *Histoire de Belgique,* 3rd ed., vol. 3; 4th ed., vol. 2. Brussels, 1923, 1947.
————. *Early Democracies in the Low Countries.* New York, 1963.
VAUGHAN, RICHARD. *Philip the Bold.* Cambridge, 1962.
————. *John the Fearless.* Cambridge, 1966.

England:
CHRIMES, S. B. *English Constitutional Ideas in the Fifteenth Century.* Cambridge, 1936.
GAIRDNER, JAMES. *Henry the Seventh.* London and New York, 1889.
JACOB, E. F. *The Fifteenth Century, 1399–1485.* Oxford, 1961.
LAPSLEY, G. T. *Crown, Community, and Parliament in the Later Middle Ages.* New York, 1951.
MCILWAIN, CHARLES H. *The High Court of Parliament and Its Supremacy.* New Haven, 1910.
MCKISACK, M. *The Fourteenth Century, 1307–1399.* Oxford, 1959.
MAITLAND, F. W. *The Constitutional History of England.* Cambridge, 1908.
STUBBS, WILLIAM. *Constitutional History of England,* 3 vols. Oxford, 1874–1878.
WILKINSON, B. *Constitutional History of Medieval England,* 3 vols. London 1948–1958.

Spain:
ALTAMIRA Y CREVEA, RAFAEL. *La Historia de España y de la civilización española,* 4 vols., 3rd ed. Barcelona, 1900–1930.
CALMETTE, J. *La formation de l'unité espagnole.* Paris, 1946.

CHAPMAN, CHARLES E. *A History of Spain.* New York, 1927. (A summary of Altamira, *Historia de España.*)

ELLIOTT, JOHN. *Imperial Spain.* London, 1963.

MARIEJOL, J. H. *The Spain of Ferdinand and Isabella.* New Brunswick, N.J., 1961.

Scandinavia:

BIRCH, J. S. H. *Denmark in History.* London, 1938.

LARSEN, K. *A History of Norway.* Princeton, 1948.

STROMBERG, A. A. *History of Sweden.* New York, 1931.

CHAPTER 4

Italy:
Home of the
Renaissance

"You may have the universe if I may have Italy," *wrote Temistocles* Solera in his libretto for Verdi's opera *Attila*. He was reflecting the sentiment not only of Huns, Germans, and Turks, but of the Holy Roman emperors themselves. At the center of the Mediterranean world, home of the mother church and heir to the grandeur that was Rome, Italy enjoyed an importance in the minds of Western men not equaled by any other land.

A vague feeling of national identity was developing in Italy, though it was less pronounced than in France, England, or Spain. Certainly an Italian consciousness can be recognized not merely in enthusiastic poets such as Dante and Petrarch, but in such a political realist as Machiavelli. In the famous Chapter 26 of *The Prince* Machiavelli penned his exhortation to the Medici prince to liberate Italy from the barbarians. Writing in 1513, Machiavelli urged Lorenzo de' Medici, grandson of Lorenzo the Magnificent, to free Italy of all barbarian domination, now that his house controlled both Florence and the papacy.

> This opportunity must not, therefore, be allowed to pass, so that Italy may at length find her liberator. I cannot express the love with which he would be received in all those provinces which have suffered under these foreign invasions, with what thirst for vengeance, with what steadfast faith, with what love, with what grateful tears. What doors would be closed against him? What people would refuse him obedience? What envy could oppose him? What Italians would withhold allegiance?

An Italian could be fiercely loyal to his own city-state, ready to die for it. The contemporaries of Machiavelli, subjected as they were to foreign invaders, were conscious of the difference between Italians and "barbarians." But few had a concept of Italy as a political entity or conceived of an alliance or confederation of city-states which would repel all invaders. The city-states proved to be too small and too selfish for such an ideal solution to the Italian problem. Moreover, geography and history worked against the unification of Italy and the rise of a national dynasty that would provide a standard to which loyal Italians could repair. Even though the Italian peninsula was clearly delineated on the map as a boot surrounded by the sea, the Apennine mountain range ran down the center like a spine, dividing the land and isolating many smaller states. Moreover, Italians learned early that the sea itself was a convenient highway for invaders, making Italy vulnerable to attack on all sides.

The south was overrun by Greeks and Moors. The Normans had set up their kingdom in Naples and Sicily, holding them as fiefs under the pope. The Hohenstaufens, as Holy Roman emperors, had moved to the two Sicilies and re-sided there virtually as local kings. Although the pope brought in the house of Anjou and destroyed the Swabian rule, the people arose in the revolt known as the Sicilian Vespers (1282) and massacred nearly all the French on the island. The house of Aragon was enthroned in Sicily by the Treaty of Caltabellotta (1302). The popes aspired to extend their temporal kingdom from Rome across the width of the Italian boot. Although the emperors from 1300 on had no real control over Italy, Henry VII, Ludwig the Bavarian, Charles IV, Frederick III, and the others did intervene in Italian affairs and had an unsettling effect upon them. In the north the Po valley was a rich land and a great prize for conquerors, contested first by Milan and Venice, then by the great powers of the north. In little Tuscany in the center, hemmed in by Rome to the south and Milan to the north, Florence had to be content with lesser ambitions—the possession of Pisa, the conquest of Lucca.

Thus history as well as geography worked against the unification of Italy during those centuries. It is ironic and one of history's notorious injustices that even though the greatest cultural and social achievements emerged from the city-states in the fourteenth and fifteenth centuries, wherever the cities were the strongest, whether in Flanders, the Hanse cities, the Rhineland, south Germany, or Italy, national unity with its obvious benefits came latest. In fact, it did not come until the nineteenth century. The city-states were very successful culturally, just as they had been in classical antiquity. Plato had favored politically small units for the full development of the individual within his closed society. Aristotle had ven-tured to say that ideally a state should be small enough so that a citizen could see across it from one side to the other. Some of the smaller Italian states, such as Urbino, with very active cultural life at their ducal courts, nearly fitted this ideal pattern, but most of them were considerably larger. Most of them also put greater stress upon the liberty of citizens (by which they meant the nobility and the successful men of commerce) than the classical city-states. Lord Acton was more right than wrong when he argued that in the classical form of the state "the passengers existed for the sake of the ship." Aristotle himself considered the worst government to be that which left men "free to live as they please." The catchwords of the Italian states, in contrast, were "peace" and "liberty." The people even accepted new despots only in the name of liberty.

In spite of their cultural glories, the city-states in the long run failed politically. No leagues of cities held up against outside pressures, and within the cities, except for Venice, regimes were constantly changing. The national states proved to be politically more successful because they managed to develop institutions representing the interests of a larger part of the population than did the oligarchic and despotic city-states, and because they had superior resources. The idea of the individual represented in a collective body as a "corporate person" was developed in Roman private law. With the revival of Roman law from the twelfth century on, this conception was once again consciously articulated. People came to look upon corporations as legal persons, entirely natural and real, not merely as fictitious persons. This concept of representation was transferred to representative bodies in the government, such as the parliament in England (1295), the estates general in France (1302), the cortes of Aragon and Castile, the estates of Naples, and the imperial diet (*Reichstag*) or territorial diets (*Landtage*) in the empire. The late thirteenth, fourteenth, and early fifteenth centuries have been called the "corporative period," following the feudal period of individual relationships and preceding the modern period, in which the state has come to be a collectivity of individuals.

In this corporative period the individual was not conceived of as an isolated atom in the body politic, but as a member of a corps, such as the church, nobility, guild, and the like. The corps then coalesced into orders, and each order or estate appeared as a unit in the representative assembly. Western Europe had its tradition of a strong monarch asserting his power from a territorial center. This period saw neither absolute monarchy nor exclusively representative government, but states operated on the basis of a functional dualism. The policy of kings was determined by their need for support and counsel (*auxilium et consilium*). The clergy, the nobility, and the third estate, which made its first appearance as a town association, could cooperate with the monarch or resist his designs, according to their own collective interest. Custom and precedent played important roles in legal thought in this period and served as guiding and restricting forces upon royalty. In Poland and the empire the estates were strong, while in the west the kings grew in power.

In the medieval commune four social elements were universally present: (1) the nobility or patricians; (2) the merchant capitalists, some of them newly enriched (*gente nuova*); (3) the petty bourgeois class, made up of members of the lesser guilds, craftsmen, and shopkeepers; and (4) the unorganized and property-less workers. The pattern of political dominance varied a great deal in the city-states and there was great flexibility during the fourteenth and fifteenth centuries. In a Hanse city such as Lübeck, the participation of nobility in government was very prominent. In Venice the merchant oligarchy ruled supreme. In Florence the patricians or magnates (*grandi*), a class formed by the intermarriage of rich merchant families and the nobility from the estates of Tuscany, dominated the commune in its formative years. But newly rich families pressed into prominence as the fourteenth century moved on. Political life was marked by the struggle of the greater and lesser guilds for power. It is fascinating to observe how the meanest guildsmen closed ranks with the upper classes in fighting off the unorganized wool workers during the Ciompi revolt of 1378. The peasants in the countryside were frequently a threat, for they were excluded from the political processes altogether; they suffered exploitation, had little hope for a better life, and thus had nothing to lose either by revolting or by joining an alien power.

The historian is bound to the concrete and must resist the temptation to construct an ideal type of Italian Renaissance city-state and to manipulate parts of the model. For whatever similarities existed, each state had its own historical background and its unique political experience. "The principal foundation of all states," Machiavelli pronounced, "is good laws and good arms." The conception of what constitutes good laws and the success of good arms varied so greatly from state to state and from decade to decade that each must be examined separately and concretely. Milan, Venice, and Florence had distinct kinds of government. But they experienced a parallel development from urban communes into very centralized territorial states. Naples differed in having a feudal monarch and in being so vulnerable to foreign domination. The situation in Rome was complicated by the presence of the papacy.

Rome

THE IDEA OF ROME as the capital of the empire and center of the Western world was very much alive throughout the Middle Ages. But as a reality the city fell far short of the grandeur that was ancient Rome's. By the fourteenth century the city had gained in population over its near pastoral state in the earlier medieval period. The people were clustered around various centers, such as the Capitoline Hill, the old Lateran Palace, and St. Peter's. The economy was sustained by the income of the ecclesiastical bureaucrats, administrative and judicial, and by the pilgrims who came to visit the sacred shrines. There was little trade and hence virtually no bourgeois class.

Power was held by the feudal magnates, families such as the Orsinis and Colonnas, with city palaces and landed estates outside Rome. The papacy contended with these families for local control, but as a result of the Babylonian Captivity in Avignon and the schism, papal authority declined enormously. The Roman mob not only intimidated the College of Cardinals during the election of a new pope, but even frightened away the pope himself, as in 1434 when they forced out Eugenius IV. Central control over the Papal States was extremely tenuous during the fourteenth century and the first half of the fifteenth. The popes had to accept the virtual autonomy of many cities nominally in their territory, such as Bologna and Ferrara, as well as lesser towns in Romagna and Emilia. Only with the Renaissance popes, from Nicholas V on, did the security of the popes in the city and their control of the communes and lesser dynasties become in any sense effective. Since the Papal States reached to the northeast well beyond the confines of Tuscany, many foreign forces that wished to avoid the Florentines found it convenient to pass through the Papal States instead. Being in the center of that strife-torn peninsula had certain advantages, but Rome was by the same token open to attack from the north and the south, as well as from the sea.

Rome's most fascinating political adventure during the Renaissance was its revival of the republic under Cola di Rienzo (1313–1354). Rienzo has captured the imagination of political as well as literary romantics. When Napoleon was taken captive after Waterloo, a life of Cola di Rienzo was found in his baggage. Lord Byron honored him with a poem and Bulwer-Lytton celebrated him with an epic. Wagner did an opera (1838–1840) on Rienzo, the "last Roman tribune." Some of his followers claimed that he was an illegitimate son of Emperor Henry VII, for he happened to have been born in 1313, when Henry had been in Italy. In reality he was the son of a laundress and a tavern keeper. Rienzo became a notary and developed an interest in Roman history and archeology. In the *Lex regia* he read how the Roman people had delegated their power to the emperors. Rienzo delivered a rhetorically powerful oration at the Forum, telling the people of Rome that they were the true source of political power and preparing them for a republican revolution.

In 1342 Rienzo became the head of a delegation to Avignon. There he first met Petrarch, the great humanist, and impressed the politically naïve poet. Petrarch addressed a series of letters to Rienzo and the Roman people encouraging them to restore Rome to its ancient glories. In 1347 Rienzo led a popular revolt and declared himself to be the tribune of the Roman people, and proved it by appearing in a tribune's garb. He claimed to rule the city and the empire "by the authority of our lord Jesus Christ." A powerful orator, he spoke of *Italia sacra* with patriotic fervor. "You will die in freedom," he declared, "so that posterity may be born in freedom." He wished a renovation, a renaissance, of the imperial rule and of the church. But Rienzo failed to win the support of the powerful Roman princely families, and the great revolt came to an ignominious end in 1349 when the Orsinis combined with the Colonnas to suppress it. Rienzo fled for refuge to the Franciscans.

Rienzo believed that he had relied too heavily upon the papacy and that the emperor might prove to be a more effective ally. In 1350 he went to Prague and was ushered into the presence of Emperor Charles IV. Charles thought him interesting but erratic, and finally imprisoned him. At the pope's request Charles IV delivered him to Avignon, where he was put on trial. Finally a new pope devised a plan to use Rienzo to pacify Italy and to prepare Rome for the return of the papacy. He appointed the papal legate Cardinal Albornoz as Rienzo's protector. Rienzo's true character was revealed in his moment of triumph, when he turned into a petty tyrant. In 1354 he entered Rome and had himself proclaimed a senator, with a banner bearing the ancient emblem SPQR (*Senatus populusque romanus*). At last the very lowest classes, on whose support he counted, turned against him. He attempted to escape wearing a disguise, but was caught and killed by a mob at the foot of the Capitoline Hill.

Rienzo foreshadowed Italian national patriotism and possessed a humanist's interest in ancient Rome. In a way, Rienzo was very much a man of the Renaissance. Exaggerated claims have been made for his role in introducing the Renaissance to the court of Charles IV and thus initiating the northern Renaissance. But at the same time he was not unlike medieval figures such as Arnold of Brescia, who centuries earlier had dreamed of restoring Rome to its ancient glory.

Naples and Sicily

THE ONLY KINGDOM in Italy with a well-established monarchy was Naples. Its history was complicated during the fourteenth and fifteenth centuries by its involvement with Sicily, its vulnerability to the conflicting claims of foreign dynasties, and the ambitions of its rulers to dominate other parts of Italy, preeminently Rome. The Angevins, who ruled during the fourteenth century, were involved in a constant struggle with the Aragonese in Sicily.

When King Robert succeeded to the throne in 1309, he was immediately involved in a war with Sicily, and sent a series of punitive expeditions into the island to lay it waste. He had more the appearance than the reality of royal power. An able man, scholarly, and a friend of Petrarch, he was unsuccessful in his attempts to control the rebellious barons at home, and before long lost his position as the leader of the Guelph party in Italy. When he died in 1343 his granddaughter Joanna, the wife of Andrew of Hungary, succeeded him. When a band of conspirators, perhaps with Joanna's connivance, murdered Andrew, Andrew's brother Louis, king of Hungary, came to Naples to avenge his death and to assert his claims to the throne. He drove out Joanna and her new husband, Louis of Taranto, but his excesses alienated all of Italy, and in 1352 the papal legate crowned Joanna and her husband in Naples. When the papal schism began in 1378, Joanna supported Clement VII, the antipope. Pope Urban VI thereupon declared the throne vacant and offered it to Charles of Durazzo. In this crisis Joanna appealed to Louis of Anjou for help, in return for which she made him her legal heir. Clement supported Louis, of course, but in 1382 Charles of Durazzo captured Naples, had Joanna put to death, and ruled in her stead as Charles III. When he died a few years later, civil war broke out between his son Ladislas, then seventeen, and Louis of Anjou. By 1400 Ladislas conquered the kingdom, occupied Rome, and even threatened Florence. He died at the right moment (1414) for Rome and Florence, but Naples sank into a state of virtual anarchy.

Joanna II, the sister of Ladislas, was involved in a maze of intrigues and assassinations that it is pointless to record here. She was eventually succeeded by her last lover, Alfonso of Aragon, whom she designated as her heir. Sicily and Naples were at last once again united under this Alfonso the Magnanimous, who proved to be a brilliant ruler and a great patron of arts and letters. When he died in 1458, his illegitimate son Ferrante succeeded him as King Ferrante I. He had the usual task of subduing the unruly barons (barons, it seems, are always unruly). In alliance with Pope Sixtus IV and Milan, he made war on Florence in 1479. It was then that Lorenzo de' Medici made his daring trip to confront Ferrante I in person and persuaded him to make peace. Ferrante died in 1494 as King Charles VIII of France was undertaking a wild invasion of Italy to assert Angevin claims to Naples. Charles VIII did take Naples and drove out Ferrante's grandson Ferrantino. When the French withdrew, Ferrantino moved back in, but he soon died and the kingdom was plunged into civil war and virtual anarchy. France and Spain fought for the spoils, and finally, at the end of the year 1502, the Spaniards seized and held the kingdom. Clearly the Neapolitan monarchy, with the many claims and counterclaims upon it and its inability to control the nobility, provided no more continuity and security than the rules of communes and *signori* were able to offer in the other states of Italy.

Milan

THE POLITICAL DEVELOPMENTS in the north were hardly more inspiring than those in the south. In Lombardy the medieval communes, with some assured civic liberties, evolved in a few decades into despotisms. By 1300 many towns were ruled by *signori* rather than by the councils of the communes. "The cities of Italy," Dante lamented, "are full of tyrants and every clown that comes to play the partisan becomes a Marcellus" (*Purgatorio,* Canto 6, lines 125–26). This development was almost everywhere the same. An able or particularly aggressive leader, whether the *podestà* (the chief executive) or the *condottiere* or *capitano del popolo* (the military commander), assumed the leadership of the state for a limited term. The term was then renewed or extended in time as the internal or external crisis persisted. His powers were enlarged and he undertook to entrench himself by manipulating opposing factions and currying popular favor. He then sought to make the succession in office hereditary. By successfully expanding the territory of the state at the expense of neighboring cities, the ruler achieved a double purpose, for he appealed to the pride and patriotism of the citizens and at the same time ensured the existence of hostile neighbors who would perpetuate the state of crisis and make a strong ruler a necessity. The people invariably accepted the new provincial despot in the name of liberty and peace. Milan provides the classic example, with the rise of the Viscontis to power and the Sforza takeover.

In the center of the rich Po valley, Milan was strategically located, and from Roman times played an important role in Italian history. During the thirteenth century the city freed itself from Hohenstaufen domination, but was torn internally by the struggle for power of the old nobility and the rising merchant class. In 1262 Otto Visconti became lord of Milan, and except for the years 1302–1310, when the rival della Torre family was in control, the Visconti family ruled from then until their line came to an end in 1447. Before his death in 1295 Archbishop Otto had his nephew Matteo elected *capitano del popolo.* Matteo secured the additional title of "imperial vicar," confirmed in 1299. Under Visconti leadership Milan expanded its territories along the Po valley to include Bologna, Parma, Lodi, Bobbio, Cremona, Brescia, Bergamo, Como, Novara, and other cities.

When Matteo's son Giovanni died, these territories were governed by three of his nephews, Matteo, Bernabò, and Galeazzo. A bit of loving family history came into play, for Matteo was murdered by his brothers in 1355. Bernabò reigned in Milan (1354–1385) and Galeazzo (1354–1378) in Pavia. Galeazzo was followed by his son Gian Galeazzo, who murdered Bernabò and ruled over the entire Milanese dominion after that. In 1395 he bought the title of duke from Emperor Wenceslas. He was an energetic, formidable ruler, who began the building of the great Gothic cathedral of Milan and the Certosa in Pavia. He also began the expansion of Milan into Tuscany, taking Vicenza, Verona, Pisa, and Siena, and threatening the encirclement and conquest of Florence itself. His death in 1402 saved Florence. Two sons succeeded him, Giovanni Maria (d. 1412) and Filippo Maria (d. 1447). The Viscontis lived the extravagant lives of petty potentates. They spent lavishly and taxed the people harshly. Filippo Maria kept a menagerie of leopards, English hounds, and falcons that cost three thousand gold pieces a month for care and upkeep. For all his grandeur, Filippo Maria died without a legitimate heir. At this juncture the Milanese, weary of their extravagant rulers, set up the Ambrosian Republic, named after St. Ambrose of Milan, and undertook to restore the old commune.

The Ambrosian Republic lasted only three years, for there was too little of the old communal spirit left to sustain it. Francesco Sforza, the military commander or *condottiere* (*condotta* was the contract for mercenary service), betrayed the republic. Venice was expanding up the valley against Milan, so the republic needed to employ mercenary forces, which were captained by Sforza. He had married Bianca, an illegitimate daughter of Filippo Visconti, and felt that he deserved special prerogatives in the city. When the council refused his demands, he went over to Venice and conquered Milan with its aid. His was a naked power grab and his success depended on the soldiery. He built the great red-brick castle that still looms formidably over Milan with its massive round towers. He declared that the 130 captains of castles throughout Milan's territories were the defense and backbone of the state.

Ludovico il Moro, who ruled from 1480 on, conducted the Milanese court with all the grandeur of a monarch. He was very anxious to ally his family by marriage with European royalty. As a political conniver he went too far. He was guilty of a fatal blunder in encouraging the French to intervene in Italian affairs, for they had claims on Milan itself. In 1499 the French king Louis XII drove Ludovico from power. Swiss mercenaries reinstated him for a short time, but in 1500 they turned him over to the French, who kept him imprisoned until his death in 1508. For a few years Massimiliano Sforza ruled as a protégé of the Habsburg emperor, for Emperor Maximilian's second wife was Ludovico's daughter Bianca. In 1515 the French king Francis I won a stunning victory at Marignano and dominated Milan until the imperial forces occupied the city in 1522. The Spanish crown controlled Milan from 1535 until 1714. Then Austria dominated the city until Napoleon placed upon his own head the iron crown of Lombardy.

Milan experienced two distinct styles of political domination during the Renaissance. The Viscontis gradually changed their magistracy into a hereditary position. They grasped power but retained the forms of legitimacy and legality, retaining in office the traditional magistrates and civic councils. The Sforzas had no real interest in conforming to legal forms. They made a straight power play and had so little regard for traditional government that the Council of Nine Hundred met very infrequently, and then merely to approve decisions already made or actions already taken. Machiavelli was fascinated by the success of the Sforzas and asked why they triumphed whereas Cesare Borgia failed.

In government Milan was typical of the city-states of northern Italy. The Scaligeri family in Verona, the Estes in Ferrara, the Carraras in Padua, the Gonzagas of Mantua, and the Malatestas of Rimini conformed to the Visconti pattern of political aggrandizement. But several of the Malatestas were sufficiently vicious and tyrannical to evoke the image of Ludovico il Moro.

Before leaving the north one must take note of an area that was to loom large in Italy's future. Savoy and Piedmont were organized into a unified state by Amadeo VI, Amadeo VII, and especially Duke Amadeo VIII (1391–1451). Its influence reached as far north as Geneva.

Genoa and Venice

IF MILAN AND VENICE engaged in a struggle on land in the fifteenth century, a far older rivalry existed on the sea between Genoa and Venice for the control of maritime routes and the lion's share of the Levant trade. At one time Pisa, too, had competed for trade in the Levant, but Pisa was being pressed by Milan and Florence and was torn by internal strife, and never recovered its former strength after being decisively defeated by Genoa in 1284. The two great rivals that remained provide a fascinating contrast in government, for Genoa represented an extreme of political instability, whereas Venice was a model of law and order. In the long run the orderly succession of governments in Venice meant that it could recover from losses and come back after reverses abroad. Venice triumphed and Genoa declined.

Located on the beautiful Ligurian coast, Genoa had ready access to the sea. Since Genoa controlled Corsica, Genoese ships could freely sail the western Mediterranean and Tyrrhenian Seas, and had ready access to rich markets also in the East. But it was torn by the struggle of rival aristocrats, the Spinolas, Dorias, and other families. Competing groups of merchants further disrupted civic life and fought in the overseas markets. The commoners were hostile to the upper classes, and the popular government during the fourteenth and fifteenth centuries was constantly in a state of uproar and rebellion. After domination by the German, Neapolitan, and Milanese rulers, Genoa finally achieved a greater measure of independence early in the fourteenth century. In 1339 it paid its rival Venice the flattery of imitation by appointing its first doge, giving him an appointment for life. This step did not in itself provide stability, however, for in one three-month period in 1393 five doges held office. The next century saw continued disturbances, especially from 1413 to 1421 and again in 1435.

The rivalry with Venice lasted from the thirteenth to the sixteenth centuries and was particularly acute during the fourteenth century, when trade suffered in general and the Ottoman Turks began to restrain trade by their military action in the Levant. The thirteenth century witnessed two major conflicts, from 1261 to 1270 and from 1294 to 1299. In one of these clashes, in 1298, Marco Polo was captured by the Genoese. It was during his imprisonment that he wrote his account of the Far East. Another great war was fought from 1351 to 1355. But the most deadly was the War of Chioggia, 1377–1381, which took its name from the bold attack made by Genoa's fleet upon the Venetian lagoon. The Venetians fought off the Genoese, but it was the closest they had come to defeat. The Genoese were in deep trouble at home, for unlike Venice, at the far end of the Adriatic, Genoa was exposed to attack by major powers. It fought Alfonso of Aragon, king of Naples, for the possession of Sardinia and lost. Then it was alternately overrun by the Milanese and the French. Finally in 1528 the great admiral Andrea Doria freed Genoa of French domination and reestablished home rule as a Habsburg satellite, a status that Genoa retained until the time of the French Revolution.

The most amazing example of political stability and governmental continuity in Italy was Venice, queen of the Adriatic. Not only did its strategic position off the mainland and its open communications on the sea keep it free from siege and conquest by enemies outside, but its unique political institutions kept it secure from rebellion and civil war at home. Venice was fortunate in not having a feudal countryside, and therefore having no need to tame or absorb a landholding nobility, as other Italian cities had to do. It was not entangled in the Guelph-Ghibelline rivalries. Basically a merchant oligarchy, the Venetian government was relatively stable, run by the patricians in the interest of their own social and economic interests. Cicero's sardonic definition of oligarchy applied perfectly to the Venetians: "When a group of men controls the commonwealth by virtue of their wealth, their birth, or any advantages they happen to possess, they form an oligarchy, but they call themselves leading citizens." From the "closing of the council" in Venice in 1297 to the fall of the republic in 1797, exactly half a millennium of history had gone by, a remarkable achievement for a city-state.

So far as the lesser nobility and the common people were concerned, liberty was virtually a myth. When Wordsworth lamented "The Extinction of the Venetian Republic" and celebrated Venice as "the eldest child of liberty, a maiden city bright and free," he was using poetic license. For the government remained firmly in the hands of the rich old families, and after 1297 no one was able to become a member of the Great Council who could not claim an ancestor who had been a council member. This meant that political authority was effectively in the hands of some two hundred or so wealthy families. Machiavelli could scoff at these hucksters who assumed the "style of nobility," but the relative prosperity of Venice is proof enough that on the whole they used their authority wisely. The constitution of Venice merits examination.

The Venetian government had a fascinating scheme for the allocation and use of power. There were three basic parts. The senate ostensibly represented all the people and served as the main legislative body. The Great Council elected the senate and eventually served the main function of assisting in the selection of the executive committees, executive officers, and lesser magistrates. The doge performed ceremonial functions and did the will of the Great Council and the senate. He was usually an older man who could be relied upon to remain ornamental and not to press his personal ambitions, although several doges in the early fifteenth century, such as Michele Steno, Tommaso Mocenigo, and Francesco Foscari, did attempt to increase their political power.

In order to prevent any one faction from securing the election of its candidate as doge, the Great Council developed an elaborate system of election by lot which went through many steps. The whole council selected by lot thirty members, from which number nine members then chose forty. Of the forty members, twelve were selected who chose forty-five. The forty-five were reduced to eleven, and the eleven chose the final group of forty-one, who elected the doge. This built-in safety device worked well and was essential precisely because the doge was elected for life. After 1335 an executive committee of ten, the *Dieci,* could assume emergency powers in times of crisis. They were chosen annually by an electoral group of twenty, ten of whom were selected by the council and ten by the doge and executive officials. The *Dieci* received anonymous charges of crime, conspiracy, or sedition, which could be slipped through a slot in the thick wall of their chamber, and they deliberated in secret. The Bridge of Sighs led from the doge's palace, where they met, to the prison on the other side of the canal.

The constitution of Venice gave every appearance of providing a system of checks and balances among the legislative, executive, and judicial branches of government. Enlightened political theorists in the eighteenth century considered Venice's stability to have been a result of this system of checks and balances. Actually, the complexly interlocking functions and the restraint of the *Dieci* in the exercise of authority are the most fascinating features of Venetian government. Any lesson on the separation of powers learned from the Venetian experience needs to be modified by consideration of Venice's history and the facts of life.

In the *Inferno* Dante has grafters in public office punished in a smoky, fiery place, sulfurous and smelling of pitch. It is a description of the arsenal at the mouth of the Grand Canal in Venice, where the great galleys were repaired and the tar boiled and bubbled for calking the ships back from battles with the enemy and storms at sea. The state galleys were the largest and were ordered by special officials. The senate supervised every detail of their construction, for on them depended the prosperity and safety of the state. Like the Florentine florin, the Venetian sequin provided one of the very few stable currencies for trade in all of Italy, which was very important for Venice's international merchants.

Near the doge's palace on the Piazzetta stand two slender columns bearing the lion of St. Mark, the patron saint of the city, whose body had been brought to the city from Egypt, and the crocodile of St. Theodore, another symbol of Venice's tie to the Near East. Following the fourth crusade in 1204, in which Venice played an ignoble part in the sack of Constantinople, Venice steadily expanded its Mediterranean possessions. Over the gate of its great seventeenth-century fortress on the hill overlooking Nauplia in Greece its great lion of St. Mark is still to be seen. Venice's policy was to set up fortresses and merchant colonies at the mouths of rivers and at ports in order to control trade, rather than occupy the territory and control political developments in the hinterland. That its fleet could take on the naval forces of mighty empires such as that of the Turks is a tribute both to the skill and to the courage of the Venetians. Venice had a responsible ministry at home and a well-trained civil service to sustain its commitments abroad.

Florence

WESTERN INTELLECTUALS have carried on a perpetual love affair with Florence, the queen city of the Renaissance. To Elizabeth Browning, Florence seemed to be "the most beautiful of the cities devised by man." Robert Browning described Giotto's campanile as "completing Florence as Florence Italy." When Jacob Burckhardt had at last made his way to the "lazy South" and come to Florence, he said, "The view from Brunelleschi's dome placed the crown on everything. This is the most beautiful thing I have seen in my life." In the fourteenth century a noted chronicler, Giovanni Villani, described the glories of Florence at the height of its prosperity in 1338. "Florence," he wrote, "the daughter and creature of Rome, was in the ascendancy and destined for great things."

In the twelfth and thirteenth centuries the social and political organization of Florence was communal. It was a natural outgrowth of the struggles of the late Middle Ages. The last of the Hohenstaufen emperors, Frederick II, had failed to maintain a hold on northern Italy, in spite of the brutalities of his *condottiere,* Ezzelino da Romano. In Florence a "republic" was established, *Il primo popolo,* from 1250 to 1260. Following bitter Guelph-Ghibelline struggles a second "republic" was established with the creation of a new executive authority in 1293, a committee of *priori,* and new "ordinances of justice." Then came the final fight of two powerful factions, the Blacks and the Whites, which ended with the exile in 1301 of the Whites, including Dante, the father of Petrarch, and other illustrious citizens.

With a population of about 90,000, Florence was the fifth largest city in Christendom. The Florentines had a mystical conception of their city, referring to the *polis* as the mystical body of Christ and to the treasury as *Christus fiscus.* During the first half of the fourteenth century Florence was ruled by the upper classes, the *popolo grasso* or "fat people." In the years 1328–1342, 71 percent of the magistrates of the republic came from three of the major guilds, wool, banking, and cloth. The seven most powerful associations or guilds, the *arti maggiori,* were the judges and notaries, the money changers or bankers, the wool cloth manufacturers, the cloth importers, the silk merchants, the physicians and apothecaries, and the furriers.

Two powerful guilds controlled the wool industry: the cloth manufacturers, the *Arte della Lana,* and the cloth finishers, the *Arte di Calimala,* who imported unfinished textiles from Flanders. The guilds were not made up of master artisans, as they were during the Middle Ages, but were really associations of merchant industrialists. They were organized in order to control the laborers, manipulate prices, maintain monopolies, and control government economic policies by the use of political pressure. A limited number of the most important members of each of these major guilds elected an executive committee for a half-year term.

The five guilds of the so-called middle crafts made up the *arti medie.* These five were the blacksmiths, the shoemakers, the carpenters and masons, the second-hand clothes dealers, and the butchers. In the course of the decades nine additional lesser guilds, the *arti minori,* came into existence to represent the lower bourgeois shopkeepers and artisans: innkeepers, bakers, armorers, and tradesmen who sold salt, oil, and cheese. The great mass of unorganized workers made up the *popolo minuto.* The "little people" were miserably paid and lived in squalid housing. It was communal policy to keep grain and meat prices low, but the guilds kept the prices of many other articles artificially high.

The board of *priori,* or *signoria,* was the keystone of the communal edifice. The six (later eight and nine) *priori* were chosen by lot, their names drawn from a purse by guild leaders. Candidates had to be Guelph citizens over thirty who were guild members and who were not noblemen or tax delinquents and had never been bankrupt. They were named for a term of two months and formed the most important governing body of the state. By 1361 over five hundred Florentines were eligible to serve on the *signoria.* Its nine members were responsible both for formulating policy and for the actual administration of the government. The very broad powers they exercised were stated in the statute of the *capitano del popolo* in these words: "The *priori* and *gonfaloniere* [standard-bearer of justice, an executive post] should work diligently for the safety, exaltation, conservation, and growth of the peaceful and tranquil state of the people and commune of Florence." They selected magistrates, initiated legislation, guided proposals through the councils, and directed foreign policy. To assure some distribution of responsibility, a *priore* could not serve again in the *signoria* until three years after the expiration of his previous term.

The years 1336–1338 saw the high point of Florentine prosperity. The great banking houses of the Bardis and Peruzzis, upon which the economic prosperity of Florence depended, were peaking, but in 1338 the first indications of their coming bankruptcy were beginning to shake the business community. The Bardis and Peruzzis had unwisely made immense political loans of around a million florins. In May 1339, King Edward III of England suspended payment on loans he had received from them. Since the Bardi bank had a highly centralized structure, it collapsed. Moreover, Florence was waging war against Lucca, which proved to be enormously costly. The chronicler Giovanni Villani estimated that the city had spent 600,000 florins on the war, that the public debt was 450,000 florins, and that the tax revenues for the next six years were committed to the reduction of the war debt. All this spelled economic disaster, and when it came, the Florentines turned to a strong man to save the state.

In September 1342 the Florentines chose the military captain Walter of Brienne, titular duke of Athens, as ruler for life. The factions within the city continued to feud and the duke proved to be totally unable to cope with the complicated economic and internal political situation. *Il popolo* screamed, "Death to the duke and his followers!" In July 1343 all classes combined to expel him. The Florentines seemed to have learned their lesson, for never again did they resort to one-man rule in a crisis, and when in the next century one man did emerge as the supreme leader, his power was at least circumscribed by the forms of republican government. During the two decades following the explusion of Brienne, Florence was in a state of perpetual crisis.

In 1348 the Black Death struck Florence. Although contemporary chroniclers estimated that three-fifths of the population died of the plague, more conservative contemporary estimates suggest losses of 30,000 to 45,000 out of a population of 80,000 to 90,000. Hardly a family escaped without a death. For the next thirty years the population seems to have fluctuated between 50,000 and 60,000. It took a century for the population to rise well above the level of 1348. One estimate is that by 1500 the population had climbed to nearly 130,000.

The disasters that befell Florence make a depressing story. The chronicler Matteo Villani (d. 1363) remarked that history is essentially a narration of the calamities and disasters that befall the human race. After the plague, famine struck the land in 1352–1353, 1369–1370, and 1373–1375. Another grave economic crisis developed in 1396. As though the buffeting of nature were not enough, Florence was involved in four costly wars: two with Milan (1351–1353 and 1369–1370), one with Pisa (1362–1364), and one with the papacy (1375–1378). Tuscany suffered from pillaging by armed bands of mercenaries. Factional strife within the city increased as pressure from the outside mounted. From 1350 on internal hostility crystallized around two rival families, the Albizzis and the Riccis. The patrician families tended to give way to the new families (*gente nuova*), who made their way into the upper echelons of the Florentine business class. "New men" (*novi cives*) who were impatient with the leisurely patrician world of the commune entered the government. They insisted upon a more rigorous rule of law, a more equitable administration of justice, and tighter fiscal control. The communal debt mounted even higher, for mercenaries were far more costly than militia. This debt grew so large that it could not be taken care of by simply borrowing from wealthy individuals or private groups. It had to be funded by the *monte communale,* which sold public shares and kept public books. The *monte communale* became a mainspring of civic life and helped to "democratize" public life. The Florentine commune developed into a territorial state, which the civic humanists then justified in their political treatises.

Perhaps the low point of Florentine fortunes was reached with the Ciompi revolt of 1378. In the winter and spring of 1377–1378 Florence suffered a severe internal crisis. Nearly a hundred Florentines fell victims to Guelph terror. On June 21 the masses rioted and burned the houses of the Albizzis and other wealthy oligarchs. In the fall the day laborers and especially the unorganized wool carders, known as Ciompi for the wooden shoes they wore, struck out against the whole oligarchy and guild system. They gathered outside the city and plotted to overthrow the *signoria* and set up a popular government. They fought for better pay and legal recognition. *"Viva il popolo!"* was the cry. But even the lowest artisan guilds with some stake in society opposed the unorganized laborers in this crisis and helped to crush them. After the Ciompi were suppressed, the innkeepers petitioned the *signoria* to proclaim the anniversary of the Ciompi downfall as a holiday.

During the brief time in which the Ciompi were masters of the city, they reformed the constitution, created three new guilds, and appointed a new board of *priori*. The new board was made up of three representatives of the major guilds, three of the lesser guilds, and three of the new guilds. Each of these classes was to have a turn at appointing the *gonfaloniere*, but the first one appointed was very naturally one of the Ciompi, Michele di Lando. By popular demand Piero degli Albizzi and other *grandi* were charged with conspiracy and executed, and many others were exiled. The Ciompi behaved badly, constantly interrupting the meetings of officials and breaking into frequent rioting, and reduced the city to near anarchy.

Their foolish excesses very naturally produced a decisive reaction. In 1382 the guilds regained power and introduced a revised constitution that provided that half of the *priori* should come from the major guilds and half from the lesser guilds. They eliminated the three new guilds set up to accommodate the lower classes. They executed or exiled the rabble-rousers and so firmly established their control over the state that they easily suppressed subsequent Ciompi strikes and riots for better pay. Florence regained internal stability just in time, for it was now threatened by a deadly enemy that was determined to subdue it and take away all of Tuscany.

By 1390 Gian Galeazzo Visconti had conquered a large part of northern Italy and was now expanding the domain of Milan southward. He had designs on Siena, Perugia, and Pisa, then the Tuscan lands around Florence, and finally Florence itself. Florence employed a mercenary captain named Hawkwood as *condottiere* with some seven thousand men to defend the city. He fought off the Milanese and a temporary peace was signed in 1392.

In 1393 a wealthy member of the powerful wool guild, the *Arte della Lana*, Maso degli Albizzi, became *gonfaloniere*. Although Maso held this office only two months, he used his position to suppress rival families, such as the Albertis, and drove many prominent citizens into exile. The Albizzis and their merchant oligarchy reigned supreme, despite minor disturbances and the intrigues of the exiles. In 1397 and 1398 Gian Galeazzo advanced once more into Tuscany and defeated the troops Florence had hired from Emperor Rupert. Florence stood alone and seemed doomed. But at that very moment fate intervened and Gian Galeazzo died in 1402.

Florence now pressed its advantage in order to gain possession of Pisa, whose location at the mouth of the Arno River made it highly desirable as an outlet to the sea for Florence's maritime trade. A Visconti still ruled in Pisa, and the Florentines failed to take the city in 1404. But they persisted, and in 1406 they besieged Pisa for six months until it fell. Florence had gained at last the port it had so long coveted.

From 1409 to 1414 the Florentines had to ward off King Ladislas of Naples, but fortunately he died before he could capture the city. The Viscontis threatened Florence once again in 1421, when Filippo Maria took Forli and moved against Tuscany. Florence declared war, even though a peace party, headed by one Giovanni de' Medici, favored negotiations. The Milanese beat them badly in several battles, and the pope in Rome was against them as well. Florence was saved when the Venetians joined the war on their side and forced the Viscontis to sign an unfavorable peace in 1427. Florence was sorely tempted by the plucky little city of Lucca nearby and made a number of attempts to capture it, but Lucca always successfully resisted. One of Florence's attacks on Lucca brought on another war with Milan in 1432–1433. The whole campaign was badly handled and brought Florence once again close to a military debacle.

The leader of the oligarchy, Rinaldo degli Albizzi, favored the war effort. The leader of the popular party, Cosimo de' Medici (1389–1464), Giovanni's son, favored peace. Although the Medicis belonged to the privileged classes, they had been associated with popular causes ever since one member of the family, Salvestro de' Medici, had been sympathetic to the commoners during the Ciompi revolt. Rinaldo drove Cosimo into exile and tightened his grip on the government. He plotted a coup d'état, but failed to gain the needed support.

Much to Rinaldo's consternation, in 1434 a *signoria* was chosen favorable to the Medicis. The *signoria* summoned Rinaldo to the Palazzo Vecchio to answer charges that he was scheming to overthrow the state. Rinaldo gathered an armed band of some eight hundred men and civil war threatened. Pope Eugenius IV, in the city at the time, intervened. The wheel of fortune turned, and Rinaldo degli Albizzi and his aristocratic supporters were sent into exile. On October 6, 1434, Cosimo entered Florence to popular acclaim. For the next three centuries the history of Florence was inseparably intertwined with the fortunes of the Medici family.

Cosimo de' Medici was a political realist of the first order. "States are not ruled by *paternosters*," he once growled. The way in which he controlled the city of Florence is well worth analyzing. The fundamental precept of government in republican Florence had been the formulation of policy through group consultation. Cosimo kept up the practice of consultation, retained all the forms of republican government, and only very cautiously took those steps necessary to establish and consolidate his power.

One source of Cosimo's tremendous power in the city was his enormous wealth. His father, Giovanni, had acquired a great fortune through his banking and trading operations. Cosimo maintained a keen personal interest in the business and based his personal power upon his financial strength. The tax records of 1457 reveal the Medicis to have been by far the wealthiest family in Florence. Cosimo was able to lend as much as 20,000 to 30,000 florins to the city in times of crisis. He could subsidize such *condottieri* as Francesco Sforza in defense of the city. He could lend money and thus place prominent citizens under obligation to him. Moreover, the three Medici textile factories, two manufacturing woolen cloth and one silk, made a great many workers dependent for their livelihood upon the success of the Medici enterprises. Cosimo was often personally present when wages were paid, so that the laborers were made aware of their benefactor. Cosimo served as an official on the board of the *monte communale*. He understood how to use the *catasto*, a form of graduated income tax introduced earlier, in order to secure tax breaks for himself and his supporters. The reform of the *catasto* in 1458 worked to the disadvantage of the older families and in favor of the party that supported Cosimo.

When Cosimo returned in 1434 he forced into exile some seventy-three of his enemies during the first two months. This was not a large number, but they were key people of great importance. Cosimo preferred indirect control and seldom held public office himself. In 1435 he became the *gonfaloniere,* but he was very moderate, dismissed the guard that the *signoria* had set up to protect the Palazzo Vecchio, and moved about the city freely and with complete confidence. Cosimo could act decisively and with a show of force when he was pressed. In 1458 there was a minor disturbance over the arrest of Girolamo Machiavelli, a prominent member of the opposition. The *signoria,* mindful of Cosimo's interests, had several citizens arrested, tortured, and exiled. They put a hundred and fifty citizens under house arrest and forbade them to appear in public until given permission. But Cosimo and the *signoria* found few occasions that required force. The longer Cosimo retained his leadership, the more families came over to his side, until those who resisted him were too few to form an effective opposition.

The key to Cosimo's control over the government of Florence was the influence he exercised over the electoral system. The ten electors, or *accoppiatori,* who appointed the *priori* for two-month terms, were favorable to Cosimo. Cosimo did not blatantly have these ten electors given permanent tenure, but as the years passed, the *signoria* repeatedly extended the length of their terms. By the time the *accoppiatori* were permanently dissolved in 1455 and a return to traditional methods of election was effected, the opposition to Cosimo was so weak as to pose no serious threat at all. Another constitutional device for the efficient control and operation of the government was the creation of a *balia* or executive council with broad powers to scrutinize the voter lists, pass tax bills, and appoint ministers of defense. At times these key officials of the state did not even bother to meet in the appropriate chambers of the Palazzo Vecchio, but met instead in the Medici palace on the Via Larga.

Another development may have been operating in favor of Cosimo's control of the city. Some historians have held that the general level of prosperity had declined below that of 1338, and that a larger percentage of the total wealth was concentrated in fewer hands than ever before. Seven *arti maggiori* in Cosimo's day held seven of nine positions in the *signoria*. These positions were largely preempted by a very few families, favorable to Cosimo. Of the 411 names on the scrutiny list of people from the *arti maggiori* who were eligible for the three highest offices in 1448, 240 were members of 25 families. Clearly the base of political power was narrowing. At the very center of political power was Cosimo, shrewdly assessing these developments and cleverly manipulating the controls of this delicate political machine. Maintaining stability among a population as volatile as the Florentines was a noteworthy achievement indeed.

Cosimo was a friend of learning and a patron of literature and art. It is said that on his deathbed he had Platonic dialogues read to him for comfort. He was given the title of *pater patriae* by his grateful countrymen. "I know my countrymen," Cosimo once commented cynically. "They will remember me a few years hence only for the buildings I have erected in Florence."

He married his son Piero to Lucrezia Tornabuoni, of a prominent Florentine family. But Piero, nicknamed "the Gouty," was not of his father's stature. He was a magnanimous man, but he was crippled by illness. Yet he surprised his enemies, such as Luca Pitti and Agnolo Acciaiuoli, by the energy he displayed in defending his interests. During Piero's brief rule (1464–1469) Florence had to defend itself against the Venetians, who used the death of Francesco Sforza as an opportunity to move against Milan and Florence. When Piero died he left behind two sons, Lorenzo (1449–1492) and Giuliano (1453–1478), who assumed the direction of the state with greater energy than their father and much more openly than Cosimo.

In 1471 Lorenzo had a *balia* formed for a five-year term, which was made up of the *signoria*, the *accoppiatori*, and 240 Medici partisans. Lorenzo was openly moving toward a position of power. In 1472 he launched a punitive expedition against the little city of Volterra, because of a quarrel over certain alum mines, and crushed it.

Fearing the growing strength of Florence and coveting Tuscan territories for the Papal States and his nephews, Pope Sixtus IV plotted against the Medicis. He seems at least to have had knowledge of the plot against their lives, though he may not have been personally involved in it. In 1478 the Pazzis too conspired against the Medicis. While Lorenzo and Giuliano attended mass and knelt before the altar rail in the cathedral, the assassins struck. Giuliano was killed. Lorenzo fled to the vestry on the right, where he barricaded himself with some retainers and fought for his life. The vengeance that Lorenzo and his followers took upon the Pazzis was fearful, and Lorenzo emerged from the crisis in a stronger position than before. Giuliano had not been particularly interested in political life, but it was Lorenzo's great love. Giuliano left behind one illegitimate son, Giulio, who later became Pope Clement VII.

Pope Sixtus IV was relentless. He excommunicated Lorenzo and joined with King Ferrante of Naples in a war on Florence. The unholy allies met with great resistance, but finally, after a number of indecisive battles, they won a victory over the Florentines at Poggio Imperiale in 1480 and threatened the city itself. At that moment of acute danger to the city, Lorenzo took a bold gamble. He believed that he could convince King Ferrante that it was not to the advantage of Naples to build up the Papal States against Florence. He hurried to Naples and appeared before the king in person to present his case and to ask for favorable terms. "He exposed his own life," wrote Machiavelli, "to restore peace to his country." Ludovico il Moro, who had just become regent of Milan with the help of Naples, urged Ferrante to make peace. After two months of diplomatic dickering, Naples made peace, and soon thereafter the triple alliance of Milan, Florence, and Naples was restored.

Lorenzo's keen political sense told him to seize the moment to consolidate his power. In April 1480 he formed a *balia* that appointed a council of seventy, made up of Lorenzo's friends, to rule the state. Although it was originally appointed for five years, the council remained a permanent institution. Lorenzo's enemies frequently accused him, not without justification, of fusing his personal fortune with public finance in order to increase his own wealth. Lorenzo was now clearly master of the state. "If Florence had had a tyrant," wrote the historian Guicciardini some years later, "she could not have found a better one than Lorenzo."

Posterity has bestowed upon him the sobriquet Lorenzo the Magnificent. This title is in part a misreading of the Italian *magnifico,* a term of honor used very generally in the *Quattrocento* and given to various of the Medicis. He was a patron of the arts and letters, although the actual extent of his generosity is still under dispute. He sponsored the artists Ghirlandaio and Botticelli, the poets Pulci and Politian, and the philosopher Marsilio Ficino, the great Platonist. He wrote vernacular poetry himself, *canzoni* and sonnets, and appreciated the Italian classics of the Renaissance. He wrote religious poetry with a Platonic cast to it, and even did a miracle play. At the same time, his *canti carnascialeschi,* or carnival songs, were extremely sensual. During his last years he came into conflict with Girolamo Savonarola, the moralistic Dominican preacher, who criticized him for his worldliness. A legend no longer accepted by historians, but intriguing nevertheless, is that when Lorenzo summoned Savonarola to his deathbed, Savonarola refused to grant him absolution for his sins, because he had destroyed the liberty of Florence and refused to restore it. When he died in 1492 at the age of forty-three, Lorenzo designated his son Piero, nearly a total misfit, to succeed him as ruler of Florence.

Lorenzo's reputation has suffered some from recent research. It is now clear that in his preoccupation with politics he neglected the family banking enterprise and allowed the Medici fortune to dwindle. Much of his energy was dissipated in handling the petty intrigues and constant threats of new hostilities from neighboring states. He sought by diplomatic marriages to ally his family with European royalty. He succeeded in placing one son, Giovanni, in the College of Cardinals at the age of fourteen, and Giovanni became Pope Leo X.

Lorenzo's elder son, Piero (1471–1503), was a wastrel and a lecherous youth with little character and even less political sense. When Charles VIII of France invaded Italy in his march on Naples, Piero allied himself with Naples, in spite of the traditional friendship of Florence and France. When Charles entered Tuscany, took Sarzana, and threatened Florence, Piero crept submissively to the French camp, begged forgiveness, and asked Charles to spare Florence. Charles agreed, but forced him to cede Leghorn, Pisa, and other Tuscan towns. The Florentines were furious, and when Piero returned to Florence on November 8, 1494, he was not admitted to the Palazzo Vecchio. Amid shouts of *"Popolo e libertà!"* the crowds frightened him away. He fled from the city with a few retainers, and his brother, Giovanni, soon followed him into exile. The first period of Medici rule in Florence was over. With the invasion of Charles VIII, domination by major foreign powers began and Italy entered its time of troubles.

Renaissance Diplomacy

JACOB BURCKHARDT proudly called Italy the first-born among the sons of Europe, for he believed that modern secular statecraft and the interstate diplomacy that has characterized European history first emerged during the Italian Renaissance. The metahistorian Arnold J. Toynbee finds in the Italian microcosm the very laws of interstate relations that have been characteristic of international relations in contemporary Europe. He finds in the Italy of the Renaissance a balance-of-power principle. This configuration of Italian city-states lay, however, in the very center, and was unable to expand territorially. Meanwhile, the giant states to the north, west, and east grew to outsized proportions. Toynbee sees an analogy to the situation in Europe before 1914. The small states of England, France, Germany, and Italy had achieved a balance of power and held each other at a standoff. France and Germany coveted tiny bits of territory such as Alsace and Lorraine. Meanwhile, on the periphery, Russia and the United States expanded eastward and westward until they became the giants that today overshadow little Europe. That there is mimicry involved and not merely coincidence is indicated by the fact that the instruments and language of diplomacy with which Renaissance statesmen directed interstate relations have been adopted and used in the same way by statesmen of modern Europe. This phenomenon Toynbee refers to as the Italianization of the West.

This style of Renaissance statesmen, the conceptions and the language of their diplomacy, make a fascinating study. In the fifteenth century an equilibrium did develop on the peninsula and the great powers did intervene to prevent Italy's domination by a single state or its possession by an outside force. Before the end of the century the term "balance of power" was used to describe the military parity of the two groups of allies among the city-states. This conception of the balance of power was the achievement of Cosimo de' Medici, who is usually credited with arranging the alliance that was the keystone of diplomacy in the second half of the century.

After the terrifying threats of Milan to Florence and the danger from Naples had passed, Cosimo brought Florence into an alliance with its recent enemies. He had hired the *condottiere* Francesco Sforza for the defense of Florence, and after Francesco's accession to power in Milan, Cosimo saw in him a potentially strong ally. In 1454 Florence and Milan signed the Peace of Lodi, which established a strong axis of power, joined also by Naples, as a counterpoise to the Papal States and Venice. The papacy and Venice, traditionally hostile because of territorial conflicts, now found cooperation to be to their mutual interest. The balance of power thus achieved facilitated an uneasy truce that lasted for forty years, until the invasion by Charles VIII in 1494. It seemed to the Florentines that Lorenzo the Magnificent was the master diplomatist who maintained peace. Lorenzo was a skilled manipulator and came through brilliantly, as in the crisis with Ferrante of Naples; but the Florence-Milan alliance was set well before Lorenzo took over the reins.

Throughout the second half of the fifteenth century the Italians were painfully aware of the fact that they were living under the shadow of the crescent. The steady advance of the Turks had not gone unnoticed earlier, with their victory at Nicopolis in 1396 and at Varna in 1444, but the fall of Constantinople in 1453 was nevertheless a traumatic event. The battle of Belgrade in 1456, the seizure of Negropont in 1470, the assault upon Rhodes in 1480, and a number of lesser raids on the Italian peninsula itself brought home to the Italians that the terrible Turk was not only at the gateway to the West, but was already marching through it. The news of

Constantinople's fall spread throughout the West during the summer of 1453. A monk at Agarathos wrote that "nothing worse than this has happened, nor will happen." Sensitive to developments in the East, the Venetians were thrown into near panic. The secretary to the *Dieci* read the news of the fall to a silent senate. The Venetians dispatched a letter the next day warning Pope Nicholas V that the Turkish triumph was as perilous as it was grievous. The West was becoming aware of the fact that the Turks now had a base for naval and military operations on the continent which posed a possibly fatal threat. The news was accompanied by rumors of the assassination of whole city populations and the abduction of Christian children into slavery.

The diplomatic response of the Italian states to the Turkish threat was anything but inspiring. The Peace of Lodi was to preserve the peace so that the Christian princes would be able to ward off the assaults of the Turks. Similarly the Holy League, formed in 1495 by Venice, the papacy, Emperor Maximilian, Ferdinand and Isabella, and Ludovico il Moro, was ostensibly intended for the defense of Christendom against the Ottoman Turks; but in reality it was directed against the French, who had invaded Italy a year before. It has even been said that the emissaries of Bayazid II listened to the discussions from behind a screen. The diplomats illustrated the myopia of most statesmen of nearly every age, who much prefer to meet short-term emergencies rather than plan policy beyond their particular interests at any given moment.

The development of a sophisticated urban culture in Renaissance Italy and the urgencies of interstate relations led to the creation of techniques and a language of diplomacy well ahead of those in use in other parts of Europe. A more secular concept of politics was essential to the new rational and calculating approach to diplomacy. The development of the resident ambassador was one of the most important innovations in Renaissance diplomacy. Traditionally an ambassador was sent by one state to another for a specific purpose and a limited time. William Durant defined a *legatus* or legate of the thirteenth century simply as "anybody sent by another." The Italians learned the advantage of having resident ambassadors who could represent the interests of their states at all times, gather and secretly transmit information about their host country, and even intervene in local affairs. Although a variety of names for these state representatives in residence was in use in the fifteenth century, such as *orator* or *nuntius* (messenger, for ecclesiastical ambassadors), it is significant that the Italian word *ambasciator* came into general use. The states soon recognized the diplomatic immunity, safe-conduct, and special protection that accompanied the post, although there were many violations and it was centuries before these special privileges were regularized and codified in international law.

"Ambassadors," wrote Guicciardini in his *History of Italy,* "are the eyes and ears of the state." They had more than a ceremonial function, for they served as intelligence agents for their states. The Venetian ambassadors were the most famous for their detailed reports. Their instructions were to send back day-by-day accounts of all the information they could accumulate about the comings and goings of political figures, whether or not it seemed significant to them, for only the "home office" had the whole picture. They reported on the political temper of the people, the likelihood of local disturbances, the condition of the market, and general economic developments. Needless to say, these *relazioni* of the Venetian ambassadors are today prize sources of information in historical research.

The diplomats were symbols of alliances and keepers of goodwill. An ambassador, according to an epigram falsely attributed to the seventeenth-century diplomat Sir Henry Wotton by a man who didn't like him very much, is "an honest man sent to lie abroad for the good of his country." Machiavelli, who represented Florence at the court of Cesare Borgia and held other assignments, once confessed, "I never believe what I say, or say what I believe." Secret dispatches soon were sent in code and the ciphering of messages developed into a fine art. Abbot Trithemius discussed the potentials of the art in his work *Polygraphiae libri sex.* Cesare Borgia heard of a cleric in Germany, Lorenz Behaim, who had many occult powers and secret devices. He sent him a letter in which he asked Behaim how to open a letter and seal it again without leaving any sign that it had been opened; how to write a letter with ink that in two weeks would turn white or with water that would turn black; how to write on skin, on a shirt, on iron; how to transmit a ciphered message by the use of dots; how to cause a message to disappear by chewing the letter; how to develop one's memory; how to secrete poisons in prison and introduce them into food; how to use slow-acting poisons so that their effects would be apparent only after four to six months; and how to induce a severe fever in a man and then give him relief again.

Behaim wrote in his own hand a recipe for a poison that gradually desiccates the body. On the reverse side of the recipe was an invocation to the devil asking his help in making the potion effective on both body and soul.

The invasion of Italy by the non-Italian powers led to the rapid spread of Italian diplomatic methods throughout the rest of Europe. Ferdinand of Aragon was the quickest to learn, and Machiavelli greatly admired both his ability and his success. Spain remained a leader in astute diplomacy. The routines of diplomacy were varied and irregular. The growth of the nation-states, each considering itself sovereign and recognizing no power as higher than its own, brought clearly into focus the need for international law, which had remained dormant as long as the unity of Christendom existed at least as a myth in the minds of men. Hugo Grotius in the seventeenth century, while not the first to write on the subject, understood the problem and urged the development of a law of nations for the good of the sovereign states themselves.

Jacob Burckhardt once ventured the opinion that the only remedy for Italy's ills would have been a union of the free cities. Such a union would have ended the costly and debilitating internecine warfare of the Italian city-states, and would also

EUROPEAN CIVILIZATION
During The Renaissance

MILES 0   50   100   200   300

———— Boundaries of approximately 1470

Location of
School of Art ———→ ⊕ ←——— Early printing
press

Important church ——→ ⊕ ←—— Library
council

• Birthplace outside city

Florence   Location of important Renaissance
building

20°   10°   0°

NORWAY

SCOTLAND

Edinburgh
John Knox,
1505

North
Sea

DENMARK

Lübeck

IRELAND

Dublin

Coverdale,
1488

Cranmer,
1489

WALES

ENGLAND

Tyndale
1490

Malory,   Oxford
15th Cent.

Colet, 1466
More, 1478

Agricola,
1443

Bremen

HOLLAND

Rotterdam
Erasmus,
1466

Leiden

Hampton Court

London

Bruges

Brueghel,
1520

Van Eyck, 1381

Luther
1483

Wyatt,
1503

Caxton, 1422

Canterbury
Linacre, 1480

Van de Wyden,
1400

Louvain
Massys, 1460

Cologne

Ulrich
von Hutten,
1488

Lefèvre d'Étaples,
1455

DOMAINS

Gossert, 1470

Rhine

Comines,
1449

OF

Berlin
Dürer

Chartier, 1392

Noyon
Calvin, 1509

Meuse

Trier
Nicholas
Cusanus, 1401

Mainz
Gutenberg,
1391

Melanchthon,
1497

Nuremberg

Pare, 1510

Fontainebleau

Seine

Paris

NATIONAL LIBRARY,
COLLEGE OF FRANCE, 1550
Boccaccio, 1313
Charles of Orleans, 1391
Villon, 1431

Reuchlin,
1455

Regensburg

Rabelais, 1490

Blois

Loire

Chambord

THE

Basel

Augsburg

Azay-le-Rideau

Amboise

Tours

Jean Fouquet,
1415   Moulins

Dijon

DUKES

BURGUNDY

Zurich
Paracelsus,
1493

Holbein,

Constance

Zwingli, 1

Bay of

FRANCE

Angoulême
Marguerite d'Angoulême
1492

Rhone

Geneva

EMPIRE

Biscay

Bordeaux

Garonne

Loyola, 1493

Pau

Milan

Po

Venice

Genoa

Bologna

AGE OF HUMANISM

**RENAISSANCE PAINTING
AND SCULPTURE**

CLASSICAL AND BIBLICAL STUDIES

FIRST PRINTED BOOKS

NAVARRE

PYRENEES

Avignon

Pisa

Siena

Ferrara

Servetus, 1511

Ebro

Marseille

CORSICA
(Genoa)

ROME
VATICAN
SOCIETY

Magellan,
1480

Duero

Ximénes,
1438

ARAGON

Madrid

Barcelona

SARDINIA
(Aragon)

Lisbon

PORTUGAL

CASTILE

Tagus

Tyrrhenian

Vasco da Gama,
1450

Guadiana

Guadalquivir

Seville
Las Casas,
1474

BALEARIC ISLANDS
(Aragon)

Mediterranean

GRANADA

40°

50°

0°   10°

THE ITALIAN RENAISSANCE

MILES 0 10 20 30 40 50   75   100

—— Boundaries after the Peace
     of Lodi, 1454

• Birthplace outside city

Map labels:

SWITZERLAND

HABSBURG LANDS

DUCHY OF SAVOY

Milan

• Titian, 1477

REPUBLIC OF VENICE

Venice
ALDINE PRESS, c. 1490
J. Bellini, 1400
Alberti, 1404

• Giorgione, 1478
o Vicenza
Mantegna, 1431

Verona o
Fra. Giocondo, 1435
Paul Veronese, 1528

Pavia o
Cardan, 1501

Cremona

Piacenza

MARQUISATE OF MONTFERRAT

REP. OF GENOA

DUCHY OF MILAN

Mantua
MANTUA
Pomponazzi, 1462

Parma o Correggio, 1494

Reggio o
Ariosto, 1474

Pico della Mirandola, 1462

o Ferrara
Savonarola, 1452

DUCHY OF FERRARA

Adriatic Sea

Genoa
John Cabot, 1450
Columbus, 1451

DUCHY OF MODENA

Bologna

STATES

• Fra. Bartolomeo, 1472

REP. OF LUCCA

Lucca
Leonardo
da Vinci, 1452

REP. OF

• Fra. Angelico, 1387

PLATONIC ACADEMY, c. 1440
Brunelleschi, 1377
Donatello, c. 1386
Fra. Filippo Lippi, 1406
Ficino, 1433
Botticelli, 1447
Lorenzo de' Medici, the "Magnificent," 1449g
Americent Vespucius, 1451
Machiavelli, 1469
Guicciardini, 1483
Andrea del Sarto, 1486
B. Cellini, 1500

o Pisa

FLORENCE

Masaccio, 1402

Arezzo
Petrarch, 1303
L. Bruni, 1370
P. Aretino, 1492

o Urbino
Raphael, 1483

• Michelangelo, 1475

THE

Siena
Francesco
Giorgio, 1439

REP. OF SIENA

• Signorelli, 1441
Aeneas Sylvius, 1405

• P. Vannuchi, 1446

ELBA

CHURCH

KINGDOM OF

CORSICA

Tyrrhenian

Sea

Rome
VATICAN LIBRARY, c. 1450
SISTINE CHAPEL, 1473
L. Valla, 1405
Lucrezia Borgia, 1480

NAPLES (Aragon)

Naples

Other map labels:

Baltic Sea

o Königsberg
Regiomontanus, 1436

Danzig

Thorn
Copernicus, 1473

POLAND

Vienna

Buda o

HUNGARY

Drave

Save

Danube

Theiss

Vistula

OTTOMAN

EMPIRE

Constantinople

Salonika

Black Sea

Aegean Sea

Ionian

Sea

RHODES
(Knights of Rhodes)

CYPRUS
(Venice)

CRETE
(Venice)

Sea

Copyright by Rand McNally & Company, Made in U.S.A.

have allowed them to build up a united defense force formidable enough to discourage other powers from their adventurous invasions of Italian soil. But the contemporary Italian historian Nino Valeri quite realistically concludes that the city-states were simply too small and too selfish to act as the times required. Sir Thomas More, whose *Utopia* appeared at about the same time as Machiavelli's *Prince,* found the problem to be human pride, which is deeply rooted in the nature of man himself. "This hell-hound," he wrote, "crept into man's heart and is so deeply rooted in man's breast that it cannot be plucked out."

Bibliography

General:
Bowsky, William. *Henry VII in Italy: The Conflict of Empire and City-State, 1310–1313.* Lincoln, Nebr., 1960.
Salvatorelli, Luigi. *A Concise History of Italy.* New York, 1940.
Simeoni, Luigi. *Le signorie, 1313–1559,* 2 vols., 4th ed. Milan, 1950.
Sismondi, J. C. L. *History of the Italian Republics in the Middle Ages.* London, n.d.
Valeri, Nino. *L'Italia nell'età dei principati dal 1343 al 1516.* Verona, 1950.

Rome:
Klaczko, J. *Rome and the Renaissance: The Pontificate of Julius II, 1503–1515.* Paris, 1926.
Partner, Peter. *The Papal State Under Martin V.* London, 1958.
Paschang, John L. *The Popes and the Revival of Learning.* Washington, D.C., 1927.
Paschini, P. *Roma nel Rinascimento.* Bologna, 1940.
Roscoe, William. *The Life and Pontificate of Leo the Tenth,* 2 vols., 7th rev. ed. London, 1878.
Vaughan, Herbert M. *The Medici Popes (Leo X and Clement VII).* London, 1908.

Naples and Sicily:
Léonard, Émile G. *Les Angevins de Naples.* Paris, 1954.

Milan:
Ady, C. M. *A History of Milan Under the Sforzas.* London, 1907.
Bueno de Mesquita, D. M. *Giangaleazzo Visconti.* Cambridge, 1941.
Fondazione Treccani degli Alfieri. *Storia di Milano,* vols. 1–10. Milan, 1955–
Muir, Dorothy. *A History of Milan Under the Visconti.* London, 1924.
Pieri, Piero. *I Visconti e l'Italia del secolo XIV.* Turin, 1952.

Venice:
Cessi, Roberto. *Storia della Repubblica di Venezia,* 2 vols. Milan, 1944–1946.
Davis, James C. *The Decline of the Venetian Nobility as a Ruling Class.* Baltimore, 1962.
Hazlitt, William C. *History of the Venetian Republic,* 2 vols. London, 1915.

LANE, FREDERICK C. *Venice in History*. Baltimore, 1966.

MOLMENTI, POMPEO G. *Venice: Its Individual Growth from the Earliest Beginnings to the Fall of the Republic,* 6 vols. Chicago, 1906–1908.

Florence:

ADY, C. M. *Lorenzo de' Medici and Renaissance Italy*. London, 1955.

ALBERTINI, RUDOLF VON. *Das florentinische Staatsbewusstsein im Übergang von der Republik zum Prinzipat*. Bern, 1955.

ARMSTRONG, E. *Lorenzo the Magnificent and Florence in Her Golden Age*. London, 1896.

BECKER, MARVIN. *Florence in Transition;* vol. 1, *Decline of the Commune;* vol. 2, *Studies in the Rise of the Territorial Estate*. Baltimore, 1967, 1968.

BOOTH, C. *Cosimo I, Duke of Florence*. Cambridge, 1921.

BRUCKER, GENE. *Florentine Politics and Society, 1343–1378*. Princeton, 1962.

———. *Renaissance Florence*. New York, 1969.

GUTKIND, KURT S. *Cosimo de' Medici, pater patriae, 1389–1464*. New York, 1938.

MARTINES, LAURO. *Lawyers and Statecraft in Renaissance Florence*. Princeton, 1968.

RODOLICO, NICCOLÒ. *I Ciompi*. Florence, 1945.

RUBINSTEIN, NICOLAI. *The Government of Florence Under the Medici: 1434–1494*. New York, 1966.

RUGGIERS, PAUL G. *Florence in the Age of Dante*. Norman, Okla., 1964.

SCHEVILL, FERDINAND. *History of Florence*. New York, 1936.

———. *The Medici*. New York, 1949.

Lesser states:

ADY, C. M. *The Bentivoglio of Bologna: A Study in Despotism*. New York, 1937.

BRINTON, S. *The Gonzaga Lords of Mantua*. London, 1927.

CRISTIANI, E. *Nobilità e popolo nel comune di Pisa*. Naples, 1962.

GARDNER, E. *Dukes and Poets of Ferrara*. New York, 1904.

HERLIHY, DAVID. *Pisa in the Early Renaissance: A Study of Urban Growth*. New Haven, 1958.

———. *Medieval and Renaissance Pistoia: The Social History of an Italian Town*. New Haven, 1967.

HUTTON, E. *Sigismondo Pandulfo Malatesta, Lord of Rimini*. London, 1906.

HYDE, J. K. *Padua in the Age of Dante: The Social History of an Italian City-State, 1256–1328*. New York, 1965.

LARNER, JOHN. *The Lords of Romagna*. Ithaca, N.Y., 1965.

SCHEVILL, FERDINAND. *Siena: The History of a Medieval Community*. New York, 1964.

Renaissance diplomacy:

MATTINGLY, GARRETT. *Renaissance Diplomacy*. New York, 1954.

MOWAT, R. B. *A History of European Diplomacy, 1451–1789*. New York, 1928.

PETRY, C. *Earlier Diplomatic History, 1492–1713*. New York, 1949.

PIERI, P. *Il Rinascimento e la crisi militare italiana*. Turin, 1952.

PONTIERI, E. *L'equilibrio e la crisi politica italiana nella seconda metà del secolo XV*. Naples, 1946.

QUELLER, DONALD E. *The Office of the Ambassador in the Middle Ages*. Princeton, 1967.

CHAPTER 5

The Rise
of Capitalism

Over the door of the beautiful Renaissance house of Jacques Coeur, "the money man," in Bourges is engraved a motto that is at the same time an egregious pun on the name Coeur (heart) and an expression of the verve of that early capitalist:

TO THE VALIANT HEART
NOTHING IS IMPOSSIBLE.

The men who built enormous fortunes under most hazardous conditions needed valiant hearts and iron constitutions. They were bold adventurers, but they could also be calculating and cautious. They were driven on by that desire to acquire which was a common characteristic of all the early capitalists.

The Origins of Capitalism

HISTORY IS NEVER INNOCENT, least of all when it offers a simple narrative or a single analysis as unadorned truth. There are a number of major theories about the origins of capitalism, theories so controversial that blood as well as ink has been spilled over them.

THE QUALITATIVE SCHOOL

The qualitative school of economic history held that the critical factor in the development of capitalism was a change in the mind and outlook of man. Whereas the medieval agrarian system had provided security, with a predetermined place for every man, and kept most people at the minimum subsistence level, capitalism resulted from the development of a strong acquisitive instinct. The desire to accumulate wealth, the self-restraint requisite for delayed satisfactions, and the mental discipline necessary for rationalizing economic activity were part of the new economic man imbued with the spirit of capitalism. One of the early leaders of this qualitative school, Werner Sombart, a German political economist writing in the early twentieth century, found this mentality in Leon Battista Alberti, the author of a work *On the Family,* which identifies and lauds the bourgeois virtues of sobriety, thrift, rational order, industry, and the desire to build a family fortune for future generations. Daniel Defoe's Robinson Crusoe was exemplary in husbanding the resources of his island, accumulating a store in his stockade, and putting his man Friday to work. Benjamin Franklin's *Poor Richard's Almanac* exuded the capitalistic spirit in its admonitions: "Time is money"; "A penny saved is a penny earned." In his *Household Book* Anton Tucher, a German capitalist, showed how accounts were to be kept to eliminate any frivolous spending and how money was to be carefully husbanded. Sombart believed that high churchmen, bureaucrats in the rising national monarchies, and aristocrats who collected rents on land, rather than tradesmen, were responsible for the primary accumulation of capital. He emphasized the importance of woman's role in the demand for luxuries and the effects of this demand on the growth of cities. He believed also that Jews were especially important to the rise of capitalism, for in accordance with the Mosaic laws they were industrious and lived orderly lives. Moreover, because of the ecclesiastical restraints upon usury, Christians left financial activity largely to the Jews.

The sociologist Max Weber, a contemporary of Sombart, argued that Protestantism and especially the ethic of Calvinism produced the kind of sober, hardworking men who pursued their vocations with zeal and considered material success a sign of God's favor. R. H. Tawney found these virtues to be a general Christian phenomenon and an inheritance from Judaism. Luigi Brentano traced the emergence of the acquisitive instinct to the early Middle Ages, and argued the futility of trying to pin down its actual beginning.

THE MARXIST SCHOOL

Karl Marx and Friedrich Engels theorized at great length on the nature, origin, and demise of capitalism. They stressed the separation of the ownership of the means of production and the producer or worker, the labor theory of value, and the rise of capitalism in the total setting of their historical dialectic. Since their day, knowledge of early economic history has so increased and economic analysis has become so refined that in contemporary scholarly discussion the views of more sophisticated Marxist theorists such as Maurice Dobb are given more weight than the historically interesting but superseded statements of Marx himself.

In his various studies of the rise of modern capitalism, Maurice Dobb raises a number of important questions. The question of causation brings up the Marxist assertion of the inefficiency of feudalism. In the onward movement of the historical dialectic, according to the Marxists, feudalism was bound to collapse because of its own internal contradictions, just as capitalism will do eventually. Dobb argues that the inefficiency of the feudal system was causally more important than blows from without, such as the incursions of merchant capitalism. He describes the money economy of the twelfth to the sixteenth centuries as a merchant capitalism, which should not be confused with industrial capitalism. The merchant capitalists were, as Marx described them, parasitical, not contributing to the total wealth by labor, but merely exploiting price differentials due to differences in market conditions. The Marxist analysis is highly complex and is not to be dismissed cavalierly, but a few questions can be raised. If the feudal agrarian economy was so inefficient, whence came the increment of value represented in the early accumulation of capital used to develop trade? If merchant capitalism was parasitical, merely siphoning off the surplus, could it have been the source of the capital that made possible the expansion of industry? If old feudal agrarian arrangements in England first declined in the counties far from the mercantile center of London and persisted near London, was this because the wealth of the city supported the inefficient agrarian system nearby? Why didn't the feudal agrarian economy decline first in Russia, far from the most active mercantile centers of western Europe? In general, most informed historians find that the Marxists do not give due consideration to multilateral causation and to mutually interdependent variables such as the effects of the money economy, the desire for luxuries, the breakup of the land-labor ratio, and the contribution of merchants in risk, labor, enterprise, and exchange of raw materials for finished products.

THE MERCHANT ENTERPRISE SCHOOL

The point of view that most Western historians find acceptable is much more complex and not compressed within a ready-made ideological structure. It is now well established on the basis of numismatic and other evidence that some trade between the West and the eastern half of the Roman Empire continued even during the Dark Ages of the Germanic invasions. Nor did the Moslem expansion and domination of much of the Mediterranean completely cut off trade and nonagrarian economic activity. From the eighth to the mid-eleventh centuries the proprietary land organization was the predominant form of economic life, with the care of the individual family as virtually the limit of its capacity. The businessmen (*negociatores*) of those centuries were petty traders who operated on a small scale and in limited localities. Even then towns were growing, some in the ruins of the old Roman cities, the ancient administrative and trading centers. Urban centers and small manufacturing enterprises developed first in Italy and the Netherlands, in such towns as Bruges and Ghent. The general stability achieved during the eleventh century made possible a striking recrudescence of trade and manufacturing during the twelfth century.

Commerce developed first along seacoasts and then at the confluence of rivers and other natural centers. Peasants moved to the urban centers to work for wages and to achieve more personal freedom. As the old German saying has it, "City air makes one free!" (*Stadt Luft macht frei!*) The pioneers of commerce came from the fringes of society: poor men, adventurers, floaters. St. Godric of Finchale was a peasant who grew rich by successively larger trading operations. His aim was profit and riches, not merely a livelihood. The merchants of the eleventh and twelfth centuries organized into associations (*caritates*). Some of the wealthy *parvenus* found security by investing in land, and made further gains in ground rents and the sale of produce for cash in the growing towns. Many factors, interacting and reinforcing, contributed to the rise of capitalism.

As cities grew, manufacturing increased, especially of textiles, and many secondary industrial localities developed. Some urban centers handled merely local trade, but others developed a European market for their products. Many of the instruments of capitalism that had developed during the Roman Empire were preserved in Byzantium and transmitted back to the West. In the major urban centers capitalistic techniques were now perfected, with banknotes, credit systems, double-entry bookkeeping, and trade fairs, as at Champagne. The thirteenth century saw the raising of restrictions by the church, guilds, and city councils in the interest of the collective welfare. New, aggressive capitalists entered the scene, and new cities, such as Antwerp, less hampered by old limitations and regulations, overtook the older urban centers and outstripped them. By the fourteenth and fifteenth centuries banker-tradesmen had built enterprises that reached throughout all Europe and into the Levant, businesses that involved assets of millions of dollars, all well before the advent of Protestantism in the sixteenth century.

This analysis of the origins of capitalism is usually associated with the name of the great Belgian historian Henri Pirenne, who based his conclusions upon archival research into the growth of Flemish cities. Other writers have objected to the anticapitalist bias of the religio-sociological and Marxist schools and have been eloquent in praise of capitalist virtues. H. M. Robertson argued that the new bourgeois individualism was not merely a product of greed. He believed it inculcated a sense of honor and justice, of liberty to act in accordance with fair rules of business. The members of the bourgeoisie held man to be sufficiently rational to prefer justice to injustice. They were sincerely convinced that the market would be more cheaply and better supplied by free competition than it would be in an economy heavily controlled by legislation. The most important school for economists in the sixteenth and seventeenth centuries was the school of business experience, Robertson held. The capitalist spirit was equivalent to the rise of economic rationalism.

In assessing capitalism in the Renaissance, it is useful to bear these varying interpretations in mind.

Capitalism in Italy

In Italy the first significant accumulations of capital took place in the seaport towns. Genoa has received the most attention, in part because it developed early and was a worthy rival of Venice, but in part for the very pedestrian reason that very fine sources for the study of this problem have survived in Genoa, such as the archives of Genoese notaries before whom contracts were registered. The Bank of St. George in Genoa was one of the most powerful financial institutions in the Mediterranean world by the early sixteenth century. It exercised great political power, and because of its large holdings in Corsica it directed and supported Genoa's efforts to hold the island against Aragonese and Neapolitan aggression. But the growth of capitalistic institutions can also be traced in Pisa, Siena, Pistoia, and other major Italian cities, and very much the same pattern emerges in all of them. A basic distinction can be made between speculative capitalism, in which financiers profited by taking advantage of the fluctuating value of currencies and bills of exchange from country to country, and methodical rational enterprise of a more stable kind. Finance capitalism was useful as an instrument of both trade and industrial development.

Historians have often conveniently forgotten one source of capital and man-power during the Renaissance: the slave trade. At the end of the Roman Empire and during the early Middle Ages the institution of slavery died out. It was no longer economically viable. Moreover, the moral force of Christianity and the conviction that it was wrong to enslave a human soul worked against it. But the thirteenth century witnessed a resurgence of slavery as the merchants of Genoa and other Italian city-states, avid for profit, entered the lively slave trade in the East. Prisoners of war and the children of starving or greedy parents were bought up and sold in the markets of Egypt and in Italy itself. The Balkans and the Black Sea area provided most of the human flesh for this traffic. In Egypt slaves were bought to fill the harems and garrisons of the Mamelukes. Orientals and captured Turks were highly prized in Italy as house servants and for lowly tasks in industry. Their sale and their exploitation as a source of labor provided another source of capital. Still, although precise statistics are not available, the main source of capital remained profit gained through trade.

At first individuals traded on a very small scale. Then the "society" or simple partnership developed, with each partner supplying equal capital and participation. A more common arrangement was for one partner to supply two-thirds of the capital and stay at home, while the other partner invested only one-third of the money but personally undertook the voyage. A further development took the form of the "accommodation," an arrangement of a company of several investors who hired an agent or a factor to carry merchandise abroad for trade, an early anticipation of the joint stock company.

With this development an adjustment in legal interpretation took place. Aristotle, whose authority loomed large in the thirteenth century, had stated flatly that money is inert and cannot of itself bring forth money. The Old Testament injunction against "taking usury or increase" from a borrower was given a literal application by scholastic theorists such as Thomas Aquinas and canon lawyers. In the agrarian culture of the ancient Hebrews a man borrowed from his neighbor or family, and then only when he was in need. The extension of this command against charging interest to an impersonal situation, in which the borrower sought capital to be utilized for his own enrichment, was not really appropriate. But taking the historical situation into account was not one of the intellectuals' habits at that time. As the practice of charging interest evolved, theory adjusted to circumstances, and the scholastic philosophers developed a number of fascinating rationalizations for it. The lender could now charge interest, not on the money as such, but as just payment for his own loss in not having the use of the money while it was out on loan, for the risk he incurred in placing his money in the hands of the borrower, and for the opportunities for enrichment that he was transferring to the borrower.

In the late thirteenth century the courts ordered restitution when a man was proved guilty of usury. If the amount of usury involved was uncertain, either because the sum was indeterminate or the exploited party was unknown, then a gift to charity could be substituted for repayment. The merchant princes gradually brought about acceptance of the idea of usury and compelled a change in the prevailing social ethic. The great banking families endowed chapels, hospitals, and other foundations to redress the grievances that society or the church might have against them, at the same time magnifying their reputations as solid citizens. Later the compensation became increasingly secular, taking the forms of fountains and statues to enhance the city.

FLORENTINE BANKS

The Bardis and Peruzzis.   In the year 1254 the first florin was coined in Florence. On one side of the coin was impressed the lily of the city and on the other side John the Baptist, its patron saint. The florin became one of the most stable currencies in an epoch of economic instability.

The most prosperous of the early Florentine banking families at the end of the thirteenth and beginning of the fourteenth centuries was the Bardi family. They were basically engaged in trade, with a banking operation on the side that facilitated the mercantile activity and brought in easy profit by taking advantage of differentials in the rates of exchange. Pope Boniface VIII used the Bardi banks throughout Christendom for the collection of papal taxes from England to Poland and the transmission of money to Rome. The Peruzzis' operations were very similar to the Bardis'.

One of the Bardi agents, Pegolotti, who worked for the family for some forty years, wrote a fascinating business manual, the *Practica della mercatura.* The handbook, a useful compilation for Bardi agents, gives information on weights, the value of monetary units, and rates of exchange, and includes a discussion of the standard currencies of Italy. Pegolotti records transit tolls and taxes; describes how items are to be packed—sugar and rose water from Cypress, for example—in order to preserve them; discusses the standard weight of wool per sack in England, the gathering of wool from monasteries, and the least expensive and most efficient transit across France, down the Rhône, and across to Florence; lists all of the feudal dues collected from the merchant transporting goods overland; describes the routes across Asia to Cathay; and lists the factors and agents in charge of the Bardi trading posts in Syria, Greece, Spain, Bruges, Ghent, Antwerp, Poland, and elsewhere throughout the empire—some four hundred in all. It is fascinating to learn that when the Bardis went into receivership, Pegolotti was one of those who took over what remained of their assets. He knew the business extremely well.

Political loans proved to be the ruination of the Bardis, as well as of many other banking houses during the next two centuries. At the beginning of the Hundred Years' War England was well behind other countries in economic development. It served almost as a colony, producing raw materials for more advanced industrial areas, notably Flanders. The Bardi bank supplied huge loans to the feudal English monarchy, which had a very inefficient revenue system and was usually at least a year behind in its collection of taxes. The government adopted the practice of anticipating income from taxes and borrowing money from the bankers, who received the tax revenues at the end of the year, usually a good deal more than the loan had been. This easy money became a trap, for the escalation from small political loans to large ones was easily made, especially when the bank had become obligated for obvious windfalls. Pegolotti tells of precious cups and other treasures given to members of the royal family, sometimes as gifts and sometimes as payment in kind. Not until 1338 and 1339, during the reign of Edward III, did the Bardis float a really large loan, guaranteed by the wool taxes. Since the Bardis had at the same time made loans in France, Naples, and other countries, they were dangerously overextended.

In 1340 Edward III, in great financial difficulty because of the war, repudiated all of his debts except those to the Bardis, whom he considered essential to his war economy, but very shortly thereafter he threw the Bardi agents into prison as well. The default of England and the Bardis' general overextension brought them to bankruptcy. In the same year some less important members of the Bardi family planned a coup in Florence, in the hope that control of the city-state's foreign policy might enable them to achieve greater security for their foreign investments. Their plan failed, although various members of the Bardi family retained important status in Florentine society even after their bank collapsed. The city-state did not provide sufficient political leverage for economic enterprises that were extended far beyond its influence.

The Medicis. The Medici family learned from the experience of the Bardis and Peruzzis. Whereas the Bardis' operations were highly centralized, so that when the English branch went bankrupt, the whole bank suffered the loss, the Medicis organized their bank on a decentralized system. From 1434 on, under Cosimo, the Medici bank operated as a system of partnerships between the central bank, managed out of the main office to the left of the grand entrance of their palace, and agents in various cities. The arrangements varied, and were drawn up as individual contracts between the bank and the agents, with the main bank holding the controlling interest but with the agent making a large personal investment, which guaranteed his energetic participation and proper caution.

The Medici bank was involved in trade as well as banking—trade in bills of exchange and trade in goods. Although Giovanni de' Medici amassed a respectable fortune, the Medici bank entered its greatest period with Cosimo, who was the senior partner in eleven enterprises. Bound to the main bank by contracts were three industrial establishments in Florence and about eight banking houses in other major European cities. The branch managers were junior partners who took a share of the profits rather than drawing salaries. They made their day-to-day decisions with complete freedom. Although they usually dealt with other Medici branches, each managed his individual branch as though it were an independent concern. Control by the senior partners in Florence on matters of policy was firm but quite general. Of course, the senior partners (among whom the principal ones were members of the Medici family) contributed most of the capital to operate the branches and drew most of the profits.

The three Medici industrial operations in Florence were a silk factory and

THE OPERATIONS OF THE MEDICIS AND FUGGERS

MILES 0   50   100   200   300

Florence ★   The Medici center
         ○   Medici branches
Augsburg ★   The Fugger center
         △   Fugger branches
         ◻   Fugger mines

two woolen cloth factories, each operated by a separate Medici-controlled partnership. The word "factory" is really a misnomer, for there were no industrial plants, and production was organized on a putting-out system. Finished goods were sold to local exporters or shipped to foreign branches of the Medici bank. These industrial enterprises were not very important in the overall Medici operation.

The banking operation was not a simple matter of lending at interest, for interest charges were taboo on religious grounds. The bankers carried on a traffic in bills of exchange, devices by which merchants bought and sold merchandise in one currency in one locality and made or received payment in another currency at another locality. Hence banking was an indispensable adjunct of commerce. Its relation to industry was very slight. The profit derived from handling bills of exchange was derived not by discounting them in advance, but by a somewhat hazardous calculation on a favorable rate of exchange. Money-market watching was the favorite indoor sport of fifteenth-century bankers.

As we have seen, there has been much theoretical speculation on the source of capital, and the answer in the case of the Medicis is interesting. The profits accumulated through trading were in part added to the capital holdings of the company. Money was invested not only by the Medicis and their junior partners, but also by outsiders. Many of the investors were Florentines, but some were not. The French politician and chronicler Commynes invested in the Lyon branch. The Medicis paid interest to its outside investors.

The Medicis' banking operations served to facilitate their trading operations. The Bruges bank, for example, bought and sold commodities like any merchant firm: wool, silk, spices, olive oil, alum, nuts, currants, citrus fruits, Venetian glass, any item for which there was a market. Just like the Bardis in their day, the Medicis in Rome acted as fiscal agents for the papacy. For a time they managed the alum mines owned by the papacy in the Papal States.

During his last years Cosimo was unable to oversee the vast operation in his customary way. Piero was so ill and unsure of himself that he could not maintain firm control. Lorenzo was involved in the cares of state and in grand political designs, and so neglected the business. The third quarter of the fifteenth century saw several reverses and an overall decline due to general mismanagement and overextension. The Bruges branch, under a reckless and politically ambitious manager, lent money to the ill-fated Burgundian duke Charles the Bold, killed at Nancy in 1477. The Medicis themselves invested ever larger sums in culture, patronage of men of letters, and artistic monuments, and plowed increasingly smaller amounts of their profits back into the business. The branches went down like dominoes: London, Venice, Bruges. Then in 1494, the year of Charles VIII's invasion, the Roman branch folded and the home office in Florence closed down.[1]

The observation of the early capitalists during the Italian Renaissance suggests both the potentialities and the limitations of their position. The small city-state seemed to be a congenial environment as a base of operations, for the capitalists were able to assert control over the political power on the local level. The city-state, however, had definite limitations, for it lacked the power to offer real protection to its merchants abroad, even in enforcing contracts, to say nothing of fighting piracy and confiscation by larger states. Even Venice, the most successful in this respect because of its great naval power, was always subject to losses. In the long run the city-state could not provide sufficiently secure coverage for the continuity of an international financial operation. In the larger states the basis for a mercantilist national economic organization was already present in the fourteenth century.

A certain myopia on the part of these early capitalists is evident. They were often apologetic about their materialism on moral grounds, and frequently suffered pangs of conscience about usurious practices. Because of the precariousness of their whole operation, they tended to be very much on the defensive. They seem

---

[1] See Raymond A. de Roover, *The Medici Bank: Its Organization, Management, Operations, and Decline* (New York, 1948) and *The Rise and Decline of the Medici Bank, 1397–1494* (Cambridge, Mass., 1963).

not to have realized the full extent of the political power that their economic strength would have permitted them to wield. It may have required more time than they had to adjust psychologically to the new reality they helped to bring into being, the power of capitalism.

The Hanse

ALTHOUGH THE EARLY emergence of capitalism in Italy is particularly striking, it was a European phenomenon, and by the fifteenth century it was fully developed in many parts of the continent. The Hanse (League) in the north was a full-blown international organization of merchant capitalists whose operations reached from the Atlantic into Russia and whose naval power grew great enough to bring a king to his knees.

Two conditions made possible the organization of the Hanseatic cities. The first was the difference in economic life between western Europe and the Baltic area. The west, with its textile manufacturing, was industrially more advanced than the east, with its basic raw materials. The Hanseatic merchants provided the essential link between them, taking cloth and fine goods to the Baltic in exchange for such products as Swedish iron, lumber, herring, amber, and furs. Furs were especially prized by the upper classes, for castles and manor houses were even harder to heat than the small cottages of the peasants.

The second condition favoring the development of the Hanse was the freedom of the German commune in comparison with those states (England, France, Aragon, Castile) where the central government was stronger than the emperor. The Hohenstaufen emperors in the thirteenth century were preoccupied with Italian affairs, and in the fourteenth century the interregnum as well as the weakness of the emperors left the German cities free to go their own way. Whole colonies of merchants emigrated to new locations. The movement into the Baltic area by German merchants in the thirteenth and fourteenth centuries was much like the colonization of Sicily and other Mediterranean areas by the Doric Greeks in antiquity. Cologne merchants went to London, where they enjoyed special privileges and participated in guild activities and in city government. Known as Easterlings in London, they even minted their own silver coins, and gave their name to "sterling" silver. The Hanse had outposts in Pomerania, Königsberg, and Riga, and on the island of Gotland, where the German merchants at Visby developed a more elaborate form of corporate organization. Merchants of the Hanse traveled as far as Novgorod in search of furs and amber and were active as far west as the Iberian peninsula. Bruges was a Hanseatic "staple": a center for the sale of certain commodities, in which any ship arriving with such commodities

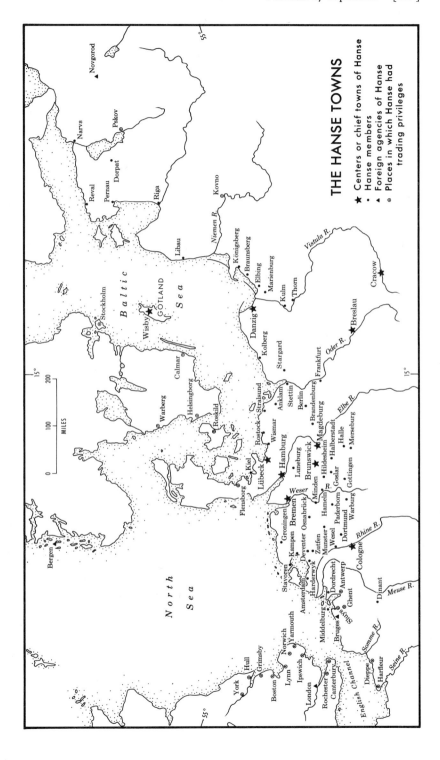

THE HANSE TOWNS

★ Centers or chief towns of Hanse
• Hanse members
▲ Foreign agencies of Hanse
⊙ Places in which Hanse had trading privileges

had to give the merchants of the Hanse the privilege of buying first, a very profitable advantage.

In the fourteenth century the Hanse rode the high tide of fortune. The Hanse met in a diet, usually at Lübeck. Visitors to Lübeck today can still see there the red-brick St. Mary's Church, the commerce building, the Hospital of the Holy Ghost for retired sea captains, and the city gate, endowed by the Hanseatic merchants in the city's heyday. The diet taxed its members and planned their military defense. The year 1370 marks the high point of Hanseatic power, for in that year, after a long contest with the Danish king, marked by naval battles and the invasion of Denmark, representatives of the Hanse dictated the terms of the Peace of Stralsund.

During the fifteenth century the Hanse declined under the pressure of larger states. As the duchy of Muscovy expanded, it took in Novgorod. In England, the Netherlands, Scandinavia, and Flanders the Hanseatic merchants encountered increasing restrictions and limitations. The tradition-bound conservatism of Hanseatic policies contributed to the decline of Bruges, which was finally ruined as a port by the silting up of the Zwyn estuary. The first great movement of foreign merchants from Bruges to Antwerp took place in 1442. Antwerp, unhampered by traditional restrictions and encouraged by Habsburg diplomacy, rose rapidly as the most important trade center in the Netherlands for silver, copper, alum, spices, and textiles. During the late fifteenth century a peculiar thing happened, still unexplained: The herring emigrated from the Baltic to the North Sea, which forced the reorganization of the fishing industry. But the main cause of the decline of the Hanse was the rise of competitive forces within a large national political structure.

Capitalism in France

A STRIKING EXAMPLE of an individual capitalist operating within the structure of a rising national state is the famous Jacques Coeur (1395–1456) of France.

Coeur was the son of a fur merchant connected with the Hanse. Young Jacques was trained for the French royal service. At an early age he took charge of the royal mint in Bourges. There he was arrested and tried for coin clipping. In the course of his trial it became clear that he had trimmed the precious metals from the coins with royal connivance, and he very conveniently escaped. He appeared next in the Near East, where he organized trade to supply the needs of the court. In a very short time Coeur had many agents and ships under his control. In the final period of the Hundred Years' War, Coeur lent money to the French king to finance his decisive victories in Normandy. He was rewarded with an appointment as the king's jeweler.

Suddenly Coeur suffered another reversal of fortune. He was arrested and tried on a number of serious charges: that he had poisoned Agnes Sorel, the king's mistress; that he had accepted gifts from the Ottoman Turks; and that he had impressed sailors into forced labor. Coeur escaped from prison and fled to the Turks, but after a time he turned against them and fell at last in a campaign mounted by the pope against the Turks after the fall of Constantinople. His beautiful Renaissance house still stands in Bourges, a tribute to the good taste of at least one of the *nouveaux riches*.

LYON

One cannot leave the French scene without taking note of at least one rising commercial center, which illustrates what the favor of the rising national monarchy could mean not merely to an individual, but to a whole city. The trading center of Lyon, even more than the international bourse in Antwerp, was the conscious and carefully tended creation of its country's rulers. After the fairs at Champagne went into decline early in the fourteenth century, France lacked a prominent trading center. King Charles VII was the first to give favorable treatment to Lyon, in order to build it up as a competitor to prosperous Geneva. Late in the fifteenth century, Louis XI, with a mercantilist economic approach, further strengthened Lyon in order to prevent the loss of bullion through trade in Geneva. Lyon developed a bourse, held four fairs, and became an important center for the new and fast-growing printing industry.

German Capitalists

LIKE ITALY, the empire was subdivided into many small states, including imperial and territorial cities with a great deal of freedom. These cities along the Rhine and especially in southern Germany became centers for feverish mercantile activity. The merchants of Augsburg, Nuremberg, Ulm, Regensburg, and other cities of southern Germany carried on a lively trade with the cities of northern Italy, through the Brenner pass and along other routes. In some places, such as Venice, part of the city was allotted to them as a center for their banking and mercantile operations. They served as a link between Italy and the Netherlands. In time they amassed such fortunes that through their international banking operations their activities reached through all of Europe.

THE FUGGERS

The growth of a family fortune through several generations is best illustrated by the fabulous Fuggers of Augsburg. Hans Fugger came to Augsburg from a small village as a fustian weaver. He became a trader on the side, selling his own textiles and those of his less enterprising neighbors, and accumulated a small fortune of three thousand florins. Jakob Fugger I, Hans's son, became master of the Guild of Weavers in Augsburg. Through his father-in-law, who was mintmaster in Tyrol, Jakob became interested in mining investments in the Tyrol, which became his second source of wealth. Jakob II, called "the Rich," began with a great deal of caution to make political loans. Since these paid a high rate of interest, his wealth grew rapidly. His loans to Maximilian I, for example, were guaranteed by the income from the royal salt mines. In an impudent letter to Charles V, Jakob Fugger once reminded the emperor that he owed his crown to the Fugger bank, which had lent the money with which he bought the votes of the electors. His marriage to a member of the Thurzo family of Austria, with mining interests in Hungary, the Tyrol, and the Sudeten mountains, increased his fortune. When urged by Thurzo to retire, Jakob Fugger made his famous statement: "I shall earn as long as I am able."

The heyday of the house came under Anton Fugger (1493–1560). During the Schmalkald War the house suffered losses by having holdings in Protestant as well as Catholic lands. (The Fuggers were Catholics.) The Fugger bank was caught again when the Spanish Habsburgs defaulted in 1575. In 1650 the Fuggers still had a claim of some 615,000 florins against the Habsburgs. The social settlement of 142 residents that Jakob II built for the poor in Augsburg, the Fuggerei, is still in service, and the indigent still pay only a few marks a month rent. He dedicated it "to the praise of God and in gratitude to Him." The chapel he built in the compound still stands. And in the rebuilt Fugger house, descendants of the family still operate a Fugger bank, though on a small scale.

The form of business combination used by the Fuggers was a family partnership, a link in a chain that led to the joint stock company. The business was centralized in the home office at Augsburg, but somewhat localized in the very distant cities such as Antwerp and Naples. Their policy was to keep control in the family, but to keep the leadership as virile and aggressive as possible. Jakob Fugger II has been called the first modern businessman, but since he did not specialize, he belonged to an order that has in the main disappeared.

OTHER GERMAN CAPITALISTS

The rapid development of the silver mines of the Tyrol around the middle of the fifteenth century induced the Fuggers and other families to leave the traditional paths of trade with Venice and to venture into mining operations. The Meuting family of Augsburg invested in Tyrolean mines as well as in silver mines in Saxony. The Paumgartner family of Nuremberg invested in Tyrolean copper mines.

The Welser family, which ranked next to the Fuggers in wealth, was an old Augsburg family. The Welsers joined with the Vöhlins to enter the Tyrolean silver business and played a prominent role in the great trade expeditions to the East Indies. They had active factories in both Antwerp and Lisbon, and eleven branch offices in leading cities. Conrad Peutinger and other humanists acted as agents for them. Like the Fuggers, however, they could not resist the temptation of easy profits on risky political loans. They made sizable loans to the Habsburgs, but regretted them during the Schmalkald War, when their money and land were confiscated by princes who grew suspicious of their imperial loans. The Welsers' claims on the French court and in the Netherlands remained unpaid. They fell into great difficulty during a credit crisis in 1562 and could scarcely meet the demands of their own creditors.

The Hochstetters were the third most important of the south German capitalist families. Ambrosius Hochstetter made a phenomenal rise and was one of the first to set up a branch in Antwerp. The Hochstetters were engaged in the East Indies trade and came very close to establishing a monopoly in quicksilver, but failed when new deposits were discovered in Hungary and Spain. They soon were beset with financial trouble with the Greshams in England and went broke in Antwerp. If their rise was rapid, their fall came early, for by around 1530 their house went into receivership.[2]

CAPITALISM AND CONSCIENCE

As time went by, the consciences of the early capitalists were bothered less and less by the charging of interest and monopolistic practices. They kept up certain pious pretentions, as when Francesco di Marco Datini headed his account book "To God and Profit." The Augsburg merchants and the Ravensburg trade association kept separate accounts captioned "Our Lord God's Capital." In their account book of 1511 the Fuggers included 15,000 florins for charity dedicated to St. Ulrich, the patron saint of Augsburg. Piety and profit were beautifully harmonized.

Preachers and moralizers might storm against them, but the merchant princes remained unperturbed and even hired propagandists to counterattack. The popular Alsatian preacher Geiler von Kaisersberg and the humanist Sebastian Brant, au-

---

[2] For a more detailed account of early German financiers, see Richard Ehrenberg, *Capital and Finance in the Age of the Renaissance* (New York, 1928), chap. 2, "The Other German Financiers," pp. 133–92.

thor of *The Ship of Fools,* boldly attacked usury and monopolies. The humanist Adelmann von Adelmannsfelden applied Plutarch's treatise *On Avoiding Usury* in a very obvious way to Jakob Fugger. The Fuggers supported the young Ingolstadt professor of theology Johannes Eck, who drew a distinction between interest and usury, and argued that the charging of interest was permissible. When the bishop of Eichstätt refused to allow a public disputation on the question, Eck traveled to Bologna, with a subsidy from the Fuggers, and there defended interest charges of 5 percent. The Dominicans adopted his position and the University of Paris favored his thesis. Although these intellectuals provided a theoretical basis for charging interest with arguments drawn from moral philosophy, the Catholic Church itself held officially to its absolute injunction against interest all through the Renaissance and Reformation period; in fact, down to the nineteenth century.

Industrial Development

IN EUROPE as a whole, the general economy picked up from the mid-fifteenth century on. The picture in Italy is unclear and is still debated. While many nineteenth-century historians believed that the great efflorescence of culture in the *Quattrocento* was a natural concomitant of a prosperous bourgeois society, some more recent historians have argued that the investments in culture were made despite hard times. It is fairly clear that in the second half of the fourteenth century the level of prosperity fell far below the heights reached around 1338. In the fifteenth century, Genoa, of course, went down, but Florence made a good recovery. It has been argued that fewer families were wealthy and that the aggregate wealth of a city like Florence was less than it had been early in the preceding century, but that is yet to be proved. Certain indices point to a higher general level of prosperity in fifteenth-century Florence. The manufacture of silk, for example, a real luxury item, increased markedly. We know, too, how the resourceful Venetians adjusted to the exigencies of the times, and that many of the most splendid palaces of the merchant princes along the Grand Canal were built during the seventeenth and eighteenth centuries. Yet with the foreign invasions from 1494 on, Italy's difficulties increased enormously, and the economies of Lombardy and Tuscany suffered.

Industry changed more slowly than commerce during the fifteenth and sixteenth centuries. Textiles had been very important during the medieval period, but from the mid-fifteenth century on other large industries developed, notably printing, mining, metallurgy, and silk manufacture. Although block printing had been in use for some time, the invention of the printing press by Johannes Gutenberg triggered the development of a major new industry. His original contribution, around the year 1450, was the development of an alloy that could be poured into molds to form letters that would not shrink or twist on cooling. This made feasible the use of movable type. From the thirteenth century on the supply of paper had increased, so that the mass production of books was now possible. Books now cost only one-twentieth as much as they had cost in manuscript. From Mainz printing establishments spread rapidly throughout Europe. In the printing establishments the owner of the press hired the printers and kept their apprentices, thus separating the workers from ownership of the means of production. They introduced standardization in production and rationalization in schedules, for they tried to time a book's production to meet set dates, such as the opening of the Leipzig and Frankfurt fairs. Labor troubles developed early in this industry, and the printers struck in Lyon. King Francis I published edicts ordering the suppression of labor disturbances and regulating the relationship of journeyman printers and apprentices. Some publishing centers had as many as five thousand of the new industrial proletariat.

Astonishing technological breakthroughs were made in the mining industry. Georg Agricola, in a treatise *On Metals*, described the new machinery and techniques for separating the metal from the ore and purifying it. Legal problems regarding the rights to underground resources had to be resolved. Theorists on Roman law held to the right of the monarch to the ownership and control of all underground minerals. But as the princes fell into financial difficulties, they transferred their titles to mineral rights to the bankers as security for loans. The financiers were quick to exploit these mineral resources, and copper, iron, and silver mining boomed.

One mining enterprise of special importance in this period was the production of alum, a sulfate that was used in textile manufacturing to fix dyes. During the Middle Ages most of the alum used in Europe came from Asia Minor. Western mining engineers and technicians had worked the deposits there, but as the Turks advanced they returned to the West, and frantic search for new alum deposits began. The ancient alum mines at Volterra were rediscovered in 1458 and at Tolfa in the Papal States in 1461. The papacy attempted to establish a monopoly on alum production as a source of funds for a crusade against the Turks. Papal agents actually used some of the funds to encourage Balkan leaders to resist. The Chigis and other bankers helped to finance and manage the papal mining enterprises. The mines employed eight to ten thousand workers.

The growth of the silk industry, especially in Italy and France, was another important industrial development of the time. Lucca in Tuscany was Italy's major silk center, but Florence and other cities also increased production of this luxury item.

From the end of the fifteenth century through most of the sixteenth century Europe experienced an inflationary spiral. The rise in prices served as a stimulus to industrial expansion, but wages, as always, rose much more slowly than prices. The laborers caught in this financial squeeze fought for better pay, and industrial relations throughout the century can hardly be described as tranquil. Europe, of course, has never been known for tranquillity in any case.

The rise of capitalism and the development of an urban society were necessary preconditions for much of the rebirth of culture during the fourteenth and fifteenth centuries. The economic factor was important for the emergence of the modern world. It helped to shape the political and social framework within which Renaissance cultural developments took place. Capitalism served as a solvent of the medieval agrarian economy by facilitating the transition from feudalism to larger territorial and national states. To state this is by no means to suggest economic determinism, for in addition to the economic component, many political, traditional, intellectual, aesthetic, and religious forces were at work which were often only remotely influenced by economic considerations. The human spirit is capable of great creative breakthroughs, and economic conditions can seldom be shown to be their prime cause.

Bibliography

General economic history:
Boissonade, P. *Life and Work in Medieval Europe: Fifth to Fifteenth Centuries.* New York, 1927.
Cambridge Economic History of Europe, 6 vols., vols. 1–3. Cambridge, 1941–1967.
Dobb, Maurice. *Modern Capitalism: Its Origin and Growth.* London, 1928.
———. *Studies in the Development of Capitalism.* London, 1946.
Genicot, Léopold. "Crisis: From the Middle Ages to Modern Times." In *Cambridge Economic History of Europe,* 2nd ed., vol. 1, pp. 660–741. Cambridge, 1966.
Glass, D. V., and Everseley, D., eds. *Population and History.* Chicago, 1965.
Gras, N. S. B. *Business and Capitalism.* New York, 1939.
———. *A History of Agriculture in Europe and America,* 2nd ed. New York, 1940.
Heaton, Herbert. *Economic History of Europe,* 2nd ed. New York, 1948.
Lopez, Robert. "Hard Times and Investment in Culture." *The Renaissance: A Symposium,* pp. 19–34. New York, 1953.
——— and Miskimin, H. A. "The Economic Depression of the Renaissance." *Economic History Review,* 14 (1962): 408–26.
Mols, Roger. *Introduction à la démographie historique des villes d'Europe du XIVe au XVIIIe siècle,* 3 vols. Louvain, 1954–1956.
Nef, John U. "Industrial Europe on the Eve of the Reformation." *Journal of Political Economy,* 44 (1941): 1–40, 183–224.
Nelson, B. N. *The Idea of Usury.* Princeton, 1949.

PERNOUD, R. *Les villes marchandes aux XIVe et XVe siècles: Imperialisme et capitalisme au moyen âge.* Paris, 1948.

PIRENNE, HENRI. *Medieval Cities: Their Origins and the Revival of Trade.* Princeton, 1925.

———. *Economic and Social History of Medieval Europe.* New York, 1937.

ROBERTSON, H. M. *Aspects of the Rise of Economic Individualism.* Cambridge, 1935.

SÉE, HENRI. *Modern Capitalism: Its Origin and Evolution.* New York, 1928.

SOMBART, WERNER. *Luxury and Capitalism.* Ann Arbor, 1967.

———. *The Quintessence of Capitalism: A Study of the History and Psychology of the Modern Businessman,* tr. and ed. M. Epstein. New York, 1967.

VON MARTIN, ALFRED. *Sociology of the Renaissance.* London, 1944.

Italy:

CONTI, E. *La formazione della struttura agraria moderna nel contado fiorentino.* Rome, 1965.

DAVIDSOHN, ROBERT. "Über die Entstehung des Kapitalismus." In *Forschungen zur Geschichte von Florenz,* vol. 4, pp. 268f. Berlin, 1908.

FANFANI, AMINTORE. *Le origini dello spirito capitalistico in Italia.* Milan, 1933.

GOLDTHWAITE, RICHARD A. *Private Wealth in Renaissance Florence. A Study of Four Families.* Princeton, 1968.

LANE, FREDERICK C. *Venetian Ships and Shipbuilding of the Renaissance.* Baltimore, 1934.

———. *Andrea Barbarigo, Merchant of Venice, 1418–1449.* Baltimore, 1944.

LUZZATO, GINO. *An Economic History of Italy.* London, 1961.

ORIGO, IRIS. *The Merchant of Prato: The Life and Papers of Francesco di Marco Datini.* London, 1957.

RICHARDS, GERTRUDE R. *Florentine Merchants in the Age of the Medici.* Cambridge, Mass., 1932.

ROOVER, RAYMOND DE. *The Medici Bank: Its Organization, Management, Operations, and Decline.* New York, 1948.

———. *The Rise and Decline of the Medici Bank, 1397–1494.* Cambridge, Mass., 1963.

SAPORI, A. *La crisi delle compagnie mercantili dei Bardi e dei Peruzzi.* Florence, 1926.

———. *Studi di storia economica medievale,* 3rd ed. Florence, 1955.

Northern Europe:

CARUS-WILSON, E. M. *Medieval Merchant Venturers.* London, 1954.

DOLLINGER, PHILIPPE. *La Hanse (XIIe–XVIIe siècles).* Paris, 1964.

EHRENBERG, RICHARD. *Capital and Finance in the Age of the Renaissance.* New York, 1963.

HERING, ERNST. *Die Fugger.* Leipzig, 1939.

KERR, A. B. *Jacques Coeur, Merchant Prince of the Middle Ages.* New York, 1927.

PAGEL, KARL. *Die Hanse,* 4th ed. Brunswick, 1965.

PLANITZ, HANS. *Die deutsche Stadt im Mittelalter.* Graz, 1954.

POWER, EILEEN. *The Wool Trade in English Medieval History.* London, 1941.

——— and POSTAN, M. M., eds. *Studies in English Trade in the Fifteenth Century.* London, 1933.

Roover, Raymond de. *Money, Banking, and Credit in Medieval Bruges.* Cambridge, Mass., 1948.

Sée, Henri. *Histoire économique de la France.* Paris, 1939.

Strieder, Jakob. *Jacob Fugger the Rich.* New York, 1932.

Thrupp, Sylvia. *The Merchant Class of Medieval London, 1300–1500.* Chicago, 1948.

Van der Wee, H. *The Growth of the Antwerp Market and the European Economy,* 3 vols. The Hague, 1963.

Von Polnitz, G. *Jakob Fugger,* 2 vols. Tübingen, 1949–1951.

CHAPTER 6

Renaissance Humanism

The most characteristic form of Renaissance intellectual life was the thought of the humanists. The term "humanism" was coined by a German pedagogue, F. J. Niethammer, who used it in 1808 to refer to a philosophy of education that favored classical studies in the school curriculum. Since then the term has been subjected to many varying interpretations. Early in the nineteenth century it was used for the so-called second humanism of Wilhelm von Humboldt and his contemporaries, who made reason and experience the sole touchstones of truth. In a very general way it was tied up with those rationalistic and humanitarian attitudes cultivated by the Enlightenment. The "new" or "third humanism" of the twentieth century, militantly anthropocentric and not infrequently antireligious, existential humanism, communist "progressive humanism," and a host of other varieties have in our day further complicated the use of the term.

Even if the historian succeeds in thrusting aside all these modern connotations and examines Renaissance humanism in its historical context, the task is difficult and dangerous, for he cannot and must not reduce such a complex phenomenon to a single formula. Renaissance humanism embraced many intellectual emphases. It was not a static thing, but underwent change and movement throughout the period. It can be understood only in relation to its historical situations in both Italy and northern Europe.

Despite the difficulties, it is possible to sketch a crude profile that will point up at least the most prominent and common features of Renaissance humanism. The German scholar Paul Joachimsen offered a clear and positive definition of it as "an intellectual movement, primarily literary and philological, which was rooted in the love of and desire for the rebirth of classical antiquity." Humanism was not merely an interest in antiquity, but a certain way of looking at antiquity and of relating it to the present. Antiquity provided the humanists not only with certain classical forms of thought, literary expression, and action, but with new norms for determining the suitability and rightness of the content of thought, word, and deed. The humanists were concerned with *humaniora,* or the humane studies. The concept of the *studia humanitatis,* the liberal arts, was taken over from Cicero, who believed that the poet or orator was best suited to communicate humane learning. These liberal arts embraced grammar, rhetoric, poetry, history, and moral philosophy. The Italian humanist Leonardo Bruni expressed a thought common to nearly all of them when he wrote to Niccolò Strozzi that these studies were best designed to perfect and ornament man. The term "humanist" was initially applied to the professional teacher of these liberal arts.

As a group of professionals the humanists were continuing the medieval vocation of the *dictatores,* men who taught the skills of letter-writing and proper style in written work and in speech. The humanists were more insistent upon the imitation of classical models, but they belonged to this medieval tradition. The twelfth-century renaissance had been an ecclesiastical affair, with its chief centers at the cathedral schools of Tours, Chartres, Laon, and Orléans in France, and to a lesser extent at Canterbury in England. The principal educational resources at hand were the Latin literary classics, late antique grammars, and the rhetorical tradition. The study of the liberal arts was the customary method of training the clerical administrators needed for the expanding ecclesiastical hierarchy. Thus John of Salisbury, perhaps the most famous humanist of his time, was bishop of Chartres at the time of his death in 1180.

In the thirteenth century the teachers of the *ars dictaminis,* epistolary techniques and skills useful to an ecclesiastical official, city secretary, or chancellor, developed rhetoric and classicism. Dante's teacher Brunetto Latini not only had an impressive knowledge of the Latin classics, but even undertook to teach the Florentines the lessons that Aristotle had to offer for running the state. To say that the Renaissance humanists stood in this older rhetorical tradition, however, is not to say that they did not differ from it. They were conscious of being different, and said so loudly, in their fervent love of the classics and in their cultivation of rhetoric as a guide to and expression of wisdom. They considered eloquence of great importance and seemed never to tire of Cicero's phrase from his treatise *On Oratory:* "For eloquence is nothing else than wisdom speaking copiously."

Wisdom must be brought to bear upon life in the most effective way possible. Wisdom must be given such rhetorical expression in language and tone that form and content fuse for maximum impact upon the hearer or reader. The Italian humanists rediscovered the ancient Greek definition of man as a "living being having the power of speech." They had tremendous faith in the power of the word. Classical languages were not merely philological tools, but living instruments that were used to give expression to man's highest culture.

Before the term "humanist" came to be used in the late fifteenth and early sixteenth centuries for the professional teachers of the humanities, they applied other names to themselves and their colleagues. The most common was "orator," for they frequently held chairs of rhetoric or spoke as advocates of their cities or princes. They also called themselves philosophers, poets, even prophets (*vates:* inspired poet-prophet). As professional rhetoricians they vied with the scholastic philosophers for the place of their discipline in the universities and even for endowed chairs. Not all of the conflict of the humanists and scholastics was intellectual. In fact, the humanists did not meet scholastic philosophy head on in debate; they declared scholastic problems trivial compared with their own pursuit of wisdom.

Two Trecento Humanists

PETRARCH, FATHER OF HUMANISM

Francesco Petrarca, or Petrarch (1304–1374), was the son of Florentine exiles, who as White Guelphs were driven from the city by the Blacks at the same time as Dante. He was born in Arezzo near Florence, but when he was still young his family moved to Carpentras, near Avignon. In the family circle his father, a notary, read Cicero's letters and orations aloud. Petrarch thought Cicero so wonderful that he had to wonder at those who did not wonder at him. Then as now, the most certain way to rise in public life was through a career in law. Petrarch spent four years at the University of Montpellier and another three at Bologna, the most famous center for the study of both civil and canon law. But the study of law failed to satisfy him and he studied classical literature assiduously on the side. When his father died in 1326, he returned to Avignon, then a lively intellectual center with the pope in residence. There he enjoyed the confidence and patronage of Cardinal Colonna and other high-ranking churchmen. He took minor orders, although he was never ordained. It was on April 6, 1327, that Petrarch first laid eyes on the woman we know only as Laura, in the church of Santa Chiara in

Avignon. She was married, a beautiful woman who became the angel of his dreams, the inspiration of his sonnets. He idealized this beauty, etherealized her, sublimated his passions. His Italian sonnets, which were greatly influenced by Provençal lyrics, established his renown. Until the second half of the fifteenth century they constituted his chief claim to fame, for his other writings were little recognized until then.

Laura, alas, was carried away in the Great Plague of 1348, and Petrarch could only await a happy spiritual reunion with her in heaven. Here on earth he fathered two illegitimate children by a less ethereal woman. Always torn between the active life and the contemplative life, he loved to withdraw to his villa in the nearby valley of Vaucluse to cultivate his studies and indulge his melancholy moods. He traveled in the Netherlands, the empire, and Italy. On the nomination of King Robert of Naples, the Roman senate crowned him poet laureate on the Capitoline Hill in Rome in April 1341, and King Robert granted him a commission "for reading [teaching], disputing, and interpreting the ancient writers both in the said poetic discipline and in the said historical discipline, and for himself composing new books and poetry." In 1347 he became a supporter of Cola di Rienzo. Petrarch accepted the hospitality and patronage of the Viscontis, the Correggios, the Carraras, and Venice, whose council gave him the use of a palace. During his last years he lived once again a life of solitude on a small farm at Arquà, where his daughter, Francesca, looked after him. He was recognized by the next generation as the founder of a new cultural period.

During the medieval centuries a strange sense of identity with the Roman Empire persisted. The political myth of the "translation of the empire" to the Germans, the religious presence of the Roman Catholic Church, and the lack of a sense of history contributed to this feeling of continuity. This conception was evident in medieval art, which portrayed Roman and biblical people in medieval costumes and ancient scenes in medieval settings. Petrarch developed a new sense of distance from classical antiquity, for he felt that the centuries preceding his own times were a dark age that broke the continuity from ancient times to the present.

Petrarch was fond of letters. His own correspondence, beginning in 1325, when he was twenty-one, rivals that of Cicero, Erasmus, and Voltaire in revealing insights into his age. He used a fictional correspondence as a literary device for expressing his inner feelings. In his *Letters to the Ancient Dead* Petrarch addressed familiar letters to his cultural heroes of antiquity: Cicero, Livy, Virgil, Horace. He reported to Cicero on the condition of Rome and the empire, and wrote an epistle to Livy, the Roman historian, expressing his wish that he could have lived in Livy's age, or Livy in his. He regretted the loss of so many ancient writings, and confided that he read Livy's histories in order to forget the present low estate of Italy and the customs of his age. "I am filled with bitter indignation," he wrote, "against the mores of today, when men value nothing except gold and silver and desire nothing except sensual pleasures."[1]

Petrarch failed to integrate the Roman virtues with his Christian values. In some treatises he celebrated the Roman values of piety, gravity, dignity, faith, probity, and honesty in the hope that they would help restore virtue "in the face of the miseries of the age." In "Concerning the Best Methods of Administering a State" (*Epistolae seniles*, book 14, epistle 1) he commended the injunction found in Roman law "to harm no one, to give to each his own, and to live honestly." Petrarch thought he would be best remembered for his *Africa*, in which he depicted Scipio as the apotheosis of republican virtues in contrast to Carthaginian malice, but it turned out to be an epic bore.

In a number of important treatises, such as *On the Solitary Life* and the *Secretum*, Petrarch developed as themes conventional Christian virtues, although not without some ambivalence. In the *Secretum*, subtitled *On the Contempt of the World*, which he had first entitled *Concerning the Secret Conflict of My Desires*, Petrarch developed his religious thought in three dialogues with St. Augustine. In the second dialogue Augustine explores Petrarch's feelings of sin and guilt. He probes the melancholy in his soul (*accidia*, melancholy; not *tristitia*, sadness). The way of despair leads to destruction. Using the analogy of a besieged castle, Petrarch depicts his soul engulfed in melancholy. His trouble, Augustine ventures to suggest, is that he has too low an opinion of himself, counsel that does not have an authentic Augustinian ring to it. The problem of melancholy runs like a black thread through the texture of Renaissance thought, much like the melancholy strain in Chateaubriand and romanticism in a later century. Perhaps melancholy was generated by the insecurity that resulted from the increased individualism of the period. Possibly it was the price paid for the broader cultural horizon, which now included a much greater knowledge and deeper appreciation of pagan antiquity. Then again, perhaps the recovery of so much material from the late classic period which was pessimistic and decadent in tone worked against the basic Christian optimism of the humanists. Certainly the famines, plagues, exilings, wars, and vendettas of Renaissance Italy were unsettling enough to infect all but the hardiest types with anxiety, fear, and melancholy.

Some of the ambiguities of Petrarch's position can be seen in his *Ascent of Mt. Ventoux*, which expresses both Christian and classical ideas. It used to be said that the *Ascent* illustrated the humanist's rediscovery of nature, after the long centuries of medieval neglect. But it is quite clear that the account is not a nature story, but rather a highly sophisticated literary piece. Petrarch describes the search for a companion attuned to his own psyche and intellect. He has difficulty finding a real

---

[1] Myron P. Gilmore, "The Renaissance Conception of the Lessons of History," in *Facets of the Renaissance*, ed. William Werkmeister (Los Angeles, 1959), p. 75.

soul mate, and so he chooses his own younger brother. They meander around the mountain rather than attempting a direct vertical ascent—apparently an allusion to the circuitousness of life. Finally he leaves his brother behind and climbs alone. On the mountaintop at last, far from merely drinking in the beauties of nature, Petrarch opens St. Augustine's *Confessions* to Book 10, in which Augustine discusses the lust of the flesh, the lust of the eyes, the pride of life, and what Christian continence prescribes for each. Christ the mediator can cure the sick soul. Petrarch has Augustine deplore the fact that "human beings go around admiring the mountain heights, the mighty tides of the seas, the broad streams of the rivers, the circle of the ocean, and the orbits of the stars, but do not care to look more deeply into themselves." In the *Ascent* Petrarch is ornamenting his own experience and transforming the whole literary treatise into an allegory.

Petrarch even wrote as an apologist for the Christian view of man and the humanists' appreciation of individual worth against certain Neo-Aristotelians whose doctrines he believed to be subversive. The Neo-Aristotelians, mistakenly referred to as Averroists, held that upon a person's death his soul is absorbed into a world soul or *intellectus,* thus being assured of immortality, but of an impersonal kind. This, plus the idea of the eternal self-sufficiency of matter, seemed to Petrarch, as it was to seem to the Platonists, to be contrary to Christian doctrine and to militate against the dignity of man. He questioned the validity of a philosophy that investigates "the nature of beasts, birds, fishes, and snakes but ignores or neglects the nature and destiny of man." For much the same reason Petrarch preferred the study of law, which is concerned with society, to medicine, which is concerned with the physical body. Petrarch touched upon some of these issues in *On His Own Ignorance and That of Many Others.* Spelling out the limitation of reason, he asserted that "the object of the will is to be good; that of the intellect is truth. It is better to will the good than to know the truth." He confessed quite frankly: "If to admire Cicero means to be a Ciceronian, I am a Ciceronian. . . . However, when we come to think or speak of religion, that is, of supreme truth and true happiness, and of eternal salvation, then I am certainly not a Ciceronian, or a Platonist, but a Christian."

In his political thought Petrarch was anything but clear and realistic. He had a vague conception of Italy as his motherland, movingly voiced in his poem *"Italia mia."* But his lack of realism could be seen in his support of Rienzo. While enjoying the patronage of Francesco di Carrara in Padua he wrote "Concerning the Best Methods of Administering a State," which expressed a sense of city loyalty. It was not a great republican document, however, for he urged the despot to mobilize the civic spirit in support of state projects. The ruler must justify his existence by ruling well.

Petrarch's conception of his own place in history was expressed in his *Letters to Posterity,* which form a kind of autobiography. Renaissance men were concerned about their reputation with posterity, for fame constituted one sure form of immortality. Boccaccio spoke of man's "great desire for perpetuating his own name." The generation of humanists at the end of the fourteenth century acknowledged Dante, Petrarch, and Boccaccio as the three founders of the new age; but during the course of the Renaissance, while Dante continued to have an important symbolic cultural significance for the Italians, he gradually came to be associated more with the Middle Ages, the "voice of ten silent centuries," as the romantic writer Johann Ludwig Tieck was to call him, because he wrote in the vernacular and in the *Divine Comedy* presented a poetic *summa* of the medieval world view. In his *Epistolae familiares* (Book 21, epistle 15) Petrarch himself, in a letter to Giovanni Boccaccio, made the gratuitous comment that from his youth he had avoided the attractions of Dante for fear they might make of him too a poet "applauded by innkeepers, dyers, and wool weavers." Petrarch was the self-conscious founder of neo-Latin literature.

When Petrarch and Dante are compared, several points of difference do stand out. Dante really was more medieval in his conception of hierarchy in political life, and in his whole world view. Petrarch's outlook was more fully integrated with classic viewpoints. The pyramidal social and political structures of Dante's conception fitted neatly into his Ptolemaic cosmology and Thomistic theology. Petrarch acknowledged the political particularism that existed in the city-state structure of Italy and the national patriotisms of the north. Dante used the vernacular and took many liberties in composition. Much of his prose and poetry, such as the *Vita nuova,* his spiritual autobiography in which he recounts his great love for Beatrice, is filled with dream visions and allegory of a spiritualized medieval cast. Petrarch used Latin for his "serious" writings and introduced classicism. Latin purists among the later humanists were highly critical of Dante for his linguistic flaws. Cardinal Bembo, an elegant Ciceronian Latinist, in his *Prose* (Venice, 1525) rebuked Dante for using base words. By the middle of the sixteenth century the judgment of the critics was entirely in favor of Petrarch and against Dante. Giraldi Cinthio compared the two in his *Discorsi* (Venice, 1554):

> But the law is not so strict for romances as not to permit more license in words than is customary for sonnets and *canzoni*. Long and serious subjects, if the conception is not to be warped, need such latitude, which must nevertheless be limited. Petrarch shows this clearly in his *Trionfi*. I will not cite Dante; for whether through the fault of his age, or because of his own nature, he took so many liberties that this liberty became a fault. Therefore I find quite judicious that painter who, to show us in a fair scene the literary value of the one poet and the other, imagined both in a green and flowery mead on the slopes of Helicon, and put into Dante's hand a scythe, which, with his gown tucked up to his knees, he was wielding in circles, cutting every plant that the scythe struck. Behind Dante he painted Petrarch, in senatorial robe, stooping to select the noble plants and the well-bred flowers—all this to show us the liberty of the one and the judgment and observance of the other.[2]

---

[2] Cited in Charles Sears Baldwin, *Renaissance Literary Theory and Practice* (New York, 1939), pp. 29–30.

Was Petrarch the first modern man, as Ernst Renan tagged him? The answer depends upon what is meant by "modern man." He was modern in his highly self-conscious individuality. This individualism was characterized less by egoism or bravado than by sensitive introversion. Even his love poems seem less concerned with the lady than with his own complicated state of mind and emotion. His self-searching dialogues reveal a concern with inner motives and questions of conscience that we commonly associate with highly psychologized modern man. In the medieval period only Abelard approaches this level of agonizing. It is telling that Petrarch chose as his partner in conversation St. Augustine, whom William James once called "the first man" because of his tendency toward sensitive introspection. Petrarch was constantly torn by the conflict between the active life and the contemplative life. The life of study, he came to believe, was really a life of action. This conflict posed problems for many of the humanists during the two centuries that followed.

Petrarch was the founder of humanism, the most characteristic expression of Renaissance culture, and as such became a symbol of the new and the "modern" element in that culture. "For who of you is unaware," wrote the sober Antonio Minturno in *De poeta* (Venice, 1559),

> that from the time when the Roman Empire, for all its power and eminence, began to totter and lean, literature was asleep, not to say overwhelmed and buried, till the time of Petrarch? From then on, it has been so steadily regaining the light that now it has been almost recalled from the rude and barbarous [medieval] teaching to its ancient cult.[3]

As a pioneer in literary culture, Petrarch was a spiritual guide and an inspiration to many generations of Western man. But he had many limitations, as do all men, and in a way he seems as far removed from our times as Cicero seemed from his. But distance in time did not prevent Petrarch from intensely admiring Cicero, just as Cicero in his day pointed to Plato, the divine mind who would free the intellects of his age. We can hardly withhold our praise from Petrarch.

BOCCACCIO, LITERARY HUMANIST

It is a mistake to make sharp distinctions among various categories of humanism, such as literary, civic, and metaphysical humanism. For some literary men—Petrarch was one—showed a modicum of civic concern and political interest, and some civic humanists, such as Coluccio Salutati and Leonardo Bruni, involved in the operation of the state, had keen literary, philosophical, and religious concerns, and even published in these areas. The labels literary, civic, educational, and philosophic humanists are introduced here for convenience in discussion, not as airtight distinctions.

---

[3] *Ibid.*, p. 4.

The third man in the great *Trecento* triumvirate, together with Dante and Petrarch, was Giovanni Boccaccio (1313–1375), a friend of Petrarch's. The illegitimate son of a Florentine merchant and a French woman of Paris, Giovanni was educated for a career in business. His father sent him to Naples to work for the Bardi bank there, but he developed an intense dislike for business routine and bourgeois taste. He preferred the court with its chivalric and aristocratic way of life, brought from France by the house of Anjou. There he developed a burning passion for Maria d'Aquino, the illegitimate daughter of King Robert. Although she was married, she finally yielded to him, and thereby won a place in literature as the Fiammetta of Boccaccio's poems and romances. When Fiammetta at last turned away from him in 1341, Boccaccio left Naples for Florence, where he sought solace in the study of the classics.

Boccaccio's fame rests primarily on the *Decameron,* a collection of one hundred short stories. Three youths and seven young ladies have fled Florence to escape the Great Plague of 1348 and found refuge in a country villa. To pass the time away in their rural retreat they tell ten tales a day. The stories are drawn from the old chivalric romances and *fabliaux,* but Boccaccio has fun with them, mocks and ridicules. Bed-hopping is a major theme and the lasciviousness of monks and nuns he finds very amusing.

There was something of the antiquarian about Boccaccio in his zeal to recover ancient manuscripts. His biographer tells the story of his visit to the ancient Benedictine monastery of Monte Cassino in search of lost classics. The account may not be authentic, but it is true to Boccaccio's spirit:

> Desirous of seeing the collection of books, which he understood to be a very choice one, he modestly asked a monk to open the library, as a favor, for him. The monk answered, stiffly, pointing to a steep staircase, "Go up; it is open." Boccaccio went up gladly, but he found that the place, which held so great a treasure, was without a door or key. He entered, and saw grass sprouting on the windows, and all the books and benches thick with dust. In his astonishment, he began to open and turn the leaves of ancient and foreign works. Some of them had lost several sheets, others were snipped and pared all around the text. At length, lamenting that the toil and study of so many illustrious men should have passed into the hands of most abandoned wretches, he departed with tears and sighs.[4]

Boccaccio made some great finds while reconnoitering: a text of Ausonius, another of Martial, a minor work of Ovid, and an important Tacitus selection. Boccaccio authored a manual of classical geography, a book *On Famous Women,* and one *On the Fortunes of Great Men,* mostly Greeks and Romans.

The work of Boccaccio that merits the most serious attention was his *Genealogy of the Gods,* an encyclopedia of ancient mythology. In Book 4 he revives the Prometheus myth in a significant new form. Prometheus defied the gods by

---

[4] J. E. Sandys, *History of Classical Scholarship* (Cambridge, 1908), vol. 2, p. 13.

stealing fire from them and as punishment was chained to a rock, exposed so that an eagle could tear the flesh away from around his heart. Boccaccio knows of a second Prometheus—that is, the learned man. Learning "makes of natural man civil man, remarkable for morals, knowledge, and virtue, whereby it becomes obvious that nature produces man and learning then forms him anew." This is a telling humanist view of man, for his dignity does not consist in his human nature as such, but in that learning which first truly makes a man human.

Boccaccio was aware of the innovations the humanists were introducing into culture. In a letter addressed to Jacopo Pizzinghe around 1370 Boccaccio wrote:

> In our age, if I observe well, more illustrious men have come from heaven, generous spirits who wish to raise up again with all their strength the oppressed art of poetry, and to recall it from exile into its former abode; and not in vain. But we see . . . that in advance of others who are worthy of note, a famous man, our Dante Alighieri, who dwelt in the house of Philosophy, had drunk the honied waters at that fount which was lost many centuries ago. . . .
>
> Then, after Dante, his fellow citizen of Florence, that illustrious man, Francesco Petrarca, my teacher. . . . For Petrarca cleansed the fount of Helicon, swampy with mud and rushes, restoring its waters to their former purity, and reopened the Castalian cave which was overgrown with the entwining of wild vines. Clearing the laurel grove of briars, he restored Apollo to his ancient temple and brought back the Muses, soiled by rusticity, to their pristine beauty. Then he ascended to the topmost peaks of Parnassus.[5]

The Cult of the Classics

THE GREAT DUTCH cultural historian Johan Huizinga, in his *Homo ludens,* said of the Renaissance humanists, "If ever an elite, fully conscious of its own merits, sought to segregate itself from the vulgar herd and live life as a game of artistic perfection, that was the circle of choice Renaissance spirits." Although Huizinga exaggerated, as historians who are remembered are wont to do, he did in this sentence put his finger upon a very important feature of humanism. It was an upper-class phenomenon and the humanists were elitists.

With its medieval communes, Italy had never genuinely fitted into classical feudalism as it developed in France, the empire, and England. With the rise of the universities Italy was again out of phase, emphasizing law and medicine rather than theology as at Paris, Cologne, or Oxford. In literature chivalric poetry, which flourished in the north, and Provençal lyrics and sonnets found a home, and then only briefly, in the court life of Naples and Sicily. In architecture, Gothic had to be

---

[5] James Ross and Mary McLaughlin, eds., *The Portable Renaissance Reader* (New York, 1965), pp. 123–25.

artificially introduced, usually by northern architects, as happened in Milan. While medieval culture in the north reached its climax in the thirteenth century, Italy lagged behind.

The late thirteenth and early fourteenth centuries witnessed a basic change in this situation. For in those decades Italy reached a new height of prosperity and developed a secular urban culture more advanced than any Europe had seen since antiquity. The new humanism, with its nearly fanatical devotion to classical culture, suited the taste of the rich laymen who dominated urban society. The humanists catered to these men, for they provided support and an appreciative audience. Moreover, many of the humanists were drawn from this stratum of society, or worked their way up into it. The middle and lower bourgeois types had no appreciation of the aristocratic humanist culture. The shopkeeper Vespasiano da Bisticci, in a gossipy book on famous men of Florence, tells of these middle-class types not interested in learning and culture. Leon Battista Alberti observed that the Florentines did not care about the liberal arts, only in making money. "They say," Alberti observed, "that it is enough to be able to sign your own name and to be able to strike a balance in a ledger." The proletariat, of course, had no interest in the new literary culture at all. The humanists, for their part, were condescending to shopkeepers and artisans and disdainful of the ignorant masses.

A brief description of the socioeconomic aspects of the situation does not at all explain the rise of humanism as an intellectual and cultural phenomenon. A dominant wealthy class does not by itself guarantee the development of a specifically humanist culture. For that, powerful ideas must come into play. Men of intellect and dedication must serve as carriers and creators of the new culture. The humanists recognized each other as brothers joined in the battle against medieval barbarism and builders of a new world of thought. Their zeal for the recovery and study of the classics made them not only intellectual elitists but virtually devotees of a cult.

It is possible to trace a concatenation of people who transmitted Petrarchan humanism to all parts of Italy. Since Petrarch spent his last years in the lands of the Carraras, his influence was powerful in cities in their domain, such as Verona and Padua. At the University of Padua, Giovanni Conversini (1347–1406) was given a chair of rhetoric in 1392. An enthusiastic Ciceronian and great admirer of Petrarch, Conversini promoted the classics as professor and then as chancellor of the university. Among the students he inspired were Poggio Bracciolini, Francesco Filelfo, Guarino da Verona, and Vittorino da Feltre, who became major figures in Renaissance humanism.

Gasparino da Barzizza (1359–1431), author of the famous text *Orthographia,* having tried in vain to find support in Venice, opened a humanist school in Padua in 1408. Filippo Maria Visconti, who read Dante and Petrarch, as well as medieval chivalric romances, invited him to open a Latin school for boys in Milan in 1418.

And so the wandering humanists carried classical culture to new courts and cities.

Florence proved very early to be open to the new culture, for had not Dante and Petrarch been her own sons, though driven from home? In Florence an Augustinian monk, Luigi Marsigli (d. 1394), a friend of Petrarch, gathered a group of intellectuals together at the Church of Santo Spirito and discoursed on the classics. Palla Strozzi (1372–1402), influenced by Petrarch and Conversini, became a patron-practitioner of humanist studies. He gave large sums of money to develop the *studia* or University of Florence. He encouraged the Greek scholar Manuel Chrysoloras (*c*. 1350–1415) to come to Florence to lecture, and founded the first public library in Florence in the Santa Trinità monastery. Very active in business and public life, he hurried home from the office in order to spend his evening hours reading the classics. Later he hired John Argyropoulos, a Greek refugee from Constantinople, to tutor him privately in Greek.

Another Florentine merchant who promoted the "new learning," as the humanists fondly called their studies, was Niccolò Niccoli (1363–1437). Niccoli showed less zeal for merchandise than for books, and attended Luigi Marsigli's lectures faithfully. He in turn opened his own house to students of the new learning. Although Niccoli became a fine classicist, he never published a line, for he was too inhibited by the glories of the classics and too firmly convinced that he was inferior to the ancients.

POGGIO BRACCIOLINI

Petrarch and Boccaccio began what was to become one of the favorite sports of the humanists, the search for ancient manuscripts. The most energetic and successful hunter was the unlovable egotist Poggio Bracciolini (1380–1459), who was a friend of Niccolò Niccoli and studied with Manuel Chrysoloras. His conduct was anything but exemplary, and when, to improve his station in life, he found it prudent to enter into the state of lawful wedlock, he was obliged to dismiss a mistress who had produced for him twelve sons and two daughters. His personal deficiencies did not keep him from being a severe critic of the institutions and ways of life of his times. An elegant Latin stylist, he served for many years as apostolic secretary and at the end of his life as Florentine chancellor. While in the service of Pope John XXIII he traveled to the Council of Constance in the papal retinue. When the hapless pope was deposed, Poggio was free to search for classical manuscripts in northern monasteries.

Poggio had a very low opinion of the monks, who had the reputation of ignorantly neglecting the precious manuscripts that had been so laboriously copied and stored in the monastic libraries from the days when Cassiodorus initiated the first *scriptorium* at Squillace in the last days of the Roman Empire. Actually the Carthusian hermits were the only monks who completely rejected nontheological or worldly learning. When the Cluniacs were asked for a pagan or secular book, they would scratch their ears like dogs, indicating their opinion that such books were lousy, but at least they preserved the books and made them available. It was in Cluny, as a matter of fact, that Poggio discovered several of Cicero's orations in the summer of 1415. The next year, in the great Swiss monastery of St. Gall, he made his greatest find, Quintilian's *Institutio oratoris,* which, together with Cicero's work on oratory, became the basis of the humanists' doctrines on rhetoric. Two years later he searched through the monasteries of Einsiedeln, Reichenau, and St. Gall once again. On this expedition he recovered copies of the work of Ammianus Marcellinus, the late Roman historian, and the skeptical poet Lucretius. Through the years Poggio also found the text of Vitruvius, whose theories were so important for Renaissance architects, nine new Plautus comedies, and the letters of Pliny the Younger. He helped recover some of the historian Tacitus' minor works, *Agricola,* the *Dialogues,* and the *Germania,* a work vastly exciting to the German humanists, for it was the only major literary source of information on the ancient Germans between Julius Caesar's *Gallic Wars* and the history of Ammianus Marcellinus. In addition to making these finds, Poggio wrote a description of the Roman ruins, *De varietate fortunae,* which revealed his appreciation of their aesthetic value as well as their importance for literary and historical documentation.

FRANCESCO FILELFO

Poggio's great rival as a collector was Francesco Filelfo (1398–1481), who studied Latin and rhetoric at Padua, and in 1417 was invited to teach moral philosophy and rhetoric in Venice. He made such an impression with his knowledge of Cicero and Virgil that two years later the Venetians made him secretary to their consul general in Constantinople. He studied Greek with John Chrysoloras, a relative of Manuel. In 1427 he brought back to Venice not only his Greek bride, John's daughter, but a very large collection of Greek manuscripts. Filelfo was a man of gross appetites and great physical energy, with a vile temper and wicked tongue. Exceedingly greedy, restless, and ambitious, he made his life into one constant chase after golden opportunities. From Venice he went to Bologna, from there to Florence. In Florence he lectured daily on major Greek and Latin authors and on occasional Sundays he discoursed on Dante in the cathedral. He also busied himself translating Greek authors: Aristotle, Xenophon, and the orator Lysias. When the Albizzis exiled Cosimo de' Medici in 1433, Filelfo urged the death penalty for him. When Cosimo later made a political comeback, there was no room in Florence for Filelfo. Filelfo even claimed that Cosimo had paid an assassin to murder him, though Cosimo really had bigger targets than this loud-mouthed professor.

Filelfo gladly accepted a post in Siena, where he lasted four years. Showered with tempting offers, he chose in 1440 to accept a lucrative position from Filippo Maria Visconti, duke of Milan, which paid seven hundred gold florins a year plus honoraria for special panegyrics and orations greeting visiting dignitaries and lamenting the honored dead. He continued university teaching, translating Greek, and heaping scorn and abuse upon Milan's political enemies and his own literary rivals in Florence. When Francesco Sforza destroyed the Ambrosian Republic, Filelfo ingratiated himself with the winner by producing a ponderous epic, the *Sforziad,* which fortunately was never published.

When Francesco died, Filelfo, now seventy-seven years old, cast about for greener pastures, and found them in Rome, where Pope Sixtus IV gave him a well-endowed chair of rhetoric. But he soon quarreled with the papal treasurer and made an ill-tempered attack on Sixtus IV himself, so that he found it prudent to return to Milan. He was ambitious, however, to make his mark in Florence. At the time of the Pazzi revolt Filelfo issued a harsh indictment of Pope Sixtus IV for his part in the plot. Gratified, Lorenzo the Magnificent invited Filelfo to teach Greek in Florence, but he died of dysentery just two weeks after he arrived. He was buried in the Church of the Annunziata at the age of eighty-three.

Filelfo was of great importance to the Renaissance, not for anything original he created, but as a wandering apostle of humanism. As a carrier of the new classical culture, he played a most important role with energy and conviction.

Humanist controversies were not always very elevating. Filelfo had attacked Cosimo de' Medici and rejoiced when Cosimo was imprisoned in the Palazzo Vecchio and exiled. With Cosimo's exile, Filelfo's rival Poggio lost his best patron and most powerful friend in Florence. Then when the Medicis returned, Filelfo became a professor in exile. In response to the invective of the jealous Poggio, Filelfo dipped his pen in gall and vilified Poggio in a bitter satire of one hundred verses:

> Poggio! ere long thy babbling tongue shall feel
> The keen impression of the trenchant steel;
> That tongue, the herald of malicious lies,
> That sheds its venom on the good and wise.
> What mighty master in detraction's school,
> Thus into knavery has matured a fool?[6]

Poggio responded in a fit of rage:

Thou stinking he-goat! Thou horned monster! Thou malevolent detractor! Thou father of lies and author of discord! May the divine vengeance destroy thee as an enemy of the virtuous, a parricide who endeavorest to ruin the wise and good by lies and slanders, and the most false and foul imputations. If thou must be contu-

---

[6] M. W. Shepherd, *The Life of Poggio Bracciolini,* 2nd ed. (Liverpool, 1837), p. 250.

melious, write thy satires against the suitors of thy wife—discharge the putridity of thy stomach upon those who adorn thy forehead with horns![7]

Poggio had a vocabulary to cover any occasion.

The Greek Revival

THE ROMAN POET Horace observed that captive Greece took her barbarian captors captive. During the fifteenth century the Renaissance too, initially a Latin literary phenomenon, experienced a reconquest by the Greeks. From Cicero, the most important single influence upon the early Renaissance, the humanists learned the keenest admiration for Greek culture. The church had not been unmindful of the value of the Greek language, and in 1312 the Council of Vienne provided for instruction in Greek at the Universities of Paris, Bologna, Oxford, and Salamanca, and at the Curial University. It also called for the study of Arabic, Chaldee, and Hebrew, but nothing came of these good intentions. The humanists took up the challenge.

Sicily and southern Italy, once known as Magna Graecia, had many Greek settlements in Petrarch's day. Even now Greek survives in the patois of some localities in Calabria. From Calabria came Petrarch's Greek teacher, Barlaam, whom he met in Avignon. Petrarch had developed a passion to read Homer and Plato in the original, but he actually made little progress in mastering the language. Boccaccio discovered the scholar Leontius Pilatus and arranged for a chair in Greek studies at Florence in 1360, but only Boccaccio and a few others came to hear his lectures. Simon Atumano, a very fine philologist, taught in Rome in 1380–1381, but he attracted only one student. Still absorbed in reviving Latin antiquity, the intellectuals of that generation had little energy in reserve for learning Greek.

There is a legend that when Constantinople fell in 1453, a stream of Greek refugees poured into the West, bringing many precious manuscripts saved from the Turks and initiating the Greek revival. It is quite clear, however, that by 1453 the humanists had already revived Greek studies in Italy, and that the refugees after the fall added little that was new, though they did lend them fresh impetus. In fact, nearly all of the important classical manuscripts that had survived the disastrous sack of Constantinople by the fourth crusade in 1204 had been brought to the West long before 1453, so that very little was lost to the Turks.

During the closing decades of the fourteenth century, the eastern emperor, under pressure from the Turks, had sought renewed contact with and aid from the

---

[7] *Ibid.*, p. 252.

West. An imperial expedition in 1374 and another in 1399 produced no help from the West. The distinguished Greek scholar Manuel Chrysoloras came to Venice in 1393. Niccolò Niccoli and Palla Strozzi asked the chancellor of Florence, Coluccio Salutati, to invite Chrysoloras to Florence, and he was appointed to lecture on the classics at the university there in 1387. In the years 1397–1399 Chrysoloras traveled with Manuel II Palaeologus through northern Italy and to Paris and London, but nowhere outside of Florence did he find a truly appreciative audience for his lectures.

One of Chrysoloras' most brilliant pupils was Leonardo Bruni (1374–1444), who succeeded Salutati as chancellor of Florence. In a moving passage Bruni tells of his excitement at the prospect of learning Greek.

> I was then studying the civil law, but . . . I burned with love of academic studies and had spent no little pains on dialectic and rhetoric. At the coming of Chrysoloras, I was torn in mind, deeming it shameful to desert the law, and yet a crime to lose such a chance of studying Greek literature; and often with youthful impulse I would say to myself, "Thou, when it is permitted thee to gaze on Homer, Plato, and Demosthenes, and other poets, philosophers, and orators, of whom such glorious things are spread abroad, and speak with them and be instructed in their admirable teaching, wilt thou desert and rob thyself? Wilt thou neglect this opportunity so divinely offered? For seven hundred years no one in Italy has possessed Greek letters, and yet we confess that all knowledge is derived from them. There are doctors of civil law everywhere, and the chance of learning will not fail thee. But if this one and only doctor of Greek letters disappears, no one can be found to teach thee." Overcome at length by these reasons, I gave myself to Chrysoloras, with such zeal to learn, that what through the waking day I gathered, I followed after in night, even when asleep.[8]

Bruni learned his Greek so well that he made valuable translations of Plato, Aristotle, Demosthenes, Plutarch, and St. Basil, the Greek church father.

In 1438 John VIII Palaeologus came to Italy with several hundred Greeks to beg the Council of Ferrara-Florence for help. He had to borrow heavily from Venice and the pope to gather the funds for the trip and to get his jewels out of hock for the occasion. Although the reunion of the churches was declared on July 6, 1439, the West sent no real aid to beleaguered Constantinople.

Among the Greeks to attend the Council of Ferrara-Florence was the Byzantine Platonist Gemistos Pletho, the author of a distinguished book on law. Pletho, together with Landino and others, played a role in the development of "theological poetry." At Cosimo's request he gave a speech on Plato in Florence and helped to inspire a Platonic revival. He urged Cosimo to establish an academy in Florence where Greek letters and Platonic philosophy would be cultivated. When Pletho

---

[8] Henry O. Taylor, *Thought and Expression in the Sixteenth Century* (New York, 1920), vol. 1, p. 36.

died in 1450 the Malatestas had his body taken to Rimini. The mortal remains of scholars were becoming as prestigious as those of saints and martyrs.

The chief negotiator for the Greeks at the council was John Bessarion (1403–1472), metropolitan of Nicea, another distinguished Platonist. He remained in the West and was elevated to the dignity of cardinal in 1439. Unlike Pletho, who was primarily interested in the pagan classics, Bessarion was a student of the Greek patristic writers.

Ambrogio Traversari (1386–1439), the prior of the Camaldese Convent of Santa Maria degli Angeli in Florence, turned the convent into a center for humanist learning and especially the study of the Greek church fathers, just as Luigi Marsigli had made the Santo Spirito a center for the study of the Latin classics. Traversari personally translated many of the Greek patristic writings. He worked for the union of the churches at the Council of Ferrara-Florence, and he influenced the pattern of Lorenzo Ghiberti's magnificent bronze doors for the Baptistery in Florence.

Meanwhile two manuscript collectors did for the East what Poggio, Filelfo, and others had done for the West. Cyriaco de' Pizzicolli of Ancona (*c.* 1391–1457), a merchant adventurer, gathered epigraphy, made drawings, and collected manuscripts, vases, and statues. His notebooks, containing descriptions of the Greek and Roman monuments he found in Greece, the Aegean islands, Syria, and Egypt, are still today a valuable source of information for classical archeologists. "I go," exclaimed Cyriaco, "to awake the dead!" Giovanni Aurispa (1374–1450) traveled to Chios in 1413 and brought home texts of Thucydides, Euripides, and Sophocles. He journeyed to Constantinople in 1421, and when he returned to Italy two years later he brought with him 238 codices, most of them containing Greek classics. After the fall of Constantinople, other Greek scholars—John Argyropoulos, Demetrius Chalcondylas, John and Constantine Lascaris—fled to the West, adding new impetus to the Greek revival and broadening the dimensions of philosophical discussion.

Education

POSSIBLY AT NO TIME in history previous to our own has so much attention been paid to educational theory as in the age of the Renaissance. The humanists had a high opinion of the rationality of the upper strata of human society and were generally optimistic about the educability of man.

Petrarch initiated the discussion of some of the issues involved with his argument about the superiority of law to medicine, for he believed that "Averroistic" science subverted moral philosophy. Salutati continued that particular debate in his discourse *On the Nobility of Law and Medicine,* in which he discussed the relative merits of studying law, which deals with human relationships, and medicine, which belongs to the world of nature. Law deals with the soul of man and involves questions of moral philosophy, whereas medicine treats man's body and is concerned merely with physical properties. Laws control medicine and the other sciences, while the reverse is not true. In the course of this rambling treatise Salutati came to the question of what constitutes true nobility. Nobility, he declared, does not depend upon relationship or blood, but upon virtue. Nobility of virtue is possible for slave and freeman, rich and poor, ruler and subject. This was, of course, a classic platitude, but for the chancellor of Florence, spokesman for the urban bourgeoisie, thus to reject openly the feudal conception of a man's worth was noteworthy. The question that such a definition of true nobility posed for educators was how to instill such virtue in the young, and how to help it develop.

Renaissance educators believed that the study of the liberal arts best served the purpose of developing true virtue in man. During the Middle Ages the liberal arts existed as a basis for later professional study in theology, law, or medicine. Little thought was given to the value of the liberal arts themselves in producing men of cultivation and character, fit to be leaders of society. Moreover, by the thirteenth century the study of logic and the authority of Aristotle had come to overshadow grammar and rhetoric and the other arts. The author of *The Battle of the Seven Liberal Arts,* a tedious medieval vernacular poem, lamented that "logic now has the students whereas grammar is reduced in numbers. . . . Aristotle strikes Priscian, our noble ancient authority, that he makes him drop to the ground. He wanted to trample him under his horse." Renaissance educators lifted grammar up out of the dust and elevated rhetoric to new dignity. The recovery of Cicero's *On Oratory* and Quintilian's *Institutes of Oratory* gave new impetus to the study of rhetoric and stirred new enthusiasm for the liberal arts.

PIETRO PAOLO VERGERIO

The most influential treatise on education during the Renaissance came from the pen of Pietro Paolo Vergerio (1370–1444). His *De ingenuis moribus* (On Morals Becoming a Free Man) drew heavily on Plato, Plutarch, and Cicero. He wrote it for Ubertino, son of the Carrara lord of Padua. Vergerio, a personal friend of Salutati and Bruni, was a student of Conversini and Chrysoloras. His career as professor of logic and rhetoric took him to Florence, Padua, and Verona. He put his Latin skill to work as secretary to Pope Innocent VII and to Cardinal Zabarella at the Council of Constance. He served later as orator at the court of Emperor Sigismund, and died in Budapest.

In discussing the ideal curriculum, Vergerio spelled out the importance of the liberal arts for teaching the secret of true freedom and developing the individual to his full potential. This is the platform he laid down for higher learning:

> We call those studies liberal which are worthy of a free man, those studies by which we attain and practice virtue and wisdom. That education which calls forth, trains and develops those highest gifts of body and of mind which ennoble men, and which are rightly judged to rank next in dignity to virtue alone. . . . Amongst these [studies] I accord the first place to History on grounds both of its attractiveness and of its utility, qualities which appeal equally to the scholar and to the statesman. Next in importance ranks Moral Philosophy. . . . History then gives us the concrete examples of the principles inculcated by philosophy. The one shows what men should do, the other what men have said and done in the past, and what practical lessons we may draw therefrom for the present day. I would indicate, as the third branch of study, Eloquence. . . . By philosophy we learn the essential truth of things, which by eloquence we so exhibit in orderly adornment, as to bring conviction to differing minds.[9]

What Vergerio worked out in theory other educators put into practice.

VITTORINO DA FELTRE

The two greatest of these practical educators were Vittorino da Feltre (1378–1446) and Guarino da Verona (1370–1460), who founded schools based on the humanist educational philosophy at Mantua, Verona, and Ferrara. Vittorino lived in Venice and Padua at the time when Greek learning was coming in from Constantinople. He felt that insufficient attention was being paid by educators to the development of individual character. He grew impatient with dialectics and scholastic disputes that he thought frustrated the principal aims of education. Gian Francesco I Gonzaga, endeavoring to make of the little court of Mantua an important center of culture, invited Vittorino to set up a school there, and Vittorino resigned his chair at Padua and created in Mantua a model for teaching the liberal arts, well supported by Gonzaga.

Although Vittorino retained the formal structure of the medieval trivium and quadrivium, he gave them an entirely new emphasis. He aimed at building character by the study of classical literary masters, such as Plutarch and the historians. He also taught the Scriptures and the works of the church fathers, above all St. Augustine. He believed that a cheerful environment was important for good learning and named his school La Casa Giocosa, the Pleasant House. He introduced such novelties as coeducation, games, and physical education, including swimming, riding, fencing, and drill. His aim was to develop a sound mind in a sound body, and to develop in the student a proper sense of form, style, and decorum. Although the school served primarily the Gonzaga princes and Mantuan

---

[9] W. H. Woodward, *Vittorino da Feltre and Other Humanist Educators* (Cambridge, 1918), pp. 102, 106.

nobility, Vittorino also admitted children of the lower classes, to provide a multi-cultural experience. Possibly with reference to Vittorino's school the humanist pope Pius II wrote:

> As regards a boy's physical training we must bear in mind that we aim at implanting habits which will prove beneficial through life. So let him cultivate a certain hardness which rejects excess of sleep and idleness in all its forms. Habits of indulgence such as the luxury of soft beds, or the wearing of silk instead of linen next to the skin, tend to enervate both body and mind. Too much importance can hardly be attached to right bearing and gesture. . . . In ancient Greece we find that both philosophers and men of affairs—Socrates, for instance . . . or Philip of Macedon—deemed this matter worthy of their concern, and therefore it may be thought deserving of ours. Games and exercises which develop the muscular activities and the general carriage of the person should be encouraged by every teacher.[10]

Vittorino's pupils proved the value of the new pedagogy, for the alumni of his school included rulers of men and scholars as well. Ludovico Gonzaga succeeded his father, Gian Francesco, as marquis of Mantua in 1444. He retained his enthusiasm for the classics and even carried a copy of Caesar's *Gallic Wars* on his campaigns. He loved art and brought the painter Andrea Mantegna to Mantua. He commissioned the great architect Leon Battista Alberti to design the beautiful Sant' Andrea Church in Mantua. Vittorino's most famous pupil was Federico da Montefeltro, duke of Urbino, who turned his tiny court into a brilliant center of Renaissance art and literature. Vespasiano da Bisticci related that Federico had Livy read aloud in Latin during the midday meal, except during Lent, when he had the Scriptures read instead. Another pupil was Giovanni Andrea di Bussi, bishop of Aleria, who edited an edition of Livy's works that was published in Rome in 1469. In his preface the learned bishop dutifully acknowledged that he owed his knowledge of Livy to his genial mentor Vittorino.

GUARINO DA VERONA

Guarino da Verona was a pupil of Chrysoloras. He had studied Greek in Constantinople and brought back many Greek manuscripts when he returned. On the invitation of the Este family he set up a court school in Ferrara, not unlike that of Vittorino in aim and program. He and his somewhat less famous son, Battista da Guarino, composed important educational treatises.

LEONARDO BRUNI

The most potent statement of the power and practicality of a humanist education did not come from a professional educator, but from a man of ready discourse

---

[10] *Ibid.,* pp. 137–38.

and action, Leonardo Bruni, chancellor of Florence in a time of crisis. He shall have the final word on the subject. In *On Studies and Letters,* written between 1423 and 1426, Bruni explained:

> That high standard of education to which I referred at the outset is only to be reached by one who has seen many things and read much. Poet, orator, historian and the rest, all must be studied, each must contribute a share. Our learning thus becomes full, ready, varied and elegant, available for action or for discourse in all subjects. But to enable us to make effectual use of what we know we must add to our knowledge the power of expression. These two sides of learning, indeed, should not be separated: they afford mutual aid and distinction. Proficiency in literary form, not accompanied by broad acquaintance with facts and truths, is a barren attainment; whilst information, however vast, which lacks all grace of expression, would seem to be put under a bushel or partly thrown away. Indeed, one may fairly ask what advantage it is to possess profound and varied learning if one cannot convey it in language worthy of the subject. Where, however, this double capacity exists— breadth of learning and grace of style—we allow the highest title to distinction and to abiding fame. . . . My last word must be this. The intelligence that aspires to the best must aim at both. In doing so, all sources of profitable learning will in due proportion claim your study. None have more urgent claim than the subjects and authors which treat of Religion and of our duties in the world; and it is because they assist and illustrate these supreme studies that I press upon your attention the works of the most approved poets, historians and orators of the past.[11]

With Leonardo Bruni we join the company of the distinguished civic humanists, who combined their love of learning with active participation in political affairs.

Civic Humanism

AFTER MANY CENTURIES during which men thought of Cicero as primarily a moral philosopher of the stature of Seneca, it came as a surprise to the humanists to discover the Cicero who was an active statesman and an apologist for the Roman Republic. With such authoritative sanction, the humanists could involve themselves with enthusiasm in the affairs of state and live the *vita activa* while cultivating the *vita studiosa* in their available leisure time. While the rhetorical discipline had been put into the service of the state by chancellors and orators long before the end of the fourteenth century, during the chancellorships of Coluccio Salutati and Leonardo Bruni in Florence a new element was added. During their terms in office Florence was involved in a struggle to the death for its freedom and for its very survival as an independent state. If Florence had become a provincial town in a Milanese territorial state there would have been no Renaissance in

---

[11] *Ibid.,* pp. 132–33.

Florence such as we know it. The humanist chancellors used their rhetorical skill and historical insight to strengthen the will of the people to defend the republic and resist tyrannous aggression.

From the time of Dante's *De monarchia* in the second decade of the fourteenth century to the treatises of Coluccio Salutati, Leonardo Bruni, and Alamanno Rinuccini (1419–1499), author of the anti-Medici dialogue *De libertate*, there is not a single work by a Florentine that can justly be called a work of political thought. The crisis of Florence galvanized the humanists into action; rhetoricians became civic humanists.

COLUCCIO SALUTATI

Florence was fortunate to have in Coluccio Salutati (1331–1406) a chancellor of superior quality, which was revealed as successive crises overtook the city. Salutati was born in Stignano, a small town in Tuscany, and spent twenty years in Bologna, where he studied law and became a notary. He worked as a notary for nearly a quarter of a century, at first in obscure posts, eventually for two years in Rome. Then in February 1374 he received an appointment as notary in the office of elections in Florence, and a year later he became chancellor, a position he held until his death, thirty-one years later. The chancellor not only played a major role in domestic decisions, but served as foreign minister as well.

Salutati showed his iron will by remaining calm during the Ciompi revolt in 1378. In spite of the street fighting and the attack on the Palazzo Vecchio, he denied that the revolt had caused much destruction or bloodshed, in a valiant though fruitless attempt to forestall excessive reaction against the defeated Ciompi. In that same year Pope Gregory XI accused him of heresy for making war on the papacy. Salutati responded with a skillful letter, done in his best Ciceronian style, declaring that Florence had not made war, but had merely defended its territory against papal attack. "In a fight for liberty," he wrote, "all will unite."

Salutati developed an intense love for Florence. He criticized all those who deserted the city in time of plague and refused to leave himself or to send his children away, for he was a fatalist and believed that no one would die before his appointed time. In an eloquent tribute to Florence he called her "the first in Tuscany, the most famous in Italy, known through all the world. Free herself, she is the mother of freedom and that is the glory of nations!" He was reelected to office again and again, with the gratitude and praise of the council and citizens.

The loyalty of the Florentines was put to the supreme test in the struggle with Gian Galeazzo Visconti, duke of Milan, who was determined to subdue the city and nearly encircled it. The war began in 1390, and Salutati rallied the people to the city's defense while he engaged in diplomatic maneuvering designed to frustrate Milan's designs. Gian Galeazzo said that a thousand Florentine horsemen did him less damage than the letters of Coluccio Salutati, and he sent assassins to kill the chancellor. When they failed, he tried a favorite trick and arranged for a forged letter, implicating Salutati in treason to Florence, to come into the possession of the council. By a similar ruse he had gotten the marquis of Mantua to behead his own wife. The marquis later used the same device against him, when the gullible duke was trapped into putting his own chancellor in prison, where he soon died. Fortunately, Salutati was able to persuade the council that the letter was indeed forged and that they were up against a ruthless and artful enemy. Though Salutati of course had nothing to do with the treasonous letter, he did write many others, and his correspondence, public and private, covering a period of fifty years, constitutes a major source of knowledge about the political and diplomatic history of the period.

Though less skilled than Petrarch and Boccaccio, Salutati had literary ambitions of his own. He wrote *On the Labors of Hercules,* an allegorical explanation of Seneca's play which was medieval in its use of allegory and in its moralizing but Renaissance in its use of quotations from the classics. In *On the World and Religion,* written about 1381, he offered arguments to persuade a monk to remain true to his calling. In another work, *On Fate and Fortune,* he took St. Augustine as his guide and assumed a basically orthodox position. But the work of Salutati that has stirred up the most discussion is his *Concerning the Tyrant,* because it seems to run counter to the republican sentiments of his civic humanism. In response to an inquiry from a young law student in Padua, Salutati wrote that a tyrant is a usurper who rules unjustly and therefore can justly be destroyed. Nevertheless, he argued, Dante was right in condemning Brutus and Cassius for assassinating Caesar, for Caesar's power had been legalized and he was therefore not a tyrant. Perhaps this specious defense of Caesar revealed a cleavage between Salutati the literary man, who felt driven emotionally to support Dante, and Salutati the civic humanist, who opposed tyranny. Then again, as a foreign minister Salutati may have wished to discourage anyone who might consider his argument as a license to attack the Carraras in Padua. Salutati was basically a very religious man, who was emerging from a medieval mentality into an early humanist frame of mind.[12] When Salutati died on May 4, 1406, he was honored with the laurel wreath. Poggio praised him as the haven and refuge of all scholars, the bright light of his fatherland, the glory of Italy.

LEONARDO BRUNI

During the decades after Salutati's death Florence was confronted by repeated crises in foreign relations. King Ladislas of Naples threatened from the south, but his designs were cut short by his death in 1414. Then Filippo Maria Visconti

---

[12] For a judicious assessment of Salutati's works, see Berthold L. Ullman, *The Humanism of Coluccio Salutati* (Padua, 1963), pp. 19–38; for a discussion of the medieval and humanistic elements in the man and his works, see *ibid.,* pp. 39–49.

took up Gian Galeazzo's ambitious plans for southward expansion from Milan at the expense of Florence. During much of this critical period the implementation of Florentine Policy was entrusted to Chancellor Leonardo Bruni Aretino (*c.* 1370–1444).

Leonardo Bruni was very much a self-made man. Born in nearby Arezzo in modest circumstances, he rose by sheer ability and determination to positions of prominence in the state and built up a sizable fortune. Early inspired by humanist culture, he caught the attention of Coluccio Salutati, who promoted his career. He was an eager student of Chrysoloras, mastered Greek, and became a tutor in the Medici household. In 1405 he became secretary to the papal chancery under Pope Innocent VII. In 1410 he was back in Florence for a brief tour of duty as chancellor. Then Pope John XXIII enticed him back to Rome by offering a career in the church. He accompanied the pope to the Council of Constance in 1414, but in March 1415 he returned to Florence, where he served as one of the *Dieci* and as a *priore* until in 1427 he again became chancellor, a post he kept until his death.

Bruni continued Salutati's application of humanist learning to social and political life, in contrast to Petrarch's constant urge to withdraw to the contemplative life. A member of the third generation of Florentine humanists, Bruni demonstrated a maturity and assurance not to be found in the early tentative phases. His dialogue *Ad petrum histrum* (1401) punned on the name of the educator Pietro Paolo Vergerio, who came from Istria; he may have intended the last word of the title to suggest "history" as well. This dialogue, a treatise on education, is an obvious imitation of the Platonic dialogues. It differs from most of the few attempts at dialogue in medieval literature in the way its characters stand out as individuals rather than as representatives of some type or class: the cleric, the knight, the scholar. The dialogue, which develops in a salon atmosphere, touches upon the value of learning and of conversation, the greatness of Cicero, the importance of Varro, and similar subjects. Near the close Bruni has Salutati speak as a representative of the old generation, venturing the opinion that Dante, Petrarch, and Boccaccio were the equals of the ancients. This opinion draws protests from three younger men, Niccolò Niccoli, Roberto de' Rossi, and Bruni himself, who prefer "a single letter of Cicero to all your moderns."

Bruni not only defended Florence diplomatically, but helped build up a patriotic tradition in order to deepen the loyalty of the upper classes to the city. His *Praise of the City of Florence* (1400) lauded the freedom of the republic, its security as an inland city, and its physical plan, with the tower of the Palazzo Vecchio in the center surrounded by four concentric circles. To Bruni, the beauty of Florence exceeded that of ancient Athens and Rome.

Bruni worked nearly three decades on his great *History of Florence*. He studied Livy, Polybius, Julius Caesar, and Thucydides, and absorbed the classic notion that history is philosophy taught by example. He could therefore introduce

Ciceronian rhetoric in driving home the lessons to be learned from historical events. He argued that Florence, a daughter of Rome, had not been founded by Caesar, as legend had it, but by Sulla, champion of the senate. From its very origins, therefore, Florence had a republican tradition. Liberty is perhaps the main theme of the *History,* freedom from tyranny and freedom from foreign domination. The twelfth and final book of this ambitious undertaking was still unfinished at the time of Bruni's death.

From the ancients he learned the legitimacy of contemporary history. In his *Commentary on Things Done in His Own Time* he explained that he felt an obligation to pass on knowledge of his age to posterity. He regretted that those who lived before his day had not done the same; if they had, men would not now find themselves in such a state of darkness and ignorance. The age of Cicero and the age of Demosthenes, he pointed out, were much better known than the period sixty years before his own time.

It is difficult to say whether Florence appreciated Bruni more as a man of action or as an intellectual. He himself had declared in 1433, "The greatest philosopher must give way to the greatest captain." When he died he was given a state funeral. As he lay upon the bier a copy of his *History of Florence* was placed upon his breast beneath his folded hands. The eloquent Giannozzo Manetti spoke the eulogy and laid upon his head the laurel crown. Bruni lies buried in the Santa Croce, where Galileo and other great Italians are enshrined. In front of the church stands a splendid statue of Dante, presiding over the noisy marketers and parking attendants.

CIVIC HUMANISM AS SOCIAL ACTION

The concept of civic humanism lends itself to a somewhat broader usage than an ideology of embattled republicanism. When it is understood as a life of action for the common good, such treatises as Leon Battista Alberti's *On the Family* and Matteo Palmieri's *On Civil Life* deserve to be included as representative expressions. But the most eloquent statement in praise of civic man's achievements came from the man who had delivered Bruni's funeral oration, Giannozzo Manetti (1396–1459), a man of a good Florence family, prominent as a statesman and diplomat. In the activist tradition of civic humanism, he once answered King Alfonso of Naples, who had asked what comprises the whole duty of man, "To understand and to act." It was to King Alfonso that he dedicated his most famous treatise, *On the Dignity and Excellence of Man.* He stressed man's achievements as evidence of his intrinsic worth. He rehearsed the triumphs of man from the building of the pyramids in ancient Egypt to the construction of Brunelleschi's dome in Florence.

> The genius of man is such that all these things, after that first new and rude creation of the world, seem to have been discovered and completed and perfected by us with

a certain unique and extraordinary acumen of the human mind. For things which are perceived are ours, that is, are human things, since they have been made by men, all houses, all towns, all cities, in short, all edifices on earth, which certainly are so great and such that they ought rightly to be considered the works of angels rather than of men, on account of this great excellence of theirs. Ours are the pictures, ours the sculptures, ours the arts, ours the sciences.[13]

Had Manetti known in 1451 and 1452, when he composed this exuberant piece, that he would soon be facing total ruin and disastrous flight from Florence, he might have felt in a somewhat less expansive mood. But if the civic humanists of the early *Quattrocento* could have known to what domestic tyranny and foreign oppression Florence would fall victim before the century was over, they might have lost their magnificent verve and become as cynical or despondent as Machiavelli and Guicciardini at the end of the Renaissance.

Humanism and History

THE HUMANISTS were keenly interested in history, especially in classical history, the history of their own times, and the place they would occupy in history yet to be written. Their beloved Cicero had declared: "History is the witness of the times, the torch of truth, the life of memory, the teacher of life, the messenger of antiquity." Paradoxically, it was the growing sense of their distance from classical antiquity, first seen in Petrarch, that contributed most to their deepened sense of history. From the classical historians, both Roman and Greek, they learned a view of history that differed from that of the medieval chronicler. A master such as Leonardo Bruni, whose *History of Florence* was a model and basic source for many later historians, derived from the reading of classic historians a feeling for coherent organization, literary style, and historical criticism. The contrast with even such late chroniclers as Matteo and Giovanni Villani is very noticeable, even though Bruni too could be needlessly detailed and tedious.

The humanists also learned from classic authors the pragmatic purpose of history. The rediscovered Tacitus, great Roman historian of the decline, had written: "The principal office of history I take to be this: to prevent virtues from being forgotten, and that evil words and deeds should fear an infamous reputation with posterity." History has the power to encourage good deeds and inhibit evil ones. It provides concrete examples for truths that moral philosophy teaches only in the abstract. The humanist historians were not at all embarrassed about introducing Ciceronian rhetoric in order to drive home a lesson suggested by the events they were narrating. They learned from the classic historians how history can serve a

---

[13] Giannozzo Manetti, *De dignitate et excellentia hominis,* in *Filosofi italiani del quattrocento,* ed. Eugenio Garin (Florence, 1942), p. 238.

patriotic cause, demonstrating the honorable course of their city-state or nation through the centuries. The writing of contemporary history, then, is respectable and a great service to posterity. But above all the humanist historians developed a sense of historical criticism, of the power of history as an instrument for the criticism of society and institutions. Educators provided an important place for history in the curriculum. It must be conceded, however, that the humanists did not contribute to what today would be known as the historical sciences, nor did they carve out a place in higher education for history as a discipline.

From Salutati to Machiavelli, author of a great *History of Florence,* and Francesco Guicciardini, author of a monumental *History of Italy* at the end of the Renaissance period, the humanists shared a wholesome respect for history. In 1392 Salutati wrote to the grand master of the order of St. John of Jerusalem praising his collection of books, especially of history. He commended him for having

> cherished the historians whose duty it is to hand down to posterity the memory of things done so that the examples of kings, nations, and illustrious men can be either equalled or exceeded by imitating them. . . . The knowledge of things done warns princes, teaches people, and instructs individuals. . . . It is the most certain basis for the conduct of affairs. History teaches us the doctrines of philosophy. What is rhetoric itself, one of the most beautiful of the sciences, but the conflict and opposition between things which have been done and things which ought to have been done?[14]

This understanding of the meaning and utility of history became so common during the Renaissance and Reformation periods as to become platitudinous.

ARCHEOLOGY

The search for ancient documents stimulated a search for ancient monuments. The founder of modern archeology was Flavio Biondo (1389–1463), who as papal secretary was well situated to study the Roman ruins. In two massive works, *Rome Triumphant* and *Rome Restored,* Biondo reconstructed the way of life and the political institutions of the ancient Romans, utilizing his knowledge of the topography of the city, its monuments, and its archeological finds. Then he broadened the scope of his studies to include all of Italy in a topographical-historical survey from ancient times and published an encyclopedic work entitled *Italy Illustrated.* These works not only were a great mine of information for historians and patriots in later years, but inspired similar efforts in other lands.

LORENZO VALLA

The man who demonstrated most powerfully the force of the new sense of history and the effective use of historical criticism was no historian at all, but a

---

[14] Myron P. Gilmore, *Humanists and Jurists* (Cambridge, Mass., 1963), p. 19.

philologist and rhetorician, Lorenzo Valla (1407–1457), perhaps the most brilliant critical mind of the Renaissance. The philosopher Leibniz, at any rate, considered Lorenzo Valla and Nicholas Cusanus to have been "the two most powerful spirits of the late Middle Ages."

Valla was born in Rome and was proud of being a Roman. A pupil of the famous pedagogue Vittorino da Feltre, he proved to be a student worthy of the great teacher. He became a superb Latinist and learned Greek so well that he did translations for the pope on commission. A real peripatetic, he moved about from Pavia to Milan to Genoa to Ferrara to Mantua, and then spent many years as secretary to King Alfonso of Naples. The last decade of his life he spent at home in Rome in the service of Pope Nicholas V, as a notary in the apostolic chancery, a position that left him a great deal of time for his literary activities.

Valla early gained a reputation as a pagan Epicurean with his dialogue *Concerning Pleasure and Concerning the True Good*. In this dialogue, directed against Boethius' quasi-Christian Stoic philosophy in *On the Consolation of Philosophy*, Valla reports the conversation of a Stoic, a Christian, and an Epicurean. The dialogue form makes it difficult to determine which of the three is expressing Valla's own opinions. The message, however, seems to be that if people could vote, they would choose happiness. For many years during the nineteenth century, when historians stressed the pagan nature of the Renaissance, they assumed that Valla was endorsing the Epicurean position. It seems, however, that he had a more subtle point to make. He was an ambitious student of the Greek church fathers, and many leading patristic thinkers held the position that Epicurus' stress upon true pleasure, which emphasized control over desire, not self-indulgence, was more readily harmonized than Stoicism with the Christian's belief in God's love for mankind and desire for man's true good and happiness. Valla was in harmony with the fathers of the Eastern church.

Valla's best-known work was the *Elegances of the Latin Language* (1444), which became a standard handbook for humanists south and north who were interested in philological precision and graceful style. Valla noted how two words could be synonymous, yet have quite different connotations. Thus the Latin words *gesta* and *acta* both mean a deed or an action, but *gesta* suggests the grand deed of a hero, a great man such as Alexander or Julius Caesar, while *acta* means any action of any man; the words *series* and *ordo* both mean a succession of things, but *series* merely suggests a sequence while *ordo* implies a grand and stable order of relationships. This work became an indispensable tool for stylists, but by scorning medieval Latin and insisting on classical precision Valla helped kill Latin as a living language.

Always a critical genius and independent thinker, Valla entered the arena of philosophy with his work *On Free Will*. He argued that predestination is not inconsistent with free will and that divine foreknowledge and human free will can be harmonized. He doubted that man has the capacity to bridge the natural and supernatural worlds intellectually or to harmonize reason and revelation rationally. "We stand," he concluded, "by faith, not by the probabilities of reason." He was here swimming against the humanist stream and speaking counter to the spirit of the times, for the theme of man's dignity and the power of his reason were shibboleths for many humanists. Small wonder, in view of his combative temperament, that his stormy career was filled with controversy, including a two-year feud with the rambunctious Poggio.

Three other works of Valla's touched upon problems that were to loom large in the controversies of the next century. His *Annotations to the New Testament* undertook to undo the textual mistakes of Jerome's Vulgate and even ventured to criticize exegetical interpretations of authorities like St. Augustine. In *Concerning the Profession of the Religious* he argued that the monastic life does not have a higher religious value than the good life of the layman, for the layman's good works spring from his own volition and do not consist merely of conformity to rules imposed from without. In his *Encomium of St. Thomas Aquinas* he subtly criticized St. Thomas for giving logic and metaphysics prominent places in theology, and for poor style, by praising the Latin and Greek church fathers. The fathers abhorred speculation and followed Paul's injunctions against following after philosophy and vain deceit, and not after Christ. In style the fathers modeled their writings after the great ancient authors and imitated Paul, a master stylist and rhetorician, whom Valla compared favorably with Demosthenes.[15]

Valla's most sensational work was his *Declamation Concerning the False Donation of Constantine,* in which he challenged the authenticity of the document that allegedly proved that Constantine, when he moved the capital to the east, had given the Lateran Palace and outlying provinces to Pope Sylvester. Valla held that this was the sole basis of the pope's claim to his temporal possessions, so that if it were discredited, the pope's worldly kingdom would collapse. Valla was in the pay at the time (1440) of King Alfonso of Naples, a foe of Pope Eugenius IV. In 1444 the pope commanded the Inquisition in Naples to bring Valla to trial, but the king frustrated its efforts.

Valla used rhetoric in this *Declamation* to appeal to his audience, playing on emotions and constructing fictitious speeches. His concern was with what one might reasonably assume to have taken place. Valla used a general historical argument: Constantine would scarcely have been likely to make the donation, nor would his sons have permitted it. What is more, Pope Sylvester would not have accepted such a gift, even if Constantine had offered it to him, for at that time the church was still pure and the saintly pope was concerned with his spiritual

15 Hanna H. Gray, "Valla's *Encomium of St. Thomas Aquinas* and the Humanist Conception of Christian Antiquity," in *Essays in History and Literature,* ed. Heinz Bluhm (Chicago, 1965), pp. 37–51.

office as shepherd of souls. The specific historical-critical and philological arguments that Valla used to prove that the document could not have been written in
the fourth century, but must have been of a later date, brought into play his remarkable linguistic talent. He showed that the word used for the papal crown was
not in use at the time of Sylvester. He pointed to the word "satraps" in the document, and exploded: "What do satraps have to do with this? Stupid! Dumbbell!
Do caesars speak that way? Has anyone ever heard of any reference to satraps in
the councils of the Romans?"

Valla was quite right, of course, for the document that was purported to have
been written by Constantine was an eighth-century compilation, backed up by
pseudo-Isidorian decretals and other documents. Wycliffe, Dante, and Cusanus
had all challenged the authenticity of the *Donation,* but they had done so from a
royalist, imperialist, or conciliarist point of view, and had used only general arguments. Valla employed the much more persuasive historical-critical method, and
he was in addition compellingly vehement and uncompromising. It is a tribute to
the tolerance of the Renaissance pope Nicholas V that he welcomed Valla to Rome
even after he had written his treatise on the *Donation.* In the Counterreformation
period Cardinal Bellarmine called Valla a precursor of Luther. Luther himself
acknowledged Wycliffe and Valla as his two great authorities. The Renaissance
and the Reformation movements had many such interconnections.

Bibliography

General:

BAKER, HERSCHEL. *The Dignity of Man.* Cambridge, Mass., 1947.

BARON, HANS. *Humanistic and Political Literature in Florence and Venice at the Beginning of the Quattrocento.* Cambridge, Mass., 1955.

———. *The Crisis of the Early Italian Renaissance, 2* vols., rev. ed. Princeton, 1966.

———. *From Petrarch to Leonardo Bruni: Studies in Humanistic and Political Literature.* Chicago, 1968.

BAYLEY, CHARLES. *War and Society in Renaissance Florence.* Toronto, 1961.

BOLGAR, R. R. *The Classical Heritage and Its Beneficiaries.* Cambridge, 1954.

BOUWSMA, WILLIAM S. *Venice and the Defense of Republican Liberty.* Berkeley, 1968.

CHASTEL, A. *The Age of Humanism: Europe 1480–1530.* New York, 1963.

EMERTON, EPHRAIM. *Humanism and Tyranny: Studies in the Italian Trecento.*
Cambridge, Mass., 1925.

FLETCHER, JEFFERSON B. *Literature of the Italian Renaissance.* New York, 1934.

GARIN, EUGENIO. *L'Educazione in Europa, 1400–1600.* Bari, 1957.

———. *Italian Humanism, Philosophy, and Civic Life in the Renaissance.* New York,
1965.

GEANAKOPLOS, DENO. *Greek Scholars in Venice.* Cambridge, Mass., 1962.

GILMORE, MYRON P. *Humanists and Jurists: Six Studies in the Renaissance.* Cambridge, Mass., 1963.

GOLDSMITH, E. P. *The Printed Book of the Renaissance.* Cambridge, Mass., 1950.

HOLMES, GEORGE. *The Florentine Enlightenment, 1400–1450.* New York, 1969.

KRISTELLER, PAUL OSKAR. *The Classics and Renaissance Thought.* Cambridge, Mass., 1955.

——. *Studies in Renaissance Thought and Letters.* Rome, 1956.

LIND, LEVI R., ed. *Lyric Poetry of the Italian Renaissance.* New Haven, 1954.

MARTINES, LAURO. *The Social World of the Florentine Humanists.* Edinburgh, 1963.

NELSON, JOHN C. *The Renaissance Theory of Love.* New York, 1958.

RICE, EUGENE F. *The Renaissance Idea of Wisdom.* Cambridge, Mass., 1958.

ROSSI, VITTORIO. *Storia letteraria d'Italia: Il Quattrocento.* Milan, 1945.

ROTH, CECIL. *The Jews in the Renaissance.* Philadelphia, 1959.

SAITTA, G. *Il pensiero italiano nell' umanesimo e nel Rinascimento,* 3 vols. Bologna, 1949–1950.

SANCTIS, F. DE. *History of Italian Literature,* 2 vols. New York, 1931.

SAPEGNO, N. *Storia letteraria d' Italia: Il Trecento,* 3rd ed. Milan, 1938.

SEIGEL, JERROLD E. *Rhetoric and Philosophy in Renaissance Humanism.* Princeton, 1968.

SPERONI, CHARLES. *Wit and Wisdom of the Italian Renaissance.* Berkeley, 1964.

TRINKAUS, CHARLES. *Adversity's Noblemen: The Italian Humanists on Happiness.* New York, 1965.

——. *"In Our Image and Likeness": Humanity and Divinity in Italian Humanist Thought,* 2 vols. Chicago, 1970.

ULLMAN, B. L. *The Humanism of Coluccio Salutati.* Padua, 1963.

VOIGT, GEORG. *Die Wiederbelebung des klassischen Altertums oder das erste Jahrhundert des Humanismus.* Berlin, 1859.

WEINBERG, BERNHARD. *Literary Criticism in the Italian Renaissance,* 2 vols. Chicago, 1961.

WEISS, ROBERTO. *The Spread of Italian Humanism.* London, 1964.

——. *The Dawn of Humanism in Italy.* London, 1959.

WILKINS, E. H. *A History of Italian Literature.* Cambridge, Mass., 1954.

WOODWARD, W. H. *Vittorino da Feltre and Other Humanist Educators.* Cambridge, Mass., 1964.

——. *Studies in Education During the Age of the Renaissance.* Cambridge, Mass., 1965.

Dante:

BARBI, MICHELE. *Life of Dante,* ed. P. Ruggiers. Berkeley, 1954.

BRANDEIS, IRMA. *The Ladder of Vision: A Study of Dante's Comedy.* Garden City, N.Y., 1961.

CHUBB, THOMAS C. *Dante and His World.* Boston, 1967.

CROCE, BENEDETTO. *The Poetry of Dante.* New York, 1922.

FERGUSSON, FRANCIS. *Dante's Drama of the Mind.* Princeton, 1953.

FLETCHER, JEFFERSON B. *Dante.* South Bend, Ind., 1965.

GILBERT, ALLAN. *Dante and His Comedy.* New York, 1963.

GRANDGENT, C. N. *Dante.* London, 1920.

SINGLETON, CHARLES S. *Dante Studies,* 2 vols. Cambridge, Mass., 1954, 1958.

——. *An Essay on the Vita Nuova.* Cambridge, Mass., 1958.

Toynbee, Paget. *Dante Alighieri: His Life and Works,* ed. C. Singleton. New York, 1965.

Wicksteed, Philip. *Dante and Aquinas.* London, 1913.

Petrarch:

Bishop, Morris. *Petrarch and His World.* Bloomington, Ind., 1963.

Nolhac, Pierre de. *Petrarque et l'humanisme,* 2 vols., 2nd ed. Paris, 1907.

Sanctis, Francesco de. *Saggio critico sul Petrarca.* Bari, 1954.

Tatham, E. H. R. *Francesco Petrarca: The First Modern Man of Letters, 1304–1347,* 2 vols. London, 1925–1926.

Whitfield, John H. *Petrarch and the Renascence.* New York, 1943.

Wilkins, Ernest H. *Studies in the Life and Works of Petrarch.* Cambridge, Mass., 1955.

———. *Petrarch at Vaucluse.* Chicago, 1958.

———. *Petrarch's Eight Years in Milan.* Cambridge, Mass., 1958.

———. *Petrarch's Later Years.* Cambridge, Mass., 1959.

———. *Life of Petrarch.* Chicago, 1961.

Boccaccio:

MacManus, Francis. *Boccaccio.* New York, 1947.

Osgood, Charles G. *Boccaccio on Poetry.* Princeton, 1930.

Scaglione, Aldo D. *Nature and Love in the Late Middle Ages.* Berkeley, 1963.

CHAPTER 7

Renaissance Philosophy, Literature, and Science

Oswald Spengler, the twentieth-century historical pessimist, was wrong on many counts in his analyses and predictions, but he showed brilliant insight in characterizing Western culture as Faustian. That mysterious German Dr. Faust emerged from the shadows during the Renaissance period, willing to bargain away his soul in exchange for forbidden knowledge. The Faustian drive, the yearning for learning, the wish to sound the depths of wisdom and even to explore the arcane and occult impelled many men onward in a phrenetic search for knowledge, human and divine. "For men are from the earth," Cicero had written in *On the Nature of the Gods,* "not as inhabitants or dwellers but as spectators of the higher and heavenly things, a view of which things belongs to no other kind of living being."

Many major figures among the Italian humanists were gone by the mid-fifteenth century or died soon thereafter: Bruni, Vergerio, Poggio, Vittorino, Manetti, Valla. The cultural Renaissance moved on into a new metaphysical phase. The relatively uncomplicated moral philosophy of the humanists was superseded by an intense preoccupation with Neoplatonic, Neo-Pythagorean, Neo-Aristotelian, Hermetic, and Cabalistic philosophies and theodicies.

Social and political conditions in Florence were altered as the Medici family tightened its hold upon the state, restricting the expression of the republican leanings of the civic humanists. As the base of wealth narrowed, there were fewer and fewer opportunities for the professional humanists to participate in significant political action and to share in the economic prosperity of the upper classes, among whom they had once moved so freely. But even more important than these social and political changes was a progression of intellectual life into a new key, a nuance of the mind. For although no dramatic social change equivalent to Florence's took place in Milan, Venice, Rome, Naples, or lesser cities and courts, they too experienced a striking intellectual change. The most powerful factor in this mid-century intellectual and cultural change was the impact of the rediscovered Hellenic philosophy and theology upon minds sufficiently well schooled and sophisticated to respond to them.

The Patristic Revival

THE MASTERY of the language, the availability of a large body of philosophical literature, the enthusiasm of Roman authors for Greek philosophers, and the Platonic component in medieval thought all contributed to the readiness of Renaissance intellectuals for the "ancient theology." But there is one aspect of this development that needs special emphasis, because it has been largely neglected until recently. The Renaissance saw the revival of Christian antiquity as well as of classic culture. Ambrogio Traversari, Leonardo Bruni, John Bessarion, Lorenzo Valla, Egidio da Viterbo, Baptista Mantuanus, and many other scholars devoted tremendous energy to the study of patristic literature. Petrarch himself had pointed to the church fathers as models:

> The Romans may imitate as leaders the Camilluses, the Fabriciuses, the Reguluses, the Scipios. Philosophers may propose to themselves Pythagoras, Socrates, Plato, and Aristotle. Poets may emulate Homer, Virgil, Menander, Terence; historians Thucydides, Sallust, Herodotus, Livy; orators Lysias, the Gracchi, Demosthenes, Tully. And now we come to our own: the bishops and priests may have as an example the apostles and men of apostolic times. . . . We, moreover, have provided as our princes Paul, Antony, Julian, Hilary, Macarius, and, as we return to the truth of the Scriptures, our prince is Elijah, is Elisha, our leaders the sons of the prophets! Thus, brothers, those who were Jerome's leaders are your leaders; further we have Jerome himself, and Augustine and Gregory, and all those anywhere who for love of Christ, by leading a solitary and eremitical life, have been known to have been distinguished by religious leisure.[1]

The patristic revival was important not only because it provided a vision of

---

[1] Petrarch, *De otio religioso*, cited in Charles Trinkaus, "Humanist Treatises on the Status of the Religious: Petrarch, Salutati, Valla," in *Studies in the Renaissance*, ed. M. A. Shaaber (New York, 1964), vol. 11, pp. 16–17.

a golden age in the past, but specifically because of the positive attitude that the Greek and Latin church fathers took toward Greek philosophy. They looked for possibilities of synthesis and areas of agreement. They developed a theory that the divine *Logos,* or principle of wisdom, had inspired pagan philosophers long before becoming incarnate in Christ. Paul's sermon on Mars Hill in Athens had cited pagan poets with approval. One of the early apologists, Justin Martyr, declared, "Whatever has been well said belongs to us Christians." In his first *Apologia* he stated explicitly:

> We have been taught that Christ was first-begotten of God and we have indicated above that He is the Word of whom all mankind partakes. Those who lived by reason are Christians, even though they have been considered atheists: such as, among the Greeks, Socrates, Heraclitus, and others like them.

Gregory Nazianzen, St. Basil, who wrote an "Exhortation to Young Men on How They Might Derive Profit from Pagan Literature," and that great syncretist Clement of Alexandria believed that the *Logos* or the Holy Spirit had inspired the pagan philosophers before New Testament times. Philosophy, Clement argued, educated the Greek people for Christ, just as the law did the Hebrews. A few rigorists, such as Tertullian, opposed classical writings as lascivious and the antique gods as demons. Tertullian called the Greek philosophers "patriarchs of heresy" and Plato a "grocery store for all heretics," and declared that Aristotle had "introduced dialectic for the benefit of heresy."

In the West, St. Jerome was an avid student of the classics. St. Augustine, whose authority loomed so large in the fifteenth and sixteenth centuries, took a basically positive position toward the utility of the classics. In his *De doctrina christiana* he explained: "If perchance those who are called philosophers have spoken things true and agreeable to our faith, especially the Platonists, not only are they not to be feared, but they should be appropriated from them as from unjust possessors for our own use." With very few exceptions the philosophers of the Renaissance took their cue from Augustine. They were less interested in a pagan revival than in working out a grand new synthesis of Greek philosophy and Christian theology. They looked for the most ancient sources of wisdom and sought corroboration of the truth of Christianity in Greek and Hebrew sources.

Neoplatonism

PARTLY BECAUSE of its contrast to the Aristotelianism of the thirteenth century, so central to Thomist scholastic philosophy, Neoplatonism seems to be the most prominent and the most characteristic form of Renaissance philosophy. It lent itself readily to the endeavor of the "academicians" to fuse the "classical ideal of beauty and the Christian ideal of moral perfection." In the *Trionfo della fama* Petrarch assigned the first place to Plato and only second place to Aristotle, since, he said, Plato was praised by the greatest authors, Aristotle only by the greatest numbers.

From the time of Petrarch until the end of the Renaissance, Platonism won an ever larger place in Western thought. Egidio da Viterbo (1469–1532), prior general of the Augustinian order and a cardinal under Leo X, thought that Platonism would bring on a golden age. In his *Commentary on the Sentences* he exclaimed, "Oh, if only Plato rather than Aristotle had come into the hands of our theologians!" Egidio considered Plato a Christian before Christ, one who discovered the secret of the Trinity by means of natural theology. The Renaissance Platonists were concerned with the traditional theological problems: the existence and nature of God, the immortality of the soul, predestination, free will. Their way of thinking was not opposed to formal theology, but it was no longer merely in the service of official theology. The nature of Platonic thought can perhaps best be seen in the key ideas of the three most prominent philosophers of the Renaissance: Nicholas Cusanus, Marsilio Ficino, and Giovanni Pico della Mirandola.

NICHOLAS CUSANUS

Perhaps the most original and significant thinker of the fifteenth century was Nicholas Cusanus (1401–1464), a German churchman who spent a good many years in Renaissance Italy. Ernst Cassirer and other scholars have pointed to Cusanus as the great pioneer of modern thought who made the transition from a scholastic synthesis to a new relativistic approach, using mathematical symbolism to express and illustrate his ideas.

Born in Cues, a small town nestled on the bank of the Moselle River, he went to school in Deventer and then studied Greek, Hebrew, mathematics, and astronomy at Padua. During the papal schism, as a representative of the archbishop of Trier at the Council of Basel, he was a convinced conciliarist, and wrote one of the great statements of conciliar thought. But he became disillusioned with the constant divisions and acrimonious bickerings of the conciliarists, and in 1437 he swung over to the papal side. He was entrusted with many missions by the pope, who sent him to Constantinople to work for the unity of the Eastern and Western churches. He was made a cardinal in 1448 and become bishop of Brixen in 1450. The Habsburg archduke of Austria attacked him and even imprisoned him for his strong defense of the rights of the church. In 1460 he retired to Rome, where he spent his last four years writing his brilliant philosophical treatises.

Cusanus, a true man of the Renaissance, discovered several classic manuscripts and was a jurist, theologian, speculative thinker, and observer of nature. He was pacific and conciliatory toward Islam and other non-Christian religions. A great synthesizer of disparate viewpoints, he considered error to be merely insufficiency of truth. His own thought was very much conditioned by medieval Neoplatonism and mysticism, and by such authors as Dionysius the Areopagite, Duns Scotus, Erigena, the Neoplatonist Proclus, and the great mystic Meister Eckhart.

He employed the negative approach to knowledge of things divine, according to which one arrived at a closer knowledge of God by describing in ever more refined negative comparisons what he is not, rather than stating positively by analogy what he is. Thus the statement "God is not a stone" is more true than "God is not a soul." But Cusanus went well beyond medieval negative theology in the consistency and radicalism of his approach.

Cusanus' basic philosophical concern was the search for unity, for the infinite One that individualizes and reveals itself in the multiplicity of finite things. "Man has actually come into this world in order to seek God," he wrote. The differences and antitheses of all finite creatures coincide in the infinity of God. God is the *coincidentia oppositorum,* the coincidence of opposites, which reveals in the world something of the invisible spiritual world. The central thesis is *docta ignorantia,* learned ignorance, the insight that the most brilliant man of reason cannot by rational principles grasp the identity of unity and infinite multiplicity. God is the nexus of all things, which are in turn the explication or unfolding of God. Cusanus applied to the world such terms as *deus visibilis* and *deus creatus,* bringing down upon himself charges of pantheism. To him the world was a living totality with great worth and value.

Cusanus illustrated his metaphysical theories with mathematical and geometrical symbolism: God is the maximum and the minimum of all finite creation, just as a straight line may be thought of as the circumference of a circle having an infinite radius. A straight line coincides with an infinitely enlarged angle, with an infinitely enlarged curve. Cusanus broke with Aristotle's categories, which assumed that the universe was finite and that the earth was its stationary center. He conceived of the universe rather as an infinite sphere with its circumference everywhere and its center at no specific point. By denying the centrality of the earth or any other point in the universe, he introduced relativity into cosmology. He even taught the rotation of the earth on its axis. His thought was important for Copernicus and Giordano Bruno in the next century.

MARSILIO FICINO

Excited by the new Greek learning, Cosimo de' Medici chose his physician's precocious young son to become a master of Greek and a Platonic philosopher. Cosimo told the boy, Marsilio Ficino (1433–1499), that as his father had cared for his body, so Marsilio was to become "the curer of his soul." The young man was far from impressive physically, for he was small and hunchbacked, but he was a mental giant whose mind embraced and harmonized whole systems of thought.

Cosimo made available a villa, built for him as a summer home by Michelozzo at Careggi, for his "Platonic Academy." It was not really a formal academy, but rather a salon where Ficino presided over the scholarly discussions of friends and visitors. He had no students, Ficino once stated, only "conversation partners." The academicians burned a candle to Plato and faithfully celebrated his birthday each year with a banquet, for Plato was said to have died at eighty-one after such a celebration.

Ficino edited the complete works of Plato and they were published by the Aldine Press in Venice, a beautiful edition. He completed a translation of Plato's *Dialogues* before 1469, the year in which he wrote his commentary on Plato's *Symposium.* He also edited and translated various Neoplatonic works of Plotinus (*Enneads*), Proclus, Porphyry, and Dionysius the Areopagite. He translated from Greek to Latin various texts dating from the second and third centuries A.D. which were ascribed to Hermes Trismegistus (Hermes the Thrice Greatest) and were typical of the gnosticism of that age. And he went on to write many impressive volumes of his own in which he developed his "pious philosophy" or Platonic theology.

After a long period of melancholy, in 1473 Ficino became a priest and wrote a work entitled *De religione christiana.* Between 1469 and 1474 he worked on his masterpiece, the *Theologia platonica,* an elaborate statement of his Neoplatonic philosophy. Ficino considered himself to be a "fisher of men," like St. Peter, and used Neoplatonism to bind intellectuals to the Christian faith. His philosophy was too comprehensive to be presented here in detail, but we can consider at least its most prominent and characteristic features.

Ficino's "pious philosophy" or "learned religion" presupposed an epistemology of poesy and faith. Divine poetry and allegory serve as a veil for true religion. The rhapsodic and the mystical express religious truth, which cannot be encompassed in simple intellectual formulae. "I certainly prefer to believe by divine inspiration," he wrote, "than to know in human fashion." Truth has been transmitted through a long tradition from the ancient philosophers, and wisdom has been revealed in many forms. Plato and the Neoplatonists encompassed in their thought all the elements of the "ancient theology of the gentiles." Ficino did not draw a clear line between the revealed truth of Scripture and the inspired wisdom of the philosophers. The structure of his arguments even suggests that Ficino derived the authority of the Christian faith from its correspondence with the more ancient wisdom, rather than the reverse. Certainly Ficino tended toward a syncretistic universalism that recognized truth, goodness, and beauty in all religious sources, wherever they might be found.

Ficino and the Florentine Platonists, drawing heavily on Plotinus' *Enneads* and other Neoplatonic sources, envisioned the cosmos and everything within it as a great hierarchy of being. Plotinus described the "One" (God) as the absolute and uncontradicted original essence, prior to the plurality of specific individual beings. God is the ultimate unity of all things. The One, which embraces within itself numberless numbers, is related to the lesser creatures through a great chain of being. By emanations proceeding from the One, the lesser orders are brought into being. A stepladder of bodies, qualities, souls, and heavenly intelligences marks the way of ascent to the eternal One. Man is at the center of this great chain of being, linked to the world of matter by his body and to the realm of spirit by his soul, which enables him to rise to reunion with God. The supposition that man is a product of a divine emanation and that God is therefore immanent in him reassures man of his own divinity.

At this point Ficino introduces specifically Christian theology into his system. Plotinus had conceived of an intermediary, a demiurge, between the pure One and the subdivided spiritual and material world. Ficino identified this intermediary with the divine *Logos,* Christ, the Word that became flesh and dwelt among us. Christ is the intermediary between God and man, the mirror image of God the Father, who leads men to love and to enjoy God and who serves as an archetype and example of the perfect man. Christ demonstrates God's great love for man and frees man's soul for the ascent to God. The church, through her sacraments and her teaching, keeps man in contact with the spiritual world. Freed of the body, man's immortal soul will someday enjoy the beatific vision of God without mediation.

Ficino believed that all parts of the universe are held together by bonds of sympathetic love. He used the imagery of a "light metaphysic" to represent this cosmology:

> Man is the earthly star in a cloudy covering and the stars are heavenly people. . . .
> To the song of the joyous heavenly spirits, as the Pythagoreans believe, the spheres
> lead the dances. . . . When the stars laugh, everything in heaven and earth laughs.
> . . . Light is the laughter of heaven and expresses the joy of the heavenly spirits. . . .
> And from the laughing stars as from the eyes of divine minds friendly and happy
> rays travel, influencing the seeds of all living things.[2]

The light metaphysic lent itself easily to astrological theories. Due in part to the popularity of late classic writers such as Macrobius, who declared that "man's fate is controlled by the seven stars," astrology had a strong hold over many men in "the star-crossed Renaissance." The light metaphysic lent plausibility to astral influence and to the notion that men of an artistic and intellectual temperament come readily under the sway of Saturnine melancholy.

Ficino's Platonic theory of love harmonized smoothly with his light meta-

---

[2] Marsilio Ficino, *Opera* (Basel, 1576), vol. 1, pp. 659, 978.

physic. Love binds all men together in their common humanity. The highest form of love, Platonic love, leads the true lover to love the other for the sake of God. Love directs man in his choice of good over evil, of the beautiful over the unlovely. In Neoplatonism the value of beauty is intimately associated with qualities of goodness and truth. Aesthetics, ethics, and epistemology are intimately united in Neoplatonic metaphysics. The standard use of allegory to convey ideas not readily tied down by precise syllogistic expression made this system very congenial to poets and men of letters.

GIOVANNI PICO DELLA MIRANDOLA

The most brilliant young philosopher of the Renaissance was without a doubt Giovanni Pico della Mirandola (1463–1494), a friend and pupil of Ficino. Pico was the youngest son of Francesco Pico, count of Mirandola and Concordia, a small principality just west of Ferrara. At fourteen he went to study at Bologna, but after two years he struck out on a "student wandering" that took him to universities throughout Italy and France. In Paris he was engrossed in the study of scholastic theology. In addition to the usual Latin and Greek, he studied Hebrew, and he was interested too in Arabic and other Near Eastern languages. He nearly burned out his eyes, he relates, reading Hebrew texts belonging to a Jew who was leaving in a few days for Spain. His Hebrew teachers introduced him to the mysteries of the Jewish Cabala, which appealed to his theosophic and mystical interest.

As ambitious as he was charming, Pico went in 1486 to Rome, where he published nine hundred *Conclusiones,* a summation of all learning, which were to serve as theses for a public disputation. He even offered to pay the way for any worthy disputant who could not afford the trip to Rome for a debate. No debate took place, however, for several of the theses were declared to be heretical and the pope prohibited the distribution of the little book. Pico wrote an *Apologia* in his defense, and Pope Alexander VI subsequently vindicated Pico's orthodoxy.

As a rhetorical introduction to the *Conclusiones,* Pico composed an "Oration on the Dignity of Man," one of the most famous writings of the Renaissance. Pico held that man is truly the king of creation, not merely the middle link in the great chain of being, but the object of a special creation. He has the ability to rise upward toward the angels or to sink downward to the level of beasts by indulging sensate appetites.

A tall, blond Lombard nobleman, Pico was as handsome as he was wealthy. He lived a free and easy life, which included such conveniences as mistresses. But in his late twenties he took a more serious turn, and three years before his premature death he gave up his share of the Mirandola patrimony and planned to give away his personal property in order to take up the life of a poor preacher. At twenty-eight he published a mystical commentary on the creation story in Genesis entitled the *Heptaplus*. He also wrote a treatise on God and creation, *Of Being and Unity,* and somber commentaries on selected psalms and on the Lord's Prayer, in which he stressed man's dependence on God and his need for grace. He came under the influence of Savonarola, and remarked that his hair stood on end and chills ran down his back when he heard the friar preach. He died in Florence of a fever on November 17, 1494, just when King Charles VIII came to Florence during his invasion of Italy and Savonarola assumed rule over the city.

Pico's great tribute to the dignity of man is a representative statement of the positive humanism of the Renaissance. But since Pico also acknowledged the shadowy side of human life, a word may be in order at this point about the darker vision of humanist thought. Eugenio Garin, the well-known scholar at the University of Florence, has remarked that the Renaissance was a splendid but not a happy age. Manetti, Fazio, and Pico, drawing upon classical sources and upon such church fathers as Nemesius of Emessa and Lactantius, the Christian Cicero, could write about the dignity of man and attempt to refute Pope Innocent III's dour treatise *On the Contempt of the World*. But the humanists were usually also acutely aware of mankind's miseries. Salutati's treatise *On the World and Religion* devoted one book to the evils of secular life and a second book to the joys of the monastic life. Leonardo Bruni penned an *Introduction to Moral Discipline* which emphasized the difficulty of achieving happiness, while allowing for the possibility of doing so. Poggio, as an old man of seventy-two, composed a work *On the Misery of the Human Condition,* which complained about everything the world might offer man. It has been argued with some plausibility that Manetti's optimistic declaration on man's dignity and excellence was just a shade removed from a fundamental pessimism, for the arguments seemed to grow from a search for reassurance rather than from conviction. Renaissance intellectuals and artists were frequently overwhelmed by a sense of melancholy. The humanists were hopeful for man, but not unrealistic about the human condition.

Neo-Aristotelianism

IN ADDITION to humanism and Neoplatonism, a third vigorous school of philosophy flourished during the Renaissance, Italian Aristotelianism or Neo-Aristotelianism, which dominated the professional circles of philosophers in the universities.

ARISTOTLE IN ITALY

Aristotelianism rose in the second half of the twelfth century and was a major influence on philosophers for four centuries. Its rise carried learning beyond the basic trivium and quadrivium of the earlier Middle Ages. Scholars such as William of Moerbeke translated texts of Aristotle, pseudo-Aristotelian writings, and the commentaries of Averroës (d. 1198) and other Arabic philosophers. The rise of modern Aristotelianism coincided roughly with the rise to prominence of the universities.

By the mid-thirteenth century Aristotle and his commentators, including Averroës, were studied in Paris and at other universities in the north. Philosophy was an independent discipline, but it was most often studied in conjunction with the liberal arts, as a preparation for theological studies. Thomas Aquinas made the great synthesis or *summa* of theology and Aristotelian philosophy, drawing immediately upon the thought of the Jewish Aristotelian Maimonides. In contrast to the northern universities, the universities of Italy cultivated medicine and law rather than theology. Where Aristotelianism became associated with medicine, as at Salerno in the late twelfth century, it served as a form of natural philosophy. During the course of the thirteenth century Aristotelianism penetrated Bologna, became well entrenched at Padua, and spread to other universities. Only at the University of Pisa did Platonism achieve official status.

The Greek revival during the Renaissance added new impetus to the interest in Aristotle and broadened its scope from his logic and natural philosophy to his moral philosophy, especially the *Nichomachean Ethics,* and rhetoric. The Byzantine Aristotelian John Argyropoulos lectured on moral philosophy at the University of Florence in 1457. His disciple Donato Acciaiuoli (1428–1478) represented an Aristotelian perspective in Florence during the years of Neoplatonist Marsilio Ficino's prominence. George of Trebizond and Theodore of Gaza further promoted Aristotle, against the resistance of such Platonists as Bessarion, who defended the divine Plato "against his calumniators."

Pietro Pomponazzi. In *The Pickwick Papers* Charles Dickens tells about a man who prepared to write about Chinese philosophy by looking up "Chinese" in the encyclopedia under *C* and "metaphysics" under *M*. The historian who undertakes to describe Renaissance Aristotelianism soon discovers that there is no such simple solution. Various schools of interpretation flourished—Averroist, Alexandrian, Thomist, and eclectic varieties. More can possibly be gained by considering the thought of a typical Aristotelian of Padua, one of the most prominent schools, than by trying in brief compass to cover the distinctions among the varieties of Aristotelians.

Born in Mantua, Pietro Pomponazzi (1462–1525) took his degree at the University of Padua, where he became a professor in 1488. He knew the writings of Pico and Ficino, read such classical works as those of Cicero and Plutarch, but was preoccupied above all with the study of Aristotle, the famous Greek Aristotelian commentator Alexander of Aphrodisias, and the Stoic philosophers.

His writing has a tortured scholastic style, with only occasional humanist elegance and subjective personal outbursts. In his *On Incantations* he offered natural explanations for strange phenomena popularly ascribed to spirits and demons. In his treatise *On Fate,* he wrestled with the problems of free will, fate, and predestination, and concluded by trying, with the Stoics, to reconcile determinism and human responsibility. His most famous work was *On the Immortality of the Soul.* After considering the opinions of Averroës, Plato, and Thomas Aquinas, Pomponazzi took a position that he identified with that of Alexander of Aphrodisias. The human soul, having only one nature, is absolutely mortal, and only in certain respects immortal. He held that the human intellect needs the body for its object and cannot act without the help of sense images. It is therefore clearly mortal. But the human intellect does not use the body as its subject, as animals do, and therefore in this respect it participates in immortality. The immortality of the soul, Pomponazzi confessed, can be neither proved nor disproved on empirical or rational grounds, but must be accepted on the authority of the church.

The excellence of man, Pomponazzi asserted, consists not in contemplation but in his moral virtue. Man cannot think outside of the sensible world and can understand his life only from within the world. What he thinks has only a relative value, therefore, and not an absolute value. Theoretical speculations must always remain unsatisfying. Man can build a harmonious existence only by limiting himself to those things that he is capable of achieving. The mark of the measured man is to be satisfied with what comes to him and with what he can have. It is vain to fear the inevitable, and a man should therefore "thank God and nature and always be ready to die and not to fear death."[3]

Sixteenth-Century Neo-Aristotelianism. Three Italian philosophers of the sixteenth century who merit special mention are Bernardino Telesio, Francesco Patrizzi, and Giordano Bruno. Telesio was most interested in physical and biological phenomena. In his work *On the Nature of Things* (Naples, 1565) he discarded traditional concepts of matter and form in favor of a dynamic theory of antithetical forces, such as heat and cold, brought into balance. He struggled to free himself from Aristotelian philosophy and to develop his own thought independently. Francesco Patrizzi was truly eclectic, drawing on Plato, Proclus, and Hermes Trismegistus, and translating Philopon's commentary on Aristotle's *Metaphysics* (1583). He wrote treatises on history and poetry, and held a chair of Platonic philosophy in Rome.

The most brilliant and original of the three was Giordano Bruno (1548–1600), who has been called the martyr of the Renaissance. A member of the Dominican order at eighteen, he developed grave doubts about the faith. When his deviation-

---

[3] On Neo-Aristotelianism and Pomponazzi, see Paul Oskar Kristeller, *Eight Philosophers of the Italian Renaissance* (Stanford, 1964), pp. 72–90.

ism became known while he was in Rome in 1576, he was charged with heresy. He escaped and began a long pilgrimage that took him through northern Italy to Geneva, Paris, Marburg, Wittenberg, Prague, Helmstedt, Frankfort, and then back to Padua and Venice. The Inquisition seized him in 1592 and transferred him to Rome, where, in spite of his attempts to recant, he was imprisoned for seven years and finally tried for heresy and burned at the stake in the Campo de' Fiori in February 1600.

Bruno's thought was very much influenced by the mysticism of Hermes Trismegistus. He derived his theory of heroic love, expressed in his work *Eroici furori,* from Ficino's doctrine of Platonic love. While one of the charges against Bruno was that he espoused the Copernican system, his ideas about the universe were actually more imaginative than Copernicus'. From Cusanus he derived the concepts of relativity and of an infinite universe containing an infinite number of solar systems. God is related to this infinite universe as its vital principle, in the same way in which the soul is related to the body.

With Telesio, Patrizzi, and Bruno, however, we are carried into the second half of the sixteenth century, after the impact of the Reformation and Counterreformation had made itself felt in Italy. Throughout the Renaissance both the humanists and the Platonists were basically hostile to the Aristotelians and often overtly critical of them. They believed that the Aristotelian philosophy militated against the dignity of man in denying the person immortality of the individual soul, in holding to the eternity of matter rather than to a special creation that places man above all other creatures, and in having a depersonalized concept of God, who is seen as prime mover rather than as divine father. The impetuous young Pico della Mirandola undertook to write *On the Harmony of Plato and Aristotle,* but he died without realizing his ambition. The endeavor to harmonize the two was not lost sight of, however, and was taken up again by Melanchthon and other intellectuals in the north.

Metaphysics and Literature

FOR A PHILOSOPHY that was not institutionalized, Platonism showed tremendous staying power and had a widespread, subtle influence. After Ficino's death, a friend and pupil of his, Diacceto, carried on the tradition of Platonic studies, and about 1540 a second "Platonic Academy," meeting in the Rucellai Gardens of Florence, developed as a kind of literary club dedicated to the cultivation of pure Tuscan Italian and Platonic studies. Platonism in Renaissance Italy remained a rather fashionable drawing-room body of ideas that colored the thought of poets and artists, theologians and scientists.

Lorenzo de' Medici not only was a grand patron of humanists and artists, but was a prolific poet himself. His volume of verse *Selva d'amore* was inspired by the Platonic theory of love and has received rather high praise from literary critics. Certain members of the Medici circle were excellent poets, especially Politian (1454-1494), author of the *Questiones carmaldulenses,* and Cristoforo Landino (1424-1504), a philologist as well as a man of letters. A very metaphysical poet, Girolamo Benivieni, in his "Song of Divine Love" gave a highly religious form to the Neoplatonic thought of Pico della Mirandola, emphasizing the immortality of the soul and the final reunion of man, a noble creature, with God.

In the latter part of the fifteenth century a cult of Dante developed in the Medici circle. Dante's *Vita nuova* embodied several basic Platonic ideas, such as regeneration by love. The circle of Dante cultists stressed his mysticism and developed it in Neoplatonic terms. Matteo Palmieri, Giovanni Nesi, and Luigi Pulci reflect this tendency. Luigi Pulci also had a mischievous side, however, for he delighted in mockery and in exposing the comic aspects of grave institutions and pretentious beliefs.

Poetry flourished also at the court of Naples. Giovanni Pontano (1426-1503) gained renown for his excellent lyrics. Jacopo Sannazzaro (1456-1530) created a pastoral idyll, "Arcadia," which moved Renaissance artists to portray the simplicity and virtues of pastoral life. In a poem "On the Birth of the Virgin" he presented the life of the Virgin Mary in a classical poetic style.

The great master at presenting Christian themes in classical dress was Baptista Mantuanus (1448-1516), the prior general of the Carmelite order. He favored constructive religious poetry, ornamented with classical figures of speech, to counteract the pagan influence of Greek and Latin literature. He was widely hailed as a second Virgil, and Pico called him the most learned man of the period. He was avidly read in the north because of the very religious nature of his poetry.

During the sixteenth century love literature became popular, vulgarized, and often very sensuous. The only really excellent love poem of this period was Leone Ebreo's *Dialoghi d'amore,* which showed philosophical depth and genuine originality. Michelangelo's lyrics, like his art, reflected a strong Neoplatonic influence. Neoplatonic ideas reached their culmination late in the sixteenth century and early in the seventeenth century in the works of Giordano Bruno and Tommaso Campanella (1568-1639). Campanella's philosophical outlook was strongly influenced by Cusanus, Ficino, and Telesio. He accepted the authority of the church in matters of faith, but, not unlike St. Augustine, he built his philosophy upon the certainty of individual consciousness. His most famous writing, *City of the Sun,* was in the area of political philosophy. In it he portrayed an ideal communism, based upon the closed society of Plato's *Republic.* He advocated a community of wives and property, universal military training, and population control by the state. Administrators, whose authority was to be in direct proportion to their knowledge, were to direct every detail in the lives of the happy citizens, so that the individual welfare corresponded to the collective good. Some Renaissance verve still comes through in Campanella's ecstatic vision: "The novelties of ancient truths, of new worlds, new systems, new nations are the beginning of a new era. Let God not make delay, and let us for our part do all we can."

Renaissance thought is frequently described as a steppingstone toward the Enlightenment. In reality, many features of Renaissance philosophy and literature are reminiscent of late eighteenth- and early nineteenth-century romanticism. Particularly striking is the tendency to spiritualize nature and to idealize thought. The stress on inner freedom, ecstatic theories of love, and an instinctive or intuitive approach to truth, a product of Platonic epistemology based on the doctrine of innate ideas, are romantic notions very prominent in Renaissance thought.

Science

IN THE GREAT DEBATE on the relation of the Renaissance to the modern world, the place of science in the Renaissance is of critical importance, for surely natural science is one of the most important aspects of modern culture. Its rise is usually dated from the seventeenth century. Historians who clearly see a renaissance in literature and art therefore have difficulty in discovering a similar renaissance in science. Some historians, in fact, argue that the Renaissance was a low period for science and that humanism retarded science by directing the attention of intellectuals away from nature and back to classical antiquity and "the pale imitation of the past." They see such scientific progress as was made during the Renaissance as the achievements of craftsmen and technicians, of artists who stood low on the social scale and used the vernacular rather than learned Latin to record their discoveries. On the other hand, some Renaissance scholars believe that the humanists' development of a critical mentality in their philological studies was very important for the rise of science. Thus Valla's textual and historical criticism and Machiavelli's social-scientific approach to politics helped to prepare the Western mind for a critical study of nature.

The humanists, it is true, were more interested in books than in nature, and in understanding man than in rediscovering the world. Petrarch typified their attitude when he spoke with scorn of popular bestiaries and travel books:

> And even if these things were true, they contribute nothing at all to a blessed life. For what, I ask, does it profit us to know about the nature of animals, birds, fishes, and serpents if we remain ignorant of the nature of mankind, to which we belong, and neither know nor care whence we came or whither we are going?[4]

---

[4] Petrarch, *Le traité De sui ipsius et multorium ignorantia,* ed. L. M. Capelli (Paris, 1906), pp. 24–25.

Natural science, like medicine, seemed to the humanists to belong to the preserve of the Aristotelians and scholastics.

FRANCISCAN AND PADUAN PHYSICISTS

The scholastics did indeed make significant contributions to science in the area of theoretical physics. Seventeenth-century scientists were so prone to think and speak of themselves as pioneers and innovators that their own great debt to earlier centuries is sometimes lost from view.

The basic idea of an experimentally grounded science appeared in Arabic Alexandrine science, based upon the study of the ancients. During the second half of the twelfth century and during the thirteenth century Aristotle's physics predominated in the West. In the area of dynamics the key axiom of Aristotle was that "no movement can continue unless it is acted upon by the continual power of a mover directly and immediately applied to it." Aristotle believed, for instance, that the power that sustained an arrow in flight was the movement of the air produced by the hand or implement that discharged it. Nearly all antiquity accepted this notion. The one exception was Philopon (John of Alexandria), who suggested that the arrow continued to move without any mover because the string of the bow generated energy that played the role of the moving force. The Arabic philosophers, true to Aristotle, had nothing but scorn for Philopon.

In 1277 the bishop of Paris, Étienne Tempier, pronounced against a number of Aristotle's theses that seemed to be antithetical to sound theology. This criticism weakened Aristotle's authority and prepared the way for a critique of his physical theories also. William of Occam attacked Aristotle's theory of motion, but he did not replace it with a positive theory of his own. Some followers of Duns Scotus, however, revived Philopon's theory, "energy" appearing now as "impetus."

Jean Buridan (d. 1358), rector of the University of Paris and a "modernist," took up this theory and founded a dynamics that "accorded with the phenomena." He believed that uniform laws apply to movement of any kind. The role that Buridan gave to "impetus" accorded very nearly with that which Galileo attributed to "impetus" or the "moment," Descartes to the "quantity of movement," Leibniz to the "living force." The correspondence was so exact that many centuries later, when Torricelli explained the theories of Galileo, he used the reasoning and almost the exact words of Buridan. The resistance of the surrounding medium counteracts impetus and explains variations in acceleration and the arc of a projectile.

Two of Buridan's pupils, Albert of Saxony (d. 1390), who taught in Paris and Vienna, and Nicolas Oresme (d. 1382), adopted and taught his theories of dynamics and kinesthetics. Albert of Saxony proposed two hypotheses: (1) the speed of a falling body is proportional to the time that has elapsed since it began its fall; (2) the speed of the fall is proportional to the path traveled. Nicolas Oresme, whose intellectual interests ranged from monetary theories to magic and astrology (he opposed them), worked out the essential principles of analytical geometry. Nicholas Cusanus in the fifteenth century knew the works of these men of the Paris school and summarized their position. Leonardo da Vinci was an avid reader of Albert of Saxony and adopted his principles.[5]

The Spanish Dominican Dominique Soto, a pupil of the Occamists, wrote in *Questions on the Physics of Aristotle* (1545) that the fall of a body or the vertical rise of a projectile is uniformly accelerated or decelerated, clearly anticipating Galileo's laws.

The essential link between the Franciscan theorists and Galileo was provided by the school of Padua, which made important contributions to the development of scientific method. During the first decade of the fourteenth century Pietro d'Abano formulated the problem of method, struggling with the two main kinds of proofs, effects through causes and causes through effects. Around 1413 Jacopo da Forli adopted these two "doctrines." Hugo of Siena defined two modes, resolution and composition, similar to Aristotle's analysis and synthesis. Paul of Venice, who around 1390 had developed an interest in scientific theory at Oxford, defended this two-step demonstration against the argument that it is circular. He and Gaetano da Thiene (d. 1465) knew and taught the theories of the Franciscan physicists at Padua. Jacopo Zabarella (d. 1589), a professor of logic, marked the culmination of the Paduan concern with scientific method, his greatest weakness being his failure to appreciate the importance of mathematics in quantitative analysis.[6]

The revival of interest in Neoplatonism, Pythagoreanism, and the Cabala quickened interest in numbers and mathematics, the indispensable and universal language of the physical sciences. Cusanus, Georg Peuerbach (d. 1461), and Regiomontanus (Johannes Müller, d. 1476) contributed to the development of mathematics. Finally the great mathematician Niccolò Tartaglia (*c.* 1506–1559), who taught at Verona and Venice, discovered the solution of cubic equations, and translated Euclid into Italian.

Recently historians of science have stressed the limitations of the Franciscans and the Paduan Aristotelians. They point out that they theorized and made observations, but were not systematic, since they did not do controlled experiments or refine their findings by a series of negative demonstrations. Nevertheless, Galileo learned essentials from them, and his work is in the Paduan tradition. He taught in Padua from 1592 to 1610. The application of the laws of physics to the universe as a means of explaining the movement of the heavenly bodies, in perpetual motion and

---

[5] The basic work on the Franciscan theorists remains Pierre Duhem, *Études sur Léonardo de Vinci* (Paris, 1906–1913), 3 vols.

[6] See John Herman Randall, Jr., "The Development of Scientific Method in the School of Padua," *Journal of the History of Ideas*, 1 (1940):177–206.

controlled by the necessary balance of forces, was one of the astounding achievements of early modern science. "Nature is very patient," Alfred North Whitehead observed wryly, "and lets us formulate whatever laws about her happen to interest us at the moment."

LEONARDO DA VINCI AS SCIENTIST

When in 1481 the brilliant artistic genius Leonardo da Vinci (1452–1519) applied to Ludovico il Moro for a position in Milan, he recommended himself first of all as a military engineer, secondly as a civil engineer, and only incidentally as an architect, painter, and sculptor. For military engineering was the great technical profession of the age, much in demand. As a military engineer for Ludovico, as well as for Cesare Borgia and King Francis I of France, Leonardo planned devices for protecting walls from assault, designed breech-loading canon, built catapults, and plotted the courses of artillery projectiles. His most important contribution to architecture was the analysis of stresses for various kinds of materials.

As an artist Leonardo was interested not only in design and the laws of perspective, but in the anatomy of human beings and of animals, especially of horses. "The singular things of nature are finite," Leonardo wrote, "and the work the eyes order the hands to do is infinite; the painter reveals this in his representation of the infinite forms of animals and vegetables, plants and places." Leonardo illustrates the contributions to natural science made by the artist and craftsman of the Renaissance. He wrote in the vernacular, and it has been remarked that his genius was spared by the fact that he did not attend a university. On the other hand, Leonardo acquired a great deal of classical and religious learning in Florence and in the court circles of Milan and France, and he counted among his friends such learned humanists as Paolo Toscanelli and John Argyropoulos.

Leonardo's *Notebooks* are studded with fascinating observations on natural phenomena, for he was interested in irrigation, lightning, statics, dynamics, geometry, and anatomy. He performed autopsies, observed hardening of the arteries in old people, and came close to discovering the circulation of the blood. He discovered the relation between the rings in a tree trunk and the age of the tree. Leonardo's notes are scattered and fragmented. The entries were never revised or edited, and few dates are given. One cannot call him a precursor of Copernicus just because he once made a brief entry: "The sun does not move." We really do not know what he meant by that. In his book *On Divine Proportion* he was concerned with the mathematical relation of things in space. He was strongly influenced by Neoplatonism and Pythagoreanism. He constantly searched for some simple general rule that would serve to unify all parts of natural science, but of course he never found one.

Ernst Cassirer, a noted twentieth-century cultural historian, was mistaken when he spoke of Leonardo as the first man to have determined with precision the methodological foundations of experimental science. Nor did Leonardo's quest for the proportions of sensory phenomena and the rules that govern them contain implicitly the scientific idea of natural law, as Cassirer argued. Leonardo was neither so systematic in method nor so consequential in his conclusions as modern scientific method requires. He was far from the standards even of Galileo. But he was of great importance to science as a symbol of genius and as an inspiration, and some of his work did enter the body of cumulative knowledge that has come to make up modern science. In the seventeenth century Nicolas Poussin included some twenty of Leonardo's drawings in a book of anatomical drawings. And what fledgling scientist of our time has not marveled at Leonardo's designs for an airplane, a parachute, a helicopter, screw propellers, locks for canals, double-deck streets, rolling mills, multibarreled weapons, and other ingenious devices?

Leonardo's self-portrait as an old man shows deep worry lines. He was only sixty-seven at the time of his death. Vasari relates in his *Lives of the Painters* that on his deathbed Leonardo reproached himself for not having done his duty to God and man in his art. He thought that he had left too many things unfinished and had accomplished too little. Actually, Leonardo was a victim of his own brilliance. As André Gide once remarked, "When one has talent one does what one wishes; when one has genius one does what one can."

The Renaissance was not, like the seventeenth century, a great age of scientific discovery. It was important, however, for the transmission of the medieval advances. Above all the Renaissance saw the development of a secular society and an urban culture concerned with this world. The humanists contributed to the maturation of culture and of Western man's mentality, an important preparation for modern science.

The Spread of Learning

THE RENAISSANCE produced two great boons to learning that put all subsequent ages in its debt. The first of these was the invention of printing and the second was the endowment of libraries. The great Venetian publisher Aldus Manutius spoke for several generations of scholar-printers when he declared in 1490:

> I have resolved to devote my life to the cause of scholarship. I have chosen in place of a life of ease an anxious and toilsome career. Cato compared human existence to iron. When nothing is done with it, it rusts. It is only through constant activity that polish is secured.

Aldus was the first to develop Greek fonts and he was the inventor of italic type.

The Aldine Press published the beautiful edition of Plato's works edited by Ficino and did fine editions of all the major Greek authors. In the course of two decades Aldus published 126 works that had previously existed only in manuscript.

The spread of printing during the half century following Gutenberg's invention was astonishing. By the end of the century there were fifty-one presses in Germany, a fact that was to be of crucial importance for the success of the Reformation. France had thirty-nine, Spain twenty-four, the Netherlands fifteen, Switzerland eight. And Italy—an important index to the vitality of Renaissance culture—had seventy-three printing establishments.

Linen paper had been introduced into Europe from the Far East and was in general use by 1300. It was cheaper than parchment and more durable than papyrus. Without it mechanical printing would not have been practicable. Paper and the press made printing big business. The great book fairs in Leipzig, Cologne, and other centers dictated publishers' deadlines. The whole syndrome of modern publishing problems and possibilities came into being. The invention of printing, Francis Bacon declared, changed "the appearance and state of the whole world." He urged men to "take note of the force, effect, and consequences" of Gutenberg's great invention.[7] It changed men's mental processes, altered communications radically, and was a major factor in making a mercantile and eventually an industrial society a practical possibility.

Information storage in great public libraries marked another important cultural advance. Vespasiano reported that the first Renaissance pope, Nicholas V, had accumulated five thousand volumes in the Vatican library, which he refounded after a lapse of many centuries. St. Mark's library in Venice contained Petrarch's library. Cardinal Bessarion enriched its holdings with a bequest of some five hundred Greek manuscripts. Cosimo founded the famous Medici library in Florence. He employed forty-five copyists, who completed two hundred volumes in less than two years. Vespasiano describes its contents as the Bible, Greek and Latin patristic writers, the major medieval authors, including the scholastic doctors, and classical Latin authors. Most libraries contained many books of devotion and other religious materials. Private libraries of individual humanists and men of wealth were impressive, from a few dozen books to over a thousand. A full-blown interlibrary loan traffic went on, with the humanists sending books along with the post, purloining books, procrastinating in returning them, and developing all the other trials of the modern world of books.

The elder Aldus expressed the feelings of all men of letters when he exclaimed, "What joy to see these volumes of the ancients rescued from the book-burners, and given freely to the world!"

---

7 Francis Bacon, *Novum organum*, aphorism 129.

Bibliography

Philosophy:

ALLEN, DON CAMERON. *The Star-Crossed Renaissance: The Quarrel About Astrology and Its Influence in England*. Durham, N.C., 1941.

———. *Doubt's Boundless Sea: Skepticism and Faith in the Renaissance*. Baltimore, 1964.

BETT, HENRY. *Nicholas of Cusa*. London, 1932.

CASSIRER, ERNST, et al., eds. *The Renaissance Philosophy of Man*. Chicago, 1948.

———. *The Individual and the Cosmos in Renaissance Philosophy*. New York, 1963.

FESTUGIÈRE, A. M. J. *La philosophie de l'amour de Marsile Ficin et son influence sur la littérature française au XVIe siècle*. Paris, 1941.

GARIN, EUGENIO. *La filosofia*, 2 vols. Milan, 1947.

———. *La cultura filosofica del Rinascimento italiano*. Florence, 1961.

———, ed. *Filosofi italiani del Quattrocento*. Florence, 1942.

GENTILE, GIOVANNI. *Il pensiero italiano del Rinascimento*, 3rd ed. Florence, 1955.

GILBERT, NEAL W. *Renaissance Concepts of Method*. New York, 1960.

KLIBANSKY, R. *The Continuity of the Platonic Tradition*. London, 1950.

KRISTELLER, PAUL OSKAR. *The Philosophy of Marsilio Ficino*. New York, 1943.

———. *Eight Philosophers of the Italian Renaissance*. Stanford, 1964.

———. *Le Thomisme et la pensée italienne de la Renaissance*. Montreal, 1967.

MARCEL, RAYMOND. *Marsile Ficin (1433–1499)*. Paris, 1958.

NARDI, BRUNO. *Saggi sull' aristotelismo padovano dal secolo XIV al XVI*. Florence, 1958.

———. *Studi su Pietro Pomponazzi*. Florence, 1965.

ROBB, NESCA. *The Neoplatonism of the Italian Renaissance*. London, 1935.

RÜEGG, WALTER. *Cicero und der Humanismus*. Zurich, 1946.

RUGGIERO, G. DE. *Rinascimento, riforma e controriforma*, pt. 3 of *Storia della filosofia*, 2 vols. Bari, 1937.

SECRET, FRANÇOIS. *Le Zôhar chez les chrétiens de la Renaissance*. Paris, 1958.

———. *Les Kabbalistes chrétiens de la Renaissance*. Paris, 1964.

WALKER, D. P. *Spiritual and Demonic Magic from Ficino to Campanella*. London, 1958.

YATES, FRANCIS. *Giordano Bruno and the Hermetic Tradition*. Chicago, 1964.

———. *The Art of Memory*. Chicago, 1966.

Science:

BOAS, MARIE. *The Scientific Renaissance, 1450–1630*. New York, 1962.

BURTT, EDWIN A. *The Metaphysical Foundations of Modern Physical Sciences*, rev. ed. Garden City, N.Y., 1954.

BUTTERFIELD, HERBERT. *The Origins of Modern Science, 1300–1800*. London, 1951.

CROMBIE, A. C. *Augustine to Galileo: The History of Science, 1400–1650*. London, 1952.

DUHEM, PIERRE. *Études sur Léonardo de Vinci*, 3 vols. Paris, 1906–1913.

———. *Le système du monde, histoire des doctrines cosmologiques de Platon à Copernic*, 5 vols. Paris, 1913–1917.

JAMMER, MAX. *Concepts of Space*. New York, 1960.

KOYRÉ, A. *From the Closed World to the Infinite Universe*. New York, 1958.

RANDALL, JOHN H. *The School of Padua and the Emergence of Modern Science*. New York, 1960.

————. *The Career of Philosophy: From the Middle Ages to the Enlightenment.* New York, 1962.

SARTON, GEORGE. *On the History of Science,* ed. Dorothy Stimson. Cambridge, Mass., 1962.

SINGER, CHARLES, et al., eds. *History of Technology,* vol. 2. New York, 1955.

STACE, W. T. *Mysticism and Philosophy.* New York, 1960.

THORNDYKE, LYNN. *A History of Magic and Experimental Science,* vols. 3 and 4. New York, 1934.

WIGHTMAN, WILLIAM. *Science and the Renaissance,* 2 vols. New York, 1962.

Printing:

BERRY, W. T., and POOLE, H. E. *Annals of Printing: A Chronological Encyclopedia from Earliest Times to 1950.* London, 1966.

BUTLER, PIERCE. *The Origin of Printing in Europe.* Chicago, 1940.

CHAYTOR, H. J. *From Script to Print: An Introduction to Medieval Literature.* Cambridge, 1945.

FEBVRE, LUCIEN, and MARTIN, H. J. *L'Apparition du Livre,* vol. 49 of *L'Évolution de l'humanité.* Paris, 1958.

GOLDSCHMIDT, E. P. *Medieval Texts and Their First Appearance in Print.* London, 1943.

————. *The Printed Book of the Renaissance.* Cambridge, Mass., 1950.

HAY, DENYS. "Literature: The Printed Book." In *The New Cambridge Modern History,* ed. G. R. Elton, vol. 2, pp. 359–86. Cambridge, 1958.

HIRSCH, RUDOLPH. *Printing, Selling, Reading, 1450–1550.* Wiesbaden, 1967.

McLUHAN, MARSHALL. *The Gutenberg Galaxy: The Making of Typographical Man.* Toronto, 1962.

McMURTRIE, DOUGLAS C. *The Invention of Printing: A Bibliography.* Chicago, 1942.

————. *The Book: The Story of Printing and Bookmaking,* 3rd ed. New York and London, 1943.

RUPPEL, ALOYS. *Johannes Gutenberg: Sein Leben und sein Werk,* 3rd ed. Nieuwkoop, 1967.

STEINBERG, S. H. *Five Hundred Years of Printing,* rev. ed. Bristol, 1961.

CHAPTER 8

The Fine Arts

Many points of similarity unite the visual arts of the Renaissance with the great literature and philosophy of the age. "A picture," Horace declared, "is a poem without words."

Giotto and the Birth of Renaissance Art

THE PERCEPTIVE POET Dante saw a decisive change taking place in his own day, as Giovanni Cimabue, the man who was held to have revived painting, gave place to the even greater Giotto:

> In painting Cimabue thought indeed
> To hold the field; now Giotto has the cry,
> So that the fame of the other few now heed.[1]

Before the thirteenth century Italy had been in low estate. "Greek" or Byzantine conventions held sway. Before there was serious talk about the revival of classi-

---

[1] Dante Alighieri, *Il Purgatorio*, canto 11, lines 94–96, in *The Portable Dante*, ed. Paolo Milano (New York, 1947), p. 243.

cal antiquity, Giotto (1266–1336) introduced a new naturalism into painting. When Giotto painted a madonna, he did not surround her with a host of saints and martyrs in order to emphasize her role as mother of God; rather he showed her as a lady of feeling and true virtue, worthy of veneration for her great spiritual quality. The world in which Dante and Giotto lived was conditioned toward Franciscan piety by the powerful preaching of the friars. Following in the tradition established by St. Francis, the Franciscans cultivated an intimate relationship with nature, which was reflected in Giotto's art. The Franciscan influence on Giotto is made explicit in his many portrayals of St. Francis. In the Church of St. Francis in Assisi, built above his tomb, Giotto painted twenty-eight frescoes depicting scenes from the life of the saint. His fresco of *The Death of St. Francis* in the Bardi Chapel of the Santa Croce in Florence is a masterpiece of composition and emotional expression.

But Giotto reserved his most moving artistry for the life of Christ. He sought to make his images of the Virgin Mary, of the Christ child, even of the angels real and palpable, showing love and compassion. His pictures were far more natural than the stiff and stylized icons of the Byzantine tradition. In his great masterpiece in the Arena Chapel at Padua, *The Lamentation,* he portrayed the love and anguish of Mary and the disciples over the death of Christ so passionately that all nature seemed lost in deepest mourning.

Giotto was indeed the founder of a new naturalistic approach to art. Boccaccio declared that Giotto could portray nature so realistically that a painting of Giotto's seemed to be not an image, but the thing itself. "Where was the painter's art," asked Matteo Palmieri in his *On Civil Life,* "till Giotto tardily restored it? It was a caricature of the art of human delineation! Sculpture and architecture, for long years sunk to the merest travesty of art, are only today in process of rescue from obscurity; only now are they being brought to a new pitch of perfection by men of genius and erudition."[2] The artist and critic Giorgio Vasari, in his monumental *Lives of the Painters,* stated as dogma that the artistic renaissance began with Giotto, for he led art back to "a path which may be called the true one."

Giotto made a beginning, but his naturalism had its limitations. He devoted himself exclusively to religious themes, and most of these were of a somber nature. Moreover, for decades after his break with tradition, although many artists tried to follow in his footsteps, none matched his achievements. His own assistant, Taddeo Baddi (*c.* 1300–1366), imitated the lively and novel aspects of Giotto's style, but could not handle the larger problems of complex spatial patterns and unity of total composition. The artists of Siena, such as Simone Martini (*c.* 1285–1344), produced more stylized work, in the manner of Gothic illuminations, with great beauty of color and line. The Sienese style influenced Florentine painters in the

---

[2] Denys Hay, *The Italian Renaissance in Its Historical Background* (Cambridge, 1961), p. 11.

half century after Giotto. Gentile da Fabriano (*c*. 1370–1427), who decorated the Strozzi Chapel, and Antonio Pisano, called Pisanello (*c*. 1395–1455), reverted to an older style and took over relatively little of Giotto's naturalism. Pisanello became famous for his medals in bronze depicting John Palaeologus and other rulers, thus renewing the ancient practice of striking off commemorative plaques and medals which has continued down to the present day.

The Artist in Practice and Theory

IN VIEW of the adulation bordering on worship bestowed upon the artistic geniuses of the Renaissance in later centuries, it comes as a shock to moderns to learn that during the Renaissance artists were the social equals of leather workers and other artisans, and could barely be considered lower middle class. As men who worked with their hands, they were socially far beneath the aristocracy and the bourgeoisie.

Artists received their training as apprentices in the workshops of the masters. Leonardo da Vinci, for example, learned his craft in the workshop of Andrea del Verrocchio (1435–1488), and Michelangelo trained for a time in the workshop of Domenico Ghirlandaio (1449–1494). The workshops or studios produced paintings and other works of art on commission for the churches of the mendicant orders, for the private chapels of wealthy families, and for private patrons who wanted murals or altar paintings to donate to churches or to ornament their homes; late in the *Quattrocento,* family portraits also became popular. The master would sometimes sketch out the scene and have the apprentices fill in the parts. In due course the beginners themselves became masters. Filippo Villani included a number of artists among his *Famous Citizens of the City of Florence* at the end of the fourteenth century. By the end of the fifteenth century, great artists kept company with renowned men of letters and were a familiar sight at the courts of Mantua, Rimini, and Milan, in the circle of the Medicis in Florence, and at the papal court in Rome.

It is easy to trace the growth of lay patronage through commissions and the migrations of the artists, but it is considerably more difficult to be specific about the influence of lay patronage upon the substance and form of art itself. Since Renaissance society was at least formally very pious, the subject matter of most Renaissance art remained religious, but secular influence was to be seen in increasing naturalism. Attempts to correlate the styles of individual paintings with the social views of the patrons who commissioned them have met with only limited success.

CENNINO CENNINI

No book affords the modern student of art a better insight into the technical methods of the Renaissance artist than Cennino Cennini's *Il libro dell'arte*. Written in the fifteenth century, this craftsman's handbook summarized the tricks of the trade and was actually used as a manual by Piero della Francesca, Leonardo da Vinci, and other artists. The book opens with a charming introduction:

> Here begins the Craftsman's Handbook, made and composed by Cennino of Colle, in the reverence of God, and of the Virgin Mary, and of St. Eustace, and of St. Francis, and of St. John the Baptist, and of St. Anthony of Padua, and in general of all the saints of God; and in the reverence of Giotto, of Taddeo and of Agnolo, Cennino's master; and for the use and good and profit of anyone who wants to enter this profession.[3]

Cennini explains that painting combines theory with skill of hand, and deserves to be enthroned next to theory and to be crowned with poetry. The poet, with his theory, is free to compose and bind together or not, as he pleases. In the same way the painter is free to compose a figure standing or seated, half man and half horse, as his imagination prompts him. Some painters are moved by a lofty spirit; others pursue art for profit, driven by poverty or domestic need. Beginners must submit themselves to the direction of a master for instruction and must deck themselves out in the attire of one who would learn: enthusiasm, reverence, obedience, and constancy.

Cennini, an "unimportant practicing member of the profession of painting," then instructs the novice in the techniques of the trade. He explains how to make glue from goat hoofs. He tells how to make life masks by smearing oil on the eyelids, inserting tubes into the nostrils, putting a frame around the face, and the like. He warns against the use of cosmetics, for they cause the loss of a good complexion, wither the skin, turn teeth black, and induce premature aging in women. He describes methods of casting statues and offers a summary of the best techniques available to the artist.

Whereas the architects of the great Gothic cathedrals of the north had introduced large glass windows that greatly reduced the wall space available for painting, most Italian churches provided ample space for "sermons in pictures." For these wall paintings, or murals, the artists painted with water colors on a layer of wet plaster (fresco), so that the pigment soaked in and became fixed as the plaster dried. While the medium did not determine the message, it did influence the style; for fresco painting lent itself well to the portrayal of large figures, but was not suited for delicate detail.

For smaller paintings, Renaissance painters applied a mixture of plaster of Paris and glue to wooden panels. The mixture filled the pores in the wood and provided a smooth, dry, nonabsorbent surface. Until the introduction of oil paints in the fifteenth century, the whites or yolks of eggs were used as binders for pigments. Panel painting allowed for finer work than was possible in murals, and

---

[3] Cennino d'Andrea Cennini, *The Craftsman's Handbook* (New Haven, 1933), p. 1.

made possible the introduction of detail reminiscent of medieval manuscript illuminations, which had so strongly influenced Flemish art. Moreover, it freed painting from its architectural setting. When paintings became mobile, artists were able to extend their techniques to portraits, nature scenes, and other subjects not appropriate to churches.

DIVINE PERSPECTIVE

Renaissance artists were excited by their discovery of a new principle in art, linear perspective. Leonardo da Vinci and other great artists were so intrigued by the laws of perspective that they wrote theoretical treatises about it. We do not know who was the first to discover the laws of perspective, but certain artists, preeminently Brunelleschi (1377–1446), by precept and practice became important exponents of the new approach.

Renaissance artists frequently conceived of the painter and the observer as existing within the space of the scene represented in the painting, rather than at some point outside of it. Linear perspective makes this illusion possible by portraying objects upon a flat surface just as they are seen by binocular vision, without reference to their relative size. A man in the background may be larger than a woman in the foreground, but he appears smaller to the eye, so the artist gives him smaller dimensions in his painting. The whole scene is valid from the observation point of the individual spectator. Mathematical proportions and rationalized geometric patterns are essential to the design of a painting done in perspective. Linear perspective ("clear seeing") brought about a clean break with the flat, floating arrangements characteristic of medieval art. Renaissance painting was far different from the static forms of thirteenth-century Byzantine mosaics and even from the more traditional Italian painting of the fourteenth century. The painter Paolo Uccello spoke for his whole generation when he exclaimed, "How sweet is perspective!"

LEON BATTISTA ALBERTI

A great genius of the Renaissance, Leon Battista Alberti (1404–1472), came closer than anybody before Leonardo to being a "universal man," the Renaissance ideal who excelled in many fields. He was not only a man of letters and learning, an artist, and an architect, but a brilliant theoretician as well. Jacob Burckhardt called Alberti the "first universal genius."

Alberti belonged to a noble Florentine family that had acquired a fortune in the wool trade. In 1387 his grandfather was banished from Florence, and in 1401 his father too was exiled. In Genoa, where the family had a branch bank, the father married a wealthy Bolognese widow, who gave birth to two sons, Carlo and Leon

Battista. In 1428 the family was allowed to return to Florence and in 1434 the last legal restrictions were removed from the family. In the preface to the Italian edition of his book on painting, Alberti expressed his surprise at seeing Florence for himself.

At twenty Alberti wrote a Latin play, *Philodoxius,* and deceived Aldus Manutius the Younger, the learned Venetian printer, into believing that it was a lost work of Lepidus. Like Michelangelo when one of his early sculptures was successfully passed off as a rediscovered antique work, Alberti found that the veneration for antiquity dulled the critics' judgment. The versatile Alberti was one of the best organists of the time. Interested in engineering problems, he developed a device for raising a sunken Roman ship. Vasari relates that in 1457 Alberti invented a device similar to Gutenberg's printing press. He studied art and architecture in Rome, where he explored the ruins for examples of classical forms. Brunelleschi was just closing the dome of the Florence cathedral, and Alberti was excited by the new trend in architecture. A canon in the metropolitan church in Florence, Alberti had leisure to devote to art, architecture, and theory. In his later years he associated with the Platonic circle at the court of Lorenzo de' Medici.

As an architect Alberti introduced classical motifs in practice and in theory. In Rome he helped to restore the papal palace for Nicholas V and to ornament the Trevi Fountain. In Rimini between 1450 and 1460 he remodeled the thirteenth-century Church of San Francesco for Sigismondo Malatesta. The tyrant of Rimini intended the church to be a hall of fame where the classical scholars in his academy and his mistress Isotta were to be buried. Alberti covered the brick building with a marble veneer. The façade featured three rounded arches and four semidetached Corinthian columns; if the upper part had been completed, the whole design would have formed an arch of triumph in the ancient Roman style. The design was, in fact, adapted from a Roman gate in the walls of Rimini. In Florence the Rucellais commissioned him to build them a palace, and also to design the principal façade of the marvelous Church of Santa Maria Novella. But even more important than his own designs were his theoretical writings on architecture, painting, and social thought.

As a humanist Alberti was captivated by the architectural theories of Vitruvius, a Roman of the first century A.D. whose major work was discovered in 1414 in the monastery of St. Gall. Alberti's own book *On Building,* which he finished around 1452, reflected Vitruvius' influence. Alberti's theory was that creative design should utilize classical forms, not merely by copying them, but by applying the proven principles they embodied. He praised architecture as a social art, for it is concerned with the health and welfare of the people. Alberti held that no structure should be designed as an isolated unit; each building should be planned in relation to its social function and its entire urban setting. He proposed that cities be planned with large squares for open space and with various foci or centers. The city planning of later centuries, important for Washington, D.C., and later for Paris, was influenced by a tradition of urban design going back to Alberti.

Alberti's treatise *On Painting* (1435) reflected Neoplatonic influence. It was the first such study done in a scientific fashion and became a prototype for a host of later theoretical studies. Dedicated to Brunelleschi, the treatise discusses problems of mathematical analysis in design and the place of geometry in painting. Alberti considered mathematical proportion to be symbolic of divine harmony and order. He analyzes the spectrum, the use of color, and the effect of reflected light rays. He discusses the "one-point perspective system" and the elements of composition. The painter, according to Alberti, should bring out the beauty implicit in the object. He should not merely reproduce nature; he should idealize it, for nature of itself is not always beautiful. Thus he should paint the eye of a king in such a way as to bring out a look of strength and dignity. The ideal painting should tell an elevating story. Figures should be sculptured rather than linear. They should be grouped in geometric forms, and the groups should be related to each other in such a way that the total composition forms a geometric design. Alberti's theories were applied by Piero della Francesca and other artists, and are clearly in evidence in Raphael's *School of Athens*. In aesthetic theory Alberti pioneered a tradition that reached down in time through Leonardo da Vinci to Sir Joshua Reynolds. Alberti's treatise *On Sculpture* was less influential.

A lifelong bachelor, Alberti nevertheless wrote a famous four-volume treatise *On the Family* (1443), in which he presented his version of home economics. In these four books of dialogues Alberti has the younger members of the family discuss life with the more experienced and mature members. He stresses the virtue of saving to build up the economic strength of the family, contrasting bourgeois thrift with the spendthrift ways of the nobility. He considers a rational ordering of one's affairs of utmost importance, even going so far as to suggest a list of activities for each day and a systematic checking off of accomplishments each night. He acknowledged that men vary greatly in knowledge and attainments, and that there will therefore always be great differences in wealth; but he held that government should minimize the harmful effects of such differences.

Alberti's whole philosophy of life, in fact, reflected all the virtues of civic humanism. "Nothing is better or more suited to the acquisition of virtue and good ethics than to read learned authors," declared the scholarly artist. "Man is born in order to be useful to man," he asserted. Man is fully developed only when he directs all his efforts toward the welfare of "the fatherland, the public good, and the benefit of all citizens." Alberti was a typical Renaissance man in his restless energy and his titanic enterprise. "I am pleased," he said, "not in the man of leisure and cessation, but of operation and action!"

Quattrocento Painting

MASACCIO

If Giotto was properly honored as the creator of Renaissance art, Masaccio was the "second Prometheus" who carried Renaissance painting into a new phase in the fifteenth century. In his brief life Masaccio (1401–1428) introduced exciting innovations to fresco painting. A master at twenty, the young Florentine painter, son of a notary, moved to Rome in 1426 or 1427, and a year later passed away in obscurity.

Masaccio was a nickname like "Sloppy Joe," given him because of his slovenly habits and careless dress. His real name was Tommaso Guidi. According to Vasari, he was not fully appreciated as an artist during his lifetime, but he was a great innovator all the same and made an important impact upon the development of Renaissance painting.

His renown rests chiefly upon the frescoes in the Brancacci family chapel of the Church of Santa Maria del Carmine in Florence. In *The Tribute Money* he depicted the disciples clustered around Jesus waiting to hear his answer to the question "Is it lawful to pay tribute to Caesar?" Among the spectators Masaccio included portraits of himself and a friend. Perhaps his most famous fresco is *The Expulsion of Adam and Eve from the Garden,* in which the grief-stricken nude figures reveal the awful pathos of the moment. Masaccio pioneered in the use of perspective, going far beyond Giotto in this respect. His figures show a true naturalism in the manner of Giotto, but they are even more individualistic, and they are related to each other and to their setting in a much more realistic fashion. Masaccio achieved a modeling and a spaciousness that excelled those of his predecessors and contemporaries. Vasari tells how the giants of the high Renaissance, Leonardo, Michelangelo, and Raphael, came to the chapel to study Masaccio's technique of perspective, his skill in composition and psychological expression.

FRA ANGELICO

Not all of Masaccio's contemporaries were ready for his innovations. Fra Angelico (1387–1455) employed naturalistic techniques, but he treated his religious subjects with a delicate other-worldliness reminiscent of an earlier period. He sought to express the inner life of the soul in the countenance of the subject. He did not simply employ traditional iconography in order to convey his spiritual message, however. His beautiful landscapes, his mastery in the use of delicate colors, his love of flora, all proved him to be an authentic Renaissance artist in the new mode.

MASACCIO. *The Rendering of the Tribute Money.* Brancacci Chapel, Santa Maria del Carmine, Florence.

FRA FILIPPO LIPPI

Like Fra Angelico, Fra Filippo Lippi (1406–1469) concentrated on religious subjects, but he gave them a new cheerful earthly reality. His madonnas, done in brilliant colors, are very real and credible young ladies, and his children are quite human. Filippino Lippi (*c.* 1457–1504), his son, also treated religious subjects in a worldly way. This approach is to be seen later in the paintings of Ghirlandaio (1449–1494), and in the works of the Umbrian painters Pietro Perugino (1441–1523) and Bernardino Pinturicchio (1454–1513), who were decorative illustrators.

PIERO DELLA FRANCESCA

The most worthy successor to Masaccio was the Umbrian painter Piero della Francesca (*c.* 1416–1492), who was born and lived most of his life in the little town of Borgo San Sepolcro. He was impressed by the principle of perspective expounded by Alberti and Brunelleschi, and even wrote a mathematical treatise himself: *On Perspective Painting.* He was inspired by Masaccio's frescoes in the Brancacci Chapel and went on to perfect the union of the spiritual and the natural in his own masterpieces. Piero's work was restrained and discriminating, learned and yet full of feeling. He did a series of masterful frescoes in the Church of San Francesco in Arezzo that still capture the attention of the viewer. But his most powerful work is probably *The Resurrection.* The risen Christ stands erect and imperious in the center against a dawn-gray landscape. Beneath his feet the armed guards slumber on, as though to suggest the dreamlike and transient nature of the power of this world compared with the triumphant life of the spirit and the world beyond.

SANDRO BOTTICELLI

An artist whose work seems to be strangely out of phase with the tendency toward realism in Renaissance art as developed by Giotto and Masaccio was Sandro Botticelli (1444–1510), a Florentine who enjoyed the continuous partonage of the Medicis as long as they remained in power. The son of a tanner, Botticelli ("little barrel") was apprenticed at fourteen to Fra Filippo Lippi and spent nearly a decade in his studio learning the trade. When Botticelli painted his earliest picture still extant, *The Adoration of the Magi,* he was so much under the master's influence that it was long ascribed to him. But once Fra Filippo left Florence for Spoleto, Botticelli developed greater independence in style. From the school of Pollaiuoli he gained a measure of realism, precision in linear representation, and a more exact knowledge of the human body and its movement. He became a favorite of the Medicis and through them came into contact with the circle of Neoplatonic philoso-

BOTTICELLI. *Primavera*. Uffizi Gallery, Florence.

phers and poets that they supported and encouraged. The poet Politian influenced him strongly and possibly inspired that dreamlike, evanescent quality of his mature work.

Botticelli did his two most famous paintings for the Medicis. Around 1477–1478 he painted the *Primavera,* or "Spring," for the younger Lorenzo's villa at Castello. Inspired by a poem of Politian as well as by the classical poets Horace and Lucretius, the *Primavera* portrays Venus, draped in a flowing translucent gown, standing in a grove of myrtle and orange trees awaiting the coming of spring. Mercury, messenger of the gods, heralds the advent of spring as Florus and Zephyr, the gentle west wind, encourage her entrance. Above Venus hovers Cupid, for spring is the season for love. In his other masterpiece, *The Birth of Venus,* Botticelli pictures the goddess of love emerging on a shell from the sea. The painting combines elements of medieval mysticism, Neoplatonic allegory, and Renaissance naturalism in a delicate and enchanting fantasy. Botticelli's great skill at linear representation and the delicacy and charm of his work, which suggests a highly spiritual quality, come to full expression in this masterpiece.

Botticelli did a number of religious paintings (his beautiful *Virgin with the Pomegranate* is outstanding), but he also did earthier pictures. When the Medicis had crushed the Pazzi revolt in 1478, they commissioned Botticelli to paint the rebels hanging by their necks on the walls of the Palazzo del Podestà, as a reminder to the people of the fate of traitors. When the Medicis were driven from power, the painting also perished. Botticelli also spent some time in Rome, decorating the walls of niches in the Sistine Chapel with papal portraits.

Botticelli's poetic fantasy, his increasingly intense religious sentiment, and his fascination with eschatological prophecy all conditioned him for Savonarola's message. He had done eighty-five illustrations for an edition of Dante's *Divine Comedy* just prior to Savonarola's emergence as a power in Florence. Thus mentally prepared, he was swept away by the somber preaching of the earnest Dominican. His *Nativity* is the painting that best illustrates the strong emotion and deep religious feeling of this final period.

ANDREA MANTEGNA

One of the greatest non-Florentine painters of the century, Mantegna (1431–1506) studied art in Padua. He had notable masters to emulate, for Giotto's frescoes in the Arena Chapel were an inspiration to him, and the sculptor Donatello worked in Padua for years and his monumental equestrian statue of the Venetian condottiere Gattamelata was already a city landmark. Mantegna was completely captivated by the art of antiquity and loved to portray in his paintings figures reminiscent of classic statuary and the columns and arches of Roman architecture. *The Circumcision,* an altar painting (1464), showing Mary and the Christ child in the temple with the priest at the moment of the cutting, tells the story dramatically. It illustrates Mantegna's special talent for precise detail that serves as a support for the major figures and the central theme.

PAOLO UCCELLO

The long-lived Paolo Uccello (1397–1475) turned his art to secular subjects. He still did a great number of religious paintings, but he also did hunting scenes and painted three battle scenes for Cosimo de' Medici celebrating "triumphs" of Florence over Siena. He did the first equestrian portrait of the period, of the English condottiere Sir John Hawkwood, who fought and died for Florence.

Renaissance art following Masaccio was marked by an increase in naturalism and in the number of secular subjects. Portraiture as such became more popular, and the inclusion of portraits of patrons and other contemporaries in large religious scenes became a very common practice. It may not be extravagant to suggest that bourgeois self-consciousness and a new individualism were here in evidence.

Sculpture

UNLIKE PAINTING, of which few classical examples had survived, ancient sculpture was represented by a multitude of models. Most examples came from the third and fourth centuries A.D. They were not the best that ancient sculptors had produced, for the most striking masterpieces of classical sculpturing, such as the Laocoön group and the Apollo Belvedere, were not unearthed until the sixteenth century. Still, those that were available to Renaissance sculptors served them well. Renaissance sculpture was not, however, merely an imitation of ancient art, but a living expression of the feeling, thought, and aspirations of a dynamic society. French sculpture of the thirteenth century reflected a decline in Gothic ideals, as sculptured figures were separated from their architectural settings and given artificial expressions and poses. Italian sculpture of the fourteenth to sixteenth centuries, while drawing on a strong classic tradition, expressed the growing naturalism, the psychological depths, and the intellectual currents of a vital Renaissance culture.

THE PISANS

The new naturalism found its first notable expression in the work of Nicola Pisano (1220–1278), whose pulpit in the Baptistery at Pisa (1260) pioneered in the new directions sculpture was to take. Vasari reports that Pisano had studied a Roman sarcophagus in the *campo santo* in Pisa, but his figures of men and ani-

mals prove that he was also a close student of nature itself. He decorated the hex-
agonal pulpit with a set of panels portraying scenes from the New Testament,
beginning with the nativity. His deeply engraved figures had the posture and
expression of Roman statuary. The Virgin Mary, for example, lies on a couch like
a Roman matron. Her head resembles that of an ancient Juno. The angel of the
annunciation is wearing a toga, and in the foreground stands an antique basin.
The crowded composition and the subject matter suggest that Pisano's work was
still basically medieval, but the seeds of the future are in evidence.

His son, Giovanni Pisano (1250–1317), worked with him on the pulpit in the
Siena cathedral, but gradually asserted independence in style. Giovanni moved
toward greater realism and naturalism, replacing static figures with dynamic ones.
In his nativity scene on a panel of the pulpit in Sant' Andrea at Pistoia, he portrayed the agitation of the angel, the maternal tenderness of Mary, the wonder
and reflectiveness of Joseph, and the concern of the busy midwives in a moving,
human fashion. The vertical lines used by Nicola are replaced with diagonal lines.
Nature is no longer merely symbolic of the spiritual world above it. Emotions are
given freer expression. Sculpture is released to serve as a vehicle for the artist's
highly individual interpretation of experience and reality as he understands it.
Renaissance sculpture developed along the lines indicated by Giovanni Pisano's
creations, not in imitation of them but as the original and vital expressions of a
great age and of artistic geniuses such as the world had never seen before and has
not equaled since.

LORENZO GHIBERTI

After a lag that lasted most of the fourteenth century, Renaissance sculpturing
picked up again at the very beginning of the fifteenth century with the work of
Lorenzo Ghiberti (1378–1455). Florence had a virtual monopoly on sculpture in
the fifteenth and early sixteenth centuries. It was fitting, therefore, that its leadership in this field should be spotlighted by a contest for the commission to create
the bronze doors of the Baptistery of San Giovanni in Florence.

The Guild of Wool Merchants endowed a pair of bronze doors for the Baptistery in thanks to God for saving the city during the plague of 1400, and the city
staged a competition in 1401 to select the artist who should receive the commission.
The task set was to prepare a panel on the sacrifice of Isaac by Abraham. The seven
competitors were given a year in which to prepare their models. The choice was
finally narrowed to the entries of Ghiberti and Filippo Brunelleschi. Ghiberti's
panel revealed beautiful linear effect, clarity of composition, and rhythmic movement, all done with restraint; Brunelleschi's displayed an almost frightening sense
of realism. Ghiberti was the victor, and it is said that this defeat was responsible
for Brunelleschi's decision to devote himself to architecture, a field in which he
was to gain great renown. The learned humanist Ambrogio Traversari prepared

the program for Ghiberti's remaining panels. Ghiberti completed the doors in 1423 and won fame and acclaim for his efforts. The next year he won a commission for a second set of doors, which he completed in 1447. The first pair was then placed in the south entrance and the second pair on the east portal. Ghiberti said he had done his very best to imitate nature, and his best, as represented by the second pair of doors, has never been equaled. A lesson in bronze, they have instructed generations of artists in the achievement of naturalism and the demands of technical perfection. Michelangelo declared the doors in the east portal worthy to serve as "the gates of paradise."

JACOPO DELLA QUERCIA

Compared with the work of Ghiberti, that of Jacopo della Quercia (1371–1438) seems to lack precision and refinement. He too had entered the Baptistery competition and lost. He imitated the classical pattern more closely than Ghiberti, virtually eliminating the background detail in order to emphasize the figures themselves. Jacopo learned much from his study of classical models, but his inadequate knowledge of human anatomy marred his work. His sculptured reliefs were not truly appreciated by his contemporaries, who failed to see in them the potential for further development of free-standing nude figures. Not until Michelangelo was this art form fully realized.

DONATELLO

The undisputed master of sculpture in the first half of the *Quattrocento* was Donato Bardi (1386–1466), best known by the affectionate diminutive Donatello. Donatello received his early training in a goldsmith's shop and worked for a time in Ghiberti's studio. When Brunelleschi left Florence for Rome after losing the Baptistery competition to Ghiberti, Donatello accompanied him. While Brunelleschi measured the Pantheon dome and other classic buildings and ruins, Donatello examined Roman statuary and fragments. His scientific study of human anatomy helped him to resolve many of the problems of portraying the human body in various poses. The true sign of his genius was that the inner quality and spirit of his subject shone through the technical perfection of the form. Michelangelo said of his St. Mark, done for one of the fourteen exterior niches of the Or San Michele, the church of the Florentine guilds, "I have never seen a figure that so thoroughly represents a man of probity."

The first two figures that Donatello did upon his return to Florence, for the north portal of the cathedral, were still Gothic in style, but he was soon experimenting with classical forms and a new realism. For the campanile he did marble statues of St. John the Baptist and Jeremiah, and the *Zuccone* or "pumpkin head," presumably of Habakkuk. As has often been the case in literature, the unlovely is emphasized in the early strivings for realistic effects. The *Zuccone* is a typical example of this phenomenon. Donatello reproduced his homely, almost repugnant model precisely, without in any way ennobling the features as Leonardo da Vinci was later to do, when he brought out the beauty in even a wrinkled old face.

The most famous achievement of Donatello's classic period was his bronze David, now in the Bargello in Florence. The David was the first (*c*. 1430) nude statue of the Renaissance. Conceived in the round, the David is a free-standing figure, independent of any architectural surroundings. David is presented as a slender youth wearing a Tuscan shepherd's hat. The figure is relaxed, resting on one leg, and has the angular boniness and awkwardness typical of adolescence. It may reflect Etruscan or Gothic influence.

In 1442 Donatello was invited to Padua to decorate the high altar of San Antonio. His bronze crucifix on the high altar was acknowledged as a masterpiece. But his greatest triumph was an equestrian statue, the Gattamelata. In the very year in which Donatello came to Padua, the powerful Venetian condottiere Gattamelata died and left a huge bequest to Padua on the condition that the city erect an equestrian statue in his memory. Donatello received the commission and remained in Padua for ten years executing it. In 1453 the Gattamelata was finished, and stands today, imperious, like a Roman emperor, dominating the square. Donatello studied the anatomy of the horse with scientific precision—the nostrils, veins, neck, and heavy frame of the armor-bearing war steed. The condottiere himself displays confidence and near repose. The understatement conveys a sense of his real strength.

Donatello returned to spend the last years of his life in his native Florence. He did the repulsive, emaciated Mary Magdalen in the Baptistery in Florence and the Judith group for the courtyard of the Medici Palace. His last important commission was the bronze reliefs for the pulpit of San Lorenzo, about 1460, which an assistant finished after his death. His efforts as an architect were not very successful, for he was overliteral in imitating antique form and style and crowded his surfaces with too many details borrowed directly from classical models.

THE LATE QUATTROCENTO

During the second half of the fifteenth century, sculpture followed three tendencies: the expression of a sweet lyric sentiment, the realistic recognition of ugly aspects of life, and a scientific emphasis worthy of Donatello himself.

The most striking examples of the lyric sentiment are to be found in the works of Desiderio da Settignano (1428–1464), who studied with Donatello. His finest productions were linear low reliefs, like large cameos, of the Madonna and child. Luca della Robbia (1400–1482) is most famous for his glazed terra cotta plaques, often done in blue and white, of Mary and the Christ child.

Antonio Rossellino (1427–1478) pursued the trend toward stark realism evident in some of Donatello's work. His bust of the humanist Matteo Palmieri presents the gross features of the unfortunate man just as he was, with a wide mouth, prominent nose, and head of unruly curly hair. Roman "unheroic" busts may well have served as models for Rossellino's work.

The two leading representatives of the scientific technique were Andrea Verrocchio (1435–1488) and Antonio Pollaiuolo (1432–1499). Verrocchio, a pupil of Donatello, was master of a workshop in Florence, made famous not only by his own work, but by the fact that Leonardo da Vinci was an apprentice there. He did many casts of live and dead subjects. Verrocchio painted the *Baptism of Christ* and produced jewelry, objects in silver plate, and dozens of statuettes in precious metals. But his personal renown rests upon his sculptures, especially his David and an equestrian statue in Venice. His bronze statue of David, which was to stand in the courtyard of the Medici Palace, is reminiscent of Donatello's David. It shows a thin lad, ribs visible, sword in one hand, the other resting on his hip in a gesture of triumph; the head of Goliath lies at his feet.

In 1479 the city of Venice commissioned Verrocchio to do an equestrian statue of the Venetian condottiere Bartolommeo Colleoni. It took Verrocchio until the year of his death to complete the model, which was then cast and unveiled in 1496. Colleoni stands in his stirrups astride his magnificent steed. His right shoulder is drawn back, but his cold, stern, commanding face is turned slightly to the left. He is alive, nervous, moving—in command. As a work of art, scientifically accurate and flawlessly executed, this equestrian statue surpasses even the ancient Roman monument of Emperor Marcus Aurelius on his mount.

Antonio Pollaiuolo's scientific interest led him to explore the problems of stress and strain in the human body. His treatment of muscular movement reveals his astonishingly close observation of human anatomy. His best-known work is his statuette of Hercules and Antaeus, representing that dramatic moment when Hercules lifted Antaeus into the air—for Antaeus received strength only from contact with the earth—and squeezed the life out of him as he writhed in mortal agony.

The achievements of the fifteenth century in painting and sculpture were praiseworthy in themselves, but beyond this they contributed to that accumulation of ideals and supporting skills that made possible the magnificent achievements of the high Renaissance during those golden opening decades of the sixteenth century.

Architecture

DURING THE FOURTEENTH CENTURY Italian architecture was somnolent, devoid of creativity and innovation. There was a great deal of building, *palazzi* for the wealthy families, public buildings, fortifications, chapels and churches. But no distinctive Italian style evolved. Byzantine and Gothic elements were intermingled with a traditional Romanesque base in an eclectic jumble that all but defies analysis. This situation changed radically during the course of the fifteenth century. The humanists envisioned an ideal city, peopled by men of high morals and civic virtue, men of learning and impeccable taste, living the good life. This model of an ideal citizenry was accompanied by an aesthetic vision of a material city worthy of such men. Leonardo Bruni idealized Florence and Matteo Palmieri described the need for spacious edifices for free citizens, suited to the needs of church and state. Alberti's great treatise on architecture had a powerful influence upon building design in the Renaissance. The prime mover in actually establishing a new style was a man of unusual genius, Filippo Brunelleschi, an architect suited to the world of humanism.

FILIPPO BRUNELLESCHI

The man who pioneered a new Roman or classic style in architecture was extremely versatile, skilled in many of the arts. Filippo Brunelleschi (1377–1446), the son of a notary, served as an apprentice in a goldsmith's workshop and joined the guild. Interested in geometry, he developed a theory of linear perspective in painting. Vasari relates how he left Florence in a huff after he lost out to Ghiberti in the Baptistery door competition in 1401. In Rome he measured the Roman Pantheon and other ancient structures to determine their mathematical proportions. He sketched arches, cornices, pillars, half-barrel vaults, and other devices of the ancient Roman architects. From classical architecture, he once observed, he learned to place empty space above empty space and solid mass above solid mass, arch above arch, pillar above pillar. In his own designs he followed the spirit rather than the letter of classical architecture. He used earlier Florentine models and examples from the territory of Venice.

Thus prepared, he returned to Florence in 1407, at the very time when the city council had decided to complete the construction of the dome on the great cathedral of Santa Maria del Fiore. Brunelleschi's plans called for a double-shelled cupola, similar to those found in earlier constructions in the East. It was not until 1419, after endless wrangling, that he was entrusted with the actual construction. He erected the vault without scaffolding, a fantastic engineering feat, pushing the dome upward to a height of approximately ninety feet. The dome—it is not actually a pure rounded classical structure, but is made of triangular sections pointing upward with a somewhat Gothic effect—is larger in some of its dimensions than that of the later St. Peter's in Rome. Unfortunately Brunelleschi did not live to see the completion of his masterpiece.

In 1435 Brunelleschi designed a palace for Luca Pitti, built across the Arno

BRUNELLESCHI. *Florence Cathedral.*

River from the Palazzo Vecchio. This huge structure, erected largely by slave and prison labor, became a model for other Tuscan *palazzi* during subsequent centuries. He designed the churches of San Lorenzo and Santo Spirito, but as in the case of the cathedral, he had to adapt classical Roman motifs to the medieval cruciform floor plan. The Pazzi Chapel was the first church structure that was Renaissance in style both inside and out, with rounded arches and all other classic effects. His Hospital of the Innocents is considered by some critics to be the most thoroughly individual, and hence the most successful, of his buildings.

MICHELOZZI

Michelozzo Michelozzi (1396–1472) deserves to be remembered forever for his splendid design of the Medici Palace in Florence. The son of a tailor, Michelozzi began his artistic career as a sculptor, working in bronze, silver, and marble. Cosimo de' Medici, impressed by his skill, moderation, and good taste, took Michelozzi with him to Venice during his exile, and upon his return to Florence commissioned the young sculptor to design a palace for him. In its graceful proportions and relatively modest design it is superior to Brunelleschi's massive Pitti Palace. Gothic influence is still in evidence, for the round arches are marked off by a smooth line rather than being keyed into the stones of the surrounding wall in a typically classical way. He built or rebuilt numerous other structures in Florence, repaired the Palazzo Vecchio, and reconstructed the Monastery of San Marco, where he himself now lies, honored by a grateful city.

BRAMANTE

Not all of the great architects of the Renaissance were Florentines. Bramante (1444–1514) was born in Urbino, apprenticed there as a painter, worked in Milan from 1476 to 1499, and around the year 1500 moved to Rome to enter the service of the popes. He painted murals in Rome, but continued an early interest in architecture by a close study of ancient Roman buildings and ruins, and served as artistic consultant in papal building projects. For Julius II he designed the two corridors joining the Belvedere and the papal palaces. But his most important assignment was his design for St. Peter's Cathedral, the capitol of Christendom. Although he died before he was able to complete the design, he did see the four central pillars rise with their connecting arches and vaults. He also finished the main chapel. But later other architects, preeminently Michelangelo, developed new and even more grandiose plans for St. Peter's.

The High Renaissance

THE CUMULATIVE EFFECT of the contributions of many individuals is less continuous and irreversible in the arts than in the sciences. Nevertheless, the pioneering work of the fifteenth-century artists, in creativity of conception as well as in the mastery of technique, did contribute directly to the supreme achievements of the geniuses of the high Renaissance.

By the end of the fifteenth century Italian artists had absorbed the technical skills of Flemish artists such as Jan van Eyck (*c.* 1380–1441), considered the founder of Flemish painting, his brother Hubert van Eyck, and Roger van der Weyden. Their mastery of minute detail, learned in part from medieval manuscript illuminations, their portraits, their interest in commonplace scenes such as domestic interiors, all impressed the Italian artists of the later *Quattrocento*.

But by the turn of the century the tide of influence was turning. Renaissance art drew northern artists to Italy, and Italian artists invaded the north. Among the northerners who came to Italy to look and to learn were Quentin Metsys (1466–1530), Lucas van Leyden (1494–1533), Bernaert van Orley (1493–1541), and the greatest of all, Albrecht Dürer (1471–1528). Dürer, of Nuremberg, was a master of woodcuts, copper etching, silverpoint, charcoal, watercolors, and oil painting. He spent two years in Venice (1505–1507), where he learned to know Giovanni Bellini and absorbed the Renaissance spirit of inquiry as well as Italian style. He was intrigued by the proportions of the human body, anatomy, and flora and fauna, and wrote treatises on *The Doctrine of Proportion* and *The Art of Measurement*. He was fascinated by the problems of linear perspective, and adopted an Italianate style during his early and most productive years.

But the rightful heirs of the rich artistic inheritance of Italy were the great Italian artists of the early sixteenth century. In Leonardo da Vinci, Raphael, Michelangelo, and Cellini, Renaissance art came into full flower. Ironically, this full bloom came during the decades of Italy's humiliation by foreign conquerors and its political disintegration.

LEONARDO DA VINCI

Vasari tells the story that while Leonardo was an apprentice of Verrocchio, he did an angel for one of Verrocchio's paintings that was so beautiful that the master, deeply impressed, resolved never to paint again. The story is demonstrably not true, for later work by Verrocchio is still extant. But the myth conveys the truth that Leonardo was a giant who towered high above his teachers.

Leonardo da Vinci (1452–1519) was the son of a Florentine lawyer named Piero and a woman of humble birth in Vinci, a fortified hill village outside Florence. His parents were married shortly after his birth, but not to each other. Piero, in fact, married four times, and had nine sons and two daughters by his last two wives. Piero raised Leonardo in his house in Florence and then apprenticed him to Verrocchio's studio, where he studied from 1470 to 1477. He became a friend of the painters Perugino and Botticelli, and at twenty he entered the painters' guild. Lorenzo the Magnificent became his patron from 1477 to 1482 or 1483, and Leonardo also received commissions from monasteries and other sources.

Leonardo had an enormous curiosity, and he made intensive studies of nature for his landscapes and of human anatomy for his paintings and sculptures of human figures. He wished to "learn the causes of things," and his early art reveals his love of nature. He painted calm, strange shapes, caves, rock formations, rare plants, faces, and was especially intrigued by the property and power of water. He excelled at *chiaroscuro,* the subtle treatment of light and shade. His early Adam and Eve in tempora reveals an exact knowledge of botany, such as Albrecht Dürer showed in his engravings three decades later. He used a bug as a model for a dragon he painted for a shield.

Unlike the moody Michelangelo, a solitary man who often withdrew into seclusion, Leonardo was relatively open and genial. He was a skilled horseman and loved good horses. Biographers have idealized him as a youth, describing him as a golden-haired lad who bought birds in the market to set them free. In Florence his friends included learned humanists and the Neoplatonic poets of the Medici circle.

At the age of thirty Leonardo left Florence for Milan to serve Ludovico il Moro, the Sforza tyrant. This first Milanese period (1483–1499) was an extremely productive one, although much of Leonardo's energies went into civil and military engineering projects. He became an apologist for Ludovico. When the mother of Gian Galeazzo, whose position Ludovico had usurped, attempted to assassinate Ludovico, Leonardo painted a political allegory in his behalf: a fierce stag, attacking Milan, is beaten off by the prudence and justice of Ludovico.

Ludovico commissioned a gigantic equestrian statue of Francesco Sforza to honor the double marriage in 1491 of Ludovico and Beatrice d'Este and of Alfonso d'Este and Anna Sforza. Leonardo did dozens of studies of horse heads and bodies (now in the Windsor Castle collection of drawings) by way of preparation. The statue was planned on a scale even grander than the equestrian statues of Donatello and Verrocchio, but it was never completed.

In Milan Leonardo painted some of his immortal masterpieces. Outstanding are *The Virgin of the Rocks* and *The Last Supper,* a fresco in the refectory of the convent of Santa Maria delle Grazie which illustrates the perspective and geometric arrangements (four groups of three disciples each) so characteristic of Renaissance art. With Pacioli, in fact, Leonardo later wrote a treatise entitled *On Divine Proportion.*

LEONARDO DA VINCI. *The Virgin of the Rocks*. National Gallery, London.

Then came for Leonardo a time of exile and wandering. He was in Milan for a while when the city was under French control, and it just may be that the Italians forced him to leave as a collaborator. At any rate, he left Milan in 1499, and in 1502 he was serving Cesare Borgia in the Romagna as chief engineer. He returned to Florence just before Cesare's fall. Over a four-year period (1503–1506) he perfected *La Gioconda,* a portrait of the twenty-four-year-old wife of an Italian gentleman, better known as the Mona Lisa. King Francis I paid 4,000 florins for the painting, and she has since smiled enigmatically upon millions of visitors to the Louvre in Paris. In Florence in 1503 the Soderinis commissioned two great battle scenes, one by Leonardo and one by Michelangelo. In Rome Leonardo served Leo X and did work for the Belvedere Palace in the Vatican. When at last he went to the court of Francis I in France, where he spent his last years, he took along three paintings: *John the Baptist; Anne, Mary, and the Christ Child;* and presumably the Mona Lisa. He also took along his notebooks and anatomical drawings, most of which he left to Francesco Melzi, his young assistant. He died in France and lies buried in a Gothic tomb in Amboise, a final irony.

RAPHAEL

When the "divine" Raphael journeyed from Urbino to Florence in 1504, he carried with him a letter from Giovanna Felicia Feltria, the sister of the duke of Urbino, introducing the young painter to Piero Soderini, *gonfaloniere* of Florence:

> Most Magnificent and Powerful Lord—
> He who presents this letter to you is Raphael, a painter of Urbino, endowed with great talent in art. He has decided to pass some time in Florence in order to improve himself in his studies. As the father, who was dear to me, was full of good qualities, so the son is a modest young man of distinguished manners; and thus I bear him an affection on every account, and wish that he should attain perfection.
> Giovanna, Duchess of Sora[4]

Raphael was a handsome young man, known for his charm and kindliness. Beloved in his own lifetime, he has remained the most universally popular artist, and is still acclaimed by many as the preeminent painter of all time. In the seventeen or eighteen working years he enjoyed before his early death, he produced a prodigious amount of work. He seemed to work calmly and with great ease, in contrast to such a tortured soul as Michelangelo.

Raphael Sanzio (1483–1520) was born in Urbino in Umbria, a lively cultural center. His father, a painter, died when Raphael was only eleven, but the boy had already learned from him much of the technical skill necessary for his calling. He studied then for five years in the studio of Perugino in Perugia. Perugino is said

---

[4] Regina Shoolman and Charles Slatkin, *The Story of Art* (New York, 1940), p. 101.

to have exclaimed upon seeing Raphael's drawings, "Let him be my pupil! He will soon become my master." From Perugino he learned the soft, gentle grace of Umbrian art and in his workshop he developed a sense of spatial relationships. Inevitably he was drawn to Florence to further his development. There from 1504 to 1508 he studied the works of Fra Bartolommeo, Leonardo, Michelangelo, and other masters. While he learned from their technique, he created his own mature ideal of beauty.

With the fall of the Medicis and the other ills that befell Florence, the city on the Arno began to lose its leadership in the arts. In 1508 Pope Julius II invited Raphael to Rome, where he remained until his death at the early age of thirty-seven.

Raphael's name will forever be associated with his beautiful madonnas. Raphael was desperately in love with the beautiful Margherita, his mistress, who served as the model for his madonnas and whom he celebrated also in his lyric poetry. In 1516 Raphael painted his *Madonna of the Chair,* in which Mary holds the round and fleshy Christ child affectionately on her lap while the little John the Baptist looks up at them in adoration. In 1517 he did his most famous painting, the Sistine Madonna, for the monastery of San Sisto in Piacenza. The Virgin Mary, a majestic maiden of great beauty, framed by green draperies and standing upon billowy white clouds, holds the infant Jesus. To the right St. Barbara and to the left St. Sixtus kneel in worship, while below two dreamy *putti* lean upon the bottom frame of the panel. The museums of the Western world are studded with Raphael madonnas (the Esterházy Madonna in Budapest is especially fine), but the Sistine Madonna remains his masterpiece.

Raphael's mastery of Renaissance artistic theory is powerfully demonstrated in his frescoes *The School of Athens* and the *Disputa,* which he did for the walls of the papal signature room in the Vatican. The two frescoes portray the classical and the medieval philosophers who contributed to Western thought. The perspective, geometric groupings, and total spatial arrangement make of *The School of Athens* a perfect exemplar of Renaissance artistic theory and technique.

In the year 1519 Cardinal Giuliano de' Medici commissioned a painting of the Transfiguration for the cathedral of Narbonne. The scene shows Christ on Mt. Tabor with three of his disciples, Peter, James, and John, while others of his followers wait below. At Christ's side are Moses and Elias. The painting catches the moment when a bright cloud overshadows them and a voice out of the cloud says: "This is my beloved son, in whom I am well pleased; hear ye him." It was Raphael's last painting. Shortly after completing it he was struck down by a fever that raged for ten days and finally caused his death. The grief-stricken Romans carried the painting behind Raphael's body to the Pantheon, where he lies buried in a simple tomb.

His early death cut off the career of one of the world's greatest masters. The esteem in which he was held by his fellow artists is attested to by Bramante's death-

bed request in 1514 that Raphael be appointed to succeed him as chief architect of St. Peter's. But Raphael's own premature death kept him from exercising any great influence upon the construction of the great cathedral.

MICHELANGELO

The Titan Michelangelo was a genius in nearly every medium of art. His creative triumphs marked the culmination of the Renaissance and a transition to the new age of mannerism and the baroque. In sculpture, painting, architecture, drawing, and lyric poetry, Michelangelo showed himself a giant in a race of tall men. His achievements were the products not of a tranquil life of ease, but of a tortured spirit and a stormy career that would have broken the will of a lesser man.

Michelangelo Buonarroti (1475–1564) was the son of a petty nobleman who could barely eke out a living on the family estate, and had an aristocrat's disdain for labor. Michelangelo's nineteen-year-old mother left her sickly infant to be nursed by the wife of a stonecutter or marble worker of Settignano. Michelangelo was fond of saying that he had sucked in a passion for art with this mother's milk. The boy showed great talent for drawing and was apprenticed to study for three years in the studio of Domenico Ghirlandaio. Upon observing Michelangelo's talent, the master commented, "This youth understands more than I do myself." After only a single year had passed, during which he devoted much time to learning the technique of fresco painting, Michelangelo was sent with another beginner to the Medicis in response to Lorenzo's request for two young sculptors.

There in the circle of the Medicis Michelangelo encountered that grandeur of spirit and high style in thought which was so important for his intellectual and artistic development. A student of Donatello served as director of the school for sculpture that Lorenzo maintained in the Medici gardens. There Michelangelo heard discourses on Neoplatonic philosophy that influenced his aesthetic theory in art and poetry. And he carried away from Lorenzo's academy yet another mark that stayed with him through life: in response to a critical remark, which came easily for Michelangelo, one of his fellow students smashed his nose so badly that it was disfigured for life. "You will be remembered," Michelangelo prophesied, "only as the man who broke my nose." And so with a single blow the sculptor Torrigiano Torrigiani made his mark on history.

Michelangelo was always given to melancholy, dark brooding, and apprehensive presentiments. He sent almost all the money he received for his commissions to his father and three ungrateful brothers, whom he set up in business. His father even warned him in a letter against damaging his health and spirit by living in want. He poured all of his strength and energy into his artistic creations. But his wretched diet and Spartan life may have contributed to his psychological difficulties. Savonarola's dark prophecies moved him to despondency and near despair.

In June 1496 Michelangelo took the well-traveled road to Rome. The occasion for his trip was trivial enough, but the move to Rome was fateful in its consequences. An agent had paid Michelangelo thirty ducats for a sleeping Cupid, and suggested that they bury it in the earth to give it the appearance of age. Michelangelo thought the idea amusing; it never occurred to him that the agent was contemplating fraud. When he learned that the agent had taken the statue to Cardinal Raffaele Riario San Giorgio, a collector of antiques, and sold it as an antique for two hundred ducats, Michelangelo traveled to Rome to adjust the matter. Once there, he stayed for five years, winning ever greater commissions and fame. He received 450 ducats from Cardinal St. Denis, the French ambassador to the Vatican, for a beautiful Pietà.

But his native city offered a new challenge. In 1501 a prominent citizen of Florence, Piero Soderini, commissioned a statue of David to be done from a block of Carrara marble eighteen feet high. Some forty years earlier another sculptor had begun work on the stone, but had given up the task, and the block had stood there ever since. Michelangelo went into seclusion with the stone and for two years devoted most of his conscious moments to the creation of his David. His Neo-platonic notion was that the beautiful form was already there, imprisoned in the marble, waiting to be liberated by the artist as he chipped away the waste material around it. Then in 1504 came the unveiling of the Giant, as the people called it. Michelangelo portrayed the young hero of Israel as a shepherd boy, frowning earnestly, as well he might, watchful, eying his adversary, sling in hand, but with no sign of fear. The David stood thereafter outside the Palazzo Vecchio as a symbol of the *signoria* and the people of Florence.

This Florentine period lasted only five years. In 1506 Michelangelo returned to Rome, where he spent the three most productive decades of his life in the service of four popes. The warring Julius II lived a spectacular life and wished to lie buried in an equally dramatic tomb. He chose Michelangelo to do a monstrous mausoleum, three levels high, to be adorned with myriad statuettes of saints and apostles, cherubs and sybils. "Let it cost any amount and you shall have it," Julius II assured him. For eight months Michelangelo supervised the selection and cutting of the best marble in the Carrara quarry. It was transported to the square behind the Vatican, and there Michelangelo began his work on the tomb. Julius II occasionally came by to see how he was getting on. Then quite suddenly the pope ordered him to suspend his work on the tomb and to begin instead to paint frescoes on the ceiling of the Sistine Chapel. Michelangelo attributed this change of plan to his jealous rival Bramante, who saw a chance to disrupt the sculpturing project and force Michelangelo into another medium in which his brilliance was not yet tested. But his genius triumphed here also, and his Sistine Chapel frescoes came to be numbered among the most famous paintings in the world.

For years Michelangelo labored on his back on a high scaffold, assisted only by paint mixers and plaster grinders. He covered over ten thousand square feet of the depressed barrel-vault ceiling with nine huge panels. The first panel depicts the dividing of light and darkness at the time of creation; the second portrays the creation of the heavenly bodies; the third, the creation of the waters; the fourth, the moment when God's hand reaches out to Adam, his new creature; the fifth, the creation of woman; the sixth, man's fall into sin and the expulsion from Eden; the seventh, the sacrifice of Noah; the eighth, the deluge; and the ninth, the drunkenness of Noah. The puzzling feature of this sequence is the fact that the seventh, eighth, and ninth panels do not stand in the chronological sequence of the biblical account. One plausible theory offered by art historians is that the whole ceiling is intended to represent the Neoplatonic theory of the ascent of man from the spiritual abyss of drunkenness and shameful nakedness through the purgation of the deluge upward to the final moment of reunion with God, depicted in the scene showing Adam's hand reaching out to touch the finger of God. Michelangelo read Dante religiously and his Neoplatonism had a medieval mystical cast. No doubt this deep piety, combined with his egoism and will to triumph, kept him at his arduous task, which left him crippled and hunched the remainder of his life.

The restless, assertive warrior pope could not even let this great work proceed uninterrupted. When Julius II had triumphed over his enemies, cleared the Romagna of foes, and entered Bologna victorious, he summoned Michelangelo to Bologna to do a colossal bronze figure of the pope, seated, robed, and mitered, with the keys of the kingdom in one hand and the other held out in a gesture of benediction. It was placed over the main door of the Church of St. Petronius, but three years later the Bolognese revolted against the papal rule and destroyed the image of their conqueror.

During this period of his life Michelangelo was at his most dynamic, restless, forceful, and tempestuous. His art reflected his *furia* and *terribilità*. With the completion of the Sistine ceiling, he returned to work on Julius' tomb. At this time too he did his immortal Moses, the stern lawgiver, and the two *Captive Slaves*. Julius died just as the chapel was completed, but the grandiose tomb had to be abandoned. Michelangelo labored on at it in later years, but on a much reduced scale.

The two Medici popes, Leo X and Clement VII, recognized Michelangelo's special genius and put him to work in their honor. Leo X commissioned him to do a statue to his own glory for the Church of San Lorenzo in Florence, but when four years later the pope died, the project was abandoned. Clement VII had Michelangelo design the Laurentian Library next to San Lorenzo. The structure illustrates how the artist's Neoplatonic philosophy could influence even architectural design. The great sweeping flight of stairs has a swirl-back effect on each side, as though the staircase symbolized a series of stages in the upward ascent of man.

Michelangelo was not enamored of his Medici masters, and during the restoration of the republic he was put in charge of the city's fortifications. But with the

MICHELANGELO. *The Last Judgment*. Sistine Chapel, Rome.

return of the Medicis, Michelangelo reluctantly entered the service of the tyrannous family once again. In this period of disillusionment and disappointment he worked on the tombs in the Medici Chapel. There emerged from the marble the four giant mysterious figures *Day, Night, Dawn,* and *Twilight,* which still today hold the reflective viewer spellbound under their magnetic power.

Pope Paul III, who succeeded Clement VII in 1534, had other plans for Michelangelo. He assigned him the task of painting on the front wall of the Sistine Chapel *The Last Judgment,* one of the best-known paintings in the world. Michelangelo labored for years, reading his beloved Dante for recreation. When the giant fresco was at last opened to public view, it overwhelmed the spectators, and it still keeps tourists gaping in astonishment today. With over three hundred figures, each in its own right a work of art, the grand design presents a panoramic view of the day of wrath, when the Son of God will sit in judgment upon the world.

As an architect Michelangelo undertook several challenging projects during the pontificate of Paul III. He built for his family the Farnese Palace in Rome and designed a cluster of buildings to adorn the Capitoline Hill, but his proudest achievement was his success as the chief architect of St. Peter's. He reworked all the designs of his distinguished predecessors and supervised the construction of the supports and the lower sections of the giant dome, which stands today as the loftiest monument to the universal genius of Michelangelo.

Now a man of sixty, Michelangelo turned to less strenuous and physically demanding labors. He did drawings and composed lyrics and metaphysical love poems. He cultivated an intimate friendship with a handsome young Roman aristocrat, Tommaso dei Cavalieri, to whom he addressed passionate sonnets. For twelve years he was also devoted to a young widow, Vittoria Colonna, a woman of great piety and intellectual power. The poetry he poured out in her honor reflected his Christian faith, his Neoplatonic mystical bent, and the tender affection of his heart. It was as though his personal emotions, so long repressed and sublimated in the interest of his art, now came into full flower in the autumn of his life. Vittoria's death was a blow that struck him at a time when he was least able to bear it. Heartbroken and physically spent, he lived out his years to an infirm old age.

BENVENUTO CELLINI

Michelangelo once called his fellow artist Benvenuto Cellini (1500–1571) "the greatest goldsmith of whom the world has ever heard." Cellini was in complete agreement with this assessment, for he was a supreme egotist, self-serving and assertive. Afflicted with a violent temper, vengeful and reckless, he made countless enemies, was involved in brawls and murders, and was often either in prison or in full flight from the law. A passionate man, he fathered eight children, only one of them legitimate, and recounted coolly how he abandoned a young French girl when he returned to Italy. He and a conjuror, he related, summoned up a legion of demons in the Colosseum in Rome in order to take revenge when one of his mistresses was spirited away by her mother. But he was such a brilliant artist and consummate craftsman that people made many allowances for his extravagant behavior. "Men like Benvenuto," Pope Paul III commented, "unique in their profession, stand above the law."

Cellini was born in Florence, the son of a musician and instrument maker, and was apprenticed to a goldsmith. From an early age he traveled about, often in flight from the police, to Siena, Bologna, Pisa, and Rome. He happened to be in Rome when the imperial troops sacked the city in 1527. In his autobiography he recalls his own heroic role in the defense of the city. He claims that he personally shot the imperial commander, Constable de Bourbon, and later killed Philibert, prince of Orange. He returned to Florence for a productive period and then for a time served at the court of the duke of Mantua. He went back to Florence and then to Rome, where in 1529 he avenged his brother's death by killing his murderer. He himself had to flee the city after wounding a constable. He was accused, probably falsely, of stealing jewels from the papal tiara. He was imprisoned, escaped, was recaptured, tortured, and threatened with hanging. Finally he put a safe distance between himself and Rome, entering the service of Francis I of France in Fontainebleau and Paris. Back in Florence he became involved in more legal difficulties when he was charged by an enemy with gross immorality. At the same time it must be noted that he supported his widowed sister and her six children. When he died, the citizens of Florence gave him a magnificent funeral and buried him with honor in the Church of the Annunziata.

Although many of his masterpieces have disappeared, perhaps because of the precious metals and jewels he used, those that remain testify to his genius. Some of his works are extravagantly ornate, but a few of them are very satisfyingly balanced. The masterpiece that the world knows best is the gold and enamel saltcellar he made for the French king. In a setting of waves, dolphins, and other creatures of the sea, a nude Neptune and a sea nymph recline. The cups on either side, intended to hold salt and pepper, are ornate and exquisitely detailed. The work is a bit grand and flamboyant for so prosaic an object as a saltcellar, even a saltcellar for a king. Art critics have suggested that the figures were modeled after Michelangelo's stone statues for the Medici tomb. But Michelangelo's figures were monumental in conception and cannot be reduced to small scale without loss of meaning. Cellini was not so great as he imagined. But Francis I was delighted, and that was of crucial importance for Cellini. When he had shown him the wax model, the king cried out, "This is a hundred times more divine a thing than I had ever dreamed of!" And when at last he saw the saltcellar itself, Cellini recounted, "He uttered a loud cry of astonishment and could not satiate his eyes with gazing at it."

The Venetian School

IN THE FINE ARTS Venice, the proud queen of the Adriatic, not only arrived upon the scene relatively late, but then developed a unique style. A materialistic and sensuous society, Venice reached a high level of prosperity in the mid-fifteenth century. Its citizens loved fine dress, sumptuous meals, elaborate state ceremonies, pageantry, and processions. Each year the symbolic marriage of Venice to the Adriatic was reenacted. The doge arranged for a weekly public religious procession to one of the city's great churches. For centuries every merchant returning from the Near East was required to bring with him an object of art with which to adorn St. Mark's Cathedral, in the heart of the city, until it was a veritable jewel box glittering with treasures from the Levant. So intent were the Venetians on their commerce and then so preoccupied with the naval defense of their eastern empire, as the Ottoman Turks increased their pressure after the fall of Constantinople, that they were slow to appreciate the new Renaissance culture in either literature or art.

THE BELLINIS

Gentile da Fabriano, an Umbrian painter, came to Venice in 1408. He so impressed a Venetian artist, Jacopo Bellini, that Jacopo accompanied him to Florence as his assistant. Jacopo broke with the conservative Siena tradition, which earlier Venetian artists had followed quite literally, and developed a new naturalism. The remarkable Bellini family established Venetian painting as an independent force.

Two innovations in Venetian art proved to be important for the development of a distinct school. The first was Venetian artists' rather early adoption, around 1475, of oils as binders for their pigments, rather than the egg whites and yolks that had been used earlier, and were still being used by artists elsewhere. The second was painting on canvas instead of on plaster-covered walls, since the dampness in Venice made plaster peel, or on wooden panels, since wood warps and cracks so readily in a humid climate. Canvas was well suited to the portable paintings done to adorn the *palazzi,* churches, and public buildings of the republic. The Bellinis made good use of both of these new techniques.

Gentile Bellini (*c.* 1429–1507), Jacopo's elder son, loved to depict the pomp of Venetian public life and religious tradition. Among his better known works are *The Procession of Corpus Domini; Miracles of the True Cross;* and *The Preaching of St. Mark.*

His brother Giovanni (*c.* 1430–1516), however, not only produced paintings of greater fame, but exercised a more powerful influence upon such leading Venetian artists as Giorgione and Titian. At the outset Giovanni was himself very much influenced by the severe linear style and austere classicism of Mantegna, who had married the sister of Gentile and Giovanni and enjoyed considerable authority

as an accomplished master. But soon Giovanni's independent genius asserted itself. His love of color, his taste for glowing tones in the glitter of jewels and rich adornment brought vibrancy to his canvases. Many of his themes are religious, but they are handled in a frankly sensuous and earthy way. Among his most famous masterpieces are the *Madonna and Saints*, the *Transfiguration*, the *Resurrection*, and the mysterious mythological *Feast of the Gods*.

Vittore Carpaccio (*c.* 1523?) learned from the Bellinis to employ luminous coloring and to portray even angelic beings as undeniably human. A perfect example is his *Angel with Lute*, which also reveals his careful attention to detail.

GIORGIONE

The short-lived Giorgio Barbarelli (1477–1510), known as Giorgione, exemplified the most distinctively Venetian traits in Renaissance painting. In his *Sleeping Venus*, *The Tempest*, and *Fête Champêtre* he placed full-bodied human figures in gorgeous landscapes. He strove for an Arcadian pastoral effect. He so blurred distant objects, while presenting natural objects in the foreground in exquisite detail, that his compositions had a unity and coherent impact unrivaled by those of other artists of the period.

TITIAN

The long-lived Tiziano Vecelli (*c.* 1477–1576), better known as Titian, is known for his voluptuous Venuses and beautiful landscapes. He was a master of perspective, coloration, shading, and composition. He was less concerned with religious, moral, patriotic, or historical messages than in the intrinsic beauty of a painting. His *Danaë* is truly representative of this aspect of his work. In 1516 he succeeded Giovanni Bellini as official state painter. In that role he received assignments to do paintings for the city's churches, such as *The Assumption of the Virgin* in the Franciscan church and the massive *Martyrdom of St. Lawrence*. He was also called upon to paint official portraits, the most celebrated of which is no doubt his Charles V, victorious astride his steed on the field at Mühlberg. For the Vatican he did the famous paintings of Pope Paul III, Cardinal Alessandro, and Duke Ottavio Farnese, thus documenting the history of the period as well as creating things of beauty.

TINTORETTO AND VERONESE

Tintoretto (1518–1594), the "little dyer," and Veronese (1528–1588) carried on the special Venetian characteristics in painting—rich colors, fleshy human bodies, gorgeous landscapes, and worldly emphases—deep into the sixteenth century.

During those decades the transition to mannerism and the baroque was already under way.

Music

IN A STRIKING PASSAGE in his *Book on the Art of Counterpoint* (1477) the Flemish musical theorist Johannes Tinctoris, who spent the greater part of his life at the court of Naples as a singer, composer, teacher, and writer, remarked: "Although it seems beyond belief, there does not exist a single piece of music, not composed within the last forty years, that is regarded by the learned as worth hearing."[5] Tinctoris, then, dated the beginnings of modern music about the year 1435. "The fountain and origin of this new art," Tinctoris explains, "lies with the English, whose leading master was Dunstable. His French contemporaries were Dufay and Binchois, who were immediately succeeded by the moderns." He held that the English had subsequently stagnated, using the same style in composition, whereas the Franco-Netherlandish composers "freshly create new works day by day."

Composers of the Netherlands dominated the scene during the third decade of the fifteenth century and for a hundred years thereafter. The rich Flemish commercial cities such as Antwerp and Cambrai and the Burgundian court could afford the luxury of professional musicians. From 1410 on the cathedral chapter in Antwerp paid skilled singers for their services with incomes from endowed prebends, even though they were not clerics. Most of the composers and performers received their training in choir schools. Famous teachers taught and inspired the rapidly growing number of composers, singers, and instrumentalists.

Although in the Middle Ages a great many musical theorists were mathematicians, and music was often controlled by "Pythagorean" mathematical considerations, most Renaissance theorists were themselves practical musicians, concerned about the pleasing quality of sound. Tinctoris himself referred repeatedly to the aural impact of the music he was discussing: such a procedure "offends the sophisticated ear"; in this procedure "the ear of the listener finds a modicum of sweetness"; "in the judgment of my ears . . . " The effect on the listener is the important criterion for the success of the composition.[6]

Choirs of skilled professional singers were a necessary precondition for the evolution of the new complicated polyphonic music with its counterpoint and harmony. In the classical medieval technique, one voice part was completed before another was added to a composition, which meant that the harmonic result turned out to be haphazard (not to say accidental). In the new Renaissance technique,

[5] Johannes Tinctoris, "Liber de arte contrapuncti," trans. Olive Strunk, in *Source Readings in Music History,* ed. William Oliver Strunk (New York, 1950), p. 199.

[6] Edward E. Lowinsky, "Music of the Renaissance as Viewed by Renaissance Musicians," in *The Renaissance Image of Man and the World,* ed. Bernard O'Kelley (Columbus, O., 1966), p. 136.

the composer planned the euphony of the whole piece in advance. For the first time dissonance was deliberately introduced to achieve a special effect. Modern counterpoint is the art of combining two, three, four, five, or more voices in such a way that each individual voice achieves optimum melodic and rhythmic freedom in a carefully regulated texture of harmonic sound. "Modern harmony is the art of concord based on the triad."[7] These conceptions of musical composition and choral performance have been dominant to the present time, just as Renaissance art and architecture established the basic norms down to the twentieth century.

In comparison with the Netherlands, Italy contributed little to musical innovation and enrichment. During the *Quattrocento* there were no Italian composers who compared with the Flemish masters. Musical performance was thought to be essential for a well-rounded man. Alberti was an excellent organist, Cellini performed on the flute for the papal court, and Pietro Bono, a brilliant lutist, was a favorite in several Renaissance courts. Musical performances became important features of gracious living at the refined courts of Mantua, Ferrara, Urbino, and other centers. Singers not only gave recitals to the accompaniment of the lute or some other instrument, but entertained with songs between the scenes or acts of the humanist plays performed at court.

Sunny Italy was given to song: popular love songs, moving religious songs, secular carnival songs, courtly songs. The *frattola,* the characteristic form of Italian Renaissance music, was a poem set to music. These *frottole* were simple songs, compared with the complex polyphony of Flemish compositions. The upper voice carried the melody and the other voices supported it with block chords in four-part harmony. The choral style, familiar from religious music, was carried over into secular songs toward the end of the fifteenth century.

The fifteenth and especially the sixteenth centuries witnessed a musical revolution. Several generations of extremely productive composers brought to society a new world of beauty. The composers seemed to be most attracted to keyboard music, in part because of the demand for organ music in the churches and in part because the range of the keyboard was enlarged at that time to allow fuller scope for music. The printing press had a tremendous impact upon music, for it made possible greater precision in the reproduction of scores and the distribution of thousands of copies.

The Renaissance in the Fine Arts

THE FINE ARTS are most certainly not peripheral to man's existence or merely an ornament to his "real life." They come close to being at the very heart of his hu-

---

[7] *Ibid.,* p. 142.

manity, at the vital center where his religious faith, his appreciation of the world, and his affection for his fellows define him as a man. In our own day Albert Camus expressed something of this feeling when he wrote: "I know with certainty that a man's work is nothing but the long journey to recover, through the detours of art, the two or three simple and great images which first gained access of his heart." The magnificent effort of the Renaissance men of art and letters to define and express their essential humanity was one of the most superb undertakings the world has ever witnessed.

The romanticist Victor Hugo declared the Renaissance "the setting sun all Europe mistook for dawn." He believed that the Renaissance had succeeded so well in establishing classical norms for the arts that the subsequent centuries merely reiterated what they saw there until all became moribund. In architecture there was merely a restatement, by classic column, entablature, and pediment, of the themes of a foreign culture that had died long ago. The truth of the matter, however, is quite different from what Victor Hugo imagined or such modern critics as Frank Lloyd Wright have been willing to acknowledge. For the fine arts during the Renaissance were not merely restatements of what the artists and theorists found in classical models. Their finest achievements expressed creatively the ideal, the highest aspirations, and the aesthetic feelings of their own age.

Their times are not ours, and we must not be guilty of merely imitating even the greatest triumphs of their intellect and skill. Still, we are not so far removed from the Renaissance that we cannot thrill to the beauty its artists created, or contemplate without a twinge of sorrow the inroads of time and trouble on the masterpieces of that great age.

Bibliography

Art, general:

Artz, Frederick B. *From Renaissance to Romanticism: Trends in Style in Art, Literature, and Music.* Chicago, 1962.

Gombrich, E. H. *The Story of Art.* London, 1956.

Hauser, A. *The Social History of Art,* 4 vols. New York, 1960.

Janson, H. W. *History of Art.* Englewood Cliffs, N.J., 1962.

Lassaigne, J., and Argan, G. C. *The Fifteenth Century, from van Eyck to Botticelli.* New York, 1955.

Mâle, Émile. *Religious Art: From the 12th to the 18th Century.* New York, 1958.

Panofsky, Erwin. *Studies in Iconology.* New York, 1939.

———. *Renaissance and Renaissances in Western Art,* 2 vols. Stockholm, 1960.

Sewall, John Ives. *A History of Western Art,* rev. ed. New York, 1961.

Seznec, J. *The Survival of the Pagan Gods.* New York, 1961.

SINGLETON, CHARLES E., ed. *Art, Science, and History in the Renaissance.* Baltimore, 1967.

SYPHER, WYLIE. *Four Stages of Renaissance Style.* Garden City, N.Y., 1955.

VENTURI, L. *The Sixteenth Century, from Leonardo to El Greco.* New York, 1956.

WÖLFFLIN, HEINRICH. *Principles of Art History.* London, 1932.

Art in Italy:

ANTAL, FREDERICK. *Florentine Painting and Its Social Background.* London, 1948.

BERENSON, BERNHARD. *The Italian Painters of the Renaissance.* New York, 1952.

BLUNT, ANTHONY. *Artistic Theory in Italy, 1450–1600.* Oxford, 1940.

CHASTEL, ANDRÉ. *The Age of Humanism: Europe, 1480–1530.* New York, 1964.

———. *The Flowering of the Italian Renaissance.* New York, 1965.

———. *Styles and Studies: Italy, 1460–1500.* New York, 1966.

CLARK, KENNETH. *Leonardo da Vinci: An Account of His Development as an Artist.* Cambridge, 1939.

———. *Piero della Francesca.* London, 1950.

CLEMENTS, ROBERT J. *Michelangelo's Theory of Art.* New York, 1962.

DVOŘÁK, MAX. *Geschichte der italienischen Kunst im Zeitalter der Renaissance,* 2 vols. Munich, 1927–1929.

FORSTER, KURT. *Pontormo: Monographie mit kritischem Katalog.* Munich, 1966.

GOULD, CECIL. *An Introduction to Italian Renaissance Painting.* London, 1957.

HATHAWAY, B. *The Age of Criticism: The Late Renaissance in Italy.* Ithaca, N.Y., 1962.

HAUSER, ARNOLD. *The Social History of Art,* 2 vols. New York, 1952.

MACCURDY, EDWARD. *The Mind of Leonardo da Vinci.* New York, 1928.

MEISS, MILLARD. *Painting in Florence and Siena After the Black Death.* Princeton, 1951.

POPE-HENNESSEY, J. *Italian Renaissance Sculpture.* New York, 1958.

SALINGER, MARGARETA. *Michelangelo: The Last Judgment.* New York, 1963.

THODE, HENRY. *Franz von Assisi und die Anfänge der Kunst der Renaissance in Italien,* 2nd ed. Berlin, 1904.

TIETZE, HANS. *Tintoretto.* London, 1948.

TOLNAY, CHARLES DE. *Michelangelo,* 5 vols. Princeton, 1943–1960.

VASARI, GIORGIO. *Lives of the Most Eminent Painters, Sculptors, and Architects,* 6 vols. London, 1878–1885.

WIND, EDGAR. *Bellini's Feast of the Gods: A Study in Venetian Humanism.* Cambridge, Mass., 1948.

———. *Pagan Mysteries in the Renaissance.* London, 1958.

WÖLFFLIN, HEINRICH. *Classic Art: An Introduction to the Italian Renaissance,* rev. ed. New York, 1952.

Art in northern Europe:

BENESCH, OTTO. *The Art of the Renaissance in Northern Europe: Its Relation to the Contemporary Spiritual and Intellectual Movements.* Cambridge, Mass., 1945.

BOYD, CATHERINE E. *The French Renaissance.* Boston, 1940.

BURKHARD, ARTHUR. *Matthias Grünewald: Personality and Accomplishment.* Cambridge, Mass., 1936.

CONWAY, WILLIAM. *The Woodcutters of the Netherlands in the Fifteenth Century.* Hildesheim, 1961.

Dehio, Georg. *Geschichte der deutschen Kunst,* 4 vols. Berlin, 1923–1934.

Dimier, Louis. *French Painting in the 16th Century.* New York, 1911.

Fraenger, Wilhelm. *The Millennium of Hieronymus Bosch.* Chicago, 1951.

Friedländer, M. J. *Early Netherlandish Painting, from van Eyck to Bruegel.* London, 1956.

Ganz, Paul. *Hans Holbein the Younger.* London, 1950.

Mâle, Émile. *The Gothic Image.* New York, 1958.

Panofsky, Erwin. *Albrecht Dürer,* 2 vols., 3rd ed. Princeton, 1948.

——. *Early Netherlandish Painting: Its Origins and Character,* 2 vols. Cambridge, Mass., 1953.

Pevsner, Nikolaus, and Meier, Michael. *Grünewald.* New York, 1958.

Waetzoldt, Wilhelm. *Dürer and His Times.* London, 1950.

Architecture:

Ackerman, James. *The Architecture of Michelangelo,* 2 vols. London, 1961.

Anderson, William J. *The Architecture of the Renaissance in Italy,* rev. ed. London, 1927.

Blunt, Sir Anthony. *Art and Architecture in France, 1500–1700.* Baltimore, 1953.

Giedion, Siegfried. *Space, Time, and Architecture,* 3rd ed. Cambridge, Mass., 1954.

Murray, Peter. *The Architecture of the Italian Renaissance.* New York, 1963.

Pevsner, Nikolaus. *An Outline of European Architecture.* New York, 1948.

Ricci, Corrado. *Architecture and Decorative Sculpture of the High and Late Renaissance in Italy.* New York, 1923.

Scott, Geoffrey. *The Architecture of Humanism,* 2nd rev. ed. London, 1947.

Wittkower, Rudolf. *Architectural Principles in the Age of Humanism.* New York, 1965.

Music:

Apel, Willi. *The Notation of Polyphonic Music, 900–1600,* 4th rev. ed. Cambridge, Mass., 1949.

Besseler, Heinrich. *Die Musik des Mittelalters und der Renaissance.* Potsdam, 1931.

Bukofzer, Manfred. *Studies in Medieval and Renaissance Music.* New York, 1950.

Einstein, Alfred. *The Italian Madrigal,* 3 vols. Princeton, 1949.

Geiringer, Karl. *Musical Instruments: Their History in Western Culture.* New York, 1946.

Haar, James. *Chanson and Madrigal, 1480–1530.* Cambridge, Mass., 1964.

Harman, Alec. *Medieval and Early Renaissance Music.* Fair Lawn, N.J., 1958.

Hughes, A., and Abraham, G., eds. *Ars Nova and the Renaissance,* vol. 3 of *New Oxford History of Music,* ed. J. A. Westrip et al. New York, 1960.

Lang, Paul H. *Music in Western Civilization.* New York, 1941.

Leichtentritt, Hugo. *Music, History, and Ideas.* Cambridge, Mass., 1938.

Lowinsky, Edward E. *Tonality and Atonality in Sixteenth-Century Music.* Berkeley, 1961.

Reese, Gustave. *Music in the Renaissance.* New York, 1955.

CHAPTER 9

The Dwarfing
of Italy

Living through Italy's "time of troubles," the Renaissance historian
Francesco Guicciardini confided in his *Ricordi:*

> Three things I would willingly see before I die. And yet, though I were to live to a
> great age, I fear I shall see none of them. I desire to see a well-ordered republic
> established in Florence; Italy free from all her barbarian invaders; and the world
> delivered from the tyranny of these rascally priests [Series I, no. 14].

Writing the history of his own times, Guicciardini had the depressing task of recording the collapse of the Florentine republic, the intervention of the great powers
in Italian affairs, and the disruptive role of a secularized papacy and shocking corruption in the church. The Italian microcosm, which had enjoyed some forty years
of relative peace (1454–1494) and had developed a false sense of its own security,
was suddenly engulfed by the forces of the European macrocosm, the great powers
beyond the mountains and across the sea. The experience of foreign invasion gave
the Italians a traumatic shock from which they did not fully recover until their own
risorgimento in the nineteenth century.

Charles VIII Invades Italy

THE PEACE OF ITALY during the second half of the fifteenth century depended
upon the delicate balance of power among the five major city-states. This precarious

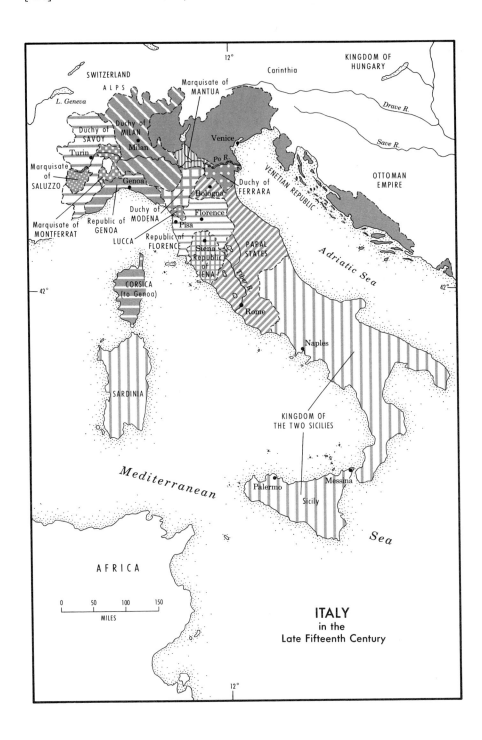

KINGDOM OF
HUNGARY

SWITZERLAND
ALPS

L. Geneva

Carinthia

Drave R.

Marquisate of
MANTUA

Duchy of
MILAN

Duchy of
SAVOY

Milan

Venice

Save R.

Turin

Po R.

Marquisate
of
SALUZZO

Genoa

Bologna

Duchy of
FERRARA

OTTOMAN
EMPIRE

Duchy of
MODENA

Florence

Pisa

Marquisate of
MONTFERRAT

Republic of
GENOA

Republic of
FLORENCE

LUCCA

Siena

Republic
of
SIENA

PAPAL
STATES

Adriatic Sea

CORSICA
(to Genoa)

Tiber R.

Rome

42°

42°

SARDINIA

Naples

KINGDOM OF
THE TWO SICILIES

Mediterranean

Palermo

Messina

Sicily

AFRICA

Sea

0	50	100	150

MILES

ITALY
in the
Late Fifteenth Century

12°

equilibrium was jeopardized during the final decade of the century by the increasing rivalry and hostility of Naples and Milan. King Ferrante of Naples, a wise and crafty old man, recognized the hazards of an open break, but his son Alfonso pressed for action against Milan. Alfonso's daughter was married to Gian Galeazzo Sforza of Milan, who was suppressed by the regent, Ludovico il Moro. When Ferrante died, on January 25, 1494, Alfonso threw caution to the winds. He lined up Pope Alexander VI and Piero de' Medici of Florence against Ludovico il Moro and prepared to deliver the coup. At this juncture Ludovico called on the French king for aid.

Young King Charles VIII of France was eager for high adventure and fascinated by the grand designs of state. From the last Palaeologue emperor he had received authorization to save the East from the Turks and to free Constantinople. He saw himself as a great crusader and considered Naples a suitable port from which to set sail for the reconquest of Jerusalem. Propaganda tracts were scattered about, depicting him as the liberator of the Holy Land. This was heady stuff for a young man of twenty-four. It blurred his vision so that he did not see how heavy a price he would have to pay for his ambition. To secure his rear and his lines of communication, he had to depart from the wise policy of Louis XI, who had worked to build up a solid territorial state and was more interested in the possession of Artois, Comté, and Roussillon than in claims to far-off lands. Charles was prepared to make concessions to his neighbors in order to free himself for adventure. He pacified Emperor Maximilian in the Treaty of Senlis (May 23, 1493), and was ready to move when Ludovico appealed to him for aid against Alfonso of Naples.

Charles built up an army at Lyon and gathered a large fleet to support the invasion. It was one of the largest French armies ever fielded up to that time. More than half the force was made up of French cavalry, knights who were professional fighting men. The infantry was largely made up of Swiss mercenaries, who had developed a formidable new tactic. They grouped into tight phalanxes with long pikes and charged an opposing line with the force of a battering ram. The French army was well equipped with heavy artillery as well. Despite the efforts of the Italian military engineers to strengthen the stone walls and to build up the tops of the parapets so that they slanted more obliquely and thus would deflect cannonballs more effectively, the citadels were increasingly vulnerable to attack by big guns. The Italians were thoroughly cowed, and Charles's march on Naples turned out to be a triumphal procession. Charles, described by a contemporary as "small, with a large head, visibly credulous and without malice," rode through Italy like a conquering hero.

Once the scalpel had cut in, all the rot in the Italian body politic lay exposed. On October 15, 1494, Ludovico il Moro arrived in Pavia to greet his deliverer and cheer him on his way. On October 21 Gian Galeazzo died suddenly—there were whisperings of poison—leaving his uncle Ludovico as uncontested master of Milan.

Venice found it prudent to remain neutral for the time being. Giovanni Bentivoglio of Bologna had warned Ludovico's ambassador against bringing the French into Italy. Now that the Pandora's box had been opened, he vacillated so long that he missed the chance to make any effected resistance against the French. Charles moved south into Tuscany.

Florence was caught in an impossible predicament. It had a long tradition of friendship with France, based in part on commercial ties. These suffered, to be sure, when Charles ruined the Medici agents in Lyon, and Lorenzo de' Medici had based his foreign policy upon an alliance with Naples. Now Piero de' Medici, dull-witted and a wastrel, had to make a critical decision, and he blundered. Initially he decided to honor his obligation to Naples, but as the French army rolled into Tuscany, Piero hurried to prostrate himself before Charles. He surrendered Pisa and the key fortresses to Charles in return for the safety of the city. When he returned to Florence he found it in open rebellion. His enemies barred his entrance, and he fled for his life to Venice, disguised as a liveryman. The republic then sued for peace and allied itself with the conqueror. On November 17, 1494, Charles entered Florence, just one week after Piero's flight. He was received with all respect, for he was the personal fulfillment of the Dominican friar Savonarola's prophecy that a king would be sent by God to give a new birth to Italy. Florence remained a French vassal until 1512, when the French were expelled from Italy.

Charles announced his intention of spending the Christmas of 1494 in Rome. The Romans, who had heard of the brutality of the French soldiery, were terrified. The Colonnas, allies of the French, occupied Ostia and threatened to starve out the city. Pope Alexander VI, who had recognized Alfonso as king of Naples, now attempted to conciliate Charles by sending him Djem, the sultan's brother, as a hostage. On December 25 the king's envoys arrived before Rome and on December 31 Charles himself led his army into the Eternal City, riding at the head of the column with his lance at rest on one side. Taking along Cesare Borgia, the pope's son, to assure the pontiff's continued cooperation, Charles marched toward Naples.

King Alfonso abdicated and left his throne to his popular son, Ferrantino. On February 22, 1495, Charles rode triumphantly into Naples, without having fought a single serious engagement. But his prize quickly slipped through his fingers. The French quickly alienated the people of Naples. The soldiers terrorized the citizenry, and an epidemic of syphilis, known to the Neapolitans as the "French disease" and to the French as the "Neapolitan disease," spread like wildfire. The French monopolized all the best public offices. King Ferdinand of Aragon, a crafty schemer who was also king of Sicily and felt his vital interest in the Mediterranean threatened by the French, organized the League of Venice (March 31, 1495) to resist them. In addition to Ferdinand, the league included Pope Alexander VI, Ludovico il Moro, who now saw the danger of French claims to Milan, Emperor Maximilian, and the republic of Venice itself. That the Spanish king and the emperor were members of the league was an ominous sign for Italian independence. Charles realized that he was overextended, and returned with the main part of his army toward France. On July 6, 1495, he fought a brief and bitter battle at Fornova with the forces of the league under Francesco Gonzaga. Both sides claimed victory, but Charles disengaged his troops and escaped to the north. The Italians had demonstrated their ability to do battle with the French and Swiss. With the aid of Spanish troops, King Ferrantino drove out the garrisons Charles had left behind and took possession of his capital. On April 7, 1498, Charles VIII died. His great adventure had come and gone, but Italy would never be the same again. Henceforth the major states of Europe were to use it as a battleground and claim its treasures as their spoils of war.

Savonarola in Florence

VERY RADICAL CHANGES in Florence resulted from the coming and going of the French. The sophisticated city on the Arno fell under the spell of a charismatic leader, the Dominican friar Girolamo Savonarola (1452–1498). So strange is this phenomenon, and so instructive, that a close look at the man and his role in Florentine life will be rewarding.

This gaunt ascetic leader of men was born in Ferrara into a family of modest means. He was to become a doctor, like his grandfather, in the hope of building up the family's prosperity. But as a youth he showed signs of nonconformity. He was given to walking alone along the banks of the Po River. He read St. Thomas and the Arabic commentators on Aristotle. Although he was brought up in a courtier household and observed at firsthand the grandeur of Borso d'Este's Renaissance court, he held only disdain for the vanities of such a life. His love for a Strozzi daughter was frustrated when her family rejected him because of his lower social status. He prayed each day, "Lord, teach me the way my soul should walk." Then, at twenty-two, he fled to the Dominican monastery in Bologna, where he wrote a treatise *On the Contempt of the World*.

Savonarola made no particular impression on Bologna and Ferrara during his early years as a preacher there. In 1482 he was transferred to San Marco in Florence, a Medici foundation, where a circle of literati who called themselves "Martians" gathered to study the classics. His reaction to Florence was both sweet and sour, for he loved its beauty but was shocked at its worldliness. In 1483 he delivered the Lenten sermons in San Lorenzo, but the multitude went to hear the elegantly rhetorical Fra Mariano da Genazzano in the cathedral. Savanarola now began to have visions of divine wrath and great tribulation soon to overtake the sinful, worldly city.

From 1487 to 1490 he was away from Florence in nearby San Gimignano, where his preaching first began to attract attention. When he was recalled to Florence, his first sermon in San Marco, on August 1, 1490, called for repentance and conversion, and was full of vague apocalyptic prophecies. His reputation grew steadily until he was the most famous preacher in Florence. He criticized tyrants and predicted they would come to a bad end. Lorenzo had no great love for this gadfly, and Piero could not abide his sharp thrusts. Savonarola became a bold advocate of the poor and oppressed. Elected prior of San Marco and invited to preach in the cathedral, the eloquent friar became a greater and greater force in the city. His *Triumph of the Cross* was a rhetorically powerful writing.

In 1494 his Lenten sermons called for the building of another Noah's ark against the floods to come. In one of his visions he saw a hand bearing a flaming sword inscribed with the words "The sword of the Lord over the earth swift and speedy." He saw the coming of Charles VIII as the fulfillment of his prophecies that the Lord would send an avenger. When news reached Florence in September 1494 that the French king had crossed the Alps and had arrived in Genoa, Savonarola resumed preaching a series of sermons on Genesis, choosing as his text Genesis 6:17: "Lo, I shall loose over the earth the waters of the flood." The terrified congregation in the cathedral burst out in sobs and cries of despair. Pico della Mirandola told later how shivers ran up his spine and his hair stood on end, and as an old man Michelangelo said that Savonarola's voice still haunted him. On November 1, with the French army nearing the gates, Savonarola mounted the pulpit and preached to a packed cathedral:

> You know that some years ago, before there was any hint or rumor of these wars which have now come from beyond the mountains, great tribulations were foretold to you. You know, too, that less than two years ago I said to you: *Ecce gladius Domini super terram cito et velociter.* Not I, but God gave you this prediction, and now it has come. It is now approaching.[1]

With Charles VIII's entry into Florence on November 17 it seemed that the flood had come. Twice Savonarola intervened with the king, and though at times it looked as though he might sack the city, Charles marched out of the gates for Naples eleven days later without having done any deliberate damage. Now that Piero and Charles were both gone from Florence, it seemed to Savonarola that divine grace had intervened in favor of the city. He now announced "this good news to the city, that Florence will be more glorious, richer, more powerful than she has ever been." Glorious in the sight of God and man, Florence would have temporal and spiritual power over all of Italy. These cheery prophecies inaugurated the new republic, which Savonarola dominated for several years.

---

[1] Roberto Ridolfi, *The Life of Girolamo Savonarola,* tr. Cecil Grayson (New York, 1959), p. 80.

Savonarola urged the adoption of a republican constitution similar to that of Venice. There was to be a grand council with some three thousand members to represent all the people, a third of the membership sitting for six months in turn. This council was empowered to create lesser councils for specific purposes. There was to be an upper council consisting of eighty members, which was to discuss delicate and confidential matters in consultation with the *signoria*. The system worked surprisingly well as long as Savonarola kept his hold on the people. He could sponsor legislation in the interest of moral improvement and convince the populace it was for the common good. In 1496 at carnival time he inspired the great "burning of the vanities," when the people made a great bonfire of their gambling equipment, jewelry, cosmetics, false hair and pads, lewd books, and trinkets. The story that many Renaissance art treasures were lost in an iconoclastic holocaust is pure fabrication. Such events and the unifying effect of the war with Pisa kept the Florentines in line for two or three years, but gradually Savonarola's hold over them weakened.

Savonarola was a severe critic of the secular interests and the gross immorality of the popes. He had even implored Charles VIII as a Christian prince to convene a council to depose the pope. He declared the independence of the Tuscan Dominican houses from the Lombard congregations, in order to purify them while they were free from the control of worldly officials. The infamous Alexander VI was unhappy over Florence's pro-French policy and its persistence in thwarting his expansionist designs northward. The pope forbade the "meddlesome friar" to preach, but Savonarola not only continued his attacks on the papacy, but intensified them. In 1497 papal emissaries excommunicated Savonarola and threatened to place Florence under an interdict if he were permitted to preach again. Although Savonarola denied the validity of the ban, since, he said, it was imposed by a pope who was the representative not of God but of Satan, the people were not convinced. Moreover, the oligarchical clans, who were accustomed to rule the city, were impatient with his theocratic rule.

The end came quickly, once the fickle populace turned against him. A conniving Franciscan challenged Savonarola to an ordeal by fire. Pressed by his fellow Dominicans, who had absolute faith in him, Savonarola accepted the challenge. But when the day of the ordeal arrived and the fires were prepared, the Franciscans managed to delay the proceedings until a rainstorm struck and they were able to hustle their champion away in the general confusion. Savonarola barely made it safely back to San Marco through the hostile crowd, angry and frustrated at missing the show. They were soon to have a bloody spectacle to their taste, for the city government arrested him and condemned him to death. On May 23, 1498, after days of torture, he and two young supporters were publicly hanged. The spot is still marked by a bronze plaque. Their bodies were burned and the ashes tossed into the Arno. It was reported that a member of the *Dieci* said on Savonarola's execution day, "Praise be to God, now we can practice sodomy."[2]

Louis XII Invades Italy

THE ITALIAN QUESTION was becoming increasingly a European question. The major states of the north and west saw their vital interests involved in the political affairs of the peninsula, and they promoted them with the two standard weapons, war and marriage. The Italian princelings in turn found it to their interests to marry their sons and daughters into wealthier and more powerful houses beyond the Alps. A Borgia married the sister of the king of Navarre, a Sforza daughter married Emperor Maximilian, a Medici daughter became the queen of France.

When Louis XII of France invaded Italy, the whole enterprise was different from the adventure of Charles VIII. Precedents had been set and the city-states could calculate their responses in advance in accordance with their particular interests. Moreover, the other major powers, especially Spain, could estimate with fair precision the counterforce necessary to clear the French out again.

Savonarola fell the day after Charles VIII died. The news of the king's death had of course not reached Florence yet, but the coincidence dramatically emphasized the dependence of the friar upon the king, of the Florentines upon the French.

Charles's successor was Louis XII, of the house of Orléans, who reigned from 1498 to 1515. Louis XII had married Jeanne, the daughter of King Louis XI, in order to establish a firm claim to the succession. But now that he was king, it seemed more useful for him to marry the widow of Charles VIII, Anne of Brittany, in order to keep her province securely attached to the French realm. Such a marital maneuver required church sanction, however, and the need for an annulment of the first marriage and dispensation for the second obligated the king to the pope. Alexander VI, seeing an opportunity to aggrandize his own family, sent his son Cesare Borgia to France as his emissary in 1498.

Cesare Borgia gave up his cardinalate in order to build up the papal territories as a frankly secular state. When he sailed for France aboard a French ship, he went as the duke of Valentinois, bringing with him the dispensation sought by Louis XII and a red hat for Georges d'Amboise, an influential churchman-politician. Cesare had marriage plans of his own, for he hoped to wed Carlotta, the daughter of King Federigo of Naples, who was being brought up at the French court. By marrying the princess, Cesare could unite southern and central Italy, a formidable

---

    2 *Ibid.*, p. 288. A fascinating sociopsychological analysis is T. C. Price Zimmermann, "Girolamo Savonarola: A Study in Mazeway Resynthesis," *Soundings*, 1 (1968):45–59.

base for even grander designs. But Carlotta found the idea of marrying the ex-cardinal repugnant. Her father did something most unusual for those days: he honored Carlotta's wishes and refused to force her into the marriage. This bit of paternal sentiment, as it turned out, cost him his kingdom. For, denied Carlotta, Cesare Borgia married Charlotte d'Albret, sister of the king of Navarre, and then joined Louis XII in an invasion of Italy that toppled Federigo from the throne of Naples.

Louis XII was not unmindful of the need to strengthen his central government and to control the feudal lords. But the lure of Italy was strong, and he could not refrain from asserting his dynastic claims to Naples and Milan. At last Ludovico il Moro was to pay the price for his folly in bringing the French into Italy. On the departure of Charles VIII, the Italian courts had returned to business and pleasure as usual. Ludovico was a big spender, for he loved tournaments and carnivals, and kept up a very elaborate and expensive court. Now that he needed financial reserves to hire mercenaries, he was nearly bankrupt.

In September 1499 Ludovico sought refuge in the Habsburg lands of the Tyrol. The following spring, when he thought conditions more favorable, he made his way back to Milan with an army of Swiss mercenaries. The people opened the gates of the city to him and received him with cheers. But the French held the mighty Castello, which a traitor had surrendered to them shortly after Ludovico's first flight. The French built up their forces, and at Novara on April 8, 1500, they captured Ludovico's army, for his Swiss soldiery would not fight against the Swiss mercenaries in the French army. Ludovico's mercenaries turned him over to the French, who shipped him off to France, where he lived out his days in a dungeon.

Louis XII moved on toward Naples. In the secret Treaty of Granada (November 1500) he and Ferdinand of Aragon agreed to partition the kingdom of Naples. Federigo was unaware of this deal until the French invasion was under way. When he realized that the Spaniards were not coming to his aid, he had to agree to an unconditional surrender. Soon the French fell out with the Spaniards and Sicilians over disputed territory. By January I, 1504, the Spaniards had driven them completely out of Neapolitan territory and Naples once again belonged to Aragon.

The French adventure in Italy worked to the immediate advantage of the papacy. Cesare Borgia used Milan as a base from which to conquer the Romagna, using Swiss infantry and French cavalry. In three campaigns he laid low the petty principalities within the papal estates which had dared to maintain or assert their independence. After Alexander VI's death and Cesare's departure from the scene, the French supported Julius II in his conquest of the north, and with their aid he even took Bologna. In 1508 the French, Pope Julius II, Emperor Maximilian, and Ferdinand of Spain formed the League of Cambrai against haughty Venice, and in 1509 defeated her decisively.

Having subdued all the papal states except Ferrara, which was a French protectorate, Julius II found it to his advantage to turn against the French, and in 1510 he helped to organize the Holy League of major powers to expel them from Italy. The Swiss meanwhile had been organized by Cardinal Matthias Schinner for an attack on the French. They came down through the Brenner Pass, put the French to flight, and in 1513 at Novara decisively defeated them. Ludovico's son, Massimiliano Sforza, was made duke of Milan, but the Swiss kept control over the duchy themselves in order to secure their mercantile interests.

After Savonarola's death the Florentine republic fumbled along with its cumbersome governmental machinery. From 1502 on, Piero Soderini served as *gonfaloniere,* which made him a kind of titular head of state, for there was to be no doge or duke. In August 1512 the Spaniards took little Prato, not far from Florence. Soderini was deposed, the republic fell, and the Medicis were restored to power in Florence. There was a brief republican revival from 1527 to 1530, but with Spanish support Duke Cosimo I de' Medici then became ruler of Florence and the call for liberty was silenced until a later century.

Machiavelli

IN THE YEAR of Charles VIII's invasion and Piero de' Medici's flight into exile, Niccolò Machiavelli entered public life. He was born in 1469, the year Lorenzo de' Medici came to power, and he was to die in 1527, the year of the invasion by the troops of Emperor Charles V and the sack of Rome. He lived through the years of Italy's ordeal and the times made a deep impression upon him.

Machiavelli belonged to a Florentine family of poor nobility. His father, Bernardo, was a jurist, who owned some landed property in addition to the modest house that still stands today at 16, via Guicciardini. Niccolò's education included a knowledge of the Latin and Italian classics, although he knew no Greek, and enough grammar and law to make him serviceable to the state. His first position was modest enough; he served as a clerk in the second chancery of the commune under Marcello Virgilio Adriani, who had taught him grammar. When in 1498 Adriani became chancellor of the republic, Machiavelli moved into his post with the title of second chancellor and secretary to the *Dieci*. The *Dieci* had independent power over war and diplomacy, as well as certain internal matters, although it was subordinate to the *signoria*. Machiavelli retained this position until the fall of Piero Soderini and the republic in 1512.

His life was totally absorbed in the affairs of his office, which included a voluminous correspondence, diplomatic missions of varying importance, and the inspection of fortifications and reforming of the militia. His more interesting assignments included a diplomatic mission to France in 1500 to negotiate with Louis XII about the problem of Pisa, for Soderini was determined that Florence should conquer Pisa and Machiavelli urged on the war until Pisa fell in 1509. From October 1502 to January 1503 he served as an emissary to Cesare Borgia, to observe his conquest and pacification of the Romagna. In 1506 he was with Pope Julius II on his campaign through Perugia into the province of Emilia. In December 1507 he was dispatched to the court of Emperor Maximilian, who was planning an expedition to be crowned in Rome. Machiavelli traveled through Switzerland and the Habsburg Tyrol to Bolzano, and returned to Florence in June 1508.

This diplomatic experience served Machiavelli as a laboratory for political science, where he could observe men and governments in action. He used his journey to France as an opportunity to observe the vigor of the northerners. Although he did not get far into German lands, he made some very shrewd observations on the Germanic peoples. After observing Cesare Borgia in action, he prepared a discourse encouraging Soderini to spend freely in defense of the state, and wrote a book on military affairs. During 1506 and 1507 he organized a new "national militia" for Florence. He divided the country districts into departments, which were to provide levies of foot soldiers for a standing army. He had a low opinion of fortresses and thought artillery relatively ineffective; infantry was the critical force, for only infantry could hold the country surrounding a city, and if the countryside fell, the state could not long survive. When the Spaniards sacked Prato in 1512, however, Machiavelli's national militia proved ineffective against Spain's professional army of mercenaries.

Machiavelli was not an imposing man. He was of medium height, with a small head, a receding hairline, and a slightly aquiline nose. The only portrait of him, by Santi di Tito, probably done from his death mask, shows him with bright dark eyes and a wary, alert look, his thin lips ready to curl back in a sardonic smile. In 1502 he married Marietta Corsini and fathered several children. They were reasonably happy, despite his frequent infidelities. He was not a strong and secure person, and consequently he was given to posturing. In 1521, when he was sent to the monastery of Carpi on a petty mission, he arranged to have armed messengers ride up to the monastery at a gallop and ostentatiously deliver to him "urgent" dispatches that required his immediate attention. The monks were enormously impressed.

When the Medicis returned to power and the republic collapsed, Machiavelli lost his position. Worse, he was unfairly implicated in the anti-Medici conspiracy of Piero Paolo Boscoli in February 1513 and was tortured on the rack and thrown into a dungeon. When Giovanni de' Medici was elected to the papacy, the Medicis released Machiavelli from prison as a gracious gesture. He retired to his small farm near San Casciano, and in a famous letter to a friend he described his life there. In the morning he did menial chores, such as supervising the cutting of wood and dickering for its sale. Then he went to the village inn to gossip and play rustic games with the townsmen. Back home in the evening, however, he took off his muddy shoes and rough clothes, put on silken slippers and fine robes, in which he had once appeared before kings and princes, and turned to reading and writing. He felt more at home communing with the ancient dead, men of quality, than with the contemporaries who were available to him as companions. "I am welcomed kindly," he confided, "and fed on that fare which is mine alone, and for which I was born; where I am not ashamed to address them and to ask the reasons for their actions."

Machiavelli was a real intellectual, reacting creatively to all that he read as well as to all that he experienced and observed. He wrote three books, three plays, a volume of poems, and a short story. His *Mandragola* is a wild, witty, and lascivious farce in which a lusty adventurer, assisted by a cynical companion, a greedy confessor, and the indulgent, worldly-wise mother of a young married woman who has caught his eye, has the girl delivered to him, reluctantly yielding, by her own cuckolded husband. The comedy played to packed houses even in the rival city of Venice. In his serious work on political science and history, he showed respect for Livy and other ancient authors, but he always weighed what they had to say against reality as he had learned to know it. "I do not know," he once wrote to Francesco Vettori, "just what Aristotle says about countries that have been destroyed. What interests me more than theory is what is, what has been, and what may reasonably happen."

"You have always been at odds with the conventional, and an inventor of new and unexpected things," wrote Guicciardini to Machiavelli in 1521. Machiavelli pioneered as a "retrospective sociologist," analyzing statecraft and military power on the basis of historical case studies and his own observations. Rodolfo de Mattei has commented that Machiavelli is still "one of the poles of . . . scientific interest in the field of political thought." In his *Discourses on the First Ten Books of Livy* Machiavelli wrote: "I have decided to enter on a path which has up to now been trodden by no one, and if it brings me labor and difficulty, it may also bring me a reward. . . ." He believed that in statecraft the examples of the ancients were more admired than imitated. If lawyers considered the precedents of Roman law and if doctors could learn from ancient medicine, then men who governed states should learn from the political experience of rulers by reading history and applying its lessons to their own situations. His discourses took the form of commentaries on Livy's history, but in reality they provided the opportunity for Machiavelli to develop his own theories about the genesis and maintenance of states. "Whoever desires to found a state and give it laws must start with assuming that all men are bad and ever ready to display their vicious nature," Machiavelli observed in the *Discourses* (53). "If their evil disposition remains concealed for a time, it must be attributed to some unknown reason."

Machiavelli's most notorious book was *The Prince,* written with great fervor and a strong sense of urgency. His intent was to instruct a prince in ways to maintain the state in desperate times. The prince must be prepared to act amorally, even immorally, to lie, dissemble, and kill in the interest of the higher good, which is the security of the state. The prince must not even trust friends, for enmity is the norm. "It is much safer to be feared than loved," he counseled, "if one of the two has to be wanting." The prince must not trust treaties, for rival princes are held in check only by threat of war. Fortune "will not help those who will not help themselves, nor will the heavens—nor can they—sustain a thing that is determined to destroy itself." Machiavelli has therefore been accused of introducing the doctrine of *raison d'état,* that where the welfare of the state is involved, the end justifies any means. In *The Prince* the rules of power have priority over normal standards of good and evil, which are reduced from absolute to very relative categories. He dedicated the book to Lorenzo de' Medici, duke of Urbino, in an effort to ingratiate himself with the Medicis and enter once again into the service of his beloved Florence.

Judgments on Machiavelli's *Prince* have differed widely. In 1576 the French Huguenot Gentillet published a collection of Machiavelli's maxims which did much to blacken his reputation. On the Elizabethan stage Machiavelli appeared as a furtive, sinister figure. Englishmen, including Francis Bacon, read Machiavelli's own works, of course. The Spanish Jesuits in the sixteenth and seventeenth centuries judged him to be very wicked. The philosopher Spinoza suggested that Machiavelli had written it as a warning, to show how evil a prince can really be. Machiavelli was not blind to personal moral standards, but the situation in Italy appeared so desperate that realism divorced from moral considerations seemed to be called for. He seems less shocking to men who have seen the degradations of the twentieth century than he seemed to men in earlier times, when the restraints theoretically imposed by religion were more seriously considered. Men no doubt will continue to debate the question. Benedetto Croce once observed that "the puzzle of Machiavelli is one that will perhaps never be solved."

Machiavelli's third major work was *The History of Florence,* to which he devoted his declining years. Many habits of thought developed during his long years of work on the *Discourses* carried over to his historical writing. At times the narrative seems essentially a work of analysis and instruction, a pragmatic use of history. He had been commissioned to do the work in 1520, and when he died in 1527 it was still incomplete. But he had dedicated it to Pope Clement VII, and had already received 120 gold ducats as a reward for this gesture of esteem to a Medici. According to his son Piero, his fatal illness was brought on by a medicine he had taken.

Machiavelli's primary concern was for the security of the state. As Leopold von Ranke observed, he wished above all to see Italy freed of barbarian invaders.

Although he was an ardent republican, he saw that under some circumstances participation of the people in the government was less vital than the survival and security of the state itself. Thus the republican Machiavelli could counsel a Medici prince on how to save the state and possibly all Italy. He conceived of *virtù* as the leader's ability to conceive a plan and carry it through: intelligent will in action. He saw religion as a vital force in early Rome, a symbol of order and a support for public morals. The people's willingness to serve the state, in the Roman army and otherwise, made it stable and strong. Machiavelli seemed to feel that there is a limited amount of *virtù* available in any given historical epoch, and that its dispersion leads to decline. Just as Tacitus contrasted the *virtù* of the strong, simple German tribes with the decadence of the imperial Romans, so Machiavelli saw in his own day the *virtù* of the barbarians outside Italy—the Spaniards, French, Germans, and Turks—as overpowering corrupt Italy, now at the bottom of history's great cycle. In these last days, he saw some hope in a prince who might unite all Italy against the foreigners. Even while acknowledging the powerful forces of fate and fortune, Machiavelli remained an activist, believing that by superhuman effort it is possible to build the dams that can keep the river's torrent out of the city. Fortune, he writes in *The Prince,* is "ruler of half our actions, but he allows the other half or thereabouts to be governed by us." It was fitting that such a patriot of the republic should be buried in the Santa Croce, not far from Leonardo Bruni, the great civic humanist. The times in which the two men lived differed more than the two men differed from each other.

Guicciardini

MACHIAVELLI'S LIFE crisscrossed the life of another great Florentine, the statesman-historian Francesco Guicciardini (1483–1540). Pope Clement VII commissioned Machiavelli to inspect the fortifications of Florence in the spring of 1526. That summer he was ordered to attend Guicciardini, the pope's commissioner of war in Lombardy. In August Guicciardini sent him to Cremona to negotiate with Venetian officials. They were together later that year in Bologna. In the spring of 1527 Guicciardini sent him to Città Vecchia, but not long after his return Machiavelli died. The political scientist and the historian had seen together the tragedy of Renaissance Italy and had been involved in some of the same political maneuvering.

The scion of a prosperous and venerable Florentine family, Guicciardini was educated in the civil law in Florence, Ferrara, Padua, and Pisa. His professional life was bound to the service of the Medicis. He began his diplomatic career in 1512, when the *signoria* sent him as its emissary to the court of Ferdinand of Aragon, and he represented the Medicis there for two years. In December 1515 he served as the Florentine envoy to Pope Leo X at Cortona. In 1518 he entered the service of Leo X as papal governor of Modena and Reggio. In 1521 he became governor of Parma. The second Medici pope, Clement VII, made Guicciardini vice-regent of Romagna in 1523. On June 6, 1526, he became lieutenant general of the papal forces.

His military career was not exactly brilliant, for he failed to prevent the sack of Rome in 1527 and was unable to rescue Clement VII from the imperial troops besieging the Castello di Sant' Angelo. That same year he failed to suppress a popular revolt against the Medicis and was expelled with them for trying. Despite this record of failure, the pope continued to rely on him. He sent him to reinstate the Medicis in Florence in 1530, which he did "by cruel but effective means," as he himself wrote in his *Ricordi*. In 1531 Guicciardini became governor of Bologna, and had to suppress a popular revolt there on the death of Clement VII in 1534. He then cast his lot with the Medicis. As a member of the Council of Forty-Eight in Florence he promoted the cause of Cosimo I de' Medici, but once Cosimo was in, the senators, including Guicciardini, were out. Guicciardini retired to his villa to write his *History of Italy*. Three years later, at the age of fifty-eight, he was dead.

In his *Ricordi,* maxims of prudential wisdom which he compiled for future generations of his family, and an eighty-page commentary on Machiavelli's *Discourses,* Guicciardini was candid and articulate, if aphoristic, about his political views. A lifetime spent in the service of the Medicis destroyed whatever republican sentiment he might have had. "To speak of the people," he wrote, "is in truth to speak of a beast; mad, mistaken, perplexed, without taste, discernment, or stability." He cynically counseled princes, "Bind the people to the ruler; employ the younger men in the service of the ruler; let men forget the responsibilities of government and concentrate on their own pleasure and profit; give men who might be troublesome honor and office and ease." Some of his passages make Machiavelli look like a naïve idealist.

His personal failures, or possibly the whole experience of Italy's debasement, developed in Guicciardini a strong pessimistic streak. "It is scarcely possible to find anything that has not somewhere imperfection or blemish," he wrote. "We must therefore be content to take things as they are, and to reckon the least evil as good." Human life as such is short, brutal, and miserable. "When I consider how many accidents and perils of infirmity, of chance, of violence, and in infinite ways, the life of man is subjected to . . ." he wailed, "I marvel all the more to see an old man or a fruitful year." When a disillusioned realist, not to say cynic, turned to write the history of those times, the result is instructive.

Guicciardini's *History of Italy* covered the period from 1492 to 1534. In his *Ricordi* he had declared that a historian should "write in such a way that men born in a distant age should have every event as much before their eyes as those in whose presence it happened; for this is the true object of history." This desire to present each event as it actually happened led him to detailed descriptions of political happenings and diplomatic situations. He wrote virtually nothing on intellectual and cultural history, but excelled at analyzing personal motivations. His assumption that history could serve the pragmatic purpose of instructing future generations rested upon his conviction that human nature remains basically the same. "Past events," he wrote, "throw light on future ones, because the world has always been the same as it is now."

He wrote his contemporary history with a remarkable detachment, almost as though it were a history of another time. The famous French historian Henri Hauser believed that modern historiography begins with Guicciardini's *History of Italy*. But the famous English historian Macaulay related that a Florentine criminal, offered a choice between the galley and Guicciardini's *History,* thankfully chose to read Guicciardini, but when he reached the point in the narrative where Guicciardini rehearses in detail the history of the wars against Pisa, he changed his mind and asked to be sent to the galley instead.

In times such as our own, we can perhaps appreciate better than the Victorians those pessimistic realists Machiavelli and Guicciardini. Looking back on the collapse of Florence and the dwarfing of Italy, Guicciardini lamented:

> All cities, all states, all kingdoms are mortal, since either by nature or by accident everything in this world must at some time come to an end. But the citizen who happens to be living when his country is in its own decline should not so much lament over its unhappy fortunes as over his own. For his country only suffers what it was fated to suffer. His is the infelicity of being born at such a time when his country has to fulfill its doom.

Bibliography

General:

Cavaignac, Eugène. *Politique mondiale, 1492–1757.* Paris, 1934.

Clark, George. *Early Modern Europe: From About 1450 to About 1720.* New York, 1960.

Ercole, F. *Da Carlo VIII a Carlo V: La crisi della libertà italiana.* Florence, 1932.

Fueter, Eduard. *Geschichte des europäischen Staatensystems von 1492 bis 1559.* Munich and Berlin, 1919.

Grant, A. J. *A History of Europe from 1494 to 1610,* 4th ed. London, 1948.

Laven, Peter. *Renaissance Italy, 1464–1534.* London, 1965.

Pieri, P. *Il Rinascimento e la crisi militare italiana,* 2nd ed. Turin, 1952.

Savonarola:

Bedoyère, Michael de la. *The Meddlesome Friar and the Wayward Pope.* Garden City, N.Y., 1958.

Naccari, Giuseppe. *Girolamo Savonarola*. Milan, 1955.

Ridolfi, Roberto. *The Life of Girolamo Savonarola*. New York, 1959.

Soranzo, Giovanni. *Il Tempo di Alessandro VI Papa e di Fra Girolamo Savonarola*. Milan, 1960.

Villari, Pasquale. *La Storia di Girolamo Savonarola e de suoi tempi*, 2 vols., 2nd ed. Florence, 1910.

Machiavelli:

Butterfield, Herbert. *The Statecraft of Machiavelli*. London, 1940.

Cassirer, Ernst. *The Myth of the State*. New Haven, 1946.

Chabod, Federico. *Machiavelli and the Renaissance*. London, 1958.

Gilbert, Allan H. *Machiavelli's Prince and Its Forerunners*. Durham, N.C., 1938.

Hale, John R. *Machiavelli and Renaissance Italy*. New York, 1960.

Meinecke, Friedrich. *Machiavellism: The Doctrine of Raison d'État and Its Place in Modern History*. New Haven, 1957.

Ridolfi, Roberto. *The Life of Niccolò Machiavelli*. Chicago, 1963.

Villari, Pasquale. *Niccolò Machiavelli and His Times*, 4 vols. London, 1878–1883.

Whitfield, J. H. *Machiavelli*. Oxford, 1947.

Guicciardini:

Gilbert, Felix. *Machiavelli and Guicciardini: Politics and History in Sixteenth-Century Florence*. Princeton, 1965.

Ridolfi, Roberto. *The Life of Francesco Guicciardini*. New York, 1968.

CHAPTER 10

Renaissance
and
Reconnaissance

On the oldest surviving terrestrial globe known, made in Nuremberg in 1492, the geographer Martin Behaim inscribed the words: "Be it known that on this globe here present is laid out the whole world according to its length and breadth in accordance with the art of geometry . . . wherefore let none doubt . . . that every part may be reached in ships, as is here seen."[1] The discovery of a wider world that dwarfed not only Italy but Europe itself was an achievement of the Renaissance. There was great excitement about the new sea routes to the East and the New World, although more than a century was to pass before the enthnocentric Europeans began to appreciate the full implications of their new global horizons.

West Meets East

THE RELATIVE ISOLATION of Latin Christendom during the high Middle Ages began to break down during the thirteenth and fourteenth centuries as the Europeans

---

[1] Charles Singleton, ed., *Art, Science, and History in the Renaissance* (Baltimore, 1967), p. 187. D. W. Waters' essay "Science and the Techniques of Navigation," pp. 189–237, discusses the importance of portable sundials, mechanical clocks, and other instruments for navigation.

established promising contacts with the Far East. The West reacted with fear to the spread of the great Mongol Empire across Asia and part of Europe. Genghis Khan (1206–1227) seemed irresistible as his barbarous hordes, reportedly clad in skins, rolled across the great land mass of Asia. But the Mongol Empire soon fell apart as the leadership fragmented, and the threat to Europe subsided. In fact, the Mongols soon were thought of as a blessing in disguise, for they had attacked the Moslem caliphate from the rear and relieved pressure on eastern Europe from that source. They proved to be quite open to cultural and even religious influence from the West, and the possibility of trade with China beckoned.

For about a hundred years, from the mid-thirteenth to the mid-fourteenth centuries, the Far East was open to Europeans. In 1245 the council of Lyon and the pope sent a Franciscan friar, John of Plano Carpini, to the khan at his head-quarters in Karakorum in what is now Outer Mongolia. In 1253 a Flemish Franciscan friar, William of Rubruck, was sent by King Louis IX of France to the Mongols. The king, St. Louis, was planning a crusade against the Moslems. Recalling the quick conversion of whole Germanic and Baltic tribes in the early Middle Ages, he hoped to win over the Mongols to Christianity in the same way and thus to box in the Moslems by encircling them from behind. William of Rubruck gave a long account of his mission (1253–1258), including his religious discussions with the great khan in Karakorum. He was impressed by the high moral standards of the Chinese. The scholars of that period tried to connect the Chinese with the true faith through their common descent from Noah, and stressed Nestorian Christian influence.

In 1256 two merchants of Venice, Niccolò and Matteo Polo, made a long trip in search of trade, which took them eventually to Peking, which the Tatar khans had made their permanent capital. The great khan, Kublai, was a man of great curiosity and philosophical flexibility, and before the Polo brothers turned toward home he asked them to come again to China and bring some churchmen who could teach him about their religion. In 1271 they returned to China with Niccolò's son Marco, then seventeen years old, and two Dominicans. Marco had an extraordinary talent for close observation, and after a journey he would relate unusual details and matters of special interest to the khan. The appreciative ruler therefore used him often as an emissary and thus afforded him many opportunities to see distant places. When the Polos at last returned again to Venice, they had been away twenty-five years. The account of Marco's travels we owe in part to the Venice-Genoa war, for he was captured by the Genoese in 1298, and while he was in prison in Genoa he had the leisure to write his famous book. Some of the more fantastic tales, and the report on Cipangu (Japan), far out to sea, he related from hearsay. He even included some legends from Greek mythology. But most of what he wrote from his own experience, such as his account of the "black rocks" that the Chinese burned for heat, proved to be quite reliable. His reports of the

wealth of the East stirred great interest in Europe, and the geographical information he brought back was incorporated into the Catalan Atlas and was of great
use to mariners and other travelers.

The relative reliability of Marco Polo's *Travels* becomes evident when his
account is compared with Jehan de Mandeville's widely read *Book of the Wonders
of the World*. This book of fantasies was supposedly written by a noble medical
professor who was born in England and died in 1371 in Liège. It was a spurious
work based on travelers' hearsay accounts, replete with stories of dog-headed island-
ers and other ancient myths. It appeared in many manuscript editions and was
printed in Italian and French around 1480. It did much to popularize the idea
that a ship could reach the East by sailing around the world toward the west.

In the early fourteenth century still more churchmen traveled to the Far East.
John of Monte Corvino was commissioned in 1315 to establish contact with the
Nestorian Christians in Asia. He accommodated himself beautifully to Chinese
customs, was well received in Mandarin circles, and became bishop of Peking.
Odoric of Pordenone traveled to India as well as to China. In a book about his
travels he gave a very superior account of Chinese customs and spiced his story
with interesting oddities and marvels. Other missionaries journeyed to the East
and wrote accounts of their experiences. Merchants as well as missionaries were
keenly interested, and their handbooks, such as that of Pegolotti around 1340,
frequently gave quite precise descriptions of the main trade routes to India.

This promising intercourse was cut off by a series of historical developments.
The Ilkhans of Persia were converted to Islam and thereby acquired a rationale
for attacking Christendom. Farther east, the Ming dynasty overthrew the Mongol
dynasty in 1368. Hostile to foreigners, they shut off the cultural communication
and trade routes to Peking. Most ominous of all was the emergence of the Ottoman
Turks, who posed a threat not only to the routes to the East, but to Europe itself.

The Osmanli or Ottoman Turks occupied a small state wedged between the
Mongols and the Seljuk Turks. In the mid-fourteenth century they emerged as
a major military power. Responding to Mongol pressure, they built a major base
of power in Asia Minor and then proceeded to conquer the Balkans. In 1356 the
Osmanli emirate set up a capital at Adrianople and pressed on through Mace-
donia to the west and through Bulgaria to the north. In the decisive battle of
Nicopolis in 1396, the Turks defeated the Christian army. Only the city of Constantinople and a bit of territory around it still held out. The Turks suffered only
one major setback, when around 1400 the terrible Tamerlaine, a Persian Mongol,
attacked them from behind and slowed down their westward movement. By 1430,
however, they pressed on into Greece, moved up the Adriatic coast, and threatened
to take the whole Danube valley. Even Italy felt exposed and vulnerable. It was
then that the Council of Florence, in 1439, declared the reunion of the Eastern
and Western churches.

In 1453, after a terrible siege, Mohammed II rode into Constantinople on his white horse through a breach in the city walls pounded out by artillery. He is said to have ridden into Justinian's thousand-year-old cathedral, the Hagia Sophia, on his horse and commanded that it be whitewashed and converted into a mosque. The Turks still show a handprint on a stone pillar where Mohammed is said to have leaned against it. During his long reign (1451–1481) the Turks moved into Serbia (1459), Bosnia (1463–1464), and Morea (1458–1460), and seized the Genoese colonies on the Black Sea and the Venetian strongholds in the Aegean.

After a long war (1463–1479) with the Venetians, the Turks took Negroponte and other Venetian trade and naval centers in the eastern Mediterranean. Sultan Bayazid II (1481–1512) resumed the war with Venice in 1499 and continued it for four more years. The Ottomans had a well-developed bureaucracy and trained special shock troops for their armies, the dreaded janissaries, made up of captured Christian children indoctrinated as fanatical Moslems. Under Selim I (1512–1520) the Turks were temporarily diverted eastward. Selim fought and defeated the Moslem shah of Persia in 1514 and fought the Mamelukes in 1516–1517, conquering Syria and Egypt. Under Suleiman the Magnificent (1520–1566) they pressed up the Danube to the gates of Vienna and all the way across North Africa to the Atlantic Ocean. It is to be noted, however, that they did not cut across all the trade routes to the Far East until long after the Portuguese had begun their search for new ways to reach India.

Ancient Cosmology

CERTAIN COSMOLOGICAL SUPPOSITIONS and technical advances were essential preconditions to oceanic reconnaissance. Much of the information as well as fortunate misinformation available to explorers in the fifteenth century was inherited from classical antiquity. Questions about the shape of the cosmos, the distance around the globe, astronomical determination of position, and the like were crucial to mariners who ventured far from land or established sea lanes. The Arabs had stayed close to shore and within the Mediterranean, or had sailed in a straight line across the Indian Ocean with the prevailing winds and back again when the winds reversed. The Europeans who braved the Atlantic confronted a whole new set of navigational problems, and on their solution depended the success of the age of exploration.

The ancient Greeks had already speculated about the shape and size of the earth. In earlier centuries they thought of the earth as a round disk tilted to the south and floating upon an immense cosmic sea. This conception was not unlike the Hebrew notion of the "four corners" of the earth; only the shape differed. The

Pythagoreans in southern Italy seem to have first suggested that the earth was a sphere. Aristotle, like Plato, believed the cosmos to be spherical, but he envisioned the solid land mass as extending a relatively short distance from the north to the uninhabitable tropics, and stretching out very far from east to west. Again like Plato, he believed that there were islands in the antipodes. The astronomer-geographers Eratosthenes, Strabo, and Ptolemy held the earth to be a sphere.

All through the Middle Ages scholars with a minimum of learning held the earth to be round like a ball. In the works of St. Augustine and that great compiler and transmitter of Latin lore Isidore of Seville (d. 636) they could read about the round earth. In a widely used schoolbook Martianus Capella had taught that the earth is round. The Venerable Bede, in his treatise *On the Nature of Things,* spoke of the world as round. John Holywood (Sacrobosco) of Halifax, a mathematician and astronomer who taught in Paris in the thirteenth century, wrote immensely popular elementary treatises in which he declared the earth to be round. When a ship approaches land, he pointed out, a man on shore sees the top of the mast first; therefore the earth's surface must be curved. In the *Divine Comedy* Dante spoke of the earth as a sphere. By the fifteenth century the idea was taken for granted.

The ancient world drew the very logical conclusion that it was possible to reach eastern Asia by going westward. The Stoic philosopher Seneca wrote: "How far is it from the farthermost coast of Spain to that of India? With a good sailing wind only a few days' sea journey." The Hellenic scientists had made some very close estimates as to the size of the earth. Eratosthenes (275–195 B.C.) calculated the circumference of the earth at 250,000 stades, which was nearly accurate.

Living in Alexandria during the second century A.D., the Hellenized Egyptian Ptolemy summarized a great store of Greek learning in his two major works, the *Astronomy* or *Almagest,* which in Arabic means "the greatest," and the *Geography.* The *Almagest* was available from 1175 on in the Latin translation by Gerard of Cremona, working in Toledo. Ptolemy went beyond Aristotle's simple picture of the planets moving in concentric paths about the earth and introduced the more complex theory of spheres and epicycles in planetary motion which was widely held until the time of Copernicus.

Ptolemy's *Geography* was also a great compilation of Hellenic learning. It served as a major source for the Arabic scholar Edrisi, who spent fifteen years making a map of the world in the mid-twelfth century and wrote a text to accompany it, the *Book of Roger,* so named because he produced it while he was in residence at the court of Roger II of Sicily. But Ptolemy's work had its major impact through a translation made around 1406 by a pupil of Manuel Chrysoloras, Jacobus Angelus. Ptolemy divided the earth into 360 degrees of latitude and longitude, and from his calculation of the length of the equator he arrived at a figure for the length of a meridian. He explained how to construct a grid of parallels and meridians for maps drawn on a conical projection, and offered a method of adjusting the length of a degree of longitude for any given latitude.[2] The problem of projection in cartography was not really solved, of course, until Mercator produced his world chart in 1569. In the second part of his *Geography* Ptolemy offered a small atlas of regional maps and a map of the world. His work contained major errors that were uncritically accepted down to the fifteenth century. He attached southern Africa to Asia, making the Indian Ocean an inland sea. His estimate of the distance around the world was one-fourth too small. He extended the land mass of Asia too far to the east, making the westward route from Europe to Asia much shorter than it really is. But it was these very errors that encouraged the Renaissance explorers in their bold attempts to round Africa and to sail westward to Asia.

The leading theoretical geographer of the fifteenth century was the famous conciliarist Pierre d'Ailly. His *Imago mundi* (*c.* 1410) was an immense storehouse of knowledge in which he brought together biblical, classical, and Arabic cosmological lore. He followed Roger Bacon's *Opus majus* (1264) in holding that both Africa and Asia extended southward across the equator and that the tropics were habitable, an opinion held in antiquity by both Polybius and Ptolemy. He also held the common error that Asia extended much farther to the east than in fact it does. The geography and cosmography of the fifteenth-century Europeans left much to be desired and were in many respects inferior to the knowledge of some of the best scientists and navigators in antiquity.

New Technology

As LONG AS the ancient mariners stayed inside the Mediterranean Sea or hugged the coastline when passing through the Strait of Gibraltar to reach England and Flanders, navigational problems were relatively simple. In the Mediterranean they seldom sailed more than twenty-four hours without sight of land. They estimated their distances by dead reckoning, their speed by watching a floating chip pass by, and their location by familiar landmarks, which were shown on the increasingly accurate regional sea maps, the *portolani*. Sailing out onto the ocean, however, required astronomical navigation and instruments of relative precision.

In antiquity the astronomers of Alexandria worked out a catalog of the stars which gave their positions within the twelve signs of the zodiac throughout the year. The astronomer Hipparchus constructed an astrolabe that enabled a navigator to measure the height of a star and thus to arrive at the latitude. The astrolabe was the first instrument available for sidereal navigation.

---

[2] J. H. Parry, *The Age of Reconnaissance* (Cleveland, 1963), p. 11.

The Arabs transmitted Greek astronomy, as well as Persian and Indian lore, and handed on the knowledge of the astrolabe and charts of the stars. Massala in the eighth century and Aben Assafar in the eleventh century described the construction of the astrolabe and its use. Their treatises were translated into Latin and incorporated into Christian manuals. The astronomer Azarquiel (d. 1100), who worked in Toledo and Córdoba, worked out detailed tables of the positions of the stars which were still used by Portuguese and Spanish navigators in later centuries. King Alfonso X commissioned a group of court astronomers to prepare an almanac of the heavenly bodies (1248–1252). The Spanish Jew Zacuto of Salamanca prepared an *Almanac perpetuum* published in 1496. In 1475 in Nuremberg the mathematician-astronomer Regiomontanus published the *Ephemerides,* tables showing the daily positions of the heavenly bodies in relation to the celestial equator. His work was widely known in Spain and Portugal.[3]

The mechanics and craftsmen of the late medieval period were tremendously ingenious and inventive. They greatly improved upon the precision of the astrolabe and developed the quadrant, a simple instrument for measuring the altitude of the heavenly bodies, which in modern times was replaced by the sextant. It consisted of a graduated arc of 90 degrees, or of 45 degrees graduated to measure 90 degrees, with a movable radius carrying sights. The use of mechanical clocks became widespread during the fourteenth century. They were used on shore for recording tidal bearings, and at sea for checking the bearing of the sun. Another instrument developed during this period was the nocturnal, for telling the time at night. It consisted of movable circles, the larger having a handle, the lesser rotating around a hollow tube with a radial arm. On the larger the months and days of the year were engraved and on the smaller the hours, so that the navigator could tell the time by the positions of the pointer stars of the Little Bear or the Great Bear relative to the polestar.[4]

No doubt the most important nautical instrument was the compass. It was discovered in China, perhaps as early as the tenth century, although the first description of it dates from 1080. By the end of the eleventh century it was in use for navigation. The earliest European reference to it was made by Alexander Neckam in 1190. In the thirteenth century the magnetic sea compass evolved from a simple iron needle and lodestone indicator into an efficient, self-registering instrument. During the Renaissance the Mediterranean eight-rayed compass card, based upon the names of the eight prevalent Mediterranean winds, was replaced by the northern system of dividing the card into thirty-two points based upon the four cardinal points, north, east, south, and west.[5]

---

[3] Richard Konetzke, "Überseeische Entdeckungen und Eroberungen," *Propyläen-Weltgeschichte* (Berlin, 1964), vol. 6, p. 547.

[4] Waters, "Science and the Techniques of Navigation," p. 194.

[5] *Ibid.,* p. 195.

The Portuguese pilots, who first used sidereal navigation around 1480, measured their location against the position of the polestar. This was not only awkward, but actually impossible if the ship was moving south toward the equator, leaving the polestar behind over the northern horizon. They switched later to determining their position in relation to the place of the sun at high noon. Astronomical navigation was not adopted in the Mediterranean until the sixteenth century. Such were the technical demands of the new improved navigation that in 1508 King Ferdinand established the office of *piloto mayor* in the *Casa de la Contratación* of Seville. No pilot could steer a ship across the Atlantic unless he had first passed an examination given by the *piloto mayor*. The first man named to this important office was the Florentine navigator Amerigo Vespucci.

As important as the instruments and the navigators who used them were the ships in which they sailed. The ships with which the Europeans braved the seas at the beginning of the fifteenth century were inferior in structure and design to those in use in east Asia. But by the end of the sixteenth century the Europeans had the fastest, sturdiest, most maneuverable ships in the world. They borrowed ideas, but contributed important improvements of their own. Living on a peninsular continent surrounded by the ocean and several seas, they took readily to a seafaring way of life.

At the end of the fourteenth century and the beginning of the fifteenth an improved ship design was introduced by the Portuguese and Castilians, the caravel, familiar to every schoolboy, for this was the type of ship used by Columbus. The lateen caravel was a small, fast sailing vessel with a high, narrow poop and three-cornered sails. Borrowing freely from Arab designs, the Iberian shipbuilders continually improved the caravel and adapted it for ocean voyages. A caravel weighed fifty to a hundred tons. The number of masts was increased from two to three in order to enlarge the sail area. On some the middlemast was equipped with a square sail, while the masts fore and aft were rigged with three-cornered lateen (Latin) sails. The caravel did not have a raised forecastle; that space was used for ropes and gear. Most caravels had full decks, where the crew slept, except when storms drove them below. Tar, foul bilge water, unwashed bodies, cockroaches, and rats must have made the stench below overpowering. The crew ate ship's biscuits, salt pork and beef, chickpeas and beans, and after the water stored in the casks was no longer potable they drank wine.

The crew worked a two-watch system, with the pilot (navigator) and sailing master alternately in charge. Light artillery was mounted on the bows and on the poop. Sometimes guns were lined up along the waist to fire over the gunwales. In the late fifteenth century embrasures were cut into the gunwales, like slits in the parapet of a castle, through which the guns could be fired. During the sixteenth century, with the development of heavier naval artillery, the guns were given permanent mounts between the decks and portholes through which they could shoot.[6] The object of naval warfare came to be sinking the enemy's ship, not killing his men, apparently a Portuguese innovation first used against the Arab fleet in the Indian Ocean. The caravels used in exploration were not, then, the discarded tubs legend would have them, but the best designed ships the technology of the time could provide.

Societal Forces Toward Expansion

INDIVIDUAL MEN in sturdy ships explored, discovered, colonized, but their actions expressed the drives of their whole society. The development of a capitalistic society and strong central governments was a necessary precondition of Europe's outward thrust. Chinese junks were strong, seaworthy ships. At one point the emperor of China sent an expedition down the east coast of Africa, but after assembling animals, black men, and other curiosities, the ship returned to China without rounding the southern tip of the continent or otherwise following up on this promising beginning. The aggressive, competitive, acquisitive nature of Western society gave impetus to the drive for overseas expansion.

GOLD

Travelers' accounts of the fabulous wealth of the Indies and Cathay stirred the imagination of the Westerners. The 25 percent customs duties charged by the Mamelukes and the threat to trade routes posed by the Turks drove them to seek new routes to the Far East. Since the goods that the Europeans had to trade hardly compared with the value of the spices, silks, and other luxuries of the East, they were obliged to pay large amounts in gold and silver to acquire them. The need for precious metals led to intensified mining at home and the search for bonanzas abroad.

The arrival of Sudanese gold during the thirteenth century had aroused curiosity about the treasures of Africa. But the interest it stirred was mild compared with the gold fever that struck in the fifteenth and sixteenth centuries. During the reign of King Manuel I of Portugal (1495–1521) twelve ships were said to have arrived in Lisbon from Guinea laden with gold. The reports of gold attracted Flemish adventurers to the African coast and Italian and German bankers to Iberia. In 1459 the cortes in Lisbon indulged in a bit of xenophobia, urging Alfonso V to expel the Florentine bankers and other foreign parasites. But the monarchs usually brushed such nativism aside and protected and used the foreigners to their own advantage.

---

[6] J. H. Parry, *Europe and the Wider World, 1415–1715* (London, 1949), pp. 21–28.

SLAVES

Africa promised black gold as well—the lucrative slave trade. After the fall of Constantinople, the price of Eastern white and yellow slaves rose, and traders turned to Africa and its blacks. The Arabs had been trading in black slaves for some time, and now the Portuguese began shipping blacks to the European slave markets. It has been estimated that one to two thousand black slaves, bought from black slave dealers, were shipped out of Rio de Oro and Guinea between 1441 and 1448. During the next few years Portuguese slave traders shipped some 3,500 human beings as slaves from Senegal and Sierra Leone. From 1450 to 1505 a total of some 140,000 slaves was shipped out of Guinea alone.

Around 1460 a trader could get twenty-five or thirty slaves for a good Moroccan horse in Rio de Oro, although in Senegal he could get only ten or twelve. On the Gold Coast the tsetse fly made horses useless, so slaves were exchanged for woolen cloth instead. They were at first sold in Portugal, Spain, and Italy, but soon a new market opened up in the Spanish colonies across the Atlantic. In 1496 Ferdinand and Isabella forbade the sale of Indians and in 1500 forbade their importation to Spain. The truth was that Indians made poor slaves. In the hot lowlands of Spanish America they sickened and died in vast numbers under the harsh conditions of slavery, and in the cooler uplands, which in any case were less suited to slave labor, they disappeared into the mountains, where it was all but impossible to find and control them. And so Africans were shipped to the New World to work the new plantations.

COLONIZATION

The drive to colonize set in early, for large landowners, frustrated in attempts to expand in Europe, sought to aggrandize themselves abroad. In 1270 the Genoese Lancelot Malocello rediscovered the Canary Islands, which had been known to antiquity. In 1402 the Norman nobleman Jean de Béthancourt conquered three of the Canary Islands, built a church and a fortress, and placed himself under the protection of the Castilian throne. Three years later he brought 160 French colonists to settle his holdings and turn them into landed estates. Through the centuries that followed the European monarchs rewarded national heroes and court favorites with patents to landed estates in newly discovered lands, and poor townsmen and villagers flocked to seek their fortunes in the New World.

MISSIONS

In most men motives are curiously mixed. In the age of European expansion the missionary zeal of the high-minded, self-sacrificing mendicants was shared at least in some small part by the grossest and most secular materialists. It is a commonplace in histories of early modern Europe to describe the overseas expansion of Spain and Portugal as a natural extension of the Catholic crusade for the reconquest of Granada and the suppression of the Moors. But the reconquest of Portugal was completed by 1250, and a mission motive is more in evidence than a hateful crusading spirit as the Spaniards explored lands free of their old Islamic foes. The mendicant orders participated in the explorations and settlements from the very beginning. Their role can be seen as an extension of the thirteenth- and fourteenth-century missions to Asia. The spirit of St. Francis quickened the devotion of many devout Latin explorers as they literally went "into all the world."

The power of myth came into play in quickening the religious zeal of Catholics. The legend of Prester John stirred the imaginations of dreamers and offered hope to adventurers of receiving a friendly reception in some fabulously wealthy Christian kingdom in Africa or Asia. The belief that St. John, the "beloved disciple" of Christ, had not died, but had lived on in some lost corner of the world, presiding over a Christian realm, rested upon a popular interpretation of John 21:21–22:

> Peter seeing him [John] saith to Jesus, "Lord, and what shall this man do?"
> Jesus saith unto him, "If I will that he tarry till I come, what is that to thee? Follow thou me."

The story of Prester John's kingdom appeared in the chronicle of Otto of Freising and was very much alive in the fifteenth century. According to an early version, Prester John was the Christian emperor of Ethiopia. The emperor was invited to attend the Council of Florence in 1439 and his emissaries actually did arrive, though two years too late. Another account held that Prester John was king of a sub-Saharan realm, possibly in the Congo. Yet another variant was that he reigned as a potentate of a (Nestorian?) Christian state in India. In minds made feverish by Franciscan mysticism, the legend of Prester John found a ready reception.

MONARCHY

One very essential precondition of the age of European expansion was the development of powerful centralized monarchies. The transformed states of Portugal, Spain, France, and England took the lead in building empires overseas. The Italian city-states contributed skilled navigators, ancient learning, maps, instruments, and capital, but they did not play major roles in the unfolding drama. The Holy Roman Empire lost prestige and power relative to the rising Atlantic states. Its bankers provided capital for financing expeditions and its cities supplied learned geographers and astronomers, but it played no other part in the outreach to India or the discovery of America. The importance to exploration of the new monarchies is brought home forcefully by the work of Prince Henry the Navigator.

Henry the Navigator and Portuguese Voyages

THE PORTUGUESE completed the reconquest of their lands from the Moors more than two centuries before the Spaniards cleared their territories. But they had internal problems and trouble with their Spanish neighbors, so that they did not embark upon overseas adventures so promptly as they might have. In 1411 Portugal ended a twenty-year war with Castile and was thus at last freed for action. But the moving force and guiding spirit for its entrance upon the world scene was its young prince Henry, known as "the Navigator." An ascetic, scholarly youth, Henry (1394–1460) spent long hours in his secluded study and in his chapel. He was impelled by a great curiosity about this marvelous world and felt a missionary urge to Christianize it. Gomes Eanes de Zurara relates in his chronicle that Henry desired "to spread the holy faith of our Lord Jesus Christ and to lead all souls to it, who wish to be saved." Henry became the grand master of the Crusading Order of Christ.

Henry was a peculiar mixture of knight in shining armor and stay-at-home mission organizer. In 1415 he took part in King John I's capture of Ceuta, a Moorish stronghold across the Strait of Gibraltar. At twenty-one he was knighted on the battlefield. Ceuta was an important trade center for the Mauritanians, a marketplace for the sale of the wares of Africa and India. The city had palaces and other beautiful public buildings, and was said to have even more bazaars and warehouses than Venice. After plundering the city and slaughtering many of its inhabitants, the Portuguese made it the first overseas outpost of their mercantile empire. The use of Ceuta established the Portuguese pattern: a trade center would be captured, then held as a key to the mercantile nexus it served.

From the Arab traders Prince Henry learned of the precious metals and other treasures brought by caravans from the heart of Africa. It is doubtful that he thought primarily, if at all, of finding a new route to India as he sponsored the nearly annual expeditions down the west coast of Africa after 1415. At Sagres, east of Cape St. Vincent on the southwest coast of Portugal, Prince Henry assembled the best cartographers, geographers, and experienced seamen he could find and founded a school for navigators, from which the African explorations were directed. In 1434 one of his men, Gil Eannes, sailed around Cape Bojador. By 1445 his ships had discovered and colonized Madeira and the Azores, rounded Cape Verde, and pressed far down the coast of Africa. By 1471 the Portuguese caravels reached upper Guinea and began a profitable trade in gold, slaves, ivory, and precious woods. In 1483 they reached the Congo and Diago Cão set up a supply and trading post at the mouth of the river.

As the Portuguese voyaged farther and farther down the African coast, the problems of supply grew acute. When Bartolomeu Dias set out from Lisbon on his great expedition in 1487, he took along a storeship to supply his two caravels. About Christmastime he transferred supplies to the caravels and left the storeship and a few men behind in Walvis Bay. The caravels then sailed south, out of sight of land, until they reached 40 degrees south latitude, well beyond the southernmost point of Africa, where they picked up the prevailing westerly winds. Sailing then north and east in search of land, they struck the southern coast on February 3, 1488, having rounded the tip of Africa. They continued eastward until the north-ward trend of the coast was unmistakable, and warm-water currents indicated that the way to India lay open. But the crew and officers alike were weary of travel now and insisted on turning back. It was on the return voyage that they first sighted the cape that Dias named the Cape of Storms, which King John II later renamed the Cape of Good Hope. Farther north Dias picked up his storeship, with only three men on board still alive. The three ships arrived back in Lisbon in December 1488. Because of the reports of Columbus' success, the death of King John II in 1495, and Dias' discouraging reports of the contrary winds east of Africa, the rounding of the cape was followed up only a decade later when Vasco da Gama undertook his long voyage to India.

In *The Wealth of Nations* (1776) the political economist Adam Smith pro-nounced the discovery of America and the journey to India around the Cape of Good Hope the two most important developments of which human history had to tell. Vasco da Gama set sail in 1497. He was a diplomat-soldier rather than a pro-fessional navigator. His fleet of square-rigged ships, equipped with twenty cannon, was outfitted under the supervision of Dias, who accompanied him part of the way in a caravel. He set sail southwest from the Cape Verde Islands, crossed the equator, and then picked up the westerly trade winds, which carried him east again. After thirteen weeks at sea out of sight of land, he reached the coast of Africa about a hundred miles north of the Cape of Good Hope. He ran into the same trouble as Dias with storms at the cape, and then worked his way up the eastern coast. Owing to Arab influence, he was received in an unfriendly and even hostile manner in most ports. But at Malindi he was fortunate in gaining the services as pilot of Ahmed ibn Majid, a skillful navigator, who knew the Indian Ocean well. On May 20, 1498, the fleet anchored off Calicut on the Malabar coast—India at last!

Vasco da Gama began immediately to negotiate with the local ruler for per-mission to trade, which was vigorously opposed by the Arab merchants. But in spite of their hostility, and the fact that the cloth and hardware he had brought along to trade were of little interest to the Indians, he did manage to get together a cargo of pepper and cinnamon, with which he sailed for home. The entire voyage took two years and cost the lives of half his men, but the returns on the spices he brought back and the appreciation of King Manuel richly rewarded Vasco da Gama for his efforts.

Determined to follow up on this sensational success, King Manuel the Fortunate sent out a merchant-war fleet of thirteen ships under Pedro Álvarez Cabral in 1500. Bartolomeu Dias was a member of the expedition. They sailed to the southwest on the now proven theory that they needed to catch the westerlies south of the equator to round Africa. But they crossed the equator too far west of the Cape Verde meridian and ended up in Brazil, which Cabral claimed for his king. Caught in storms, Dias and the captains of three other ships were lost at sea. Cabral eventually rounded Cape Horn, crossed the Pacific, and reached Calicut, where his reception was anything but friendly. The Arab merchants stirred up a murderous mob against him, and forty of his men were killed. But at Cochin and Cannamore he was able to trade. When he returned to Lisbon, despite the loss of five ships, he made a 100 percent profit on the voyage.

In 1505 King Manuel appointed Francisco Almeida as first viceroy of East India. An ominous combination of foes was beginning to coalesce: the Arab traders, who feared the competition of the Portuguese; the Mamelukes of Egypt, who felt the loss of custom revenues on goods transported through Suez and Alexandria; and the merchants of Venice, who saw the lucrative eastern trade slipping through their fingers. Venetian spies in Lisbon sent word east so that Arab pirates could be ready to intercept Portuguese ships as they entered the Indian Ocean. In 1509 Almeida fought a naval battle with a large Arab fleet off Diu in the Mohammedan sultanate of Gudjarat. Portuguese gunners concentrated on sinking the Arab ships rather than on trying to grapple and board them or shoot down their men. The Arab ships lacked maneuverability and the Portuguese victory was decisive. Almeida and the able Alfonso d'Albuquerque, who succeeded him as viceroy, established the Portuguese empire in India and eastward.

Columbus and the Spanish Voyages

A WEATHER-BEATEN MARINER stood among the crowd watching the return of Dias to Lisbon in 1488. He was a widely traveled Genoese sailor named Christopher Columbus, who was already dreaming of surpassing Dias' feat. If he was not the first European to see the New World, his was the discovery that had the greatest consequences.

There are many theories about pre-Columbian explorations of the New World. There is a Chinese tale of a trans-Pacific expedition in the fifth century and there are advocates of Phoenician and African claims. But European claims have been

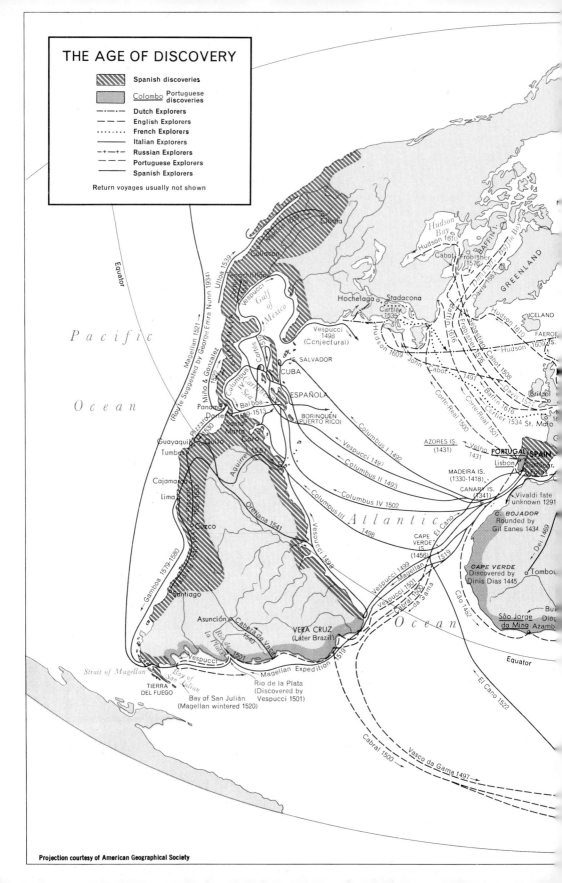

THE AGE OF DISCOVERY

Spanish discoveries

Colombo Portuguese discoveries

—·—·— Dutch Explorers

— — — English Explorers

········· French Explorers

———— Italian Explorers

—+—+— Russian Explorers

— — — Portuguese Explorers

———— Spanish Explorers

Return voyages usually not shown

Equator

Pacific

Ocean

Hudson
Bay
Hudson 1610

BAFFIN

Cabot Frobisher
1576

GREENLAND

ICELAND

FAEROE
IS.

Hudson 1610
1609 IS.

(Route Suggested by George Emra Nunn 1934)

Ulloa 1539

Miño & Gonzalez

Magellan 1521

Cíbola

Culiacan

Tenochtitlan

Vespucci

*Gulf
of
Mexico*

Cortés

Hochelaga
Stadacona
Cartier
1535

Vespucci
1498
(Conjectural)

Hudson 1609
John Cabot

Cartier
1535

Sebastian Cabot 1508

Baffin 1616

Frobisher 1576

Davis 1581

Hudson

S. SALVADOR
CUBA

ESPAÑOLA

Cortés

Columbus
IV
Caribbean
Sea

Panama
Darien
Balboa
1509–1513

BORINQUÉN
(PUERTO RICO)

Corte-Real 1500

Corte-Real 1501

Cartier 1534 St. Malo

Bristol

Davis 1585

Santa
Marta
Coro

Guayaquil
Quito
Tumbez

Aguirre

Columbus I 1492

Vespucci 1497

Columbus II 1493

Columbus IV 1502

Columbus III
1498

AZORES IS.
(1431)

Velho
1431

PORTUGAL SPAIN
Lisbon Sanlúcar
1519

Cajamarca

Pizarro 1530

MADEIRA IS.
(1330–1418)

CANARY IS.
(1341)

Vivaldi fate
unknown 1291

Lima

Cuzco

Orellana 1541

Vespucci 1499

El Cano

C. BOJADOR
Rounded by
Gil Eanes 1434

Diel 1469

CAPE
VERDE
IS.
(1456)

1519

Atlantic

CAPE VERDE
Discovered by
Dinis Dias 1445

Tombou

Gamboa 1579–1580

Santiago

Vespucci 1499

Magellan 1501

Vespucci 1501

Cabral 1500

da Gama

Cão 1482

São Jorge
da Mina

Bu
Dio
Azamb

Ocean

Asunción
Cabeza de Vaca
1540

Rio de la Plata

VERA CRUZ
(Later Brazil)

1519

Equator

Vespucci

Magellan Expedition

Strait of Magellan

Bay of
San Julian

TIERRA
DEL FUEGO

Rio de la Plata 1501

Rio de la Plata
(Discovered by
Vespucci 1501)

El Cano 1522

Bay of San Julián
(Magellan wintered 1520)

Cabral 1500

Vasco da Gama 1497

El Cano 1522

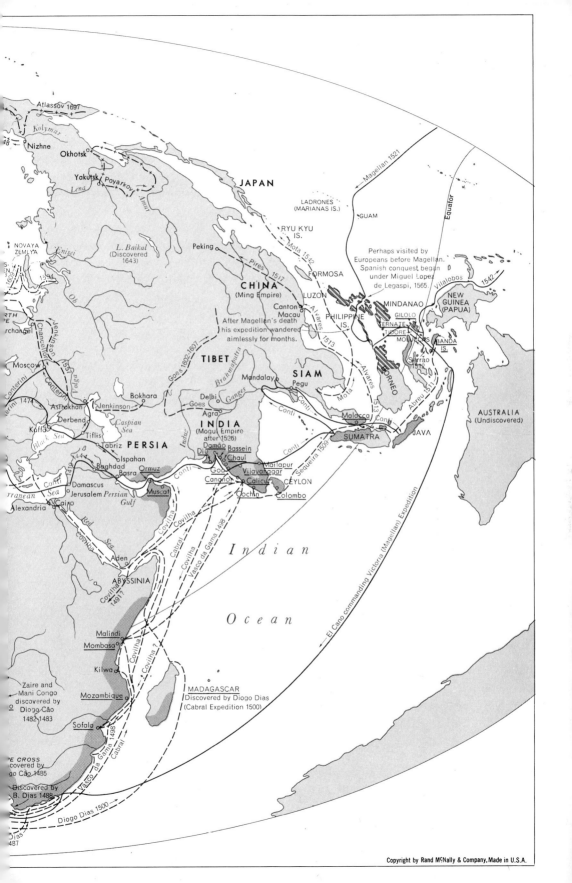

Atlassov 1697
Kolyma
Nizhne
Okhotsk
Yakutsk
Poyarkov
Lena
Amur

NOVAYA
ZEMLYA
Enisei
Ob

JAPAN

LADRONES
(MARIANAS IS.)
GUAM

Magellan 1521

Equator

RYU KYU
IS.

Mota 1542

Peking

Pires 1517

FORMOSA

Perhaps visited by
Europeans before Magellan.
Spanish conquest began
under Miguel Lopez
de Legaspi, 1565.

Vitalobos 1542

NEW
GUINEA
(PAPUA)

CHINA
(Ming Empire)

Canton
Macau

LUZON

Alvares 1513

MINDANAO
GILOLO
TERNATE
TIDORE

PHILIPPINE
IS.

MOLUCCAS
BANDA
IS.

After Magellan's death
his expedition wandered
aimlessly for months.

Goes 1602-1607

TIBET

Brahmaputra
Mandalay

SIAM
Pegu

BORNEO

Serrão
1512

Abreu 1511

L. Baikal
(Discovered
1643)

Moscow

Conterini
Conterini 1474

Astrakhan
Derbend
Koffa
Black Sea
Tiflis
Tabriz PERSIA
Ispahan
Baghdad
Basra Ormuz
Damascus
Jerusalem Persian
Cairo Gulf
Alexandria

Jenkinson

Bokhara

Delhi
Goes
Agra

INDIA
(Mogul Empire
after 1526)
Damão
Diu Bassein
Chaul
Goa Mailapur
Canano Vijayanagar
Calicut
Cochin
Colombo

Ganges

Conti

Conti

Malacca

SUMATRA

JAVA

CEYLON

Sequeira 1509

Conti

AUSTRALIA
(Undiscovered)

Caspian
Sea

Mediterranean Sea
Red Sea

Conti

Covilha
Covilha
Cabral
Vasco da Gama 1498
Covilha

Indian

Ocean

El Cano commanding Victoria (Magellan) Expedition

Aden

ABYSSINIA
Covilha
1497?

Malindi
Mombasa
Covilha ?
Kilwa

Covilha ?

Zaire and
Mani Congo
discovered by
Diogo Cão
1482-1483

Mozambique

MADAGASCAR
Discovered by Diogo Dias
(Cabral Expedition 1500)

Sofala

Vasco da Gama 1498
Cabral

PE CROSS
covered by
go Cão 1485

Discovered by
B. Dias 1488

Diogo Dias 1500

Dias
487

taken most seriously. Certain islands on Battista Beccario's map of 1435 were once thought to represent the Antilles, but it was later decided that they were the Azores, moved west. Martin Behaim, the geographer, reported a voyage of western discovery in 1415. A claimant for Portuguese priority alleges that Portuguese sailors reached Newfoundland in 1452. A Copenhagen scholar tried to demonstrate that the Danes visited America around 1472–1474. But the Portuguese and Danish advocates lack any tenable evidence.[7]

On the other hand, material evidence for the claims of an earlier Viking exploration is building up in an impressive fashion. The Norse sagas relate how a party led by Bjarni Herjulfson was driven off course while sailing from Iceland to Greenland around the year 986. Blown west and south, they saw a wooded shore, and during subsequent days saw land repeatedly. They made no landing, but when they had made their way back to Greenland they recounted their experiences to Bjarni's friend Eric the Red and his son Leif. Around 992 Leif Ericson set out in Bjarni's ship with thirty-five men to search for the coast Bjarni had seen. They came first to Helluland (Stoneland), then sailed south till they came to an inviting wooded land. They found many wild grapes, and so named the new land Vinland. Fish and game were plentiful. After wintering there, they returned to Greenland. The Norsemen, including Leif's brother Thorwald, made several subsequent voyages to the New World in the years—perhaps centuries—that followed. As recently as 1963 archeologists discovered the remains of a Norse settlement in Newfoundland. A 1440 map now in Yale University's library shows North America and refers to the expeditions of Bjarni and Leif Ericson. Though the map has its critics, it seems to be authentic. The Kensington Stone, found on a Minnesota farm in 1898, bearing runes that purport to tell of a Norse expedition from Vinland into the interior, has been discredited. In any case, no Norse settlement led to permanent colonization or changed the history of the world. The honor for this must go to Columbus.

Sources for the first forty-one years of Columbus' life are very sparse and are questioned on nearly every point. He was born in Genoa in 1451, the son of a wool weaver, Domenico Colombo. A Spanish historian has recently asserted that the family name, Colón in Spanish, is Jewish, and that his parents were probably Spanish Jews who emigrated to Genoa. Another theory, recently advanced by the Spanish historian Fernando del Valle Lersundi, is that Columbus was the nephew of the French Basque freebooter Guillaume de Casenove-Coullon, a vice-admiral of Louis XI. Casenove-Coullon may well have been a relative, for Columbus is said to have fought under him in the service of Portugal against a fleet of Genoese ships off Cape St. Vincent, near Lisbon, in August 1476—an incident that, if true, certainly suggests no patriotic ties to Genoa. Other sources claim that he was fighting with

---

[7] Charles E. Nowell, "The Columbus Question," *American Historical Review,* 44 (1939):802–22.

the Genoese. At least there is agreement that he was there. Columbus' second son, Ferdinand, born to Beatriz Enríquez de Arana, a Spanish woman with whom Columbus had a love affair, wrote a biography of his father which was published in Venice some thirty-two years after Columbus' death, but its authenticity has been questioned on the ground that it may have been largely written by Luis de Colón, Columbus' dishonest grandson. The account of Columbus' life written by the Spanish bishop Bartolomé de Las Casas in his *Historia de las Indias* agrees with Ferdinand's biography, but there is no way of knowing whether this agreement brings Las Casas into question or supports Ferdinand. Enough has been said to suggest that we are far less well informed about Columbus than we would like to be. The great authority on naval history Cecil Jane thought Columbus to be illiterate at least as late as 1492, but this seems very unlikely, for he was a well-traveled man, could converse effectively with kings and scholars, and had a collection of very learned books, so that if he learned to read after forty, he must have been remarkably talented.

Although Columbus began as an apprentice in his father's shop, at fourteen he took to the sea. His first voyages were in the Mediterranean, but he soon sailed into the Atlantic. In the battle off Cape St. Vincent his ship was lost and he clung to an oar until he reached land. The fact that he was not detained suggests that he was probably not fighting on the side of Genoa. He made his way to Lisbon, where his brother Bartolomé had settled and had a small shop in which he sold maps. Columbus signed up shortly thereafter with a Portuguese ship that sailed north to England or Ireland; some sources say Iceland. He may also have sailed south to Africa on a Portuguese trading vessel. In 1478 he married a Portuguese woman, who bore his first son, Diego.

During this period of his life Columbus thought out his plan to reach the Far East by sailing west. One cannot with certainty establish that the books in the Columbus library in Seville which bear careful marginal notations in Spanish in the hands of the Columbus brothers were actually read prior to 1492, but it seems likely that he would have studied the authorities before rather than after his voyage. He knew Ptolemy's theories about the small circumference of the earth and the great extension of Asia eastward. He annotated Marco Polo's *Travels* in detail and thought the great island of Cipangu to be located about where Florida actually is. He also annotated extensively Cardinal Pierre d'Ailly's *Imago mundi*. A very controversial matter is the business of the Toscanelli letters. The learned Florentine humanist, physician, and geographer Paolo Toscanelli (1397–1482) prepared a map of the world and sent it with an accompanying letter to the Portuguese cardinal Fernâs Martins de Roriz. The letter tells of the islands on the way to Guinea and the way across the ocean to "India and the islands." Martins may have handed it on to Columbus, for when Ferdinand was preparing his father's biography, he found it among his papers. Ferdinand claimed that Toscanelli had sent a duplicate of this letter to Columbus. In any case, if Columbus did see it prior to 1492, Toscanelli's message must merely have reinforced an opinion he already held. A second "Toscanelli letter" is clearly forged.

Columbus' motivation was primarily glory and gold, but many of his statements suggest that he was also a religious visionary with a sense of mission. He once wrote to the Spanish monarchs that whoever has gold can do what he wants in the world, and can even bring souls into paradise. He invested in his own voyage, paying an eighth of its costs, which he borrowed from Italian bankers in Seville and from the Pinzón brothers, seamen and shipowners of Palos, who had befriended and encouraged him when it seemed no one would back the voyage he proposed. He offered to send the Spanish rulers as many Indians as they should demand, and actually did several times send Indians for sale as slaves. On the other hand, he had a considerable measure of Catholic piety. According to Las Casas, he was "especially devoted to the honor of St. Francis." He spoke of "Prester John of India." He wrote of his first voyage that he wished to tell about the princes and people of India in order to show how to "spread our most holy faith abroad there." Before his second voyage the Spanish rulers instructed him to be concerned about bringing "the inhabitants of the named islands and lands in all ways and by every means to the point of converting to our holy Catholic faith." He suggested that the Catholic monarchs could use the profit from the Indian spice trade to finance a crusade for the liberation of Jerusalem. Perhaps misled by older maps that showed Jerusalem at the center of the world, he believed that if he kept going west, he could arrive at Jerusalem and strike at the Moslems from behind. It is impossible to tell how much of all this was conventional piety and how much was personal zeal.

Columbus was completely obsessed by his great idea and carried it to the thrones of Portugal and Spain. King John II of Portugal heard him patiently and sympathetically, then referred the matter to a commission for study. When the commission reported unfavorably, the king dismissed him. In Spain Queen Isabella granted him an audience. She received him graciously and listened sympathetically, but then she too referred the matter to a commission, which also reported unfavorably. The Spanish monarchs, however, were intrigued by the dream and fascinated by the earnest conviction of Columbus. Since Portugal could claim control of the eastward route to India, a westward route seemed to be Spain's only chance of sharing in the wealth to be found there. Ferdinand and Isabella put him on a pension to hold him in Spain until they were in a position to do something further about his project. Years passed, but when in January 1492 they completed the conquest of Granada, they were free to take up Columbus' project again. They decided in his favor.

On August 3, 1492, Columbus set sail from Palos as admiral of a fleet of three ships: the flagship *Santa María,* under Columbus; the *Pinta,* under Martín Alonso Pinzón, with Martín's brother Francisco as pilot; and the *Niña,* under another

Pinzón brother, Vicente. They sailed to the Canary Islands and then headed straight west. Columbus used an astrolabe, a quadrant, and a compass as navigational aids, and he proved to be an expert sailor. The complement of ninety men was not the crew of criminals and cutthroats of legend, but able and experienced seamen who had fallen on hard times and hoped to win or recoup their fortunes. But their faith in Columbus' great idea began to fail after several weeks at sea with no sight of land, and on October 10 they demanded and received Columbus' promise that if they did not sight land within three days, they would turn back. Two days later Rodrigo de Triana on the *Pinta* sighted land. The island was very likely the one known today as Watling Island. That very morning Columbus dressed in his finest and, accompanied by the Pinzón brothers and most of the crew, carried ashore the flag of Spain. They knelt upon the shore, kissed the ground with tears of joy, gave thanks to God for the great mercy received, named the island San Salvador, and took possession of it in the names of Ferdinand and Isabella.

When they reached Cuba, Columbus believed he had reached China, and sent a party ashore to greet the great khan. When he was not to be found, the expedition sailed on and next discovered Hispaniola, the island now divided by Haiti and the Dominican Republic. On November 21 the *Pinta* disappeared before a strong wind, and on Christmas Day the *Santa María* was wrecked on a reef, so Columbus decided to return to Spain with news of his discovery and as many of the men and stores as he could crowd aboard the *Niña*. The rest—some forty men—were left behind to establish a settlement called Villa de la Navidad (Christmastown).

On the return voyage the *Pinta* was sighted, and although the two ships were later separated again, both of them arrived back in Palos on the same day, March 15, 1493. Five days later Martín Pinzón died.

Columbus' reception by the Spanish court in Barcelona was all he could desire. He displayed his trophies—six Indians, gold trinkets, cotton, unknown plants and birds, and other curiosities—and received from Ferdinand and Isabella the titles of Admiral of the Ocean Sea and Viceroy of the Indies, a coat of arms bearing royal symbols, and wealth appropriate to these honors.

On September 25, 1493, he set sail on his second voyage with three galleons, fourteen caravels, and a complement of 1,500 men. The search for China in the West Indies continued to be fruitless. He found the settlement of La Navidad wiped out, and established a new settlement at another site on Hispaniola. After sailing among the islands for two and a half years, accomplishing little beyond the stirring up of anger among the Spaniards and the enmity of the Indians, he returned to Spain in 1496 and was kindly received by the Spanish monarchs.

On his third voyage, in 1498, he reached the mainland of South America, but, still clinging to the illusion that Cuba was the Chinese mainland, decided that this was Marco Polo's great island to the southeast, and without exploring further sailed back to his colony on Hispaniola. The complaints of the colonists reached the ears of the monarchs back in Spain and Columbus lost favor, especially with Ferdinand. The king appointed a new governor, Francisco de Bobadilla, who arrived in Hispaniola on August 23, 1500, to find Columbus and his brothers Bartolomé and Diego engaged in hanging those Spaniards who were displeased with Columbus' rule. Bobadilla freed the prisoners not yet hanged and returned the Columbus brothers to Spain in irons.

But by the time Columbus appeared in court on December 17, 1500, the tide had turned once more in his favor, and he was received with honor. On his third voyage he had heard of the ocean to the west of Panama, and now he persuaded the monarchs to send him on a fourth voyage to find a passage through the "islands" to the sea beyond. On May 9, 1502, he sailed with four caravels and 150 men. After profitless reconnoitering in the Caribbean and a fruitless attempt to found a colony, he returned in November 1504 for the last time, ill and disoriented. On May 20, 1506, he died without ever realizing the magnitude of his accomplishment. Unable to admit his failure to find Asia, he could not appreciate his achievement in discovering a new world. After many removals and reinterments, he now lies buried in the cathedral of Seville.

In May 1493 the Spanish pope Alexander VI, at the urging of Ferdinand and Isabella, laid down a line of demarcation between the Portuguese and Spanish possessions. He gave the Spaniards everything that lay one hundred leagues or nautical miles "west of the islands of the green foothills," or the Cape Verde Islands and the Azores. Portugal was less than happy with this demarcation, and opened direct negotiations with Spain. These negotiations culminated in 1494 in the Treaty of Tordesillas, which moved the line to 370 leagues west of the Cape Verde Islands. They were thinking less of dividing up the newly discovered land than of defining and limiting the two ways to India—south and east for Portugal, west for Spain. Effectively this secured Brazil to Portugal and the rest of the New World to Spain.

So great is the fame of Columbus that other illustrious men and glorious deeds are sometimes forgotten. Thus Amerigo Vespucci (1451–1512), a Florentine merchant sent to Spain as a Medici agent around 1491, became inspired by Columbus and in 1497 joined an expedition to the Indies, serving as navigator. In 1499 and 1500 he sailed along the coast of Central and South America until he reached the Amazon. In 1501 he sailed again, this time with a Portuguese expedition. In a series of letters written in 1504 he described these lands as a continent, as though he fully realized the true nature of the discovery. It is not entirely unfair, then, that the New World came to be known as America rather than Columbia. In 1507 Martin Waldseemüller, a German cartographer, published Vespucci's letters in Latin in a volume entitled *Introduction to Cosmography*. On a map of the newly discovered lands he labeled the South American continent "America," a name that came very quickly to be used for North America as well.

Other explorers followed, notably Vasco Núñez de Balboa, who crossed the Isthmus of Panama and in 1513 discovered the Pacific Ocean. Ferdinand Magellan, a Portuguese navigator in the employ of Spain, set sail westward in 1519 on a journey that led to the circumnavigation of the globe. He passed through the straits at the southern end of South America and sailed across the Pacific. Unfortunately he was killed by the natives of the islands later named the Philippines, in honor of the Spanish king Philip II, but one of his ships sailed on and finally arrived home again. There could now be no doubt about the nature of Columbus' discovery. Moreover, Europeans now had a clear idea of the size of the earth and the relation of the major continents to each other. By a treaty in 1529 Spain took possession of the Philippines but confirmed the Portuguese claim to the Moluccas or Spice Islands.

The Spaniards' first attempts at colonization were very modest, but with the adventures on the mainland of such *conquistadores* as Hernán Cortés, Francisco Pizarro, and Juan Ponce de León, Spanish overseas expansion entered a new phase of conquest and colonialism.

The Ancient and the New Worlds

IN THE DAYS when Jacob Burckhardt's description of the rediscovery of the world and of man in the age of the Renaissance was still taken quite literally, it was possible to see the voyages of discovery as but one more expression of the spirit of the Renaissance. Yet it is quite obvious that the contributions of Italy, the home of the Renaissance, were very modest compared with those of "medieval" Portugal and Spain. The humanists helped to revitalize the knowledge of the ancients and enthusiasm for their learning, but the texts crucial for exploration, such as those of Ptolemy, owed scarcely anything to the humanists for their great influence, nor did the technological advances that made it possible. Much more important were the societal factors, the economic drives of a competitive capitalism, the expansive impulses of the national dynasties, the missionary drive still operative in the kingdoms of Iberia. Italy supplied mapmakers and navigators, Vespucci and Columbus, but they had to make their fortunes with the Portuguese and Spaniards.

The new discoveries caused some stir, but in retrospect it seems strange that those sensational finds did not arouse greater excitement than they did. It was more than a century before the full implications of the new geography and ethnography were fully appreciated. Engrossed in their studies of the ancient world, some of the most powerful intellects of the day scarcely took note of the new. Yet a few did get into the spirit of the modern world. The Italian humanist Pietro Martire d'Anghiera exclaimed, "What has been done and written since the beginning of the world is still little, as I see it, when we compare it with these new lands and seas, those manifold peoples and languages, those treasures of precious metals and discoveries of pearls!"[8] But Pietro had already emigrated to Spain and had no intention of ever returning to Italy.

On May 4, 1503, Johann Kollauer, royal secretary to Emperor Maximilian and member of the Augsburg sodality of northern humanists, wrote a letter from Antwerp to Conrad Celtis, the German humanist who was titular head of the Rhenish and Danubian sodalities, about the exciting reports he had heard from Portuguese sailors who had returned from voyages of discovery, and urged Celtis to join him there so he could hear for himself of the wonders of the New World from men who had actually seen them. But Celtis was no more interested in the New World than were Marsilio Ficino, Niccolò Machiavelli, Desiderius Erasmus, or Martin Luther.

Bibliography

Abbott, W. C. *The Expansion of Europe,* 2 vols. New York, 1918.

Arciniegas, Germán. *Amerigo and the New World.* New York, 1955.

Baker, J. N. L. *A History of Geographical Discovery and Exploration.* London, 1931.

Baker, Nina. *Amerigo Vespucci.* New York, 1957.

Beazley, C. R. *Prince Henry the Navigator.* New York, 1894.

———. *The Dawn of Modern Geography,* 3 vols. London, 1897–1906.

Blake, J. W. *European Beginnings in West Africa, 1454–1578.* New York, 1937.

Boxer, Charles. *Four Centuries of Portuguese Expansion, 1415–1825.* Johannesburg, 1961.

Cipolla, C. *Guns and Sails in the Early Phase of European Expansion, 1400–1700.* London, 1965.

Hakluyt, R. *The Principal Navigations, Voyages, Traffiques, and Discoveries of the English Nation,* 3 vols. London, 1599–1600.

Hart, Henry H. *Sea Road to the Indies.* London, 1952.

———. *Marco Polo: Venetian Adventurer.* Norman, Okla., 1967.

Hay, Denys. *Europe: The Emergence of an Idea.* Edinburgh, 1957.

Heers, J., et al. *Les grandes voies maritimes dans le monde (XVᵉ–XIXᵉ siècles).* Paris, 1965.

Jane, Cecil, trans. *The Journal of Christopher Columbus.* New York, 1960.

Jensen, De Lamar, ed. *The Expansion of Europe: Motives, Methods, and Theory.* Boston, 1967.

Morison, Samuel E. *Portuguese Voyages to America in the Fifteenth Century.* Cambridge, Mass., 1940.

———. *Admiral of the Ocean Sea: A Life of Christopher Columbus,* 2 vols. Boston, 1942.

---

[8] Konetzke, "Überseeische Entdeckungen," p. 538.

NEWTON, A. P., ed. *The Great Age of Discovery*. London, 1932.

PARRY, JOHN H. *The Spanish Theory of Empire in the Sixteenth Century*. Cambridge, 1940.

———. *The Establishment of the European Hegemony, 1415–1715*. New York, 1961.

———. *The Age of Reconnaissance*. Cleveland, 1963.

———. *The Spanish Seaborne Empire*. New York, 1966.

PENROSE, BOIES. *Travel and Discovery in the Renaissance, 1420–1620*. Cambridge, Mass., 1952.

POHL, F. H. *Amerigo Vespucci, Pilot Major*. New York, 1944.

PRESTAGE, E. *The Portuguese Pioneers*. London, 1933.

SANCEAU, E. *Henry the Navigator*. New York, 1947.

SAUER, C. *The Early Spanish Main*. Berkeley, 1966.

SCHWOEBEL, ROBERT. *The Shadow of the Crescent: The Renaissance Image of the Turk, 1453–1517*. Nieuwkoop, 1967.

WILLIAMSON, J. A. *Maritime Enterprise, 1485–1558*. New York, 1913.

———. *The Voyages of the Cabots and the English Discovery of North America Under Henry VII and Henry VIII*. London, 1929.

CHAPTER 11

Humanism
Beyond Italy

"Thank God we are out of the Gothic night!" exclaimed François Rabelais, the French wit and humanist. It took northern Europe longer than southern Europe to emerge from medievalism precisely because the Gothic culture was northern. Gothic architecture and scholastic philosophy had to be artificially introduced into Italy, and that very late. Conversely, the Renaissance, based on a revival of classical learning, could hardly have occurred spontaneously in a land where classical learning had never flourished. In the lands that had once been the northern provinces of the Roman Empire and in the other areas that had lain beyond the borders of ancient Rome, there was less a genuine renaissance in the fifteenth and sixteenth centuries than the development of a humanist literary culture and some artistic adaptation. It seems more appropriate to speak of northern humanism than of a northern renaissance.

Social change came slowly to northern and western Europe, and urbanization was limited in comparison with the growth of cities in northern and central Italy. The feudal nobility was not so easily absorbed into the moneyed mercantile class in other areas as it was in Italy; it retained its hereditary cast and social status longer in the wooded north. As the military and political power of the feudal lords ebbed away, they clung all the more tenaciously to their traditional way of life.

The northern humanists poured scorn upon the nobles who took greater pleasure in drink and the hunt than in learned discourse and books. The rich merchants of the northern cities adapted themselves to the literary standards of the feudal aristocracy, preferring chivalric romances and lyrics to classical works or humanist writings. Moralizing treatises, golden legends, lives of saints, and other traditional materials suited the taste of the provincial nobility and of the urban middle class. Even after the invention of the printing press, many of the books issued in the second half of the fifteenth century were of the chivalric and devotional kind. But that half century saw the beginnings of the new humanist culture as well.

"A man who has not been in Italy," Dr. Samuel Johnson pronounced three centuries later, "is always conscious of an inferiority." He was reflecting a convention of high society formed during the Renaissance. In 1549 the English author William Thomas commented in his *History of Italy* on the number of foreigners in that country, "specially of gentlemen, whose resort thither is principally under pretense of study." During the late fifteenth and the sixteenth centuries there was a two-way traffic of men and ideas. Italian humanists and artists traveled north as diplomatic emissaries, ecclesiastical legates, secretaries to northern princes and cities, lecturers in the universities, or business representatives. Northerners went to Italy either as students, primarily of law and medicine, or simply as admirers of the learned Italians, whose wisdom they hoped to absorb.

As capitalism grew and the cities of the north developed, an atmosphere more congenial to humanist culture evolved. The princes and courts gradually learned to admire the elegance of the Italian Renaissance courts, the wit and charm of their ladies, and the skill of their humanist chancellors in diplomacy and domestic politics. Even the ecclesiastical potentates, the prince-bishops, began to emulate the fashions of Italian courts and churchmen. Humanism, promoted by poets and orators, began at last to penetrate even the universities.

Once humanist culture began to take hold in the north, enthusiasm for the classics sometimes went wild. When a second-rate Italian humanist, Aleander, gave a series of lectures on a third-rate Roman poet, Ausonius, in Paris one hot summer, two thousand culture seekers listened for two and a half hours to his initial lecture, and on the third day the house was packed at eleven for a lecture that was not scheduled to start until one. But humanist culture was not the same in northern Europe as in Italy, for humanism fused with the indigenous cultures of the various peoples that embraced it, producing in each area a unique cultural amalgam.

There might very well have been an efflorescence of culture in northern Europe in the late fifteenth and early sixteenth centuries even without Italian influence. The Hundred Years' War over, relative peace returned. As trade expanded, the urban centers prospered and an economic base strong enough to support higher culture developed. But even more important than political and economic factors was the emergence in the north of an educational movement of major importance.

The Brethren of the Common Life, founded by Gerard Groote (d. 1384), were concerned essentially with deepening inward religious faith and with cultivating practical Christian living, but they saw education as the major instrument for promoting these concerns. They established schools, opened hospices for indigent students in university towns, and operated printing presses for the publishing of devotional literature, grammars and textbooks, Bibles, and the moral treatises of classical philosophers. Since they found the "safe classics," such as the ethical treatises of Cicero and Seneca, to be of great value in instructing the young and favored a pure Latin style, they became instrumental in promoting a classical revival in the north. The houses of the Brethren spread from Deventer and Zwolle in the Netherlands along the Rhine through Westphalia, Hesse, and Württemberg, and along the North and Baltic seas into Saxony and as far as Kulm. Many famous men of letters were either directly educated or supported by them. Alexander Hegius (1433-1498), the learned master at Deventer, was a friend and correspondent of Agricola and the teacher of Erasmus. But while there might well have been a flowering of culture in those decades in any case, without Italian influence it would not have taken the classical form it did.

German Humanism

IN THE YEAR 1507 Nicholas Gerbellius, a young humanist, wrote, "I congratulate myself often on living in this glorious century in which so many remarkable men have arisen in Germany." The first two decades of the sixteenth century marked the high tide of German humanism. The new culture came earlier to the Germanies than to the other countries of the north. There were many close political ties between the empire and Italy, and a lively trade prospered between the Italian cities and the German cities along the Danube and the Rhine. The old medieval tradition of student wandering brought literally thousands of German students to the Italian universities each year. The "German nations" at the universities of Bologna, Padua, and Pavia were large and active. The transition from wandering student to roving humanist was not hard to make.

PIONEERS AND MORALISTS

The migratory birds of German humanism appeared in the north during the second half of the fifteenth century. Peter Luder (*c.* 1415–1474) was a typical pioneer of the movement. He went as a cleric to Rome, wandered around Italy, and joined the German students in Padua. In 1444 the elector of the Palatinate appointed him a lecturer in classical languages and literature at the University of Heidelberg. An aggressive, free-wheeling, hard-drinking man, Luder battled conservative professors for a larger place in the curriculum for classical rhetoric and poetry. A combination of academic hostility and the plague drove him away from Heidelberg, and he returned to study medicine in Italy and later taught at Basel and Vienna. Besides loose-living poets such as Luder, there were schoolteacher humanists like Johannes Murmellius and Rudolf von Langen, scholastic humanists like Conrad Summenhart and Paul Scriptoris, and moralistic critics of society like Heinrich Bebel and Jacob Wimpfeling.

Jacob Wimpfeling (1450–1528), the cathedral preacher at Speyer, stood in an ambivalent relationship to Italian humanism, for he admired classical form but disliked pagan morals. Invited to join the Rhenish sodality of humanists, he responded with the shy demurrer that he would only be a crow among nightingales or an owl among falcons. He attacked simony and concubinage, and his major work, *De integritate,* was designed to help priests learn to abhor the pernicious love of women. As an Alsatian, Wimpfeling was a strong German patriot, and he warned against the designs of the French king on the pearl of the empire. He founded in Schlettstadt a small sodality of humanists. Two of his friends, Sebastian Brant (1457–1521) and Johann Geiler von Kaisersberg (1445–1510), were the same sort of reformers. Brant's popular book of satiric poetry, *The Ship of Fools,* holds up to ridicule lazy students, pedantic professors, and the high and the mighty. Geiler von Kaisersberg, a powerful penitential preacher, carried the same earnest message to the people from the pulpit.

RUDOLF AGRICOLA

Rudolf Agricola (1444–1485) was clearly the most important representative of the older generation. "It was Rudolf Agricola," Erasmus declared, "who first brought with him from Italy some gleam of a better literature." He believed that "Agricola could have been the first in Italy had he not preferred Germany." Agricola's power lay not in his pen, but in his personality. He wrote relatively little, but he inspired many younger humanists, especially at Heidelberg, and became a symbol of the new wave of humanism.

Born near Groningen in Frisia, Agricola studied at Erfurt, Louvain, and Cologne. He spent ten years in Italy, from 1469 to 1479, and while there wrote a *Life of Petrarch* to honor the "father and restorer of good arts." "We are indebted to Petrarch for the intellectual culture of our century," he wrote. "All ages owe him a debt of gratitude—antiquity for having rescued its treasure from oblivion and modern times for having with his own strength founded and revived culture, which he has left as a precious legacy to future ages." Drawn homeward in 1479, he found, as Albrecht Dürer was to do when he returned from Italy, that he "froze after the sun." He lamented to Alexander Hegius that he was losing his capacity for thought and ornamented style. His spirit would not respond.

Bishop Johannes von Dalberg and the Palatine elector brought Agricola to

Heidelberg, where he presided informally over a circle of young humanists. "I have the brightest hope," he said, "that we shall one day wrest from haughty Italy the reputation for classical expression which it has nearly monopolized, so to speak, and lay claim to it ourselves, and free ourselves from the reproach of ignorance and being called unlearned and inarticulate barbarians; and that our Germany will be so cultured and literate that Latium will not know Latin any better." His major work was an introductory manual, *On Dialectical Invention*, primarily intended for teachers in the arts, in which he sought to demonstrate that the true function of logic, as an element basic to rhetoric, was to produce conviction through straight thinking and effective style.

CONRAD CELTIS

Among Agricola's disciples at Heidelberg was a young student named Conrad Celtis, who became the best lyric poet among the German humanists. Celtis (1459–1508), a runaway son of a peasant, studied at Cologne, Heidelberg, Rostock, and Leipzig.

On April 18, 1487, Emperor Frederick III crowned Celtis the first German poet laureate of the empire at Nuremberg. "O sacred and mighty work of the poets," Celtis declaimed, "you alone free all things from fate and lift up mortal ashes to the stars!" In the four volumes of his *Amores* he celebrated four of his loves, symbolizing the four parts of Germany. In his *Odes* he wrote eloquently of life, love, and learning. From Cicero and Horace he learned the sophist-rhetorical theory of the art of poetry as a passionate and rousing power, the motif of poetic madness and intoxication. He liked to think of himself as a *vates*, a term restored to favor by Virgil, meaning a poet-philosopher, a prophet or sage.

Later in 1487 he crossed the Alps for a rapid trip through Italy, visiting Venice, Padua, Bologna, Florence, and Rome. After unpleasant encounters with the "superior" Italians, he hurried back to Cracow, where he studied mathematics and poetry, and moved on from there to Nuremberg and then to Ingolstadt, where he became a professor of rhetoric.

In his inaugural address at the University of Ingolstadt he summoned his fellow Germans to cultural rivalry with Italy. "Take up again, O German men," he cried, "that old spirit of yours with which you so many times were a terror and specter to the Romans!" Romantic cultural nationalism was one of the major themes of German humanism. To demonstrate that the Germans too had a literary past, he published the plays of Roswitha, a tenth-century nun of Gondersheim, and the epic poem *Ligurinus* in praise of Frederick Barbarossa. Celtis organized the Rhenish and Danubian sodalities, loose associations of local societies of humanists which sprang up under his aegis in Linz, Ingolstadt, Augsburg, and other cities, and recruited their members as contributors to his *Germany Illustrated,* a topographical-historical work modeled on Biondo's *Italy Illustrated* and on his own *Norimberga,* which described the past and present glories of Nuremberg.

In 1497 he accepted Emperor Maximilian's invitation to the University of Vienna. There he founded the College of Poets and Mathematicians, wrote poems and plays, and taught until he died of syphilis at the age of forty-nine. He was buried in St. Stephen's Cathedral.

COURTS AND CITIES

By 1520 humanism had penetrated the courts of Germany to a much greater extent than historians have realized. This was true not only of the imperial Habsburg courts in Linz and Vienna, but of the courts of the many territorial princes and the powerful ecclesiastical prince-bishops in Mainz, Trier, and Cologne. The advantages of having a skilled Latinist as secretary and a rhetorician as orator came to be recognized, and with the introduction of Roman law, legists who coupled a humanist interest in letters with a knowledge of civil law became commonplace.

Aeneas Silvius Piccolomini spent the years 1442 to 1445 at the court of Emperor Frederick III (1440–1492) as the emissary of Pope Eugenius IV. His description of Germany, blessed by the presence of the Roman church, helped to kindle national pride among the German humanists, while Sabellicus and other Italians who ridiculed the Germans as barbarians stimulated their competitive instincts. The humanists looked to young Emperor Maximilian (1493–1519) as the hero who would restore the empire to greatness and introduce a new golden age. Celtis and the rest wrote plays to ornament his court and poems in his honor. Maximilian himself sought immortality as a patron of poets and artists. He commissioned a long poetic allegory, the *Theuerdank,* to celebrate his courtship of Mary of Burgundy, and he dictated *Der Weisskunig,* or *The White King,* which related his own daring deeds. For Maximilian the Nuremberg artist Albrecht Dürer did the woodcut *Triumphal Arch* and a portrait.

The prosperous cities of south Germany served as focal points of humanist and artistic activity. In Augsburg, home of the Fuggers, Welsers, Paumgartners, and other wealthy families, Conrad Peutinger (1465–1547) became a highly influential legist and humanist. While studying law in Italy he developed a passion for classical learning, and he collected coins, artwork, and classical manuscripts. His stylistic ability made him of special value to the city government and he served as a privy counselor for Emperor Maximilian as well. He owned the important *Tabula Peutingeriana,* a military map of the Roman Empire which Celtis had discovered and presented to him.

The historian Johann Turmair, known as Aventinus (1477–1534), served in Ingolstadt as tutor to the two younger sons of the duke of Bavaria. Encouraged by

Duke William IV, he undertook to write *The Annals of Bavaria,* which he completed in 1521.

In Nuremberg the city councilor Willibald Pirckheimer (1470–1528) presided over humanist intellectual life. A friend of Celtis and of Albrecht Dürer, Pirckheimer was a scholar in his own right. He was educated in Italy, read and wrote Greek, composed a history of the Swabian-Swiss war, and took part in the sacramental controversy during the Reformation period. Luther was a guest in his home on one occasion, but Pirckheimer remained within the Catholic Church. His sisters, especially Charitas, a nun, were so well educated that Erasmus compared them in his *Colloquies* with the brilliant daughters of Sir Thomas More.

THE REUCHLIN CONTROVERSY

The humanists were virtually unanimous in their attack upon scholastic theology. They believed the language to be barbarous, the dialectic religiously ineffective, the emphasis upon logical formulation and demonstration of dogma misplaced. They favored an ethical interpretation of Paul and a spiritualization of dogma. One of the humanists most concerned with reinvigorating Christian doctrine by exploring new sources of religious knowledge was Johannes Reuchlin, a pioneer in Hebrew studies. In his *Rudimenta hebraica* he wrote, "I reverence St. Jerome as an angel, I prize Nicholas de Lyra as a great master, but Truth I worship as God."

Johannes Reuchlin (1455–1522) was educated by the Brethren of the Common Life and at northern universities. On two trips to Italy he came to know Marsilio Ficino and Giovanni Pico della Mirandola, and he was an avid reader of Nicholas Cusanus. A professional lawyer, he served most of his life as chancellor to the duke of Württemberg, but spent his last years as a professor at Ingolstadt and Tübingen. The university was his natural habitat, for he was a genuine intellectual who lived for ideas.

Reuchlin believed that Hebrew brought him closer to God than any other language. Moses, after all, was more ancient than the Greek philosophers. Reuchlin's *Rudimenta hebraica* was the first fairly reliable manual of Hebrew grammar by a Christian scholar. But through the years, as his knowledge of Hebrew deepened, he became intrigued by Jewish mysticism. He believed that Moses and the prophets had transmitted many divine truths orally through the seventy wise men in unbroken tradition until they were embodied by the medieval Jewish mystics in the Cabala. Because of the references in the Cabala to the Messiah, Reuchlin believed that the Cabala corroborated Christian revelation. From Pico he received the suggestion that the ideas of the Cabalists paralleled the philosophy of the Pythagoreans. "Marsilio [Ficino] produced Plato for Italy. Lefèvre d'Étaples restored Aristotle to France. I shall complete the number and . . . show to the Germans Pythagoras reborn through me!" he boasted. The numerological mysticism of the Cabalists was related, he held, to the mysterious power and quality of numbers which Pythagoras developed in the mid-sixth century B.C. He wrote two major works, *On the Wonder-Working Word* and *On the Cabalistic Art,* in which he sought to demonstrate the way in which Pythagoreanism and Cabalism harmonize with and support Christian revelation.

Ironically, this Christian apologist became the target of a vicious obscurantist attack. In 1506 a Jew named Pfefferkorn had renounced Judaism for Christianity. With the zeal of the convert he wrote *A Mirror for Jews,* in which he argued that all Hebrew books should be confiscated. The Dominicans of Cologne backed his outrageous demand, and in 1519 the emperor issued a decree ordering the Jews to turn in their books. In response to an inquiry from the archbishop of Mainz, Reuchlin offered the opinion that Hebrew books should not be destroyed. Pfefferkorn attacked Reuchlin in a scurrilous pamphlet entitled *The Hand Mirror,* accusing him of ignorance. Reuchlin loathed controversy, but he felt that he must defend his position, and did so in *The Eye Mirror.* He also published a collection of testimonials in his favor under the title of *Letters of Famous Men.* The case dragged on until in 1520 the pope finally condemned Reuchlin's *Eye Mirror.*

This attack on the humanists' idol was more than they could bear in silence. While the controversy was at its height, two young students, Crotus Rubeanus and Ulrich von Hutten, published *Letters of Obscure Men,* a biting satire on the "obscurantists" of Cologne and the would-be book-burners who supported them. It set Europe to laughing on the very eve of the Reformation.

ULRICH VON HUTTEN

Ulrich von Hutten (1488–1523), a militant critic of scholasticism and of abuses in the church, was a fighter. A German knight, he belonged to a class that was rapidly losing its social utility. When the Reformation broke out and Luther was summoned to appear before the diet at Worms in 1521, Hutten called to him, "Long live liberty!"

Hutten was born in the fortress of Steckelberg, on the border of Franconia and Hesse. At the age of eleven he was sent to the ancient monastery of Fulda to begin life as a religious. At seventeen he fled from the monastery, only a few weeks before Luther entered one at Erfurt. He studied at Cologne, Erfurt, and Frankfort on the Oder, where he took his A.B., then went on to Leipzig, Greifswald, and Rostock. During the course of his wanderings he became an enthusiastic humanist, and he dedicated his life to poetics and polemics. "Behold, posterity," he wrote, "the songs of Hutten the poet, whom you are rightly able to call your own."

He saw the hypocritical priests and superstitious monks as the implacable foes of learning. Only gradually did he come to regard the pope as the *bête noire* leading the forces of reaction. His goal was to free the fatherland of the forces of ignorance and to elevate culture in Germany above that of Italy. Hutten was an angry young man who poured out polemical tracts from the depths of a choleric soul. In his *Trias Romana* Hutten had a character named Ernholdus offer what really was his own program: "Truly it is a great and excellent deed to bring it about by persuading, exhorting, inciting, driving, and impelling that the fatherland come to recognize its own debasement and arm itself to win back its ancient liberty." "Even if it cannot be attained," Hutten responds in the dialogue, "there is merit in having tried!"

Hutten's writings were like a broadside of grapeshot, all the more devastating for being fired at close range. He attacked the whole catalog of evils in the church—simony, nepotism, benefice-hunting, immorality, neglect of duty, clerical pride and insolence. He called for the abolition of celibacy, and caricatured Cardinal Cajetan as a dissolute papal lackey who pretended to be collecting money for defense against the Turks when he had really come to cheat the Germans out of their money so that the Romans could live in luxury. He attacked the sale of indulgences as exploitation.

Hutten's attitude toward the papacy became increasingly hostile. At first he considered the pope to be an enemy of the emperor, but finally he pronounced him to be an enemy of Christ himself. In 1517 he published a new edition of Lorenzo Valla's *On the Donation of Constantine,* which exposed the false foundation of the papal claim to temporal power. In a letter to Pope Leo X in December 1520 he concluded with the biblical phrase: "Let us break their chains asunder and cast their yoke from us."

Hutten died in August 1523 of syphilis, the same disease that had claimed the life of his foe Pope Julius II. He was buried on the island of Ufenau in Lake Zurich. His only remaining possession was his most powerful weapon, his pen.

Humanism in Eastern Europe

HUMANISM PENETRATED rather feebly into eastern Europe. King Matthew Corvinus of Hungary invited Italian humanists to Buda, built up a sizable library, and ornamented his court with Renaissance art; John Vitez and his nephew Janus Pannonius, humanists in their own right, invited Conrad Celtis to visit Buda from Vienna, and he came with much fanfare; Marius Nizolius contributed to rhetorical theory. But the advance of the Turks up the Danube and their conquest of Hungary cut off this promising beginning of Hungarian humanism.

Bohemia was so torn up by the Hussite wars during the fifteenth century that it could not participate very fully in the Renaissance. Fierce nationalism and its separation from Italy by the territory of the empire had a further negative influence. The nobleman Bohuslav Hasištein of Lobkovice (1460–1510) spent seven years in Italy and upon his return organized a literary circle. Some of the writings of Petrarch and Erasmus were translated into Czech. But that is about all there is to say about humanism in Bohemia, which in the days of Emperor Charles and Cola di Rienzo had been a cradle of Renaissance culture in the north.

Students traveled to Italian universities from Poland as they did from Germany, but in much fewer numbers. The Italian humanist Philip Buonacorsi, known as Callimachus (1438–1496), came to Poland as an exile. He had belonged to the Roman Academy of Pomponius Laetus, which Pope Paul II suspected of pagan proclivities and closed down. Callimachus became tutor to the children of King Casimir and taught at the University of Cracow. Largely because of his influence, Cracow became an important center for mathematics, astronomy, and humanistic studies. But the most important developments took place in western rather than eastern Europe as the Renaissance moved over the Alps into new territory.

French Humanism

VESPASIANO DA BISTICCI remarked disparagingly of the northerners, "These *ultramontanes* generally have little spirit." From an Italian point of view, this observation was essentially true of fifteenth-century French humanism, but it hardly did justice to the major figures of the sixteenth century. The French Renaissance showed most of the general characteristics of the German movement, including its deep religious concern, although romantic cultural nationalism was less in evidence and criticisms of ecclesiastical abuses were less pronounced.

The flowering of neoclassical culture in France was delayed by the Hundred Years' War and by France's duel with Burgundy. Only two major figures truly qualify as humanists in the first half of the fifteenth century. The chancellor Jean de Montreuil (1354–1418) acquired from his many Italian contacts an enthusiasm for Petrarch and Renaissance culture, and the great preacher Nicholas de Clemanges (1367–1437) admired Cicero and was mindful of the utility of rhetoric in his calling. But these promising beginnings were not followed up until the very end of the century.

Historians at one time liked to date the French Renaissance from the time of Charles VIII's invasion of Italy. We now appreciate more fully that ideas, books, and men such as Pico della Mirandola had made their influence felt in France before the troops returned from Italy. But no doubt the adventures of Charles VIII, Louis XII, and Francis I did focus renewed attention upon Italy. Local styles of art and architecture flourished, particularly in the Loire valley; outstanding examples can be seen in the châteaux of Amboise and Blois. Flemish and German artists, Jan Van Eyck and Hans Memling in particular, were important influences on French art until the time of Francis I. But during Francis' long reign (1515–1547) Italian influence became much more pronounced. The king brought Italian artists to France as a regular policy: Leonardo da Vinci, Benvenuto Cellini, Andrea del Sarto, Il Rosso, and Francesco Primaticcio. The Flemish artist Jean Clouet and his son François also came, and combined Flemish realism with French delicacy. The palace of Fontainebleau, built during Francis' reign, betrays Italian neoclassical design in many of its features, but the Château Chambord, also built for Francis I, is an interesting composite of the Italian and French traditions.[1]

During the reign of Francis I French literary culture came alive. In his *Commentaries on the Latin Tongue* Étienne Dolet (1508–1546) boasted of the progress literature was making and appealed for increased support from the court, the aristocracy, and other men of means. Dolet himself lived in Lyon and was a friend of François Rabelais. He placed his hope in the power of secular scholarship, believing that if men know the truth, they will act in accordance with it. He was burned as a freethinker in Naples, the "martyr of the Renaissance."

GUILLAUME BUDÉ

The man whom Dolet called the chief captain of the French humanists, Guillaume Budé (1468–1540), was indeed a scholar of substantial achievement, an intellectual of many serious interests, and an indefatigible worker. He represented all the basic motifs of French humanism: devotion to the classics, religious thought, and the reformation of society.

Budé's family had a tradition of government service, and he seemed destined for a government career himself. But he left the study of law at an early age, captivated by the classical revival, and at twenty-six took up the study of Greek with such zeal that the story went around that he spent several hours on his wedding day studying Greek grammar. When a servant burst into his study one day to tell him the house was on fire, he was said to have replied, "Tell my good wife *she* is in charge of housekeeping!" If these stories are apocryphal, it is at least true that Budé often stayed up all night reading and writing Greek. He wrote a good many letters in Greek to Erasmus and to others less able to reply in kind.

Budé's literary career was notable for the breadth of his interest. He wrote a commentary on the *Pandects* or digest of Justinian's law (*Annotationes*, 1508). In 1515 he published *De asse*, a treatise on coinage and money in which he applied historical analysis to the study of the ancient monetary system. His most important work, however, was his *Commentaries on the Greek Language* (1529), in which

---

1 Catherine Boyd, *The French Renaissance* (Boston, 1940), pts. 1 and 2.

he offered several thousand critical analyses of grammatical and syntactical questions, providing examples from Greek texts. His work was rambling and undisciplined, but readers of that century were patient with savants who felt a compulsion to display all the erudition at their command.

Francis I esteemed Budé highly and considered him an ornament to his court. Budé and Jean du Bellay, bishop of Narbonne, persuaded the king to found the Collegium Trilingue (1530), which developed into the Collège de France. Budé also induced the king to establish a library at Fontainebleau, from which grew the Bibliothèque Nationale in Paris. After his death he was suspected of having had Protestant leanings, for his widow retired to Geneva and openly professed the Reformed faith. Erasmus declared Budé to be the "marvel of France"—but Erasmus was given to easy compliments.

LEFÈVRE D'ÉTAPLES

Lefèvre d'Étaples (1455–1529) had tremendous influence on the course of events in the Reformation period. He took his doctorate at Paris, dutifully made an intellectual pilgrimage to Italy, and studied at Florence, where he encountered Ficino's Neoplatonism, and at Padua, where he read Aristotle with Ermolao Barbaro. He also read voraciously the works of Meister Eckhardt, Johannes Tauler, and other German mystics, and was intrigued by Raymond Lull's philosophy, which was designed to win the Moslems to Christianity. In 1514 Lefèvre published an edition of Nicholas Cusanus' works. Lefèvre's thought was synthetic, an amalgam of Aristotelianism, Neoplatonism, and mysticism. He delivered a series of lectures in Paris on Aristotle, in which he tried to interpret Aristotle's texts in accordance with their historical contexts. But his deepest concern was theological.

Lefèvre applied to religious thought the good humanist principle of returning to the sources. He was intrigued by the synthesis of philosophy and theology achieved by the Eastern church fathers. In 1505 he published an edition of John of Damascus in which he enunciated the principle that the Scriptures must be the sole source and authority for man's statements about God. In 1509 he published his *Quintuplex Psalter,* in which he placed five Latin versions of the Psalms in parallel columns in order to show the variant readings and make clear the philological problems involved in textual studies.

In 1512 he published his *Commentary on the Epistles of St. Paul,* in which he offered the Vulgate texts, his own translation based on the Greek texts, and his commentary on their meaning. Like Paul, he held that man is saved only by God's grace and forgiving mercy, which are achieved by faith alone and cannot be won by good works or human merit. He worked out a system of rigid predestinarianism, drawing heavily upon Paul's Epistle to the Romans. Lefèvre believed that the Scriptures were intended by the Holy Spirit to convey a spiritual message, and that this spiritual message therefore constituted the basic literal meaning, rather than any literal interpretation in a historical-critical sense. When Luther was preparing the lectures on the Epistle to the Romans which he delivered at the University of Wittenberg in 1515 and 1516, he used Lefèvre's commentary and observed in his marginal notations Lefèvre's emphasis upon grace and faith. Lefèvre's influence was thus of crucial importance not only for French Protestantism but for the Lutheran Reformation as well. In the belief that authentic texts of the sources would serve as useful tools for the purification of belief and the reform of the church, he published in 1522 his *Commentary on the Four Gospels*. He then did his own French translation of the New Testament and of the Psalms, based essentially upon the Vulgate.

Under pressure from the conservatives and in search of a more congenial environment, Lefèvre joined the circle of Guillaume Briconnet, bishop of Meaux, son of Charles VIII's worldly-wise adviser. Bishop Briconnet not only reformed abuses in his own diocese, but wished to renew Christian faith and piety by general church reform. He appointed Lefèvre as his vicar general to establish discipline among the clergy and to inspire them with his spiritual and mystical insights. At one point official hostility to Lefèvre was so great that he had to take temporary refuge in Strassburg. Gerard Roussel, Guillaume Farel, and John Calvin knew him personally and were influenced powerfully by his thought.

MARGUERITE D'ANGOULÊME

Women figured less prominently in the north than at the Italian Renaissance courts. The attitude of most northern humanists toward women was not exactly flattering. Erasmus, for example, owned a tapestry cautioning against the power of women. Aristotle, with a bit in his mouth, serves as a mount for lovely Phyllis, who says, "He who would pay homage to beautiful women must allow them much!" An exception to the general rule was Marguerite d'Angoulême, who protected the group at Meaux and was a brilliant intellectual in her own right.

Marguerite, the sister of Francis I, was the wife of Duke Charles of Alençon and later of Henry d'Albret, king of Navarre. Her mother, Louise of Savoy, taught her sufficient Italian to read Dante and Petrarch's sonnets, which stimulated her poetic interest and talent. She read Latin and possibly even had the rudiments of Greek. Although she was beautiful and vibrant, the belle of the court, she was not content to let her physical attributes overshadow her intellect.

Her literary output was phenomenal, covering a wide range from poetry and short stories to intense religious mystical treatises. Obviously influenced by Boccaccio's *Decameron*, Marguerite wrote the *Heptameron*, a collection of seventy short stories, some risqué, even crude. But the popular *Heptameron* reflected the society in which she lived more than her inner self, for Marguerite was a sensitive religious person with a strong inclination toward mysticism. Her religious poetry and her *Mirror of a Sinful Soul* expressed her deep mystical piety.

Marguerite used her position as the king's sister to protect the reforming humanists at Meaux. When the Sorbonne, then the theological faculty at the University of Paris, condemned Clément Marot, the translator of the French Psalter, Marguerite intervened in his behalf with Francis and won him a reprieve. She interceded for Lefèvre and Briconnet as well, and like them she died in the Catholic faith. The French humanists were unwilling to press for reform so urgently as to become schismatic or overtly heretical. They shied away from leading a popular movement and wished under no circumstances to disrupt the unity of the church.

FRANÇOIS RABELAIS

"To laugh is proper to man," wrote François Rabelais (*c.* 1495–1553), wit and satirist. He was a complicated personality, a monk but hardly an ascetic, a classicist who preferred to write in the vernacular, a mocker who was a true believer.

Tonsured as a child, Rabelais spent his early years as a Franciscan friar and used his leisure to study the Latin and Greek classics. Unhappy with the mendicants, he transferred to the Benedictine order, which had a longer tradition of learning. But he was dissatisfied with them too, and after a time he abandoned his Benedictine garb for that of a secular priest, which freed him for a life of wandering. He enrolled in the school of medicine at the University of Montpellier in 1530 and took his A.B. the same year. The next year he lectured on Galen and Hippocrates. In 1532 he moved to Lyon, which had an enlightened society interested in publishing and literary activities. There Rabelais began writing the works to which he was to return from time to time throughout his life, *Gargantua* and *Pantagruel*. In 1533 and 1535 he traveled to Rome with Jean du Bellay, who was made a cardinal. Upon his return Rabelais rejoined the Benedictines and became a canon of St. Maur. In 1537 he took his doctorate in medicine at Montpellier. During the period of repression at the end of Francis I's reign, Rabelais found it prudent to serve as a physician in Metz, an imperial city. The Sorbonne censured his major work and the parlement suspended its sale. Controversy about the proper interpretation of his work still continues. Possibly posterity has taken his books more seriously than he intended, for he wrote them in time left over from other activities that he seems to have considered of greater importance.

Rabelais took the names Gargantua and Pantagruel from minor literary pieces already extant. His Gargantua is a giant whose parents, also giants, celebrate his arrival into the world with a fantastic feast at which the guests gorge on food and drink in a most immoderate way. As a young man Gargantua founds the Abbey of

Thélème, the ideal monastery: it welcomes both sexes and its motto is "Do what you wish!" Pure spirits all, its members shun vice and cultivate virtue, learning freely and without constraint.

Gargantua's son, Pantagruel, goes to Paris to study and there he encounters Panurge, an intellectual who is also a lecherous rascal, a heavy drinker, and a coward. Panurge announces his intention of marrying, but he feels the need of advice, and together with Pantagruel and some other companions sets sail for the Land of the Lanterns to consult the Oracle of the Bottle. When finally they arrive, the oracle tells Panurge, "Drink a toast!" This is taken as sanction for his marriage. At this point the book breaks off. The whole work is replete with digressions, amplifications, satires, puzzling and seemingly irrelevant incidents. It is a catchall for the intellectual currents of French humanist society in the final two decades of Rabelais's life.

Rabelais has so puzzled interpreters that they have described him variously as a skeptical freethinker, a forerunner of Voltaire, a crypto-Protestant, and an Erasmian humanist. His real message seems to be the need for candor about and sympathy for the human condition. Man must bear life with as much humor as he can muster and not lose faith in God or love for man. If grossness and coarseness are recognized as common in the sixteenth century, Rabelais seems less out of line than men in the Victorian age thought him to be. There is really no good evidence to support the hypothesis that he was a Protestant; he belongs rather to the tradition of Christian humanism. His work is an Erasmian "praise of folly." His wit is dependent upon the medieval *fabliau* tradition and the *facetiae* of the Italian Renaissance.[2] Rabelais wrote in the vernacular and is really only the best known of a very respectable number of literary figures in early sixteenth-century France who were strongly influenced by Italian Renaissance thought.[3]

Spanish Humanism

IT HAS BEEN QUESTIONED whether Spain experienced a renaissance at all before the time of that giant of Spanish literature, Miguel de Cervantes (1547–1616), who lived during the reign of Philip II. There were beginnings, however, during the reign of Ferdinand and Isabella. But a reform movement led by Cardinal Francisco Ximénez de Cisneros (1436–1517) so strengthened the Spanish church that Spanish culture remained virtually impervious to Erasmian and Lutheran influences,

---

[2] See Lucien Febvre, *Le problème de l'incroyance au XVIe siècle: La religion de Rabelais,* 2nd ed. (Paris, 1947).

[3] Jean Festugière, *La philosophie de l'amour de Marsile Ficin* (Paris, 1941).

though the effect of Erasmus' thought was felt to a limited extent before the time of Cervantes.

Ximénez, the son of a poor member of the minor nobility, studied law and theology at the University of Salamanca and spent some time in the service of the curia in Rome under the first Borgia pope. He was rewarded by the papacy with a major benefice in Spain, against the opposition of the Spanish clergy, who had become such fierce defenders of the faith during nearly eight centuries of Moslem rule that they were—and remained—disinclined to bow gracefully before any authority outside Spain, even the authority of Rome. But Ximénez possessed such force of character and intellect that he nevertheless moved up the ecclesiastical ladder from vice-general to bishop before deciding to withdraw to the disciplined life of a Franciscan monk, and even then success sought him out. After the fall of Granada in 1492, Queen Isabella brought Ximénez to her court as her private confessor. In 1494 he was made provincial of the Franciscan order; in 1495 he became archbishop of Toledo and primate of Spain. On occasion he served as regent for Ferdinand and Isabella, and in 1508 was made grand inquisitor. Ximénez used his power as a means toward one end: the reform of the Spanish church.

As captain of the ark of salvation, Ximénez ran a tight ship. He favored the Observantine Franciscans over the Conventuals, who were more casual about their interpretation of the rules. He forced the canons of the cathedral chapters to honor their obligations. He insisted upon strict discipline among the secular clergy. As grand inquisitor he was in a position to control every detail of church discipline. In order to upgrade the intellectual and moral level of the clergy, he founded the University of Alcalá, not far from Madrid. The university was made up of a number of colleges, one of them a trilingual college for the study of Latin, Greek, and Hebrew. Professors were paid by student fees, and Ximénez instituted a generous retirement plan as an attractive fringe benefit.

Ximénez envisioned a Christian humanist reform program that would enlighten the clergy by means of education and a return to the pure sources of religion. With this latter end in mind, Ximénez directed the publication of the Complutensian Polyglot Bible, with the Hebrew, Latin, and Greek texts in parallel columns. Although the edition was based upon a respectable number of manuscript sources and took over fifteen years to complete, the level of critical scholarship left something to be desired. Ximénez thought also of those who knew no Latin, and had Ludolf the Saxon's *Life of Christ* and Thomas a Kempis' *Imitation of Christ* translated into Spanish.

Ximénez so strengthened the Catholic Church in Spain that none of the heterodox influences of the Reformation period gained a firm foothold there. At the same time he shut Spain off from many creative ideas and enlivening impulses that could have enriched Spanish culture and spiritual life.

English Humanism

BOCCACCIO ONCE CALLED the English "thickheads" who could not master humanistic learning. This remark referred less to the proverbial English cultural insularity than to the status of classical studies in England in the fourteenth century. Even the fifteenth century has generally been depicted as an intellectually barren time, with England's energies expended on the Hundred Years' War and the Wars of the Roses. Actually, however, the English scene was not so dismal as many have supposed.

As humanism began to penetrate English thought during the fifteenth century, it was absorbed into traditional scholastic learning and was not considered to be a new intellectual system incompatible with scholasticism. The majority of the English humanists were ecclesiastical civil servants whose interests in classical learning were those of the amateur or dilettante with theological leanings. Clerics fairly well monopolized the civil service, the diplomatic corps, and the universities during the fifteenth century. They were busy with practical affairs and cultivated classical studies merely for relaxation. They were neither professional scholars nor teachers of rhetoric. They did not pursue antique learning with abandon, nor did they burn to teach it.

During the course of the century Italians of various callings came to England—churchmen, artists, merchants—and brought some Renaissance ideas with them. Five successive bishops of Worcester were Italians. In 1418 Poggio came to England as the secretary of Henry Beaufort, bishop of Winchester, and searched English monasteries for classical manuscripts. Polydore Vergil was a papal subcollector who wrote a noteworthy *History of England*. There were Italian physicians at court. The Italian sculptor Torrigiano—the fellow who had broken Michelangelo's nose when they were students together in Florence—prepared the tomb of Henry VII. Henry VIII kept a whole coterie of Italian artists. Italian merchants and bankers such as the Bardis, Peruzzis, and Frescobaldis operated in England until the government defaulted on debts or appropriated their holdings, or until English merchants squeezed them out.

The English, in turn, made some direct contacts of their own with Italian Renaissance culture. Duke Humphrey of Gloucester, a brother of Henry V, employed Italian secretaries, promoted humanistic studies at Oxford, and bequeathed a fine manuscript collection to the university. John Tiptoft, earl of Worcester, allowed his humanist studies to affect his political attitudes, and was executed as a Yorkist at the Lancastrian restoration in 1470. But more churchmen than laymen had ties with Rome and Italy, and thus it was the upper clergy that took the lead in advancing humanist studies. William Grey, bishop of Ely and treasurer of Edward IV, was a student of Guarino and a friend of Poggio and Bessarion. George Neville, archbishop of York, who was ousted to Calais by Edward IV in 1472, appointed his secretaries with an eye to their Latin style and hired Emanuel of Constantinople to teach him Greek. John Shirwood, bishop of Durham and ambassador to Rome, was himself a fine Latinist and could read Greek. Clerics, usually Oxford educated, with such abilities were useful servants at home and respected diplomats abroad.[4] William Caxton, who set up England's first printing press at Westminster in 1477, helped to stimulate intellectual life.

Serious study of the classics began at Oxford at the end of the century with Thomas Linacre (*c.* 1460–1524), William Grocyn (*c.* 1466–1519), and William Latimer (*c.* 1460–1543). All three studied in Florence, where they acquired the rudiments of Greek. Grocyn taught Thomas More, John Colet, and Erasmus. Three Christian humanists stand out in the first phase of the English Renaissance: John Colet, Thomas More, and the Dutch-born Desiderius Erasmus, who became known as the Oxford Reformers.[5]

JOHN COLET

John Colet (*c.* 1467–1519) was an exceedingly earnest man, moved by the religious concerns of the Italian Platonists and by a passion for the reform of theology and church life. Of the twenty-two children sired by Sir Henry Colet, a London merchant who at one time was lord mayor of London, John was the only one to survive to adulthood. He was educated in the traditional subjects, mathematics, grammar, rhetoric, and dialectic, and took his M.A. degree at Oxford. There he heard the lectures of Grocyn and Linacre, who taught him some Greek and inspired him to pursue further studies in Italy.

There in 1493 Colet fell under the spell of Florentine Neoplatonism. He corresponded with Ficino, although he seems not to have had a close personal relationship with him, and he was much influenced by Augustinianism and by the mystical writings of Dionysius the Areopagite. In 1496 he returned to Oxford and began immediately his famous lecture series on Paul's Epistle to the Romans, which differs significantly from Ficino's commentary. The Englishman puts much greater emphasis on sin as a basic component of human nature. Natural man is a "stench in the nostril of God." God's grace is achieved by the study of the Scriptures, which opens man's mind to divine inspiration and imbues him with trust in Christ the Redeemer. In his exegetical method, Colet departed from the traditional fourfold interpretation of the text, the literal, allegorical, tropological, and anagogical. Like Lefèvre d'Étaples, he pressed instead for the literal meaning of the text, by which

---

[4] See Roberto Weiss, *Humanism in England During the Fifteenth Century,* 2nd ed. (New York, 1957); Lewis Einstein, *The Italian Renaissance in England* (New York, 1902).

[5] However unsuitable, the name given them by Frederic Seebohm in his book *The Oxford Reformers* (London, 1896) persists in the literature.

he meant not the historico-critical meaning, but its spiritual content. He was a "Paulinist"; that is, he stressed man's sin and the need for God's grace and mercy.

As Colet's Christian humanist concern with the return to the Scriptures and to the church fathers matured, he became increasingly impatient with scholastic theology. "Twenty doctors expound one text in twenty days," he sneered, "and with an antitheme of half an inch some of them draw a thread nine days long. They usually look on no more Scriptures than they find in their Duns [Scotus]."[6] Even Thomas Aquinas drew his fire, though Aquinas' moderate realism and admiration for Aristotle usually made him less offensive to the humanists than Scotus, Occam, and the later scholastics. Once when Erasmus had spoken kindly of Aquinas, Colet replied, "Why do you preach up that writer to me? For, without a full share of presumption, he never would have defined anything in that rash and overweening manner; and without something of a worldly spirit, he would never have so tainted the whole doctrine of Christ with his profane philosophy."[7] The English humanists joined the continentals in the war against scholasticism.

Colet was an intimate friend of Thomas More and of Erasmus, who was a frequent guest in his house. Colet had many a serious theological discussion at the dinner table with Erasmus. He extracted a promise from Erasmus that he would turn to theological studies and apply his great talent to biblical and patristic scholarship, although for some time after his first visit to England Erasmus protested that he was not well prepared for such work.

Colet won his doctorate and in 1505 was made the dean of St. Paul's Cathedral, against his own wishes. In 1508 he inherited his father's considerable fortune, which he used, together with his own private income, to found St. Paul's School, modeled after the humanist schools in Italy. As headmaster he chose William Lilly, who taught classical Latin and Greek. Control of the school was vested in the London Company of Mercers, as lay trustees. Colet combined the humanist interest in education with a high moral purpose and religious aim. He himself preached boldly against abuses in society and in the church, attacked England's continental wars as costly adventures, and even spoke pointedly, on the occasion of Cardinal Wolsey's installation, on the duties of a cardinal.

THOMAS MORE

Thomas More (1478–1535) is best remembered as a man of conscience who paid with his life for opposing the divorce of King Henry VIII and England's break with Rome. But he was also a distinguished man of letters, and his *Utopia* was the best-known book produced by an English humanist.

Thomas More was born in London, studied at St. Anthony's School, and was

---

6 Cited in *ibid.*, pp. 17–18.
7 Cited in Ernest Hunt, *Dean Colet and His Theology* (London, 1956), p. 9.

then placed in the household of Cardinal Morton, archbishop of Canterbury, for tutoring and to learn good manners. His father planned a legal career for him, and after studying some Greek with Linacre at Oxford he embarked on the study of law. When More was about twenty, however, he underwent an acute spiritual crisis and seriously contemplated renouncing the world and withdrawing to a monastery. Although he never took vows, he lived for some years at the London Charterhouse (the Carthusian monastery) and voluntarily adopted the discipline of the monks, wearing a hair shirt, beating himself each Friday in remembrance of Christ's scourging by the Roman soldiers, and sleeping on the floor with a block of wood for a pillow. Although he gradually resumed his original career aims, he never lost his "religious nonchalance" about the bourgeois success syndrome. His Christian awareness of man's sinfulness and the evil that dwells in human hearts served him well during his later service in the government.

In 1502 he became undersheriff of the city of London, representing the city's interest in court. In 1504 he was so bold as to oppose Henry VII's demands for higher revenues in the House of Commons. His very daring and strength of character later attracted the attention of Henry VIII and his chancellor, Cardinal Thomas Wolsey, and they sent him on a number of diplomatic missions to Calais and the Netherlands.

In 1505 More married Jane Colt, a lady of good family, and their children were raised as paragons of gentility and learning. Their daughter Margaret in particular was known for her wit and her knowledge of the classics. More came to know Erasmus on his first trip to England, in 1499, and when Erasmus returned to England from Italy he stayed at More's house. It was there that he wrote his *Praise of Folly* (*Encomium moriae,* which can also be translated as "Praise of More"). More's second wife, Alice, was not particularly fond of the little Dutchman, who spoke no English and made jokes in Latin, which she did not understand. More's contact with Erasmus and with Colet spurred him to cultivate the humanist interests that had already been awakened in him at Oxford.

The best of More's literary output, which was substantial, was his *Utopia.* In the first book he criticizes the political and social abuses of his times. Harsh punishments in the criminal code, hardship resulting from the enclosure system, wars between Christian states, and other outrages are critically examined. The second book describes the social arrangements of the island called Utopia. Its principal city, Amaurote, has houses with glass windows and fireproof plaster roofs. Each house has a garden and vineyard. The water supply is clear and unpolluted. The markets are hygienic, the hospitals sanitary, the streets wide and clean. Conditions on the island seem to be the precise opposite of those with which More was familiar.

Reason and righteousness rule the land. There is no private property and therefore no stimulus for greed or self-aggrandizement. The state provides for every individual. But there is no idleness, for support is withheld from any recalcitrant person until he does the required amount of work. Even part of the profit taken in trade with another state is returned to it for care of its poor. Religion is undogmatic, ethical, and flexible. The island is heavily armed for defense; even the women receive military training. But there is no war of conquest, except for the purpose of taking possession of unused land, for natural law requires that land be used, since nature abhors overpopulation. Possibly at this point a bit of the white man's imperialism emerges from More's subconscious.

So creative and imaginative is More's *Utopia* (and the Renaissance inspired several such efforts) that scholars have warred over its meaning ever since. For one it is a bourgeois criticism of society, for another it is a precocious expression of socialism, for still another it is an idealization of the medieval values of a closed society called forth by the individualism emerging in early modern times. Still another interpretation emphasizes More's basic religious concerns. He was realistic about man and thought that institutions should be so devised as to minimize man's propensity for sloth, greed, and pride.[8] He did not believe that society could be made perfect, since men are themselves imperfect, though his description of Utopia leaves little doubt that he had given serious thought to ways in which it could be improved.

In 1521 More became treasurer of the exchequer; in 1523 he was elected speaker of the House of Commons; and in 1529, when Cardinal Wolsey lost favor because of his failure to secure a papal annulment of Henry's marriage to Catherine of Aragon, he was named to succeed Wolsey as lord chancellor, against his judgment and desire. Henry finally rid himself of Catherine by staging a divorce trial in England, which left him free at last to marry Anne Boleyn. Thomas More, unable to reconcile his conscience with his king's rejection of papal supremacy, resigned as chancellor on May 16, 1532. Two years later the Act of Supremacy made the English monarch the "supreme head" of the English church, and when More refused to take an oath acknowledging Henry's ecclesiastical supremacy, he was convicted of treason. He was executed on July 7, 1535, and his severed head was displayed on London Bridge as a warning to any who might put conscientious loyalty to the pope above obedience to the king in religious matters.

Erasmus, Prince of the Humanists

DESIDERIUS ERASMUS (1469–1536) belonged to all nations of the north, and he belonged to none. He was born and received his early education in the Netherlands, studied in France, visited and taught in England at various times, traveled and

---

[8] For this insight I am indebted to that indefatigable scholar J. H. Hexter (*More's Utopia: The Biography of an Idea* [Princeton, 1952]).

published in Italy, spent some time in Louvain, and lived for two decades on the upper Rhine, in Basel and Freiburg. He spoke fondly of "our Germany." He could cite urbane Cicero with approval: "Where you fare well, there is your fatherland!" But in an intellectual sense he belonged to all nations, for his program of Christian humanism represented the loftiest thoughts and highest aspirations of a whole generation of northern humanists. Young and old alike acknowledged him as their leader. The universities of Oxford, Cambridge, Louvain, Vienna, and Basel tempted him with offers. Oecolampadius, the Basel reformer, had a framed letter from Erasmus hanging over his desk, until another admirer stole it.

Not only men of intellect but men of power sought him out. King Henry VIII wrote a personal letter inviting him to England, and King Francis I invited him to Paris. Prince Charles of the house of Habsburg put him on a pension. The king of Hungary invited him to grace the Danube with his presence. Both Pope Leo X and Pope Adrian (who was Dutch) would have been happy to welcome him to Rome and reward him with the red hat. The archbishop of Canterbury and the primate of Spain would gladly have kept Erasmus in their company.[9] His massive correspondence compares with that of Cicero or Voltaire in size and as an index to the temper of the times. "Every day," he once exclaimed, "letters come to me from the most distant regions, from kings, princes, prelates, from learned men, and even from people of whose very existence I did not know!"

What was the secret of Erasmus' popularity? "His manner and his conversation," wrote his young student Beatus Rhenanus, "were polished, affable, and even charming." Beyond his personal qualities, he deserved renown for his tremendous erudition. No one could match his knowledge of the classical and patristic writings. Few men were so prolific in scholarly publication or so able in a variety of literary forms. But above all else, Erasmus' Christian humanism spoke to his generation of intellectuals, who were weary of scholastic quibbles over picayune details.

Erasmus was born in Gouda in the Netherlands, probably in 1469 (although Erasmus gave the date as 1466), the son of a priest, Rogerius Gerardus. Schooled under the Brethren of the Common Life at Deventer from 1475 to 1483, he acquired their simple piety and mystical devotion along with an invincible love of the classics and high regard for such church fathers as Jerome and Augustine. In 1483, when his father died, his guardians sent Erasmus and his brother Peter to school at 's Hertogenbosch. But the funds left by their father dwindled rapidly, and the best hope for further education appeared to lie with a monastic order. Erasmus entered the Augustinian community at Steyn, and in 1492 was ordained a priest. His treatise *On the Contempt of the World,* despite a disclaimer of serious intent when it was published years later, suggests that at the time the leisure provided for study by the monastic life was not entirely displeasing to him. Nevertheless, two years

[9] See Roland H. Bainton, *Erasmus of Christendom* (New York, 1969), pp. 3–4.

after his ordination he grasped an opportunity to travel as secretary to the bishop of Cambrai. In August 1495 he enrolled in the Collège de Montaigu in Paris. The curriculum was scholastic and traditional, and Erasmus was repelled by it. He began to develop secular interests, and first broke into print with a small piece published with one of the historical volumes of Robert Gaguin, a French humanist.

In the spring of 1499 he made his first trip to England as tutor to William Blount, Baron Mountjoy. During the two months he spent at Oxford he heard Colet's lectures on Paul's Epistle to the Romans. Colet urged him to turn to theology, and at the age of thirty he took up the study of Greek as a key to the New Testament. Five years later he could write Colet that he was eagerly "pursuing sacred letters and chafing at every hindrance and delay." In 1500 he published an edition of eight hundred Latin adages in France. In 1504 he came across a manuscript of Valla's *Annotations on the New Testament,* and the following year he published an edition of it.

On a visit to England he was offered an opportunity to travel to Italy as tutor to the two sons of Henry VII's physician, and in September 1506 they left for the homeland of the Renaissance. He spent a year as tutor in Bologna, then went to Venice, where he worked with Aldus Manutius, the great publisher. They did an enlarged edition of the *Adages,* including some in Greek. "Together we attacked a work," Erasmus recalled, "I writing while Aldus gave my copy to the press." Then with a new protégé, Alexander Stuart, the illegitimate son of James IV of Scotland, he journeyed to Siena and Rome before returning to England, where, as a guest in the home of Thomas More, he wrote his *Praise of Folly*. He then spent a miserable time in Cambridge, the cold relieved by the gift of a porcelain stove, but his hunger poorly assuaged by English cooking.

In 1514 Erasmus moved to Basel in order to be near the publisher Johannes Froben. The year 1516 saw Erasmus, at the height of his powers, enjoy two major publishing triumphs. In March his critical edition of the New Testament in Greek, with a substantially new Latin translation attached, was published, and in the autumn his nine-volume edition of Jerome appeared. After a brief period in Louvain, which proved to be uncongenial because the monks and "sophists" pressured him to take a stand against the Reformation, he returned to Basel and remained there for many years. In 1524 he yielded at last to the pressure of his ecclesiastical patrons and attacked Luther in his treatise *On Free Will*. Although he had no wish to support the Protestant cause, his own feelings were moderate at a time when moderation was unpopular on both sides of the controversy.

When the Reformation triumphed in Basel in 1529, Erasmus left for Freiburg. The quiet and seclusion of that beautiful city in the Black Forest suited him, but in 1535 he returned to Basel to see his work on Ecclesiastes through the press and to finish his edition of Origen. He was not well, and he died there in June 1536.

Erasmus had a reform program of his own, which envisioned a Christendom in which men would follow the Master in faith and love, in which the church would return to the purity and simplicity of New Testament times, and in which nations would learn to live together in peace and harmony. He hoped that through Christian scholarship and wholesome instruction the philosophy of Christ could be so clearly portrayed that plowboys and prelates, citizens and kings would at last understand the meaning of the gospel and would be moved to revive the whole darkening world. "I dreamed," he wrote, "of a golden age and the fortunate islands; and then, as Aristophanes said, I awoke."

Erasmus' reform program called for an end to the obscurantism of the scholastics, the paganism of some Ciceronians, and the attempt to ensure salvation by doing prescribed good works—fasting, going on pilgrimages, maintaining vigils, and the like. He was, as his biographer Johan Huizinga observed, most brilliant and profound when he was being ironically humorous. In his witty and entertaining *Praise of Folly,* which has appeared in over six hundred editions, he poked fun at the weaknesses and follies, the fetishes and vices of men in all walks of life. "We have praised Folly," he says to More in the preface, "not quite foolishly!" In his *Colloquies,* which has seen over three hundred editions, he mocked the superstitious veneration of relics, repetitive prayers, pilgrimages, social fopperies, and especially monkish ignorance. In his *Method of True Theology* he attacked the "frigid and perplexing" theology of Scotus and Occam.

In his drive to strip Christianity of its latter-day accretions, Erasmus went well beyond the achievements of any other humanist, Italian or northern. He worked feverishly, "standing on one foot," as he once put it, at his writing desk. He called his study in Basel a "mill" where he ground out prefaces, translations, learned editions, and commentaries for eight years in his period of peak productivity. "The eagerness for writing grows with writing," he observed.

The work that contains the most characteristic expression of his "philosophy of Christ" was his *Enchiridion, or Handbook of a Christian Knight,* which he wrote in 1501 and published two years later. In this treatise, written to instruct a hot-tempered and rowdy soldier in a better way of life, Erasmus emphasized an undogmatic ethical piety based on genuine love, in contrast to the ritualistic forms of religion. In the introduction to his edition of the New Testament he described his philosophy of Christ in these words:

> This kind of philosophy is situated more truly in the emotions than in syllogism, it is a life rather than a disputation, an afflatus rather than erudition, a transformation rather than reason. To be learned is the lot of only a few; but no one is unable to be a Christian, no one is unable to be pious, and I add this boldly, no one is unable to be a theologian. For that which is most of all in accordance with nature descends easily into the minds of all. But what else is the philosophy of Christ, which he himself calls a rebirth, than the instauration of a well-founded nature?

The coming of the Protestant Reformation was an intense personal tragedy for Erasmus. No longer the intellectual arbiter of Europe, he now became, as he put it, "a heretic to both sides." At the same time that he hoped for reform within the church, he was horrified at Luther, who could cite with gusto Paul's words (2 Corinthians 6:4–5): "Let us approve ourselves . . . in tumults!" Erasmus, who at one time hailed "the dawn of a golden age," came in the end to think his century the worst since the time of Christ. History played strange tricks on Erasmus. But viewed in the light of his own philosophy, his personal efforts at reform must be recognized as an idealistic and courageous endeavor worthy of mankind's respect and gratitude.

One cannot, in fact, leave the great age of the Renaissance without reflecting at least a moment upon the debt Western man owes to those who shouldered the cultural burden of our civilization. For better or for worse, men make history move.

Bibliography

German humanism:

ANDREAS, WILLI. *Deutschland vor der Reformation: Eine Zeitenwende,* 5th ed. Stuttgart, 1948.

GEIGER, LUDWIG. *Renaissance und Humanismus in Italien und Deutschland.* Berlin, 1882.

HOLBORN, HAJO. *Ulrich von Hutten and the German Reformation.* New Haven, 1937.

———, ed. *On the Eve of the Reformation: "Letters of Obscure Men,"* trans. F. G. Stokes. New York, 1964.

NAEF, WERNER. *Vadian und seine Stadt St. Gallen,* 2 vols. St. Gall, 1944–1945.

NAUERT, CHARLES G. *Agrippa and the Crisis of Renaissance Thought.* Urbana, 1965.

NEWALD, RICHARD. *Probleme und Gestalten des deutschen Humanismus.* Berlin, 1963.

PEUCKERT, WILL-ERICH. *Die grosse Wende.* Hamburg, 1945.

RUPPRICH, HANS. *Humanismus und Renaissance in den deutschen Städten und Universitäten.* Leipzig, 1935.

———. *Die Frühzeit des Humanismus und der Renaissance in Deutschland.* Leipzig, 1938.

SPITZ, LEWIS W. *Conrad Celtis, the German Arch-Humanist.* Cambridge, Mass., 1957.

———. *The Religious Renaissance of the German Humanists.* Cambridge, Mass., 1963.

STRAUSS, GERALD. *Sixteenth-Century Germany: Its Topography and Topographers.* Madison, Wis., 1959.

———. *Historian in an Age of Crisis: The Life and Work of Johannes Aventinus, 1477–1534.* Cambridge, Mass., 1963.

French humanism:

CHAMARD, HENRI. *Les origines de la poésie française de la Renaissance.* Paris, 1932.

CHAMPION, P. *Histoire poétique du 15ᵉ siecle,* 2 vols. Paris, 1923.

DENIEUL-CORMIER, ANNE. *A Time of Glory: The Renaissance in France, 1488–1559.* Garden City, N.Y., 1968.

FEBVRE, LUCIEN. *Le problème de l'incroyance au XVIe siècle: La religion de Rabelais,* 2nd ed. Paris, 1947.
———. *Au coeur religieux du XVIe siècle.* Paris, 1957.
GUNDERSHEIMER, WERNER. *The Life and Works of Louis Le Roy.* Geneva, 1966.
JEANROY, A. *Les origines de la poésie lyrique en France,* 3rd ed. Paris, 1925.
LEBLANC, PAULETTE. *La poésie religieuse de Clément Marot.* Paris, 1955.
PLATTARD, JEAN. *La Renaissance des lettres en France de Louis XII à Henri IV.* Paris, 1925.
RENAUDET, AUGUSTIN. *Préréforme et humanisme à Paris pendant les premières guerres d'Italie, 1494–1517.* Paris, 1916.
SAULNIER, VERDUN L. *La littérature française de la Renaissance, 1500–1612,* 6th ed. Paris, 1962.

Spanish humanism:
BATAILLON, MARCEL. *Érasme et l'Espagne: Recherches sur l'histoire spirituelle du XVIe siècle.* Paris, 1937.
BELL, AUBREY F. G. *Luis de León: A Study of the Spanish Renaissance.* Oxford, 1925.
CIONE, EDMONDO. *Juan de Valdés: La sua vita e il suo pensiero religioso,* 2nd ed. Naples, 1963.
GREEN, OTIS. *Spain and the Western Tradition,* 4 vols. Madison, Wis., 1963–1966.
HIRSCH, ELIZABETH. *Damião de Gois: The Life and Thought of a Portuguese Humanist, 1502–1574.* The Hague, 1967.
LONGHURST, JOHN E. *Erasmus and the Spanish Inquisition: The Case of Juan de Valdés.* Albuquerque, N.M., 1950.
MENÉNDEZ Y PELAYO, MARCELINO. *La Historia de los heterodoxos españoles.* Madrid, 1932.
NIETO, JOSÉ C. *Juan de Valdés and the Origins of the Spanish and Italian Reformation.* Geneva, 1969.
STARKIE, WALTER F. *Grand Inquisitor, Being an Account of Cardinal Ximenes de Cisneros and His Times.* London, 1940.
TOBRINER, SISTER MARIAN LEONA, ed. *Vives' Introduction to Wisdom.* New York, 1968.
VILLANOVA, A. *Erasmus y Cervantes.* Barcelona, 1949.
WATSON, FOSTER, ed. *Vives and the Renascence Education of Women.* New York, 1912.

English humanism:
BAKER, HERSCHEL. *The Race of Time.* Toronto, 1967.
BALDWIN, CHARLES SEARS. *Renaissance Literary Theory and Practice.* New York, 1939.
BUSH, DOUGLAS. *The Renaissance and English Humanism.* Toronto, 1939.
BUXTON, JOHN. *Sir Philip Sidney and the English Renaissance.* London, 1954.
CASPARI, FRITZ. *Humanism and the Social Order in Tudor England.* Chicago, 1954.
CRAIG, HARDIN. *English Religious Drama of the Middle Ages.* Oxford, 1955.
EINSTEIN, LEWIS. *The Italian Renaissance in England.* New York, 1902.
HALE, JOHN R. *England and the Italian Renaissance.* London, 1954.
HUNT, ERNEST W. *Dean Colet and His Theology.* London, 1956.
JAYNE, SEARS. *John Colet and Marsilio Ficino.* London, 1963.
LEHMBERG, STANFORD E. *Sir Thomas Elyot, Tudor Humanist.* Austin, Tex., 1960.
LUPTON, J. H. *A Life of John Colet.* London, 1887.

Nugent, Elizabeth M., ed. *Thought and Culture of the English Renaissance: An Anthology of Early Tudor Prose, 1483–1555.* Cambridge, 1954.

Seebohm, Frederick. *The Oxford Reformers: John Colet, Erasmus, and Thomas More* 3rd ed. London, 1896.

Spingarn, Joel E. *History of Literary Criticism in the Renaissance.* New York, 1912.

Weiss, Roberto. *Humanism in England During the Fifteenth Century,* 2nd ed. Oxford, 1957.

Thomas More:

Ames, Russel. *Citizen Thomas More and His Utopia.* Princeton, 1949.

Campbell, W. E. *Erasmus, Tyndale, and More.* London, 1949.

Chambers, R. W. *Thomas More.* New York, 1935.

Hexter, J. H. *More's Utopia: The Biography of an Idea.* Princeton, 1952.

Kautsky, Karl. *Thomas More and His Utopia.* New York, 1927.

Marc'hadour, Germain. *The Bible in the Works of Thomas More,* vol. 1. Nieuwkoop, 1969.

Surtz, Edward, S. J. *The Praise of Wisdom.* Chicago, 1957.

Erasmus:

Allen, P. S. *The Age of Erasmus.* Oxford, 1914.

Bainton, Roland H. *Erasmus of Christendom.* New York, 1969.

Huizinga, Johan. *Erasmus.* New York, 1924.

Hyma, Albert. *The Youth of Erasmus.* Ann Arbor, 1930.

Kaiser, Walter. *Praisers of Folly: Erasmus, Rabelais, Shakespeare.* Cambridge, Mass., 1963.

Phillips, Margaret Mann. *Erasmus and the Northern Renaissance.* New York, 1950.

Smith, Preserved. *Erasmus: A Study of His Life, Ideals, and Place in History.* New York, 1923.

CHAPTER 12

The Age
of the
Reformation

"We are at the dawn of a new era!" exclaimed Luther more
prophetically than he himself imagined. For the final consequences of the Reformation movement for all of Europe went far beyond what Luther expected, and in
many ways were very different from what he hoped for. "Rarely is a work undertaken out of wisdom and precaution," he declared, "but everything is undertaken
out of ignorance." The man who initiates creative action can seldom know where
his steps will lead him and what effect his actions will have on himself and others.
Luther knew this, and was willing to leave the result to God. "God has led me as
a horse having blinders so that I cannot see those who come up against me," he
confessed. As an outsized historical figure, Luther cast a large shadow across the
events of early modern times. But if Luther was a prime mover, the forces that
soon set all Europe in motion were stronger than any single man.

Europe entered the sixteenth century at least nominally unified by the Catholic
Church; it emerged from the Reformation with a variety of evangelical communities and Protestant groups competing with the old church and with each other for
the faith and devotion of men. At the outset Europe still conceived of itself as
Christendom, a body of believers with common goals to match their common faith;
by the end of the period it openly acknowledged the particularist interests of the
new monarchies and territorial principalities, and witnessed the bursting of its long-

DUTCH ENGRAVING OF THE SEVENTEENTH CENTURY. *The Candelstick: The Light of the Gospel Was Rekindled by All the Reformers.*

established bounds by colonial expansion into nearly all parts of the world. At the beginning of the century Europe had a lively but geographically limited capitalist economy on a broad agrarian base; at the end of the era its capitalism was vastly expanded and its mercantile enterprises circled the globe. Europe came to the Reformation epoch with a certain uniformity of ecclesiastical culture and still aglow with the artistic and literary triumphs of the Italian Renaissance, and at the close was moving rapidly toward new secular cultural foundations and the world of modern science. If it is no longer fashionable to refer to the Reformation, as did the historian James Froude in the nineteenth century, as "the hinge on which all modern history turns," its tremendous importance in the shaping of modern Europe must still be acknowledged. "I perceive a certain fatal change in human affairs," wrote Erasmus at the time. But the change he apprehensively saw as fatal was characterized rather by an enormous new vitality and by drives that carried European culture into new geographical and intellectual worlds.

A major historical happening like the Reformation is difficult to describe in detail, and no analysis of it can hope to be complete and final. The great historian Jacob Burckhardt, in the sixth book of his masterful work *The Civilization of the Renaissance in Italy,* candidly conceded the near impossibility of the undertaking:

> Mighty events like the Reformation elude, as respects their details, their outbreak and their development, the deductions of the philosophers, however clearly the necessity of them as a whole may be demonstrated. The movements of the human spirit, its sudden flashes, its expansions and its pauses, must forever remain a mystery to our eyes, since we can but know this or that of the forces at work in it, never all of them together.

History as the realm of freedom and of meaning is always difficult to describe and to interpret, but a movement in which the most delicate inward spiritual concerns of men are involved requires special sensitivity, a proper balance between objectivity and sympathy.

The task of understanding the period has been made more difficult by the great simplifiers, who have fixed in the popular mind clichés and half-truths that must first be cleared away. The eighteenth-century philosophers missed the real importance of the Reformation. Voltaire, for example, praised Luther only as one who resisted the Roman Catholic Church, and saw the Reformation as a squabble of monks in a corner of Saxony which plunged thirty nations into misery. Montesquieu appreciated the Reformation for its cultural by-products. Many of the nineteenth-century historians saw it as a seedbed of ideas congenial to themselves, whether they were liberal or conservative. Thus the French statesman and historian François Guizot called the Reformation an expression of the desire of the human mind for freedom and a "great effort to emancipate human reason." The German poet Heinrich Heine declared that when Luther defied the pope, Robespierre decapitated the king, and Immanuel Kant disposed of God, it was all one insurrection against the same tyrant under different names. The Prussian historian Heinrich Treitschke proclaimed in 1883 that Luther broke the shackles of "that crowned priest the pope" and became the founder of the modern secular state. And the famous nineteenth-century thinker Bertrand Russell, who lived on far into the twentieth century, once said that the Reformation had freed men religiously, but they have yet to free themselves politically and economically.

But if one were to ask the reformers themselves what gave their work its special memorable character, they would declare their service to have been the restoration of Christian truths that had been forgotten or only half remembered in the church: the sovereignty and graciousness of God, the meaning of Jesus Christ as the redeemer of estranged man, the power of faith, the essence of the Word, the freedom of the Christian, and the pure teaching of these truths against the false accretions of tradition and an erring papacy. Though the Reformation brought about social, political, and economic change, the reformers themselves concentrated predominantly on theological and religious matters. "My affair is not a joint program," Luther asserted. The study of the Reformation in its full dimensions, then, must take the religious issues seriously. "The deepest theme in history has been posed by the conflict between faith and disbelief," wrote Goethe.

During the first years of the Reformation many humanists viewed it as the religious expression of the general cultural Renaissance. The Erasmian humanist Johann von Botzheim, a canon at Constance, praised Luther as the man who, "after all the other disciplines have been renewed, is now renewing theology itself." In Augsburg another Erasmian, Bernhard Adelmann, equated the terms *doctus* and *Lutherus,* learned man and Lutheran. Erasmus' own alter ego, the young humanist Beatus Rhenanus, responded to the Reformation with the cry: "I see the whole world reviving!" And Luther himself viewed the Renaissance revival of learning as a kind of John the Baptist serving as a forerunner for the advent of the pure gospel. "No one knew," he wrote, "why God allowed the study of the languages to come forth until it was finally realized that it was for the sake of the gospel which He wished to reveal thereafter."

Many ties bound the Reformation to the Renaissance: the drive back to the pure sources, the reaction against scholastic philosophy, the criticism of formalism in religious practice, and the concern with an educational and religious revival. The humanists had sought their model in the golden age of classical letters, the reformers in the early church and the Scriptures. This drive to the sources was recognized as a characteristic mark of the Reformation by Francis Bacon, who wrote in his *Advancement of Learning* (Book 1):

> Martin Luther, conducted (no doubt) by an higher providence, but in discourse of reason finding what a province he had undertaken against the Bishop of Rome and the degenerate traditions of the church, and finding his own solitude, being no ways aided by the opinions of his own time, was enforced to awake all antiquity,

and to call former times to his succours to make a party against the present time: so that the ancient authors, both in divinity and in humanity, which had long time slept in libraries, began generally to be read and revolved.

The humanists made basic contributions to the recovery of Christian as well as classical antiquity. The new philology and linguistic studies, the discovery and editing of patristic texts as well as new critical editions of the Scriptures in the original languages, the new historical sense of distance from the pure and more perfect age, all these belonged to the Renaissance inheritance of the reformers.

The reformers shared with the humanists a low assessment of the centuries just past. If Petrarch and the humanists evolved the concept of a dark age separating them from antiquity, the reformers viewed the three preceding centuries as the nadir of the church's history, a period of corruption in the hierarchy, of abuses, ignorance, and indifference among the lower secular clergy and monks, and of gross superstition and "work righteousness" on the part of the laity. They reserved special scorn for medieval scholastic philosophy. Like the humanists, they were critical of the "barbarous" Latin of the scholastics, and elevated rhetoric above dialectic as a method for ascertaining and expressing truth. Luther's young lieutenant Philipp Melanchthon thus described medieval learning as a barbaric mixture of two evils: ignorant yet garrulous philosophy and the cult of idols. The English reformer John Bale, popularly known as "bilious Bale" for his talent for invective, declared that the mere description of this sordid, obscure, and ignoble kind of writing was enough to move generous and wellborn minds to nausea. Luther opposed scholastic logic as unsuitable to religious study. The objection of the reformers to scholastic learning went far beyond criticism of its language and dialectic to rejection of the religious presuppositions of scholastic theology, propositions they considered to be semi-Pelagian, stressing man's contribution to his salvation rather than his total dependence upon God's grace and forgiveness. The reformers' drive against the church's religious teaching and practice proved to be a far more radical and revolutionary force than Renaissance religious philosophy had generated. From 1520 on, the Reformation began to derail humanism in the religious realm.

How revolutionary was the Reformation? Edward Gibbon observed toward the end of the second volume of his monumental *Decline and Fall of the Roman Empire:* "After a fair discussion we shall rather be surprised by the timidity than scandalized by the freedom of our first reformers." Luther recognized in himself and others the difficulty of overcoming inertia and undertaking something that challenged established custom. "How very true is the saying 'To leave behind customary things is difficult and custom is second nature,'" he reflected. Moreover, the magisterial reformers viewed their program as a restoration of the ancient and honorable faith, not as an innovation or novelty. Melanchthon, in fact, believed that their moderate reforms had prevented tumults that would have been much more serious. A movement that was not revolutionary by intent, then, nevertheless turned out to have very revolutionary consequences. Revolutions are not created, they are unleashed. Controversy drove Luther to take positions more radical than any he had anticipated. Much of Europe was ready for that historical change to which the reformers gave actual form and shape. Leopold von Ranke, the great founder of modern critical history in the past century, described the Reformation as the most profound spiritual revolution ever experienced by a people in so short a period of time. Paradoxically the Reformation was moderate in intent and radical in consequence.

The Reformation was the first major historical movement of the post-Gutenberg era, and the printing press was a major instrument in its mass appeal. The printing press had an impact on two levels, among the learned and among the commoners. The printers, many of whom, such as Johannes Froben, Johannes Amerbach, and Aldus Manutius, were intellectual humanists and patrons of learning, made available to scholars a flood of classical, patristic, and medieval texts, especially devotional materials, and above all Bibles. More than one hundred editions of the Scriptures were published between 1457 and 1500. After the first printing the Bible was reduced to one-twentieth of its former price. It has been estimated that by 1500 A.D. some forty thousand works had been published, totaling around ten million precious volumes. This meant a great diffusion of knowledge, of course, but perhaps of equal importance was the improvement of textual accuracy and general consistency for the benefit of philological study. While the printed book inaugurated that phase of Western civilization which the metahistorian Oswald Spengler characterized as our "book and reading culture," and may have unduly exalted the authority of the written word, with peculiar consequences for later Protestantism, its immediate effect was a powerful impact by the reformers upon the masses through ideas that trickled down from the learned classes and through tracts and flyers distributed directly to the people. From 1500 to the start of the Reformation, German publishers issued an average of forty books a year, but once the Reformation began this number rocketed to five hundred titles a year. Beatus Rhenanus wrote to Zwingli that Luther's books were not so much sold as snatched from the hands of the booksellers. Within a fortnight after their appearance Luther's ninety-five theses had been printed and carried into all parts of Europe. Luther viewed the printing press as the ultimate gift of God by which the gospel was to be propagated. In his *Book of Martyrs* the English Protestant John Foxe praised the invention of printing as the "admirable work of God's wisdom," through which by God's grace "good wits" were stirred up "aptly to conceive the light of knowledge and judgment, by which light darkness began to be espied and ignorance to be detected, truth from error, religion from superstition to be discerned." Protestants and their opponents were very quick to seize upon this revolutionary instrument.

BROSAMER. *The Seven Heads of Martin Luther*. Title page for Cochlaeus' blast against Luther. One head is a fanatic with wasps in his hair.

Why the Reformation Happened

WHY DID the Reformation originate in Germany? Why, for that matter, did it happen at all?

A common elementary explanation of the occurrence of the Reformation is that it came as a reaction against abuses in the church. "The church" was hopelessly corrupt, arousing the wrath and indignation of right-minded men. This simple argument, which appeared in much early humanist and Protestant polemical historiography, was matched on the Catholic side by assertions that Luther acted as a wicked or misguided and rebellious son of mother church, a grand example of what the philosopher Alfred North Whitehead has described as "the fallacy of misplaced concreteness." Actually an explanation on this level is not without some truth, for there were gross and offensive abuses in the church, and Luther and the reformers did seek to bring about changes while remaining within the fold.

A second explanation, a variation of the first, is that the Reformation was a result of doctrinal deviation. On the eve of the Reformation the church was, so the argument goes, wallowing in theological uncertainty. Doctrine was imprecisely defined, allowing as legitimate many theological statements that were no longer really Catholic, since they were not compatible with the Roman missal or liturgy. This uncertainty was heightened by the battle of the *viae* in scholastic theology— that is, the philosophy of the nominalist followers of William of Occam, known as the *via moderna,* and that of the moderate realist supporters of Thomas Aquinas, known as the *via antiqua.* The Occamists are said to have pressed their nominalist epistemology to the extreme of skepticism and nearly to the point of the doctrine of double truth: that some things are true in theology that are not true in philosophy and vice versa. They put such emphasis on God's will and sovereignty that they made him seem arbitrary and unaccountable. Yet man's role in attaining salvation and a stress upon the authority of the church were paradoxically elevated to new heights. Luther studied *via moderna* theology in the works of Gabriel Biel (d. 1485), the last significant Occamist. The opposition by Johannes Eck and other poor representatives of the faith also schooled in nominalism led to the doctrinal deviations of the Reformation. Against this negative interpretation of scholasticism it may be argued that the scholastics from Robert Holcot (d. 1349) to Gabriel Biel did not press Occam's presuppositions to extremes of skepticism or basic doctrinal deviation, and that Luther criticized the tendency of both scholastic *viae* to stress man's contribution to his own salvation in contrast to reliance on God's grace alone. Thanks to the schism and the conciliar movement, the primacy of the pope and his monarchical episcopate were no longer so securely fixed in the popular mind. But beyond the debates that still remained within the bounds of ecclesiastical permissiveness lay the acknowledged heresies of the Cathari, Waldensians, Wycliffites, Hussites, and a welter of other sects and mystic cults, many of which persisted into and beyond the first decades of the Reformation and contributed to radical deviation.

Behind the medieval variations in theology and the Reformation leap into new dimensions of religious thought lay what seems to be a characteristic of the collective mind. Systems of thought such as the great *summa* of St. Thomas seem to have certain limits of extension and longevity; when these are reached, the restless intellect presses beyond them. This has been true of all dogmatic systems as well as of the great synthetic philosophies. Perhaps, too, there is something worth pondering in Carl Jung's suggestion that the great archetypal configurations in the collective unconscious lose their hold upon man after a time and are replaced by others.

Still another and more prosaic explanation of the Reformation looks to its sociological roots. Europe in 1500 had between 65 million and 80 million people and possibly sixty or more kings, princes, archbishops, and other rulers in strategic positions of power. New social forces such as capitalism and the bourgeois classes that rose with it, the new technology in printing, mining, shipping, and other enterprises and the new working classes that maintained it, and the further growth of the cities were changing the real lines of power and dependency. Some classes, such as the lower nobility, were losing their traditional status and, except for a relatively few individuals of extraordinary adaptability, were being pushed aside. The church, which had adapted all too well to feudalism—some bishops, for example, were little more than feudal overlords—found it necessary to adopt new capitalist devices in order to support her hierarchy and the bureaucracy that had developed to meet the exigencies of curial government. The papacy's desperate and frustrated attempts to increase its income from the time of the Avignonese popes through the Renaissance popes gave the church the appearance of rapacious avarice, contributed to its loss of prestige and moral influence, and enraged the moralists, humanist critics, and reformers.

Finally, by one of those peculiar developments that precipitate cataclysmic events in history, at the very time when the official church was least able to provide moral leadership and a satisfying spiritual experience for the people, a new wave of religious devotion broke over Europe. For a century and a half before the Reformation, an increase in religious fervor was in evidence throughout most of Europe, including Italy. This increasing religiosity, principally touched off by the horrors of the Black Death and fear of the Turks, was evident in the growing number of shrines and pilgrimages, new prayers and increased use of candles, a renewed popularity of the rosary promoted by the Dominican Alain de la Roche (d. 1475), and the appearance of the stations of the cross in churches.

The veneration of saints increased, and each craft and trade guild adopted its own patron saint. St. George and St. Martin were popular with soldiers, St. Dorothea with gardeners, St. Barbara (who had been imprisoned in a tower)

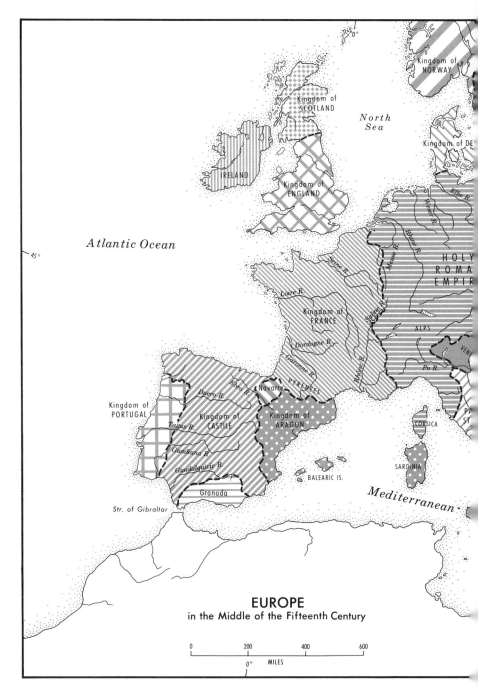

EUROPE
in the Middle of the Fifteenth Century

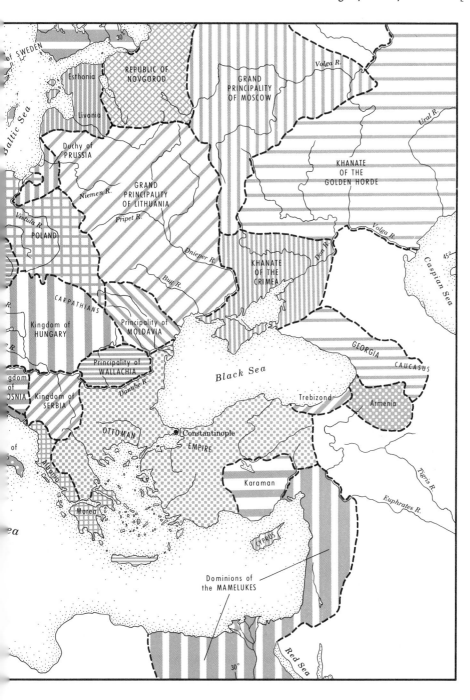

of SWEDEN

Baltic Sea

Esthonia

Livonia

Duchy of
PRUSSIA

Niemen R.

Vistula R.

POLAND

30°

REPUBLIC OF
NOVGOROD

GRAND
PRINCIPALITY
OF LITHUANIA

Pripet R.

Dnieper R.

Bug R.

CARPATHIANS

Kingdom of
HUNGARY

Principality of
MOLDAVIA

Principality of
WALLACHIA

Danube R.

gdom
of
OSNIA

Kingdom of
SERBIA

OTTOMAN

Albania

Morea

ea

GRAND
PRINCIPALITY
OF MOSCOW

Volga R.

KHANATE
OF THE
GOLDEN HORDE

Ural R.

Volga R.

KHANATE
OF THE
CRIMEA

Don R.

45°

Caspian Sea

GEORGIA
CAUCASUS

Black Sea

Trebizond

Armenia

EMPIRE

Constantinople

Karaman

Tigris R.

Euphrates R.

CYPRUS

Dominions of
the MAMELUKES

30°

Red Sea

with cannonaders, and St. Bartholomew, skin in hand, with butchers. In Germany saints' names superseded all but the most popular old German names for children during the fifteenth century. The cult of St. Anne, Mary's mother, was widespread during that century and at the start of the next. Devotion to Mary increased enormously during the late fourteenth and fifteenth centuries. New masses were established commemorating every detail of her life, piety, and seven sorrows. The Franciscans, with the support of many of the humanists and against the opposition of the Dominicans, promoted the doctrine of the immaculate conception of Mary, an idea destined to become Catholic dogma many centuries later. Scores of new churches, especially in the new lands in northeast Germany, from Lübeck eastward, were named in her honor.

Endowed brotherhoods were organized for the pooling and sharing of good works. The Brethren of St. Ursula in Cologne in the sixteenth century amassed a spiritual fortune of 6,000 masses, 3,000 psalters, 20,000 *Te Deums,* and 100,000 rosaries, paternosters, and *Ave Marias.* Grotesque collections of relics in various parts of Europe attested to the gullibility and superstition of the people as well as to the commercial advantage of such attractions. Two such treasures, which played a direct part in setting the stage for the Reformation, were the collection of Frederick the Wise in Saxony, which included among its five thousand relics such gems as straw from the manger in Bethlehem, wood from the true cross, and the thumb of St. Anne, and the collection in the cathedral chapter at Noyen in Picardy (where John Calvin spent his childhood), which boasted a fragment of the crown of thorns and a lock of John the Baptist's hair. Pilgrimages to the shrines at Canterbury in England and Compostela in Spain remained popular, and newer shrines such as those in Regensburg and Alt-Ötting in Bavaria drew increasingly large numbers, including many crippled and sick people looking for cures.

The sale of indulgences multiplied, allegedly for church building or crusades against the Turks, though often for debt reduction by higher clergy or the papacy. The fact that they were sold and bought on such a grand scale is an index of the admixture of piety and superstition that proved to be such an explosive compound. Many new churches were built in the fifteenth and sixteenth centuries, first in an elaborate late Gothic style and then in the Renaissance style. The success of such popular preachers as John of Capistrano (d. 1456) and Johann Geiler von Kaisersberg (d. 1510) in swaying tens of thousands of people was an indication of the surcharged spiritual atmosphere and the response awaiting a clear call and more certain trumpet.

The great irony, indeed the great danger, of the situation was that in this time of increased religious fervor, the church was in no position to provide inspiring leadership or a constructive channel for this new force, but was itself the object of criticism and even ridicule. In religion, Dean Inge observed, nothing fails like success. At the Council of Nicea in 325 A.D. the Spanish bishops were reprimanded for being too worldly and too concerned with material things. In 1215, at the height of the Middle Ages, the great pope Innocent III charged the Fourth Lateran Council with introducing reforms. *Ecclesia semper reformanda* (the church which must always be reformed) was a phrase perennially applicable to a human institution of such wide scope. During the fifteenth century the slogan formulated by William of Durand during the conciliar movement, calling for a "reformation in head and in members," was repeatedly heard. Signs of discontent and disaffection were everywhere.

When the church appeared to be most opulent, it actually stood most in need of money to finance its burgeoning bureaucracy, elaborate juridical processes, and ambitious building programs and activities. It has been asserted that one-third of the landed wealth of Europe was held by the church, by means of a legal fiction known as the incorporation of the church, whereby the title was vested in God while the property was administered by churchmen. It was widely believed that two-fifths of the German income was siphoned off to Rome through ecclesiastical channels. Great ingenuity was employed in devising new sources of ecclesiastical income. From the thirteenth century on, by canonical provision, if the holder of an ecclesiastical post died while in Rome, his benefice was reassigned by the pope (not by the bishop in whose see the post was located). The practice of reservations, or payments for nominations to vacant benefices, and the collection of annates, the first year's revenue from a benefice, increased opportunities for simony, the buying of church offices. Nepotism in ecclesiastical appointments seemed to be on the increase. Under Pope Leo X (1513–1521) the number of church offices available for purchase rose to an all-time high, and he employed his Medici talent in founding new offices for financial gain. The acrostic *Radix Omnium Malorum Avaritia* (the love of money is the root of all evil) = ROMA was popular. Conrad Peutinger, the Augsburg city secretary sent to Rome during the pontificate of Innocent VIII, wrote in 1491 of the shocking venality in the capital of Christendom:

> I see that everything here can be bought from top to bottom. Intrigues, hypocrisy, adulation are highly honored, religion is debased; vulgarities occur without number; righteousness sleeps. Whenever I see the ruined monuments of antiquity, I deplore the fact that this famous city is ruled by a foreign race which under pious pretenses practices every deed of violence and other unheard-of outrages, and they wish thereby to be praised instead of the deserved censure. When I rebuke them they say that fate has so ordained it![1]

In marked contrast to the splendor of many of the upper clergy in key positions, a great many priests, especially in rural areas, were wretchedly provided for. The income from many prebends was so small that a cleric either held several of them, which involved him in the abuse of plurality of incomes, or lived in poverty

---

[1] Peutinger to Valentin Eber, August 5, 1491, in *Konrad Peutingers Briefwechsel,* ed. Erich König (Munich, 1923), p. 9.

as great as any monk's. Vicars of parishes attached to monasteries had extraordinarily small incomes. In Scotland over half the vicars were extremely poor. In Flanders the priests were so poorly paid that many had to work at other jobs. The bishop of Clermont reported to the Council of Trent in 1546 that of eight hundred parishes in his diocese, only sixty had regular parish priests, and the rest were cared for by vicars, whose incomes amounted to a mere ten or twelve guldens a year.

The education of a majority of priests was minimal. Most of them had learned the elements of Latin and basic catechismal theology and the rite of the mass as apprentices to local priests; only a few were privileged to attend cathedral and monastic schools prior to ordination. A very small proportion of priests studied theology at a university, although the number increased during the second half of the fifteenth century. Felix Faber was exaggerating, though not greatly, when he wrote in his *Chronicle of Ulm* at the end of the fifteenth century that in his youth, of a thousand clergymen there was hardly one who had so much as seen a university town, and the holder of a degree was stared at as a prodigy. Of course, this was an unfair thrust, for ever since the high Middle Ages it had been the custom for most local clergymen to be educated in local houses of study that served the purpose, though they never claimed to produce scholars. In some dioceses candidates for the priesthood were required by their bishops to study in the diocesan schools of the regular clergy. The social status of the common clergy was depressingly low. These conditions help to explain not only the poor morale of the clergy on the eve of the Reformation, but also the fact that recruits for the evangelical movement came by the thousands from the secular and regular clergy of the church itself.

One of the abuses most corrosive of the spiritual life of the church was the absenteeism of key clergy. The holding of multiple prebends and offices was necessitated in part by the low income produced by endowments in the depressed economy and in part by the extravagant living by higher clergy, many of whom were actual feudal overlords or functionaries of civil government. Cardinal Wolsey, the butcher's son who rose to be Henry VIII's chancellor, was also archbishop of York, bishop of Durham and Winchester, deputy for nonresident alien bishops at Worcester, Salisbury, and Llandaff, and abbot of St. Albans. As a boy his bastard son was already dean of Wells and archdeacon of York and Richmond, with two rectories, six prebends, and one appointment as chancellor. Even Henry VIII's humanist physician Thomas Linacre had been a canon of three cathedrals, rector of four parishes, and precentor of the York cathedral prior to ordination into the priesthood. Government was exploiting church income for the monarch's political or personal ends, but the church as keeper of the public conscience suffered the moral opprobrium of a situation not always of its own making. A scandalous instance in France was the case of Antoine Duprat, a diplomat who was rewarded with the archbishopric of Sens, but entered the cathedral there for the first time on the occasion of his own funeral. In Italy Cardinal Ippolito d'Este, who was archbishop of Milan, never once visited this important diocese in thirty years. In Germany the most blatant case of plural offices was that of Albert of Brandenburg, who was not content to be merely archbishop of Magdeburg and bishop of Halberstadt, but in addition purchased the archbishopric of Mainz, since this office made him both one of the imperial electors and secretary of the Holy Roman Empire. The clergy, said the preacher Johann Geiler von Kaisersberg, had become fishers of prebends rather than of souls. Because the rewards of high church offices were great, the aristocracy preempted them. Many enterprising young men took degrees in both canon and civil law, so that they would be prepared for any opportunity. The social requirements of some cathedral canons were so severe that Erasmus commented that Christ himself could not have become a member of the chapter at Strassburg.

A peculiar dichotomy existed in the general attitude toward the clergy. The late scholastic Gabriel Biel placed priests higher than the angels, for in the blessed sacrament they were dispensers of a mystery and could allow or prohibit God to come into being, which angels could not do. The father of German humanism, Rudolf Agricola, in his *Exhortation to the Clergy at Worms,* waxed eloquent over the majesty, mystery, and glory of the priesthood. But these very decades witnessed a marked increase in the immorality of the clergy and a widespread breakdown of celibacy as a viable system. Sixteenth-century visitation reports reveal that one-fourth of the clergy in the Netherlands and one-third of all Catholic clerics in the lower Rhine region were living with concubines. In rural areas a woman was considered a natural and necessary helpmate to the working priest. The reform-minded bishop of Constance decreed that priests' children were not to serve as altar boys or take walks with their fathers. Bishop Christoph von Stadion composed a long report on the clergy's loss of virtue. Archbishop Albert of Brandenburg kept a house of courtesans in Halle until it was stormed and dismantled by a mob of Protestants. As late as 1539 Luther had to admonish him for smuggling a mistress into the archepiscopal palace inside a relic box. In the popular mind corruption was seen to be spreading from Rome outward, subverting the simple, purer people across the Alps. "The nearer to Rome, the worse the Christians," they said. The author of *The Ship of Fools,* Sebastian Brant, a half-medieval humanist, summarized much popular sentiment in his foreboding couplet:

> Saint Peter's ship I fear I'm thinking
> May very shortly now be sinking!

The medieval religious principles of the virtue of self-denial and the spiritual value of the ascetic life remained the theoretical ideals of society into the sixteenth century. On this basis the regular clergy (those who lived by the *regula,* or rule, of a monastic order) were the truly "religious," bound by their threefold vows of poverty, chastity, and obedience. "To become a priest is worthy of honor," wrote Trithemius, abbot of Sponheim, "but to become a monk out of love of God means to achieve a greater perfection." But this same Trithemius who held such high regard for the monastic way decried the pride, power drive, and corruption of the orders and their houses. He attacked the abbots who ruled as feudal overlords of the vast possessions of the monasteries:

> Dare we believe, my brothers, that St. Benedict had such expensive horses and mules as we now see many an abbot possess? Certainly not! And do we not read of St. Martin that he rode in on a lowly donkey using a cord for a rein, not on such a proud steed as our heads of orders today, who dash about here and yon on their noble horses holding in their hands a bridle with silver and gold ornamentation! O vanity of vanities, what does this pride mean?[2]

Preachers such as Johann Geiler von Kaisersberg were critical of the worldliness and lack of spirituality of the monks. "The walls do not make a monastery!" he exclaimed. "It must be within the heart." Popular humor often turned on the theme of monastic corruption. "She longs for the cloister for she wants a lover" was a standard witticism.

The humanists assaulted especially the mendicants for their tyranny, which made even popes fear them, and for their obscurantism. Because of their reputation for mendacity and lechery, they were depicted in popular art as foxes and wolves wearing cowls. The controversy over Johannes Reuchlin defined the issues clearly in the humanists' minds. They saw the Dominicans of Cologne as treacherous re-actionaries intent on martyring Reuchlin, who had achieved so much for Hebrew studies and the cause of scholarship. There was clearly a loss of élan, a displace-ment in the heart of the medieval ascetic system, due to a corrosion in the monastic and mendicant orders themselves and to a shift away from the ascetic ideal as an expression of the good life and of religion's highest worth.

Yet the reputation of the orders, thanks to the exaggerations of the humanists, Protestants, and later Whiggish historians, was certainly much worse than the actual conditions warranted. The orders, in fact, made repeated efforts at funda-mental reforms. The Carthusians had a near-perfect record of adherence to their rule. The Benedictines had such centers of reform as Melk on the Danube. The Dominican reform effort began in Italy under Cajetan, the master general of the order. A Franciscan "observant" movement began in France, and in 1517 Pope Leo X allowed two independent orders to organize: the Observantines, who be-lieved in strict observance of the rule of St. Francis, and the Conventuals, who fol-lowed a modified rule. The Augustinian hermits developed an Observantine group of houses, organized by the Saxon Andreas Proles and continued by Johannes Staupitz, Luther's confessor, after Proles's death in 1503. It was in connection with

---

2 Cited in Willi Andreas, *Deutschland vor der Reformation: Eine Zeitenwende,* 5th ed. (Stuttgart, 1948), p. 126.

a dispute about bowing to a nonreformed provincial that Luther was sent to Rome to represent the Observantine Augustinians in 1510. The lay order of the Brethren of the Common Life, founded by Gerard Groote (d. 1384), established many houses from Utrecht and Deventer across northern Europe and up the Rhine in the course of the fifteenth century. The Brethren, closely associated with the more mystical Augustinians, showed tremendous vitality, maintained dozens of famous secondary schools where the "safe" classics were taught, kept hospices for poor students, and educated a surprisingly large number of men who later became famous, among them Desiderius Erasmus and, it seems, Martin Luther. They were so useful and enjoyed such an excellent reputation that even after the church was wrenched apart, Luther and Melanchthon defended them, and they were allowed to teach in such Protestant lands as Brandenburg. Recent research has revealed that moral conditions had not deteriorated so badly in the English monasteries as had been popularly believed since their closing by King Henry VIII. The same is true of monasteries on the continent. And yet all the evidence suggests that in much of northern Europe the monastic system was played out as a vital religious force. In city after city, as in Nuremberg and Augsburg, the same mothers who had tearfully delivered their unmarried daughters to the cloisters descended upon these establishments to free them again when the Reformation erupted. More than coincidence is involved in the fact that literally thousands of evangelical preachers and teachers were recruited from the ranks of the monks, friars, and hermits; Luther himself was only the first of many.

The church missed its last big chance at a general reform that would have met the demands for restoration and renewal when, at the opening session of the Fifth Lateran Council (1512–1517), the general of the Augustinian order, Egidio da Viterbo, a distinguished Platonist, called for an inner spiritual reform that would be reflected in an outward improvement. His approach was in the tradition of the Christian humanist program, but the council failed to respond to this or to any of the other demands for reform. It was comprised mostly of Italian prelates, and thus fell somewhat short of being ecumenical, even though a New World bishop from Santo Domingo did attend. It called for perpetual peace among Christian princes and made a loud clamor for a financial assessment on all kingdoms and states for a crusade against the Turks, even permitting the taxation of the clergy in some lands. But the response was cynical, for the Venetians, for example, declared that the money would be used by Pope Leo X to finance his war against Urbino, where he hoped to gain territory for the Medici family. In the final session, which ironically came in the year in which the Reformation began, the council reaffirmed the bull *Unam sanctam* (1302), in which Pope Boniface VIII had asserted his claim to a fullness of spiritual power and real, though indirect, authority over all rulers. The ecclesiasts had, it seems, forgotten nothing, but they were about to learn a great deal.

After the outbreak of the Reformation the earnest Dutch pope Adrian VI instructed Chieregati, his legate to the Diet of Nuremberg in 1522 and 1523, to confess:

> God has let this persecution of His church occur because of men and especially because of the sins of the priests and prelates. The Holy Scriptures loudly proclaim that the sins of the people have their origin in the sins of the religious leaders. We know all too well that also in the case of this Holy See for many years many reprehensible things have taken place: abuses in spiritual things, breaking of the commandments, yes, that everything has taken a turn for the very worst! We therefore have no cause to wonder that the disease has been transplanted from the head to the members, from the popes to the prelates.[3]

If the disappointing pronouncements of the Fifth Lateran Council and the failure to implement even these was a matter of too little, too late, the public confession of Pope Adrian was a matter of too much, much too late, for by 1523 the Protestants simply used his statement to prove the truth of their allegations against Rome. The church entered the Reformation with its spiritual power sadly diminished.

Why the Reformation Happened in Germany

LEOPOLD VON RANKE formulated the postulate that ecclesiastical and political history are indissolubly connected. In the case of the Reformation this truism is even more obvious than usual, for the political conditions in the Germanies contrasted in many essential ways with those in other lands. The special circumstances in Germany constituted preconditions favorable to the success of the Reformation movement. Certainly they do not of themselves offer a causal explanation for the Reformation or for its religious nature and theological substance.

The Holy Roman Empire was not yet so effete as it was to become in the seventeenth century, when the political philosopher Samuel Pufendorf called it a ghost, but its claim to universality was already empty and its ancient members could hardly bestir themselves to effective action. The very name Holy Roman Empire did not come into widespread use until the twelfth century, and the fact that the empire's jurisdiction was really limited to the German lands was at last acknowledged when the qualifying phrase "of the German Nation" came into semiofficial use during the reign of Emperor Maximilian I (1493–1519). Various efforts at the constitutional reform of the empire, such as those of its secretary Archbishop Berthold von Henneberg, who hoped to make it a more effective political force in the late fifteenth century, failed because of the particularist interests of the territorial principalities and the dead weight of tradition. Von Henneberg pressed for

---

[3] Carl Mirbt, ed., *Quellen zur Geschichte des Papsttums und des römischen Katholizismus,* 4th ed. (Tübingen, 1924), p. 261.

an executive college of electors, an effective imperial supreme court, and a common imperial tax to promote centralization. But the princes were unwilling to sacrifice any sovereignty, and neither Maximilian nor Charles V succeeded in getting any reforms through the diet. In 1519 the elector of Mainz referred to the empire as a princely aristocracy with the diet as the actual sovereign.

The historian can argue with some plausibility that the last real chance for a unified Germany under effective imperial rule was lost at the time of the investiture controversy in the late eleventh and early twelfth centuries, when in his struggle for "the right order of things in the world" Pope Gregory VII freed the feudal vassals of their oaths of allegiance to the emperor and gave the princes their chance at virtual autonomy. The empire had failed as a political force long before the Reformation; there is no truth in the old cliché that Luther did what Pope Innocent III and Emperor Frederick II had failed to do—break up the Holy Roman Empire and the Holy Roman Church. The very most that can be said is that the Reformation accelerated a process of dissolution already far advanced. By the end of the eighteenth century Goethe's whimsical query in *Faust* could be understood by all: "The dear old Holy Roman realm, how does it hold together?" The ignominious end came at last in August 1806, when a diminutive Corsican corporal pronounced its demise, speaking as Emperor Napoleon of France.

During the fifteenth and sixteenth centuries the Holy Roman Empire of the German Nation moved in a direction precisely opposite to the trend in western Europe. While England, France, and Spain moved toward national consolidation under strong dynastic monarchies, the empire experienced a strengthening of the territorial principalities, the social upsets of a dying feudalism, and a further weakening of the emperor's position. The very universality of the Habsburg dynastic holdings kept them from concentrating their efforts upon the Holy Roman Empire as such. Charles V was Charles I of Spain, though his first language was French, part of his Burgundian heritage and upbringing. His election as emperor in 1519, secured with loans from the Fugger banking house and the manipulation of the electors, brought to him a decentralized state with virtually none of the instruments of government that could serve as centripetal forces. For revenue and military power he was almost entirely dependent upon his dynastic lands. The *Reichstag* or diet was composed of the usual three estates, but it was dominated by the nobility, with lesser influence wielded by the upper clergy and especially the prince-bishops with great landed holdings, such as the three episcopal electors, the archbishops of Mainz, Trier, and Cologne; little or no power was exercised by the cities. For such enterprises as defense against the Turks the emperor was dependent upon voluntary contributions voted ad hoc and seldom paid when they were due.

Like the territorial principalities, the cities of the empire were in the ascendancy. In 1521 the imperial registry listed some eighty-five cities, of which sixty-five were directly under the empire. Governed by city councils and mayors who were

Der Buchdrucker.

Der Teppichmacher.

Der Papyrer.

Der Organist.

Der Schrifftgiesser.

Der Uhrmacher.

Der Apotecker.

Der Buchbinder.

really controlled by the merchant oligarchies, with some influence being exercised by lesser guilds, the cities enjoyed a large measure of freedom and independence. During the fifteenth and early sixteenth centuries they enjoyed great prosperity, especially those in southern Germany and along the Rhine. Augsburg, Nuremberg, Constance, Freiburg, Strassburg, Mainz, Cologne, and Erfurt hummed with commercial activity. They were veritable beehives, observed the humanist Conrad Celtis, where German merchants returned from Italy and the north to store their honey. But the cities were not organized to protect their mutual interests and had little collective political power, no matter how prosperous they became.

While the princes and cities rose to new eminence, the knightly class lost its military utility and went into decline as a vestigial remain of feudalism. Some of the nobility adjusted to the new society, but many turned to robbery and pillage, making raids upon merchants, towns, and monasteries until their castles were reduced to rubble by artillery fire or they were hanged or imprisoned in city dungeons. Goethe has immortalized in a play one such robber baron, Goetz von Berlichingen, the man with the iron arm, who struck fear into the hearts of prince-bishops and merchants until he was finally captured while leading a peasant revolt. There were many like him. To this superfluous class belonged also the humanist Ulrich von Hutten; perhaps his class background goes far to explain the bitterness of his attacks upon the ecclesiastical establishment.

Much of the empire, especially in the central and northern territories, was still agrarian and feudal in economic organization and mentality. While the peasants had less personal freedom than in many parts of France and England, they had greater independence than they had enjoyed in earlier centuries. They still shouldered many of the traditional burdens: annual dues, tithes, death taxes, restrictions on hunting and fishing, and limitations on personal movement. But payment in kind was increasingly commuted to payment in money, so that more and more peasants became renters rather than serfs. In a money economy their position seemed unenviable compared with that of the city dwellers, even though on an absolute scale they were much better off than ever before. Paradoxically their very prosperity and gains in personal liberties made the remaining restrictions more irksome. And in the southwest upper Rhineland, where the position of the peasants was better than elsewhere, their unrest was greater. It was in these regions that the dreaded *Bundschuh,* a secret revolutionary society of peasants, had its greatest strength. With social tensions mounting, the empire was a tinderbox ready for the revolutionary spark.

Ironically, much of the resentment of various social classes was directed against the church. The princes, who needed ever larger revenues for their modern weapons, mercenary troops, law courts, and finery, eyed the property and income of the church and coveted the wealth that was siphoned off to Italy. The cities struggled to wrest power away from neighboring overlords who were often prince-bishops, as much feudal rulers as churchmen. The city councils, like the princes, were opposed to the juridical privileges and immunities of the clergy, who were subject only to ecclesiastical courts and could carry their cases out of the empire all the way to Rome. The knights harbored hostility against the prince-bishops and exploitation by foreigners. Why should German gold be used to build churches in Rome, asked Ulrich von Hutten, when so many churches in Germany needed rebuilding? The peasants hated the ostentatious bearing of silk-clad prelates. When they labored on church lands, the abbots and bishops were themselves the hated oppressors, and it was very easy to identify the church with feudal exploitation.

The Roman church was much less restricted in Germany than in neighboring France. The Pragmatic Sanction of Bourges, agreed to by the French king Charles VII in 1438, had given the Gallican church many special privileges, among them the right to forbid judicial appeals to Rome, to restrict the papal control of benefices, and to substitute voluntary contributions for official dues. In 1516 King Francis I concluded the Concordat of Bologna with Pope Leo X, securing to the French king the right to make nominations to vacant bishoprics and abbacies in his realm, while granting the pope the right to collect the annates or first years' incomes from these offices. The emperor had no such privileges. He could never act with the force and effectiveness of the French king, to say nothing of the English monarch Henry VIII on his tight little island.

On the other hand, for a century and a half prior to the Reformation the rising new powers in the empire, the princes and the cities, had been strengthening their control over the church on the local level. In their drive to establish centralized control over their territories the princes introduced where they could the newly revived Roman law, which elevated the absolute power of the *princeps,* for it had, after all, been codified under Justinian. It is true that arguments from Roman law could be used to limit the power of princes, as in the frequent citations in the treatises on the right of resistance in the sixteenth century, but officially it was usually exploited in behalf of princely power. Humanist chancellors and secretaries worked with Roman legists to strengthen the authority of the prince at the expense of the traditional rights of the territorial estates and in opposition to the loosely organized bodies of common law such as the *Sachsenspiegel,* or Saxon folk law. Long before the Reformation some jurists of the territorial courts decided that the *princeps,* after the example of the *pontifex maximus* in ancient Rome, should be concerned also with religious affairs. Thus the old Germanic *Eigenkirche,* or proprietary church tradition, reinforced by the Renaissance legal development, grew into a system of princely control over the church in the princes' territories. The domination of church life by the princes was most thorough in the larger states: Austria, the Palatinate, Bavaria, Brandenburg. In Ducal Saxony the two archbishops took their fiefs from Duke Georg and paid him feudal dues. When Lutheranism threatened to penetrate Ducal Saxony, it was one of Georg's lawyers,

Melchior von Aussa, who first enunciated that principle so important in later centuries: *Cuius regio, eius religio*—whoever rules the realm, his shall be the religion. In tiny Jülich and Cleves the dukes had the right of visitation as though they were bishops. And in Electoral Saxony Duke Frederick the Wise made ecclesiastical and academic appointments. Though he saw Luther only once, at the Diet of Worms in 1521, as a good German ruler he would not tolerate Roman persecution of his professor.

In the imperial cities a very similar pattern of secular control developed. The city councils preempted one prerogative of the hierarchy after another until they were virtually in control of the church. The councils took over the administration of charity, sick care, hospices for the aged, the ordering of church and cloisters, regulations on ethical questions, and punishment for blasphemy, swearing, religious disturbances, and superstitious excesses. Education too became the concern of secular authorities: the cities and princes founded eighteen of the twenty universities established in Germany before the Reformation, including the University of Erfurt, a city foundation, and the University of Wittenberg, established by Frederick the Wise. The political fragmentation of the empire, coupled with the proprietary church situation, made the Reformation possible in the Germanies.

Lay control opened the door further to ecclesiastical abuses, so that, ironically, animosity against the Roman Catholic Church increased sharply in these decades. Erasmus wrote of the common hatred of the name of Rome among the Germans, intensified by the cultural nationalism of the German humanists. Year in and year out the imperial diets were flooded with complaints about exploitation, false jurisdiction, immorality, and other abuses. From 1415 to 1521 the *gravamina,* or grievances of the German nation against the Roman church, were voiced at the diets. In 1452 the archbishop of Mainz, as secretary of the Holy Roman Empire, drew up the first official statement of such grievances. In 1493 the nobles submitted their own list of grievances. The din grew loud and shrill. When at the Diet of Nuremberg in 1522 the papal legate Chieregati asked why the Edict of Worms of 1521 had not been enforced against Luther, he was answered with a list of a hundred grievances against the church about which nothing had been done either. Years later Cardinal Contarini had to tell Pope Paul III that if all the Protestant divines, including Luther himself, were reconciled to the church, the situation would in no way be affected, and the rebellion would go on as bitterly as before.

The religious situation in the Germanies in the early sixteenth century, however, does not bear an easy causal relationship to the outbreak of the Reformation. Quite the contrary, it offers rather the startling paradox that when disenchantment with the Roman hierarchy was most complete and resentment against abuses burned most fiercely, religious fervor and popular piety were most intense. Philosophers and historians have noted this phenomenon and have speciously attributed it to some quality in the Germans themselves. The German philosopher Hegel

ALBRECHT DÜRER. *Knight, Death, and the Devil.* Grey Collection, Fogg Art Museum, Harvard University.

ascribed the force of the Reformation to an "ancient and constantly preserved in-wardness of the German people." The Swiss Protestant historian Merle d'Aubigné wrote of "the peculiar character of the Germans, which seemed especially favorable to a religious reformation, for they had not been enervated by a false civilization."

Certainly there is nothing peculiarly Teutonic about religious intensity. For most people life was grim. As a result of poor diet, repeated outbreaks of the plague, and feudal warfare, life expectancy was not much over forty years, and many men of that age referred to themselves as "old men." The Germans, moreover, stood directly in the line of advance of the fearful Turks as they pressed up the Danube. A somber mood predominated, perhaps best illustrated in Albrecht Dürer's wood-cut of the four grinning horsemen of the apocalypse riding roughshod over hu-manity, or in his portrait of a knight in armor accompanied by death and the devil. The most striking characteristics of the German people in the years that ushered in the Reformation were a deep piety, a concern with the afterlife, and a zealous loyalty to the church as keeper of spiritual treasures. Heresies seemed ac-tually to be in decline and church activities increased, from the building of chapels to the publication of a great volume of religious literature. Mysticism gained a new power through the spread of tracts and treatises. The heartfelt tenderness of per-sonal religious faith is reflected in the one major contribution of the Germans to late medieval art, the Pietà, the representation of Mary holding in her lap the life-less body of her crucified son. The traditional economy of salvation was firmly held to and a genuine concern for the restoration of the church to its primal purity was everywhere in evidence among the humanists as well as among popular preachers. Matthias Grünewald's Isenheim altar painting of the suffering Christ on the cross was a typical expression of German faith in the crucified Redeemer. Germany was in the medieval religious mold in a way unique among the larger lands of Europe.

The churchmen, both German and Italian, failed to respond to this renewed piety. Not only did they fall behind lay humanists in culture and lay devotees in faith and ethics, but they continued as before to use the church for material gain and for political ends. They employed the dreaded ban or power of excommunica-tion to force payment of debts and to gain political concessions, and were insensitive to the giving of offense. The hostility to the Roman church that poured forth when the floodgates were opened by Martin Luther was largely the bitterness of the dis-appointed lover.

Luther, the Man of the People

SELDOM HAS ONE MAN so shaken the world as did Martin Luther as leader of the Reformation movement. In his own person he embodied both of the major re-

formatory drives surging through the German people: a demand for external reform to end abuses and pressure for a genuine spiritual renewal on the deepest level.

As an orator and publicist who enjoyed extraordinary rapport with his public,
he became the spokesman for all of their pent-up feelings of frustration, moral indignation, and downright anger at the Roman hierarchy, from the pope to the exploiting clergy and ignorant monks. The people were carried away with his powerful thrusts at the greedy "tyrants." His declarations ring with revolutionary force,
as do these lines from his "Address to the Christian Nobility of the German
Nation" in 1520:

> How is it that we Germans must put up with such robbery and extortion of our
> goods at the hands of the pope? If the kingdom of France has prevented it, why do
> we Germans let them make such fools and apes of us? . . . And we still go on
> wondering why princes and nobles, cities and endowments, land and people grow
> poor. We ought to marvel that we have anything left to eat![4]

The people could not resist a voice so tuned to their thinking. Alfonso Valdés,
secretary to Emperor Charles, reported that the Germans were generally exasperated against the Roman see. The people did not seem to attach great importance
to the emperor's edicts, he observed, for Lutheran books were sold with impunity
on every street corner and marketplace.

But even more important than the negative attack was Luther's own evangelical religious fervor. A religious genius of profound faith and theological insight,
he had made a deeper plunge into the meaning of the gospel than perhaps any other
man since St. Paul. As a prophet he reached the heart of a people longing for purity
and spiritual renewal. The great artist Albrecht Dürer wrote to Georg Spalatin in
January or February of 1520: "If God helps me to see Dr. Martin Luther, I shall
diligently make his portrait and engrave it as a lasting memory of the Christian
man who has helped me out of great anxieties!"[5] And Hans Sachs, the simple
cobbler and *Meistersinger* of Nuremberg, saw a new stirring and a new hope, and
hailed Luther as the "nightingale of Wittenberg." The Reformation was under
way, and no one could possibly know where it would lead Western man.

Bibliography

ATKINSON, JAMES, ed. *The Great Light: Luther and the Reformation,* vol. 44 of *Luther's
Works,* ed. Jaroslav Pelikan and Helmut T. Lehman. Grand Rapids, Mich., 1968.
BAINTON, ROLAND H. *The Reformation of the Sixteenth Century.* Boston, 1952.

---

[4] *Luther's Works,* ed. James Atkinson (Philadelphia, 1966), vol. 44, pp. 142–43.
[5] Edwin Panofsky, *The Life and Art of Albrecht Dürer* (Princeton, 1955), p. 198.

————. *The Age of the Reformation.* New York, 1956.

BRANDI, KARL. *Deutsche Geschichte im Zeitalter der Reformation und Gegenreformation,* 3rd ed. Leipzig, 1941.

BÜHLER, JOHANNES. *Deutsche Geschichte: Das Reformationszeitalter.* Berlin and Leipzig, 1938.

CHADWICK, OWEN. *The Reformation.* Baltimore, 1964.

DICKENS, A. G. *Reformation and Society in Sixteenth-Century Europe.* New York, 1966.

DILLENBERGER, JOHN, ed. *Martin Luther: Selections.* Garden City, N.Y., 1961.

ELTON, G. R. *Reformation Europe, 1517–1559.* Cleveland, 1963.

————, ed. *The Reformation, 1520–1559,* vol. 2 of *The New Cambridge Modern History.* Cambridge, 1958.

GRIMM, HAROLD J. *The Reformation Era, 1500–1650,* rev. ed. New York, 1965.

HARBISON, E. HARRIS. *The Age of the Reformation.* Ithaca, N.Y., 1955.

HARTUNG, FRITZ. *Deutsche Geschichte im Zeitalter der Reformation, der Gegenreformation und des 30 Jährigen Krieges,* 2nd ed. Berlin, 1963.

HILLERBRAND, HANS J. *The Reformation: A Narrative History Related by Contemporary Observers and Participants.* New York, 1964.

————. *The Protestant Reformation.* New York, 1968.

————. *Men and Ideas in the Sixteenth Century.* Chicago, 1969.

HOLBORN, HAJO. *The Reformation,* vol. 1 of *A History of Modern Germany.* New York, 1959.

HULME, E. M. *The Renaissance, the Protestant Revolution, and the Catholic Reformation in Continental Europe.* New York, 1921.

HURSTFIELD, JOEL, ed. *The Reformation Crisis.* New York, 1966.

JOACHIMSEN, PAUL. *Die Reformation als Epoche der deutschen Geschichte.* Munich, 1951.

KOENIGSBERGER, H. G., and MOSSE, G. L. *Europe in the Sixteenth Century.* New York, 1968.

LAU, FRANZ, and BIZER, ERNST. *A History of the Reformation in Germany to 1555.* London, 1969.

LÉONARD, ÉMILE G. *A History of Protestantism,* vol. 1, *The Reformation,* ed. H. H. Rowley, trans. Joyce M. H. Reid. London and Camden, N.J., 1965.

LINDSAY, THOMAS M. *A History of the Reformation,* 2 vols. New York, 1951.

LORTZ, JOSEPH. *How the Reformation Came.* New York, 1964.

————. *The Reformation in Germany,* 2 vols. New York, 1969.

LUTHER, MARTIN. *Luther's Works,* ed. J. Pelikan and H. Lehmann, 56 vols. St. Louis and Philadelphia, 1958– .

MOUSNIER, R. *Les XVIᵉ et XVIIᵉ siècles,* vol. 4 of *Histoire générale des civilisations.* Paris, 1954.

SMITH, PRESERVED. *The Age of the Reformation.* New York, 1920.

SPITZ, LEWIS W., ed. *The Reformation: Material or Spiritual?* Boston, 1962.

————, ed. *The Protestant Reformation.* Englewood Cliffs, N.J., 1966.

THULIN, OSKAR. *Illustrated History of the Reformation.* St. Louis, 1967.

WHALE, J. S. *The Protestant Tradition.* Cambridge, 1955.

WHITNEY, J. P. *The History of the Reformation.* London, 1940.

CHAPTER 13

Luther's
Evangelical
Thrust

About six o'clock in the evening of April 18, 1521, the imperial
herald led a pale and inwardly fearful and trembling Augustinian brother into the
crowded torchlit episcopal hall next to the towering Romanesque cathedral of
Worms in Germany. There Martin Luther stood before Emperor Charles V, the
princes and estates of the diet, the cardinals and the powers of this world, to attest to
his other-worldly faith. It was hardly a fair judicial trial, for he had been cited to
recant publicly, or, as Luther put it, to "rechant," or sing a new song. A day earlier
Luther had been asked whether he acknowledged the books placed before him to
be his and whether he was willing to retract and recall them. Much to everyone's
surprise, Luther had requested twenty-four hours in which to consider his reply.
Now his time was up, and as a great throng milled about outside, everyone within
strained to hear his decision. In a high, clear voice he spoke for ten minutes in
German and in Latin, acknowledging his books and declaring his loyalty to the
word of God. When the emperor's spokesman then demanded a simple answer declaring whether or not he would recant, Luther answered:

> Since then your serene majesty and your lordships seek a simple answer, I will give
> it in this manner, neither horned nor toothed: Unless I am convinced by the
> testimony of the Scriptures or by clear reason (for I do not trust either in the pope
> or in councils alone, since it is well known that they have often erred and contra-

dicted themselves), I am bound by the Scriptures I have quoted and my conscience is captive to the word of God. I cannot and I will not retract anything, since it is neither safe nor right to go against conscience.

I cannot do otherwise, here I stand, may God help me. Amen.

This simple declaration changed the state of Christendom and the course of human affairs. "Luther at Worms," wrote the Catholic historian Lord Acton, "is the most pregnant and momentous fact in our history.... The great fact which we have to recognize is that with all the intensity of his passion for authority he did more than any single man to make modern history the development of revolution."[1] But the twenty-one-year-old emperor Charles V was not impressed by this Saxon monk; "He will not make a heretic out of me!" he declared.

Luther left the hall with German soldiers muttering approval and the Spanish horsemen at the street gate shouting, "Into the fire!" Some witnesses reported that as Luther made his way out of the hall, he held his hand over his head like the victor in a tourney and cried out, "I am finished!" But what he thought to be the end turned out to be only a beginning.

Luther was warned to leave by friends who remembered the fate of Jan Hus at Constance. On April 26 he left Worms by a side gate and was spirited away by retainers of Elector Frederick of Saxony to a hideaway in the Wartburg Castle. Emperor Charles had the papal legate Girolamo Aleander prepare the famous Edict of Worms against Luther as an obstinate schismatic and manifest heretic. It was passed by a small group of delegates after the diet had officially adjourned and was signed by Charles on May 26, joining to the church's excommunication the great ban and overban of the secular arm and making Luther an outlaw who could be seized at will. But could the edict be enforced?

Luther's trip from Wittenberg to Worms had turned into a triumphal procession. He had left home on April 2, and on entering Erfurt he was greeted by his old friend Crotus Rubeanus, the rector of the university, with a large delegation of faculty and students, who hailed him as a righteous judge come to redress the grievances of the nation. He was repeatedly warned not to enter Worms. People held up to him pictures of Savonarola, a sobering reminder. At the last minute Elector Frederick himself, through the chancellor Spalatin, urged him not to enter Worms, for he had already been condemned. But Luther declared he would enter the city if there were as many devils in it as tiles on the roofs. As the procession moved along, Luther riding in a simple wagon with two or three companions, preceded by the imperial herald Kaspar Sturm in ceremonial costume and accompanied by a troop of a hundred armed men, thousands of people poured out to cheer the man who had become a national hero. In the dispatches that Aleander sent to Rome he estimated that three-fourths of the common people were on

---

[1] Lord Acton, *Lectures on Modern History* (London, 1906), pp. 101, 105.

Luther's side. The trip to Worms had been tense and fearful, but Luther's long road from his early years to Wittenberg had been even more arduous.

Luther's Religious Reformation

LUTHER'S ANCESTRAL HOME was Moehre, a small village of some fifty families on the western slope of the Thuringian forest. His forebears had emigrated to this region of Saxony from western Germany centuries before and had become free peasants. His grandfather Heinrich owned considerable property, including a small estate. The family lived in comfortable circumstances, but according to Saxon custom the younger son inherited the land and the eldest, Hans, had to make his own way. He moved to Eisleben, and there on November 10, 1483, Hans's second son, Martin, was born. Hans worked as a miner and rose first to foreman and then to renter. In 1491, when Martin was only eight, Hans borrowed money and became a member of a firm of copper miners. Two decades later he owned shares in six pits and two smelting companies. He supported his family of eight children well and sent Martin all the way through the university.

Martin attended school in Mansfeld to the age of fourteen, when he was sent to secondary school at Magdeburg for a year, possibly in the care of the Brethren of the Common Life. In 1498 he transferred to a similar school in Eisenach, where for three years he studied with the well-known grammarian Trebonius. He entered the University of Erfurt in 1501 and received his A.B. degree in the fall of 1502, thirtieth in a class of fifty-two. On January 7, 1505, he took his master's degree, second in a class of seventeen. As a graduation present his father sent him the expensive *Corpus iuris,* for he was to enter the legal profession, a sure ladder to wealth and social preferment. On May 20, 1505, Luther entered law school. On July 16 he threw a party for a group of university friends and as his guests were leaving after an evening of beer and high-spirited song he said to them, "After today you will never see me again." He gave away all his books, except for a copy of Virgil and one of Plautus, and the next day he entered the Augustinian monastery. Why did he take this dramatic step?

Luther was a typical product of the fear-motivated medieval piety. His home discipline had been severe, although not unusually so, and the religious training in the schools had been more somber than joyous. The way to be assured of salvation was to flee the temptations of the world, overcome the appetites of the flesh and the assaults of the devil, do the best one could to obey the commandments of God and the precepts of the church, and with the initial gift of grace work toward perfect holiness. The ideal life of perfection was the ascetic life of the hermit or monk, given over to contemplation and religious duties away from the world. Toward this end Luther chose the strict Observantine Augustinian house, and while he was there he was a perfect monk, outfasting, outpraying, and outworking the other brothers in his search for assurance that God was merciful and forgiving.

To be sure, some events in the months preceding his decision had precipitated the act. As he was returning to Erfurt after spending Easter at home he accidentally cut a blood vessel in his leg and nearly bled to death. The plague swept through Erfurt and took one of Luther's classmates. Immediately before he entered the monastery Luther made another trip home and was caught in a storm. When lightning struck a tree near him he vowed to St. Anne that if she would spare his life he would enter a monastery. But the underlying reason was really a long spiritual struggle for religious certainty and assurance. "Doubt makes a monk" was an old medieval saying. In September 1506 he was admitted to the order and was assigned an unheated cell seven feet wide by nine feet long with a window looking out over the anticipated site of his future grave in the monastic cemetery.

On the vicar general's order Luther was ordained into the priesthood in 1507, and on May 2 he celebrated his first mass, trembling as he held the sacred host in his hand. His father came with two wagonloads of friends and provisions for the customary banquet, and gave the monastery a very large cash gift. But at the end of the banquet Hans concluded his speech as host with the remark: "But have you not read 'Thou shalt honor thy father and thy mother'?" Luther commented later that this note of parental disapproval raised in him his first misgivings about the course he had chosen.

Luther's theological studies tended to reinforce the basic religious presuppositions upon which the monastic life was based. The scholastic theology at Erfurt was taught according to the *via moderna* or nominalist system. Though he did not study William of Occam himself, he did study intensely one of the late Occamist theologians, Gabriel Biel, especially his exposition of the mass. Biel and the Occamists stressed on the one hand the mighty sovereign will of God and on the other man's ability to contribute toward his own salvation. They stressed the limitations of human reason when man searches the tremendous mystery of the Divinity and emphasized the authority of the church in defining matters of dogma. God would not withhold grace from anyone who did the best that was in him. Man thus obtains a conditional merit, and with the gift of prevenient grace is enabled to lead a holy life. On the basis of his sanctified life and good deeds, his fully sufficient merit, man becomes fit to receive salvation. When Luther was unable to obtain peace of mind through his most energetic monkish works or from the sacrament of penance, his confessor, Johannes Staupitz, conceded to him the futility of attempting to attain the perfect love of God through these methods and urged him to commend himself to God's grace and forgiving love.

Staupitz saw in Luther a young man of intellectual brilliance and religious earnestness, and he recommended him to Elector Frederick for the new University of Wittenberg, founded in 1502. Luther arrived there in 1508 as an instructor of philosophy, and lectured on Aristotle's ethics. In March 1509 he received his bachelor of divinity degree and proceeded to lecture on the scholastic Peter Lombard's dogmatic *Sentences*. He returned to teach at Erfurt from 1509 to 1511, but then was reassigned to Wittenberg, where he remained for the rest of his life. The journey he made to Rome in the winter of 1510–1511, as a representative of the Observantine Augustinians, had no particular effect upon him. Pope Julius II was away from Rome on one of his many campaigns. Luther visited churches and went up the stairs to the praetorium of Pilate on his knees in order to gain indulgences for his grandfather, but the story told years later by his son—that halfway up he heard a voice saying, "The just shall live by faith," rose, and walked back down—is surely a false legend. Luther left Rome as he came, an ardent papist and obedient son of the church.

In Wittenberg again Luther rose to new positions of leadership in the order and in the university. On October 18, 1512, Luther received his doctorate, and a few days later he assumed the chair for biblical studies, taking an oath to protect and expound the word of God to the best of his ability. He lectured first on the Psalms and then in 1515–1516 on Paul's Epistle to the Romans. During the course of his exegetical studies he seems to have achieved an evangelical breakthrough, an insight into the all-encompassing grace of God and all-sufficient merit of Christ. The turning point came in connection with the exposition of Romans 1:17: "For therein is the righteousness of God revealed from faith to faith: as it is written, The just shall live by faith." This passage he understood in the light of Romans 3:24: "Being justified freely by his grace through the redemption that is in Christ Jesus." Formerly Luther had understood this "righteousness of God" as an active, retributive, punishing, essential righteousness that demands that a man keep the whole law of God. Now he understood the "righteousness of God" (*justitia*) as a passive, imputed righteousness that God gives freely to man through Christ. "I pondered night and day," he related many years later, "until I understood the connection between the justice of God and the sentence 'The just shall live by faith.' Then I grasped that the justice of God is the righteousness by which, through grace and pure mercy, God justifies us through faith. Immediately I felt that I had been reborn and that I had passed through wide-open doors into paradise!" Luther had emerged from his tremendous struggle with a firmer trust in God and love for him. This doctrine of salvation by God's grace alone, received as a gift through faith and without dependence upon human merit, was the measure against which he judged the religious practices and official teachings of the church of his day and found them wanting. He had, as Lord Acton once put it, a "lever of wonderful strength with which he moved the world." In his exegetical lectures on Galatians in 1516 and 1517 and on the Epistle to the Hebrews in 1517 and 1518, he expounded his theology with a new clarity and began to attract the attention of students and colleagues.

Luther's "theology of the cross and suffering" represented not so much a new theological system as a new way of thinking theologically. In the treatise *De servo arbitrio* he laughs at himself as a *rusticus,* but he was actually as capable of the greatest theological sophistication as he was skilled in making the most elementary catechetical explanation. He was a great scholar, not in the sense of excelling in scholarship for its own sake, but in using his gifts fully, in reading his sources carefully, in employing new humanist methods, in practical philology and the mastery of languages, his own German as well as Latin, Greek, and a respectable amount of Hebrew. Compelled by a strangely concrete dynamism, he approached theological problems directly rather than as an abstract speculative systematician. He owed something to mysticism, the stress on the necessity of inward appropriation of religious belief and experience, but he was critical of the mystics' assumptions about the divine scintilla in man and his ability to mount the heavenly ladder to reunion with God. He owed much to the discipline of scholastic theology, but he objected to the scholastics' suppositions about man's ability to keep God's law and even to Thomas Aquinas' formula of "faith fashioned by love" rather than "trust inducing love." He owed much to Renaissance humanism for its stress on languages and critical method. Halfway through his commentary on Romans, for example, he switched to Erasmus' edition of the Greek New Testament text (1516). But he sensed an excessive anthropocentrism and stoic moralism in the humanists' religious thought. He was indebted to Augustine and of course to Paul for his basic theological orientation, but he allied himself with their thought creatively, and his theology had the ring of relevance and made a powerful impact.

Luther had a Hebraic rather than a Hellenistic view of God, reinforced by many years of exegetical studies of the Old Testament. He believed that metaphysical speculation about God leads merely to a formal concept of God, such as God as pure being. To define God thus abstractly is to make him unreal, a scarecrow for timid souls. God can only be addressed, not expressed. God's will is the only truly free will, itself the rule of all things without exterior cause or reason or external norms. In 1520 Luther spoke of God as an active power and continual creativity. God is noted for willing and acting and is known by what he has done. In the *Commentary on Genesis* he wrote: "God is heroic without a rule." God's omnipotence is not that power by which he can do anything he may choose to do, but the actual doing of all that he does. His power exerts itself concretely and imbues all that exists with actuality. The world is what it is according to the contingent will of God. God willed to reveal himself in the historic Christ portrayed in the Scriptures. God in nature and in history is an awesome God, both hidden and exposed, whose intentions toward us are not known. Among unbelievers in the world he remains silent. In Christ God becomes the revealed God who shows himself to be full of grace and love. God works in a hidden way and by contrasts rather than directly, revealing lofty truth in lowly form. God's true intentions toward us can be known only if, like a man approaching us in the gathering dusk, he stops and talks with us. In his word he reveals himself to be a glowing God of love, one who deplores sin and overcomes it, abhors death and triumphs over it, and by his grace transforms alienated people into trusting men of faith. He is gracious and merciful toward man, a forgiving God.

Man stands in need of God's grace, for without God's forgiveness man remains in a state of sin. Luther heightened the conception of sin beyond the notion of sins as specific transgressions against particular commandments of God. Sin is the root condition of natural man, who is in the state of unbelief until he is acted upon by the Holy Spirit, who calls him to faith through the gospel. Sin is not, then, related to things of the body as opposed to higher things of the spirit. Luther saw man whole, as a unity, not divided by the body-soul dichotomy or body-soul-spirit trichotomy. "In my temerity," he said, "I do not distinguish body, soul, and spirit, but present the whole man unto God." The "whole man" is flesh insofar as he lives his life without God and is alienated or hostile to him, and spirit insofar as he loves God and has come to trust in him. The law is the word of the God of justice to man. He gives man commandments that man does not fulfill, such as "Be ye therefore perfect" and "Thou shalt love the Lord thy God with all thy heart and with all thy soul and with all thy mind" and "Thou shalt love thy neighbor as thyself." The gospel is the word of God in man, Christ in the heart of man, promising forgiveness to all who accept the offer. Grace in this context is not a spiritual power extended to man, but a benignity, a specific act by which God forgives a particular man at a specific point in time. Faith in God is the "life of the heart," which unsettles poise and insists on transformation. Faith is active in love and produces good works. The forgiven man, justified in God's eyes, does good works. On this earth man attains perfection only in hope, not in reality.

Certain existential emphases in Luther's theology are very striking. While he remains formally an ontologist, his distrust of metaphysical abstractions and his emphasis upon the concreteness and immediacy of religious experience indicate the new thrust of his teaching. The most important words in religion, he stressed, are the personal pronouns he, I, and you (my brother). There is no salvation by affiliation or through implicit faith in what the church teaches, but only through explicit faith in Christ. "Everyone must do his own believing just as everyone must do his own dying," he wrote. An either/or quality in Luther's theology points toward modern dialectical theology and existentialism. There is, finally, a bold facing up to the harshest realities of life, wickedness, transiency, irrationality, and death itself. For the smooth Latin rational "therefore" (*ergo*) of scholastic theology he substituted the paradoxical German agonizing "nevertheless" (*dennoch*), for it is only in spite of everything that a man can with the help of the Holy Spirit say, "*Credo*," I believe. The kingdom of God, he once said, is like a besieged city surrounded on all sides by death. Each man has his place on the wall to defend and no one can stand where another stands, but "nothing prevents us from calling encouragement to one another." Luther's evangelical message made a tremendous impact upon a generation searching for religious assurance. He was the Copernicus of theology, who with his high Christology pointed to a Son-centered universe.

The conflagration began over a relatively simple issue, Luther's attack upon abuses in the sale of indulgences and his questioning of their validity. The granting of indulgences had undergone a considerable development since the early days of the church, when the congregation granted permission (*indulgentia*) to relax or commute the penance imposed upon a repentant sinner as an outward sign of sorrow. The power to impose private penance in place of public penance was gradually taken over by priests, bishops, and popes. The church assumed the power of remitting the temporal punishment for sins after the guilt had been forgiven on the basis of sincere repentance and by application of the merits of Christ, Mary, and the saints. Indulgences were promised to crusaders, pilgrims, and donors to the church. In 1457 Pope Calixtus decreed that indulgences were valid for the relief of souls in purgatory. The papal bull *Salvator noster* in 1476 extended the remission of temporal punishment in purgatory to include both the living and the dead. In promulgating indulgences the popes were careful to distinguish between guilt and temporal punishment, insisting that those who received indulgences must be of contrite heart and must have made oral confession. These requirements, however, were glossed over in actual practice, and often the sale of indulgences became routine huckstering.

Ironically, one of the grandest monuments in Christendom, St. Peter's Cathedral in Rome, became the occasion for and the lasting reminder of the division of the church. Pope Julius II in 1507 issued a plenary indulgence to obtain funds for building St. Peter's. In 1513 Pope Leo X renewed this indulgence and made Archbishop Albert of Brandenburg the high commissioner of the sale in the archbishoprics of Magdeburg and Mainz, promising him half of the take to help him repay the Fugger bankers some 29,000 gulden. The Fuggers had advanced this sum to Albert so he could pay for papal dispensation to assume the archbishopric when he was underage (he was only twenty-three at the time) and to hold a number of offices simultaneously, and to pay the annates and the fee for the archbishopric itself. The supersalesman of indulgences was a fat Dominican named John Tetzel. When in April 1517 Tetzel approached the borders of Electoral Saxony and many members of the Wittenberg congregation swarmed over to buy letters of indulgence, Luther urged various bishops to intervene. When they failed to act, he prepared his ninety-five theses on indulgences and sent copies to Bishop Jerome of Brandenburg and, naïvely, to Archbishop Albert of Brandenburg. According to

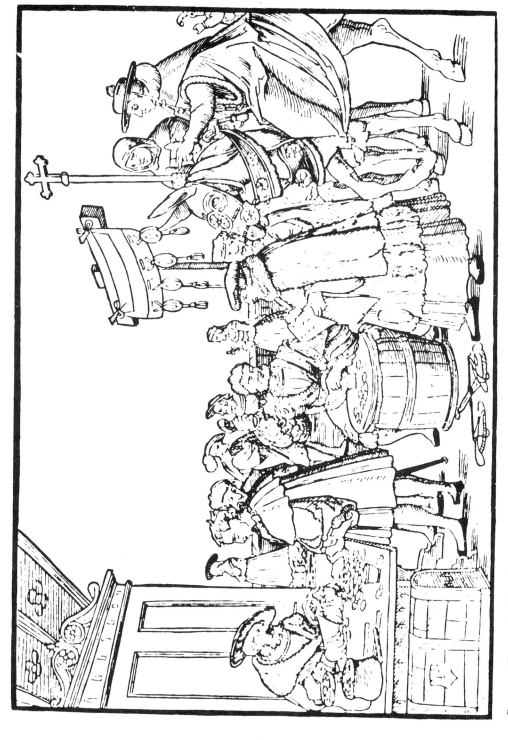

BREU THE ELDER. *Proclamation of the Indulgence.*

Melanchthon's account many years later, he posted them on the north door of the Castle Church on All Saints' Day, challenging any comer to an academic disputation. "When our Lord and Master Jesus Christ said, 'Repent' (Matthew 4:17), he willed the entire life of believers to be one of repentance," he wrote. Repentance in the New Testament meant a change of heart, not to do penance, and if God forgives the guilt of sin, why should punishment remain? The storm unleashed by this act surprised Luther most of all, for within weeks his theses were carried to the farthest corners of Europe. Luther had ruined the sale and had unknowingly launched the Reformation.

The wheels of the ecclesiastical machinery began to grind, beginning with a squeak from Tetzel, who threatened to have the heretic in the fire within three weeks. Tetzel's fellow Dominicans in Saxony preached from the pulpit that Luther would soon be burned. On February 3, 1518, the Dominicans in Germany officially denounced him to the pope. In July 1518 the Dominican master of the sacred palace, Prierias, prepared a citation summoning Luther to Rome. On August 25, 1518, the head of the Augustinian order in Germany was instructed to arrest and imprison Luther. Under pressure from Emperor Maximilian, Pope Leo, whose first reaction had been to view the theses as the irresponsible work of some drunken German who would sober up eventually, authorized Cajetan, the papal legate to the diet at Augsburg, to arrest Luther. He demanded that Frederick the Wise surrender this "son of iniquity" to Cajetan, but Luther appealed to Frederick for protection as a German citizen. Since at that time Pope Leo favored Frederick over Charles as a candidate for election as emperor after the death of the aging Maximilian, Leo agreed to a mere meeting of Cajetan and Luther at Augsburg, which took place from October 12 to 14, but left Luther unmoved. In December the papal chamberlain Miltitz arrived with the Golden Rose for Frederick and a bull against Luther. The Golden Rose was a coveted decoration blessed by the pope on the fourth Sunday in Lent and awarded only once each year to some Christian king or prince. But nothing came of the pope's maneuvering. During the course of a debate in Leipzig with Dr. Johannes Eck of Ingolstadt University, held from June 27 to July 15, 1519, Luther reminded his listeners that popes and councils had often erred and contradicted each other. The decision in points clearly went to Dr. Eck, but in preparing for the debate Luther plunged into a furious study of canon law, church history, and the church fathers, and became even more firmly convinced that the church had departed far from its early teachings.

Luther's power as a publicist now came into full play. As early as February 14, 1519, the humanist publisher Johannes Froben in Basel wrote to Luther:

> We sent six hundred copies of your collected works which I published to France and Spain. They are sold in Paris, read and appreciated at the Sorbonne. The book dealer Clavus of Pavia took a sizable number to Italy to sell them everywhere in the cities. I have sent copies also to England and Brabant and have only ten copies left

in the storeroom. I have never had such good luck with a book. The more accomplished a man is, the more he thinks of you![2]

Luther was a prolific writer, producing over four hundred treatises, an average of more than one a month, between 1516 and 1546. Charles and Aleander could not believe that Luther had singlehandedly written all the books that lay on the table before them at Worms.

In a burst of unparalleled creativity he wrote his three famous treatises of 1520. "I deliver as soon as I conceive!" he exclaimed. At one point in his career he was keeping three presses busy. He sent the first pages of his *Address to the Christian Nobility of the German Nation* to the printer while he was still writing the last pages. In it he called upon the emperor and princes as Christians in authority to reform the church, since the clergy had defaulted. The *Address,* which has been called a "cry from the heart of the people" and a "blast on the war trumpet," was Luther's first publication after he was convinced that the breach with Rome was all but irreparable. He assaulted the "three walls of the Romanists," the arguments that secular force has no jurisdiction over them, that only the pope is competent to expound Scripture, and that no one but the pope can summon a council. In *The Babylonian Captivity of the Church* he attacked the abuses in the sacramental system, through which he believed the "Roman tyranny" had exercised its control over all Christians. He discussed all seven sacraments, holding only baptism, communion, and penance to have been instituted by Christ, but paid most attention to the Lord's Supper. He held the first "captivity" to be the withholding of the cup from the laity, the second the doctrine of transubstantiation, and the third the conception of the mass as a sacrifice rather than as a spiritual communion with the Lord. The third famous treatise of 1520, *On the Liberty of the Christian Man,* was more devotional in nature and, as he put it, contained the "whole of Christian life in brief form." In it he described the liberating effect of faith in Christ upon the Christian man, for faith frees man from spiritual slavery and moves him to a life of love and service to his fellows. This treatise, conciliatory in tone, was accompanied by an open letter to Pope Leo reassuring him that Luther's intention had been to attack the corruption and false doctrine surrounding the papacy, not Leo's own person.

But Leo was not to be appeased, for by now the affair had moved far beyond the point of reconciliation. On June 15, 1520, Leo had published the bull *Exsurge domine,* citing forty-one heresies in Luther's writings, giving him sixty days in which to recant, and demanding that his books be burned. That fall the papal legate Girolamo Aleander and Johannes Eck staged a burning of Luther's books. In retaliation the Wittenberg University faculty and students gathered on Decem-

---

[2] Froben to Luther, February 14, 1519, in *D. Martin Luthers Werke: Briefwechsel* (Weimar, 1930), vol. 1, p. 332.

CRANACH THE YOUNGER. *The Last Supper of the Lutherans and the Fall to Hell of the Catholics; in the Center Luther Preaching.*

ber 10, 1520, outside the Elster gate to build a bonfire and burn copies of scholastic writings and the canon law. Luther, shaking with emotion, stepped out of the crowd and threw upon the flames the papal bull, saying softly, "Because you have destroyed God's truth, may the Lord destroy you today in this fire." Luther had spoken his final farewell to Rome. On January 3, 1521, the pope issued the bull of excommunication *Decet romanum pontificem,* declaring Luther a heretic outside the law. It remained now for Charles V, who had become emperor in 1519, to enforce the excommunication through the imperial ban, which meant death for the heretic. Luther was summoned on March 6, 1521, to appear before the emperor and the diet of the Holy Roman Empire meeting in Worms. Luther went to Worms and there took his stand.

On the way home from Worms to Wittenberg, Luther's party detoured to Moehre so that Luther could visit his grandmother and preach in the church there. In the evening of May 4 a troop of armed horsemen ambushed the wagon train near Altenstein. Luther's companions fled into the underbrush, and when they returned Luther was gone. The horsemen took him on roundabout paths for half the night, till morning found them at the Wartburg Castle, up the hill from Eisenach. Elector Frederick had instructed his men not to tell him where they took Luther, so that at the diet he could truthfully profess no knowledge of his where-abouts. Only the warden and a few trusted troopers knew the identity of the hostage. As Knight Georg, Luther wore a knight's necklace and trappings, let his beard and hair grow long, and sent letters with such mysterious addresses as "the Realm of the Birds," "the Region of the Air," and "the Isle of Patmos." Rumors ran wild that Aleander had arranged to have him assassinated, that he had been found dead in a silver mine, that he had fled to Sickingen; but there were some who suspected Elector Frederick of protecting him.

Removed from the public arena, Luther was extremely restless during his ten months at the Wartburg. He suffered from severe nervous exhaustion and attacks of indigestion after his ordeal. He wrote a number of treatises, the most important of which was *On Monastic Vows,* dedicated to his father, in which he argued that celibacy and monastic asceticism were contrary to Scriptures and contributed less to God and man than a useful life in society. But the great achievement of his enforced "idleness" was his masterful translation of the Greek New Testament into German, which he accomplished from December to the end of February 1522. Later he and his "sanhedrin" at the university translated the Old Testament from the Hebrew, completing the entire work in 1534. It was a linguistic triumph important for its direct religious impact, for its formative power in the development of New High German as the standard language of the people and of literature, and for its influence on translations of the Bible into other vernacular languages, including English.

Social Unrest and Revolts

IN WITTENBERG MEANWHILE affairs took a radical turn. Gabriel Zwilling, an Augustinian friar, and Andreas Carlstadt, a university professor, made a violent attack upon the form of the mass, favoring communion in both kinds (communicants' receiving both the bread and the wine), and upon celibacy and images. Carlstadt married the daughter of a poor nobleman, and many monks followed him in taking wives. Zwilling led an iconoclastic attack upon altars, images, and pictures in churches. On December 21 the "prophets" of Zwickau arrived in Wittenberg: Thomas Müntzer, a religious mystic with radical social ideas; Nicholas Storch, an illiterate clothmaker; and Mark Stübner, a student. These charismatic spiritualists made claims to private revelations, opposed the use of external sacraments, and preached the setting aside of all authorities. There was some talk of communism in property and in wives. Philipp Melanchthon, who assumed the role of leader in Wittenberg during Luther's absence, however timidly, was initially favorably impressed by them. Luther's reaction was that no private revelation could be valid unless it was in agreement with the Scriptures, and he quipped, "They have swallowed the Holy Ghost feathers and all."

On February 1, 1522, there was a great tumult in the town, and the city council, unable to contain it, appealed to Luther to return. He did so on March 6 and preached eight sermons on the need for moderation, the duty to proceed with love toward one's neighbor, and the need to avoid giving offense to weaker brethren not yet converted, for all eyes were on Wittenberg. The situation quieted down and changes were then made gradually: the abrogation of private mass, the change of the public mass into a reformed communion, and in the fall of 1523 the introduction of Luther's own revised liturgy.

Unrest is contagious, and since feuding was an endemic disease of the knightly class, the outbreak of the Knights' War of 1522–1523 was almost predictable. The knights had three possibilities open to them as their class lost its social utility. They could turn to farming or estate management, as they did east of the Elbe; they could adjust to the new forces of the time and serve as functionaries of the more powerful princes; or they could turn renegade and live by robbery and pillage. Franz von Sickingen, a little man with big ideas, chose the third alternative. When he was born, in the fortress of Ebernburg in 1481, his father read his horoscope and saw that the child would achieve a considerable reputation but would come to a bad end. Franz had great ability and amassed considerable wealth from the mines on his lands and by plundering merchant wagon trains; at one point he even loaned the emperor 50,000 gulden. He put himself at the service of the French king and made punitive and plundering raids with a thousand armed men all the way into Lorraine. He declared a feud with the city of Worms. His heart was with the German empire, however, and he supported Charles V, though he was disappointed when Charles failed to lead Germany to new triumphs. "Franz is a man such as Germany has not had for many a day!" wrote Ulrich von Hutten, as propagandist for the German knightly cause.[3] Sickingen fortified Ebernburg with thirty-six cannon, including a three-and-a-half-ton piece called the Nightingale.

On August 27, 1522, Franz declared a feud with the semifeudal archbishop of Trier, starting what has mistakenly gone down in history as the Knights' Revolt. He declared that he would free the people from the yoke of the priests and bring them evangelical liberty. Lutheranism had indeed penetrated far into the knightly class, but Franz's motives were as mixed as he himself was ideologically confused, for in secularizing the archbishop's territory he hoped to gain land for himself. On September 7 he attacked the city, but was defeated after an eight-day siege. Then three princes combined forces and on April 30, 1523, besieged Sickingen in a fortress called Landstuhl. Franz was mortally wounded by a missile and a broken beam finished him as the stone walls collapsed under artillery fire. The Swabian League of princes and towns in southern Germany then fielded an army under Georg Truchsesz von Waldburg which assaulted the strongholds of the Swabian and Franconian knights, destroying thirty-two castles within six weeks.

Ulrich von Hutten had at first thought Luther's cause a mere battle of the monks, and chortled, "Devour and be devoured in turn!" But without ever really appreciating Luther's theology, he soon identified himself with his cause as an anti-Roman ally. He addressed Luther as "You my dear brother!" and wrote, "They tell me that you have been excommunicated. How great, O Luther, how great you are, if this is true!" He was ready to attack the "priestly tyranny" with letters and with arms. From 1520 on he wrote a steady stream of pamphlets attacking the Roman hierarchy. His *Febris* and *Inspicientes* assaulted Luther's interrogator and judge, Cardinal Cajetan. In his glosses on *The Bull of Leo X Against The Errors of Martin Luther* he attacked the pope as the Antichrist. His tract *Bulla* was a discussion of Leo's bull, German liberty, Hutten, Franz, and other Germans. In his *Monitor I* and *Praedones* (Robbers) he identified Christian liberty with freedom from Rome. He switched from Latin to the vernacular and reached the masses with a great number of German tracts. But Luther could not condone Hutten's appeal to the sword in defense of the gospel and refused his suggestion that he take refuge with Sickingen. On January 16, 1521, Luther wrote to his friend Spalatin:

> You see what Hutten wishes. But I do not desire to do battle for the gospel with violence and murder, and I wrote him as much. Through the power of the Word

---

[3] William R. Hitchcock, *The Background of the Knights' Revolt, 1522–1523* (Berkeley and Los Angeles, 1958), p. 46.

the world is conquered, through the power of the Word the church has been created—and through the Word it will also be restored.

Hutten, too sick to fight in Sickingen's campaign, fled to Switzerland, but Erasmus refused him sanctuary in Basel. He was finally befriended by Zwingli in Zurich and died there in August 1523, still a young man.

Scarcely had the Knights' War ended than a more terrifying uprising occurred, a series of peasant revolts that racked southern and central Germany from May 1524 to July 1526. The astrologers had predicted a deluge and horrendous things for 1524 and 1525. Half of Germany was torn apart by rioting bands of peasants numbering up to twelve thousand men in some regions. In the south the revolt spread into Austria as far as Salzburg and Styria; only Bavaria was spared major uprisings. Caught up by the revolutionary spirit, interpreting Luther's Christian liberty as social freedom, urged on by erratic "prophets," and led by inept military men, the peasants rose up against their feudal overlords, ecclesiastical and secular. The uprisings were spontaneous, regional, and in no way coordinated.

In the Black Forest the peasants were stirred up and led by a soldier-agitator named Hans Müller von Bulgenbach, who was joined by an Anabaptist preacher, Balthasar Hubmaier. In Swabia Sebastian Lotzer, a tanner from the city of Memmingen, framed the famous Twelve Articles, which illustrated the concrete nature of the peasants' demands, for it was not liberty in the abstract that they demanded. They wanted the restoration of common lands to the community, the abolition of arbitrary feudal services and the death tax, elimination of the "small" or cattle tithe, the right to choose their own pastors, a return of hunting, fishing, and forest rights preempted by the nobles, an end to increases in rents and services, and the restoration of the good old law in the administration of justice in place of the Roman law codes. The demands were moderate enough, but once the revolt was under way it produced mob excesses—burning, pillaging, lynching, murder, and at Weinsberg the massacre of all the defenders of the castle after they had surrendered. The count of Helfenstein was run through with a spear before the eyes of his wife and child. The Swabian League fielded against them a veteran of the Knights' War, Georg Truchsesz von Waldburg, who killed and captured thousands at Leipheim, east of Ulm. He confronted a large army of peasants at Weingarten and induced them to sign a treaty, whereupon they disbanded and lost further bargaining power. In Franconia the peasants, led by an innkeeper, recruited the knight Goetz von Berlichingen for campaigns against Bamberg and Mainz. They even succeeded in forcing the archbishop of Mainz to accept the demands of the Twelve Articles.

In Thuringia the peasants rioted and pillaged Erfurt. In central Germany alone over forty monasteries and castles were destroyed by the rebels. Under the leadership of the fanatical spiritualist Thomas Müntzer, who made his headquarters in Mühlhausen, the peasants made the wildest assaults and suffered the most tragic slaughter imaginable. Müntzer was more a chiliastic religious extremist than a social revolutionary. He preached the imminent coming of the kingdom of God, in which all men would be equal and all property would be held in common. He encouraged the masses to kill the rulers and destroy their castles. He urged his League of the Elect to wipe out the unregenerate. "Do not listen to the cries of the godless," he exhorted in 1524. "On while the fire is hot! Do not let the blood cool on your swords!" On his banner he displayed the rainbow as a reminder of God's covenant with man. The overwrought peasants went into battle singing, "Come, Holy Ghost, God and Lord!" On May 15, 1525, Duke Georg of Saxony and Count Philipp of Eisenach attacked. One volley of artillery fire threw the peasants into a panic and the cavalry cut them down. In one of the worst massacres of the war, the princes' troops killed several thousand peasants and took hundreds of prisoners, allowing few to escape. Müntzer fled, but he was captured feigning illness in a bedroom, and was quartered. Thus ended the bloodiest and most dramatic episode of the revolts, on an eschatological note of Armageddon.

These peasant revolts fitted the pattern of such rebellions in the late Middle Ages. They swept across Flanders, France, England, and Bohemia, and there were at least a dozen such uprisings in German lands before the major one of 1525. As during the fourteenth-century revolts, the condition of the peasants was better than it had been earlier. Again improvements in their lives led to visions of greater improvements still, and to resentment against the increased wealth and growing power of princes, towns, and bishops. The crushing defeat of the knights in southwest Germany, those bullies who had despoiled and terrified the peasants for centuries, released the peasants from one group of foes, though remnants of them, including Hutten's brother and Sickingen's son, now fought in the armies against them. Population pressure was greatest in the hilly Swabian southwest, that fountain of German emigration throughout the centuries. There the only well-organized peasant movement, called the *Bundschuh,* after the sandal worn by the peasants, arose under the leadership of the skillful Joss Fritz, who was more effective as a propagandist than as a military tactician but always avoided capture. Luther's evangelical proclamations of Christian liberty led to a coalescing of economic and religious ideas which triggered revolution. During the night between his appearances before the diet at Worms the sign of the *Bundschuh* had appeared on the walls. From the beginning Luther had consistently opposed the use of force and violence in the defense either of his person or of his theology. He attacked the tyranny of the rulers, secular and ecclesiastical, but warned against mob terror. "Had I wanted to start trouble," he once boasted, "I could have brought great bloodshed upon Germany. Yes, I could have started such a little game at Worms that even the emperor would not have been safe. But what would it have been?

Petrarca-Meister. *Von Adeligem Ursprung.* The peasant foundation of medieval society.

A mug's game. I did nothing. I left it to the Word!" Sensing the dangerously charged atmosphere while in refuge at Wartburg Castle, he wrote *A Faithful Exhortation to Christians to Keep Themselves from Riot and Revolution.*

That his position on armed rebellion was widely understood is evident from the famous tract of 1521 by the Swiss humanist Vadian entitled *Karsthans* (Hans the Hoeman; just as all French peasants were called Jacques by their betters, German peasants were called Hans). In this tract Mercury, Murner the Franciscan monk, and Karsthans are discussing the Leipzig debate. When it is announced that Luther is coming, Murner leaves the scene. Luther complains of persecution and Karsthans promises the protection of the peasants. But Luther denounces all "fighting and killing" and takes his leave. Luther never gave up the principle that only constituted authority had the power of the sword. A month after the appearance of the peasants' platform he wrote *An Exhortation to Peace in Reply to the Twelve Articles of the Swabian Peasants* (April 1525), in which he admonished both sides, boldly attacking the princes and bishops, against whose tyranny God's word and all history threatened a catastrophic end, and warning the peasants that God's word and all experience showed that rebellion and anarchy made conditions worse rather than better, citing Christ's warning, "All they that take the sword shall perish with the sword." Luther went personally to centers of disaffection in Thuringia at the risk of his life to mediate between the peasants and Elector Frederick, who was willing to make concessions, but his preaching was in vain. When he heard outrageous and probably exaggerated reports of mob rapine and murder and saw the peasants follow Müntzer into battle, he wrote his harsh pamphlet *Against Robbing and Murderous Peasant Bands* (May 1525), urging that the rebels be struck down, strangled, and suppressed. When the crisis passed he wrote letters and pamphlets urging clemency and moderation toward the peasants, and expressing regret for his harsh language earlier.

The peasant revolts actually had only the remotest possibility of success because of their sporadic nature, lack of organization, poor military leadership, and small staying power. The position of the peasants in reality remained little altered. The fines imposed upon them were gradually reduced or left uncollected. Not even the disarming of the peasants was everywhere insisted upon. Many lords saw that concessions to the peasants were to their own economic advantage. Only after the failure of the revolts did the peasants turn to Luther's evangelical religion en masse, as evangelical preachers became willing to man the pulpits of country parishes. They seemed to understand the consistency of Luther's position and few charged him with betraying a cause he had never really embraced. The Reformation continued to spread into new areas of Germany as a spontaneous popular movement after 1525 as it had before. On the other hand, the suppression of one more major sociological group that could serve as a counterforce made the way to princely absolutism much easier. It has often been alleged that the peasant revolts alarmed the rulers and drove them closer to Catholicism out of shock at the effect of Lutheranism on the masses, but this is manifestly untrue in view of the continued spread of the evangelical church to many additional territories and countries.

The Reformation to the Diet of Augsburg, 1530

SELDOM IN HISTORY has there been such rapport and resonance between a university and the broad mass of people as existed between the new and vigorous University of Wittenberg and the Germans. The heart of the Reformation movement was a center of learning and its leader was a professor of theology who had come from among the people, which gave it a special character. "Learning, wisdom, and writers must rule the world," Luther pontificated in one of his *Table Talks*. "If God out of his wrath would take away from the world all the learned men, people would become beasts and wild animals. Then there would be no wisdom, religion, or law, but only robbery, theft, murder, adultery, and all kinds of evil!" Luther was a professor to the core, lecturing twice a week to the crowds of theological students who came for education or reeducation from all parts of Germany. One of them has given us this description of Professor Luther the exegete:

> He was a man of middle stature, with a voice which combined sharpness and soft-ness: it was soft in tone; sharp in the enunciation of syllables, words and sen-tences. [Typical Saxon!] He spoke neither too quickly nor too slowly, but at an even pace, without hesitation and very clearly, and in such fitting order that each part flowed naturally out of what went before. He did not expound each part in long labyrinths of words, but first the individual words, then the sentences, so that one could see how the content of the exposition arose and flowed out of the text itself. . . . For this is how he took it from a book of essential matter which he had himself prepared, so that he had his lecture materials always ready at hand—con-clusions, digressions, moral philosophy, and also antithesis, and so his lectures never contained anything that was not pithy or relevant. And, to say something about the spirit of the man: if even the fiercest enemies of the gospel had been among his hearers, they would have confessed from the force of what they heard that they had witnessed, not a man, but a spirit, for he could not teach such amazing things from himself, but only from the influence of some good or evil spirit.[4]

Luther felt gratified and a bit surprised that not only the students but the whole learned world listened to what he had to say. "We wished out of respect," wrote the humanist Irenicus in 1518, "to call Luther the leader of all the Germans on account of the excellent erudition possessed by such a man."

Luther led the movement for reform of the arts curriculum at the university,

---

[4] Cited in E. Gordon Rupp, *Luther's Progress to the Diet of Worms* (New York, 1964), p. 44.

supporting humanist discipline, languages, rhetoric, and history against the traditional dialectic and scholastic disputation. He accomplished reform also in the theological curricula, challenging the Thomist dictum that without Aristotle it is impossible to be a theologian. In a letter to Matthew Lang in 1517 he wrote: "Our theology and St. Augustine are beginning to prosper. . . . Aristotle is coming down little by little." The students and the young instructors at the university rallied to his ideas for educational reform and his evangelical theology, while his older colleagues for the most part opposed both. The Reformation was a young man's movement, for at thirty-four Luther had a following at Wittenberg, at other universities, and among the humanists of men thirty years old or younger. Conversely, nearly all of his major opponents except Dr. Eck were fiftyish or older. The very radical treatise that estranged some of the older humanists, *On the Babylonian Captivity of the Church,* attracted the support of the young humanists. Many students now changed their vocations from law to theology, and a stream of monks and clerics turned to the new ministry. Luther was active in organizing congregational life whenever localities turned to him for help. He recommended students for pastorates and schools, and carried on a tremendous correspondence totaling over four thousand letters.

Luther's young lieutenant Philipp Melanchthon (1497–1560), a grandnephew of Reuchlin, was already renowned as a precocious young humanist when he came to Wittenberg as professor of classics in 1518. His inaugural lecture, "On the Improvement of the Studies of Youth," called for the recovery of the wellsprings of classical literature, the ancient languages, and Christian piety. Melanchthon was a slightly built, bookish, professorial type. Urban Balduin observed in a letter to a friend, "I saw Melanchthon dance with the dean's wife and it was marvelous to behold!" Melanchthon lectured on the Greek and Latin classics as well as on the Scriptures throughout his career. At one point he was lecturing to a class of over nine hundred students. Luther, fourteen years his elder, thought him the greatest theologian who had ever lived, and declared that his *Loci* or *Commonplaces* on Christian doctrine should be esteemed next to the Bible. He was a clear systematic thinker, the primary author of the Protestant Augsburg Confession and many other systematic, rhetorical, and confessional writings. After Luther's death he became titular head of the movement, working in a conciliatory humanist fashion for concessions leading to the unity of the church.

The break between Luther and Erasmus in 1524–1525 must have been particularly painful to Melanchthon, who so keenly admired the prince of the humanists and kept up a correspondence with him even after the great debate. The older humanists had at first been favorably inclined toward Luther, believing him to be a critic and renovator of theology according to their program. Reuchlin exclaimed, "God be praised that now the monks have found someone else who will give them more to do than I!" Georg Spalatin wrote to Mutian in 1519:

I have written to you about your doctor Martin Luther, the Augustinian, toward whom I know you to be much too favorably inclined to wish him ill, that he is such a Christian that he would truly rather suffer all human danger than deny Christ and his truth and teaching. God be praised that the best learned disciplines still are so coming to life, together with that true and holy theology, that we may hope shortly to have all the fine arts and sciences clean and purified.[5]

Luther himself was perfectly clear in his own mind that although the humanities represented the flower of man's creativity and culture, they had no redemptive power. "True it is," he wrote, "that human wisdom and the liberal arts are noble gifts of God. . . . But we never can learn from them in detail what sin and righteousness are in the sight of God, how we can get rid of our sins, become pious and just before God, and come to life from death." Luther sensed the relative relaxation of religious intensity among the humanists as early as March 1517, when he wrote, "The human avails more with Erasmus than the divine." Erasmus recognized his own weakness when he commented that God had not given all men the strength to become martyrs—but he added that Christianity had had many martyrs but few scholars. They were, moreover, men of different temperaments. Zwingli shrewdly compared Luther with the heroic young Ajax and Erasmus with the wily Odysseus. The poet Eobanus Hessus observed that Erasmus had pointed out what needed to be done but that Luther took the ax and did the pruning.

When they came to grips it was a battle of giants, and Luther congratulated Erasmus on avoiding peripheral issues and aiming for the jugular. Erasmus, who would gladly have remained aloof from the dispute, as he had done during the Reuchlin controversy, was caught in the crossfire. When at last he was pressured into writing against Luther, he argued that man's will is conditionally free, that deeds of a conscious ethical character can be meritorious in God's eyes, and that the commandments to do good would be meaningless unless man had the ability to act as God requires. For Erasmus the way into God's presence was a compound of grace and good works by which man can climb "from the body to the spirit, from the visible to the invisible, from the letter to the mystery, from the sensible to the intelligible, from the compounded to the simple, up as on the rungs of Jacob's ladder" (*Enchiridion*). Erasmus made some damaging admissions, such as that on certain matters he would be a skeptic if the church had not defined such beliefs as necessary. To this Luther replied in his *De servo arbitrio* (*On the Bondage of the Will*), "The Holy Spirit is not a skeptic!" Luther followed Paul in stressing the divine initiative in man's salvation. God's grace is a benignity, and the giver of grace himself is always present. Grace is the divine act of full, free, and final forgiveness which justifies man, not merely an element of spiritual power to be infused and combined with man's natural free will. Man cannot of his own reason

---

[5] Spalatin to Mutian, May 17, 1519, cited in Irmgard Höss, *Georg Spalatin, 1484–1545: Ein Leben in der Zeit des Humanismus und der Reformation* (Weimar, 1956), pp. 79–80.

or strength believe in Jesus Christ. The debate, then, was not one of free will versus determinism in the content of man's life on earth. Like Erasmus, Luther believed that human reason was the greatest of God's creations and that man was quite free to decide things of an earthly nature. He did not, however, believe that man could unaided keep God's law, to love God above all things and his neighbor as himself, even though God commanded it. He did not believe that man could come to faith in Christ, which ran basically counter to reason, unless enlightened by the Holy Spirit. Only the will of the regenerate man is free in spiritual things. This great debate marked a divide between the older humanists and the reformers. From that point on Luther publicly ignored Erasmus, although he continued to read his writings. Ironically, many of Erasmus' Catholic contemporaries thought he was defending his own positions rather than the doctrine of the church. His old friend Aleander once commented that Erasmus had damaged the church more than Luther ever could.

Luther dominated his age as few other men have done, but at the same time there was an unaffected naturalism about him. Open and frank, he displayed his innermost sentiments for all to see.

In the very year in which Luther wrote *On the Bondage of the Will* (1525), he married. Luther's marriage almost caught even him by surprise. He had long resisted the idea of taking a wife, although he had energetically recommended marriage as an excellent estate—for others. He feared that if he married, his opponents would malign his intentions as a reformer. On August 6, 1521, he wrote to Spalatin, "They will never force a wife upon me." In 1524, he was of the same mind, though several of his friends in the religious life had married. He himself lived on in the Black Monastery in Wittenberg with the sole surviving monk, the prior, in real bachelor style—beds not made for as much as two years at a time, irregular hours, poor food. By springtime of 1525 his attitude was changing. Then one day his friend Wenceslas Linck received a letter from him: "Suddenly, and while I was occupied with far other thoughts, the Lord has plunged me into marriage." It may have happened suddenly, but apparently "other thoughts" had not completely crowded the idea from his mind, for he had written to another friend, "If I can manage it, I shall take my Kathie in marriage to spite the devil before I die. I trust they won't deprive me of my joy and courage!" Katherine von Bora was one of nine nuns who had fled the cloister of Marienthron under the influence of Luther's writings and had come to Wittenberg for refuge. She had a lively spirit and somewhat aristocratic bearing. The wedding took place in the evening of June 13, 1525, in the Black Monastery. The bride was twenty-six and the groom forty-two. "Thank God," Luther said years later in one of his rambling *Table Talks*, "it has turned out well, for I have a pious, faithful wife, on whom a man may safely rest his heart."

Martin and Kathie Luther had six children during their two decades of mar-

MARTHIN EVTHER.   CATHARINA.

CATHOLIC SATIRE. *Luther and His Wife Carrying and Wheeling Home the Expelled Protestant Preachers.*

ried life, and Luther spent many happy hours in the family circle. He loved music, played both the lute and the flute, and led in the singing of songs by Flemish and German masters, and occasionally of his own composition. Luther prepared a book of family devotions (*Hauspostille*), the *Small Catechism* and the *Large Catechism* (1529) for the instruction of children and the use of the clergy, and wrote hymns to be sung in congregational worship. The best known became the "marching song" of the Reformation, "A Mighty Fortress Is Our God." The house was always full of indigent students, friends, and visitors from all parts of Europe, so that only Kathie's careful household management kept them from bankruptcy. Luther learned, too, a father's sorrow at the death of a child. His daughter Elizabeth died in infancy, and when thirteen-year-old Magdalena passed away in her father's arms, he turned aside to conceal his tears and said, "Whether we live or die, we are the Lord's." His faith was tested experientially.

The ancient Spartans said of Philip of Macedon after the fall of Thebes, "To destroy a city he is able, but to build another lies beyond his power." Rebuilding the reformed church along the lines of an evangelical church order consumed much of Luther's energies during the last decades of his life. He prepared a new German order of worship (1526) for the church in Wittenberg which retained the traditional responses. The sermon, in the language of the people, was given the central place in the service, with communion in both kinds celebrated after it. Baptism was retained as the second dominical sacrament, through which infants were regenerated and engrafted into the church. He applied his idea of the priesthood of all believers, as far as it proved to be practicable, to the re-creation of a congregational form of church life on the New Testament pattern. The congregation was to exercise judgment in matters of doctrine, call pastors and teachers, manage finances, care for the needy, and exercise the office of the keys, or admonition and excommunication. The authority of the pastor to preach and to administer the sacraments was derived from the congregation that called him to his office.

In actual practice this ideal was only partially realized, for the pattern of control of the physical properties and external affairs of the church by the princes and city councils was so deeply rooted that in many areas Luther was forced to depend on them for the organization and supervision of the church. He would not, however, concede the principle, and referred to them as "Christians in authority" and as "emergency bishops" until such time as educated men were available to assume control and leadership as evangelical bishops free from the control of secular authority. In Saxony Elector John (1525–1532) appointed a visitation commission consisting of two electoral councilors and two theologians, Luther and Justus Jonas, to look into the spiritual condition of the congregations. The monastic properties and endowments for masses were now to be used for educational and charitable purposes. The next year Melanchthon prepared for the elector an *Instruction for the Visitors to the Pastors,* which outlined evangelical doctrine, provided for supervision of the clergy in four separate districts by a superintendent, and demanded an improved level of education for pastors and laymen. In the preface to this *Instruction* Luther stressed again that "his Electoral Grace" was to act "out of Christian love, for he is not responsible as secular overlord, and for God's sake for the good of the gospel and for the benefit and welfare of distressed Christians." The visitation, he wrote, was called for because of the great need of the church; it was to be undertaken as by a Christian brother, out of love, and was to be temporary, until an improved situation or better plan evolved. Luther strove manfully to preserve the distinction between the spiritual and the secular authorities. He was caught in the dilemma of choosing between the congregation as a small group of confessing believers and the idea of the people's church, embracing all members of the community, even those who were only formally Christians. In 1539 Elector John Frederick established a consistory or civil court to handle cases of ecclesiastical discipline. While Luther lived, matters of spiritual concern were still regularly referred to him for disposition, but after his death the consistory and its four commissioners became increasingly the instruments of the territorial government.

The Lutheran movement gained in strength with the addition of new cities and territories during the decade following the Diet of Worms. In 1526 Emperor Charles decided to enforce the Edict of Worms, but he was unable to attend the diet at Speyer that summer. There the evangelical estates, supported by some Catholic princes, managed to postpone action until a national council or an ecumenical council, to meet within a year and a half, could take up the question. Meanwhile each estate should act in response to its own sense of duty toward God and the emperor. The emperor was prevented by his constant preoccupation with his wars against the French, the pope, and the Turks from acting freely against Luther. But when at Speyer in 1529 he demanded that the resolution of 1526 allowing the estates discretion in the Lutheran question be rescinded, the evangelical estates, Electoral Saxony, Brandenburg, Hesse, and Anhalt, and fourteen free imperial cities under the leadership of Strassburg became "protesting estates," the origin of the name Protestant.

The emperor resolved to attend the next diet at Augsburg in 1530. Luther could not be present because of the ban, and even the city of Nuremberg did not dare give him sanctuary. He therefore stayed in the fortress of Coburg, the Electoral Saxon castle nearest to Augsburg, impatiently awaiting news from the diet; would the edict now be enforced against him? On the wall of his room high over the castle ramparts he inscribed for his own comfort the words of the psalmist: "I shall not die, but live, and declare the works of the Lord!" He kept up a steady barrage of letters to Melanchthon and the evangelical party, telling them to stand fast and be courageous. Melanchthon wished to do nothing to perpetuate the schism and would gladly have restricted the Protestant statement to criticism of abuse, but he was forced by Luther's opponents to make a doctrinal statement of the evangelical position. His Augsburg Confession, read to the diet and emperor on June 25, 1530, became the classical statement of the Lutheran faith. There was no thought of founding a new church, but an effort toward the reform of the whole Christian church on earth. "I cannot walk so soft and gently," Luther said admiringly when he read Melanchthon's words. Still hoping for unity, Melanchthon omitted from the Confession such controversial subjects as the veneration of saints, purgatory, transubstantiation, and the priesthood of all believers. Luther shared Melanchthon's concern, but he no longer believed that unity was possible while the pope remained at the head of the hierarchy. The emperor and Catholic majority rejected the Confession and would not even consider Melanchthon's *Apology* for the Augsburg Confession. On October 2, 1530, two days before he left Coburg, Luther preached a final sermon in the chapel on the events at Augsburg:

> If they are willing to be merciful toward us, then they are so in God's name. If not, then let them do as they will—what do we care? Heaven is greater than the earth, and things will hardly be so turned around that the earth rules heaven. If they have plans, they must first ask our Lord God whether it is pleasing to him. If it does not suit him, let them deliberate and resolve what they will; it is written: "He that sitteth in the heavens shall laugh, the Lord shall hold them in derision."

At Worms Luther stood alone; at Augsburg he was represented by a chorus of evangelicals, and the Confession was signed by some of the most powerful and energetic rulers in the empire.

Luther's last years were marked by restless activity and prodigious labor. He continued lecturing, began his last great commentary on Genesis in 1535, served as dean of the theological faculty, made church visitations, and prepared the Schmalkald Articles as his theological testament for a meeting of the Schmalkald League of Protestant princes in 1537. At that meeting he fell ill with kidney stones and gallstones and was brought back to Wittenberg a very sick man. But he still had nearly nine years of life in him, and devoted much of them to writing nearly 165 treatises and as many as ten letters a day. He examined doctoral candidates and staged "doctor feasts" with beer and venison for the lucky candidates. Sick and constantly apprehensive about the danger of war, he became short-tempered and even harsh, though in behalf of the cause and not from personal peevishness. In response to Kathie's chiding, "Dear husband, you are too rude," he retorted, "They teach me to be rude!"

His life came to an end where it had begun, in the town of Eisleben. An activist to the last, concerned with social issues, he traveled there in midwinter to settle a legal dispute between the counts of Mansfeld. He suffered a heart attack on arrival, but recovered and directed the negotiations for three weeks. On February 17 the affair was settled, but Luther was exhausted and suffered a series of further heart attacks. When one of his friends at the bedside asked him, "Dearest father, do you confess Christ, the Son of God, our Savior and Redeemer?" he answered with a clear "Yes!" Thus about two-thirty in the morning of February 18, 1546, there passed into history the man about whom more has been written than about any other person with the exception of Jesus. Was he an event-maker or merely a man whose life was eventful? His own last written words, jotted on a slip of paper two days before his death, reflect his appreciation of both the greatness and the limitation of every human being:

> No one who was not a shepherd or a peasant for five years can understand Virgil in his *Bucolica* and *Georgica*.
>
> I maintain that no one can understand Cicero in his letters unless he was active in important affairs of state for twenty years.
>
> Let no one who has not guided the congregations with the prophets for one hundred years believe that he has tasted Holy Writ thoroughly. For this reason the miracle is stupendous (1) in John the Baptist, (2) in Christ, (3) in the Apostles.
>
> Do not try to fathom this divine *Aeneid*, but humbly worship its footprints. We are beggars. That is true. [*Wir sind Pettler. Hoc est verum.*][6]

Luther may have had his own fascinating theories about wondermen and healthy heroes in history, but he saw himself as a humble instrument in the hands of God, not as a mere piece of driftwood thrown up by indifferent waves of history upon the sands of time.

Bibliography

Luther:

BAINTON, ROLAND H. *Here I Stand! A Life of Martin Luther.* Nashville and New York, 1950.

BOEHMER, HEINRICH. *Road to Reformation.* Philadelphia, 1946.

DICKENS, A. G. *Luther and the Reformation.* London, 1967.

ERIKSON, ERIK H. *Young Man Luther.* New York, 1958.

FIFE, ROBERT H. *The Revolt of Martin Luther.* New York, 1957.

GERRISH, BRIAN, ed. *Reformers in Profile.* Philadelphia, 1967.

GRISAR, HARTMANN. *Martin Luther: His Life and Work.* Westminster, Md., 1950.

KOOIMAN, W. F. *By Faith Alone: The Life of Martin Luther.* New York, 1955.

McGIFFERT, A. C. *Martin Luther.* New York, 1917.

MACKINNON, JAMES. *Luther and the Reformation,* 4 vols. London, 1925–1930.

OLIN, JOHN C., ed. *Luther, Erasmus, and the Reformation: A Catholic-Protestant Reappraisal.* New York, 1969.

RITTER, GERHARD. *Martin Luther: His Life and Work.* New York, 1963.

---

[6] Heinrich Bornkamm, *Luther's World of Thought,* trans. Martin H. Bertram (St. Louis, 1958), p. 291. The reference to the *Aeneid* is a quotation from the Roman poet Statius (d. *c.* 96 A.D.), *Thebaid,* XII, 816f., cited in *ibid.,* n. 4.

Schwiebert, Ernest G. *Luther and His Times*. St. Louis, 1950.

Simon, Edith. *Luther Alive: Martin Luther and the Making of the Reformation*. Garden City, N.Y., 1968.

Thiel, Rudolf. *Luther*. Philadelphia, 1955.

Todd, John M. *Martin Luther: A Biographical Study*. Westminster, Md., 1964.

Luther's religious reformation:

Althaus, Paul. *The Theology of Martin Luther*. Philadelphia, 1966.

Bluhm, Heinz. *Martin Luther: Creative Translator*. St. Louis, 1966.

Bornkamm, Heinrich. *Luther's World of Thought*. St. Louis, 1958.

———. *Luther and the Old Testament*. Philadelphia, 1969.

Elert, Werner. *The Structure of Lutheranism*, vol. 1. St. Louis, 1962.

Forell, George W. *Faith Active in Love*. New York, 1954.

Gerrish, Brian. *Grace and Reason: A Study in the Theology of Martin Luther*. New York, 1962.

Headley, John. *Luther's View of Church History*. New Haven, 1963.

Kadai, Heino. *Accents in Luther's Theology*. St. Louis, 1967.

McSorley, Harry J. *Luther: Right or Wrong?* New York and Minneapolis, 1969.

Meyer, Carl S. *Luther for an Ecumenical Age*. St. Louis, 1967.

Pelikan, Jaroslav. *Luther the Expositor*. St. Louis, 1959.

Pinomaa, Lennart. *Faith Victorious: An Introduction to Luther's Theology*. Philadelphia, 1963.

Prenter, Regin. *Spiritus Creator*. Philadelphia, 1953.

Preus, James S. *From Shadow to Promise: Old Testament Interpretation from Augustine to Luther*. Cambridge, Mass., 1969.

Rupp, Gordon. *Luther's Progress to the Diet of Worms*. London, 1951.

———. *The Righteousness of God: Luther Studies*. London, 1953.

Siggins, Ian D. Kingston. *Martin Luther's Doctrine of Christ,* Yale Publications in Religion no. 14. New Haven, 1970.

Vajta, Vilmos. *Luther on Worship*. Philadelphia, 1958.

Watson, Philip. *Let God Be God!* Philadelphia, 1948.

Wingren, Gustaf. *Luther on Vocation*. Philadelphia, 1957.

Ziemke, Donald. *Love of Neighbor in Luther's Theology*. Minneapolis, 1963.

Social unrest and the progress of the Reformation:

Althaus, Paul. *Luthers Haltung im Bauernkrieg*. Basel, 1953.

Bax, E. B. *The Peasants' War in Germany*. London, 1903.

Cranz, F. Edward. *An Essay on the Development of Luther's Thought on Justice, Law, and Society*. Cambridge, Mass., 1959.

Engels, Friedrich. *The German Revolutions: The Peasant War in Germany; and, Germany: Revolution and Counter-Revolution,* ed. Leonard Krieger. Chicago, 1967.

Franz, Günther. *Der deutsche Bauernkrieg,* 7th ed. Darmstadt, 1965.

Gritsch, Eric W. *Reformer Without a Church*. Philadelphia, 1967.

Kautsky, Karl. *Communism in Central Europe in the Time of the Reformation*. London, 1897.

Smirin, M. M. *Deutschland vor der Reformation*. Berlin, 1955.

CHAPTER 14

The Empire
in Crisis

The young emperor Charles V who sat upon the throne in the presence of the diet at Worms in 1521 was in every respect a remarkable person. The product of ancient historical forces, he had inherited from his Habsburg fore-bears the Netherlands, Luxemburg, Burgundy, Alsace, Castile, Aragon, Naples, Sicily, Austria, and the Spanish dominions in the New World, and three years earlier he had been elected Holy Roman emperor as well. He had the largest hold-ings of any ruler of his time, more than twice the realm of France, which his posses-sions now encircled. Through his veins flowed the royal blood of Christendom's oldest dynasties, mostly Hispanic, but also Burgundian, French, and German.

The young man whom Luther addressed as his "most gracious lord and em-peror" had light brown hair, a long, rather thin and melancholy face, alert eyes, and a jutting Habsburg jaw. On the walls in Worms these words appeared mys-teriously during the night of April 17: "Woe to the land whose king is a boy!" Before Charles stood Luther, the lowly Augustinian, who by sheer spiritual power had broken out of a monastery onto the stage of history. By a strange irony the forces he unloosed helped to wear down the emperor until in his last years he him-self retreated to a monastery. He was a lay brother there when he died. The reign of Charles V was for him frustrating but it was in no sense futile, for he molded

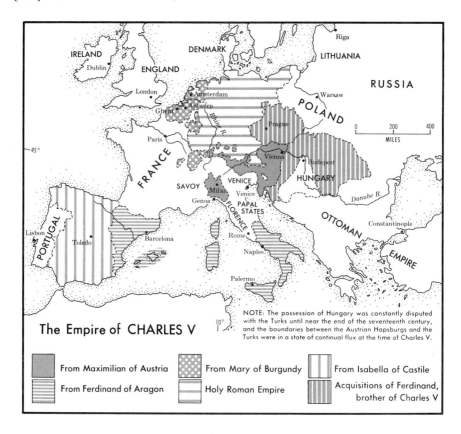

Riga

IRELAND   DENMARK   LITHUANIA
Dublin   ENGLAND

London   RUSSIA

Amsterdam   Warsaw
Ghent   Antwerp   POLAND

Prague   0   200   400
Paris   MILES

45°

Vienna   Budapest
FRANCE   HUNGARY
SAVOY   VENICE
Milan   Venice   Danube R.
Genoa   PAPAL
STATES   OTTOMAN
FLORENCE   Constantinople
Lisbon   Rome
Toledo   Barcelona   EMPIRE
PORTUGAL   Naples

Palermo

NOTE: The possession of Hungary was constantly disputed
with the Turks until near the end of the seventeenth century,
The Empire of CHARLES V   10°   and the boundaries between the Austrian Hapsburgs and the
Turks were in a state of continual flux at the time of Charles V.

From Maximilian of Austria   From Mary of Burgundy   From Isabella of Castile

From Ferdinand of Aragon   Holy Roman Empire   Acquisitions of Ferdinand,
                                                                brother of Charles V

inherited ideas of power, behavior, and belief into new universal forms that have
shaped both reality and the vision of mankind down to the present.

Born at Ghent on February 24, 1500, to Philip the Fair, son of Emperor
Maximilian and Mary of Burgundy, and Joanna, later called "the mad," daughter
of Ferdinand of Aragon and Isabella of Castile, Charles grew up in the Netherlands imbued with Flemish piety and Burgundian chivalric notions, which remained his two most outstanding personal characteristics throughout his life.
While Charles was still an infant his parents went to Spain, leaving him in the
care of Margaret of York, the widow of Duke Charles the Bold of Burgundy,
who had been killed at Nancy in 1477. In 1507 Margaret of Austria moved to
Malines and assumed the roles of regent and mother to Charles. From early
childhood he had a high sense of his calling and the dignity and supremacy of
kingship as a divine regency; it never left him. One of his tutors was Adrian of
Utrecht, a pious man who later became pope. During his boyhood his policy was
aimed at the recovery of Burgundy from the French. With a change of advisers
and his election as Holy Roman emperor in 1519, his interest shifted to Italy.

Operating mainly from Spain after 1521, he reasserted the old imperial claims to the territories of Milan, Tuscany, and Naples and assumed the imperial responsibilities of shielding Italy from the French and dominating the papacy. With a new Madrid-Rome axis established, he reawakened a vision of European unity.

Charles was completely dedicated to dynastic policy as a means of achieving a European hegemony and world empire. To establish Habsburg rule by marriage or conquest was a solemn religious duty owed in piety to his ancestors and in conscience to his descendants. He held to the medieval ideal of one pope as the supreme spiritual head and one emperor as the highest secular power in Christendom. He was deeply hurt by the pope's betrayal and by the alliance of the Christian king of France with the Turks. His interest in the New World was centered on the extension of Christianity to the heathen and the resources that the new treasures of Mexico and Peru provided for his continental enterprises. His dream of a universal dynastic empire raised the sights of feudal and urban authorities to higher political conceptions and goals. The great lords were beckoned away from their petty personal rivalries to larger policies of empire and a statecraft based upon more lofty principles.

For over forty years Charles waged war after war and negotiated treaty after treaty in order to achieve his goals or redress losses. His campaigns were often quixotic, planned and executed like some feudal chess game or tournament. Though slightly built, he was athletic, and he directed many battlefield encounters well armored and mounted on a white horse. He sent tens of thousands of state letters, often in his own hand; many still survive, evidence of his passion for affairs of state and his devotion to duty. He left the image of a most dedicated monarch to kings for centuries to come, but his own master plan as a design from Charlemagne floundered and failed. His very strength was his weakness, for the vast extent of his holdings meant they were correspondingly exposed and vulnerable. The encircled French had the advantage of centrality and interior lines of communication. The extreme eastern lands, farthest away from his main base of strength in Spain, lay directly in the path of the advancing Turks. Above all, Charles's widespread commitments and the shift in the seat of his power to the west proved to be disastrous for the Holy Roman Empire itself, which now entered a period of severe crisis.

The imperial election of 1519 was of crucial importance to the princes and people of the empire and to all Europe. Even before the death of Maximilian on January 12, 1519, political maneuvering for the election was under way. On January 1, 1515, twenty-one-year-old Francis I had ascended the throne of France. He was a handsome, proud, somewhat vain, free-spending Renaissance king who generously supported humanists, artists, and pleasing women at his magnificent court. "A court without beautiful women," said the king, "is like a spring without roses." His fairy-tale Château Chambord still stands as one of the architectural pearls strung along the Loire valley, and the deer still roam through his hunting grounds in the woods of Boulogne. Personally courageous, he loved a campaign. He had more than a touch of bravado about him, as when he said to the Venetians, "I will come, and I will triumph or die." After his victory at Marignano in 1515 over Swiss soldiery he enjoyed a military reputation that was totally undeserved, for he was a poor strategist and an impulsive field commander. According to the Treaty of Brussels (1516), France was to receive Milan and Spain was to control southern Italy. Francis I now feared that if Charles I of Spain were to be elected emperor, his own interests in northern Italy would be jeopardized. He believed that his own election as emperor would countermand the growing Habsburg ascendancy, and from 1517 on he worked to secure the votes of a majority of the seven electors. The months prior to the election of the new emperor were filled with conniving. Archbishop Richard of Trier committed himself to Francis and Frederick the Wise of Saxony followed an independent course; but the other five electors took fantastic bribes from both sides. The Habsburgs were reduced to borrowing bribe money from the German bankers. Pope Leo X favored the French king, in line with Medici policy and out of fear of the Spaniards, and he used his influence, promising a cardinal's hat and appointment as permanent papal legate to the archbishop of Mainz for the right vote. Francis promised to make Joachim I of Brandenburg his regent for all Germany. Both Leo and Francis would have preferred any German prince to Charles, but the only likely candidate was Luther's patron, Elector Frederick the Wise, and Frederick realized that his family and Electoral Saxony lacked the resources in men and money to keep peace in the empire. Pope Leo's agents reported back their suspicion that the electors were taking French gold but would not choose a French king. Then just before the election Frederick came out forcefully for Charles I of Spain, and on June 28, 1519, the electors choose Charles with a unanimous vote. The grandson of the popular Maximilian had been chosen. To the great rejoicing of all the Germans, the Habsburg eagle had soared above the Gallic cock. On October 22, 1520, Charles rode into Aachen on a beautiful stallion for his coronation.

The Germans could not yet foresee how Charles's international policies would work to the disadvantage of their empire. But it gradually became apparent to them that Charles was shifting the main base of his power away from Germany and Burgundy to the west. He always put Spain first and gave to the Spanish branch of his dynasty a preponderance that was to last for a century and a half. He achieved an ephemeral unity of Iberia through his fifteen-year marriage with Isabella of Portugal. The control of the Habsburg Danubian lands he transferred to the younger branch of his family. He skillfully glued together the Habsburg-Jagellon lines by arranging for the marriage of his younger brother Ferdinand with Anne, sister of King Louis II of Hungary and Bohemia, and of his sister Mary to Louis himself. He made Ferdinand regent of Austria and of the adjoining lands, Tyrol,

Vorarlberg, and Württemberg, and also turned over to him Alsace, Pfirt, and Hagenau with the proviso that on Ferdinand's death they should revert to the Burgundian inheritance.

In moving his own base of power to Spain, Charles made the western Mediterranean his own sphere of interest, which involved him in dramatic sea battles with the Tunisian pirates. He tied the Netherlands in with his Spanish nexus, thus cutting them off from a more natural union with the empire. He suppressed the north German Hanse cities and accelerated their decline. He opposed Christian II of Denmark, husband of his unhappy sister Isabella, and frustrated his attempt to build a strong state in the north. By shutting France out of Italy, he diverted its expansive drives into Lorraine and toward the empire, to the discomfiture and at times the terror of the German Rhineland. By his relative neglect of the empire, he allowed the Protestant princes in the north and the Catholic princes in the south to further the development of their territorial autonomy and particularist interests. After the Diet of Worms in 1521 Charles left for the Netherlands, hurried then to Spain, and did not return to the empire again for eight long years. Three enormous challenges confronted him: the wars with France, the invasion by the Ottoman Turks, and the test of strength with the Lutherans.

The Habsburg-Valois Wars

CHARLES V found the enemy of his life in King Francis I of France. The emperor had a dual role to play in his statecraft, for he strove toward that universal dominion which would ensure the unity and the security of Christendom against all foes, and he forged a dynastic chain of Habsburg states designed to throttle France. Much was at stake, for the control of the Mediterranean, the Atlantic, and the New World would be the prize of the victor in this struggle. The Italian cities and smaller states became mere pawns in this chess game of kings. The new superstates now swallowed up many small principalities.

In Francis of Angoulême, of a second line of the house of Orléans, the emperor found a worthy opponent, brash, colorful, determined, a gambler who thoroughly enjoyed ruling his nation. When Francis learned that Louis XII would be childless, he called together his friends and celebrated with a tournament, and when the king died Francis succeeded to his throne. His mother, Louise of Savoy, had imbued him with an exalted sense of his royal worth. "I went," she once related, "on foot to Our Lady of Fontaines in order to commend to her him whom I love more than myself, my son, the glorious and triumphant caesar, conqueror of the Helvetians." The growing French feeling of cohesion and national pride worked to his advantage. He exercised all the control he possessed and found a powerful response in the people. Emperor Maximilian once commented that he was a king of kings, for no one felt obliged to obey him. The king of Spain was a king of men, for people voiced objections but did not withhold obedience. But the king of France was like a king over animals, for no one dared think of refusing obedience. When the Venetian ambassador related Maximilian's *bon mot* to Francis I, he laughed out loud, for he recognized the truth in it. He ruled with a certain flair for grandeur and worked with vigor at governing, meeting his *conseil des affaires* in his bedroom each morning shortly after he awoke. He wished desperately to establish his family firmly on the throne, and when his oldest son suddenly died at a time when the imperial armies had occupied Provence, he was in despair. But he had other heirs, including his second son, Henry, who was married to Catherine de' Medici and perpetuated the Valois line.

Once the imperial election of 1519 was decided in favor of the Habsburg, Charles and Francis jockeyed diplomatically for a favorable position and then squared off for a duel that went through four wars and lasted four decades. In August 1521 the representatives of the emperor, Francis I, the pope, and Henry VIII met in Calais, ostensibly to assure peace but in reality to win England over to one side or the other. The Spanish diplomats succeeded in isolating Francis and winning over Henry VIII to a mutual-assistance pact with promises of the return of the old Angevin holdings, while Charles would take everything in the east and south of France that once belonged to the empire, as well as Navarre north of the Pyrenees. Pope Leo X made an alliance with Charles V in order to strengthen him against the Lutherans. Leo even prepared a bull that would have empowered Henry VIII to absolve French subjects of their oaths of loyalty to Francis. Francis gave sufficient provocation to Charles, aiding rebels in Castile, trying to detach the kingdom of Navarre from Spain, and encouraging Robert von der Mark to attack the empire on the western front. When Charles heard of Robert's aggression he exclaimed, "God be praised! It is not I who starts the war! God is giving me an opportunity to defend myself!"

Georg von Frundsberg, Franz von Sickingen, and an imperial army under the count of Nassau pressed into France, but were held off with the loss of only a few forts. Italy was destined to be the main theater of action. The imperial forces, opposed by French, Swiss, and Venetian troops, took Milan on November 19, 1521. Then Georg von Frundsberg brought in twelve fresh contingents of soldiers in support of the imperial general Pescara and together they took Genoa on May 20, 1522. The following year a great French magnate, Constable Charles of Bourbon, turned against Francis I, whom he considered a threat to his land and prospects, and in July 1524 he invaded southern France and besieged Marseilles with the help of imperial troops. Francis I now made an all-out effort to retake Milan. The French were well entrenched in the park of Mirabello near Pavia, but their impetuous king, spoiling for the encounter, moved out of his protected position. "Today," he exclaimed, "I shall name myself duke of Milan!" He gambled everything in one desperate battle at Pavia and lost. Before the battle the German troops knelt until the enemy was very close, then sprang to their feet shouting, "Forward! Now is the time! In God's name!" The Spanish arquebus proved to be a formidable weapon, and hand-to-hand combat raged for an hour and a half. French losses ran to over ten thousand men. Francis I himself was surrounded and captured.

The battle took place on February 24, 1525, and at the close of the day the imperial commissioner, the abbot of Najera, sent a dispatch to Charles in Spain: "Today is the feast of the Apostle St. Matthew, on which your majesty is said to have been born twenty-five years ago. Twenty-five thousand times thanks and praise be to God for his grace! From this day on your majesty will be able to pre-scribe laws as you will to Christians and to Turks!"

The effect upon France of the capture of Francis I and his imprisonment in Madrid was traumatic. The leaderless troops wandered about aimlessly, shouting for Bourbon or Burgundy. The nobility had suffered heavy losses and the cities now began to assert greater independence. Francis himself indulged in posturing, de-claring that honor and duty had led him into captivity, but his heart remained free. But he fell ill and became for a time demoralized. Popular opinion in France fixed the blame for the debacle more on Queen Mother Louise and Chancellor Duprat than on the king himself. A note widely distributed in the churches of France in March 1525 read: "Do you wish to know who is to blame for all this evil? It is Dame Pride and her chancellor. Through stubbornness and desire for revenge they have brought the king and his realm into this misfortune, and it will become worse if the chancellor is not punished!"

Charles V was astounded at the capture of his archrival; he was completely unprepared for such a turn of events. Henry VIII urged him to render Francis permanently harmless, but this advice did not take into account the strength of French national feeling for the young king and the terrible reaction such a step would have produced. A churchman urged him to release Francis immediately and unconditionally as a gesture of magnanimity that would elicit gratitude and friendship forever after, but this kindly approach did not take into account Francis' own Machiavellian propensities. Charles chose the middle course of releasing Francis on certain conditions. People should not say of him, he declared, that he was like Hannibal, who knew how to conquer but not how to use the victory. The Treaty of Madrid (January 14, 1526) was a severe but not an unreasonable resolu-tion. Francis was to renounce his claims to Burgundy, the Netherlands, and Italian territories. Charles of Bourbon was to be restored to his own lands. Francis was to marry Charles's sister Eleanor. Francis' two oldest sons were to be sent to Madrid as hostages to ensure the honoring of the treaty. The treaty was signed with due ceremony, but quickly came unglued. The marriage did nothing to ensure peace between the brothers-in-law, for Francis did not allow Eleanor to influence his policy. She was ill at ease at the brilliant French court and failed to produce a child. Francis very predictably took the first opportunity to renounce the treaty on the grounds that he had signed it under duress.

The European powers now turned against Charles, fearing his power. They joined forces in the League of Cognac on May 22, 1526, with the Medici pope Clement VII, Florence, Venice, Duke Sforza of Milan, and Francis I lined up against Charles. They were bolstered further by Henry VIII, who anticipated England's later policy of maintaining a balance of power on the continent by opposing the leading force. Moreover, he was already disenchanted with his inherited wife, Catherine, who happened to be Charles's aunt. Charles was enraged at the duplicity of Pope Clement VII. He addressed a letter to him asking how the vicar of Christ on earth could justify shedding one drop of blood for the sake of worldly possessions. The pope was damaging the Christian religion, for as emperor he could not now protect Christendom from the Turks or suppress the heretics. If the pope continued to act as a factional leader rather than a father, as a robber rather than a shepherd, the emperor would appeal to a council. In less than a year the emperor had his revenge.

In November 1526 an army of fifteen thousand German troops crossed the Alps under the command of Georg von Frundsberg, the old campaigner. In February 1527 Charles of Bourbon joined him with five thousand French dissidents and Spanish soldiery. The commanders ran out of money and Frundsberg died of a stroke after a confrontation with his rebellious troops. The army stormed on toward Rome, living on loot and plunder. On May 6 they began an assault on the walls of the eternal city. Bourbon was killed by a bullet as he mounted a scaling ladder. By midnight the troops were in the city and began the sack of Rome, which still lives in Italian memory as one of the most terrifying experiences in the city's long history. Clement VII took refuge in the fortress Sant' Angelo, while on the streets below drunken soldiers paraded a comrade crowned with a triple tiara and dispensing blessings with his wineglass. Now, they shouted, they would make Luther pope! But Emperor Charles allowed the pope to keep his secular power in exchange for a promise to work for peace and to call a council.

Francis recovered his stamina and was ready for a second try at realizing his ambitions. He developed a defensive system of fortresses in two lines, employing the latest techniques in earthworks and stone construction developed in Italy against artillery fire. He organized a rudimentary system of provincial militias. In August 1527 he made peace with Henry VIII, now in love with Anne Boleyn and hostile to Charles V. With the home front secured, he plunged into another Italian adventure and the second Habsburg war. The imperial army suffered the fate of countless forces that had invaded Italy through the long millennia, debauchery and demoralization. The French retook Genoa and went on to besiege Naples on land and, with a Genoese fleet under Andrea Doria, by sea. But then the French were hit by a plague, Andrea Doria defected to the emperor over the French treatment of Genoa, and an imperial army occupied Lombardy and relieved Naples.

In the Peace of Barcelona (June 29, 1529) Pope Clement confirmed the imperial claim to Naples and guaranteed free passage of imperial troops across the Papal States in exchange for the emperor's promise to oppose the Lutherans. With the Treaty of Cambrai, or "Ladies' Peace," as it was called, because Queen Mother Louise and Charles's aunt Margaret of Austria initiated negotiations, the second war was officially ended on August 5, 1529. The terms of Cambrai were basically the same as those of the Treaty of Madrid, with Charles renouncing attempts to recover Burgundy and Francis renouncing his overlordship of Flanders and Artois and promising never again to invade Italy or the empire. Pope Clement VII saw the "great value" of the treaty in the return of Francis' sons for a huge ransom in a single gold payment, for the emperor would now be free to go to Germany and personally oppose the Turks and Lutherans. On February 25, 1530, he crowned Charles emperor in a festive ceremony in Bologna, the last time in history that a pope would crown an emperor.

Though he had obviously signed the treaty freely, Francis again claimed that he had signed it under duress and maneuvered for a resumption of hostilities. The marriage in 1533 of his second son, the future Henry II, to Catherine de' Medici, the pope's niece, cemented relations between king and pope. The gift of Francis to Pope Clement on this grand occasion aroused considerable comment: a unicorn's horn that, when placed upon a banquet table, would reveal the presence of any poison in the food or drink by breaking into a cold sweat. Charles tried repeatedly during these years to find a basis of agreement with Francis. But a sinister development was in the making, an alliance of the most Christian king of France with the infidel Turks against the most Catholic emperor.

While a prisoner in Madrid, Francis had contrived to communicate with Sultan Suleiman I, presumably urging him to invade Hungary, which he did the next year. An official French embassy was sent to the Turks in 1535. In that year Francis explained this act to the Venetian ambassador: "Orator, I cannot deny that I hope the Turks appear mighty on this sea; not that I find pleasure in their advantages, for they are infidels and we are Christians, but they keep the emperor preoccupied and thereby effect greater security for other rulers." In February 1536 he made a formal alliance with the Turks, to the general horror of Christendom. The following month Francis suddenly invaded Savoy and moved on into Italy while the Turks attacked the Habsburg lands along the Danube and the Venetians at sea. The French pressed into the Netherlands, while imperial troops invaded Piedmont and Provence. Pope Paul III, fearing the Turks, was relieved to be able to mediate a peace between the two Christian monarchs on June 18, 1538.

The fourth and last attempt of Francis to break the Habsburg power nearly ended in disaster for his own kingdom. He renewed his alliance with Sultan Suleiman, who responded by a new invasion of Hungary. A combined French and Turkish fleet ruled the Mediterranean and attacked the cities along the coast, avoiding those in France. In the summer of 1542 Francis' armies attacked Spain and Luxemburg simultaneously. Charles again made an alliance with Henry VIII against France and then launched a massive counterattack. He sent a force down the Rhine to crush an ally of the French, William of Cleves, a rebellious Protestant prince. Then in June 1544 an imperial army of some 35,000 men penetrated deep into France, coming within fifty miles of Paris by September 8. At that point cautious Charles, near exhaustion and not willing to risk a reversal, offered peace terms. Charles once again invoked his dynastic principle and agreed that if the king's third son would marry the emperor's daughter, he would give her the Netherlands or Milan as a dowry. Thus ended the fourth and final Habsburg-Valois war.

Both sides, having devoted blood and money to a massive exercise in futility, were near bankruptcy and collapse. On March 31, 1547, Francis I died and was succeeded by Henry II. Charles V retired in 1555 and the task of arranging a more lasting peace with France fell to his successors. The Treaty of Cateau-Cambrésis (April 1–3, 1559), which came just forty years after the election of Charles as emperor and less than a year after his death, formalized the relationship between Spain, the empire, and France for decades to come. According to its terms France once again renounced her claims to Italy (except for five fortresses), yielded Savoy and Piedmont, but retained the income from those fateful bishoprics in the east, Metz, Toul, and Verdun. Italy suffered a new division, with western Lombardy going to Savoy, the south and east to the Farneses and Gonzagas, and Siena to the Medicis. The fact that this peace endured was due less to the good faith of the contracting parties than to the Spanish preponderance of power in the second half of the sixteenth century. Beset by civil war and domestic troubles, the French were in no position to challenge the Habsburgs for a long time to come.

The Ottoman Turks Attack

WHAT THE GERMAN EMPIRE really needed for its own well-being was a new location. In the center of a troubled continent and with no substantial natural barriers for defense, it was constantly caught between pressures from alert, advanced forces in the west and massive, brutal powers in the east. Charles V was caught in the middle of a two-front war with an opponent in the east as colorful and as worthy as his enemy to the west. Suleiman the Magnificent (1520–1566), the only son of Sultan Selim I, succeeded to the golden throne in the same year in which Charles V was crowned emperor, and remained his lifelong opponent. Suleiman, it was widely believed, was of a quiet and calm disposition, not well versed in affairs of state. But once in power he became a ruler without peer, a lawgiver, administrator, builder, patron of letters, and military leader of enormous energy and daring. He is remembered in history and legend for his style of governing, for the "marvelous grandeur" of his face, as the Venetian Navagero observed, and for a unique combination of wisdom and ruthlessness.

When King Francis I declared war in April 1521, Suleiman I saw his chance to realize the ambition of Mohammed II and of Bayazid II, Selim's predecessor, who had made assaults on Belgrade, the key to the Hungarian plain, but had failed to take it. A tremendous force of janissaries, regular troops, siege guns, and the sultan with his personal regiments moved out of Istanbul up the Danube. Light cavalry raided the countryside and cut off Belgrade to the west and north. A heavy bombardment and assault drove the garrison of defenders into the citadel, while Ottoman boats controlled the river. The Serbian and Hungarian defenders quarreled over tactics, and on August 29 the fortress surrendered. Suleiman followed up this victory the next year with a triumphant assault on the island of Rhodes. The Knights of St. John on Rhodes received no help from the west, for the Dutch pope Adrian VI seemed not to realize the strategic importance of Rhodes, in the eastern Mediterranean. They fought until exhausted and then surrendered on condition that they be allowed to withdraw to the west. The Mediterranean was now open to Turkish galleys.

The Persians provided a temporary distraction, but in April 1526 Suleiman's armies moved out again, this time to crush Hungary. King Louis II of Hungary led his brave but badly outnumbered Magyars against the Ottoman forces on the plain at Mohács on August 29, 1526. The Danube flowed to the east, and wooded hills to the west and south screened Ottoman forces from view. The Hungarian heavy cavalry charged the center of the Turkish line and threw it back. But at a critical moment Ottoman troops came down from the woods to the west and hit the Hungarian right flank. Murderous fire from the Ottoman artillery cut down thousands and the Hungarians were routed. Those not massacred by the Turks drowned in the marshes of the Danube, among them King Louis II. While noble Magyars died at Mohács on that fateful day, the governor of Transylvania, John Zapolya, stood aside with a large army. He was rewarded by being made king of Hungary under Suleiman's protection. The claim was disputed, of course, by Ferdinand, the younger brother of Charles V, on whom the emperor had bestowed the Habsburg Danubian lands.

Rebellious Turks distracted Suleiman, but in 1529 he was ready to take another slice of Europe. Having taken Buda and gained control of most of Hungary, Suleiman set his sights on Vienna. Time and distance were now his great foes, for the campaign season lasted only from April to the end of October, and the long lines of supply and communication compounded his logistics problems. His forces moved out of Istanbul on May 10, and on September 21 the first Turks appeared before Vienna. Within a week the 20,000 defending troops within the city were surrounded by a force estimated at more than 200,000. The Turks tunneled under the walls and mined them. On October 9 they blew up a large section of wall between the Carinthian gate and the fortress and began to storm the gap. The defenders filled the breech with cannons, guns, and lances, and held off the attackers. Two days later the Turks blew up another section of wall, and Spanish and German troops fought them off in fierce hand-to-hand combat. The Turks launched three new attacks, but the scimitar could not cut through the imperial shields and heavy double-edged swords. On October 12 a third section of wall fell and two days later the Turks made their final assault, suffering heavy losses from artillery fire at close range. Suleiman decided to withdraw, for Count Frederick of the Palatinate, field marshal of the empire, had gathered a relief force in Linz, the Austrians were collecting troops in Moravia, the Swabian League was stirring, and the nights were getting longer and colder. Suleiman retreated through the snow to Belgrade and Vienna was saved. The cross and not the crescent was to glisten on the tall tower of St. Stephen's Cathedral.

In the summer of 1532 Suleiman was back in Hungary with a huge army ready for another try at Vienna. But this time the emperor and his brother Ferdinand were better prepared. The pope sent a hundred thousand gold guldens to support Hungarian and Italian troops. By the end of September the emperor had an army of eighty thousand men. The Turks failed to take the small fortress of Güns, sixty miles south of Vienna, lost some fifteen thousand men in the woods outside Vienna, and turned south toward Graz. Only a final effort was needed to drive the Turks out of Hungary, but Charles now left Vienna for Italy to negotiate with the pope, and the German Protestant princes had no interest in freeing Hungary so that Ferdinand could re-Catholicize it, so the opportunity was lost.

The struggle at sea was equally dramatic. In 1532 an imperial fleet under the great admiral Andrea Doria scored a triumph over the Ottoman fleet in the eastern Mediterranean. In 1535 Charles assaulted the Moorish city of Tunis and took it. The next summer, 1536, Charles planned to attack the Turks' stronghold of Algiers and free all of Tunis. He even planned a great naval operation from Naples against Istanbul itself, but more prudent counsel prevailed. In October 1541 Charles's fleet attacked Algiers, but only part of his landing forces had hit the beach when a storm destroyed many ships and forced a retreat. To the disgust of Christendom, the Ottoman fleet wintered securely in the French harbor of Toulon. The dramatic blow at sea was to be struck not by Charles, but by his illegitimate son, Don Juan of Austria, in the battle of Lepanto in 1571. In 1574, however, the Ottomans conquered Tunis and fixed their hold on the southern coast of what Charles had hoped would be a Spanish sea.

The Expansion of Lutheranism

THE "INFIDEL TURK," by keeping Charles and Ferdinand constantly off balance and periodically on the defensive, quite unintentionally provided the evangelical movement in the empire with the respite from repression needed for continued growth. The year in which the Turks won their great victory at Mohács, 1526, was the year in which Charles made his concession at the Diet of Speyer, when he guaranteed the security of Lutheranism for the time being by endorsing the principle of a conciliar solution to the problem of Protestantism. The pope's suspicions of Charles and opposition to a council, together with Habsburg involvement with the French in Italy and fear of the Turks in Hungary, gave to Lutheranism precious time for consolidation and expansion. The emperor's alarm at the rise of Lutheranism and his determination to deal with it, made evident at the Diet of Speyer in 1529, came late in the year of Suleiman's siege of Vienna, before the danger was entirely past. The doom pronounced against the heretics by Ferdinand and the Catholic princes at the Diet of Augsburg in 1530 was never executed, for rumors of the major Turkish offensive of 1532 were already in circulation. The religious Peace of Nuremberg, agreed to at the diet in that same year, postponed a religious settlement until the meeting of a general church council and ordered that the processes against the Lutherans in the imperial supreme court be thrown out. The Protestants responded by supporting the war effort against the Turks. The Lutherans gained such strength in those years that even their defeat in the Schmalkald War in 1546 was not fatal, and in 1555, in the religious Peace of Augsburg, they achieved legal recognition of their existence as ecclesiastical bodies. The evangelicals viewed their deliverance as the working of Providence, with Suleiman cast in the role of King Cyrus of Persia, whom God used to free Israel although he knew Him not.

The evangelical movement spread through the empire by many channels and in unseen ways. From workmen to princes, Lutherans testified to their renewed faith. By word of mouth, through tracts and books the ideas spread. Merely charting the advance of Lutheranism on a political map state by state or listing the cities and territories by the dates of their conversion does not reveal the true human story of the struggles of conscience, the strife and uproar, the sacrifices and suppression, the martyrdoms.

The establishment of the Reformation in the cities and territorial states followed a pattern. Usually there was a general spirit of criticism or hostility to the Roman church and the local bishop and hierarchy. Sometimes there was in addition an active reform group already in existence, which then metamorphosed into a Lutheran group. This was true in Nuremberg, for example, where the followers of Johannes Staupitz, Luther's confessor, turned to Luther's program, and in Augsburg and other cities. The city council or the prince would appoint or tolerate evangelical preachers, who prepared the people for the radical changes subsequently introduced. Thus in Nuremberg the council and the city secretary, Lazarus Spengler, worked with the preacher Wenceslas Linck for evangelical reform. The preacher Johannes von Zwick played a key role in the conversion of Constance, though the Habsburg armies soon took the city and reestablished Catholicism by force. The roster of cities that turned Lutheran included Esslingen, Reutlingen, Memmingen, Lindau, Augsburg, Nuremberg, and Regensburg in the south, and Magdeburg, Erfurt, Halberstadt, Danzig, and Bremen in the north.

A key city in Reformation history was Strassburg, because of its central location at the commercial crossroads on the Rhine and its moderate theological tradition, midway between the Lutheran and Swiss reformed positions. At the Strassburg cathedral the great preacher Geiler von Kaisersberg had denounced the evils of the day and called for reform. Strassburg had its sodality of humanist reformers, led by the earnest moralist Jacob Wimpfeling. Its city secretary, Jacob Sturm, a political leader of great ability, became a Lutheran. The printers published many editions of the works of Luther and Melanchthon. The earliest leaders of the Reformation in Strassburg were Matthew Zell, a priest and penitentiary who preached in a side chapel of the cathedral in 1521, and his wife, Catherine, whom he married in 1523. An eloquent folk preacher, he attacked abuses and delivered evangelical sermons to large congregations. He and Catherine were consistently protective and hospitable to sectarians such as the Anabaptists and were open to the mystical inner-light ideas of religious thinkers such as Caspar Schwenkfeld.

In 1523 Martin Bucer (1491–1551) arrived in the city, a virtual unknown who quickly assumed the leadership of the movement. He had become a Dominican while still a boy, studied in the Schlettstadt Latin school in Alsace, and associated with Erasmus' alter ego, the young humanist Beatus Rhenanus. In 1518 he heard Luther defend his theological theses before the Augustinians in Heidelberg and was completely won over. As chaplain to von Sickingen he was a participant in the Knights' War. In 1523 the Strassburg city council authorized evangelical preaching in the pulpits of the city's churches, and the next year the parishes were reorganized with new orders of church discipline under the guidance of evangelical preachers. With the public conscience thus prepared for reformed prescripts of public law and the religious precepts of the biblical reformers, Bucer worked to establish a model Christian community, ably assisted by Wolfgang Capito (1478–1541), an Erasmian humanist turned reformer. In the tradition of the Zells, the city was unusually tolerant and hospitable toward Protestant refugees of all kinds. An edict of June 27, 1527, was designed to protect the city against disturbances by fanatics.

At Augsburg in 1530 four south German cities, Strassburg, Constance, Lindau, and Memmingen, presented a doctrinal statement, the *Confessio tetra-politana,* which Bucer and Capito had written. Swiss reformed tendencies were evident in it, including a reluctance to follow the Lutheran insistence on the real presence of Christ in the Sacrament and a consequent discretionary attitude toward the question; severe criticism of ceremonies; and stress upon the authority of Scriptures over that of the church. And yet in 1536 the Strassburg reformers traveled to Saxony and worked out the Wittenberg Concord on doctrinal matters, including the Lord's Supper, to which both Luther and Melanchthon were able to subscribe. With John Calvin and Melanchthon, Bucer attended the colloquies with Catholic theologians at Worms and Regensburg in 1540 and 1541, always seeking unity. His second wife, the merry widow Wibrandis, who had outlived two husbands, the reformers Oecolampadius and Capito, kept up his morale. When the city was forced to accept the emperor's doctrinal interim after the triumph of the imperial armies in 1546, and Jacob Sturm on bended knee begged for Charles's clemency, Bucer left his city for the England of Edward VI and lived out his days as regius professor of divinity in Cambridge. His earnest book *De regno christi* described that ideal community of Christ's kingdom on earth for which he had worked with such fervor in Strassburg.

The new pattern of Protestant education emerged clearly in Strassburg. Whereas pupils formerly went directly from the cathedral, monastic, or city schools to the universities when they were only twelve to fifteen years old, under the leadership of Luther and Melanchthon a secondary school, or *gymnasium,* was established, combining studies in arts and letters with evangelical religious instruction as preparation for university work. Melanchthon was personally active in founding such a school in Nuremberg; a life-sized statue of him still stands before its front door. Nicholas von Amsdorf, who assisted Luther in translating the Old Testament, helped found a school of this type in Magdeburg, where he was pastor and reformer. In Strassburg the founder and director of the humanist-evangelical school was Johannes Sturm, Jacob's brother, who published an influential treatise on *The Correct Exposition of Letters in the Schools* in 1537. New Lutheran universities were founded as well at Marburg, Tübingen, Königsberg, and later Jena, complete with evangelical theological faculties to train a new generation of Protestant leaders.

One of the first major territorial gains of Lutheranism came when Albert von Hohenzollern, the grand master of the Teutonic Knights, on Luther's advice secularized his holdings in East Prussia into a duchy under the overlordship of the king of Poland. His marriage to the daughter of King Frederick I of Denmark was important for the spread of the Reformation to that country. The decade of the 1530s saw the addition of powerful new territories to the Lutheran side. In Württemberg Duke Ulrich, who had been driven out in 1519 and replaced by the Habsburgs, reestablished himself in power in 1534 with the help of Philipp of Hesse and the French. He turned the territory Protestant under the leadership of Johannes Brenz, who worked out a program of school and church reform, including a new liturgy. That same year Pomerania turned Lutheran and in 1535 was given an evangelical church order prepared by Johannes Bugenhagen. Elector Joachim II (1535–1571) reformed Brandenburg in 1539, although he was so conservative that he kept the episcopal constitution intact until 1543. But perhaps the greatest joy to the Wittenberg reformers was the conversion of Ducal Saxony to Lutheranism in 1539. In that year Luther's implacable foe Duke Georg died, and his successor, Duke Henry (1539–1541), quickly introduced the Reformation. One can imagine Luther's satisfaction at preaching the festive Reformation sermon in the same hall in Leipzig in which he had debated Dr. Eck just twenty years before.

Other noteworthy Protestant gains within the empire came with the conversion of Brunswick-Wolfenbüttel and part of the Palatinate. The entire northwestern part of the empire came very close to turning Protestant when the archbishop of Cologne, Hermann von Wied, called on Bucer and Melanchthon to reform the archdiocese, but he was deposed and the Protestant duke William of Cleves was forced by the armies of Charles to re-Catholicize his territories. In that part of Germany the process was reversed and the area remained firmly Catholic.

EXPANSION IN NORTHERN AND EASTERN EUROPE

The Reformation movement reached beyond the borders of the empire to the Scandinavian countries as early as the 1520s and 1530s. The Reformation in the north was imposed from the top, with very limited spontaneous response from the people. The Danish king Christian II (1513–1523), who had executed more than eighty Swedish foes in one bloodbath, attempted to introduce the Reformation into Denmark in the hope of joining with Sweden to form a strong consolidated state, but the opposition of the Danish clergy and nobility and of the Swedish aristocracy was too strong, and in 1523 the king was forced to flee. In exile he visited Wittenberg and gave Kathie Luther a beautiful ring that she always cherished—a kind act by an unscrupulous and reckless man. Frederick I (1523–1533), who succeeded him, was well disposed toward the Reformation and had the example of his successful son-in-law Duke Albert of Prussia always in mind, but he had to promise the conservative nobility not to move against the old church. In his own duchies of Schleswig and Holstein he allowed evangelical preaching, and appointed as court chaplain the evangelical preacher Hans Tausen, who had studied at Wittenberg. In 1527 he persuaded the diet at Odense to allow toleration for Lutherans pending the convening of a council. In 1529 Christian Peterson published a Danish translation of the New Testament which was very influential in the formation of the modern Danish language. A full-scale reformation was not possible until 1536, when the next king, Christian III (1533–1559), introduced the new evangelical church order prepared by the itinerant statesman of Protestantism, Luther's "Dr. Pommer," the preacher Johannes Bugenhagen of Pomerania and Wittenberg. The seven bishops became superintendents, although the title of bishop was later reintroduced in the new context. The king became the head of the church as supreme bishop, and in due course the Augsburg Confession was accepted as the official credal statement.

Christian III's success in introducing the Reformation in Denmark coincided with his political and military victory over Norway. Since the Norwegians had supported Danish dissidents in a civil war against Christian, he forced them now to surrender their independence and compelled them to accept Lutheranism as their official religion. Iceland, formerly a Norwegian province, fell under the same legislation.

By a strange turn of events, Lutheranism was allied with nationalism in the Swedish drive for independence from the Danes between 1521 and 1523. The new king, Gustavus Vasa (1523–1560), led the resistance movement against the Danes and was crowned by the Swedish diet at Strengnäs on June 7, 1523. He was personally inclined toward Lutheranism, and in addition believed that its introduction would strengthen the independence movement. In 1527 at Westerås he forced the diet to sanction the transfer of church property to the king and to allow evangelical preaching. He was greatly aided in the dissemination of Lutheran ideas by two brothers, Olaf and Lars Petri, who had been educated in Wittenberg, and by Lars Andersson. They produced a Swedish translation of the Bible based on Luther's German Bible and led in the educational reform of the country. The Swedish Reformation was very conservative, retaining the episcopacy and a claim to an apostolic succession together with many traditional Catholic rites and ceremonies, such as the elevation of the host, prayers for the dead, and exorcism. It took another generation for Lutheranism to saturate the country. That Sweden became and remained Lutheran was to be of great political significance during the following century.

As a territory of Sweden, Finland followed along into the Lutheran Church. The most able of the Finnish reformers, Michael Agricola (1508–1557), had studied and taught at Wittenberg. He translated the New Testament, the Psalms, and some of the prophets into Finnish, and thus helped to develop Finnish as a literary language.

The chief center of Lutheranism in the Baltic states was the city of Riga. German Lutheran merchants in the Baltic were among the most active missionaries of the new movement. There had been evangelical influence in Riga as early as 1523, and in 1539 an evangelical archbishop was elected. Livonia and Esthonia followed Riga's lead. In 1561 the master of the Livonian Brethren of the Sword in Courland turned Lutheran, secularized his land into a duchy, and held it as a fief under the king of Poland.

The Poland of the Jagellon dynasty extended from west of the Vistula River to east of the Dnieper, reaching nearly to the Black Sea. Ethnically and religiously heterogeneous, the land included, besides the Poles, Roman Catholic Lithuanians, Greek Orthodox Ruthenians, and in the cities of western Poland many German merchant colonies and Jews, who were very important to the economic life of the country. The king had little effective power, for the landed nobility was virtually autonomous, and the Polish diet of 1505 had passed a law providing that only with the consent of all three estates could any new business be considered by that body, and another forbidding the king to maintain a standing army. Since the state was so thoroughly decentralized, a conversion of the whole state by the king in the familiar pattern was an impossibility. With such a poor power base, King Sigismund II Augustus (1548–1572) could not help losing ground on all fronts, falling back before Ivan IV of Muscovy, tolerating the union of Brandenburg and East Prussia under the Hohenzollerns, and making ever new concessions to the gentry, especially in "Little Poland," or the southwestern lands of the Vistula valley.

It was in this province that Protestantism took strongest root, and there were reportedly some 265 reformed congregations there, compared with 120 in "Large Poland" of the northwest. Whereas in western Prussia and "Large Poland" congregations of Lutherans and Bohemian Brethren were in the majority, in "Little Poland" a church in the Calvinist style developed, with anti-Trinitarian groups breaking off from them. The anti-Trinitarians—or Socinians, as they were also called, after their leaders, Lelio Sozzini and his nephew Fausto (1539–1604)—were centered in Racow, where they had their own church school and published their own catechism and confession of faith (the second Racow catechism of 1605). In 1638 their school was destroyed and in 1658 they were driven out of Poland as an "Arian sect." The multicolored Protestant movement prospered in Poland for only some sixty years. Eventually Roman Catholicism as a national faith seemed a necessary bond of unity to differentiate the Poles from the Russian Orthodoxy of the threatening power in the east and the Lutheranism of the Prussian complex to the north and west.

At the very outset of Luther's career his ideas were often associated with those of Jan Hus, the Bohemian heretic burned at Constance. At the Leipzig debate Luther had declared that not all of Hus's propositions condemned by the Council were false. Luther even dedicated a book to the Prague city council in 1523 and encouraged it to break with Rome. It seemed natural to expect that Lutheranism would find a foothold in Bohemia. In actual fact, however, it prospered mainly among the Germans in the north and in Moravia. While the Bohemian Brethren of the Unity, the more radical Hussites, looked with favor on Lutheranism, the more conservative Utraquists, who had made their peace with the Catholic Church, effectively frustrated movements toward a union with the new Protestantism. Conrad Cordatus, a student of Luther's who recorded his *Table Talk,* brought the evangelical religion to the miners in Slovakia, where a Lutheran church was to persist during the centuries that followed.

In view of Ferdinand's determined opposition and persecution, the spread of Protestantism in the Habsburg Danubian lands is most surprising. It was not only the cities of upper Hungary, with large German populations, that turned Lutheran; so did most of the Magyar landed magnates, including eventually the family of John Zapolya, the erstwhile king under the Turkish hegemony. The most influential reformer was Matthias Biró (Dévay), a Wittenberg student and friend of Melanchthon. After his exile to Switzerland he returned in 1543 to lead the Protestant movement in the direction of the Swiss reformed Helvetic Confession. In Austria, too, many leading members of the landed nobility turned Lutheran, but the chief centers of the movement were in cities such as Graz and Klagenfurt. For a time it seemed that all Austria might move into the Protestant camp, slipping right through the fingers of the Habsburgs, until they slowly tightened their grip once again.

THE STRUGGLE FOR SURVIVAL

Luther was a fighter who recognized the inevitability of conflict between the new and the old. He prophesied the worst:

> To wish to silence these tumults is nothing else than to wish to hinder the word of God and to take it out of the way. For the word of God, wherever it comes, comes to change and renew the world. . . . You do not see that these tumults and dangers increase through the world according to the counsel and the operations of God. And therefore you fear that the heavens may fall about our ears. But I by the grace of God see these things clearly, because I see the other tumults greater than these which will arise in ages to come, in comparison with which these appear but as the whispering of a breath of air, and the murmuring of a gentle brook.[1]

Nevertheless, Luther adamantly opposed the use of force or shedding of blood in defense of his theology or his life. It was years, in fact, before the jurists could convince him that the Protestant princes had the right to fight in their own defense when the emperor sent troops against them in an aggressive war that went beyond the prerogatives of his office. In any case, the actual decision to organize defensively against the Habsburgs and the Catholic princes was not for Luther to make.

The ominous maneuvering began as early as July 1525, when several Catholic princes, notably Duke Georg of Saxony, Albert of Mainz, Joachim I of Brandenburg, and Erich and Henry of Brunswick, organized the League of Dessau to root out evangelical doctrine. The young evangelical ruler Philipp of Hesse responded by forming with Elector John of Saxony and several lesser princes the League of Gotha, also called the League of Torgau, after the town where the

---

[1] Cited in E. Gordon Rupp, *The Righteousness of God* (London, 1953), p. 273.

alliance was ratified in February 1526. That same year both Hesse and Saxony organized territorial churches with Protestant constitutions. Tension mounted when in 1528 an official of Duke Georg of Saxony, Otto von Pack, was reported to have discovered a treaty signed by Catholic princes, pledging to exterminate the Lutherans. Even though the letter allegedly substantiating the existence of the treaty was proved to be a forgery, suspicion and rancor lingered on. In February 1531 a larger group of Protestant princes organized the Schmalkald League to prevent the enforcement of the decree of the Diet of Augsburg, condemning Luther and the evangelical movement to extinction. They developed the legal fiction that the territorial princes received their power directly by divine ordination, whereas the emperor's power was merely derivative, since he was appointed by the princes through the electors. A decade of relative security and continued Lutheran advances followed.

Protestant solidarity received a body blow in the scandal of Philipp of Hesse's bigamy and his separate treaty with the emperor. Philipp's wife, Christina of Ducal Saxony, it seems, could not satisfy the volcanic prince. The *femme fatale* of the drama was Margaret von der Saal, a court beauty, whose mother held out for a proper marriage. In earlier days Philipp had been an accomplished fornicator, but now his Protestant conscience would not allow him to step so freely outside the law—or at least this particular law. His wife agreed to the second marriage, and Luther, Melanchthon, and Bucer gave the confessional counsel that bigamy was preferable to divorce, since it enjoyed Old Testament precedents. Strange as this counsel seems, it was the same that Pope Clement VII gave to Henry VIII as an escape from his dilemma. Luther naïvely believed that Philipp's pangs of conscience were real and severe, and that the second marriage would be the lesser of two evils. When the second marriage was consummated in March 1540, a great uproar arose. Philipp had violated solemn imperial law and thereby made his title and lands subject to seizure by the emperor. On June 13, 1541, recognizing his vulnerability, Philipp made a separate nonaggression treaty with the emperor. His son-in-law, Maurice of Ducal Saxony, subscribed to this pact and eventually left the Schmalkald League to side with the emperor, a mortal blow to Protestant defenses and to the balance of power in the empire. Charles prepared to strike at his foes.

A general council was summoned to assemble at Trent in 1545. On February 18, 1546, Luther died. All signs seemed propitious for the final solution of the problem of heresy in the empire. With Pope Paul III, Duke Ferdinand, Duke William of Bavaria, Maurice of Saxony, and some lesser evangelical princes as allies, Charles fielded his armies in 1546. He overran southern Germany within the year and forced the south German Protestant cities and states to capitulate. Then he moved into north Germany, and at Mühlberg on April 24, 1547, thoroughly defeated the Lutheran forces, taking captive Elector John Frederick of Saxony and Landgrave Philipp of Hesse. In the Wittenberg capitulation of May 19, 1547,

Maurice took over the electoral right from John Frederick and much territory, including Wittenberg.

In June 1548 Charles had a basically Catholic doctrinal statement prepared, known as the Augsburg Interim, which he attempted to impose upon the Germans. Melanchthon and the Catholic bishop Pflug of Naumburg worked out a substitute doctrinal formulation known as the Leipzig Interim, which they hoped would be more satisfactory to the Lutherans, but resistance was strong and many Protestant cities and estates openly defied it. At this juncture the Machiavellian Maurice, who was besieging the Lutheran stronghold of Magdeburg, saw his opportunity. He deftly insinuated himself into a position of leadership in the Schmalkald League. The league now sacrificed Metz, Toul, and Verdun to King Henry II of France in return for aid against the emperor. Emperor Charles suffered a military setback and loss of prestige when he failed to take Metz. In a surprise attack on Charles, Elector Maurice surrounded the imperial troops near Reutte and forced them to surrender. He almost captured the emperor himself near Innsbruck. Charles fled through the Brenner Pass to the south, falling back to Lienz and Villach. The disaster was a shock from which he never recovered. In the Peace of Passau, in August 1552, the emperor agreed to free Philipp, as he had John Frederick, and allowed the Lutherans to practice their religion until the next diet.

At the Diet of Augsburg in 1555 the emperor's final failure to suppress Protestantism in the empire was legally acknowledged. The Protestant princes at the diet represented a whole spectrum of particularist interests, from conservative Saxony,

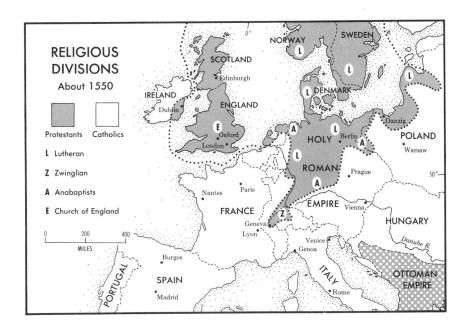

most concerned with securing a permanent peace, to Duke Christoph of Württemberg, who wanted concessions that would assure further Protestant gains. After tedious negotiations that lasted from February into September, the provisions of the celebrated Peace of Augsburg were agreed upon. The Lutheran cities and states were to be guaranteed security and all pledged themselves to an eternal and unconditional peace. The principle *cuius regio, eius religio* was to be applied to Lutherans as well as to Catholics, each estate to have the privilege of choosing its official religion. Ecclesiastical property taken by the Protestants prior to the Peace of Passau was to remain theirs, but any ecclesiastical prince who turned Protestant thereafter was to lose his title, lands, and privileges—the so-called ecclesiastical reservation. The peace also made real a privilege that Luther had urged in his day: Christians were to be permitted to move freely from one principality to another more congenial to their religious convictions. When the peace was announced the bells rang out throughout the Lutheran lands, for the right of peaceful coexistence had been won at last. And for all its compromises and weaknesses, the Peace of Augsburg did bring relative tranquillity to the land until the outbreak of the horrendous Thirty Years' War more than half a century later, a near record for Europe.

Emperor Charles was thoroughly weary and demoralized. In a dramatic and emotional scene in 1556 he renounced his worldly titles and, having made careful provision for the succession of his son Philip to the thrones of Spain, the Netherlands, and Spanish Italy and of his brother Ferdinand as emperor, he retired to a villa adjoining the monastery of San Jerónimo de Yuste in Spain to prepare for the world to come. There he died in September 1558. He had brought Habsburg power to the greatest heights it was ever to know. And yet a deep sense of tragedy and melancholy lay like a shadow upon the emperor. In victory as in defeat, the thought of the transiency of this earthly life and the hope of a better life to come had kept him from overweening pride or bottomless despair. He was a man of tremendous character, sincere and well intentioned. He has been compared, ironically enough, with Luther, who intended to reform the old church but founded a new one, and with Columbus, who searched for the ancient East but discovered the New World. For Charles was dedicated to the renewal of the medieval ideal of universal monarchy, but in reality he let the empire sink into impotence and became instead the founder of the Spanish imperium and the Spanish hegemony in Europe.

Bibliography

Habsburg-Valois wars:
BABELON, JEAN. *Charles Quint.* Paris, 1947.

BRANDI, KARL. *The Emperor Charles V*, trans. C. V. Wedgwood. New York, 1939.

CARSTEN, F. L. *Princes and Parliaments in Germany, from the Fifteenth to the Eighteenth Century.* Oxford, 1959.

CLASEN, CLAUS PETER. *The Palatinate in European History, 1559–1660.* Oxford, 1966.

FRANÇOIS, M., et al. *Charles Quint et son temps.* Paris, 1959.

FUETER, EDUARD. *Geschichte des Europäischen Staatensystems von 1492 bis 1559.* Munich, 1919.

MOUSNIER, ROLAND. *Les XVIᵉ et XVIIᵉ siècles.* Paris, 1956.

RITTER, GERHARD. *Die Neugestaltung Europas im 16. Jahrhundert.* Berlin, 1950.

ROSSOW, PETER. *Karl V: Der Kaiser und seine Zeit.* Cologne, 1960.

Ottoman Turks:

FISCHER-GALATI, STEPHEN A. *Ottoman Imperialism and German Protestantism, 1521–1555.* Cambridge, Mass., 1959.

LEWIS, B. *Istanbul and the Civilization of the Ottoman Empire.* Norman, Okla., 1963.

LYBYER, A. H. *The Government of the Ottoman Empire in the Time of Suleiman the Magnificent.* Cambridge, Mass., 1913.

MERRIMAN, R. B. *Suleiman the Magnificent, 1520–1566.* Cambridge, Mass., 1944.

ROUILLARD, C. D. *The Turk in French History, Thought, and Literature, 1500–1660.* Paris, 1939.

WITTEK, P. *The Rise of the Ottoman Empire.* London, 1938.

Expansion of Lutheranism:

CHRISMAN, MIRIAM. *Strasbourg and the Reform.* New Haven, 1967.

EELLS, HASTINGS. *Martin Bucer.* New Haven, 1931.

FRAENKEL, PETER. *Testimonium Patrum: The Function of the Patristic Argument in the Theology of Philipp Melanchthon.* Geneva, 1961.

HARTFELDER, KARL. *Melanchthon als Praeceptor Germaniae.* Berlin, 1899.

HOPF, C. *Martin Bucer and the English Reformation.* New York, 1946.

KITTELSON, JAMES. "Wolfgang Capito: Humanist and Reformer." Ph.D. dissertation, Stanford, 1969.

MANSCHREK, CLYDE. *Melanchthon, the Quiet Reformer.* New York, 1958.

POLL, GERRIT JAN VAN DER. *Martin Bucer's Liturgical Ideas.* Assen, 1954.

SPERL, ADOLF. *Melanchthon zwischen Humanismus und Reformation.* Munich, 1959.

STEPHENS, W. P. *The Holy Spirit in the Theology of Martin Bucer.* Cambridge, Mass., 1970.

STUPPERICH, ROBERT. *Melanchthon.* Berlin, 1960.

Northern and eastern Europe:

BENZ, ERNST. *Wittenberg und Byzanz.* Marburg, 1949.

BERGENDOFF, CONRAD. *Olavus Petri and the Ecclesiastical Transformation of Sweden, 1520–1552.* New York, 1929.

DUNCKLEY, E. H. *The Reformation in Denmark.* London, 1948.

FOX, PAUL. *The Reformation in Poland.* Baltimore, 1924.

HALECKI, OSKAR. *A History of Poland.* Baltimore, 1924.

LARSEN, K. *A History of Norway.* Princeton, 1948.

MECENSEFFY, GRETE. *Geschichte des Protestantismus in Oesterreich.* Graz, 1956.

MURRAY, ROBERT. *Olavus Petri.* Stockholm, 1952.

WADDAMS, H. M. *The Swedish Church.* London, 1946.
YELVERTON, E. E. *The Manual of Olavus Petri.* London, 1951.

Protestantism's struggle for survival:
BERGENDOFF, CONRAD. *The Church of the Lutheran Reformation.* St. Louis, 1967.
BRANDI, KARL. *Der Augsburger Religionsfriede, 1555,* 2nd ed. Göttingen, 1927.
FABIAN, EKKEHART. *Die Entstehung des Schmalkaldischen Bundes und seiner Verfassung.* Tübingen, 1962.
HARTUNG, FRITZ. *Karl V und die deutschen Protestanten, 1540–1555.* Halle, 1910.
MENTZ, G. *Johann Friedrich,* 3 vols. Jena, 1903–1908.
SCHLINK, EDMUND. *Theology of the Lutheran Confessions.* Philadelphia, 1961.
WINTERS, R. L. *Francis Lambert of Avignon.* Philadelphia, 1938.

CHAPTER 15

Zwingli
and the
Radicals

An enemy soldier looked down at the mutilated body of the reformer Ulrich Zwingli as it lay on the battlefield at Cappel on October 11, 1531, and exclaimed, "You were a rotten heretic, but a damned good Swiss!" Zwingli was indeed Swiss to the marrow of his bones, and in turn he impressed his own personality upon the national character as few Swiss have done. His reform program determined the direction of Swiss history, and the Alpine state became a microcosm presaging the way divided Europe was to go.

Although in Zwingli's day Switzerland was nominally still a part of the Holy Roman Empire, it had long since achieved very real political independence. The original union in 1291 of three forest cantons, Uri, Schwyz, and Unterwalden, had grown into a confederation of thirteen cantons in all. The confederacy was held together by mutual defense treaties and by a diet that met to discuss common problems, although it had little authority over the virtually autonomous cantons. In the Swiss War—or the Swabian War, as the Swiss preferred to call it—in 1499, the Habsburg emperor Maximilian I made a final feeble attempt to force the Swiss back under the imperial yoke. The fiction of imperial rule was maintained until Swiss independence was legally acknowledged in the Peace of Westphalia in 1648. A pattern of urban resistance to the rule of feudal episcopal authorities outside the cities developed even before the Reformation, as the bourgeois city councils assumed an ever greater authority over ecclesiastical administration within the cantons. In this unique urban republican setting the German Swiss Reformation developed under the leadership of Ulrich Zwingli.

Zwingli the Reformer

THE KEY to Zwingli's preeminence lay not in his social position but in his native ability and superior education. Ulrich Zwingli (1484–1531), the "third man" of the Reformation (after Luther and Calvin), developed from a learned humanist into an ecclesiastical reformer of great historical stature. His father, a free peasant and an official of the village of Wildhaus in the Toggenberg valley of St. Gall canton, was very ambitious for his son and kept him in the best schools available. At eight Ulrich went to school in Wesen, where an uncle of his was dean, and at ten transferred to Basel, where he studied Latin, dialectics, and music for three years under Gregor Bünzli in the School of St. Theodore. At thirteen he moved on to a school in Bern for two years (1496–1498) under the formative influence of a noted teacher, Heinrich Wölflin, a man thoroughly dedicated to Renaissance humanist educational ideals, who inspired him with a love of the classics and an appreciation for music. The Dominicans in Bern recognized in Zwingli a youth of extraordinary gifts and urged him to enter their monastery, but he had barely begun his probationary year with them when his family forced him to withdraw, and soon afterward sent him to Vienna for university study.

The Vienna of Maximilian's brilliant reign made a tremendous impression upon the young Swiss student during his two-year stay (1500–1502). The matriculation book indicates that he was expelled at one point (his name is struck out and an *exclusus* written in the margin), possibly for expressing anti-Habsburg sentiments. The liveliest spirit at the university in those years was Conrad Celtis, the German arch-humanist, active as a teacher of the classics, head of the college of poets and mathematicians, and director of humanist plays. Zwingli cultivated further his classical learning and musical prowess and was able to play a variety of instruments: lute, harp, flute, viol, reed pipe, and cornet. He became a close friend of Heinrich Glareanus, later renowned as a leading musical humanist in Switzerland. But as a good Swiss Zwingli returned to Basel, where he took his A.B. degree in 1504 and his M.A. degree in 1506. At Basel he came under the direct influence of Dr. Thomas Wyttenbach, an Erasmian reform-minded scholar who favored the study of the New Testament and the church fathers and was hostile to scholasticism, monastic vows, indulgences, and the mechanical use of the sacraments. Zwingli taught the classics at the School of St. Martin and purchased an edition of Pico della Mirandola. At the age of twenty-two he was ordained into the priesthood by the bishop of Constance. He said his first mass among his own people in Wildhaus.

Zwingli's decade as the people's priest at Glarus provided a solid foundation for his later reform activities. At the very outset he encountered a problem typical of the chicanery that characterized all too many church positions. When Zwingli was elected priest at Glarus over Heinrich Goldi, who had been appointed by the pope, he found it necessary to buy Goldi off with a hundred guldens. Zwingli was pulled in two directions during his Glarus ministry, toward scholarship and toward a real pastoral concern for his people. His library of over 350 volumes covered subjects ranging from geometry and geography to philosophy, theology, philology, and the classics. He studied Greek assiduously and began Hebrew, and read widely in patristic literature. His friends soon began referring to him as "the Cicero of our age." He was naturally attracted to Erasmus, who repaid his admiration with chillingly superior and patronizing letters. Zwingli even made a trip to Basel to meet the prince of the humanists in person. When Erasmus' edition of the New Testament appeared in 1516, Zwingli memorized Paul's epistles in Greek from his own copy. At the same time, he was devoted to his pastoral duties. He established a school for children and taught in it himself.

Zwingli accompanied Swiss mercenary troops as chaplain in such lost battles as Novara in 1513 and Marignano outside of Milan in 1515. He conducted himself on the battlefield with honor and courage, his biographer Heinrich Bullinger related, but saw clearly the evils of the mercenary system, which enriched but corrupted young Swiss, when it did not cripple and maim them. He wrote political rhymed allegories or fables and preached sermons against the degrading practice of selling blood for money. His opposition to the lucrative mercenary business, and to a treaty with France which obligated the Swiss to the French in return for financial aid, turned powerful pro-French interests against him and forced him out of Glarus.

In 1516 Zwingli was called to the monastic church in Einsiedeln, where the shrine of the Black Image of the Virgin attracted many pilgrims. But Zwingli soon began to criticize the plenary indulgence granted for the pilgrimage to Einsiedeln, and in August 1518 he managed to block the activities of the Franciscan monk Bernardin Samson, who had come to sell indulgences like Tetzel in Saxony. Late in October 1518 the possibility of a pulpit far more influential opened up in Zurich, but two things worked against Zwingli's chances of obtaining it: the rumor that as a musician he was frivolous and unreliable and the report that he had been guilty of immoral conduct. Zwingli met the charges head-on by writing a letter defending his music making but confessing his guilt of misconduct. A wanton young woman had tempted him and he had unwisely embraced the opportunity and the girl, as others had before him; the child she awaited in Zurich might indeed be his. He denied that he had violated a virgin or a woman of high standing, although, as he said ironically, her father was one of those powerful men who could even touch the emperor's beard without risk, since he was a barber. On December 11, 1518, the canons elected Zwingli to the pulpit in Zurich over a Swabian competitor who had a concubine, six children, and many benefices. It was at the Great Minster in Zurich that Zwingli was to undertake the reformation of German Switzerland.

Zwingli had an attractive personality and a warmhearted way with him, along with a quick mind, a beautiful voice, and tremendous rhetorical power. He already enjoyed a reputation as a powerful preacher. He was also keenly perceptive and had an acute sense of the right moment for action. He carefully prepared the council and the congregation before undertaking any major change. On New Year's Day of 1519, his birthday, he preached his first sermon in the great church at Zurich and announced that the following Sunday he would begin to interpret the gospel according to Matthew according to divine truth, not human vanity. Zwingli had the Greek text before him in the pulpit and presented a straightforward explication of the text. The impact was sensational. A young humanist in the congregation, Thomas Platter, recorded that when he heard the word of God proclaimed from the very source, as he put it, he felt as though he were being drawn up by the hair of his head. After this treatment of the life of Jesus, Zwingli went on to portray the early church on the basis of the Acts of the Apostles and Paul's epistles. It took him six years to go through the entire New Testament.

During his first year in Zurich Zwingli underwent an agonizing experience that almost took his life. The dreaded bubonic plague swept through the Swiss confederacy and struck Zurich in August. It has been estimated that as much as a third of the population died. Often when the plague struck in those centuries, the doctors who recognized the symptoms were the first to leave. Zwingli was away at the time, taking the waters at Bad Pfäfers, but he returned immediately to minister to the sick and dying. Death claimed his own brother Andreas, and in late August or September Zwingli himself fell sick. In November rumors of his death circulated in Basel and Constance. But after a long struggle he recovered, although it was the following summer before he fully regained his strength. In gratitude he wrote his "Song of Pestilence" or "A Christian Song, Written by Huldrych Zwingli as He Was Attacked by the Plague," and set it to music. This brush with death left him in a more serious mood and led him to search even more earnestly into the deeper dimensions of the Christian faith.

The actual break with the old church was precipitated by a purely external breach of church law, the canonically enforced abstention from the eating of meat during Lent. Zwingli had taught from the pulpit that the word of God clearly allows the eating of all food at all times, and that papal prohibition ran counter to the liberty proclaimed by the gospel. On Ash Wednesday in 1522 a number of prominent citizens, including Zwingli and Leo Jud, the people's priest at Einsiedeln, met at the house of Christopher Froschauer, a printer. They cut up two fried sausages and everyone ate some, except for Zwingli, who refrained for fear of giving offense to parishioners not yet ready for such a drastic step. The city council reacted quickly by punishing several with imprisonment and fines. Zwingli responded from the pulpit less than three weeks later in defense of those who had broken the fast, and in April he published the sermon under the title *Concerning Choice and Freedom of Food.* The same year he published a key reformatory writing, *Archeteles* (The Beginning and the End), in which he argued for spiritual freedom from the control of the bishops. Only the Holy Spirit is needed to make God's word intelligible, he now argued; no definitions by church, council, or pope were necessary or proper. With Luther's Leipzig debate in mind, Zwingli pressed for a public disputation in which the issues could be publicly discussed, and the city government agreed. The debate was to be held on January 29, 1523.

Over six hundred men, friends and foes, assembled at the town hall for the disputation. The bishop of Constance was represented by Zwingli's erstwhile friend John Faber, now diocesan chancellor and vicar general. Zwingli sat front and center with his Hebrew, Greek, and Latin Bibles open before him. As a basis for discussion he had prepared and published *Sixty-seven Articles,* which summarized most succinctly his theological platform for reform. The first sixteen articles presented his positive doctrines, proclaiming the meaning of the gospel, the all-sufficiency of the teaching and work of Christ, who made known to man the will of his heavenly father and with his innocence released men from death and reconciled them with God, and the true nature of the church as the communion of saints or company of all believers in Christ. The rest of the articles spelled out his objections to the assumption of high priestly powers by the pope, the celebration of the mass as a sacrifice rather than as a remembrance, prayer for the intercession of saints, compulsory fasting, pilgrimages, monastic vows, clerical celibacy, the misuse of the ban, gabbled prayers, the sale of indulgences, the doctrines of penance and purgatory, the priesthood, the role of the state in religion, and other teachings and practices.

> Let no one undertake here to argue with sophistry of human foolishness, but come to the Scriptures to accept them as the judge (*foras cares!* the Scriptures breathe the spirit of God), so that the truth either may be found, or if found, as I hope, retained. Amen.
> Thus may God rule.

The main thrust of Zwingli's argument in the debate that followed was that the reformers were engaged in restoring the church to its ancient purity; it was the medieval church that was the innovator, not the reformers.

The disputation resulted in a resounding victory for Zwingli's teachings and an order from the city council that all priests of the canton should promote them.

Six months later Froschauer published Zwingli's *Interpretation and Substantiation of the Conclusions,* in which he contrasted church practices with the law of Christ and expressed his dissatisfaction with traditional forms of worship and liturgical music. In September the council passed an ordinance providing for changes in the statutes of the Great Minster, reducing the number of clergy, lowering the fees for spiritual services such as baptism and the Sacrament, and providing for daily instruction in the Scriptures.

In view of the favorable result of the first disputation and the growing tensions within the city, Zwingli pressed for a second debate to deal with the question of the mass and the veneration of images. The second disputation, attended by about eight or nine hundred priests and laymen, began on October 26, 1523, and lasted for three days. This time Zwingli and Leo Jud were opposed more ably by Martin Steinli of Schaffhausen. The council voted to retain the mass, to restrain those who wished to carry images into the church or to remove them, and to appoint a commission, which included Zwingli and Jud, to instruct the people in evangelical teachings. The council was clearly moving toward reform, but it preferred to move gradually.

For the enlightenment of the clergy in the canton, Zwingli wrote *A Brief Christian Introduction,* a sharp attack on the use of images. Zwingli's ideas reflected the influence of an eighteen-page pamphlet written by Ludwig Hätzer, a priest educated at Basel in classical humanism, *The Judgment of God Our Spouse as to How One Should Hold Oneself Toward All Idols and Images, According to the Holy Scriptures.* On Monday, December 28, a third and more limited debate was held with the canons and clergy of Zurich together with the members of the small and great councils to discuss once again the problem of images and the mass, but further action was deferred until another debate could be held early the next year.

The years 1524 and 1525 witnessed the culmination of the drive toward reform with the resolution of the three vexing questions of the veneration of images, the celibacy of the clergy, and the celebration of the mass. The fourth disputation, held on January 19 and 20, 1524, marked a critical turning point, for the intellectual poverty of the defenders of the "old belief," as opposed to proponents of the new "right belief," left the field to the reformers and cleared the way for the subsequent official decrees of the council sanctioning change. The debate was conducted by fourteen men: six members of the council, five cathedral canons, and the reformers Engelhard, Jud, and Zwingli. Only Rudolf Hofmann spoke at length for the iconophile position, formulating twenty-three theses drawn almost entirely from nonscriptural sources: tradition, the church fathers, medieval scholastics, conciliar decrees, and canon law. The council was easily moved to follow Zwingli's iconoclastic recommendations. After temporizing interim decrees, on June 15 the council announced its final decision, authorizing the removal of all remaining images from the churches. The council now acted swiftly and appointed a committee of twelve, each man from a different guild, to remove the "idols" from the temples and whiten the walls, an operation that took from June 20 to July 2. The myopic Zwingli had never had the appreciation for the visual arts that he had for music, and so had few regrets about the loss of medieval art. Yet his personal tastes seem to have had little influence on his reform program, for it also required the elimination of choir singing, congregational singing except for psalms, organ music, and any other features not expressly authorized by the Scriptures. On December 9, 1527, after years of silence the organs of the Great Minster were removed and chopped up. Zwingli regarded this removal of images and organs as a triumph of the spirit over things corporeal and sensual, a very Puritan point of view. "In Zurich," he exclaimed in triumph, "we have churches which are absolutely luminous; the walls are beautifully white!"[1]

In 1522 Zwingli and other clerics had petitioned the bishop of Constance for permission to marry, and when they were summarily rebuffed, he was married secretly to a pious widow, Anna Reinhard Meyer. Two years later, on April 2, 1524, when the tide in Zurich was clearly moving in his favor, he made the most of it by celebrating his marriage in the Great Minster, thus publicly practicing what he had preached about the honorable estate of marriage for clergymen and the invalidity as well as the futility of the Catholic decrees on celibacy. When Zwingli once made the dramatic charge that out of a hundred or even a thousand monks, priests, and nuns, hardly a chaste one could be found, a local canon expressed regret at such public accusations but acknowledged that they were all too true.

A third major controverted dogmatic issue was the Catholic doctrine of the mass. In 1215 the Fourth Lateran Council had given official sanction to the doctrine of transubstantiation, which held that the "elements," the bread and wine used in the Sacrament, were changed in substance into the real body and blood of Christ, although the "accidents," or external appearance, remained the same. The Sacrament itself had taken on the character of a bloodless sacrifice by which the priest repeated the original sacrifice of Christ on Calvary. Participation in the mass by the faithful believer was no longer indispensable, since endowed private masses could be said by a priest, even for the benefit of souls already presumably in purgatory. Finally, communion "in one kind," with only the bread distributed to the communing laity while the priest drank the wine, was the universal practice. Zwingli objected on biblical grounds to all of these aspects of the mass, viewing them as departures from the Lord's institution as recorded in the New Testament. To the mass he opposed the reformed conception of the Lord's Supper as a memorial or spiritual communion with Christ, with the bread and wine as symbols of the body and blood of Christ. Like Luther, he objected to the doctrine of transub-

---

[1] See Charles Garside, Jr., *Zwingli and the Arts* (New Haven, 1966), pp. 146–60.

stantiation on the grounds that the distinction between essence or substance and accidents was metaphysical and not scriptural. He viewed the elevation of the host and adoration during Corpus Christi processions as the idolizing of a material object. He opposed the idea of the mass as sacrifice on the ground that Christ's original sacrifice was valid once and for all time, and because of sacerdotal misuse of the magical power of transformation and sacrifice. He believed that private masses without the congregation of believers and without the presence of communicants were invalid and misled the laity into a work-righteous or mechanical view of the Sacrament.

Zwingli carefully educated the congregation and council to his views. During Holy Week in 1525, on April 16, to be precise, communion was celebrated in Zurich for the first time according to the new form, the Lord's Supper in both kinds as a remembrance of the Last Supper and a spiritual communion of the believer with his Lord. Once again Zwingli's drive to elevate the spiritual over the material triumphed, this time in a matter of very essential doctrine. Only a month earlier he had published his *Commentary on the True and False Religion,* dedicated to King Francis I of France, in which he clearly stated his interpretation that by faith alone the Lord's presence could be received in a feast that was designed to be commemorative and symbolic.

The influence of Erasmian humanism upon Zwingli's religious thought was very evident during Zwingli's earlier years as a reformer and remained a permanent part of his theological orientation. He was deeply impressed with the humanist emphasis upon deriving truth from the original sources, so that the formal principle of his theology required the derivation of the knowledge of Christ from "the very fountains," the Scriptures themselves. The Erasmian slogan of "gospel simplicity" and the nonscholastic nature of revelation are recurrent themes in Zwingli's writing. Until around the year 1522 phrases familiar from Erasmus' "philosophy of Christ" as he had taught it in his *Enchiridion* and *Paraclesis* recur frequently in Zwingli's program for a renaissance of Christendom. The humanist's easy association of "good letters" with Christianity and with Christ the teacher is also a major emphasis in Zwingli's writing. Humanist pedagogical ideals are reflected in his treatise *On the Education of Youth* (1523).

The basic content of the theology of the young Zwingli is the "doctrine of Christ." He refers to sin more as a blindness or infirmity of the flesh than as a basic evil and the root condition of man. His Christocentrism is normative, not existential, the result of a gratifying intellectual enlightenment rather than the result of a spiritual struggle that led him to cast himself entirely upon the mercy of Christ. Zwingli preached the most extreme doctrine of divine double predestination of any of the major reformers—the doctrine that God not only had predetermined at the time of creation the souls he would save, but had also made a deliberate selection of the souls he would cast into hell. But Zwingli's writings on the point leave the impression that he embraced the doctrine simply because he believed Paul had taught it, not because he had himself trembled before the terrible decree of God. Even his assurance that God would save Heraclitus, Plato, Aristotle, Cicero, and other good pagans comes rather easily, compared with Luther's mere hope that God might find a way to save Cicero. But the most characteristically Erasmian aspect of his thought is the constant contrast of the law of the spirit and the law of the letter or flesh. The distrust of the material constitutes the basic reason for his puritanical reaction against images and ecclesiastical art, sensuous music, and the real presence of Christ in the Sacrament. The conception of the religious life as the triumph of the spirit over the flesh explains the moralistic emphasis of his "evangelical teaching" during the early years. Nevertheless, Zwingli's teaching underwent a marked change as he became ever more deeply involved in the theological issues of the Reformation and more thoroughly steeped in Pauline theology.

The Sacramentarian Controversy

When in October 1529 Zwingli and Luther met at last face to face in the magnificent castle of Landgrave Philipp of Hesse in Marburg, towering high above the river Lahn, Luther summarized the fundamental difference between them with words addressed directly to Bucer but intended for Zwingli and the rest as well: "You have a different spirit!" The meeting, intended by the landgrave to unify the evangelicals for the anticipated Catholic assault, served only to clarify the differences among them and to render permanent the division between the German and Swiss reform movements.

In later years Zwingli liked to think of his Einsiedeln period as the time when he broke through to a true evangelical understanding of the Scriptures. How limited his advance was can be seen from the fact that as late as 1517 he personally participated in a pilgrimage as a meritorious act. Nevertheless, Zwingli was not entirely mistaken in claiming that he was preaching a reformed interpretation of the gospel before anyone in Switzerland knew anything at all about Luther. His conception of the gospel in those early years, however, was a kind of Erasmian Christocentric ethic of love, the "philosophy of Christ." It was only during his Zurich period, while he was studying Paul's epistles under the influence of Luther's writings, that he shifted his emphasis to the "law of Christ" or a higher Christology, eventually preaching with fervor of God's full, free, and final gift of salvation in Jesus Christ, bestowed upon man by God's grace alone. For this conception of the gospel, or "good news," he was clearly heavily in debt to Luther. There is no evidence that Zwingli was aware of the initial flurry of excitement over Luther's ninety-five theses in 1517, strange as it may seem in view of the fact that the humanist circles in Basel and other south German cities were so excited about the event. But it is clear that by late 1518 Zwingli knew of and corresponded about Luther's writings and thereafter assiduously read them. By 1523, however, Zwingli was protesting his own originality, declaring that he had preached the new interpretation of the gospel before he had heard of Luther, claiming to have read little of Luther, and expressing resentment at being called a Lutheran. From Luther, Zwingli averred, he had learned only the courage to do what he had already come to believe was right. Zwingli was clearly not inclined to defer to the Wittenberg reformer. The parting of the ways came over their different interpretations of the nature and significance of the Sacrament of the Altar.

Zwingli believed that the Sacrament of the Altar, or the Lord's Supper, was merely a sign or seal of divine grace already bestowed upon the communicant. The bread and wine were mere symbols of the body and blood of Christ, who was locally present in his own physical person in heaven and not on earth. The man of faith who communes in remembrance of the last supper of the Lord with his disciples gains the benefit of a spiritual communion with his Lord. Zwingli derived his conception of the Sacrament as a memorial from a Dutch humanist physician, Cornelius Hoen, who wrote to Zwingli in 1523 from The Hague that the words of institution, "This is my body," were really a figure of speech, a trope, and that the word "is" must be understood to mean "signifies." "We need to differentiate," wrote Hoen, "between the bread which is received by the mouth and Christ who is received by faith." Zwingli was impressed by Hoen's interpretation, and called it "the precious pearl" by which he found clarity in this difficult matter. It was indeed a rational solution, but was it consonant with other facets of biblical theology? Luther received a similar letter from Hoen and replied that while he was naturally inclined toward a symbolic interpretation, he could not escape the clear words of Scripture, which plainly stated, "This is my body," with no hint that a figure of speech was being employed.

Luther's catechetical definition of a sacrament, taken from St. Augustine, reads: "The Word comes to the element and makes of it a sacrament." The Sacrament, like the message of the gospel, offers to man the benefits of Christ, Luther taught, and is essentially a means of grace by which men's faith is strengthened. Christ is truly present in the Sacrament, and his real presence is assured not only by his ubiquity, since the glorified Christ is not limited by spatial dimensions, but also by virtue of his express promise in the institution of the Sacrament. It is evident that Luther felt bound by the words of Scripture, but not simply as a literalist, for the conception of the communication of attributes between the human and divine natures in Christ and the thrust against demeaning the material, as in Zwingli's doctrine, were also involved in his definition.

The sacramentarian controversy soon became a public issue. Andreas Carlstadt, the expelled Wittenberg professor with marked Puritan tendencies, brought his sacramental theories to Strassburg. Although he was not permitted to stay in the city, some of the reformed theologians there were inclined to accept a spiritual interpretation and held Christ's real presence in the Sacrament impossible because of his presence in heaven. Oecolampadius in Basel, Bucer in Strassburg, the humanist Pirckheimer in Nuremberg, and others joined in the fray until at last Zwingli and Luther themselves were drawn into the great debate. In 1526 Luther published his *Sermon on the Sacrament of the Body and Blood of Christ, Against the Fanatics.* In February 1527 Zwingli attacked his position in his *Friendly Exegesis.* In April Luther responded with a heated but substantial reply, *That These Words "This Is My Body" Still Stand, Against the Fanatics.* In June Zwingli reacted sharply in his treatise *That the Words "This Is My Body" Still Have Their Original Meaning.* In March 1528 Luther published his *Great Confession Concerning the Lord's Supper,* striking a condescending tone. Zwingli was furious and announced that he did not like being "treated like an ass." In a rage he wrote on August 30, 1528, to Conrad Saum at Ulm:

> That rash man Luther keeps killing human and divine wisdom in his books, though it would have been easy to restore this wisdom among the pious. But since the heretics, that is, his followers, together with the wicked, have become so deaf to all truth that they refuse to listen, I was for a long time doubtful about expending this enormous labor which I knew would be vain. . . . May I die if he does not surpass Eck in impurity, Cochlaeus in audacity, and, in brief, all the vices of men!

Some years before, Luther had written to a certain Gregory Casel: "In a word, either they or we must be ministers of Satan! There is not room here for negotiation or mediation." And yet on the first three days of October 1529 Luther sat with Zwingli at a massive oak table in the landgrave's castle at Marburg for a colloquy aimed at a resolution of outstanding differences in the interest of evangelical unity. The year 1529 was a hazardous one for the Protestants, who had to speak out at the diet at Speyer against the emperor's determination to nullify the temporary concessions made at the diet in 1526. Landgrave Philipp of Hesse, an energetic evangelical, who had dined on steak on a Friday at Speyer in 1526 to demonstrate his Christian liberty, was a political activist determined to unite the Protestant forces for a common defense. Luther disapproved of this political and potentially military motive for the unification efforts, since he would not condone the use of force in religious matters. But to oblige Philipp, he and Melanchthon traveled to Marburg together with Justus Jonas, Johannes Brenz, Caspar Cruciger, Andreas Osiander, and several other theologians to meet with Zwingli, Johannes Oecolampadius, Martin Bucer, Wolfgang Capito, and Johannes Sturm, the Swiss and Strassburg theologians. They quickly came to a general agreement on fourteen articles, dealing with doctrines such as the person of Christ, justification by faith, baptism, and the like.

There was also a surprising amount of agreement on a fifteenth article, dealing with the Sacrament of the Altar. They rejected transubstantiation and the conception of the mass as sacrifice and favored communion in both kinds. Luther conceded that the Sacrament had symbolic character and presupposed spiritual eating and drinking, but when he insisted upon the real presence of Christ in the Sacrament, Zwingli could not concede. Melanchthon at this point seems to have opposed concessions to the spiritualists, since he was still hopeful of reunion with the Catholics. After the session ended Luther worked out a statement on the presence of Christ's body in the Sacrament "essentially and substantively," though not "qualitatively, quantitatively, or locally." But Zwingli rejected the formula and insisted upon his views of the purely spiritual and symbolic nature of the Sacrament. Perhaps Erasmus' most effective blow at Protestantism was not his frontal assault on Luther in the *De libero arbitrio,* but his subtle infusion of spiritualism into Zwingli, making him susceptible to his fellow humanist Hoen's highly rational solution to a mystery of faith. Brenz and Bucer found Luther's formula satisfying and it became the basis of the Württemberg Concord of 1534 and the Wittenberg Concord of 1536, signed by the Strassburg theologians who traveled to Wittenberg to consult with Luther. The debate between Zwingli and Luther at Marburg was not exactly a model of irenic theological discussion. At one point Zwingli buttressed his argument by referring to Christ's statement on the bread of life in John 6. "There," Zwingli exclaimed, "is an argument that will break your neck!" Luther replied, "Ah, but don't forget you are in Hesse, not in Switzerland. Necks are not so easily broken in Germany."

Sincerity and earnestness are in evidence in their colloquy. Neither would make concessions against conscience, not even for political gain or in the interest of sheer survival. Zwingli was about to pay with his life for the failure to secure a united Protestant front, or at least good allies. Luther's land of Saxony was to be despoiled and Philipp of Hesse imprisoned by the Habsburg allies of Zwingli's Catholic opponents.

Zwingli's Leadership and Civil War

ZWINGLI'S REFORMATORY ACTIVITY in Zurich served as a catalyst for the Swiss Protestant movement, even in those cantons where the beginnings were already under way. The city of Bern is a case in point, for there Berchthold Haller, strongly influenced by Luther's theology, served as a teacher and from 1519 on as preacher in the cathedral. But it was not until the marathon nineteen-day public disputation during January 1528, in which Zwingli, Oecolampadius, Capito, and Bucer presented Reformation doctrines, that the city moved into the Protestant fold.

The city of Basel was of pivotol importance both for its location on the upper Rhine and for its preeminence as a center of humanism and publishing. The printers Froben and Amerbach were leaders in the book trade. The conciliar movement had left its mark upon the city, for the second of the major church councils had met at nearby Constance (1414–1418) and the long session of the schismatic third council had met in Basel itself (1431–1449), leaving behind a residue of conciliar and antipapal feeling and a general sense of the urgent necessity for reform. Zwingli's Erasmian humanist professor Wyttenbach had urged reform, and the presence of Erasmus himself from 1521 on attracted many reform-minded men of the Christian humanist type to the city. Wolfgang Capito was active there for a while before he moved to Strassburg. But the real reformer of Basel was the Swabian whose statue still stands in front of the cathedral, Johannes Oecolampadius (1482–1531), a man influenced by both Wittenberg and Zurich. As a young humanist he was a promising student of the classics, but he turned to biblical studies and became an Erasmian reformer, then fell under the influence of Melanchthon and Zwingli and evolved into an evangelical reformer. As pastor of St. Martin's Church and professor at the university he laid the groundwork for a more radical reformation of the church. He participated in the Bern disputation in 1528 and led the popular movement that pressured the city council in February 1529 to cut off relations with the hierarchy and inaugurate a Zwinglian reformation in Basel. As superintendent, Oecolampadius saw to the reform of the churches throughout the canton. He would have been only too happy to keep the great Erasmus in the city, but Erasmus now saw that the reform had taken a radical and schismatic turn, and he left in 1528, escorted to the river boat in grand style, for Freiburg-im-Breisgau, safe Habsburg Catholic territory.

In St. Gall, Zwingli's home canton, Vadian (1485–1551) led the reform. Vadian or Vadianus, a Latinized version of his Germanic name, Joachim von Watt, was one of the most attractive personalities among the Swiss reformers. As a young man he was both a student and a professor of classical studies at the University of Vienna. Through a study of the Scriptures he was brought quite independently to an evangelical conviction. He became the wise and revered reformer of St. Gall, where a giant statue in his honor still dominates the marketplace. He was under Zwingli's spell, though he was more moderate and less belligerent than Zwingli. Zwingli's successor at Glarus, Valentin Tschudi, also worked for a reform more generous and tolerant of Catholic convictions, though Zwinglian in essence. Zwinglianism spread also to Schaffhausen, Constance, Memmingen, and other south German cities, down the Rhine to the Netherlands, and into East Frisia. It made a considerable impact also upon the English Reformation, contributing especially to its Puritan component.

Unlike the cosmopolitan Erasmus, Zwingli was a fierce patriot who wished to see all Switzerland freed from the yoke of the papacy. The forest cantons, however, remained loyal to the Catholic Church. Uri, Schwyz, and Unterwalden were jealous of Zurich's rise to prominence and were eager to preserve their traditional pre-eminence in the confederacy. They, together with Lucerne and Zug, cast about for support, and in April 1529 made an alliance with the archenemy of the Swiss, the Austrian Habsburg duke Ferdinand. On the theory that the best defense is a good offense, and without the support of his cantonal allies, Zwingli led the Zurich troops to Cappel in June 1529 for an attack on their enemies. But Swiss fraternal feelings asserted themselves, and the troops on both sides exchanged bread, milk, and banter. Bern refused to join in an offensive war at all. Zwingli had to be satisfied with the First Peace of Cappel (June 26, 1529), which called for the severance of the Catholic cantons' alliance with Ferdinand and toleration of evangelical congregations in common administrative circuits.

Zwingli now was drawn into a diplomatic design, devised by Philipp of Hesse, for a grand anti-Austrian alliance, to include Denmark, Venice, Saxony, and France. But no one could be induced to become involved, not even the German Protestant principalities, as the breakdown of the unity efforts at Marburg in 1529 should have made evident. That year was a critical one for the empire, and the new imperial pressure on the evangelicals at the Diet of Speyer put them on the defensive. Zwingli was reduced to a basic alliance with Bern and Basel in league with Strassburg, and an assistance pact between Philipp of Hesse, Zurich, and Basel. Arrangements were completed by January 1530. The Catholic cantons had not carried out their agreement to dissolve their Austrian alliance, and Zwingli, convinced they were planning some treachery, favored striking first. The session of the confederacy diet held in January 1531 was stormy with charges and counter-charges. Zwingli was extremely nervous, expecting an attack. He maneuvered economic sanctions against the Catholic cantons, blocking the sale of wheat, salt, wine, and iron to them. The forest cantons struck back, and with a force of eight thousand men invaded the canton of Zurich at Cappel on October 11, 1531. When word reached the city, about fifteen hundred men, Zwingli among them, marched out to meet the attackers. Seeing the badly outnumbered Zurich troops giving way, Zwingli moved into the middle of the battle and took a fatal thrust in the throat. Enemy soldiers found his body on the field, quartered and burned it, and scattered the ashes. Zurich lost over four hundred dead in that battle, including twenty-six councilmen and twenty-five pastors. The Catholic cantons knew that the city of Zurich had considerable manpower in reserve and did not press their military advantage. The Second Peace of Cappel (November 20, 1531) provided that the Protestant lands were to remain as they were, the Catholic but not the Protestant minorities were to be tolerated, all entangling foreign alliances were to be abrogated, and St. Gall was to restore the ancient Benedictine monastery to its former status. The Swiss civil war was a tragedy according to Hegel's definition: "a conflict of right against right." It was an Alpine preliminary to the avalanche of misery and destruction that was to engulf all Europe during the decades that followed.

In Swiss Reformed Protestantism Zwingli left an important legacy to his own land and to the world. He gave to his followers an example of political activism coupled with religious legalism and extreme spirituality. The cultural ties with Protestant Germany remained strong even after the growth of Calvinism over-shadowed the Zurich-centered reform. Under his successor, Heinrich Bullinger (1504–1575), his own son-in-law and biographer, the German-Swiss reform move-ment was turned more exclusively to ecclesiastical concerns and lost its political drive, although Zwingli's hostility to the Habsburg emperor left its mark in the continued estrangement of the Swiss from the empire. The Swiss remained aloof from the later wars of religion for the very good reason that they had experienced one of their own and had been the first among the people of Europe to do so. Luther had disapproved of Zwingli's belligerence, and he considered Zwingli's death a divine judgment upon him.

The Radical Reformation

THE TREMENDOUS CONVULSION of the Reformation movement had the effect of free-ing millions of people from traditional norms and relationships at a time when time-honored and sacrosanct institutions were in the process of disintegration. Great numbers of people sought reassurance in the most improbable proclama-tions of bizarre prophets, or in cultlike associations that provided the company that misery seeks. These borderline individuals and marginal groups frequently had insights into dimensions of the Christian faith not at all appreciated or empha-sized by the magisterial reformers.

For centuries the role of the radicals in the Reformation was largely neglected, and they were treated as Christendom's stepchildren. But in recent years they have come into their own. Unlike the major reformers, most of the radicals founded no lasting church bodies whose members were interested in promoting the study of their teachings. But now some religious groups generically or sentimentally re-lated to Reformation sects have come of age, turned against their former anti-in-tellectual bias, and abandoned a largely self-imposed isolation. Scholars of smaller denominations are beginning to contribute significant knowledge about the move-ment. Moreover, since the Marxist historians have fastened upon Thomas Müntzer and radical religious types as the theological epiphenomena of social revolution, countless volumes have appeared interpreting the radical Reformation in the light of those remarkable scholars Engels, Marx, and Lenin. New knowledge is stream-ing in from all sides.

Protestantism very quickly took on the appearance of a banyan tree, sprouting a maze of roots and branches. The problem of authority as a basis of institutional or credal unity proved to be the Achilles' heel of the movement. One might have expected an infinite proliferation of splinter groups, but in reality a few major evangelical churches embraced the vast majority of Protestants. The minority was badly fragmented into small sects and even isolated individuals. A few of these were offshoots of the parent stock, but most developed as independent responses to the same basic problems as those with which the leading reformers were concerned.

The German historian and sociologist of religion Ernst Troeltsch (d. 1922) suggested that there were three main religious types in the sixteenth century. The first was the sect, a new collectivity or association in which those who could not conform to the larger society gathered to formulate their own norms. The sectarian groups aimed at holiness, though they were seldom perfectionists, and usually believed in a time-line progress toward an *eschaton,* or apocalyptic consummation of history, which would usher in the millennium, the thousand-year rule of Christ and the saints. Plotted on a right triangle, the sect would form the base line, moving out from the point indefinitely to the right. The Anabaptists belonged to this type of sect.

Then there were the religious individualists. The mystic caught up in his private system or method strove for vertical ascent through contemplation and meditation, experiencing the dark night of the soul before breaking through to momentary union with God. The whole spectrum of mystics, spiritualists, and ethical theists devoted to the inner life of the soul were of this kind. The evangelical rationalists too were often individualistic, although some of the anti-Trinitarians, such as the Socinians or Polish Brethren and the Lithuanian and Transylvanian Unitarians, formed associations or churches. Plotted on our right triangle, this second type forms the vertical line, moving upward toward individual perfection and union with the Infinite.

Between these two extremes were the church members, both those who remained in the Catholic Church and those who followed the major reformers. The ecclesiastical reformers sought to embrace the emphases of both the sects and the mystics, accommodating collective social and ethical progress along with personal religious expression. Plotted on our right triangle, the main reformed churches constitute sector lines, some inclining more toward the base line of the sectaries and others more toward the vertical line of the mystics.

Although formerly some sociologists of religion argued for the radically Protestant nature of the Reformation sectaries, scholars have come increasingly to recognize many ties between the radical reformers and medieval heretical currents of thought. In a history of pietism published in 1880, the historian Albrecht Ritschl pointed to the similarity of ecstatic sectarian ideas of the sixteenth century to the heretical notions of the Spiritual Franciscans. The localization of the sectaries in the Rhine valley and the Netherlands, the precise areas that had witnessed a proliferation of late medieval heretical groups—the Brethren and Sisters of the Free Spirit, the Beguines, the Beghards—cannot be explained as mere coincidence.

THE ANABAPTISTS

There was an important tie between some of the leaders among the Anabaptists and Renaissance humanism, for some of the most important of them came to their radical evangelism from Erasmian religiosity. The influence of the more volatile reformers, such as Luther's erstwhile colleague Carlstadt, upon radicals in Strassburg and elsewhere is also evident. Moreover, the impact of such a wild man as Thomas Müntzer, with his call for a war of extermination against the godless by his League of the Elect, had a detectable, if embarrassing, influence even upon peace-minded Anabaptists. The fact that a pejorative association of all Anabaptists with this militant leader was used to defame them should not obscure the definite relationship between them. From the very outset the Anabaptists had a bad press. They were considered by both Catholics and evangelicals to be heretical and by the magistrates to be subversive.

In Zwingli's Zurich Conrad Grebel (1448–1526), the leader of the Swiss Brethren, performed the first adult baptism, or rebaptism. On January 21, 1525, he administered the sacrament to Georg Blaurock in the home of Felix Manz. In a way, this act was a tribute to Zwingli's rhetorical impact and to his powers of persuasion, for these Swiss Brethren, as members of Zwingli's reform movement, took very seriously his injunction to search the Scriptures independently of tradition and authority. They found no warrant there for infant baptism, and concluded that baptism was a sign or symbol of the regeneration or coming to faith of adults who had reached the age of accountability and discretion. They were carrying Zwingli's own sacramental theory to its logical extreme. Grebel was a member of a fine patrician family and was a well-educated classical humanist who, like Zwingli, had studied at the University of Vienna. He was therefore able to counter the arguments that church fathers of the third to the fifth centuries, such as Cyprian, Tertullian, Gregory Nazianzen, Origen, and Augustine, had testified to the apostolic origins of infant baptism. Why are the Scriptures silent, he asked, if this is an essential aspect of the dominical sacrament, and why is there no evidence for it from the first two centuries? In opposition to the state church and the people's church, Grebel and the Brethren favored a free confessional church, a visible communion of saints living holy lives, excluding the faithless or immoral, following the injunctions of Matthew 18 literally. They tried to revive the simple forms of the apostolic church, using a low-liturgical order of worship and celebrating the Lord's Supper in private homes in the evening as a meal of solemn remembrance. In separating from the godless world they sought to live out the commands of Christ's Sermon on the Mount very literally, offering no resistance to evil treatment, refusing to take oaths, and rejecting military service. They even cultivated the concept of a suffering church in emulation of the "suffering servant" prophesied by Isaiah and embodied in Jesus.

Zwingli was amazed and distressed at this turn of events. He preached vehemently against the Anabaptists, for he opposed their rejection of infant baptism and their attitude toward civil government, and he believed the scurrilous reports of their social disorder and dissolute behavior. He directed a special blast *Against the Tricks of the Katabaptists.* The Zurich city council decided that the Anabaptists were subverting law and order in the state, and should be forced to conform or emigrate. Grebel, Manz, and Blaurock left the city, but undertook the propagation of their views elsewhere. Arrested near Zurich, they were tried and given life sentences, but escaped. Grebel died of the plague in 1526 and Manz was executed by drowning in 1527 (an imaginative sentence reminiscent of baptism by immersion). Blaurock managed to carry his message to Austria, but he was arrested in the Tyrol and burned at the stake in 1529. Their fates were a portent of the persecution that awaited their suffering churches.

Popular Anabaptist preachers were recruited from the ranks of the evangelical clergy as well as from the Catholic regular and secular clergy. The Swabian Balthasar Hubmaier (1485–1528), a Protestant minister in Waldshut, Austria, shocked his congregation in January 1525 by proclaiming that he had received a divine command to reject infant baptism. On Easter Day he had himself rebaptized together with most members of the congregation. His book on *The Christian Baptism of Believers* became an influential presentation of the Anabaptist view that baptism was to follow a profession of faith. The Zurich authorities arrested him and forced a recantation. Thereupon he set out upon a wandering mission eastward, preaching in Constance, Augsburg, Regensburg, and Nikolsburg in Moravia, where he converted the Lutheran congregation to Anabaptism and established a shelter for religious refugees from all over the empire. The Habsburg government could not tolerate such a disturbance in a well-ordered realm. So the lords of Liechtenstein turned Hubmaier over to Duke Ferdinand's officials, who burned him at the stake on March 10 outside Vienna and drowned his wife in the Danube. One hundred and five Anabaptists were executed in Vienna alone.

An even more pathetic, if heroic, case was the trial and martyrdom of Michael Sattler, a saintly man who was converted by evangelical preaching, gave up his position as prior of St. Peter's in Breisgau, went to Zurich, and there joined the Swiss Brethren. Driven out of Zurich, he became a refugee in Strassburg, and then moved to Horb in the Black Forest to do mission work for his cause. In 1527 he presided at the Schleitheim Conference of Anabaptists and was the main author of the Schleitheim Confession of Faith, which was adopted on St. Matthew's Day (February 24). The Confession was widely circulated and was perhaps the most representative statement of distinctive Anabaptist teachings. It elicited refutations from Zwingli and many years later from Calvin. The Confession established seven main points: (1) Baptism was to be given to all those who had learned repentance and amendment of life and who truly believed that their sins were taken away by Christ. (2) All those who, having professed the Anabaptist faith and been baptized, fell into error and sin, even though inadvertently, were to be excommunicated. (3) All those who wished to take part in the Lord's Supper had first to be baptized. (4) The baptized were to separate themselves from the evil and wickedness that the devil planted in the world. (5) A pastor in the church must, as Paul prescribed, be one who had a good reputation among those outside the faith. (6) No member of the church was to bear arms in any cause. (7) No member of the church was to take an oath.[2]

For this confession Michael Sattler was to die a horrible death. Arrested for sedition by the Austrian authorities, he was tried in Ensisheim. Tilman J. van Braght's *Martyr's Mirror* (1660) records the sentence passed upon this gentle person and the manner of his death:

> "In the case of the attorney of His Imperial Majesty vs. Michael Sattler, judgment is passed that Michael Sattler shall be delivered to the executioner, who shall lead him to the place of execution and cut out his tongue, then forge him fast to a wagon and thereon with red-hot tongs twice tear pieces from his body; and after he has been brought outside the gate, he shall be plied five times more in the same manner. . . ."
>
> After this had been done in the manner prescribed, he was burned to ashes as a heretic. His fellow brethren were executed with the sword, and the sisters drowned. His wife, also after being subjected to many entreaties, admonitions and threats, under which she remained steadfast, was drowned a few days afterward.[3]

Society has usually understood how to protect itself from its little people. Hans Denck called a conference of Anabaptist leaders in Augsburg in 1526, which was subsequently known as the Martyrs' Synod, since virtually everyone who attended was hunted down and judicially murdered. It was not only their beliefs that outraged the more conventional citizens; some mentally unbalanced extremists brought further discredit to the movement. One Anabaptist emulated the Old Testament prophet Isaiah by placing a red-hot coal to his lips, intending to confess with him, "Woe is me, I am undone, for I am a man of unclean lips!" but the burn left him speechless. Some eccentrics in the Netherlands ran around naked, also in emulation of Isaiah, who had done so as a sign. There were even cases of radicals indulging in sexual intercourse while lying on an altar, no doubt to demonstrate the triumph of pure spirit over the flesh. Storming the pulpit and ejecting an

---

[2] The full text of the Confession may be found in John C. Wenger, "The Schleitheim Confession of Faith," *Mennonite Quarterly Review*, 19, no. 4 (October 1945):247–52.

[3] See George H. Williams, ed., *The Library of Christian Classics* (London, 1957), vol. 25, *Spiritual and Anabaptist Writers*, pp. 138–44.

unregenerated minister was a common occurrence. One somber fellow marched through Zurich crying, "Woe! Woe! The day of judgment is at hand!" Another traveled from city to city wearing a wooden sword at his side by way of rebuke to the secular government. The persecution of the Anabaptists had the effect of producing a diaspora of religious refugees with tremendous mobility and a remarkable network of international contacts and intelligence.

The Anabaptist ideology of brotherhood and egalitarianism appealed to the poor and lowly, the dispossessed. Since they were attempting literally to reestablish the pattern of the New Testament church, a number of the leaders were almost inevitably attracted by the voluntary communism practiced by some of the early Christians. Jakob Hutter (or Huter) organized a communal society, nonviolent and collectivist, in Nikolsburg, that city of social ferment in Moravia. About fifteen thousand brethren, mostly artisans and peasants, were organized into communes of two hundred people in about eighty localities. Although the Austrian officials burned Hutter at the stake in 1536, several communities of the Hutterite Brethren survived. Hutterite settlements are still to be found in Russia and North and South America, models of cooperative and pacific living.

A strong strain of millennialism ran through the Anabaptist movement, as erratic and even hysterical eschatological types prophesied the imminent second coming of Christ and his thousand-year rule upon earth before the final destruction of this universe by fire. Luther too believed that he was living in the last age of the world, but he managed to keep a certain sense of balance about it. Once when a friend asked him what he would do if he knew for certain that the world would come to an end the next day, he replied, "I would plant an apple tree today." Unfortunately, all too many of the half-educated or highly emotional sectarians precipitated panic situations by their wild interpretations of the prophecies of Daniel and the Book of Revelation, those two main sources of apocalyptic visions. Three such millennialists were Hans Hut, David Joris, and Melchior Hofmann, who succeeded in gaining mass followings and stirring up social unrest.

Hans Hut, a Franconian bookbinder and dealer, was an important member of the Augsburg circle of Anabaptists. Rebaptized in Augsburg on Pentecost Day, 1526, he was one of those who preached the imminence of the kingdom of God. In Nikolsburg he debated with Balthasar Hubmaier, arguing for complete nonresistance to violence on the part of Christians, while Hubmaier defended a man's right to defend himself and his family. Hut was arrested in Nikolsburg in 1527, but escaped to Vienna, where he baptized fifty people. He then wandered westward to Linz, Melk, and Steyr, baptizing and proclaiming the coming of Christ to judgment. Christ would deliver into the hands of the saints the double-eged sword of justice to be wielded against priests and false prophets, the nobles and kings. Then Christ and the saints would rule in peace for a thousand years. Charged with preaching free love and communism, Hut was arrested in 1527, jailed in Augsburg, and killed during an attempted escape.

David Joris (1501–1556), a radical visionary in the Netherlands, wrote prolifically in Dutch, escaped execution, and went underground to direct his movement. The son of a shopkeeper and an artisan himself, he was influenced by Luther, but Lutheranism became only a halfway house on his road to Anabaptism. He attacked the pope as Antichrist, and on Ascension Day of 1528 he violated the sacramental host being carried in a procession. The authorities seized him, pilloried him, had his tongue bored, and exiled him from Delft for three years. He was rebaptized in 1533 and wandered about Europe as an Anabaptist missionary. The execution of his own mother as an Anabaptist in 1537 shocked him profoundly and may have been the occasion for the release of a stream of pent-up visions and prophecies. Like Joachim of Flora, he saw the history of the world divided into the three great dispensations of Father, Son, and Holy Spirit. As "Christus David" he proclaimed the last revelation, which was to supersede that of "Christus Jesus." a historical role that the Pontius Pilates of the Habsburg regime could not accept with equanimity. Joris left for Basel, which was to be the New Jerusalem, and lived there for the remainder of his life under the alias of Jan van Brugge. He continued his contacts with the Anabaptists of Frisia and the Netherlands, but kept his identity secret until his death in April 1556. Three years after his burial in St. Leonard's Church, his own son-in-law denounced him to the city officials, who had his body disinterred and burned.

A religious enthusiast of the same stripe as Joris was Melchior Hofmann, a Swabian furrier who wandered through northeastern Europe and the Rhineland proclaiming the approaching end of the world. Attracted to Luther's teaching, he combined missionary work with business trips to Sweden, Livonia, and Riga. He visited Wittenberg and impressed Luther favorably on his first visit, but on his second visit Luther began to fear the worst. There Hofmann wrote an apocalyptic exposition of the twelfth chapter of Daniel (1527). At Kiel, where King Frederick I of Denmark had appointed him preacher, he indulged in wild proclamations. At a colloquy of preachers in Flensburg in 1529 he defended the Zwinglian doctrine of the Sacrament and was subsequently banished, taking refuge in Strassburg. He moved now progressively toward a more radical theology, under the influence of Carlstadt and Caspar Schwenkfeld. In East Frisia he founded a community of regenerate artisans. In 1533 he returned to Strassburg to make that lucky city his New Jerusalem, for his study of the Apocalypse revealed that he was to reestablish apostolic Christianity. But Strassburg did not appreciate the honor, and though efforts were made to rehabilitate Hofmann to calmer ways, he languished imprisoned in a cage in a tower for a decade until finally he died late in 1543. Through his preaching and books of prophecy he influenced many people, especially in the Netherlands, who came to be known as Melchiorites.

The wildest adventure of the militant Anabaptists was the proclamation of the Kingdom of Münster. The anatomy of the revolution followed the classical pattern: repression by the prince-bishop, a revolt against the bishop and a moderate change in favor of Lutheranism, a more radical Anabaptist takeover, a Jacobean reign of terror, and a dictatorship, followed by the suppression of the revolution and a Thermidorian reaction. In Münster, as in other ecclesiastical estates in Westphalia, there was constant friction between the city and the prince-bishop over feudal and canonical dues. General economic distress caused by crop failures, the loss of manpower to the plague, and high prices created much unrest and a populace receptive to the Lutheran preaching of Bernard Rothmann, a persuasive pulpiteer. In the year 1532 the city council, under popular pressure, appointed Lutheran preachers to all churches in the city, and the next year the bishop recognized Münster as an "evangelical city."

Münster had already taken in the Anabaptist refugees from nearby Jülich-Cleves, and when news of its Protestantization spread, the rootless and disaffected came pouring into the city from all around. The volatile Rothmann himself turned radical and was rebaptized by two Melchiorites sent to Münster as apostles by Jan Matthys, a baker in Haarlem. Like Müntzer, Matthys was a militant radical who preached that the elect had to wield a bloody sword against the ungodly in preparation for the rule of the saints in the millennium. Persuaded by the rhetoric of Rothmann and influenced by a prominent cloth merchant and guild leader named Bernt Knipperdollinck, who had traveled in Sweden with Melchior Hofmann himself, over fourteen hundred people were rebaptized in a short time.

The arrival of a Dutch apostle, Jan Bockelson, better known as John of Leiden, marked a turning point for the movement. This handsome and eloquent young man of twenty-five had just been rebaptized by Jan Matthys and had the fervor of a convert. On February 8, 1534, John and Knipperdollinck ran up and down the streets of Münster crying out for all to repent of their sins, unleashing a flood of religious hysteria. Masses of women and men too screamed and writhed madly on the ground. At this point the Anabaptists staged a spontaneous revolt and took over the marketplace and city hall. Horrified by these excesses, many of the middle-class Lutherans moved away and were replaced by thousands of sectarian proletarians who streamed into the city from everywhere. Münster was declared the New Jerusalem, which would be spared when all the rest of the world was destroyed, before Easter of that year.

The election on February 23 of an Anabaptist city council coincided closely with the arrival of Jan Matthys in person from Holland. He immediately urged the execution of all Catholics and Lutherans remaining in the city, but they were instead driven out during a fierce blizzard. Those who refused or were unable to go were forcibly rebaptized in the marketplace. When the bishop undertook a partial siege of the city, Jan Matthys assumed dictatorial powers and began a reign of terror. He declared a communist state, and when a blacksmith protested the confiscation of private property, Matthys stabbed and shot him as an example to the crowd in the marketplace. All money and valuables were taken by the state, all houses were to be open at all times and were to be owned in common, all books except the Bible were burned, each laborer was to be paid according to his need and only in kind, and the armed men were fed at public kitchens. At this point Matthys received a vision that like Gideon of old he was to choose a handful of men and go out to destroy the army of the godless bishop. The gaunt, fierce-eyed fanatic sallied forth and was promptly cut down by the enemy.

John of Leiden's hour had come. This bastard son of a Dutch mayor and a peasant woman was a proletarian rabble-rouser, a megalomaniac with the wild imagination of an unbalanced fanatic and the peculiar lucidity of the mad. Early in May he ran naked through the streets of the city and fell into an ecstatic trance that lasted three days. When at last he roused himself he seized power, pronounced an automatic death penalty for insubordination, and established a bodyguard, a chain of command, and a system that held the whole city of ten thousand inhabitants cowed in terror. He declared that in a vision he had been commanded to establish polygamy, and, having married the beautiful young widow of Matthys, he collected a harem of fifteen wives. In August 1534, after beating off an attack of the bishop's mercenary army, John had himself proclaimed king of the New Jerusalem and the Messiah or anointed one of the last days foretold by the prophets of the Old Testament. He ruled from a tall throne covered with gold cloth in the marketplace. Rothmann, who published pamphlets significantly entitled *Restitution* and *Announcement of Vengeance,* became court orator, and Knipperdollinck became his prime minister. The royal court dined in splendor and dressed in gorgeous robes while the subjects of the king lived in want. One of John's wives, the beautiful Divora, was named queen.

The tragicomedy turned into a horror story when the bishop's army, supported by money and troops from Hesse and other states of the empire, began to besiege the city in earnest in January 1535. They surrounded it with earthworks, infantry troops, and cavalry, cut it off completely from the outside world, and settled down to wait for time to take its toll. Fierce famine raged in the city as the months dragged on; people were reduced to eating vermin and even the dead. After a siege lasting nearly half a year a few skeletal escapees from the city revealed to the besiegers vulnerable points in the defenses. On June 24 they stormed the city and captured King John and his court. He was led about on exhibition like a dancing bear on a chain as an object lesson to revolutionaries. Then in January 1536 he, Knipperdollinck, and a third man were put to death with red-hot irons. In shock or in a catatonic state, King John made no motion or sound during his torture. Their bodies were hung in cages from the Lambert Church tower in Münster, which still serves as a reminder to the city and the world of the human potential for both folly and vengeance. The city walls were torn down and the surviving inhabitants returned to the Catholic fold.[4]

---

4 Norman Cohn, *The Pursuit of the Millennium: Revolutionary Messianism in Medieval and Reformation Europe and Its Bearing on Modern Totalitarian Movements* (New York, 1961), pp. 272–306.

The disaster at Münster thoroughly discredited militant communal and eschatological Anabaptism. The cause was rehabilitated largely by a peace-minded Anabaptist in the Netherlands, Menno Simons (1496–1561), who had lost a brother to the executioners after the fall of Münster. He had moved from the priesthood to Lutheranism and from there to Anabaptism. He believed that the biblical or apostolic church pattern called for the organization of individual congregations of the regenerated, men moved by the Holy Spirit to lead lives of peace and service. Manifest and impenitent sinners should be excluded from the congregation. The sacraments were symbolic memorials of Christ's death and of the believer's rebirth. He believed that oaths, military service, and participation in worldly government were contrary to the Lord's will. His basic beliefs were summarized in his highly influential book published in 1539, the *Book of Fundamentals*. Mennonite congregations spread from his native East Frisia through the Netherlands into northern Germany and from there into Russia and the New World.

Through their vigorous effort to return to the practices of the primitive church in the ancient Roman world, the Anabaptists actually contributed enormously to the development of principles characteristic of liberal societies in the modern world. Their insistence upon a voluntary or confessional church as opposed to an official church embracing all members of the civic community was an important step in the development of religious pluralism within the state. The separation of believers from an officially sanctioned church made a marked contribution to the modern constitutional principle of the separation of church and state. Finally, the perseverance of the Anabaptists under fierce persecution impressed even their oppressors. The Anabaptists made the gift of their own blood to the cause of religious toleration and liberty. These principles anticipated the later developments made explicit in American constitutional democracy and propagated by the French revolution.

SPIRITUALISTS AND THE EVANGELICAL RATIONALISTS

If the forty or more varieties of Anabaptists were inclined toward sectarian group organization, the Reformation also liberated many individuals who sought an independent religious life. Some of these nonconforming individuals were spiritualistic, cultivating an inwardness of religious life, while others of a more questioning or rationalistic bent became radical critics of received theological traditions and orthodoxies.

An intertwining of the various trends and tendencies can be seen in the case of Hans Denck, a spiritualist who was involved for several years with the Anabaptists. A student of the classics, he was rector of the famous school of St. Sebaldus in Nuremberg. He was attracted by the stress placed by the German mystics and Christian Neoplatonists upon the spirit and the inwardness of true religion. He believed in the coincidence of the interior word inspired by the indwelling of the

Holy Spirit and the external word recorded in the life of the spirit, and showed universalistic tendencies. The Nuremberg reformer Osiander had him expelled from the city on January 21, 1525, the same day that the first rebaptism was taking place in Zurich. In Augsburg he met Hubmaier, who won him over to Anabaptism, and in 1526 he summoned the famous Martyrs' Synod to plan the missionary efforts of the regenerate. He was soon disillusioned with the Anabaptists' undisciplined activism, however, and left them before his death in 1527, turning "the eye of his mind inward" once again. His movement merged with that of the Swiss Brethren.

A man of a very similar stripe was the Lutheran Sebastian Franck (1499–1543), best known for his historical *Chronicles*. His own form of spiritualistic mysticism showed definite pantheistic and universalistic tendencies. Though he did not approve of Anabaptism, he urged toleration in a striking statement:

> I have listed them [the Anabaptists] among the heretics that they may perceive that their church is not the true church, that they may turn to genuine unity in spirit and in truth, but I warn their persecutors not to play the part of Caiaphas and Pilate. The Anabaptists are not entirely right nor is anyone else and from each we should take the best.[5]

One of the most prolific authors of spiritualistic and mystical treatises was a Silesian nobleman, Caspar Schwenckfeld (1489–1561). Captivated by Luther's teachings, he understood faith in a highly interiorized spiritual manner. From German mysticism he learned that faith must be a moving inner experience and that regeneration must be felt within the heart. His emphasis upon the spirit over the flesh led him to stress the inward baptism of the spirit and to accept a Zwinglian interpretation of the Lord's Supper, but in a highly spiritualistic mode. Eventually he left his own estate and became a traveling evangelist, preaching to small groups of followers who huddled together under the protection of benign landed nobles of his own class.

The evangelical rationalists varied even more widely from the norm and from one another. More intellectual and critical than the spiritualists, these men tended toward radical deviations such as anti-Trinitarian tendencies and low ecclesiology. An older scholarly view once held that Anabaptism fostered anti-Trinitarianism, but this position is no longer widely held. It is true that Menno Simons avoided Trinitarian terminology, since he did not find it used in the Scriptures themselves, and in Adam Pastor or Ludwig Hätzer one can possibly find traces of the tendency, but the Anabaptists were almost all orthodox in their doctrine of God and in their Christology. The evangelical rationalists were Latin scholars and learned men, and they arrived at their ideas by the study of the sources and the patristic writers rather than through the influence of the sectaries. The greatest luminary in

---

5 Sebastian Franck, *Chronica, Zeytbuch und Geschychtbibel* (Strassburg, 1531), cited in *The Recovery of the Anabaptist Vision*, ed. Guy F. Hershberger (Scottdale, Pa., 1957), p. 318.

this constellation was clearly Michael Servetus, who, as the American church historian Roland Bainton once put it, had the singular distinction of being "burned by the Catholics in effigy and by the Protestants in actuality."

Michael Servetus, born in Spain in 1511, the son of a royal notary, was gifted with a brilliant intellect and cursed with an argumentative and obstreperous personality. He studied law and later medicine, but became caught up in the theological turmoil of the time. His intellectual interests carried him to many parts of Europe—Toulouse, Bologna, Basel, Strassburg, Paris, Lyon, and finally to Geneva. During his law studies at Toulouse he had a moving religious experience in discovering in the Scriptures the historical person of Jesus of Nazareth, who became the object and center of his faith. He turned against the traditional credal formulations of the Trinity and of the divine and human natures of Christ. He came to hold that such theological terms as persons, substance, and essence represented a historical development, and had been imposed upon biblical conceptions from Hellenistic metaphysics. As Greek philosophical terms they were abstract, artificial, speculative, and unrelated to the living God.

When at the age of twenty he failed to convince the reformers in Basel and Strassburg of the propriety of his views, this precocious but obstinate and conceited young man proceeded to publish his treatise *On the Errors of the Trinity,* and gained an immediate and lasting reputation for religious deviationism. He argued that traditional scholastic theology introduced Greek philosophical terms and non-biblical categories into the definitions of the Trinity. His own formulations, however, created the impression that he was reviving the ancient Arian heresy that Jesus Christ was not the preexistent *logos* or word, a person of the Trinity who was with God the Father from eternity. His book was greeted with a storm of disapproval and was nearly everywhere condemned and suppressed. In order to make his position clear, he published in 1553 a large rambling book entitled *The Restoration of Christianity,* which failed, however, to improve upon the clarity of the first work or to restore the author's reputation for orthodoxy. A fascinating part of this omnibus work was a section dealing with his theory of the pulmonary circulation of the blood. If the work had not been so thoroughly suppressed by the book burners, this section might have established Servetus as a pioneer in early modern biological science.

Servetus found it discrete to take the alias M. de Villeneufve and to travel in disguise, but his was an ill-kept secret. He was tricked into giving medical attention to prisoners in Vienne, and there in jail was himself made prisoner. Happily he escaped over the wall, discarding a nightcap and bathrobe that he had donned for a walk in the prison yard. He was condemned in absentia by a civil tribunal in Lyon on evidence in part supplied by John Calvin. Unhappily he resolved to stop in Geneva on his way to practice medicine in Naples. In Geneva the French reformer John Calvin was enjoying new prestige as the spiritual leader of the reformed city. He was a long-standing opponent of Servetus; he had tried to convince him of the errors of his ways, had written against him, and sixteen years before in Paris had invited him to a debate for which Servetus failed to appear. Now Servetus went to hear Calvin preach and was recognized, denounced, and brought to trial before a state court for blasphemy, a capital offense. Calvin argued and pleaded with him in vain to change his erroneous opinions. Finally, when he was sentenced to be burned, Calvin sought for him the less painful execution by beheading, but the law was upheld. The hunted heretic was burned at the stake on October 27, 1553. He was a victim of a misguided zeal for truth on the part of his foes, who seem to have believed that they were acting in the best interest even of Servetus himself.

One man, perhaps the greatest liberal in an intolerant age, defended Servetus and decried his oppression: Sebastian Castellio of Savoy. Castellio went as a religious refugee to Strassburg, where he met Calvin in his home. In 1541 he accompanied Calvin to Geneva and taught in the academy there, but was rejected for ordination because of his nonconformist views. He moved on to Basel, where he expected to live out his days in peace as a professor of Greek. He was an intellectual, professorial type who, unlike Servetus, did not really relish controversy. In his work *On the Art of Doubting and Being Sure, of Knowing and Being Ignorant* he argued that of the three sources of knowledge—experience, revelation, and reason—the first two must be subjected to the third. Since many traditional dogmas are not subject to reason, they must be considered matters of faith. The written word of God is the treasure-house of divine thought, to which man's inward spirituality provides the key. He shifted the emphasis away from inerrancy to sincerity as the precondition for divine favor. Defining sincerity as a man's interior loyalty to that which he believes to be true, he argued that integrity is the indispensable factor in the quest for truth. Truth must be sought with passion and utter transparency. No one, not even Calvin, has the right to sit in judgment on another; Servetus had been a martyr for the truth as he saw it.

Castellio had differed with Calvin over the credal statement on Christ's descent into hell and on the allegorical interpretation of the *Song of Solomon*, which he took to be a love song; now the Servetus affair brought them to the breaking point. In 1554 Calvin wrote his *Defense of the Orthodox Trinity Against the Errors of Michael Servetus*. That same year Castellio, using the pseudonym of Martin Bellius, wrote his most famous work, *Concerning Heretics, Whether They Are to Be Persecuted and How They Are to Be Treated*, a book that has appeared in 133 editions through the years. In the preface, addressed to Christoph of Württemberg, he asked the prince how he would feel if he were to leave his subjects and instruct them to await his return clad in white garments, and then found them, when he came back, quarreling and even stabbing each other. So will Christ be displeased to find his followers fighting and even putting one another to death, he wrote. In the text Castellio presented many quotations in favor of liberty of conscience and toleration taken from the works of Erasmus, Luther, Sebastian Franck, and many others. He decried the persecution of the Anabaptists in a moving passage: "They were miserably slain, even those who were not in arms, and what is still more cruel, the suppression was carried on not only by the sword but also in books, which reach farther and last longer, or rather forever perpetuate this savagery."[6] His thesis that tolerance and mutual love constitute a Christian imperative, however, ran counter to contemporary notions of the absoluteness of orthodox formulations. Calvin considered him a Pelagian monster and he was finally brought to trial for heresy. But he died in 1563 during the proceedings, a death that Calvin's understudy, Theodore Beza, viewed as a punishment from God.

Montaigne believed that all posterity owed Castellio a great debt. The Anabaptists, spiritualists, and evangelical rationalists, though relatively few in number, contributed enormously to some of the finest modern liberal traditions. Many heroic deeds of passive resistance to oppressive authority and much intellectual cultivation were necessary for the development of true toleration and genuine religious freedom. The Anglo-American philosopher Alfred North Whitehead once observed that the impractical ethics of Christianity constituted one of the most remarkable instruments of human progress ever devised. In trying to live out literally some of the most impractical injunctions of the Sermon on the Mount, the Anabaptists confronted society with an embarrassing image reflected in the mirror of the evangelical law. The authorities understood well how to fight this threat to their complacency and security, but failed to suppress all nonconformists or to root out their ideas. The concept of the necessity of religious uniformity within a state was to enjoy a period of dominance in the second half of the sixteenth century and a good part of the seventeenth century. But eventually the ideas of toleration and religious liberty broke through and became a basic part of the Western liberal inheritance. There are direct lines of influence from the spiritualists and evangelical rationalists to the *philosophes* of the eighteenth century. When a modern man reads the *Martyr's Mirror* or Foxe's *Book of Martyrs* and reflects on the price in human misery and blood paid by many religious folk for the limited progress made by mankind toward genuine brotherly love, he is moved to ask with Bernard Shaw's St. Joan, "O God that madest this beautiful earth, when will it be ready to receive thy saints? How long, O Lord, how long?"

Bibliography

Zwingli and Bullinger:
BOUVIER, ANDRÉ. *Henri Bullinger: Réformateur et conseilleur oecumenique.* Paris, 1940.
BROMILEY, G. W. *Zwingli and Bullinger,* vol. 24 of *Library of Christian Classics.* London and Philadelphia, 1953.

---

[6] Cited in *ibid.,* pp. 318–19.

Courvoisier, Jacques. *Zwingli: A Reformed Theologian.* Richmond, Va., 1963.

Farner, Oskar. *Huldrych Zwingli,* 4 vols. Zurich, 1943–1954.

———. *Zwingli the Reformer.* New York, 1952.

Fast, Heinold. *Heinrich Bullinger und die Täufer.* Weierhof, 1959.

Garside, Charles. *Zwingli and the Fine Arts.* New Haven, 1966.

Jackson, Samuel M. *Huldreich Zwingli.* New York, 1901.

Köhler, Walther. *Das Marburger Religionsgespräch.* Leipzig, 1929.

———. *Huldrych Zwingli,* 2nd ed. Stuttgart, 1952.

Locher, Gottfried. *Die Theologie Huldrych Zwingli im Lichte seiner Christologie.* Zurich, 1952.

Rich, Arthur. *Die Anfänge der Theologie Huldrych Zwinglis.* Zurich, 1949.

Richardson, C. C. *Zwingli and Cranmer on the Eucharist.* Evanston, Ill., 1949.

Rilliet, Jean. *Zwingli: Third Man of the Reformation.* Philadelphia, 1964.

Rupp, E. Gordon. *Patterns of Reformation: Oecolampadius, Karlstadt, Müntzer.* Philadelphia, 1969.

Staedtke, Joachim. *Die Theologie des jungen Bullinger.* Zurich, 1962.

Stähelin, Rudolf. *Huldreich Zwingli: Sein Leben und Wirken,* 2 vols. Basel, 1895–1897.

Walton, Robert C. *Zwingli's Theocracy.* Toronto, 1968.

Anabaptists and Mennonites:

Armour, Rollin S. *Anabaptist Baptism: A Representative Study.* Scottdale, Pa., 1966.

Bax, Belfort. *The Rise and Fall of the Anabaptists.* London and New York, 1903.

Bender, Harold S. *Menno Simon's Life and Writings.* Scottdale, Pa., 1936.

———. *The Life and Letters of Conrad Grebel,* vol. 1. Goshen, Ind., 1950.

Bergsten, Torsten. *Balthasar Hubmaier: Seine Stellung zu Reformation und Täufertum.* Kassel, 1961.

Blanke, Fritz. *Brothers in Christ: The History of the Oldest Anabaptist Congregation, Zollikon near Zurich.* Scottdale, Pa., 1961.

Dyck, Cornelius J. *The Legacy of Faith: The Heritage of Menno Simon.* Newton, Kans., 1962.

Friedmann, Robert. *Mennonite Piety Through the Centuries.* Goshen, Ind., 1949.

———. *Hutterite Studies.* Goshen, Ind., 1961.

Gratz, Delbert. *Bernese Anabaptists.* Scottdale, Pa., 1953.

Hershberger, Guy F., ed. *The Recovery of the Anabaptist Vision.* Scottdale, Pa., 1957.

Hillerbrand, Hans. *A Bibliography of Anabaptism, 1520–1630.* Elkhart, Ind., 1962.

Horst, Irvin. *A Bibliography of Menno Simon (c. 1496–1561).* Nieuwkoop, 1962.

Keeney, William. *The Development of Dutch Anabaptist Thought and Practice, 1539–1564.* Nieuwkoop, 1968.

Krahn, Cornelius. *Dutch Anabaptism: Origin, Spread, Life, and Thought, 1450–1600.* The Hague, 1968.

Littell, Franklin H. *The Anabaptist View of the Church.* Chicago, 1952.

Oyer, John S. *Lutheran Reformers Against Anabaptists.* The Hague, 1964.

Peachey, Paul. *Die soziale Herkunft der Schweizer Täufer in der Reformationszeit.* Karlsruhe, 1954.

Smith, C. H. *The Story of the Mennonites,* 3rd ed. Newton, Kans., 1950.

Smithson, R. J. *The Anabaptists.* London, 1953.

Vedder, H. C. *Balthasar Hubmaier: The Leader of Anabaptists.* New York, 1905.

VERDUIN, LEONARD. *The Reformers and Their Stepchildren*. Grand Rapids, 1964.
WILLIAMS, GEORGE H. *The Radical Reformation*. Philadelphia, 1962.
———— and MERGAL, ANGEL M., eds. *Spiritual and Anabaptist Writers,* vol. 25 of *Library of Christian Classics*. London and Philadelphia, 1957.

Spiritualists and evangelical rationalists:
BAINTON, ROLAND H. *The Travail of Religious Liberty*. Philadelphia, 1951.
————. *Hunted Heretic: The Life and Death of Servetus*. Boston, 1953.
COHN, NORMAN. *The Pursuit of the Millennium*. New York, 1957.
COUTTS, A. *Hans Denck, Humanist and Heretic*. Edinburgh, 1927.
FAST, HEINOLD, ed. *Der linke Flügel der Reformation: Glaubenszeugnisse der Täufer, Spiritualisten, Schwärmer, und Antitrinitarier*. Bremen, 1962.
FULTON, JOHN F. *Michael Servetus, Humanist and Martyr*. New York, 1953.
HILLERBRAND, HANS J. *A Fellowship of Discontent*. New York, 1967.
KOT, STANISLAS. *Socinianism in Poland: The Social and Political Ideas of the Polish Antitrinitarians*. Boston, 1957.
MAIER, PAUL L. *Caspar Schwenkfeld on the Person and Work of Christ*. Assen, 1959.
WILBUR, EARL MORSE. *A History of Unitarianism*. Cambridge, Mass., 1945.

CHAPTER 16

Calvin
and
Calvinism

The great gift of France to the Reformation was her brilliant son John Calvin. In France he was born, educated, attracted to the evangelical faith, arrested, driven into exile, and finally supported by a militant minority of followers ready to fight and die for their beliefs. The campaigns of the third Habsburg-Valois war forced Calvin to take an indirect route in his flight from Paris to Strassburg. In a hotel room in Geneva, where Calvin intended to stay no longer than a single night, the fiery red-haired and red-bearded French reformer Guillaume Farel, who with Pierre Viret had driven "popery" from that city, prevailed on him to stay and help in the reform of Geneva. Farel threatened the curse of God upon Calvin's retirement and the tranquillity of his studies if he should refuse to assist in the cause. "Guillaume Farel detained me at Geneva," Calvin wrote years later in the preface to his *Commentary on the Psalms,* dated July 22, 1557, "not so much by counsel and exhortation as by a dreadful imprecation, which I felt to be as if God had from heaven laid His mighty hand upon me to arrest me." Calvin in his innermost being felt himself to be God's man, a conviction that, combined with his extraordinary abilities, raised him above the ranks of ordinary men. He became one of the truly formative influences upon Western history and the character of Western man. "To omit Calvin from the forces of Western evolution," wrote the British author and statesman Lord John Morley, "is to read history with one eye shut."

Calvin—The Man and the Message

CALVIN WAS ONE of those strong and consistent men of history whom people either liked or disliked, adored or abhorred. Shortly before his death he observed that the people of nearby Bern "have always feared me more than they have loved me." The two things that even the most untutored man of our day will presume to know about him are that he had a bad temper and that he taught the predestination of many men to hell. In actual fact, both the man and his doctrine were far more subtle and complex than the popular image would suggest.

When Calvin was born on July 10, 1509, in Noyon in Picardy, northeast of Paris, Luther had already spent four years in the monastery. While Calvin was learning to read, Luther was delivering his lectures on the Psalms, Romans, and Galatians. He was a boy of eight when Luther published his ninety-five theses. The generation that separated them explains the novel emphases in Calvin. Luther's volcanic theological affirmations needed now to be systematized and set in order. Amorphous and ineffective Protestant church organizations needed to be given a form and structure that would enable the movement to maintain itself against a militant Catholic majority and crushing blows by hostile states. Calvin and Luther were temperamentally quite different. The younger man was shy to the point of diffidence, precise and restrained, except for sudden flashes of anger. He was severe, but scrupulously just and truthful, self-contained and somewhat aloof. He had many acquaintances but few intimate friends. The older man was sociable to the point of volubility, free and open, warm and cordial with people of all stations of life. But in spite of their differences in personality, Calvin and Luther retained a mutual respect for each other that was rooted in their confessional agreement.

In 1539 Luther was tremendously pleased with Calvin's *Open Letter to Cardinal Sadoleto on Why the Reformation Was Necessary*. In a letter of October 14 in that same year Luther expressed his joy that Calvin was serving in Strassburg at the side of his other friends. Melanchthon reported that Calvin stood high in Luther's favor. In April 1545 Luther took a copy of Calvin's *Instruction and Confession of Faith* from the shelf of a Wittenberg bookstore, perused it, and observed: "The author is certainly a scholarly and pious man. If only Oecolampadius and Zwingli had been as clear from the beginning, such a terrible quarrel would never have happened." He thought Calvin to be as thorough as Zwingli was superficial. Calvin, for his part, warmly defended Luther against detractors and once wrote to counter Heinrich Bullinger's criticisms of the older reformer:

> Remember what a great man Luther is. How marvelous are his gifts, how bravely, how firmly, how ably, how scholarly, how effectively he has constantly labored in the destruction of the Antichrist in the spread of the doctrine of salvation. I hold

to what I have repeatedly said, "Even if he would call me a devil, I would yet honor him and call him an excellent servant of God."[1]

In the Frenchman Calvin the German reformer had a successor of a quality, stature, and strength worthy of himself. It was ironic that their followers did not appreciate the extent of their agreement.

Calvin's development into the second man of the Reformation was in no way predictable, for the initial influences on his young life seemed to head him in quite the opposite direction, and his evangelical conversion seems almost to have caught Calvin himself by surprise. His father, Gerard Cauvin, was a procurator and then an apostolic notary to the cathedral chapter in Noyon, where John was born as the second of five sons in their house off the grain market in the center of town, under the very shadow of the church. Gerard guided his son toward an ecclesiastical career. When he was only eleven John was appointed to a chaplaincy attached to the altar of La Gésine in the cathedral and received the tonsure, although of course he was not ordained. Following a common practice of the time, his father hired a qualified substitute to say mass for him for a small percentage of the benefice. He went to live and study with a noble family, the Hangest de Montmors, where he learned not only grammar but a certain aristocratic bearing that he always retained. Years later, when a French refugee addressed him as "Brother Calvin," Calvin put him off with a chilly "Monsieur Calvin to you!" In August 1523 Calvin went with the young Montmors to Paris, where he lived with an uncle and attended the Collège de la Marche as a day student. One of the best Latin teachers of the time, Mathurin Cordier, there developed in fourteen-year-old Calvin that stylistic clarity and precision which became marks of his writing. When, twenty-seven years later, Calvin dedicated his *Commentary on the First Epistle to the Thessalonians* to Cordier, a "man of excellent piety and learning," he declared that his instruction had been so helpful that it was responsible for all his subsequent progress. "I wish to witness to posterity that if any should profit from my writings, they ought to recognize that it derived in part from you!" Cordier followed his pupil into exile, taught in later years in Neuchâtel, and died in the same year as Calvin in Geneva.

Calvin transferred to the Collège de Montaigu, more scholastic and ecclesiastical in nature, and remained there until 1527. Erasmus and Rabelais had studied in this college and complained of its stultifying atmosphere. There Calvin was enrolled in an elementary arts course. Among his personal friends, besides the Montmors, were the sons of the king's Swiss physician, Michel and Nicholas Cop, and his cousin Pierre Robert, better known by the sobriquet Olivetan, earned by his habit of burning the midnight oil. Calvin left the school about the time that Ignatius Loyola arrived, but Calvin was then only eighteen, while Loyola was thirty-

---

[1] Calvin to Bullinger, November 25, 1544, cited in Emanuel Stickelberger, *Calvin: A Life* (Richmond, Va., 1954), p. 70.

six, and they probably had little or no contact. In September 1527 the canons of Noyon rewarded Calvin's progress with the curacy of St. Martin de Marteville, which he exchanged two years later for the curacy of Pont l'Évêque, a town near Noyons. Though not ordained, he preached a number of sermons and seemed on his way to taking orders in the church. "I was," he commented many years later, "obstinately devoted to the superstitions of popery."

At this very point, however, Calvin began moving in the direction of a secular career. His father had a falling out with the canons and came to favor a more remunerative law career for his gifted son. The fact that his father was under the ban of excommunication at the time of his death in 1531 must have had an unsettling effect upon the son as well. Olivetan had begun serious study of the Scriptures, which led to his pioneering translation of the Bible into French. Olivetan's studies also raised problems in his mind about the nonbiblical foundation of Roman Catholic teachings and practice, problems that he may have discussed with Calvin. In March 1528, at his father's suggestion, Calvin began the study of law at Orléans under Pierre Taisan de l'Étoile, a renowned jurist. He worked furiously and at the same time was captivated by the humanistic study of the classics. In the fall of 1529 he transferred to Bourges to study Roman law under the Italian legist Andrea Alciati. Melchior Wolmar, a German teacher and friend, taught him to read the New Testament in Greek and possibly introduced him to Lutheran theology. Though devoted now to classical scholarship, Calvin remained serious about religion, and he was deeply impressed by an inscription that he read in a church in Bourges: "Fear God, succor the poor, and bear in mind the end." Following the death of his father Calvin left Bourges for the Collège Fortet, where he read Greek and began the study of Hebrew. In April 1532 he published his first work, a commentary in Latin on Seneca's *De clementia*. It was a pedantic piece exhibiting a great deal of erudition. As a good young humanist he sent a copy to Erasmus.

Only eighteen months later Calvin was a convinced evangelical fleeing Paris for his life. In his preface to the *Commentary on the Psalms* Calvin related:

> God by a sudden conversion subdued and brought my mind to a teachable frame, which was more hardened in such matters than might have been expected from one at my early period of life. Having thus received some taste and knowledge of true godliness, I was immediately inflamed with so intense a desire to make progress therein, that although I did not altogether leave off other studies, I yet pursued them with less ardor.

Precisely when this profound change in Calvin occurred remains a mystery. After publishing his book on Seneca he went back to Orléans for a year, visited Noyon in August 1533, and by October returned to Paris. On All Saints' Day his friend Nicholas Cop delivered his inaugural address as the new rector of the university, written under Calvin's influence, in which he praised all the sciences for their usefulness but declared that they mean little next to the time-honored philosophy that "God's grace alone redeems from sins." There was much head-shaking during the oration, and within a matter of hours Cop was summoned before the parlement and had to flee to sanctuary in Basel. Friends warned Calvin and he too escaped, though his room was searched and his books and incriminating letters were taken. Around New Year of 1534 he took refuge under an assumed name with a friend, Louis du Tillet, in Angoulême, and made use of the library of the elder Tillet in preparation for the first version of his *Institutes of the Christian Religion.*

While in the southwest Calvin visited the venerable French humanist Lefèvre d'Étaples, who was spending the evening hours of his life under the protection of Marguerite d'Angoulême, queen of French Navarre and sister of Francis I. Their conversation was symbolic of the confrontation of Christian humanism and the Reformation:

LEFÈVRE: For heaven's sake, be moderate, so that you won't tear down the house of God which you intend to purge!

CALVIN: The building is too rotten to be patched up. It must be torn down and in its stead a new one must be built!

LEFÈVRE: Take heed that you may not be killed by the cracking walls. . . . You are chosen to be a mighty instrument of the Lord. Through you God will erect his kingdom in our land![2]

Calvin had received his great commission from the man who had urged everyone *"Christum ex fontibus praedicare,"* to preach Christ from the very fountains themselves, the Scriptures.

Thereafter, when not in jail, Calvin was on the move. He resigned his prebend in Noyon, was briefly imprisoned twice, went to Paris, and visited Orléans and Poitiers, where in a grotto near the city he celebrated the Lord's Supper according to a reformed rite for the first time, using a slab of rock for a communion table. The situation in France was tense and the Affair of the Placards brought things to a boil. On the morning of October 18, 1534, radical Protestants posted placards headed "True Articles on the Horrible Abuse of the Papal Mass" in Paris and other cities. One was even found tacked to the king's bedroom door in Amboise. Francis I dramatized his horror and outrage by accompanying a solemn procession to Nôtre Dame Cathedral, with tapers burning, to cleanse the city of Paris after this abomination. At a banquet held in the episcopal palace he pledged to purge this poison from the realm. Capitalizing on the subsequent upsurge of popular anger, he imprisoned hundreds of Protestants, burned thirty-five of them, executed

---

[2] Theodore Beza, *Vita Calvini*, cited in Stickelberger, *Calvin*, pp. 23–24.

one of Calvin's own brothers, and the following year, to please Pope Paul III, issued a royal decree commanding the thorough suppression of heresy. Calvin fled with Louis du Tillet to Strassburg and then to Basel.

In Basel in March 1536 the printer Thomas Platter published Calvin's *Institutes*. It has recently been argued with some plausibility that although Calvin was under Lutheran influence while still in France, his personal conversion experience did not take place until after his arrival in Basel, and that it was in Basel that he actually wrote the *Institutes*. He wrote it, he said, "first that I might vindicate from unjust affront my brethren whose death was precious in the sight of the Lord, and, next, that some sorrow and anxiety should move foreign peoples, since the same sufferings threatened many." He dedicated the work to King Francis and warned him to desist from persecuting the faithful lest God avenge his own. He made a brief visit in April 1536 to the court of Renée, duchess of Ferrara, a cousin of Marguerite d'Angoulême, whose support he hoped to enlist. The attempt was futile, thanks to the duke's hostility, and Calvin later commented, "I only went to Italy in order that I might have the pleasure of leaving it." He returned to France incognito to arrange his affairs. On the way to sanctuary in Strassburg with his younger brother Antoine and his half sister Marie, he was importuned by Farel into staying in Geneva, his city of destiny.

Like the introduction of Bacon's *Novum organum,* Newton's *Principia,* and Kant's *Critique of Pure Reason,* the publication of the *Institutes* by the twenty-six-year-old John Calvin was an epochal event. Few scholars in Christendom have written so much as Calvin, except perhaps Augustine, Thomas, and Luther. Fewer still have written so much with such tremendous consistency. There is an awesome homogeneity in his writings, though they were produced over three decades. To know Calvin well requires extensive study of his sermons (of which some 2,025 are still extant in the public library in Geneva), his treatises, biblical commentaries, and correspondence, for he could write with anger and gentleness, in sorrow and exultation. And yet in a very special sense Calvin was a man of one book—the *Institutes.* As a systematic presentation of Christian theology it became the handbook of militant Protestantism and exercised an enormous influence upon Western thought, among friends and foes alike. In its French version (1541), done by Calvin himself, it had a formative influence upon the French language. All his life Calvin worked at improving the *Institutes.* The second edition of 1539 was twice the size of the first and the eighth edition of 1559 was twice the size of the seventh. Through these editions and some twenty-five impressions there is amplification but very little change; its theological core remained substantially unaltered. His biographer Theodore Beza relates how Calvin ate frugally, stayed up till midnight, and rose early in the morning to meditate on what he had studied. Calvin, like Dr. Johnson, was a man "born to grapple with libraries."

A "masterpiece of luminous argument," the *Institutes* presented a statement of faith of the persecuted Protestants and served as a manual of instruction for neophytes. The first edition was divided into six books on (1) the law, (2) faith, (3) prayer, (4) sacraments, (5) false sacraments, and (6) Christian liberty, ecclesiastical power, and civil liberty. The centrality of Paul and the influence of Augustine and Luther are evident throughout, although Calvin's comprehensive knowledge of the Scriptures and patristic writers also comes through in force. The law, or the commandment of God to love him above all things and one's neighbor as oneself, reveals to man his complete spiritual inadequacy. In the mirror of God's law man recognizes that he is hopelessly lost when confronted with God's command to be perfect, even as he is perfect. The law strikes fear in the hearts of sinners and is a schoolmaster leading men to Christ. Faith or trust in the promises of God and the benefits of Christ's sacrificial and atoning death is itself a gift of God. Faith is instilled by the Holy Spirit into the hearts of the elect, who approach God in prayers of supplication and thanksgiving and without spiritual pride. With the later Luther he reduced the sacraments to the two dominical institutions of baptism (for infants as well as adults) and the Lord's Supper, both of which are symbolic acts and means of grace because of the promise associated with them. Christ is spiritually present in the Lord's Supper, which is a true communion with him and not a renewed sacrifice of the transubstantiated bread and wine or merely a symbolic memorial. The final two books were highly polemic, attacking the Catholic sacramental-sacerdotal system, assaulting the episcopal hierarchy as unbiblical, and arguing that in the New Testament church the preachers and overseers, who were called shepherds, bishops, and elders or presbyters, served with the consent of the Christian congregations. He followed Luther's views on Christian liberty: that the Christian is the freest of all in being above the law but is the servant of all in acting willingly in love for the good of his fellow man. In the heat of controversy with Catholic foes and more latitudinarian or universalistic Protestant opponents during the decades following the publication of the *Institutes*, Calvin forged more forceful arguments, more rigorously logical and extreme positions, and more refined statements of his basic tenets, but the tenets themselves remained the same.

Melanchthon called Calvin *ille theologus,* the theologian. This tribute from the author of the *Loci communes* must puzzle those who know merely the familiar caricature of Calvin's theology symbolized by the mnemonic TULIP: *t*otal depravity, *u*nconditional election, *l*imited atonement, *i*rresistible grace, and *p*erseverance in faith. To see Calvin's theology in perspective, it is necessary not simply to define its component parts, but to proceed from its fundamental affirmation to its logical extensions. If Luther's central concern was the question of man's justification in the eyes of God, bestowed in mercy through Christ, Calvin's concern was to proclaim the power, grace, and glory of God, who has revealed himself to man in Christ. This order of priority is evident from the table of contents of the final edition of the *Institutes,* in which Book 1 treats of God the Father, Book 2 the Son, Book 3 the Holy Spirit, and Book 4 the Holy Catholic Church. Calvin's entire doctrine was intended to affirm the sovereignty of God and to vindicate his honor. The answers to the opening questions of the Westminster Shorter Catechism, though written a century after Calvin, faithfully reflect his spirit:

> Question 1. *What is the chief end of man?*
> Answer: Man's chief end is to glorify God, and to enjoy Him forever.
> Question 2. *What rule hath God given to direct us how we may glorify and enjoy Him?*
> Answer: The Word of God, which is contained in the Scriptures of the Old and New Testaments, is the only rule to direct us how we may glorify and enjoy Him.

God's providence embraces all reality, is cognizant of the least happening, and directs every occurrence in the natural and spiritual worlds. He who numbers the very hairs of a man's head and knows when a sparrow falls leaves nothing to blind fate or chance, but works in all and through all. Before the great majesty of God natural man stands helpless and uncomprehending. In a passage reflecting the influence of Augustine's phrase *finitum non est capax infiniti,* the finite cannot grasp the infinite, Calvin declared that man the creature cannot fathom the Creator, for to do so "would be to measure with the palm of his hand a hundred thousand heavens and earths and worlds. For God is infinite and when the heaven of heavens cannot contain Him, how can our minds comprehend Him?"[3] Before the great holiness of God sinful man is "brought to nothing by the incomprehensible brightness."[4] If God would "institute no medium of intercourse, and call us to a direct communication with heaven, the great distance at which we stand from Him would strike us with dismay and paralyze invocation."[5] In his favorite allegory of the labyrinth, Calvin described the fatal limitations of man's natural knowledge of God, which perceives "certain symbols of his presence" but can attain to no saving knowledge of him, and underlined the need for special revelation. T. H. L. Parker recapitulates Calvin's labyrinth imagery in this way:

> Man is lost in a maze of which he does not possess the plan, and however much he may attempt to find his way out, he always fails. He can never know God by himself, for his sin has led him into ignorance and a wrong-mindedness that prevents him from thinking his way through to the true idea of God. His mind is a veritable maze, with passages leading off to the worship of this or that idol. He has to worship some god, and he will invent a god, or perhaps many gods, to worship. "Men's conceptions of God are formed, not according to the representations He gives of Himself, but by the inventions of their own presumptuous imaginations. . . .

---

[3] John Calvin, *Commentary on Ezekiel* (1:28), in *Corpus Reformatorum,* ed. J. W. Baum *et al.,* 59 vols. (Halle, 1863–1900), vol. 40, col. 60.

[4] Calvin, *Commentary on Exodus* (33:20), in *ibid.,* vol. 25, col. 111.

[5] Calvin, *Commentary on the Psalms* (132:8), in *ibid.,* vol. 32, col. 346.

They worship, not God, but a figment of their own brains in His stead." For all his capabilities, man is a puzzled, groping creature, surrounded by that which is mysterious to him. He not only does not understand about God, but nor does he understand the world in which he lives; he does not even understand himself—whence he has come, why he lives or whither he goes. If help does not come to him from without he will never know God or find His kingdom.

But God, in His loving concern for man, reaches right to him where he is wandering imprisoned in the labyrinth, and gives him the guidance of the Holy Scriptures, which are like a thread, leading him through this maze of ignorance to the knowledge of God. "The light of the Divine countenance, which the Apostle himself says no man can approach unto, is like an inexplicable labyrinth to us, unless we are directed by the thread of the Word."[6]

Natural reason, even when aided by all the arts and sciences, cannot lead man to faith in the God who reveals himself in Christ. The Holy Spirit must move men's minds to understand that the humanity of Christ was "like a veil by which His divine majesty was concealed," but that in this person God's true nature, both just and loving, is revealed. Jesus Christ is called the image of the Father, Calvin explained, because "He sets forth and exhibits to us all that is necessary to be known of the Father.[7] For the naked majesty of God would, by its immense brightness, ever dazzle our eyes. It is therefore necessary for us to look on Christ, that is to come to the light." In Christ God has taken on mortal flesh, the source of blessing has been made subject to the curse, so that men might be redeemed from spiritual death and become partakers of righteousness and immortality.

Calvin viewed the church in dynamic terms, not merely as an institution or collection of believing individuals, but as God's covenantal people for whom and through whom God's eternal purposes are realized within the development of the total historical process. God's people in ancient times were running a race toward the goal of the full manifestation of God in Christ. God's chosen people, the spiritual Israel of the New Testament, conform to his will as instruments in his grand design for building a holy commonwealth on earth, culminating in the New Jerusalem hereafter.

It is against this background of daring and overpowering religious assertions that Calvin's doctrine of divine predestination must be understood. Only in the final edition of the *Institutes,* as a reaction to the polemical situation, did he spell out with complete clarity his definitive position on this fearful doctrine. The problem of "Why some and not others?" was implicit in the Old Testament concept of the chosen people. In preparing his powerful *Sermons on Deuteronomy* Calvin encountered the Mosaic pronouncement in Deuteronomy 7: 7–8:

It was not because you were more in number than any other people that the Lord set his love upon you and chose you, for you were the fewest of all peoples;

---

[6] T. H. L. Parker, *Portrait of Calvin* (Philadelphia, 1954), pp. 50–51.

[7] Calvin, *Commentary on 1 John* (2:22–23), in *Corpus Reformatorum,* vol. 55, col. 325.

but it is because the Lord loves you, and is keeping the oath which he swore to your fathers, that the Lord has brought you out with a mighty hand, and redeemed you from the house of bondage, from the hand of Pharaoh king of Egypt.

St. Augustine was a high double predestinarian. St. Thomas acknowledged the universality of God's prescience or foreknowledge and his election of a minority among men to salvation. Zwingli had stressed God's absolute right to choose and to reject whomever he willed. Luther found assurance in the belief that the faith of the elect was determined by God's eternal counsel and did not depend upon man's own weak will, but, except for some polemical passages in his treatise *On the Bondage of the Will* in which he overstated his own case, he left the question of why some were lost open, holding with the Scriptures that "the Lord is not willing that any should perish but that all should come to repentance." Men were lost necessarily through some fault of their own under God's permissive or secondary will. Calvin found such a paradoxical position untenable and pressed on to a logical solution that would exalt the sovereignty of God and reduce men to a state of absolute dependence. "It must remain a first principle with us," he wrote, "that there is no event which He has not ordained. Therefore if He has brought us to the saving knowledge of Himself, we must not doubt that His particular providence is watchful for our preservation, never permitting any event which it will not overrule for our eternal benefit." This tenet allowed the later Calvinists to sing with such bold confidence:

> The Lord our God is good,
> His mercy is forever sure;
> His truth at all times firmly stood
> And shall from age to age endure.

Most of Calvin's theological predecessors were perplexed, embarrassed, or anguished over the question of why some men were lost. Some clung to the universalistic hope suggested by Paul's Epistle to the Romans, Chapters 9–11, that just as Adam in the fall plunged all men into sin and death, so Christ will raise all men to righteousness and life. But Calvin was not one to mince words, and he made his meaning so clear that no one could misunderstand him:

Predestination we call the eternal decree of God by which He has determined in Himself what He would have to become of every individual of mankind. For they are not all created with a similar destiny, but eternal life is fore-ordained for some and eternal damnation for others. Every man, therefore, being created for one or the other of these ends, we say is predestined either to life or to death.[8]

Calvin did not shrink from the consequences of the double predestination theory. He held that since God does not really will all men to be saved, Christ's death on

---

[8] Calvin, *Institutes of the Christian Religion,* trans. John Allen, 7th ed. (Philadelphia, 1936), vol. 2, bk. 3, chap. 21, p. 176.

the cross must have been intended for the salvation only of the elect and a sign of judgment upon the condemned. God created many men whom he had in his eternal counsels appointed for destruction. God could rightly condemn all men, and his decrees could not therefore impudently be called into question by sinful man. In Calvin's teaching even God's love seems to be but an instrument of his justice. This is that "horrible decree," as Calvin himself labeled it, which proved to be so fascinating to his later followers. Starting with Theodore Beza, they gave to it a position of prominence it never held in the total body of Calvin's own homiletical or exegetical writings. Quite tiresome in the English Puritans, it became absolutely terrifying from New England pulpits and in the preaching of the Scottish Presbyterians. The lines of Robert Burns catch the sulfurous odor of the double predestination doctrine:

> O Thou, wha in the heavens does dwell,
> Wha, as it pleases best Thysel',
> Sends one to heaven an' ten to hell
> A' for Thy glory
> And no for any gude or ill
> They've done afore thee.

Calvin cannot be fairly impugned for the games that later Calvinists played with his teachings. In commenting upon even such a ruthless enemy and persecutor of the Reformed Church as the French duke of Guise, Calvin expressly denied that any man could know here and now who belonged among the reprobate. Nor could a man know absolutely whether he himself belonged to the elect, although Calvin proposed three presumptive tests: a man's heartfelt profession of his faith, a decent and godly life, and participation in the sacraments of baptism and communion. Certainly he did not ever suggest that worldly success or material wealth was a sign of election to be coveted or demonstrated. The practical psychological effect of the doctrine was to inspire the children of light with an unshakable fortitude and invincible courage, for a favorite Bible passage of Calvin's read: "Because God is my defence I will not fear what man can do unto me." Calvin spawned a race of stalwart activists.

Calvin's Geneva

THE CITY OF GENEVA to which Calvin came almost by chance was destined to become his model Christian commonwealth and the center of militant Protestantism. Situated at the crossroads of French and Italian trade, the lovely city on Lake Leman was in a borderland position between the Swiss confederacy, still under the nominal overlordship of the empire, and the kingdom of France. During the first decades of the sixteenth century, Geneva, with the help of Catholic Fribourg and Protestant Bern, carried to a successful conclusion its long struggle for independence from its feudal and episcopal masters, the duke of Savoy and the bishop of Geneva, who was related to the house of Savoy. By 1519 the commune had checked the feudal forces repressing its urban development and depressing its commercial enterprise. By 1534 the city had succeeded in permanently exiling the notoriously immoral bishop and repudiating the house of Savoy. On a pattern of city government familiar at that time, the patrician class ruled through the Council of Two Hundred; the Little Council, with twenty-five members, exercised certain executive functions; and four syndics plus the city treasurer were elected by the general assembly. The council announced that it wished to see no changes made in the old religion. Its aristocratic conservative members declared that they wished to possess truth with no admixture of human fables and inventions. While they showed some openness toward new and fresh religious ideas, they wanted no changes in church organization. In his *Life of Calvin* Theodore Beza commented that although the Genevans had staged a political revolt against Savoy, they were still "very imperfectly enlightened in divine knowledge and had as yet scarcely emerged from the filth of the papacy."

Farel, Olivetan, and young Antoine Froment changed all that by undertaking a preaching and propaganda mission in Geneva. When the hapless bishop opened an attack on the city, he also opened up the possibility of allying the evangelical cause with the struggle for freedom and security. In a marathon debate on dogma in June 1535, Farel and Viret routed the incompetent Catholic defenders of the faith, then boldly occupied various churches, including the cathedral. Iconoclasts broke church windows and threw statues of saints down wells. In August the large council suspended celebration of the mass, and in subsequent months the Catholic clergy abandoned the city to the Protestant leaders. In January 1536 Protestant Bern defeated Savoy and occupied Geneva, but after much dickering agreed to independent status for the city. On May 21, 1536, in an exercise of Swiss democracy, with the male heads of families voting, the general assembly congregated in the cathedral and voted unanimously in favor of the evangelical form of worship. The councils undertook the proprietary supervision of the church, and it seemed that a state-church solution reminiscent of Zwingli's Zurich was in the making. At that moment Farel prevailed on John Calvin to remain in Geneva to assist in the reform of the city.

Calvin began his work in Geneva by expounding Paul's epistles in the church of St. Pierre, and a year later the magistrates, with the consent of the people, elected him preacher. He demonstrated his brilliance by defining his position between the Catholics on one side and the radicals on the other in a disputation with Catholic defenders in Lausanne in October 1536 and with the Anabaptists in March 1537. This debate turned into such a rout that the Council of Two Hundred stopped the verbal battle and drove out the hapless Anabaptists. Aiming at good order, the city government legally established the *Articles Concerning the Governance of the Church* on January 16, 1537. When Farel and Calvin drew up twenty-one articles as an *Instruction and Confession of Faith* directed against the radicals, the citizens were required to appear in groups of ten and swear adherence to this statement of belief. The climax to these reformatory efforts came with the adoption of the famous *Ordinances* of 1537. Although Calvin held to the divine sanction of secular authority, he sought to prevent government from encroaching upon the prerogatives of the church and interfering in its purely spiritual concerns. He therefore began moving toward a structure of church government that could be independent of the state. The question of morals, which had traditionally been legislated by the city council through sumptuary laws and moral regulations, he believed to be properly within the domain of the church. He therefore proposed that key people be appointed in every section of the city to oppose immorality and to report vice. Following the steps of admonition outlined by Christ in Matthew 18, the *Ordinances* urged first fraternal remonstrances to the erring brother himself, and then if there was no evident improvement his fault was to be told to the church. If the sinner continued to offend, he might then be publicly denounced by the minister and excluded from the Christian congregation. The visible church of Christ on earth was to preserve the high public morals of her members.

But forces of reaction and opposition were gathering strength. Many Genevans resented the leadership of Frenchmen and the growing number of French refugees within the city. Pierre Caroli, an emotionally unstable convert, as pastor in Lausanne sought to discredit the work of Viret in that city. Caroli held prayers for the dead to be of value, and in the ensuing controversy charged Calvin with anti-Trinitarian tendencies. The Bern city council decided in Calvin's favor and refused to allow Caroli to preach again in its territories, whereupon he returned to France and eventually to Catholicism. But the controversy had weakened Calvin's prestige and helped to undermine his position in Geneva.

In Geneva itself a strong opposition party developed under the leadership of a certain Jean Philippe, who resisted the innovations, the control of morals by the ministers, and the forced confessions of faith. In February 1538 Calvin's foes won election to office and the ministers denounced the victors from the pulpit. The government of Bern, meanwhile, sought to have the Bernese liturgical and sacramental rites introduced throughout its territories, including the use of unleavened bread in communion and the retention of baptismal fonts. Calvin and Farel were reluctant to accede to this demand in Geneva, where they had suspended the Bernese practices. They preached on Easter Day of 1538, although they had been forbidden by the Little Council to do so, but they refused to administer the Sacrament while such an uproar was going on. The next day the Council of Two Hundred met and ordered Calvin and Farel to get out of town within three days.

They left for Bern and from there went to a synodical meeting in Zurich, where they explained their views on ecclesiastical structure and discipline and received general approbation. Farel returned to Neuchâtel, and the leader of the evangelical movement in Strassburg, Martin Bucer, persuaded Calvin to become the pastor of a congregation of some four hundred French refugees there. They were barely able to support him, but Calvin lived modestly and worked conscientiously as both minister and scholar. Bucer's moderation and concern for Protestant unity impressed Calvin very favorably. Calvin prepared a French liturgy, drawing heavily on Bucer's, which became a prototype for Calvinist services. For church music he favored the singing of psalms rather than chants or organ music, and prepared an edition of eighteen psalms set to music. He revised the *Institutes* (1539), did a *Commentary on the Epistle to the Romans,* and published a *Tract on the Lord's Supper,* which showed the influence of Bucer's views on the spiritual presence of Christ in the Sacrament. He lectured on theology at Johannes Sturm's famous secondary school for the liberal arts. He also reflected Bucer's ecumenical concern and accompanied him to the conference on Christian reunion at Frankfort sponsored by Charles V in 1539. The next year he attended the colloquies at Hagenau and Worms, and in 1541 he was sent as an official representative of Strassburg to the colloquy at Regensburg, where he saw the conciliatory Catholic cardinal Contarini and Melanchthon in action.

His tremendous labor so exhausted his strength that Bucer and other friends urged him to marry so that he would be better cared for. He resisted the idea: "I shall not belong to those who are accused of attacking Rome as the Greeks fought Troy, only to be able to take a wife." But soon thereafter Melanchthon commented, "Well, well! It seems to me that our theologue is thinking of taking a future spouse." Calvin came to concede that his friends might have a good idea, and co-operated in the search for a bride. She should be, as he put it quite unromantically, "modest, decent, plain, thrifty, patient, and able to look after my health." History had moved on; whereas Luther had married a former nun, Calvin chose a widow with three children. She was Idelette de Bure, widow of a radical from Liège whom Calvin had converted from Anabaptism. Calvin was an affectionate and considerate husband, though quite prosaic, and the marriage was successful. In a letter largely concerned with other things he referred matter-of-factly to the birth of their only child, Jacques, who was born prematurely on July 28, 1542, but lived only a few days. Idelette never regained her health and died in 1549—of weakness, and not, as some of Calvin's latter-day detractors have asserted, of boredom.

Geneva, meanwhile, had not forgotten Calvin. The city was torn with dissension, for one party, known as the Guillermins after Guillaume Farel, led by a prominent citizen named Ami Perrin, refused to acknowledge the new preachers who had replaced the exiled reformers. The Catholics had renewed hope of regaining the city. At that point, in May 1539, the Erasmian bishop of Carpentras,

Cardinal Jacopo Sadoleto, composed his famous appeal to the people of Geneva to return home to Rome. In the colorful prose of Theodore Beza, Sadoleto, "observing his opportunity in the circumstances which had occurred, and thinking that he would easily ensnare the flock, when deprived of its distinguished pastors, under the pretext of neighborliness . . . sent a letter to his so-styled most Beloved Senate, Council, and People of Geneva, omitting nothing which might tend to bring them back into the lap of the Romish Harlot." Sadoleto argued the inerrancy of the Catholic Church, since the "Holy Spirit constantly guides her public and universal decrees and councils." He saw the key question for the Genevans as "whether to accord with the whole Church, and faithfully observe her decrees, and laws, and sacraments, or to assent to men seeking dissension and novelty." The Little Council referred the letter to Bern and the Council of Bern asked Calvin to reply, which he did, composing his answer in six days during mid-August. Calvin's response reflected the impact of his own conversion to evangelical Christianity and argued especially for the conception of the church as the communion of all believers in Christ and in favor of the doctrine of justification by faith alone.

Calvin's remarkable performance made a great impact in Geneva and helped to strengthen the Guillermins. Internal strife increased when the anti-Calvin party in power made too many concessions in legal negotiations with Bern. A riot in June 1540 precipitated the arrest and execution of Jean Philippe on the charge of having killed a citizen in a street brawl. The Guillermins quickly gained control and invited Calvin to return to Geneva. Reluctantly he yielded to pressure and went back to Geneva on September 13, 1541, a fateful step for Christendom. He was welcomed back with public acclaim.

Calvin had matured a great deal during his three years in Strassburg. A man of medium size, he had a pallid complexion and dark hair and beard. Contemporaries commented upon his alert, clear, and lustrous eyes. He dressed simply, ate little, and slept less. He was quick-witted, observant, and gifted with a remarkable memory. He could be lighthearted and even facetious, and he had a special penchant for puns. "We are nowhere forbidden to laugh," he wrote in the section on Christian liberty in the *Institutes,* "or to be satisfied with food, or to annex new possessions to those already enjoyed by ourselves or our ancestors, or to be delighted with music or to drink wine." But his manner was usually grave and he spoke simply and directly, with deliberation and great weight. After his death the Little Council observed that God had given him "a character of great majesty."

The historian Merle d'Aubigné called Calvin "*the* legislator of the renovated church." On his return to Geneva Calvin set about almost immediately to reorder the church. The *Ecclesiastical Ordinances* of 1541 developed a mature Presbyterian polity. The *Ordinances,* which were approved by both councils and by the general assembly on November 20, provided for the rule of the church by four sets of officers. (1) The pastors were the ministers of the gospel; they were coopted by the venerable Company of Pastors, approved by the council, and presented to the people and clergy for approval. (2) The doctors held the very important position of teachers in charge of Christian education. (3) The elders, or presbyters, were twelve outstanding laymen chosen to assist the pastors in looking after the spiritual welfare of the congregations, and with them made up the governing consistory, which came to be known also as the presbytery. (4) The deacons administered civic charities. A city treasurer handled salaries and city councilors supervised the physical plant. Laymen, usually elders, were also chosen to serve as morals police in each of the three parishes; in this capacity they admonished sinners and reported the impenitent or intransigent ones.

Meanwhile Calvin continued his work on a reformed order of worship. He published an edition of fifty psalms in metrical translation by Clément Marot and a revised liturgy and catechism, in which he declared, "For the worship of God we have not found better songs, nor any more suitable for use, than the psalms of David, which the Holy Spirit Himself writ and wrought."

Thanks to his tremendous prestige and imposing personality, Calvin unofficially controlled the consistory, which was primarily a morals court. The consistory exercised the power of excommunication independently of the secular government, and struggled to prevent interference by the government in matters of doctrine and church discipline. It was the central switchboard for the network of morality intelligencers in the city. The minutes of the consistory, preserved from February 16, 1542, on, reveal how it reviewed and judged the most minuscule offenses. Vestigial remains of Catholic folkways and superstitious practices were reviewed and punished. One woman possessed a copy of the *Legenda aurea,* or lives of the saints; a barber had given a tonsure to a priest; a goldsmith had made a chalice for the mass; a man had called the pope a good man; a woman had tried to cure her sick husband by tying a walnut shell with a spider in it around his neck. Lewdness or breaches in strict morality were ferreted out and punished; the investigators even went so far as to question children about their parents. Indecent dancing, a dress with a low neckline, card playing, and drunkenness drew stiff penalties. Calvin was particularly adamant against prostitution, for which Geneva had enjoyed a considerable reputation. Although he urged a stronger punishment, the council decreed in 1558 that second offenders should be marched through the streets wearing a red hat, the strumpet to be heralded by a trumpet. Calvin succeeded in having the taverns closed and replaced by decent and orderly cafés, with a French Bible on the premises for reference during serious discussions, but after a time he had to yield to consumer demand and allow the taverns to be reopened. Serious cases of witchcraft, heresy, adultery, blasphemy, and sedition that threatened the public order were referred to the civil authorities. There is even a story of a citizen jailed for naming his dog Calvin. In one four-year period these cases, which not infrequently involved confessions extorted by torture, resulted in fifty-eight executions and seventy-six sentences to exile. Because of his legal training and civic-mindedness, Calvin was consulted by the syndics and councils on many purely secular matters. But Geneva was far from being the theocracy historical legends have made it. The Company of Pastors was more nearly an administrative body than was the consistory, but it was always subject to the city councils.

Opposition to Calvin and the rule of the consistory naturally arose. One group of foes, whom Calvin labeled the Libertines, reacted against the moralistic regime, and another group, whom he considered heretics, challenged his doctrinal positions. The first real test of strength developed in January 1546, when a playing card manufacturer, Pierre Ameaux, who faced financial losses and possible bankruptcy, denounced Calvin as a foreign meddler, a wicked man, and a purveyor of false doctrine. Calvin was not satisfied when the council sentenced Ameaux to kneel before Calvin in front of the council and ask his forgiveness, for the offense had been made public, he argued, and therefore the punishment should be public; so the council forced the hapless fellow to march through the city streets in a shirt, holding a taper, and imploring divine mercy. When a placard denouncing and threatening the ministers was found on the pulpit of the church of St. Pierre in June 1546, a prime suspect was seized by the councils, tortured, and beheaded. Calvin's erstwhile supporter Ami Perrin, who had helped bring him back to Geneva, turned against Calvin when the consistory disciplined his father-in-law, brother-in-law, and wife, who were members of one of the best families of Geneva. Perrin became a syndic in 1553, a year that saw many Libertines elected to office, and headed a movement to abrogate the consistory's power of excommunication and to restore it to the council. At that point the Servetus case developed and Calvin emerged with his escutcheon unsullied and his prestige and authority thereafter virtually unchallenged.

The Servetus incident was also the last of the major challenges to Calvin's doctrinal definitions. Understandably it was his extreme solution to the predestinarian problem that stirred up the most serious criticisms against him. A Catholic, Albert Pighius, conditioned to the doctrine of prevenient grace and subsequent cooperation in achieving justification before God, questioned Calvin's teaching. But in the subsequent exchange Calvin absolutely overwhelmed Pighius and convinced him of the correctness of his own more Augustinian teaching. It was this same issue that roused the Parisian Jerome Hermes Bolsec, a former Carmelite friar, to oppose Calvin in 1551. Bolsec had renounced his Catholic faith and had fled to Veigny, a village not far from Geneva, in order to practice medicine. It is fascinating to note how many medical people became doctrinal deviationists and heretics in this period, just as many Renaissance humanists and reformers had studied law before turning to classical letters or theology. Bolsec tried to convince the Genevan ministers that Calvin's doctrine made God the author of sin, which was repugnant and false. Calvin denounced Bolsec to the Little Council as a contumelious slanderer and heretic. After consultations with other Swiss city councils, which revealed no consensus on the matter, the council exiled Bolsec from Geneva. He returned to France and to the Catholic Church, taking vengeance on Calvin with a vicious and slanderous biography of him, published in 1577, after Bolsec's death.

Calvin's strength of character never stood out more clearly than during his last illness and death. Though weakened by years of overwork, anxiety, and concern for the church, he continued to labor long hours. "Would you that the Lord should find me idle when he comes?" he asked of friends who urged him to rest. When he was so sick that he could not carry out his duties, he refused to receive his regular clerk's stipend for work he could no longer do. His estate, in fact, amounted to very little, for although his income had been substantial, he had given much of it away to charities. On February 6, 1564, he preached his last sermon. On May 2 he wrote his last letter—to Farel, who hurried from Neuchâtel to be with him during those final days. He was working on a *Commentary on Joshua* at the time of his death and with this he entered into the promised land. At the end, wrote Theodore Beza, "nothing seemed left but his spirit." On May 27, in his fifty-fifth year, he died quietly in Beza's arms. The next day, in accordance with his own wish, he was buried in an unmarked grave in the common cemetery of Plain-palais.

Calvin was indeed a man of great courage and complete dedication. Beza wrote, "I have been a witness of him for sixteen years and I think that I am fully entitled to say that in this man there was exhibited to all an example of the life and death of the Christian, such as it will not be easy to depreciate, such as it will be difficult to emulate." For all his faults, his willful tenacity, his impatience and sudden flares of temper, his lack of spontaneity, generosity, and openness, Calvin stands out as a spiritual giant in a time of great turmoil. "Calvin succeeded," the mild nineteenth-century skeptic Ernst Renan concluded, "because he was the most Christian man of his age." Calvin would have considered this a false or at best an ambivalent judgment.

Calvinism in Europe

CALVINISM IN FRANCE

One of Calvin's devoted followers, François Hotman, wrote to him in 1556 that in Geneva was engendered that spirit which raised up a new race of "martyrs in Gaul, whose blood is the testimony of thy doctrine and thy church." Calvin's heart was with his fellow Frenchmen. His hopes were high that France might someday become a truly Christian commonwealth as he conceived it, and he wished that meanwhile the reformed churches and evangelical Christians would be allowed to worship in peace according to their consciences. From Geneva he sent out an army of missionaries inspired and educated to serve the reformed congregations coming into being throughout France. Calvin carried on a mountainous correspondence with the burghers, nobles, and princes sympathetic to the evangelical cause or already convinced believers. He wrote to such powerful men as King Antoine of Navarre, the prince of Condé, and Admiral Coligny. He wrote as well to young ministers and martyrs, such as the five prisoners of Lyon, who were arrested while they were on their way from Geneva to undertake a ministry in France, and sealed their devotion to the cause with their own blood. No one who asked Calvin's intervention went without aid; he wrote to help the unemployed find jobs, to recommend tutors for the children of gentlemen, to secure admission for pupils to boarding schools, to find aid for the poor, and to encourage evangelists to be mighty in the spirit. His correspondence would easily fill thirty-five volumes. Calvin confided to a friend, "I do not have time to look out of my house at the blessed sun, and if things continue thus I shall forget what it looks like. When I have settled my usual business, I have so many letters to write, so many questions to answer, that many a night is spent without my bringing any offering of sleep to nature."

In the earliest phase of French Protestantism the lines were not very clearly differentiated between Erasmian or mystical reform impulses and Lutheran evangelicalism infiltrating from Germany. By the decade of the 1550s, however, French Protestantism had taken on a Genevan cast as French exiles returned to their homeland to propagate their faith and as Calvinist literature was spread in increasingly wide circles. Small groups of the faithful would meet secretly in private homes or barns, in fields or groves, in caves or any conceivable hideaway. As the nucleus grew into a larger congregation, they often petitioned Calvin to send them a minister, and some prospered to such an extent that they even requested assistant ministers. Calvin sent as many as he could. They traveled by night, hid in attics and false rooms behind chimneys, and used secret routes. They carried with them copies of the Olivetan Bible in French, the Genevan psalter, and Calvin's treatises.

The year 1559 was of tremendous importance for Calvinist expansion, owing to the founding of the Geneva Academy. Once again the influence of Strassburg made itself felt, for the pioneer humanist-reformed gymnasium headed by Johannes Sturm served as a model for the academy. The college offered humanistic training in Latin, Greek, and Hebrew, as well as in philosophy and theology. The consistory, with the approval of the council, appointed the faculty, and it recruited top men from the Lausanne Academy who had been expelled from the canton of Vaud by Bern, such as Pierre Viret and the Greek scholar Theodore Beza, who became the head of the academy. The institution, known today as the University of Geneva, immediately attracted young men from all parts of Europe, who returned home as bearers of Calvin's message. In 1561 the French government lodged a formal protest with the city of Geneva for aiding and abetting Protestant agents in French territory. In that same year the Protestant admiral Coligny estimated that France had some 2,150 Calvinist congregations. The term Huguenots, as the French Calvinists came to be called, perhaps was a corruption of *Eidgenossen,* the Swiss "confederates." The *Aignos* were the Genevan supporters of the rebellion against Savoy, who were friendly to the *Eidgenossen.* The name was later applied to the Genevan Protestants. This etymology appears as early as 1562.

Calvinism made such tremendous advances in France that in the year 1559 a synod met in Paris to organize a nationwide church. As in Geneva, the local congregation was to be governed by a consistory, the district by an assembly or colloquy, and the province by a synod, with the provincial synods organized under a national synod. Calvinism made its greatest progress in Navarre, Dauphiné, eastern Provence, Normandy, Orléans, and Orléanais. But it was unable to consolidate its gains and realize its plans for a national organization, for the French monarchy opposed the movement with ever greater consistency, rigor, and effectiveness. That the monarchy could strike with the fervor and abandon of a medieval crusade was demonstrated in 1545, when it launched a bloody attack on the Waldensians in southern France, taking the lives of hundreds of people who espoused the ideals of poverty and humility taught by Peter Waldo centuries before. The new heretics were to fare no better. King Francis I persecuted the Protestants, fiercely at times but sporadically, for his wars with the Habsburgs kept him preoccupied much of the time. His successor, Henry II (1547–1559), had a sadistic streak, and especially in his last years loved to watch the burning of heretics, though when his own tailor was being burned the man fixed him with a look of such reproach that his majesty was unable to sleep for several nights afterward. In 1548 he set up a special tribunal to try heretics, the *chambre ardent.* In 1551 the Edict of Chateaubriand codified the laws designed to suppress the Protestants. All Protestantism breathed a sigh of relief in 1559 when Henry II breathed his last. He died a few days after a shattered lance pierced his right eye in a tournament. But the death of Henry II coincided with the peace of Cateau-Cambrésis between France and the empire, which was soon followed in the kingdom of France by the wars of religion and in the rest of Europe by the onset of the Counterreformation.

CALVINISM IN THE HABSBURG LANDS

In the year 1543 Calvin admonished Emperor Charles V himself:

> The Reformation of the church is God's work and is as independent from human hope and intention as the resurrection from the dead or any other wonder of this kind. One must therefore, in view of the possibility of doing something for it, not wait for the good will of the people or for a change of circumstances, but one

must break right through the middle of despair. God desires to have his Gospel preached. Let us obey this command and go where he calls us! What the result will be is not for us to ask.[9]

But the one thing Charles V had in common with Francis I was an implacable hostility toward Protestantism. Charles opposed Protestantism because it ran counter to the century-old allegiance of his dynasty to Rome. Francis suppressed it because it threatened the unity of his kingdom, which had moved further than other national monarchies toward consolidation. In the Habsburg Netherlands Charles was able to exert enormous pressure upon the young Calvinist movement, but in the empire it developed under the aegis of favorably disposed princes against the opposition of the established Lutheran churches as well as the Catholics.

The seventeen provinces of the Netherlands belonged immediately to the Habsburg dominions. There Charles V had managed to hold the Lutheran and Anabaptist movements in check by inquisition and execution. But the more militant Calvinism made real headway after it first penetrated into the Walloon or southernmost French-speaking provinces. A Geneva-educated missionary, Guy de Brès, prepared a Calvinist confession that was adopted in 1566 by a synod at Antwerp. The movement gained strength as French refugees came across the border and later as English Protestants arrived, especially in the northern Dutch provinces, where Calvinism became more firmly established than in the south. With the accession of Charles V's son, the narrow and fanatically Catholic Philip II (1555–1598), who was in residence in the Lowlands the first four years of his reign, more systematic repression of the Calvinists began. The cause of religious liberty in the Netherlands coincided with the desire for political freedom. Militant Calvinism paid the Habsburgs back in their own coin by contributing to the fervor of Dutch resistance to Spanish rule.

The empire was an essentially different matter, for there the princes stood as a buffer between the Habsburgs and the people. That Lutheranism became static or dormant after the Peace of Augsburg (1555) is a myth, for it made some striking accessions even after that date, including the Strassburg of Bucer and Calvin, which subscribed to the Lutheran Formula of Concord in 1580. But here and there in the empire Calvinism made gains against established Lutheran churches as well as in Catholic territories. The name Reformed Church was, in fact, first used to distinguish the Calvinist congregations from the more conservative Lutheran establishments. Penetration was evident in Württemberg, lying close to Switzerland in the lower Rhineland; somewhat later in Brandenburg, where the ruler turned Calvinist, although most of the people remained Lutheran; but especially in the Palatinate.

In the Palatinate the elector Frederick III (1559–1576) became convinced that

---

[9] *Corpus Reformatorum*, vol. 6, cols. 510–11.

Calvin's sacramental doctrine was the true interpretation. He appointed Calvinist theologians, educated in Geneva, to professorships at Heidelberg University. In 1563 they prepared the Heidelberg Catechism, Calvinist in essence but moderately formulated, which was widely used both for instruction and as a doctrinal statement by the Reformed churches in the Germanies and in the Netherlands as well. Calvinism in the Palatinate ran into the problem of the proprietary church arrangement, according to which the prince was accustomed to assume the legal governance of the church. A certain Thomas Lüber (*c*. 1524–1583), the elector's physician, better known by his Latinized name, Erastus, argued that the civil government should exercise the power of excommunication. His writings were published posthumously in England (1589), and the term Erastianism was forever after in that country applied to political theories that favored state domination of the church.

CALVINISM IN EASTERN EUROPE

In eastern Europe Calvinism made its most notable gains during the second half of the sixteenth century in Poland and Hungary. Although Lutheranism had made slow but steady progress up to the accession of Sigismund II Augustus in 1548, from then on Calvinism forged ahead until it gained a dominant position in Lithuania and Little Poland. King Sigismund corresponded with Calvin and greatly admired the *Institutes*. In 1554 Calvin sent him a plan for the reform of the Polish church under an evangelical archbishop and Calvinist bishops. For the middle and lower Polish nobility, Calvinism had certain appealing features that Lutheranism lacked. It was not so closely associated with the Germans as Lutheranism was, and in its presbyterian organization it provided for lay participation in the consistories and lay leadership at the provincial and national levels, analogous to the participation these classes were seeking in political government. As a more militant form of Protestantism, Calvinism was opposed both to papal authority and to absolute monarchy, and therefore proved to be congenial to the landed gentry.

In Lithuania the powerful Lithuanian magnate Nicholas Radziwill, Sigismund's chancellor, converted to Calvinism and brought with him all his feudal estates and dependencies. In Little Poland the leading figure was a clergyman of noble descent named John à Lasco. Lasco had been converted to Lutheranism, helped to organize the church in Ducal Prussia, and served refugee congregations in Frankfort and Emden, meanwhile veering over toward Calvinism. For three years he was a pastor of an émigré congregation in England during the reign of Edward VI. Then in 1557 he returned to Poland and there worked without success to establish a united Protestant church with a Calvinist theology and polity. Under his leadership Calvinism as such made considerable headway. But Protestantism eventually failed in Poland, and in the seventeenth century Catholicism won a nearly complete and bloodless victory, because the power of the Catholic clergy was firmly rooted in the state and the kings remained loyal to the old church. Because the kings nevertheless made concessions on freedom of worship, the Protestants were never able to combine their cause with a revolt of the gentry against the kings. After failing to place a Protestant candidate on the throne in any of the three sixteenth-century interregnums, they lost the initiative, and one by one the landed magnates returned to the Catholic Church so that their families would not be excluded from preferred appointments in the kingdom.

The development of Calvinism in Hungary was analogous to that in Poland. Until the middle of the century the Lutherans had a virtual monopoly on evangelizing the kingdom, but then Calvinism developed a powerful appeal for the Magyar landed magnates. Matthias Biró turned the city of Debrecen into a Hungarian Geneva. In Transylvania, where Zapolya had been mighty, the "Transylvania Saxons," or Lutherans, were challenged by a strong Calvinist movement, and a rule of local autonomy was established according to which villages or cities could choose preachers congenial to them, an arrangement celebrated euphemistically as "Transylvanian toleration." Although Calvinism maintained itself better in Hungary than in Poland, the great preponderance of people and of power remained with a resurgent Catholicism.

PROTESTANTISM IN SPAIN AND ITALY

French-speaking Geneva provided a strategic location from which the penetration of Latin or Romance-language Europe could be attempted. Calvin made heroic efforts to launch an evangelical invasion of these Catholic strongholds, but Spain under its most Catholic Habsburg kings remained almost completely impervious, and Italy, though rocked from head to toe with dissent, deviation, and disputes, was saved for the papacy largely by the strong hand of Spain, which dominated the peninsula throughout most of the century.

The church in Spain was extremely well organized and disciplined, primarily because of the work of Cardinal Francisco Ximénez de Cisneros, confessor to Queen Isabella, primate of the Spanish church, humanist founder of the University of Alcalá, and, above all, founder of the Spanish Inquisition in 1480. When he died, in the same year in which Luther posted his ninety-five theses, he left behind a strong church prepared to work hand in iron glove with Charles V and Philip II, who made Spain the main power base of their dynastic empire. Moreover, the successful conclusion of the crusades against the Moors had left the Spaniards with a fanatic zeal in behalf of Catholicism, which in their minds was as inextricably a part of the Spanish identity as Islam was of the Moorish, and with an endemic hostility toward all foreign influences.

Nevertheless, some humanist and Protestant books did penetrate, smuggled in by merchants, hidden in bales of hides, in colporteurs' luggage, in casks or cargo. Even though Erasmus' books were proscribed, his ideas filtered through. The Spanish inquisitors either could not or did not bother to distinguish between Erasmians and Lutherans, and fiercely suppressed them all as heretics. When these "Lutherans" went into exile, they generally ended up as Calvinists. Attempts have been made, however, to trace the influence of Erasmus on Spanish thought all the way down to Cervantes. Even the mystical movement of the *Alumbrados,* who stressed the inwardness of religion and the indwelling of Christ in the hearts of men, centering in a Benedictine monastery nestled high up on a craggy cliff at Montserrat, fell suspect to the prying eye of persecutors. In 1555 Pope Paul IV specifically condemned the *Espiritualistas* of Spain. Small groups of Lutherans gathered clandestinely at Seville and Valladolid, but were ferreted out and tortured, or fled. Some of Spain's best minds chose exile. Juan Luis Vives (1492–1540), a distinguished Erasmian humanist and educational philosopher, lived out his life in France, England, and the Netherlands. The Erasmian Juan de Valdés (1500–1541) and his twin brother, Alfonso, left Spain. After writing *The Dialogue of Mercury and Caron,* Juan moved to Naples in 1530 in fear of the Inquisition; Alfonso turned to politics and served in the entourage of Charles V in the empire, where he died in 1532 in Vienna. Spain has yet to recover from this suppression of the intellectuals and the consequent loss of independent thinkers.

The case of Italy, with Rome and the Papal States in its heartland, was far more complex. Suffering repeated foreign invasions, serving as the battleground of Spanish and French armies, and politically fragmented into small warring states, Italy experienced in the first decades of the sixteenth century a waning of its Renaissance culture and the virtual end of its world of humanism, except in Venice, which enjoyed an Indian summer of civic humanism and an artistic afterglow. In the early years evangelical religion made sporadic headway in various Italian city-states, although it is difficult to distinguish individuals of Protestant and Erasmian Catholic reform leanings, and Lutheranism from native anticlericalism or anti-curialism. Moreover, the extent to which Anabaptism and other sectarian beliefs penetrated the masses needs to be explored further, for there is evidence of Anabaptist congregations in Vicenza and Venice, and of Anabaptist activity elsewhere. Protestant Europe was rapidly dotted with Italian refugee congregations. With the year 1542 Protestantism in Italy entered upon a new phase, for in that year Pope Paul III, under pressure from the zealous Cardinal Caraffa, established the Holy Office of the Roman Inquisition. The Inquisition hounded many free spirits out of the country, most of them gravitating now toward Geneva and western Europe.

In cosmopolitan, antipapal Venice, blessed with at least a modicum of toleration, some of Luther's and Zwingli's works were published. There too appeared Benedetto Luchino's *Most Useful Treatise on the Benefit of Jesus Christ Crucified,* the most widespread Italian Protestant tract, primarily a compilation of translations of Calvin. At the University of Padua in the Venetian domain, as at the University of Bologna, the German students in residence made active Protestant propaganda, and for a long time the local authorities did not intervene for fear of losing revenue. In Padua, too, transpired a poignant human tragedy that epitomized the spiritual agony of many men in that generation. The distinguished lawyer Francesco Spiera was converted to the evangelical faith, and began to preach and distribute literature. After being arrested and tried, he recanted, for he thought that his eleven children would otherwise be disinherited. But then he feared that in denying Christ as the sole author of his salvation he had committed the sin against the Holy Ghost, and sank into a deep melancholy that lasted until he died in despair two years later.

The northeast presented Protestantism with a stalwart advocate in the person of Matthias Flacius Illyricus (1520-1575). Orphaned early, he worked his way through school and studied with the humanist Baptista Egnatius, a friend of Erasmus, in Venice. An uncle who was sympathetic to the Reformation, although he was a provincial of the Franciscans, dissuaded him from becoming a monk and directed him toward university study. He attended the universities of Basel, Tübingen, and Wittenberg, where he was warmly welcomed by Melanchthon and Luther. There in 1544 he was appointed professor of Hebrew. He subsequently feuded with Melanchthon over the compromise Leipzig Interim, and thereafter wandered from Jena to Regensburg, Antwerp, Strassburg, and Frankfort until his death. He was almost Manichaean in his stress on the substantive nature of sin and evil in man. But through his exegetical *Clavis,* or key to the Scriptures, and his historical schema in the *Magdeburg Centuries,* both designed to prove that the papacy rested on false foundations, he had a strong influence upon Protestant thought.

In Naples a second major center of unorthodox belief developed in the literary and religious circle around the Erasmian and mystical Juan de Valdés. Valdés had moved from Naples to Rome in 1531 and served as an attendant to Pope Clement VII. In the fall of 1533 he returned permanently to Naples, where a group of intellectuals gathered around him to study the Scriptures. He translated parts of the Bible from Hebrew and Greek into Spanish and wrote brief commentaries on the epistles of Paul to the Corinthians and the Romans. Pietro Carnesecchi (1508-1567) ascribed to the influence of Valdés his acceptance of the doctrine of justification by faith. Bernardino Ochino and Peter Martyr Vermigli came under his spell, and two remarkable women, Vittoria Colonna and her sister-in-law Giulia Gonzaga, belonged to his coterie. With his death in 1541 the spirit of religious freedom also ebbed away.

The Roman Inquisition lost no time in swinging into action as soon as it was organized. The impatient Caraffa set up instruments of torture in his own house until more spacious quarters could be found. One of the Inquisition's most prominent victims was Valdés' disciple Pietro Carnesecchi. Protonotary to the curia and first secretary to the pope, he was led by Valdés to accept a Pauline view of justification by faith. He fled to Paris but later returned to Venice. When he was summoned to Rome in 1557, he fled to Geneva. Under Pius V pressure was less intense than it had been under Paul IV, and he felt secure in Florence, but in 1565 the Inquisition renewed its activity. Betrayed by Duke Cosimo of Florence, who wished to ingratiate himself with the pope, Carnesecchi was condemned to die. On October 1, 1567, he was beheaded and then burned. He went to his death like a gentleman, Cosimo's agent reported from Rome, "as though to his wedding," wearing a "white shirt, with a new pair of gloves and a white handkerchief in his hand."

A man of great eminence forced into permanent exile was Bernardino Ochino (1487–1564), an earnest religious who rose to become general of the Observantine Franciscan order. In 1534 he joined the new, more austere order of the Capuchins, and four years later was elected vicar general. In 1539 he preached a series of sermons in Venice, at the invitation of Cardinal Bembo, in which a decided emphasis on justification by faith was evident. No sooner had Caraffa established the Inquisition than Ochino was summoned to appear in Rome. Warned by Cardinal Contarini, he fled to Geneva, where Calvin received him with open arms. He published six volumes of tracts defending his conversion to the evangelical faith. In 1545 he became pastor of an Italian refugee congregation in Augsburg and barely escaped when Charles V's troops took the city. He fled through Strassburg to England, where Edward VI gave him a pension. There he published *A Tragedy, or Dialogue of the Unjust Usurped Primacy of the Bishop of Rome* (1549), a prolix piece in which Lucifer, angered at the spread of Christ's kingdom, assembles all the fiends and enthrones the pope as Antichrist. Just when Satan and Antichrist are about to triumph, Ochino exults, God raises up Henry VIII and his "illustrious" son and succeeds in overthrowing them. Queen Mary drove Ochino out of her earthly kingdom. He became pastor of an Italian congregation in Zurich, but in his *Thirty Dialogues* he seemed to make a case for polygamy and to hold unorthodox views of the Trinity, so he was driven out of there too. He fled to Poland, but was banished again, and died toward the close of 1564 in Moravia.

Other men of quality, such as Vergerio, Vermigli, and Acontius, were also driven out of Italy by the Inquisition and were attracted as though by a magnet to Swiss Protestantism. Pietro Paolo Vergerio (*c.* 1498–1564), a man of unusual religious sensitivity, stood high in the ecclesiastical hierarchy. A Venetian trained in canon law, he rose to become a reforming bishop of Capodistria and a papal legate. In 1535 he was sent to Wittenberg to negotiate with Luther about an ecumenical church council and was deeply impressed by the reformer. In Italy he visited Spiera to observe his acute soul struggle. In 1548 Vergerio became convinced of the truth of the evangelical faith, and the next year he left Italy to become pastor of a congregation of Italian Lutherans in Switzerland. As councilor to Duke Christoph of Württemberg, Vergerio, who remained essentially Lutheran in doctrinal outlook, had a powerful influence on the course of religious development.[10]

Peter Martyr Vermigli (1500–1562) and Giacomo Acontius moved from Italy through Switzerland to Protestant England. Vermigli was born in Florence, the son of a devoted follower of Savonarola. He was educated in the Augustinian cloister at Fiesole and in a Paduan monastery, and became a preacher at Brescia, Pisa, Venice, and Rome. In 1530 he became the abbot of an Augustinian monastery at Spoleto and three years later became prior of a convent in Naples. But he meanwhile steeped himself in biblical studies, read Zwingli and Bucer, fell under the suspicion of the Spanish viceroy in Naples, and in 1541 moved to Lucca, where a nucleus of Protestants was in formation. Ordered to appear before his order in Genoa, he consulted with Ochino in Florence and then fled to Zurich, Basel, and Strassburg. In 1547 Thomas Cranmer offered him a pension in England, and the next year he was made regius professor of theology at Oxford. He fled back to Strassburg on the accession of Queen Mary, and ended his days as a professor of Hebrew in Zurich, where his sacramental views blended with Zwinglian teaching.

Giacomo Acontius (1492–1560?) was a real pioneer of religious toleration. Like Vermigli and Ochino, he turned to a more radical form of protest than Lutheranism. His line of flight took him through Switzerland and Strassburg to England, where he arrived soon after the accession of Queen Elizabeth. As an engineer he drained marshes and inspected fortifications; as a religious intellectual he wrote two books, upon which his lasting fame rests. In his *De methodo* he discussed the correct way of investigating the Scriptures. In his *Stratagemata satanae* he argued that dogmatic creeds are the divisive stratagems of Satan and that the least common denominator or fundamentals of the various creeds should be determined and all other disputable matters ruled out as immaterial, a daring thought for that era and one that was generally repudiated.

It seems that the dogmatic line and harsh action of the church and state in Spain and Italy produced an opposite if not equal reaction, for Spain produced Servetus and Italy a company of anti-Trinitarians. Possibly, too, the impact of Neoplatonic philosophy carried over from the Renaissance to condition religious thinkers. The relation of anti-Trinitarians to such radical groups as the Italian Anabaptists is a question still in need of scholarly investigation. Most prominent among the anti-Trinitarians were Lelio Sozzini (1525–1562) and his rambunctious nephew Fausto (1539–1604). Lelio, a jurist, told Melanchthon that his drive toward the *fontes juris* had led him to search also for the pristine fountains of religion and to renounce the "idolatry of Rome." He was a constant wanderer, moving

---

[10] See Anne Jacobson Schutte, "Pier Paolo Vergerio: The Making of an Italian Reformer" (unpublished Ph.D. dissertation, Stanford University, 1969).

through Switzerland, France, England, Holland, Germany, Austria, Bohemia, and Poland. Calvin welcomed him in Geneva and concealed his suspicions of Lelio's speculative flights. He was in Zurich when he died. His family back in Italy was persecuted by the Inquisition, and several of his relatives were imprisoned. His nephew Fausto was perhaps a bit influenced by Lelio's papers, which he claimed in Zurich, but for the most part he was an independent thinker. In his *Explicatio* of the proem of the gospel of John, Fausto ascribed to Christ an official, not an essential, deity. He expressed doubt about the natural immortality of man. For twelve years he was in the service of Isabella de' Medici, but in 1575 he fled to Basel. He then played a role in the anti-Trinitarian movement in Transylvania and in Cracow, Poland, where a mob wrecked his house. He died in retirement on an estate east of Cracow.

John Calvin was intensely interested in the "progress of the gospel" in the papacy's Italian homeland. His extensive correspondence reveals that he hoped, through the conversion of princes by the mysterious power of the word, to win Italy for the evangelical cause. He continued to write to the French duchess Renée of Ferrara, whom he had visited in 1537. But Duke Ercole II opposed him, and in 1559 her own son Alfonso drove her out and back to France, for the Estes family could not afford to alienate the pope or bring Spanish troops down upon them. Calvin, perhaps with Carnesecchi in mind, constantly warned the Italian Protestants not to be like Nicodemus, the young aristocrat who came to Jesus by night for fear of the rulers, but to confess their faith openly. It is easy to fault Calvin on many counts, but there can be no question of his dedication to the cause and his concern for all his brothers in the faith. Goethe once commented that when we elect to find fault with a great man of the past, we should, to be just, do so on our knees.

Bibliography

Calvin:

BENOIT, JEAN D. *Jean Calvin: La vie, l'homme, la pensée,* 2nd ed. Paris, 1948.

BRATT, JOHN H. *The Rise and Development of Calvinism,* rev. ed. Grand Rapids, 1964.

BREEN, QUIRINUS. *John Calvin: A Study in French Humanism,* 2nd ed. Grand Rapids, 1968.

CADIER, JEAN. *The Man God Mastered: A New Biography of John Calvin.* Grand Rapids, 1960.

DOUMERGE, ÉMILE. *Jean Calvin, les hommes et les choses de son temps,* 7 vols. Lausanne, 1899–1927.

HARKNESS, GEORGIA. *John Calvin: The Man and His Ethics.* New York, 1958.

HUNT, R. N. *Calvin.* London, 1933.

PARKER, T. H. L. *Portrait of Calvin.* Philadelphia, 1955.
STAUFER, RICHARD. *Calvins Menschlichkeit.* Zurich, 1964.
STICKELBERGER, EMANUEL. *Calvin: A Life.* Richmond, Va., 1954.
WALKER, WILLISTON. *John Calvin, the Organizer of Reformed Protestantism, 1509–1564.* New York, 1906.
WARFIELD, BENJAMIN. *Calvin and Calvinism.* New York, 1931.

Calvin's theology:
BIÉLER, ANDRÉ. *The Social Humanism of Calvin.* Richmond, Va., 1964.
BOISSET, JEAN. *Sagesse et sainteté dans la pensée de Jean Calvin.* Paris, 1959.
DOWEY, EDWARD A. *The Knowledge of God in Calvin's Theology.* New York, 1952.
FORSTMAN, H. JACKSON. *Word and Spirit: Calvin's Doctrine of Biblical Authority.* Stanford, 1962.
GANOCZY, ABBÉ ALEXANDRE. *Calvin: Théologien de l'église et du ministère.* Paris, 1964.
HOOGLAND, M. P. *Calvin's Perspective on the Exaltation of Christ.* Kampen, Netherlands, 1966.
JANSEN, JOHN F. *Calvin's Doctrine of the Work of Christ.* London, 1956.
McDONNELL, KILIAN, O.S.B. *John Calvin: The Church and the Eucharist.* Princeton, 1968.
NIESEL, WILHELM. *The Theology of Calvin.* Philadelphia, 1956.
NIXON, LEROY. *John Calvin's Teachings on Human Reason.* New York, 1963.
PARKER, T. H. L. *The Doctrine of the Knowledge of God: A Study in the Theology of John Calvin,* rev. ed. Edinburgh, 1959.
QUISTORP, HEINRICH. *Calvin's Doctrine of the Last Things.* Richmond, Va., 1955.
STROHL, HENRI. *La Pensée de la Réforme.* Paris, 1951.
TORRANCE, THOMAS. *Calvin's Doctrine of Man.* London, 1940.
WALLACE, RONALD S. *Calvin's Doctrine of Word and Sacrament.* Grand Rapids, 1957.
WARFIELD, BENJAMIN. *Calvin and Augustine.* Philadelphia, 1956.
WENDEL, FRANÇOIS. *Calvin: The Origins and Development of His Religious Thought.* New York, 1963.
WILLIS, EDWARD D. *Calvin's Catholic Christology.* Leiden, 1966.

Calvinism and the French Reformation:
DAKIN, ARTHUR. *Calvinism.* London, 1941.
HAUSER, HENRI. *La Naissance du Protestantisme.* Paris, 1940.
IMBART DE LA TOUR, PIERRE. *Les Origines de la Réforme,* 2 vols., 2nd ed. Melun, 1948.
LECERF, A. *Études Calvinistes.* Neuchatel and Paris, 1949.
LOVY, RENÉ. *Les Origines de la Réforme française: Meaux, 1518–1546.* Paris, 1959.
MACKINNON, JAMES. *Calvin and the Reformation.* London, 1936.
McNEILL, JOHN T. *The History and Character of Calvinism.* New York, 1954.
VIENOT, JOHN. *Histoire de la Réforme française des origines à l'Édit de Nantes.* Paris, 1926.

Geneva and the spread of Calvinism:
BERGIER, J. F. *Genève et l'économie européenne de la Renaissance.* Paris, 1963.
BERTHOUD, G., et al. *Aspects de la propagande religieuse.* Geneva, 1957.
CHOISY, E. *La Théocratie de Genève au temps de Calvin.* Geneva, 1897.
GRAHAM, W. F. *Calvin and His City.* Richmond, Va., 1970.

HALKIN, LÉON. *La Réforme en Belgique sous Charles Quint.* Brussels, 1957.

HIGMAN, FRANCIS L. *The Style of John Calvin in His French Polemical Treatises.* Oxford, 1967.

HUGHES, PHILIP E. *The Register of the Company of Pastors of Geneva in the Time of Calvin.* Grand Rapids, 1966.

HUNT, G. L. *Calvinism and the Political Order.* Philadelphia, 1965.

KINGDON, ROBERT M. *Geneva and the Coming of the Wars of Religion in France, 1555–1563.* Geneva, 1956.

———. *Geneva and the Consolidation of the French Protestant Movement, 1564–1572.* Madison, Wis., 1967.

MONTER, E. W. *Calvin's Geneva.* New York, 1967.

NAEF, HENRI. *Les origines de la Réforme à Genève,* 2 vols. Geneva, 1968.

Protestantism in Spain and Italy:

BREZZI, P. *Le origini del Protestantesimo.* Rome, 1961.

CANTIMORI, DELIO. *Bernardino Ochino: Uomo del Rinascimento e Riformatore.* Pisa, 1929.

———. *Eretici italiani del cinquecento.* Florence, 1939.

——— et al. *Ginevra e l'Italia.* Florence, 1959.

CHURCH, FREDERICK. *The Italian Reformers, 1534–1564.* New York, 1932.

LEMMI, FRANCESCO. *La riforma in Italia.* Milan, 1938.

LONGHURST, JOHN. *Luther and the Spanish Inquisition: The Case of Diego de Uceda.* Albuquerque, N.M., 1953.

McNAIR, PHILIP. *Peter Martyr in Italy: An Anatomy of Apostasy.* Oxford, 1967.

RODOCANACCHI, F. *La Réforme en Italie,* 2 vols. Paris, 1920–1921.

ROSSI, PAOLO. *Giacomo Aconcio.* Milan, 1952.

RUFFINI, FRANCESCO. *Studi sui riformatori italiani.* Turin, 1955.

SCHUTTE, ANNE J. "Pier Paolo Vergerio: The Making of an Italian Reformer." Ph.D. dissertation, Stanford, 1969.

TEDESCHI, JOHN A. *Italian Reformation Studies in Honor of Laelius Socinus.* Florence, 1965.

CHAPTER 17

The Reformation
in England
and Scotland

British historians have long been convinced that the Reformation in Great Britain represented one of the great turning points in modern history. Some with Protestant and progressivist Whiggish prejudices have indeed declared it to be the crucial event in Western history. James Froude, for example, wrote: "I believe the Reformation to have been the greatest incident in English history; the root and source of the expansive force which has spread the Anglo-Saxon race over the globe, and imprinted the English genius and character on the constitution of mankind."[1] In spite of its supposed universal significance, the English Reformation is said to have had a special stamp of its own. That peculiar characteristic was the moderation with which an official reformation was carried out. David Hume asserted that the English Reformation represented the *via media* between papalism and radicalism.[2]

The near-ecstatic appreciation of the English Reformation by Britain's patriotic sons has been quite evenly balanced on the other side by an absurd reduction of the Reformation to a matter of the "King's Great Question" and the bright eyes of Anne Boleyn. The mischievous Voltaire quipped that "England separated from

---

[1] James Froude, *The Divorce of Catherine of Aragon* (New York, 1891), p. 18.
[2] David Hume, *The History of England* (Boston, 1854), vol. 4, p. 115.

the Pope because King Henry fell in love." Somewhere between adulation and denigration lies the truth about the English Reformation. Sorting out the essential facts, presenting a narrative as true as brevity allows, distinguishing those features that the English Reformation had in common with the continental Reformation and those that were unique to it, and, finally, assessing its historical significance are no simple matters.

Ironically, the strong desire of the English people for peace and security played a large part in precipitating the disorder of the Reformation. For after the protracted bloody struggle of the Wars of the Roses between the Yorkist and Lancastrian factions, the English longed for quiet and prosperity. But the security of the state depended upon masterful rule by the sovereign and an orderly succession, a fact that explains the widespread acceptance of Henry VIII's moves to assert and to increase the royal power and the general acquiescence in the king's maneuvering to secure a male heir by one queen or another. The English greeted the coronation of vigorous young Henry VIII in 1509 with unrestrained enthusiasm. Expectations ran high.

His father, Henry VII (1457–1509), was the founder of the Tudor dynasty. Henry VII invaded England with French aid and landed at Milford Haven, among his Welsh allies. In the famed battle of Bosworth field, aided at this critical juncture by the noble Stanley's treason to Richard III, he defeated and killed the Yorkist king on August 22, 1485. He was ceremoniously crowned in Westminster on the following October 30. He married Elizabeth, the oldest daughter of King Edward IV, thus uniting in the marriage bed the red and white roses and eliminating all pretexts for further civil war. Nevertheless, conspiracies and insurrections persisted, and Henry VII's reign was far from peaceful. By way of matrimonial diplomacy Henry VII married his oldest son, Arthur, to Catherine, the daughter of King Ferdinand and Queen Isabella of Spain. One of his daughters, Margaret, was married to James IV of Scotland, and another, Mary, was bestowed as wife upon Louis XII of France, gentle private hostages to international security.

The Rule of Cardinal Wolsey

ERASMUS WAS MUCH IMPRESSED with the brilliance of young Prince Henry (1491–1547), whom he saw as a boy at the court in 1499. Educated under the influence of Renaissance tutors, such as the poet John Skelton, Henry was a remarkable young scholar, a gifted linguist, a talented musician, a remarkably learned amateur theologian, and an athlete and horseman who loved to ride to the hunt. He was idolized as a child and became a willful, opportunistic, assertive egotist. After the death of his older brother, Arthur, in 1502, Henry became the hope of the dynasty. On the death of his father on April 22, 1509, Henry succeeded to the throne. He was, as the historian Bishop William Stubbs said, "a man of unbounded selfishness; a man of whom we may say . . . that he was the king, the whole king, and nothing but the king; that he wished to be, with regard to the church of England, the pope, the whole pope, and something more than the pope."[3] When he was only twelve he had been betrothed to his brother Arthur's widow, Catherine of Aragon, nearly seven years older than he. Church law forbade marriage between a man and his brother's widow, but Pope Julius II granted a special dispensation so that the marriage could take place. Erasmus lauded the marriage of Henry and Catherine as an ideal example of love and chastity.

During the first two years of Henry's reign, mild Richard Foxe and Archbishop Warham managed affairs of state, while Henry amused himself. But soon one of the most spectacular statesmen Britain has ever had, the clever and ruthless Cardinal Thomas Wolsey (1471–1530), rose to prominence and proceeded to dominate the whole first half of Henry's reign. An ambitious, arrogant, masterful man, Wolsey combined magnificent style with a flair for the dramatic. Local records in Suffolk reveal that Wolsey was the son of a cheating butcher, periodically in trouble with the law for giving short weight, selling spoiled meat, and keeping a disorderly house. Wolsey was saved by those sturdy ladders of upward social mobility, the church and Oxford University. His enemies could say of him without charity, but not without justice:

> Born by butcher, but by bishop bred,
> How high His Highness heaves his haughty head!

A precocious student, Wolsey became bursar of Magdalen College, and early demonstrated unusual administrative skill. Urging a foreign policy actively directed against France in cooperation with Ferdinand of Spain, Wolsey attracted the attention of young King Henry, who named him chancellor in 1515. In 1518 Leo X named Wolsey, who was already archbishop of York and a cardinal, *legatus a latere,* that is, the pope's representative, in the church provinces of both York and Canterbury. As chancellor and legate Wolsey held in his hands the combined powers of state and church, although King Henry VIII always played a very important role in determining policies.

Game for adventure in private life, Wolsey advocated an adventurous foreign policy for the realm. Working in alliance with his father-in-law, Ferdinand, Henry joined Pope Julius II's Holy League (1511), designed to force France out of Italy. He put pressure on France to divert its troops from Navarre, which Ferdinand

---

3 William Stubbs, *Seventeen Lectures on the Study of Medieval and Modern History,* 3rd ed. (London, 1900), pp. 300–1.

was invading. In 1513 Henry crossed the channel with his army, personally led the successful sieges of Thérouanne and Tournay, and took part in the battle of Guinegate. Wolsey managed the campaign efficiently and manipulated a truce with France in August 1514. Meanwhile James IV of Scotland took advantage of Henry's involvement in France to invade the north, but he died in the battle of Flodden.

The accession to the throne of France of the young Renaissance king Francis I in 1515 led to renewed antagonism between England and France and, naturally, a renewed entente between England and Spain. In 1516 Ferdinand died and in 1519 Emperor Maximilian died, so that their grandson Charles V became heir of all the Habsburg holdings. Now Wolsey maneuvered to make Henry the arbiter who would preside over the balance of power between the Habsburgs and Valois. Charles came to court Henry's favor in Kent before proceeding to his coronation at Aachen. Francis sought his friendship at the meeting on the Field of the Cloth of Gold in 1520, although Francis injured Henry's pride by throwing him in a wrestling match on that occasion. At a conference at Calais in 1521 Henry enjoyed his finest moment playing umpire in Europe. In 1522 and 1523 he sponsored another pointless and unpopular expedition into France, but the support he gave to Charles V upset the fine balance of power, and within a few years Charles came out on top and took Francis captive at Pavia (1525). Spanish fortunes rose to new heights, to the discomfiture of Henry, whose marriage to Charles V's aunt Catherine was beginning to cloy. Henry gradually came to view Wolsey's foreign policy with a more skeptical and finally jaundiced eye.

Wolsey's domestic difficulties were compounded by the economic consequences of his continental adventures. The economy was caught in a squeeze between a decline in the demand for wool (offset somewhat by an increase of textile production and export) and rising prices for commodities. In its incipient stages in the early 1520s, this economic condition became aggravated as the decade wore on. "Money is the sinew of war," said the ancients. Wolsey's cross-channel adventures had to be financed. In 1523 the chancellor found it necessary to summon parliament to ask for subsidies. Sir Thomas More was then the speaker of the House of Commons. Parliament refused to grant the money and Wolsey was reduced to making forced loans, which did not increase his popularity. In 1526 he resorted to recoinage and debasement to relieve the money situation.

As a churchman Cardinal Wolsey had splendid plans for reform. He dissolved some twenty-eight small and understaffed religious houses in order to divert their wealth to the founding of his own college at Oxford, which came later to be known as Christ Church, and to a new school at Ipswich. He could not personally provide much inspiration for reform, however, for he was himself a notorious example of one of the church's greatest abuses, the holding of multiple benefices. He was archbishop of York, bishop of Durham and Winchester, deputy for nonresident alien bishops at Worcester, Salisbury, and Llandaff, and abbott of St. Albans. He made his bastard son dean of Wells and archdeacon of York and Richmond, with two rectories, six prebends, and one appointment as chancellor. But at the same time Wolsey had his good personal qualities: he often protected people of no personal influence against the exploitation of the powerful, attempted to slow the enclosing of common lands, which was forcing the peasants off the land, and exhibited a good deal of tolerance for unorthodox opinions. While he was at the height of his power no one was burned for heresy.

Wolsey was finally undone through no real fault of his own, but because he was not able to obtain a papal annulment of King Henry's marriage. Catherine had had a number of children, but the only one who lived was a girl, Mary. With the exception of Queen Matilda, long before, whose reign had been disputed by Stephen, no queen had yet reigned in England. There was talk of a "divorce" as early as 1514, when relations with Ferdinand were strained. By 1526, when Catherine was forty-one and Mary ten, it was evident that Henry would have no male heir by Catherine. The peace of the realm appeared endangered, since peace depended on an orderly succession. Henry meanwhile had developed a regal passion for dark-eyed Anne Boleyn, one of the queen's ladies-in-waiting. But he was more concerned about the succession than with lust; plenty of outlets for that could be found at the court.

Wolsey undertook to secure from Pope Clement VII an annulment of Henry's marriage to Catherine. The grounds for the annulment were to be the laws of consanguinity, the same laws from which Pope Julius II had exempted them in order to make the marriage possible in the first place. According to Leviticus 18: 6–18, marriages were not to be contracted within five or even six degrees of relationship. Leviticus 20:21 reads: "If a man takes his brother's wife, it is impurity; he has uncovered his brother's nakedness; they shall be childless." Wolsey convinced Henry that Rome would grant the divorce, and at first Pope Clement was inclined to do so. Cardinal Campeggio was dispatched to England with the necessary power. Then suddenly things took a turn for the worse, for Charles V laid Francis low and in 1527 his troops stormed Rome. Under pressure from Charles, who was Catherine's nephew, the pope now refused to annul the marriage. When Campeggio was recalled from England and the case remanded to Rome, Henry had his marriage secretly dissolved by an English tribunal and Cardinal Wolsey fell.

Ironically, Wolsey was arrested under a writ of *praemunire,* accusing him of acting as a papal legate, a foreign agent. He died on the way to his trial, a broken man. The tragedy of his fall is perhaps best expressed by the lines Shakespeare gives him to speak in *Henry VIII:*

> Had I but serv'd my God with half the zeal
> I serv'd my king, he would not in mine age
> Have left me naked to mine enemies.

Popular Protest and Heresy

WOLSEY'S NAME served as a catalyst for an outpouring of anticlerical feeling among the masses. In the popular mind he symbolized the higher clergy's worldly disregard for spiritual values. For throughout England the level of religiosity was higher among the people than among the clergy—a paradoxical and potentially explosive situation. In time the forces of dissidence would have produced a crisis in religion even if King Henry's eyes had never lighted upon the daring décolletage of Anne Boleyn. A look at the church in any part of England reveals many people passionately devoted to religion. The parish church was the center of the people's religious and social life, and was tied in with the details of administration of the local community. To secure the welfare of their souls, people made bequests to provide ornamentation or additions to their beloved churches. But the more they loved the church, the more indignant they became at the obvious faults of the churchmen. This popular protest was predominantly secular or ethical rather than evangelical or theological.

A number of scandalous cases of clerical tyranny stirred up anger against the privileges of the clergy, clerical immunities, and the special ecclesiastical courts. The Convocation of the Clergy had the time-honored right to pass ecclesiastical (canon) laws and fix penalties independently of the will of king and parliament, even though these acts affected laymen. The ecclesiastical courts had jurisdiction over the probating of wills, and often charged excessive fees. The case of Richard Hunne, a London tailor, focused the public eye upon this scandalous situation. In the year 1514 Hunne was imprisoned on a charge of heresy in the Lollards' Tower at St. Paul's. He was found hanged from a beam in his prison cell. The investigating jury at the coroner's inquest leveled a murder charge against Bishop Richard Fitz-James' chancellor. The bishop promptly petitioned Cardinal Wolsey to remand the case to a special board of inquiry, for he was convinced that if the chancellor were to be tried by a jury of "any twelve men in London, they be so maliciously set in favour of heretical depravity that they will cast and condemn my clerk, though he were as innocent as Abel." A special board of inquiry was set up and the chancellor and his men were declared not guilty. It is quite possible that they were in fact innocent. At any rate, Sir Thomas More, who attended the inquiry, firmly believed that Hunne was a heretic who died in despair by his own hand. But the incident does illustrate the distrust of the laity felt by the higher clergy. And of course the special handling of the case added to the popular fury against the clerical class.

The Hunne case was a national scandal; more typical was the case of a butcher, James Hardcastell of Barwick-in-Elmet. The case involved elements of both heretical sentiment and personal hostilities within the parish. On September 24, 1540, a former curate of Barwick, Sir Thomas Mettringham, accused Hardcastell of saying that "there was nothing in the church that could do him good, and he would believe in none of them." There was some talk of burning. Later in the investigation, when Myles Walker, a priest, asked Hardcastell if he did not believe in the Blessed Sacrament of the Altar, the butcher replied, "Yes, marry, that do I believe in." With that he doffed his cap and declared that he had said what he had about the church "to prove what a drunken priest would say thereto."

Rabble-rousing agitators were ready to whip up a furor among the masses with incendiary tracts. Simon Fish, an Oxford student, joined a circle of young men in London who were extremely critical of the hierarchy, and especially of Cardinal Wolsey. A vicious anticlerical pamphleteer, he stirred up the populace against churchmen as early as 1529 by circulating his *Supplication of Beggars*. Dedicated to the king, the *Supplication* spewed out pure venom on the clergy.

Many expressions of anticlerical feeling in these early decades of the sixteenth century were very difficult to distinguish from vestigial remains of Lollardy and other forms of medieval dissent and heresy. By this time the meaning of the term Lollard had become so vague that it was applied quite arbitrarily to any undesirable. The court records, moreover, are not easily analyzed, for the charges and the evidence against the accused were presented in such a way that the defendants' beliefs appeared to conform to the definitions of heresy, so that they would stand little chance of escaping conviction and condemnation under traditional statutes. Evidence does suggest, however, that some Lollardy remained in the back country of Yorkshire, and a good deal in Kent.

The Lollards were followers of John Wycliffe (1320–1384), a sharp critic of the Roman church. While a lecturer at Oxford Wycliffe criticized the wealth and worldly power of the church, soon found fault with sacramental doctrine, and with his disciples undertook the translation of the Scriptures into English. Wycliffe commissioned his Poor Preachers, the Lollards, to bring the gospel into the highways and byways of England. The Council of Constance in 1415 declared Wycliffe's teachings to be heretical and demanded that his books and his body be burned. But Wycliffe died in bed because his English sovereigns were involved in a struggle with the Avignonese papacy and could exploit Wycliffe's ready pen for their own cause, and his ideas were not easily rooted out. Lollardy persisted in the midlands and home counties into the sixteenth century and gradually fused with other strains of anticlericalism and Protestantism. Most of the Lollards belonged to the lower middle and working classes. The key to the movement was the English translation of the Bible, circulated in thousands of manuscript copies, and with many passages ardently memorized and recited at secret meetings of Lollards. There seem to have been regular contacts between various groups of Lollards. The Lollards questioned the veneration of saints, the sacramental doctrine of transubstantiation, the value of pilgrimages, the necessity for confession to priests, and indeed the need for a priesthood at all.

Some ideas of the continental reformers were so similar to these heretical views of the Lollards that there was a natural fusion between them. The high theological treatises of the reformers seem to have had no direct impact on the lower-class Lollards. The Lollards lacked positions of power and could not have launched a reformation of their own. But they welcomed the new English editions of the Bible by Tyndale and Coverdale which were smuggled in from the continent, and they provided a ready audience for the Protestant message. Periodically Lollards would be brought to trial at episcopal courts. A few were burned at the stake during the reigns of Henry VII and Henry VIII, but the great majority of the accused recanted and were made to do penance by carrying a faggot as a reminder of the punishment that might have befallen them.

Erasmian Humanists and Early Protestants

JUST AS STRANDS of anticlericalism were woven tightly together with threads of medieval heresy among the common people, Erasmian humanism was intimately fused with proto-Protestantism among the learned. The name of Erasmus was associated with English humanism from his first visit to England in 1499. His Christian humanism, with its stress upon the Scriptures, upon the wisdom of the church fathers, upon right living, and above all upon moderation and toleration, had a tremendous impact on English intellectuals of both conservative and liberal leanings. The energetic translation of his works, especially during the critical third and fourth decades of the century, indicates that many intellectuals saw some special relevance of his ideas to English problems. One might argue, in fact, that the Erasmian *via media* was the real basis of the English religious settlement in the early years of Henry's son and successor, Edward VI, and the final resolution in the Elizabethan settlement under Henry's younger daughter, Elizabeth I. On the one hand, Erasmian humanism moderated the orthodoxy of the conservative episcopal party of Warham, Tunstall, Foxe, Longland, Pole, Gardiner, Thomas More, and John Fisher; on the other, it contributed to the repeated failure of dogmatic Protestantism to take deep root and helped to produce a generation of young moderates, such as Thomas Starkey and Richard Morison, to frame Tudor policy. In the widespread infusion of Erasmian humanism into Reformation thought, English developments were much closer to those on the continent than they have traditionally been portrayed.

Through the patronage of Italian humanists by Henry VII and Henry VIII, the crown had itself promoted humanist culture in the realm. Aristocratic patrons such as Lord Mountjoy, the pupil and patron of Erasmus, nurtured the movement further. The Erasmian program for reform and the mild moralism of Erasmus' *philosophia Christi* soon made converts, and an indigenous English movement developed. During the first three decades of the sixteenth century the English universities underwent profound changes. The influence of humanism at Cambridge and Oxford, particularly in extra-official teaching, was stronger than has been commonly supposed. At Cambridge, where Erasmus himself taught, the active humanist enterprise clearly began with the foundations of Lady Margaret Beaufort, mother of Henry VII, and Bishop John Fisher, Christ's College and St. John's. Two years before Luther's attack on indulgences, a student activist at Cambridge denounced Leo X's proclamation of indulgences, posted on the doors of the schools on orders from Bishop Fisher, the chancellor. Fisher excommunicated the boy and he fled to the continent. At Oxford Richard Foxe endowed Corpus Christi College and provided for public lectures in Greek.

The fusion of Christian humanism and Pauline theology in a single mind can be seen in that notable Oxford reformer John Colet. Colet made his break from Oxford in 1504 and became dean of St. Paul's in London. He was an avid student of Paul and an earnest reformer, and he inspired Erasmus to turn more seriously toward theology. In a famous sermon to the Convocation of the Clergy on the appointment of Archbishop Warham in 1512 he laid down a platform for reform. Colet cited St. Bernard's dictum that the wicked life of the clergy damages the church more than heretics. He called for the "reformation of the church's estate, because that nothing hath so disfigured the face of the church as hath the fashion of secular and worldly living in clerks and priests." He chastized the clergy for ambition and greed, criticized the large fees charged by ecclesiastical courts, the worldliness and pomp of the hierarchy, the ignorance of the regular clergy. He spoke so openly, he confessed, because of "very zeal" and as "a man sorrowing the decay of the church."

From reforming humanists such as John Colet to humanist reformers of evangelical conviction was but a short step. England's earliest Protestants were a race of martyrs, some dying at the hands of Henry VIII's ministers and others surviving to fall into the hands of Bloody Mary. In the preface to *The Flower of Godly Prayers* Thomas Becon paid them tribute:

> God, once again having pity on this realm of England, raised up His prophets, namely William Tyndale, Thomas Bilney, John Frith, Doctor [Robert] Barnes, Jerome [Barlowe], [Thomas] Garret, with divers others, which both with their writings and sermons earnestly labored to call us unto repentance that by this means the fierce wrath of God might be turned away from us. But how were they entreated? How were their painful labors regarded? They themselves were condemned and burnt as heretics, and their books condemned and burnt as heretical. O most unworthy act![4]

Although the ideas of Luther, Zwingli, and other continental reformers made little impression on the English masses, their tracts and pamphlets did infect the

---

[4] Cited in Marcus Loane, *Pioneers of the Reformation in England* (London, 1964), p. vi.

merchants who carried on their trade between the east coast and north Germany. Even in Devon and Cornwall the seaports showed signs of Protestant activity. But the critical development was the infiltration of Reformation ideas into the universities, where Lutheran pamphlets were circulated as early as 1519. In March 1521, only a few weeks before Luther made his stand at the Diet of Worms, Archbishop Warham, chancellor of Oxford, wrote to Cardinal Wolsey of subversive influences in the university. "I am informed," he warned, "that divers of the university be infected with the heresies of Luther and others of that sort, having a great number of books of the said perverse doctrine." Wolsey responded by ordering the burning of Lutheran books on Market Hill in Cambridge and at St. Paul's Church in London. There he had a new pulpit and a scaffold built. While John Fisher preached against Luther's "pernicious doctrine," Wolsey graced the platform with an assemblage of bishops and abbots to view the burning of basketsful of Luther's books. He was dressed, Protestants noted, in purple, like a "bloody antichrist."

King Henry VIII now threw the full weight of his theological erudition into the balance. He had written a treatise designed to refute Luther's ninety-five theses, which were known in England even before Erasmus sent a copy to Sir Thomas More on March 5, 1518. Now, enraged by Luther's treatise *On the Babylonian Captivity of the Church,* Henry wrote a defense of the seven sacraments, *Assertio septem sacramentorum,* dedicated to Leo X. Ever since he "knew of Luther's heresy in Germany," the king assured the pope, he "made it his study how to extirpate it." The authorship of the *Assertio* was doubted then and since. Some said John Fisher, Richard Pace, or even Cardinal Wolsey wrote it. In Germany some charged that Erasmus wrote it for the king, and in England some said that Erasmus wrote Luther's reply. "If only they would change sides," Erasmus sighed, "that is, if only the English suspected what the Germans suspect!" Luther was quite convinced that Edward Lee was the true author, but he declared that he would treat it as the king's, for either a fool wrote it or a fool let it go out under his name, so it was all the same. Henry, for his part, doubted that his book would bring the heresiarch to repentance, declaring: "Alas! The most greedy wolf of hell has surprised him, devoured and swallowed him down into the lowest part of his belly, where he lies half alive, and half in death. And whilst the pious Pastor calls him and bewails his loss, he belches out of the filthy mouth of the hellish wolf these foul inveighings which the ears of the whole flock do detest, disdain and abhor." On October 11, 1521, the pope conferred upon Henry the title *defensor fidei, defender* of the faith.

When in the year 1525 Johannes Bugenhagen, pastor of the city church in Wittenberg, addressed a letter to the English people urging them to accept Luther's teachings and not to be misled by slanders against him, he had some reason to hope for a positive response. In those same years a group of fifty or sixty scholars was meeting at the White Horse Inn in Cambridge, known as "Little Germany," to discuss the new evangelical theology of the continental reformers. This company included names prominent in the Protestant movement and martyrology, such as

Robert Barnes, John Frith, perhaps William Tyndale, Hugh Latimer, Thomas Bilney, Nicholas Ridley, John Bale, and John Foxe, the chronicler of their catastrophes. One converted another, as in the early days of Christianity. When in 1524 Latimer presented a denunciation of Melanchthon as his bachelor of divinity thesis, Bilney took him aside and persuaded him that evangelical theology was true. Foxe reported that it was through Tyndale that Frith "received into his heart the seed of the Gospel and sincere godliness." When Cardinal Wolsey recruited Cambridge scholars to man his new college at Oxford in 1526, six of the eight who went were reform-minded. The story of two of England's earliest Protestants, even briefly related, tells us volumes about the movement.

Robert Barnes was a stormy petrel, bold and reckless when he had the ear of a crowd, less daring when alone with antagonists who could exploit his fears and misgivings. His attempt at swift reform failed miserably. Barnes was not in the humanistic avant-garde, even though he and Erasmus were at Cambridge at the same time. While he did not know Greek and Hebrew, he did cite the Latin fathers, schoolmen, and canonists. On Christmas Eve of 1525 he preached a sermon containing heretical statements and twenty-five criticisms of the church. Cardinal Wolsey had his rooms in Cambridge searched for Lutheran books, but he had hidden them elsewhere. Barnes was taken to London, and on the advice of Bishops Gardiner and Foxe he renounced his preaching "against the worldliness of the church." His penance was to kneel during Bishop John Fisher's long sermon at St. Paul's on Sunday, February 11, 1526, and to carry a faggot in procession around the church. In 1528, under house arrest, he decided to flee, but first he wrote a letter to Wolsey, tipping him off as to where he had gone to drown himself, and another to the mayor, reporting that he would find a parchment sealed in wax on his body, advising all men to submit to Wolsey. Then, dressed in layman's clothes, he shipped out to Antwerp, and arrived eventually at Wittenberg.

At Wittenberg, Foxe relates, Barnes was "made strong in Christ and got favor with the learned in Christ," such as Luther, Melanchthon, and Bugenhagen. In 1531 the Wittenberg theologians sent him as their emissary to King Henry, whose chancellor, Thomas More, sought to arrest him as a heretic and apostate monk after his safe-conduct ran out. More charged him with selling the books of the heretics George Joye and William Tyndale as well as his own. Barnes escaped detection by shaving off his beard and disguising himself as a merchant. But finally he fell victim to the conservative reaction during Henry's last years, and was condemned to die for opposing Bishop Gardiner and Henry. He was burned at Smithfield on July 30, 1540. Allowed to speak while he prepared himself for his ordeal, he asked God's forgiveness for his sin and confessed his faith. "I trust in no good works that ever I did," he said, "but only in the death of Christ. I do not doubt but through him to inherit the kingdom of heaven." Thus died "St. Robert," as Luther called him fondly.

The most remarkable of England's earliest Protestants was clearly William

Tyndale, a man whose name will forever be associated with the English Bible. Born about 1495 in Gloucestershire, he took his M.A. at Oxford in 1515 and then studied at Cambridge. While serving as a tutor in Sir John Welsh's household at Little Sodbury, Tyndale encountered opposition to his preaching from local priests whose knowledge of the Bible was sketchy at best, and thus saw clearly the need to make the Scriptures available to the laity in their own language. He decided to do the translating himself, "because," he recounted later, "I had perceived by experience how that it was impossible to establish the lay people in any truth except the Scripture were plainly laid before their eyes in their mother tongue, that they might see the process, order and meaning of the text."[5] Once resolved, he set about laboriously to perfect the linguistic tools needed for the task. Turned down by the bishop of London, Cuthbert Tunstall, he received support from a rich cloth merchant in London named Humphrey Monmouth, a member of the Christian Brethren, a secret society of merchants influenced by Lutheranism and Lollardy. In 1524 he made a pilgrimage to meet Luther in Wittenberg, and his translation of the New Testament, based upon the Greek text of Erasmus, was greatly influenced by Luther's German version. He tried most conscientiously to render a faithful translation. "I call God to record," he wrote, "against the day we shall appear before our Lord Jesus, to give a reckoning of our doings, that I never altered one syllable of God's Word against my conscience: nor would this day, if all that is in the earth, whether it be pleasure or riches, might be given me." In 1525 he started publication of his work in Cologne, but had to flee to Protestant Worms, where he finished the job. Through the years, beginning in March 1526, copies of this and later editions, as well as the Pentateuch and other parts of the Old Testament, streamed into England despite all the frantic efforts of the authorities to dam the flow. At length Tyndale even found an English publisher, John Day, who was willing to publish his work. Day thought it a great joke to arouse his printers and apprentices each morning by calling out, "Arise, 'tis day!" But it was for heresy that he was eventually sought, during Mary's reign, and he too had to flee abroad.

In his later years Tyndale lived for the most part in the English house of the Merchant Adventurers at Antwerp, where he enjoyed immunity from arrest by Habsburg imperial officers. But in May 1535 a traitor named Henry Phillips, posing as a convert, tricked him into leaving the house. He was arrested and imprisoned in the castle of Vilvorde, near Brussels, where he languished for sixteen months before being brought to trial for heresy. On October 6, 1536, he was strangled at the stake and his body burned to ashes. His last words were said to have been: "Lord, open the king of England's eyes." The acerbic preacher known to posterity as "bilious John Bale" wrote of these early Protestant martyrs: "I think within this realm of England . . . the spirit of Elias was not at all asleep in good William

---

[5] A. G. Dickens, *The English Reformation* (London, 1964), p. 70.

Tyndale, Robert Barnes, and such other more whom Antichrist's violence hath sent hence in fire to heaven, as Elias went afore in the fiery chariot."[6]

Cromwell and the Reformation Parliament

WHEN DURING THE SUMMER of 1529 Henry VIII despaired of bringing Pope Clement VII to annul his marriage to Catherine, he turned from persuasion to menace. There was a fourteenth-century precedent for asserting English independence of papal domination. In 1351 the Statute of Provisors had been directed against papal authority within the realm, followed in 1353 by the Statute of Praemunire, which forbade appeals to Rome not sanctioned by the king. Henry saw the possibilities of using parliament to blackmail the pope into permitting him virtual independence from Rome and supremacy in his own land.

Wolsey had always feared Thomas More, but he recognized his abilities and his conservative bent, and recommended him as his successor as lord chancellor. The great seal was transferred to More on October 25, 1529, with nearly universal popular approval. In his initial address to parliament as speaker, More referred to Wolsey most bitterly as "the grete wether which is of late fallen as you all knowe." As a devout layman, More was speaking for all who felt the need for reform, and reform was to be the main concern of this parliament. But events now took a turn that left Thomas More himself in a desperately vulnerable position.

After Wolsey's fall the Cambridge theologian Thomas Cranmer suggested that Henry consult the universities on the question of his divorce, hoping for a consensus that would strengthen the king's case. The result of this inquiry proved disappointing, for even antipapal Wittenberg recognized the legitimacy of his marriage, and Luther later announced how mightily he was praying for Queen Catherine. It was now clear that strong legal measures had to be taken.

At the end of 1530 the king accused the clergy of having violated the Statute of Praemunire, as had Wolsey, and the Convocation of the Clergy agreed to pay over £100,000 rather than risk the loss of all church goods through confiscation. They were forced, moreover, to grant to the king the title of "singular protector, only and supreme lord, and as far as the law of Christ allows even supreme head of the English church and clergy." The House of Commons meanwhile passed a series of bills regulating the fees payable for probate, burials, and other services, and more drastic measures were on the way.

The mastermind behind all this critical legislation was a *parvenu* named Thomas Cromwell, soon to emerge as the strong man of the English Reformation.

---

[6] Cited in Loane, *Pioneers of the Reformation*, p. 48.

Cromwell's design was to exclude the pope from the realm and to deliver a centralized control to the king and parliament. Born around 1485 in Putney, he was the son of a roustabout brewer, fuller, and blacksmith. While still in his teens Cromwell set out to make his fortune, first as a French mercenary and then as a clerk for the Frescobaldi bankers in northern Italy. After two years or so he moved on to become an economic adviser to English merchants in the Netherlands, reporting on developments in the Antwerp market. An urbane man, with a knowledge of Latin and Italian literature, Cromwell approached practical affairs of state with a rationalistic Renaissance flair. He was inspired by Marsiglio of Padua's radical *Defensor pacis* rather than by Machiavelli's *Prince,* as Cardinal Reginald Pole later charged, and was schooled in the practical art of politics in the household of Wolsey himself. Wolsey used him to carry out the liquidation of the monasteries that he had marked for dissolution in the interest of his education fund. When Wolsey fell, Cromwell was visibly shaken. They say he even cried. But soon he dried his eyes and rode off to London to court the king's favor. He held minor offices, and by January 1531 he was sworn into the king's council. He worked on the king's finances and in 1534 became his principal secretary, extending his control to all of his majesty's business.

It is not true, as has often been alleged, that Cromwell attempted to make an absolute monarch of Henry. Schooled in the common law, Cromwell worked through the House of Commons, and thus the legislation of the Reformation Parliament (1529–1536) proved to be decisive. Thomas Cranmer was able to write to the Strassburg reformer Wolfgang Capito in 1537 that Cromwell "had himself done more than all others together in whatever had hitherto been effected respecting the reformation of religion and of the clergy." In five years the juridical reformation effected the complete transformation from papal supremacy over the church in England to royal supremacy over the Church of England.

Cromwell's drive to void the legislative independence of the church began with the Supplication of the Commons Against the Ordinaries, which cleverly combined restrictions on the power of the Convocation of the Clergy to pass ecclesiastical laws without the agreement of the Commons and attacks upon the arbitrary and unjust actions of the ecclesiastical courts, often unfair to the laity. The king spoke to the speaker of the House about his displeasure with the oath of obedience to the pope taken by prelates on their consecration. On May 15, 1532, the convocation adopted the Submission of the Clergy, appealing to the king for his protection against the Commons and giving him control over their legislative functions in return for his protection of their ecclesiastical courts. The next day Thomas More resigned as chancellor. Toward the end of the year an act suspending the payment of annates to Rome was passed, a threat that forced the pope to consecrate the king's candidate, Thomas Cranmer, as archbishop of Canterbury.

In March 1533 Cromwell secured the passage of the most decisive legislation of all, the Act in Restraint of Appeals. Its famous preamble read: "This realm of England is an Empire . . . governed by one Supreme Head and King having the dignity and royal estate of the imperial crown of the same, unto whom a body politic, compact of all sorts and degrees of people divided in terms and by name of spirituality and temporalty, be bounded and owe to bear, next to God, a natural and humble obedience." The act provided that matters involving the king's business were to go to the Upper House of Convocation, which had final jurisdiction without any recourse to appeals outside the realm—to Rome, for example.

One bit of royal business was daily growing more urgent. In January of 1533, nearly six years after Henry's secret divorce from Catherine, he had secretly married Anne Boleyn. Although he and Catherine had separated, the divorce had not been made public, and he was not certain its legality would be upheld. Now Anne was obviously pregnant, and the king needed to ensure the child's legitimacy before it was born if it was ever to be able to succeed him. With the passage of the Act in Restraint of Appeals, Archbishop Cranmer could pronounce the divorce from Catherine and the marriage to Anne valid. In June Anne was crowned queen, and a few days later Henry was excommunicated by the pope. By this time the country was disinterested in papal actions, and Henry boasted that he would not care a straw if the pope promulgated ten thousand excommunications. In September Princess Elizabeth was born. Parliament then obligingly passed the Act of Succession, which established the heirs of Henry and Anne as legitimate successors to the crown. All subjects were required to swear an oath in support of this act. Later in 1534 the Act of Supremacy fully defined the royal headship over the church and authorized royal visitations. The Treason Act of November 1534, designed to protect his majesty and his loving family from subversive opposition, completed the legislative breastworks of the national church and the house of Tudor.

The resistance to Henry's ecclesiastical revolution from the top was surprisingly small, but two prominent martyrs were offered up as token sacrifices: a clergyman, Bishop John Fisher, and a devout layman, Sir Thomas More, who had once considered entering the monastic life and wore a hair shirt to humble his flesh. Fisher and More were unable in good conscience to swear the oath required by the Act of Supremacy, for in effect it repudiated the authority of the pope. Fisher had already been imprisoned for alleged collusion with the so-called Nun of Kent, who had prophesied Henry's perdition for marrying Anne. Now Fisher and More were taken to the Tower and held there for more than a year before being brought to trial. Fisher was marked for the martyr's red when Pope Paul III bestowed on him the cardinal's red. Henry is reported to have sneered, "Well, let the pope send him a hat when he will; but I will provide that whensoever it cometh, he shall wear it on his shoulders, for head he shall have none to set it on." On June 22, 1535, Fisher was beheaded.

Sir Thomas More earned his sainthood by resisting all temptations to yield.

His second wife urged him to think of all the preferments and comforts of life he could enjoy by acknowledging the king's religious supremacy, a temptation he easily rejected. His daughter urged him to consider that he was pitting his single opinion against that of many churchmen who had denied the papal primacy, and that he had turned against his own king, an argument that sorely tried his conscience. "Daughter," responded More firmly, "I never intend to pin my soul to another man's back!" He had a great fear that under the laws of treason he might be disemboweled, not merely beheaded. In prison More, who had been a harsh polemicist against Tyndale and the Protestants, wrote beautiful nonpolitical religious treatises, such as his *Dialogue of Comfort Against Tribulation*. More managed to retain his dry humor to the end. His son-in-law Roper, though he was not present himself, relates that when More mounted the scaffold he said, "I pray you, Master Lieutenant, see me safe up, and for my coming down let me shift for myself." He is said to have asked the executioner to spare his beard, for it had committed no treason. In contrast to More, Reginald Pole chose exile, and was rewarded in due course with a cardinalate.

In February 1536 the Reformation Parliament received reports on the monasteries from Cromwell's inspectors and passed the first Act of Dissolution. Economic necessity combined with religious motives and the anticlerical spirit of the Commons to bring Henry to undertake the suppression of the monasteries. By the act of 1536 parliament suppressed the smaller houses that had incomes of less than £200. The larger monasteries surrendered to the king, most of them under duress; the last to submit was Waltham Abbey in Essex, which capitulated on March 23, 1540. The monasteries were really in much better moral condition than Cromwell's propaganda and later historians supposed. Some orders, such as the Carthusians, had high morale and an exemplary record. They even provided some martyrs to Henry, including the prior of the London Charterhouse. In 1539 the abbots of Glastonbury, Reading, and Colchester were hanged, but they were victims of circumstances rather than heroes or willing martyrs. The monasteries were closed more for expediency than for principle, although even these spoils, which increased the crown's annual income by more than £100,000 by the 1540s, did not provide resources adequate for Henry's needs. With the dissolution of the monasteries the shock troops of the old church were gone, and there could never be a return to things as they had once been.

The monastic lands that passed into the hands of the gentry contributed to the further rise of this class and its participation in national government, while on a lower level the enriched squires increasingly dominated local government. The revenue from the sale of lands and other properties went as pensions to some former monks and nuns, to endow new sees, to support new schools and colleges, and to enrich the king's purse.

The dissolution contributed to a disaffection among the masses which led to the group of uprisings known collectively as the Pilgrimage of Grace. It is difficult to say precisely to what extent the four uprisings were anti-Reformation in character. For in the Lincolnshire rebellion, in the main pilgrimage under Robert Aske in Yorkshire, Lancashire, and the northeastern counties, and in two separate Yorkshire rebellions between October 1536 and January 1537, many bitter local and economic grievances were mixed with religious conservatism, irrational superstitions, and even apocalyptic elements. The pilgrimage can hardly be considered a desperate crusade to confound the heretics, reestablish the monasteries, or restore the papal dominion. The rebellions were easily suppressed.

The Emergence of Anglicanism

THE RENOWNED BRITISH HISTORIAN Thomas Babington Macaulay described the Church of England as "the fruit of the union" between the government and the Protestants, the result of compromise by both parties to its conception. The alliance of the crown and the Protestants was an uneasy one, marked by periods of tension and regression. Henry VIII seems to have believed it possible to dissolve the ties to Rome without changing the doctrine and worship of the church. He remained personally conservative in theology, and from 1532 to 1540 he was caught between the radical group, led by Cromwell and Cranmer, and the conservative group, headed by the duke of Norfolk and Stephen Gardiner, bishop of Winchester. At first the radicals and then, after Cromwell's fall in 1540, the conservatives had their day at court. Henry strove to preside over the rival factions, much as his daughter Elizabeth was to maintain a position above the Anglican and Puritan parties later in the century. As a result, the Reformation followed the comprehensive *via media* in England as it did nowhere else on the continent, except perhaps in Sweden.

The "middle way" of Anglicanism was comprehensive territorially, for it embraced all the inhabitants of the realm except for a few diehard Catholics, who were very much in hiding, and doctrinally, for it sought to include both the conservatives and as many of the radicals as could be accommodated without public scandal and offense. One of the most representative statements pleading for the middle way was the treatise of Thomas Starkey, *An Exhortation to Unity and Obedience*. Starkey, an Erasmian humanist and formerly a member of Reginald Pole's Padua circle, argued that all citizens were bound by God's law and by all good civility to embrace the middle way between "superstition" on the one hand and division, controversy, and sedition on the other. He employed Melanchthon's teaching on *adiaphora,* or things indifferent, to urge that matters of belief or practice that are not specifically defined in the Scriptures and not essential to salvation should not be made binding upon consciences or insisted upon as necessary to orthodoxy. This idea proved to be a seed of toleration that bore fruit in due course. Ironically, however, the *adiaphora* concept was double-edged, for later on, in Elizabeth's reign, instead of leading to a tolerant, comprehensive Anglicanism, the doctrine was used to justify the retention of the episcopal hierarchy, the ceremonial rubrics, and the like, which were then backed up by enforced conformity and submission. In this and other ways Starkey, Richard Morison, and other young humanists contributed to the ideological foundations of Tudor policy.

Even the conservatives had a lofty notion of the divine right of kings, related to the ancient concept of thaumaturgical or sacramental kingship. Stephen Gardiner, for example, in his *On True Obedience* (1535), was close to Marsiglio of Padua in his conception of the obedience owed by true Christians to the king as God's representative on earth, a father to his children and a master to his servants. Since the king and parliament had decreed that the English people should be separated from Rome, all should obey, for theirs was the rightful authority. Poor Gardiner was hard pressed to explain away this book when Catholic Queen Mary ascended the throne. His lame explanation then was that he had written it out of fear that he would suffer the fate of Fisher and More.

The leading role in religious reform was played by Thomas Cranmer (1489–1556), a complex personality of gentle birth, with a kindly disposition and a mind open to change, though he was no great creative thinker or very forceful leader. As a fellow at Jesus College he took priest's orders, earned the degree of doctor of divinity, and seemed headed for the life of a scholar until the king's business intervened. After several missions for the king to the Lutherans, among whom he met and married the niece of Osiander, the reformer in Nuremberg, and to the emperor in Vienna and northern Italy, he was made archbishop of Canterbury in 1533, with the expectation that he would be the king's pliant instrument. With the enthusiastic support of Cromwell, Cranmer promoted the publication of the English Bible and the introduction of an English litany. He received royal permission for the publication of Matthew's Bible in 1537. The text was basically Tyndale's and the polemical notes proved to be so offensive that Miles Coverdale was asked to revise it. This Great Bible appeared upon the lecterns in 1539 and proved to be the surest foundation for the building of Protestantism. Cranmer's theological views moved by gradual stages from a position close to Luther's, on the sacrament, for example, to Swiss interpretations close to those of Oecolampadius. He moved slowly and deliberately in the direction of less conservative Protestant convictions. He was one of the more dependable of Cromwell's partisans.

Cromwell's overthrow by Norfolk and Gardiner was due to his hapless selection of Anne of Cleves, the "Flemish mare," for Henry's fourth sally into matrimony, as well as to his failure to check a dangerous deterioration in the political and religious situation. Anne Boleyn fared no better than Queen Catherine, for she too produced a daughter and no male heir to the throne. She was beheaded for adultery in 1536, the same year that Catherine died. Henry then married colorless Jane Seymour, who gave birth to Edward VI and died in 1537. Henry made some approaches toward the Protestants in authorizing the English Bible and accepting the Ten Articles, which mentioned only three of the seven sacraments, although they did not formally abolish or deny the other four. Fearing a hostile combination of Charles V and Francis I against England, Henry followed Cromwell's diplomatic maneuvering for allies among the German Protestant states, and thus became ensnared in the marriage with Anne, daughter of the Erasmian duke of Cleves. When the Franco-Spanish crusade against England proved to be fictitious and Anne proved to be all too repugnant a reality for Henry, the king reacted by divorcing her and beheading Cromwell on July 28, 1540.

The triumph of the conservative party under Norfolk and Gardiner was celebrated by Henry's marriage to Catherine Howard. The very Catholic Six Articles (May 16, 1539) were intended to restore basic Catholic teachings on transubstantiation, communion in one kind, the celibacy of the clergy, vows of chastity, private masses, and compulsory auricular confessions. The punishments prescribed for violations were so savage that the articles were known as the "whip with the six bloody strings." Spasmodic outbursts of persecution claimed the lives of Protestant martyrs, but the conservatives failed to dislodge Cranmer from his position as archbishop of Canterbury. Luckless Henry sent Catherine Howard to the block for adultery in 1542, and in his final years found solace in the learned company of Catherine Parr, the only one of his six wives to survive him. He died on January 27, 1547, ministered to by Cranmer, in whom he trusted to the very end. In his will, however, Henry provided that many masses were to be said for his soul.

The Edwardian Reformation

UPON THE ACCESSION of Henry's son, Edward VI (1537–1553), the prophets of doom again intoned one of their favorite texts, "Woe to the land whose king is a boy!" Even though Holbein's portrait of Edward at the age of two shows him as a healthy child, he was really very frail and was never expected to live many years. His childhood was plagued by tutors such as Roger Ascham, who schooled him so thoroughly in Latin and Greek, as well as French, that by the age of thirteen he was able to read Aristotle's *Ethics* in Greek and to translate Cicero's *De philosophia* into Greek. All factions sought to control him in their struggle for power. During his first three years as king real power was in the hands of his uncle, the handsome, affable, sincere Protestant Edward Seymour, earl of Hertford, who took the title duke of Somerset and was known as Protector Somerset. During Edward's remaining years that crafty intriguer John Dudley, earl of Warwick, who became duke of Northumberland, dominated him. The course of the Reformation under Edward VI was determined primarily by social and domestic considerations rather than by issues of foreign policy.

A few hours after nine-year-old Edward was proclaimed king, the council voted Hertford protector. After a few weeks the protector received a patent that enabled him to act with great personal power. He nevertheless proceeded with considerable moderation, and Cranmer, who now enjoyed more freedom of action than he had for years, proceeded to promote Protestantism with surprising restraint. In a session of parliament the new government indulged in what has been called a "self-denying orgy," rescinding Henry's harsh additions to the old treason laws, repealing the Six Articles Act, removing all restrictions on the printing, sale, and expounding of the Bible, and annulling the act that gave royal proclamations the force of law.

In a move that affected the life of the people more directly than the dissolution of the monasteries had done, Edward's first parliament passed a new chantries act, which transferred to the crown all chantries, which were essentially endowments for masses for the souls of the dead, and all free chapels, colleges, fraternities, and guilds. This broad-scale secularization reached into the life of nearly every parish. It coincided with the Protestant rejection of intercession for the souls of the dead in purgatory. It contributed to a reshuffling of wealth in many communities, and brought into question the motives of some Protestants, including the protector, who displayed an inordinate interest in the building of his great house. But even these new resources failed to meet the needs of the royal treasury.

Further religious change came about with official blessing and on the popular level, although it is safe to say that only a minority of the people had real Protestant convictions during Edward's reign. Cranmer's *First Prayer Book* was a brilliant piece of studied ambiguity, sufficiently traditional in form to pacify the Henrician Catholics—although in English, of course—and yet so phrased, even in respect to the Eucharist, as to allow its use in good conscience by the Protestants. An act of uniformity provided sufficiently severe penalties to ensure use of the prayerbook by all the clergy. Calvinism had begun to make inroads during Henry's last years, and Protestant propaganda became even more strident and insistent during the reign of King Edward.

Somerset fell to his enemies in October 1549, helpless before the social, political, and religious unrest, having at the outset given away many instruments of strong government he now desperately needed. By skillful maneuvering the earl of Warwick gathered the dissident forces about him, and the council sent Somerset to the Tower and to eventual execution in 1552. The price of failure in Tudor politics was often death. Warwick, who adopted the title of duke of Northumberland in 1551, was thoroughly unscrupulous. Having deceived the Catholic faction into supporting him, he proceeded to promote the Reformation more radically than Somerset had ever done.

From his initial suggestion early in his career that Henry consult the universities about his "great question," Cranmer had been concerned with England's ties to continental Protestantism. He invited Melanchthon to England, and though the Wittenberg reformer could not accept, other Protestant leaders came in a steady stream from Strassburg, Zurich, and Geneva. The most notable among them was Martin Bucer of Strassburg, the charitable mediating theologian, forced out of his home city by the Interim imposed by Emperor Charles V. Bucer arrived in 1549 and through Cranmer's influence was given the regius chair at Cambridge. He finished writing his *On the Kingdom of Christ* there and contributed to the second Edwardian prayerbook, but his strength was spent and he died in February 1551. In the fall of 1548 the Polish nobleman John à Lasco arrived and consulted with Cranmer. In 1550 he returned from Friesland to become superintendent over four ministers to foreign Protestants. Holding an amalgam of Calvinist and Zwinglian views, Lasco developed a refugee congregation of some five thousand members along Puritan lines, with rule by elected presbyters or elders, rigorously enforced church discipline, and an emphasis upon edification (two-hour sermons) and the Christian life. Two Italian refugees came to England for a time by way of Strassburg, Peter Martyr Vermigli and Bernardino Ochino, as well as a militant Protestant from Scotland, the rambunctious John Knox. The radical Anabaptists, however, were as unwelcome in England as they were elsewhere.

The Edwardian bishops who shouldered the main burden of the Anglican reform covered a somewhat narrower spectrum, from the Puritan-like John Hooper to the more main-line Nicholas Ridley of Rochester and London. Clerical marriage was a subject of considerable controversy. A statute of February 1549 permitted the clergy to marry, and those who did so generally suffered little or no unfavorable reaction from the public, which as usual resolved the problem by condemning the women involved; prejudice against the wives of bishops and priests lasted into and beyond the Elizabethan period. With the introduction of a more distinct Protestant liturgy, the government felt justified in confiscating church plate, vestments, and other valuables. But Northumberland was building up a deep black pool of ill will that was soon to engulf him.

Edward's health began to fail markedly in 1552, and by May 1553 everyone realized that the king was dying, though he did not oblige until July 6. Intent upon securing his personal domination of the government, Northumberland married his son to the sixteen-year-old Lady Jane Grey, grandniece of Henry VIII and a Protestant, and then persuaded Edward to name Jane as his successor in place of his older sister Mary, who was Catholic. But when Edward died, Northumberland committed a fatal blunder in not having Mary in a secure prison. She slipped away to

East Anglia, and the people rallied around her as the heiress designated in law by Henry. Lady Jane, appalled at finding herself queen, reigned just nine days before she and her young husband were imprisoned for treason. Northumberland too was committed to the Tower, and right up to the day of his execution he made frantic last-minute efforts to save his skin by admonishing everyone within earshot to eschew heresy and embrace the Catholic religion. But he could save neither himself, his son, nor Lady Jane. Eventually all three were beheaded.

The Marian Reaction

QUEEN MARY was a high-spirited woman with more than her share of Tudor obstinacy. Her entire life was tragic. When she was still an infant she was used as a pawn in the marriage designs of Francis I and then of Charles V. Her own father had forced her to acknowledge herself a bastard, though later, in the Act of Succession, he had made a place for her as successor to Edward. As the daughter of a Spanish princess, she was brought up an ardent and narrow Catholic. Worse still for her political prospects, she thought of herself not as English, but as Spanish. She further alienated the English by marrying her cousin Philip II, the king of Spain, instead of a sturdy Englishman. In her persecution of heretics, Mary was not inherently cruel, merely fanatical. History has done her an injustice by tagging her with the sobriquet "Bloody Mary."

No sooner was Mary acclaimed queen than she turned Edward's Protestant officials out and returned to office Bishops Gardiner, Tunstall, Heath, Bonner, and Day. Cardinal Reginald Pole came as papal legate to absolve the kingdom of disobedience to the Holy See, and for so renowned a Christian humanist he proved to be a severe and uncompromising leader of reaction. When Mary announced her intention of marrying Philip of Spain, British national resentment ran high. The Commons sent a deputation to beg her not to marry a foreigner, and a series of insurrections broke out. The most serious threat was the rebellion led by young Sir Thomas Wyatt, who stirred up the county of Kent with hatred for the Spaniard and led some four thousand men to the gates of London before he was repulsed. It was this rebellion that determined Mary to have Lady Jane Grey's head. Up till then, though Lady Jane remained in prison, her hopes for a pardon were not unrealistic. Now Mary saw that as long as a Protestant contender for the throne, however unwilling, remained alive, there would be men who would try to put her there. After Wyatt's failure, Mary's second parliament revoked all statutes that had been enacted against papal authority since 1529.

Mary's marriage to Philip was a disappointment all around, and it eventually became clear that she would not succeed in having children by him. Embittered, all but ignored by her husband, she then turned to the suppression of Protestantism. Many prominent Protestant divines were imprisoned: John Rogers, Hugh Latimer, Nicholas Ridley, John Hooper, Miles Coverdale, and others. John Foxe in his *Book of Martyrs* recorded the lurid details of the executions and the courage of those who were ready to die for the faith by which they had lived. Dour Hurrell Froude once remarked that the best that was to be said of the reformers was that they burned well. John Rogers, editor of Matthew's Bible, was the first to go, burned on February 4, 1555. Hugh Latimer, formerly bishop of Worcester and a great Reformation preacher, was led with Ridley to the stake in the great ditch opposite Balliol College, Oxford. Latimer, a man of humility and moderation, died like a saint. He cheered Ridley with the heroic words: "Be of good comfort, Master Ridley, and play the man; we shall this day light such a candle by God's grace in England as (I trust) shall never be put out." He "received the flame," the martyrology recounts, "as it were embracing it. After he had stroked his face with his hands, and (as it were) bathed them a little in the fire, he soon died (as it appeared) with very little pain or none." A recent list numbers the victims of Mary's persecution at 282. Many of those burned for heresy were lowborn artisans; the rich bought their way clear. Some lucky Protestants were merely jailed or flogged. Edmund Bonner, bishop of London, answered a critic who had chided him for having an old man whipped in a "pelting chafe": "If thou hadst been in his case, thou wouldst have thought it a good commutation of penance to have thy bum beaten to save thy body from burning."

Thomas Cranmer was now put to the ultimate test. Philip and Mary requested that his case be reserved for papal disposition. He was ordered to appear in Rome within eighty days, but his trial was finally held in the university church of St. Mary the Virgin at Oxford. Pope Paul IV's representative, Bishop Brooks, sat on a platform ten feet high before the altar, while the royal prosecutors below charged Cranmer with blasphemy, incontinency, and heresy. Found guilty, he was stripped of his insignia of office in a humiliating ceremony and condemned to death. After his degradation, Cranmer, desperately afraid of the fire awaiting him, signed seven submissions and recantations. But the authorities were adamant: he must burn. On March 21, 1556, he was placed on a stage opposite the pulpit in St. Mary's. There he stood, the "very image and shape of perfect sorrow," with tears streaming down his cheeks. When it was his turn to speak he exhorted all men to true obedience toward rulers and to love toward all men. Then he astonished everyone present by reading a recantation of all his recantations:

> And now I come to the great thing, that so much troubleth my conscience, more than anything that ever I did or said in my whole life; and this is the setting abroad of a writing contrary to the Truth; which now here I renounce and refuse, as things written with my hand, contrary to the truth which I thought in my heart, and written for fear of death, and to save my life, if it might be; and that is, all such bills

and papers which I have written or signed with my own hand since my degradation; wherein I have written many things untrue and forasmuch as my hand offended, writing contrary to my heart, my hand shall first be punished therefore; for, may I come to the fire, it shall be first burned.[7]

Then he denounced the pope and acknowledged his own book on the Sacrament as representing his true belief. Cranmer was pulled off the stage, dragged to the ditch where Latimer and Ridley had died, and burned. The martyrologist recounts:

> When the wood was kindled and the fire began to burn near him, stretching out his arm, he put his right hand into the flame, which he held so steadfast and immovable (saving that once with the same hand he wiped his face) that all men might see his hand burned before his body was touched. . . . Using often the words of Stephen, Lord Jesus receive my spirit; in the greatness of the flame he gave up the ghost.

Although the conservative north and west seemed to support Mary quite strongly, the Protestant underground maintained itself in London and elsewhere. Reginald Pole was not a forward-looking leader; he rejected, for example, Ignatius Loyola's offer to train seminarians as ideological shock troops. Mary's Catholic restoration had a backward-looking, medieval, even monastic cast to it, and did not realistically take into consideration the fact that England had undergone fundamental changes in outlook. All the portents pointed toward evil days during the final months of Mary's reign. As the childless queen maneuvered to perpetuate her will in religious matters, nature intervened with disease and pestilence to decimate the number of bishops and lesser ecclesiasts. The Marian exiles were waiting on the continent to fill the vacancies. But Mary died in the early morning hours of November 17, 1558, and her strong man, Archbishop Reginald Pole, died in his sleep just twelve hours later. Young Queen Elizabeth, who succeeded her, was "pure English," and her succession to the throne was greeted with bonfires and revelry in London and throughout the realm.

The Reformation in Scotland

THE SCOTTISH REFORMATION was a Johnny-come-lately in the Reformation movement. By 1560 over four decades had passed since Luther initiated the Reformation and nearly a generation since Henry VIII broke with the pope. An act of parliament in 1525 forbade the importation of Lutheran books into Scotland, but they continued to come in through port towns. The burning of Patrick Hamilton for evangelical preaching in 1528 precipitated a number of executions and iconoclastic

---

[7] F. E. Hutchinson, *Cranmer and the Reformation* (London, 1951), p. 157.

incidents. Cardinal Beaton burned the bold evangelist George Wishart at St. Andrews in 1546 and was himself waylaid and murdered three months later in his own castle at St. Andrews. Much animosity built up before the dam burst in Scotland.

The direction in which Scotland moved was of vital importance to British and European history. A Protestant Scotland would mean a rapprochement with Protestant England. A Catholic Scotland meant a continuation of the alliance with France and intermittent hostilities with England. Scotland was relatively backward economically and was dominated locally by clans of lesser nobility. Certainly there can be no talk of a middle class inclined toward Protestantism or of Protestantism as an expression of class interest, giving impetus to the rise of capitalism. Rather there was a strong current of protest against the ignorance and lewdness of the secular clergy during the decades preceding the critical year 1560. The monks seem to have played little part, either as objects of scorn or as leaders of reform, although the canons regular were a constructive force.

The hero of the Scottish Reformation was the "thundering Scot" John Knox (1513–1572), a strong, stocky, swarthy priest of peasant lineage, who stood guard with a two-edged sword while Wishart preached. After Wishart's death Knox joined the Protestant garrison defending the castle at St. Andrews against French troops determined to preserve the power and the religion of their countrywoman Mary of Guise, widow of James V of Scotland and regent for their young daughter, Mary, queen of Scots. In August 1547 the French captured the defenders of St. Andrews, and for nineteen months Knox was forced to work as a galley slave, chained to a rowing bench, which was his only shelter from the weather. He finally reached England in April 1549, no little embittered against the Catholic French. When King Edward died, Knox fled to Calvin's Geneva. In 1556 he wrote to a Mrs. Locke of his new spiritual haven, "whair I nether feir nor schame to say is the nearest perfyt school of Chryst that ever was in the erth since the dayis of the Apostillis."

In 1559 the Scottish Protestants sent a delegation to Geneva to urge Knox to come home. Calvin declared that Knox must heed the call "unless he would declare himself rebellious unto his God and unmerciful to his country." Knox had attacked Catholic Mary of Guise, calling her an "unruly cow saddled by mistake." In 1558 he had published his *First Blast Against the Monstrous Regiment of Women,* declaring that to "promote a woman to have rule above any realm is repugnant to nature, contumely to God, a thing most contrarious to His revealed will and approved ordinance, and finally it is the subversion of good order, of all equity and justice." Now Knox returned to Scotland, and the English sent an army to help the Protestants drive out the French. Mary of Guise died during the war, and the Treaty of Edinburgh, July 6, 1560, assured the triumph of Protestantism. An act of parliament on August 24 outlawed Catholicism in the land.

John Knox preached in St. Giles' Cathedral with great energy. His student

James Melville related how Knox in the pulpit "behoved to lean at his first entry; but ere he had done with his sermon, he was so active and vigorous that he was like to ding that pulpit in blads [pieces] and fly out of it." When he lectured on the prophet Daniel, Knox made Melville shudder and tremble so much that he "could not hold a pen to write." Knox's Calvinist Presbyterianism is reflected in each of the three basic documents of the Scottish Reformation, the *Confession of Faith,* the *Book of Common Order,* and the *First Book of Discipline.* Knox also impressed his image of what had transpired upon posterity with his *History of the Reformation in Scotland.*

In 1561 Mary, queen of Scots, age eighteen, returned from France on the death of her husband, King Francis II. At first conciliatory, she reverted to a hard line against the Protestants, and was forced to flee to England in 1567. The triumph of Knox and the Reformation was astonishing for both its suddenness and its durability. Watching the outcome of the struggle from Geneva, John Calvin commented, "As we wonder at success incredible in so short a time, so also we give great thanks to God, whose special blessing here shines forth."

Bibliography

The Reformation in England:
CHILD, G. W. *Church and State Under the Tudors.* London, 1950.
DICKENS, A. G. *Lollards and Protestants in the Diocese of York.* Oxford, 1959.
———. *The English Reformation.* London, 1964.
GAIRDNER, JAMES. *Lollardy and the Reformation in England,* 4 vols. London, 1908–1913.
GASQUET, F. A. *The Eve of the Reformation.* London, 1900.
GEORGE, CHARLES, and GEORGE, CATHERINE. *The Protestant Mind of the English Reformation.* Princeton, 1961.
HUGHES, PHILIP. *The Reformation in England,* 3 vols. London, 1950–1954.
KNOWLES, DOM DAVID. *The Religious Orders in England,* 3 vols. Cambridge, 1948–1959.
LOANE, MARCUS. *Masters of the English Reformation.* London, 1954.
McCONICA, JAMES K. *English Humanists and Reformation Politics under Henry VIII and Edward VI.* Oxford, 1965.
MAITLAND, S. R. *The Reformation in England.* London and New York, 1906.
PARKER, T. H. L., ed. *English Reformers,* vol. 26 of *Library of Christian Classics.* Philadelphia, 1966.
PARKER, T. M. *The English Reformation to 1558.* New York, 1950.
POWICKE, MAURICE. *The Reformation in England.* New York, 1941.
THOMPSON, A. H. *The English Clergy and Their Organization in the Later Middle Ages.* Oxford, 1947.
WOODWARD, GEORGE. *Reformation and Resurgence, 1485–1603.* London, 1963.

Henry VIII:
BAUMER, F. L. *Early Tudor Theory of Kingship.* New Haven, 1940.
CONSTANT, G. *The Reformation in England: Henry VIII, 1509–1547.* New York, 1934.

DOERNBERG, ERWIN. *Henry VIII and Luther*. Stanford, 1961.
ELTON, G. R. *England Under the Tudors*. London, 1955.
――――. *The Tudor Revolution in Government: Administrative Changes in the Reign of Henry VIII*. Cambridge, 1962.
INNES, A. D. *England Under the Tudors*, 9th ed. London, 1929.
JACOBS, H. E. *The Lutheran Movement in England During the Reigns of Henry VIII and Edward VI*. Philadelphia, 1894.
MACKIE, J. D. *The Earlier Tudors, 1485–1558*. Oxford, 1952.
MATTINGLY, GARRETT. *Catherine of Aragon*. Boston, 1941.
PICKTHORN, K. *Early Tudor Government*. Cambridge, 1934.
POLLARD, A. F. *Henry VIII*. London, 1913.
――――. *Wolsey*. London, 1929.
READ, CONYERS. *The Tudors*. New York, 1936.
SCARISBRICK, J. J. *Henry VIII*. Berkeley, 1968.
SMITH, HERBERT M. *Henry VIII and the Reformation*. London, 1948.
SMITH, LACEY BALDWIN. *Tudor Prelates and Politics*. Princeton, 1953.
TJERNAGEL, NEELAK. *Henry VIII and the Lutherans*. St. Louis, 1966.
ZEEVELDT, W. G. *Foundations of Tudor Policy*. Cambridge, Mass., 1948.

Cranmer and other churchmen:
BROMILEY, G. W. *Baptism and the Anglican Reformers*. London, 1953.
――――. *Thomas Cranmer, Theologian*. New York and London, 1956.
BROOKS, PETER. *Thomas Cranmer's Doctrine of the Eucharist*. London, 1965.
CHESTER, ALLAN G. *Hugh Latimer, Apostle to the English*. Philadelphia, 1954.
CLARK, FRANCIS, S. J. *Eucharistic Sacrifice and the Reformation*. Westminster, Md., 1960.
CLEBSCH, WILLIAM A. *England's Earliest Protestants, 1520–1535*. New Haven, 1964.
DUFFIELD, G. E., ed. *The Work of William Tyndale*. Philadelphia, 1965.
DUGMORE, C. W. *The Mass and the English Reformers*. New York, 1948.
HUTCHINSON, FRANCIS E. *Cranmer and the English Reformation*. New York, 1951.
MAYNARD, THEODORE. *The Life of Thomas Cranmer*. Chicago, 1956.
MEYER, CARL S., ed. *Cranmer's Selected Writings*. Greenwich, Conn., 1961.
MOZLEY, J. F. *William Tyndale*. London, 1937.
PERRY, E. W. *Under Four Tudors*. London, 1940.
POLLARD, A. F. *Thomas Cranmer and the English Reformation, 1489–1556*. New York, 1904.
RICHARDSON, CYRIL C. *Zwingli and Cranmer on the Eucharist*. Evanston, Ill., 1949.
RIDLEY, JASPER G. *Nicholas Ridley: A Biography*. London, 1957.
――――. *Thomas Cranmer*. Oxford, 1962.
RUPP, E. GORDON. *Six Makers of English Religion, 1500–1700*. New York, 1957.
SMYTH, C. H. *Cranmer and the Reformation Under Edward VI*. Cambridge, 1926.
WILLOUGHBY, H. R. *The First Authorized English Bible and the Cranmer Preface*. Chicago, 1942.

Edward VI:
CHAPMAN, HESTER W. *Last Tudor King: A Study of Edward VI*. New York, 1959.
JORDAN, WILBUR K. *Edward VI: The Young King*. Cambridge, Mass., 1968.
POLLARD, A. F. *The History of England from the Accession of Edward VI to the Death of Elizabeth (1547–1603)*. London, 1910.

PRIMUS, JOHN HENRY. *The Vestments Controversy*. Kampen, 1960.

Mary Tudor:
GARRET, CHRISTINA H. *The Marian Exiles*. Cambridge, 1938.
HARBISON, E. HARRIS. *Rival Ambassadors at the Court of Queen Mary*. Princeton, 1940.
MULLER, J. A. *Stephen Gardiner and the Tudor Reaction*. New York, 1926.
OXLEY, JAMES. *The Reformation in Essex to the Death of Mary*. Manchester, 1965.
PRESCOTT, HILDA, F.M. *Mary Tudor*. London, 1952.
SCHENK, WILHELM. *Reginald Pole, Cardinal of England*. London, 1950.

The Reformation in Scotland:
BURLEIGH, JOHN H. *A Church History of Scotland*. New York, 1960.
DICKINSON, W. CROFT, ed. *John Knox's History of the Reformation in Scotland*. London, 1949.
DONALDSON, GORDON. *The Scottish Reformation*. Cambridge, 1960.
GORE-BROWNE, R. *Lord Bothwell and Mary Queen of Scots*. New York, 1937.
HENDERSON, T. F. *Mary Queen of Scots,* 2 vols. New York, 1905.
HURLBUT, S. A. *The Liturgy and the Church of Scotland,* 4 vols. Charleston, S.C., 1944–1952.
KNOX, JOHN. *The History of the Reformation in Scotland,* ed. William C. Dickinson. New York, 1950.
MACGREGOR, G. *The Thundering Scot*. Philadelphia, 1952.
McROBERTS, DAVID, ed. *Essays on the Scottish Reformation, 1513–1625*. Glasgow, 1962.
MAHON, R. H. *Mary Queen of Scots*. Cambridge, 1924.
PERCY, LORD EUSTACE. *John Knox*. London, 1937.
RIDLEY, JASPER G. *John Knox*. New York, 1968.
WATT, HUGH. *John Knox in Controversy*. New York, 1950.
WILLOUGHBY, H. R. *The First Authorized English Bible and the Cranmer Preface*. Chicago, 1942.

CHAPTER 18

The Catholic
Reformation

Pope Clement VII, who faced the shock of the Reformation and suffered the trauma of the sack of Rome, had a medal struck depicting Christ bound to a column and below him the foreboding device *Post multa, plurima restant:* After many things, even more remain. Clement, in a dark apocalyptic mood, believed that the last days of the world were at hand. Just before his own days came to an end he commissioned the great Michelangelo to portray the Last Judgment on the front wall of the Sistine Chapel. And yet only a few decades later baroque artists delighted in portraying the church as triumphant over her enemies. The change in mood was a result of the astonishing success of the Catholic Reformation in spiritually invigorating the old church and in stemming the tide of Protestantism.

It took shock treatment to restore the mental and spiritual health of the church. From the intellectual, religious, and institutional crisis of the Renaissance and Reformation movements the church emerged chastened and scourged, but purer and more vital than she had been for centuries. The increased knowledge, especially derived from new Greek sources, the doctrinal challenges of the evangelicals based upon the Scriptures, and the defection of half of Europe threatened to engulf the ark of the church. For years the church seemed completely impotent, too paralyzed to react to the blows that fell upon her. Good churchmen interpreted the

[469]

sufferings of Rome as a punishment for her sins. In 1528 Bishop Stafileo declared that the city had been laid low "because all flesh had given way to corruption and because we are no longer the inhabitants of the holy city of Rome, but of the perverted city of Babylon." Many believed that if only the Fifth Lateran Council had responded to Aegidius da Viterbo's admonitions to reform in 1512, the church might have been spared the scourging of the Almighty. But the supreme pontiffs were themselves too confused, stunned, or inept to respond effectively to the thrusts of the reformers.

The Reformation Popes

THE LATERAN COUNCIL in 1512 reaffirmed the full power of the pope, condemned conciliarism, and denounced the tendency toward independence of the national clergies. But the popes of the Reformation era were not the inspired and incisive monarchs needed to act in such a crisis. Some time was lost under Leo X before the full danger of the schism was fully appreciated. But by the time Leo X died, on December 1, 1521, the cardinals recognized the gravity of the situation. On January 9, 1522, they elected a Dutch cardinal with a spotless reputation, Adrian Floriszoon, to lead the church in its own reformation. Adrian VI, as he styled himself, had studied with the Brethren of the Common Life and taught theology at Louvain, and he was a friend of Erasmus and the tutor of young Charles V. In Spain, as archbishop of Tortosa and papal legate in Castile and Aragon, he encountered the severe discipline of the Spanish church. He was no stranger to politics, for he had served as regent of Spain in the absence of Charles. He established a severe discipline upon the prelates under him and had all the makings of an earnest and zealous reformer. But Adrian VI proved to be completely ineffective as pope, for the Italians despised him for his rude Latin, his indifference to art, and his naïveté, by Italian Renaissance standards. He died disappointed and frustrated on September 14, 1523, and his epitaph is an apt commentary on his brief pontificate: "Alas! How the power even of a most righteous man depends upon the times in which he happens to live!"

The cardinals, impressed by the futility of Adrian VI's reform efforts and relieved by the brevity of the reign of the last non-Italian pope, on November 18 proclaimed as the new pope a cousin of Leo X, Giulio de' Medici, who adopted the name Clement VII. Giulio was the son of Lorenzo's brother Giuliano, who had been murdered in the cathedral of Florence at the time of the Pazzi revolt. Clement VII was a witty, easygoing, urbane churchman, a patron of the arts. He had no really ostentatious vices, but he had one basic constitutional flaw: he was indecisive and given to procrastination. He was politically adroit, but not sufficiently forceful for the desperate times in which he ruled. The pope's involvement in Italian intrigues and the conflicts of the major powers—the price that had to be paid for possession of the Papal States—reduced the spiritual prestige and moral influence of the papacy in the eyes of the faithful and foes alike. Clement shared Erasmus' view that sending the supercilious Cajetan and the overbearing Aleander to cope with the Lutheran situation had been a mistake. He sent instead as nuncio to the Diet of Nuremberg in 1524 the moderate, learned, and good-humored Cardinal Campeggio, who went prepared to make such important concessions as allowing the sacramental cup to the laity and marriage to the clergy. But no real progress toward reconciliation was made, for the doctrinal differences ran too deep to be glossed over by offers of wine and women. The Catholic princes of Austria and Bavaria ordered their students to leave heretical universities and return home. It became increasingly clear even to Clement VII that only a church council could possibly cope with the Protestant rebellion. Early in May 1532 he consented to a council, but on September 25, 1534, he died without having actually convoked one.

The new pope, Paul III, was more serious and resolute about reform and a council. In some ways Alexander Farnese was a typical Renaissance prelate. He had a family of illegitimate children, and shortly after his accession to the papal throne he made cardinals of his fourteen- and fifteen-year-old grandsons, Ascanio Sforza and Alexander Farnese, as "props for his old age," as he put it. He encouraged conversations with moderate evangelical theologians such as Martin Bucer and Melanchthon. He bestowed red hats upon a number of Erasmian churchmen between May and December 1536: Gasparo Contarini, Pietro Bembo, Jacopo Sadoleto, Giampietro Caraffa, Jean du Bellay, and Reginald Pole.

During the spring of 1536 the consistory in Rome mastered its fears of conciliarism and consented to the calling of a general church council. Paul III convoked the council to assemble in Mantua on May 23 of the following year. By way of preparation he appointed a commission of nine cardinals, including Contarini, Caraffa, Sadoleto, Pole, Aleander, and Giberti, who were Erasmians. Under the chairmanship of Contarini the commission met almost daily from early in November until mid-February 1537. On March 9 Contarini presented to Paul III their *Counsel . . . Concerning the Reform of the Church*. The *Counsel* scored the abuses of nepotism and simony, pluralism and absenteeism, the immorality of secular and regular clergy, easy dispensations, and rampant venality; but it did not come to grips with the basic theological issues raised by the reformers. In the matter of indulgences, for example, the cardinals merely recommended that they should not be given oftener than once a year in each of the larger cities. Through an indiscretion the *Counsel* was revealed prematurely and confirmed the Protestants in their opinion of the corruption of the church. Luther himself published a German edition of the *Counsel* embellished with his own ironic comments.

In spite of Paul III's reluctant but honest intention to assemble a council, he was continually forced to postpone it. In 1537 Mantua proved to be an unsuitable place because of the duke's opposition; in 1538 the delegates did not appear in Vicenza, in Venetian territory; and in 1542 the renewal of the war between Charles V and Francis I prevented all but a few prelates from coming to Trent, and these left shortly thereafter. This tragicomedy of errors at last came to an end in 1545, when the Council of Trent, convoked for March 25, finally convened on December 13 for its first session. Paul III died of old age in 1549. A conclave of cardinals convened to elect his successor was deadlocked for months, but eventually, on February 7, 1550, elected Cardinal del Monte, who took the name Julius III. The new pope was a relaxed Tuscan who lacked strong convictions, but he was persuaded to reconvene the Council of Trent for its second session. He was succeeded upon his death in 1555 by Pope Marcellus II, who died shortly after his election. Then with the election of Cardinal Caraffa as Pope Paul IV (1555–1559) a new spirit of dogmatic rigidity and intransigence asserted itself in the Holy See.

Giampietro Caraffa embodied the spirit of the Counterreformation and in his own person represented the new direction that the church's reaction to Protestantism was taking. He had belonged to a mystical group known as the Oratory of Divine Love, and he was early closely associated with churchmen of an Erasmian Christian humanist type. But his own convictions were narrower than theirs, and he was increasingly offended by their liberal views. As nuncio in Madrid in 1536 he saw the Inquisition move efficiently against the Erasmians and effectively root out their influence in a matter of months. Caraffa was convinced that the hard line alone would be effective, and with his pontificate the repressive Counterreformation moved ahead.

Catholic Spiritual Renewal

THE JESUIT HISTORIAN Pallavicino referred to the era of the Renaissance popes as an age of iniquities "the memory of which cannot be recalled without horror and indignation." And yet even in this dark period of the church, there were signs of new spiritual life not only in the north, where the Brethren of the Common Life were making their tremendous impression upon education, but also in the south and in Rome itself. Italy contributed many first-ranking Renaissance humanists, such as Marsilio Ficino and Pico della Mirandola, whose most earnest desire was to reinvigorate Christian theology with life from new Greek and Near Eastern sources.

Erasmian Christian humanism inspired a number of prelates to write in favor of reform and to improve the administration of their own dioceses. Cardinals such as Pole, Sadoleto, Giberti, and Contarini believed that if learning were improved, if piety were taught and practiced, if the simple teachings of the gospels were made

clear, a renewal could be effected in the church. There were many interior corre-
spondences between the teachings and practices of the late medieval church and the
tenets of Christian humanism—optimism about the educability of man, respect for
ancient or received traditions, the strength of man's will in achieving piety, the
meritorious nature of good works. A certain religious superficiality and inability
to grapple with the theological issues raised by the reformers was evident in Cardinal Jacopo Sadoleto. He addressed an admonishing letter to the people of Geneva,
but when Calvin published a reply, Sadoleto let the matter drop. But Sadoleto
nevertheless hoped that the blows of the reformers would have a therapeutic
effect upon the body of the church. To Pope Clement he wrote: "If we satisfy
God's wrath and justice, if those terrible punishments open the way for purer
manners and juster laws, perchance our misfortune will not have been so great."[1]

Cardinal Gian Matteo Giberti (1495–1543), the natural son of a Genoese sea
captain, was admitted to the household of Cardinal Giulio de' Medici, where he
proved to be a brilliant student of Greek and Latin and was admitted to the
Accademia Romana, the famous classical school. He became the cardinal's secretary and an emissary to Charles V. As Pope Clement VII, Giulio appointed Giberti
bishop of Verona. Resident in Rome, Giberti advised Clement politically, promoted
peace between Francis I and Charles V at Pavia, urged papal support of Francis,
and engineered the League of Cognac (1526). After the sack of Rome in 1527 the
imperial forces imprisoned him, but he escaped and fled to Verona. There he became a model reform bishop, upgrading the learning and morals of the clergy, sponsoring a printing press that issued splendid editions of the Greek church fathers,
and laying down edicts for reform. His dissertation on the restoration of ecclesiastical discipline became the basic platform for the reformatory acts of the Council
of Trent. Post-Tridentine churchmen studied his example closely.

Gasparo Contarini (1483–1542), of a noble Venetian family, was a member of
the Great Council in Venice, a Venetian ambassador at the court of Charles V,
and a celebrant at the coronation of Charles V at Bologna in 1530. In 1535 Pope
Paul III made Contarini a cardinal and the next year appointed him to the reform
commission. He was of an Erasmian temperament, diplomatically talented, and
knew the strength of the Protestants in the empire. When Emperor Charles summoned imperial diets at Worms and at Regensburg in 1540 and 1541, at which
theologians of both persuasions were to be present for a discussion of theological
points of difference, Contarini and the Erasmians strongly favored participation in
spite of Pope Paul III's fears that the emperor might follow the path of Henry
VIII to a national church. At Regensburg the discussions were based upon some
twenty-one articles largely drawn up by the Lutherans. Melanchthon, Martin
Bucer, John Calvin, and other eminent reformers represented the evangelical point
of view. Melanchthon and Contarini worked out a verbal formulation of the doc-

---

[1] Cited in Pierre Janelle, *The Catholic Reformation* (Milwaukee, 1963), p. 47.

trine of justification by faith, which pleased the emperor enormously when word of the agreement leaked out. But hopes for unity sank as the discussions proceeded, for questions regarding transubstantiation and the authority of the papacy led to an impasse. When Melanchthon returned to Wittenberg, he found Luther adamant against the compromise formula on faith, and when Contarini returned to Italy, he was accused of heresy. Mercifully he died the next year. The failure of the Erasmians to work out peaceful solutions to the schism in the church opened the way for the militant program of the intransigents.

The religious vitality of the church, especially in Italy, was further evidenced by a renewal within the old monastic orders and the founding of new orders during the first decades of the Reformation. Ascetic renunciation, mystical contemplation, and the religious life of the regular clergy retained strong power to attract the devout. Well before the advent of Luther, Baptista Mantuanus had worked for the reform of his Carmelite order. Among the Franciscans there arose a reformer of Italian peasant stock, Matteo de Bascio (d. 1552), who worked for a restoration of the primitive simplicity of St. Francis. He later became an itinerant evangelist himself. His followers were known as the Capuchins, distinguished by their four-pointed hoods. The Capuchins were recognized by the pope in 1528. In spite of the opposition of the Observant Franciscans, the Capuchins were second in power only to the Jesuits. They survived even the crisis precipitated by the defection to Protestantism of Bernardino Ochino in 1542, though they came close to being suppressed. They gained formal independence in 1619. The Dominicans, too, produced a notable spiritual reformer, Battista da Crema, who through his life and writings exercised a profound influence upon his times.

In 1516 a reformatory movement began close to the heart of Leo X's court in Rome. Certain clerics and laymen met frequently at the Church of Saints Sylvester and Dorothea for prayer, meditation, and mutual encouragement. Under the direction of Gaetano da Thiene, a disciple of Battista da Crema, and Giampietro Caraffa, the group was organized as the Oratory of Divine Love, counting among its members Sadoleto, Giberti, Contarini, and other Erasmian reformers. Later in the century (1575) St. Philip Neri raised the organization to a new prestigious form of religious expression by founding a new community of secular priests who lived a life of obedience for mutual strengthening, but were bound by no vows.

The whole history of monasticism was characterized by gradual decay and a weakening grasp on the original difficult and purist standards, followed by reform within the orders. The evolution of the monastic ideal moved steadily away from hermetic isolation to involvement in the world. The development went from single hermits to cenobitic groups, then to monastic living, such as the Benedictines practiced, apart from the world and behind walls, but for the good of the world through agricultural improvement, the copying of manuscripts, and schools to promote learning and culture. The mendicants emphasized the ideal of poverty, but deliberately entered the world and trod the dusty streets in their sandals. The most important new foundations of the sixteenth century, those of the Theatines and the Jesuits, not only afforded stellar examples of intramundane asceticism, but deliberately entered into contact with the most influential and powerful classes of society, into the courts, patrician houses, and universities. In the world and in the mission field they engaged Protestants and pagans in a contest for the religious allegiance of mankind.

From the Oratory of Divine Love emanated a spirit of devotion that led Gaetano da Thiene, Paolo Consiglieri, Bonifacio da Colle, and Caraffa to found the order of the Theatines, named after the city of Chieti (Theate) in southern Italy, where Caraffa was bishop. On September 14, 1524, the feast of the Exaltation of the Holy Cross, they made their solemn profession before the altar of St. Peter's in Rome. Their main objective was to recall the clergy to an edifying life and all Christians to the practice of virtue. They founded oratories and hospitals, evangelized, and by good example sought to inspire others to virtuous lives. They soon counted many members of the aristocracy among their congregations. They were the first order to undertake foreign missions in the Near East and in the East Indies. Other new foundations, such as the Somatians (1532) and the Barnabites (1533), emulated their example of sincerity and devotion.

Further evidence of sincere lay piety is to be found in such religious brotherhoods as the School of St. George and the School of St. Rochos in Venice. The School of St. Rochos was supported by extremely wealthy and devout merchants and was heavily endowed through testamentary bequests. It supported the painter Tintoretto for life in return for three lavish paintings of biblical scenes each year to ornament the school, a veritable jewel box with its classical Corinthian columns.

Just as Christian humanism and renewed monasticism gave evidence of Catholic vitality, so the appearance throughout the sixteenth century of genuine religious mystics, who combined vision and practicality in the best medieval tradition, provided proof that Catholicism, though suffering, was far from dead. The Spanish milieu seemed most conducive to the mystical life, and in Spain flourished those Carmelite saints who were the finest flower of the mystic garden, St. Teresa of Avila (1515–1582) and St. John of the Cross (1542–1591). St. Teresa grew up in a pious home within the ancient walled city of Avila. As a child she once set out with her younger brother to convert the Moors. At twenty she joined the Carmelite order, devoted herself to its reform, and directed the Discalced (unshod) Carmelites, who established an amazing number of reformed convents all over Spain. It was said that it would be easier to establish four new orders than to reform one old one, but St. Teresa succeeded by skillful administration and tremendous practicality. "The Lord walks among pots and pans" was a favorite expression of hers. Her autobiography was an amazingly sensitive and perceptive account of her early life and inner struggles. Her *Way of Perfection* was intended as a guide to the ascetic life for nuns in the reformed convents. Her masterpiece of mystical writing, however, was *The Interior Castle* (1577), in which she explored the secrets of the contemplative life, the mystical techniques of the soul's communion with God.

St. John of the Cross (1542–1591) was St. Teresa's most celebrated disciple. He led a rigorous life as a Discalced Carmelite, but somehow found the time to write great treatises on the highest reaches of the mystical experience, such as *The Ascent of Mount Carmel* and *The Dark Night of the Soul*.

A mystical poet less fortunate than St. John was Luis de León (1527–1591), who wrote commentaries on the Scriptures, a metrical version of the Song of Solomon, and original odes. But in 1572 he was arrested by the Inquisition on grounds of heresy and disrespect for the Vulgate and was imprisoned at Valladolid. He was eventually exonerated and a few days before his death even appointed provincial of his Augustinian order. The repression of the Inquisition, however, gradually squeezed the life out of Spanish mysticism, which steadily degenerated into a form of quietism.

France also contributed intellectually and spiritually to the Catholic revival. A fascinating French contribution was the slightly mad William Postel (1510–1581), a noninstitutionalized representative of the Catholic Reformation. Postel was in the tradition of Raymond Lull (1232–1315), who over two centuries earlier had undertaken to convert the Moslems by making missionary journeys, writing some three hundred esoteric apologetic works, and establishing a college to teach missionaries the languages and lore of the Near East. Postel studied at the University of Paris and learned Greek, Hebrew, Spanish, Portuguese, and Arabic. He wrote a work on the harmony of the world, *De orbis terrae concordia* (1544), intended to refute Mohammed and win Moslem converts to Christianity. That same year he traveled to Rome and joined the Jesuits, who were happy to have a scholar of such distinction. But very shortly he began to show erratic tendencies, advocating that the papacy be moved from Rome to Jerusalem and that the king of Rome should be the king of France, with his capital in Paris. He was ejected from the Society of Jesus and his works were put on the Index. Still he went to the Council of Trent and undertook to expound his theories to the churchmen there. The Inquisition declared him to be mad, imprisoned him for four years, and then had him held in informal custody in Paris for the final eighteen years of his life. Postel has been all but forgotten by historians, but the Inquisition, the Index, and the Jesuits have gone down in history as characteristic instruments of the Counterreformation.

The Counterreformation

HISTORIANS in these ecumenical days very much prefer the term "Catholic Reformation" to the term "Counterreformation," for the move toward reform within the church had its own spiritual wellsprings within the old church and was not merely a negative response to the Protestant revolt. Nevertheless, in certain important respects the Catholic Reformation was predominantly a reaction, and it did turn to forms of reprisal and repression that the modern church can in retrospect only regret. The major impulses toward the hard line came from Spain, the "hammer of heretics" and "sword of Rome."

Thanks to the centuries of combat with the Moslems and the crusade to drive them out of Iberia, Spain developed a very strong militant orthodoxy and a fanatical spirit. Ferdinand and Isabella had established powerful institutional controls against deviation in any form. Cardinal Ximénez not only had strengthened the hierarchy in Spain by a rigid moral rearmament, but had himself served as a grand inquisitor (1508). Charles V allowed the Inquisition to enlarge its jurisdiction from preventing Moors and Jews from proselytizing to judging questions of faith, not even exempting the regular clergy from its authority. In 1531 Pope Clement VII subjected the episcopacy in Spain to the Inquisition and refused any right of appeal from its sentences. From 1538 on, the Inquisition became very active in combating heretical religious propaganda and suppressing the Erasmians and Lutherans.

Cardinal Caraffa had been very favorably impressed by the effectiveness of the Inquisition in Spain, and suggested introducing its methods into Italy. Popular resistance had held back the Inquisition in the Spanish domains in Italy, so that it did not function in Sicily until 1518, and then primarily in controlling the Jews, and in Naples it even tolerated the followers of Valdés for many years. Caraffa believed that papal support was necessary, and he urged the pope to establish a new congregation in Rome which would reinvigorate the old Dominican tribunal for action against heretics. Paul III was hesitant, for he feared the hostility of the people. But as the number of heretics increased and the mediating efforts of the moderates failed, he reluctantly gave Caraffa a free hand. Caraffa was so impatient to get on with it that he set up interrogation chambers and instruments of intimidation in his own house until the tribunal could be organized. "If our own father were a heretic," he exclaimed, "we would carry the faggots to burn him!" Another time he intoned: "No man is to lower himself by showing toleration toward any sort of heretic, least of all a Calvinist!" The Roman tribunal was given jurisdiction over all Italy, with the same power and organization as the Spanish Inquisition. The judges were by custom Dominicans, and they were subordinated to a congregation of six cardinals who were appointed by the pope to serve as inquisitors general, including Caraffa. On July 21, 1542, Paul III formally sanctioned the Roman Inquisition and extended its authority to all of Christendom. With this step Rome regained the initiative from the reformers.

The cooperation of the reinvigorated monastic orders and especially of the civil authorities made the Inquisition an effective instrument for the suppression of heretics. In March 1547 the Inquisition had the Spanish nonconformist Juan de Enzinas burned at Rome. It summoned Pietro Paolo Vergerio from Venetian territory to Rome. Excommunicated on July 3, 1549, Vergerio fled to safety in Grisons. The narrow-minded grand duke of Florence, Cosimo I, enthusiastically supported the Inquisition in Tuscany, and from 1542 on, it also operated in Milan. In Ferrara it brought pressure on Hercules d'Este to move against the evangelicals whom the duchess Renée was protecting. They fled, and Renée, abused by her fanatical son, retired to France. The Spanish government now felt free to act in its Italian domains. Caraffa became archbishop of Naples on February 22, 1549, and encouraged the final dissolution of the Valdés circle.

The advent of inquisitorial justice in France coincided with the resolution of an embittered King Francis I to suppress the Huguenots. The Inquisition claimed victims in Rouen, Toulouse, Grenoble, and Bordeaux. The royal courts handled heresy in Paris. Even Meaux, where Bishop Briconnet had once sheltered such free spirits as Lefèvre d'Étaples, was no longer a sanctuary, for on October 4, 1546, the authorities arrested sixty-one evangelicals at an assembly and subsequently burned fourteen of them for heresy. The next year a special tribunal of the parlement of Paris was given exclusive authority in the burning issue of heresy. It established such a record of executions by fire that it came to be known as the *chambre ardente*. King Henry II (1547–1559) was very narrow-minded and encouraged restrictive legislation on books, professorships, and communication with Protestant centers. A royal edict in 1549 defined the legal competence of the ecclesiastical and civil authorities in matters of heresy. Throughout Europe there was a direct correlation between the success of the Inquisition and the willingness of the monarchs and lesser rulers to cooperate.

For effective thought control it is essential to burn the books as well as their authors, a point that was not lost upon the zealous Paul IV. From 1521 on, lists of forbidden books were circulated; the theological faculties at Paris and Louvain figured prominently in the compilation. The first complete list, valid for the entire church, was the *Index librorum prohibitorum,* promoted by Paul IV during the last year of his pontificate and published in 1559. This list of prohibited books, however, included titles that less excitable minds than Caraffa's considered harmless, and it was modified by the Index of Trent in 1564. Not only were heretical Protestant writings proscribed, but also humanist classics thought to be injurious to morals, such as Boccaccio's *Decameron*. The works of the prince of the Christian humanists, Erasmus, who had once nearly been given a cardinal's hat, were forbidden and subsequently published in a bowdlerized version. The Renaissance was now clearly a thing of the past.

The Jesuits

THE SHOCK TROOPS of the Counterreformation were the Jesuits. In addition to the traditional monastic vows of poverty, chastity, and obedience, they took a fourth vow of absolute obedience directly to the pope. So efficient and effective was the newly founded Society of Jesus in polemics, politics, education, and mission enterprise that it has been associated too exclusively with the thrust against Protestantism. In reality the Jesuits were an expression of that reservoir of religious sentiment from which a variety of new orders welled up in the first decades of the century. A product of Spanish spirituality, the Society of Jesus considered itself primarily a force for the rejuvenation of the church and the Christianizing of the heathen, rather than a combat force against Protestantism. That it served so well also in the new offensive is a tribute to the genius of its founder, Ignatius Loyola, and to the dedication of its first members.

Ignatius Loyola (1491–1556) was one of the most dramatic figures in the history of Christendom, a man of war who became a soldier for the Prince of Peace. His father was a Basque nobleman and as a boy he served as a page at the court of King Ferdinand. Schooled in courtly manners and military strategy, he served with two brothers in the army of their feudal overlord, the duke of Najera. On May 21, 1521, Loyola was defending a breach in the city wall at Pamplona during an invasion by the troops of King Francis I when a French cannonball smashed his right leg and wounded his left one. A French doctor made a crude attempt to set his leg, but it had to be rebroken and reset twice, and he was lame for life. While recuperating in the family castle he read lives of the saints and Ludolph the Carthusian's *Life of Christ*. Caught up in a vivid religious experience, similar to the conversion struggle and release of Luther and Calvin, Loyola transferred his chivalric ideals to the realm of faith. He envisioned the Christian life as devoted service to Our Lady. The knights in shining spiritual armor formed the army of the righteous King engaged in deadly combat with the forces of Satan. With a flair for the dramatic, Ignatius made a symbolic gesture to mark his change of life. Traveling along the road discussing religion with several companions, he had been unable to convince one of them of Mary's virginity. Furious, he had been momentarily tempted to use his dagger on the insolent fellow. Shocked at his own impulse, a few days later Loyola hung the weapon in the church of Montserrat and dedicated it to the Virgin. He gave away his rich garments to the poor and put on a cloak of sackcloth reaching to his feet. Loyola thus chose a religious solution within the church.

Loyola spent a year in seclusion outside of Manresa, near Barcelona, where he underwent an intense spiritual struggle, wrestling with the question of the ability of man, with the aid of grace, to control his free will in such a way as to make salvation possible. He worked out a sketch of his famous *Spiritual Exercises,* although he did not give them their final form till 1541. He formulated "Rules for Thinking with the Church," even indulging in a bit of hyperbole with the statement: "If we wish to proceed securely in all things, we must hold fast to the following principle: What seems to me white, I will believe black if the hierarchical

Church so defines" (Rule 13). The "first principle and foundation" of the *Spiritual Exercises* expresses the heart of Loyola's religious feeling:

> Man is created to praise, reverence, and serve God our Lord, and by this means to save his soul.
>
> The other things on the face of the earth are created for man to help him in attaining the end for which he is created.
>
> Hence, man is to make use of them in as far as they help him in the attainment of his end, and he must rid himself of them in as far as they prove a hindrance to him.
>
> Therefore, we must make ourselves indifferent to all created things, as far as we are allowed free choice and are not under any prohibition. Consequently, as far as we are concerned, we should not prefer health to sickness, riches to poverty, honor to dishonor, a long life to a short life. The same holds for all other things.
>
> Our one desire and choice should be what is more conducive to the end for which we are created.[2]

Following an honored tradition, in 1523 he made a pilgrimage to Jerusalem. He returned to study at the Alcalá, the university founded by Cardinal Ximénez. There he gathered a group of like-minded followers, but came under the surveillance of the Inquisition and ironically was briefly imprisoned on suspicion of heresy.

In 1528 he moved to Paris, where he studied, as had Erasmus, at the Collège de Montaigu, and later at the Collège de Sainte Barbe. He took his licentiate in theology in 1534 and his M.A. in 1535. He was in Paris at the same time as John Calvin, but there is no evidence that they met. In Paris Loyola was once again denounced by the Inquisition but escaped prosecution. In 1534 Loyola's religious society accepted its first six members, including Diego Lainez, who was to succeed him later as general of his order, Alfonso Salmerón, and Francis Xavier, the great missionary to the Far East. They swore an oath to dedicate themselves to the conversion of the Moors, a further indication that the movement was an efflorescence of the medieval Spanish crusading spirit. It took Loyola several years to persuade the Roman curia of the orthodoxy and the great value of his proposed new order for the propagation of the faith and the support of papal authority, but finally, on September 27, 1540, Pope Paul sanctioned the Society of Jesus with the bull *Regimen militantis ecclesiae*. The Jesuits were an elitist corps. They accepted as members only the most intelligent, physically strong and attractive, energetic, and dedicated men of good character. After two trial years the novices took the usual three monastic vows of poverty, chastity, and obedience. After an additional year of general studies and three years of philosophy, they taught philosophy or grammar to the younger members. Then after studying theology for four years they were admitted to the priesthood, publicly renewing the three vows. They then devoted

---

[2] Louis J. Puhl, S.J., ed., *The Spiritual Exercises of St. Ignatius* (Westminster, Md., 1957), p. 12.

a year to the study of practical theology, preaching, and spiritual exercises. After a second year of proving themselves they were at last admitted to the special obedience to the pope and incorporated into the Society of Jesus. Ignatius spent his last years in semiretirement, handling the order's vast correspondence with its members throughout the world. He passed away peacefully while saying his prayers. At the time of Loyola's death the society numbered around a thousand members. He lived to see the establishment of a hundred colleges and seminaries, and within a century and a half the society had founded over seven hundred schools; today its schools are numbered in the thousands.

The Jesuit order was the last major flowering of monasticism in the Western world. The excellence of its constitution, which reflects Ignatius' organizational talent, explains in part the tremendous efficiency of the society. The exchange of information from the lowest echelons to the general was a model of smooth communication. The discipline emphasized the maintenance of spiritual vitality. The Jesuits advocated frequent communion, individual confessions, and spiritual direction, evidencing special concern for the conscience of each member. Although Jesuitism and Calvinism are usually portrayed as antithetical archetypes of Catholic and Protestant thought, in certain essential ways they were two sides of the same coin. Both were ascetic and inclined toward intramundane asceticism. Both emphasized the importance of education for higher culture and for the promotion of right religious knowledge. Both developed theories to justify resistance to secular authority, pointing toward the contractual political theory. Both had a pessimism and a rigidity in their anthropology that were foreign to the optimism of Christian humanists such as Erasmus. Both believed that the natural will of man must be bent and disciplined, made malleable to receive religious truth. And yet both were fundamentally optimistic regarding the ground of being, seeing the universe created and ruled by a just but merciful God. The differences in their theories of salvation, church doctrines, sacramental teachings, and other theological questions are obvious enough.

The Jesuits were most successful in the areas of education and missions. They set up excellent schools with a curriculum or *ratio studiorum* that incorporated much humanist educational philosophy, although they stressed dialectic at the expense of history for apologetic reasons. They supplied learned tutors for the instruction of princes, a successful strategy, for in this way they exercised powerful influence over future rulers such as Ferdinand of Styria and Sigismund of Poland. An interesting incident in the story of Jesuit influence is the case of the pretender to the Russian throne known to history as the first False Dimitri, who won the support of the Poles and the Jesuits when he converted to Roman Catholicism and married the daughter of a Polish nobleman. After the death of the ruling tsar, Boris Godunov (who is credited with having murdered the real Dimitri, son of Ivan the Terrible), he seemed well on his way to establishing his claim to the throne when he was murdered. He had planned an alliance with the Holy Roman emperor, the pope, Poland, and Venice against the Turks, and if he had lived and succeeded in establishing himself as tsar he might well have replaced the Russian Orthodox Church with a Jesuit-guided Roman Catholic Church.

Jesuits operating in lands where Protestantism was strong utilized all existing resources, libraries, and monastic grounds. Peter Faber and Peter Canisius made tremendous inroads into Protestant areas in the Germanies, training young priests, writing a catechism, and establishing colleges, such as the Jesuit academy in Vienna. The German College in Rome, later directed by Cardinal Bellarmine, was an important center for the reconquest of German lands. William Allen founded a seminary at Douay directed toward the infiltration of England by priests sent in as secret agents. It was there that the Douay English version of the Bible was prepared. This college, as well as the English College in Rome, was of the same type as those of the Jesuits, with whom Allen was on very good terms. The transition from princes' tutors to rulers' confessors was easily made. But Jesuit involvement in politics led to their expulsion from a number of countries, and later even to their suppression for a time by the pope.

During the sixteenth and seventeenth centuries the Jesuits undertook world missions that were perhaps their greatest achievement. In spreading Christianity to all corners of the earth, in serving as a partial counterbalance to the materialistic imperialism of the European merchants and soldiers, in bringing to Europe eye-witness reports of foreign lands and scholarly accounts of their history and geography, the Jesuit missionaries contributed to the European outreach that has been one of the most important features of modern history. This mission endeavor was in line with Christ's commission to "go into all the world and preach the gospel." It was the same generic type as the missionary activities of the fourteenth-century Franciscans and not unrelated to the desire of Vasco da Gama, Columbus, and other explorers to carry the cross to foreign shores.

Although the Franciscans, Dominicans, and Augustinians were the most active in Christianizing Mexico and Peru, the Jesuits played the leading role in Brazil, where Father José de Anchieta directed the early efforts, and in Paraguay. While conditions in Latin America favored the wholesale conversion of the Indian populations, the work was much more difficult in Asia, where more complex ancient cultures with established higher religions were encountered.

Though the older religious orders accompanied the Portuguese explorers to India and the East Indies, the great Jesuit missionary Francis Xavier towers above all the rest as the "apostle of the Indies and of Japan." Xavier was born in his noble family's castle below the Pyrenees in 1506. At eighteen he went to study philosophy at the Collège de Sainte Barbe in Paris, where he met Loyola. Ignatius recognized in this handsome, bright, and cheerful young Spanish nobleman a rare spirit, and won both Xavier and his friend Peter Faber as disciples. Xavier went with Loyola to Venice, where he worked in a hospital for incurables, then to Rome, and then back to Venice, where he was ordained as a priest. When King John III of Portugal asked Pope Paul III to send six Jesuit missionaries to the East Indies, Ignatius named Xavier as one of the two ready to go. Xavier went to Lisbon and then traveled to southern India, where he preached for three years in the Portuguese colonies at Goa, Cochin, San Thomé, and along the coast of Travancore. Then he moved on to the Portuguese colonies in Malacca, Malaya, the Moluccas, and other islands of the East Indies, where he evangelized for two and a half years. His most remarkable undertaking was his mission to Japan, from 1549 to 1551, where he had astonishing success in winning converts at Kagoshima, Yamagutsi, and elsewhere, founding a Christian community that still survives, in spite of severe persecutions in earlier centuries. He died of a fever when only forty-six while attempting to penetrate China with the Christian gospel.

Father Matthew Ricci (1551–1610) undertook to convert the Chinese by starting at the top, winning the mandarins first and then working down. Learned in astronomy and mathematics, he was well received in Peking and favored by the emperor. His adaptations to native customs and traditional beliefs went far, and offended the Dominicans and more conservative parties in the church.

The reports of the Jesuits, known as the Jesuit relations, brought volumes of new knowledge about Asia, Africa, and America to the Europeans. They stressed the great variety of custom and belief, the different standards of aesthetics, and the rule of reason and morality of the noble heathen. Father Ricci so admired the Chinese that he believed that God had endowed them with superior reason and knowledge of natural law. These reports had an unsettling effect upon the European mind, precipitating a real crisis of conscience. They became arsenals for the eighteenth-century European philosophers who developed theories of aesthetic and moral relativity, which have ever since been characteristic of Western thought.

The Council of Trent

THE REFORMATION prompted the convening of the Council of Trent (1545–1563), the most important church council since that of Nicea in 325 A.D. After its adjournment, no other council was held for three hundred years, until the First Vatican Council in the nineteenth century—a span of time between councils without precedent in the history of the church. "It was the answer of the church," writes the contemporary historian of the council, Hubert Jedin, "to the confessional schism and an act of self-definition and self-renewal of this same church." Two simple questions may serve to bring into sharp focus the historical importance of the Council of Trent: If the council had been held in 1525 instead of 1545, would everything have been different? If the council had not been held at all, would anything have been different? It can be argued that a council held before the full force of the Protestant revolt had been deeply felt would have varied little from the bland results of the Fifth Lateran Council (1512–1517). It can also be asserted that the council represented no basic reform, but rather a reaffirmation of accepted positions. Bossuet chided Leibniz, who had urged the suspension of the canons and decrees of the Council of Trent in the interest of Christian unity, with the reminder that this would do his cause no good at all, because every assertion of the Council of Trent was to be found authorized in earlier papal and conciliar documents. That the council was convoked at all, in view of papal suspicion of conciliarism, seems surprising to some observers. Others find it inexplicable that it was delayed so long, in view of the pressure for a council throughout much of Christendom.

Pope Pius II had capped the triumph of the papacy over councils in the year 1460 with his bull *Execrabilis,* in which he declared it "useless, illegal, and wholly detestable" to appeal over the head of the pope to a council, and declared anyone who did so automatically excommunicated. That this decree was not universally accepted is evident from the fact that the Fifth Lateran Council, meeting under Leo X during the greater part of its tenure, found it necessary to reassert the thesis of the *Execrabilis.* Conciliarism was far from dead during the half century following the pronouncement of Pius II. Ulrich von Hutten dared to publish a pamphlet bearing on its title page the refrain "Consilium! Consilium! Consilium!" Girolamo Aleander, the papal legate to Germany and the dedicated foe of Erasmus and Luther, writing from Worms in 1520, complained, "All the world cries out, 'Council, council!'"

Luther was ambivalent about a council. He appealed earnestly for an ecumenical council to effect the reform of the church, but at the same time realism compelled him to expect little of any council called in the prevailing circumstances. On November 28, 1518, he made a stirring appeal for a council, but the next year at Leipzig he argued for the authority of the Scriptures over that of popes and councils, for councils too have often erred and contradicted each other. In his *Address to the Christian Nobility* in 1520 he outlined the worst abuses with which a council would have to deal. When a council had still not been convened by 1539, Luther wrote a treatise summarizing his views *On the Councils and the Church.* "We cry out and appeal for a council and beseech all of Christendom for its advice and help!" he exclaimed. "You say that there is no hope for such a council any longer; I suppose I agree with you." Many people concluded that the popes were merely procrastinating and evading a council in order to save themselves from reform. Luther spoke for a large part of the public when he compared Pope Paul III with the medieval rogue Markolf, who could not find a tree anywhere on which he wanted to be hanged.

The character of the Renaissance papacy, it is true, lent plausibility to the worst construction that could be placed upon the papal opposition to a council. But there were pressing political conditions that dictated such a course, for the kings and emperors of the day exploited the threat of a council to bend the papacy to their will. The French kings Louis XI, Charles VIII, and Louis XII, with their special interest in Italian affairs, made constant use of such threats. Louis XII went so far as to have five cardinals summon a council to convene in Pisa in September 1511, but Julius II outmaneuvered him and in July of that year called the Fifth Lateran Council to meet in Rome in April 1512. Even though Julius died after the first session, this council continued sporadically under Leo X until the fateful year 1517, when it finally adjourned with little accomplished. In 1517 the University of Paris advocated the calling of a general council in protest against the abolition of the Pragmatic Sanction of Bourges. John Major (1470–1550), a professor of philosophy and theology at Paris, who returned to his native Scotland in 1518 to teach first at the University of Glasgow and then at St. Andrews, consistently appealed for a council and even wrote a *Disputation on the Authority of a Council.*

Even the lethargic emperor Frederick III and the quixotic Maximilian resorted to threats of a council and unilateral reform for political ends. But when the Habsburg empire, spanning all of Europe, came into the hands of Charles V, the papacy was placed in a really precarious position, for it was caught between the French and Spanish interests during the course of the Habsburg-Valois wars and was forced to vacillate wildly in order to maintain its own temporal interests.

Charles V, who had to get along with the evangelicals in the empire, insisted upon the calling of a council as one condition for support of the papacy. The Spanish preponderance, following the defeat of Francis I of France at Pavia in 1525 and the sack of Rome by the imperial troops in 1527, dictated the acceptance of Charles's demands. But Pope Clement VII, a Medici, in alliance now with France, still delayed in calling a council, even though the emperor threatened a national council for the empire only, with the Protestants participating. In 1542, after futile attempts to convene a council at Mantua and Vincenza, Paul III convoked a council to meet at Trent, or Trento, in northern Italy but technically on German soil—a concession he made unwillingly. But the Habsburgs had still not reached an accommodation with the French, and it was only after the Peace of Crépy (September 18, 1544) that Charles accepted the pope's proposal. A bull of November 30 announced a meeting for the following March, but the *Bull of Convocation of the Holy Ecumenical Council of Trent* did not arrive until December 11, 1545. The council opened two days later. The *Bull of Convocation* took cognizance of the "evils that have long afflicted and well-nigh overwhelmed the Christian commonwealth," of the princes "filled with hatreds and dissensions," of the "schisms, dissensions, and heresies," of the delays in the assembling of a council due to the plots of "the enemy of mankind," and warned that all who opposed the summons would "incur the indignation of Almighty God and of His blessed Apostles Peter and Paul."

Owing to the halo effect of religious assemblies, there is a natural inclination for the historical imagination to conjure up a scene of sanctity when reflecting on a council like the one that met at Trent. Cardinal Madruzzo, bishop of Trent, who alone represented the empire, had to wrestle with some very earthy problems in providing for the physical needs of the delegates and their entourages. Room rents skyrocketed, the price of wine rose 30 percent, Venice was asked to grant free transit of wheat and oats from the Papal States, oxen and cattle were imported from Germany, and "everything was exceeding dear."

The human element played a predictable part in the proceedings. One skeptical father at the council observed that the Holy Spirit would no doubt come to them from Rome in the courier's bag. After a Spanish prelate had orated interminably, one of the delegates rose and asked, "Is this the Council of Toledo?" When a French delegate had criticized the abuses of the Roman church very harshly, an Italian took the floor and said, *"Ecce!* Behold how the *gallus* [cock] crows!" The Frenchman slashed back with "But in the Scriptures it says that when the cock crowed, Peter roused himself and repented in tears." There were even physical encounters, as when an angered prelate yanked a fistful of hair from the beard of a Greek representative. But for the most part the sessions were conducted with the dignity and ceremony due the occasion.

Attendance was scanty for an enterprise of such significance; when the first session opened it included only four archbishops, twenty bishops, four generals of monastic orders, and a few theologians. The Italians were best represented, with a dozen prelates present, compared with only five Spaniards, two Frenchmen, and one bishop from the empire. The Spaniards turned out to be a difficult quotient, for while they were intransigent in dogma, they were sensitive to the emperor's wishes, and pressed conciliar arguments to put the curia on the defensive. Since the Greek Orthodox and Protestant churches did not take part in the council, it could not really pretend to be ecumenical.

In his opening address the president of the council, Cardinal del Monte, cited as the two main reasons for the convening of the council the growth of heresy and the need for the reform of abuses. He attributed both to the negligence of the bishops, and called on the bishops present (the bishop of Rome not being among them) to confess and to beg God's pardon. All knelt and prayed for forgiveness, although it became clear later that a good number of them resented being singled out in this way while the curia was omitted from censure. The cardinal read the collect and gospel lesson for the day, the choir sang *"Veni, Creator Spiritus"* and the *Te Deum,* and the Council of Trent was declared to be in session.

The council met, as it was summoned, under papal auspices. In deciding to

The Council of Trent. British Museum, London.

debate the issues of reform and dogma simultaneously, the fathers at Trent acknowledged the basically twofold nature of the problem confronting the church, the loss of spiritual idealism reflected in the growing number of abuses and the theological uncertainty and religious degeneration in matters of doctrine. The seventh and fourteenth sessions issued major decrees concerning reform, touching upon such matters as incompetency in cathedral churches, plurality of offices, plurality of benefices, plurality even in positions involving the cure of souls, neglect of visitations, and the like. The twenty-first session struck at illiteracy and the ignorance of the clergy. In matters of dogma, the fourth session pronounced upon the canonical Scriptures and their authority. In the decree *De canonicis scripturis* the council imposed the authority of the Vulgate upon the church. The statement on tradition failed to explain the full sense of its meaning and the extent of its authority. The conclusion was simply that Scripture and tradition were to be considered equally valid, without spelling out clearly whether religious truth is to be found partly in Scripture and partly in tradition or whether the whole truth is to be found in each, with the Scripture as the norm that determines acceptable tradition. The fifth and sixth sessions defined the orthodox position on original sin and justification; many of the remaining sessions were devoted to the number, nature, and celebration of the sacraments. They reaffirmed transubstantiation, the sacrificial nature of the mass, the legitimacy of private masses, and the efficacy of the seven sacraments, which were declared to be efficacious in themselves, independently of faith.

In developing their dogmatic definitions the fathers simply followed the statements in the Lutheran Augsburg Confession of 1530, opposing them with orthodox definitions and adding anathemas. The most acrimonious debates developed around the central problems of original sin and justification. Conciliatory Cardinal Contarini, in his *Epistola de justificatione* (1541), had distinguished an "inherent justification" of a man before God, which results from right action, and an "imputed justification," which the merits of Christ provide when they are appropriated by a man through faith. The righteousness thus acquired constitutes the supreme end of faith. The moderates at Trent wished to subordinate works to faith, without being indifferent to the necessity of good works. Jacopo Seripando, general of the Augustinians, pressed for a solution that would not be entirely offensive to the evangelicals. On instructions from Loyola, the Jesuit theologians Lainez and Salmerón had remained more or less in the background up to that point in the discussions. But now they intervened energetically, insisting on the absolute necessity of good works for justification, and adamantly refused to accept any conditions or to subordinate works to faith. In the end the assembly adopted a statement in harmony with the definition of St. Thomas Aquinas. Chapter 7 of the decree concerning justification promulgated on January 13, 1547, reads in part as follows:

In what the justification of the sinner consists and what are its causes: This disposition or preparation is followed by justification itself, which is not only a remission of sins but also the sanctification and renewal of the inward man through the voluntary reception of the grace and gifts whereby an unjust man becomes just and from being an enemy becomes a friend, that he may be an heir according to hope of life everlasting. The causes of this justification are: the final cause is the glory of God and of Christ and life everlasting; the efficient cause is the merciful God who washes and sanctifies gratuitously, signing and anointing with the holy Spirit of promise, who is the pledge of our inheritance; the meritorious cause is His most beloved only begotten, our Lord Jesus Christ, who, when we were enemies, for the exceeding charity wherewith he loved us, merited for us justification by His most holy passion on the wood of the cross and made satisfaction for us to God the Father; the instrumental cause is the sacrament of baptism, which is the sacrament of faith, without which no man was ever justified; finally, the single formal cause is the justice of God, not that by which He Himself is just, but that by which He makes us just, that, namely, with which we being endowed by Him, are renewed in the spirit of our mind, and not only are we reputed but we are truly called and are just, receiving justice within us, each one according to his own measure, which the Holy Ghost distributes to everyone as He wills, and according to each one's disposition and cooperation. . . .[3]

The scholastic structure of the definition is very striking. But in order to leave nothing ambiguous, the council spelled out thirty-three canons on justification, condemning Protestant positions as the fathers understood them. The definitions of the council hardened and rigidified Catholic dogma where some room for variation and maneuvering had existed before. But in removing theological ambiguity or uncertainty, it presented a dogmatic platform on which the church of the Catholic Reformation could take its stand.

The council was making genuine progress when once again the wheel of fortune upset the political balance and the fathers adjourned in a panic. Charles V had engaged the Schmalkald League of Protestant princes and cities in war and triumphed over them. The Spaniards at Trent began at once to assert themselves with new authority, and Cardinal Cervini feared the emperor might arrive in person with his armies to enforce his will on the council. A serious epidemic provided an occasion for transferring the council to Bologna, where the Italian delegates held the eighth session. Charles V protested violently, demanding that the council return to Trent, and in November the Diet of Augsburg refused to recognize the legality of the council's debates. On February 15, 1548, Pope Paul III ordered the council to recess. Toward the end of 1549 Paul III died without having reconvened it.

The new pope, Julius III (del Monte), was elected on February 7, 1550, and

---

[3] H. J. Schroeder, O.P., ed., *Canons and Decrees of the Council of Trent* (St. Louis and London, 1960), p. 33.

before the year was out he had summoned the council to reassemble at Trent on April 29, 1551. The Italian and Spanish delegates were in the majority, with the Spaniards hostile to the Italian pope, though conservative in dogma. Charles V was apprehensive about his control of the German Protestants, who were secretly negotiating with Henry II for support, and rejected the decisions of the council in advance for not giving their views a fair hearing. Julius III chose the Jesuits Lainez and Salmerón as his spokesmen. Once again reform and dogma were to be discussed simultaneously. Once again the fathers took up the question of the Eucharist, declared for a Thomist definition, and reasserted the legitimacy of the adoration of the host. In the matter of penance they reasserted the necessity of making oral confession before a priest and doing penance or giving satisfaction for sins repented of in the heart and orally confessed. They reaffirmed the time-honored forms in the administration of the last unction.

In October the council met the demands of the emperor and issued safe-conducts to German Protestant delegates. Melanchthon wished to attend but was unable to do so. But other representatives arrived in January 1552 from Saxony, Württemberg, and evangelical cities of south Germany. They were incensed that the council had decided the essential questions before they arrived and would allow them to discuss only communion in both kinds and the marriage of the clergy, which the emperor had already conceded to them in the Interim. At this juncture the wheel of fortune took one more complete turn, when Maurice of Saxony turned against the emperor and nearly captured him. Maurice reorganized the Schmalkald League, gained support from Henry II, and struck fear into the hearts of the fathers at Trent, who expected another invasion of German troops such as that of 1527. On April 28, 1552, Julius III precipitously adjourned the council for two years, but nearly a decade was to pass before it met again. In the meantime the Peace of Augsburg (1555) guaranteed the Protestants their legal right to exist in the empire, and the Treaty of Cateau-Cambrésis (1559) established a new international settlement.

Pope Pius IV (1559–1565) reconvoked the council for April 8, 1561. Called in part to head off a French national settlement, it included for the first time a significant French representation. It became increasingly clear as the debates went on that the papacy had emerged from the struggle with new prestige and authority. The papal representatives initiated proposals for action by the council and the council referred important questions to the pope for decision. The Jesuits were active proponents of papal power. The curia temporized as long as it could in the matter of reform, while pro-imperial churchmen worked desperately for it in order to quiet the criticism of the Protestants. Any question of dogma that was discussed—communion in both kinds, the mass as sacrifice, ordination—was always decided in favor of the traditional interpretation. When the council adjourned at the end of 1563, with fitting ceremony, and the canons and decrees received the formal signatures of the prelates present, 189 of the 255 signatories were Italian churchmen.

Protestant reaction was one of bitter disappointment, though not of surprise, for most of them shared Luther's skepticism about the "irreformability of the church." Even before the first session Luther had written: "Thus the council is settled before it even begins. Nothing is to be reformed, but everything is to be retained in accordance with past usage. What a fine council that is!" The council had a negative effect upon Christian unity, for with its scholastically refined definitions and its canons with anathemas attached, it burned the last bridges to the Protestant side of the stream. But by elevating the papacy anew, by improving the efficiency of the church's organization, and by clarifying dogma, the Council of Trent gave to the Catholic Church a clear-cut confession that it could embrace and for which it could battle in the wars of religion that lay ahead.

Post-Tridentine Reform

ON JANUARY 26, 1564, Pius IV (1559–1565), in the bull *Benedictus Deus,* confirmed the canons and decrees of the council, as it had petitioned him to do, and forbade any commentary on them without papal authority. On August 2, 1564, he created a congregation of cardinals for an authentic interpretation, a renewed assertion of the authority of the teaching office of the church. His bull *Iniunctum nobis,* of November 13, 1564, promulgated the *Professio fidei tridentinae,* which included the Nicene Creed, to which all to whom it was addressed were pledged. In addition the bull demanded, among other things, consent and adherence to apostolic and ecclesiastical traditions and to Holy Scripture, "according to the sense which the Holy Mother Church was held and holds whose right it is to judge regarding the true sense and interpretation of the Holy Scriptures." The pledge demands acknowledgment of the Roman church as the mother and mistress of all and true obedience to the Roman pontiff as the successor of Peter and vicar of Jesus Christ. Finally, it demands acceptance and profession of all sacred canons, particularly of the Tridentine Council, to which on January 20, 1877, was added a decree concerning the primacy and infallible magisterium of the Roman pontiff.

Charles Borromeo, nephew of Pius IV, may serve as a living model of the Tridentine spirit. As archbishop of Milan, he took for his model St. Ambrose, who more than a thousand years before had won sainthood in the corrupt times of the declining Roman Empire. Borromeo renovated and restored desecrated and deserted churches, reformed the law and the clergy, restored discipline in the religious orders, and established schools and colleges. Without the labors of men like Borromeo the resolutions of the Council of Trent would have been of little value to the church.

Pius V (1566–1572) provided all the bishops with an official edition of the council's decrees for their guidance. Peter Canisius took them to Germany, and they even reached America and the Congo at that early time. In 1566, for the benefit of parish priests, Pius published the Roman Catechism as an introduction to the council's resolutions. This he supplemented with a revised breviary and missal, for which, as well as for the catechism, the council had already made provision.

Gregory XIII (1572–1585) instructed the papal nuncios to ensure the execution of the Tridentine decrees in their respective areas. In response to the council's wish, Sixtus V (1585–1590) and Clement VIII (1592–1605) published a revised text of the Vulgate. The popes were not everywhere successful in their efforts to obtain immediate recognition of the council's acts. They succeeded in Spain, Poland, and the Italian states, but failed in France and Germany. Today the council's decisions are, within the widened borders of later papal definitions, definitive for the Roman Catholic Church everywhere.

The Roman Catechism, composed under Thomist influence, did not meet with favor among the Jesuits, who preferred the triple catechism of their fellow Jesuit, Peter Canisius. Even the catechism of Robert Bellarmine, authorized by Clement VIII and published in 1603 as a true exposition of the Roman Catechism, could not compete with that of Canisius. Canisius' beatification by Pius X (1846–1878) as one "who stemmed the Reformation" and his canonization by Pius XI (1922–1939) are indications of the continued Jesuit influence in the Roman Catholic Church. (But Pius XI also canonized Bellarmine, thus laying to rest at last a number of controversies that had seemed irreconcilable in their time.)

The issues debated at the Council of Trent were so crucial and its resolutions so decisive for the course of Western history that the events stimulated two great histories that have brought diametrically opposed interpretations into the literature. In 1618 Paolo Sarpi, a Venetian priest, published his *History of the Council of Trent,* the "Iliad of our age." Sarpi was a late Venetian version of the fifteenth-century *uomo universale,* skilled at mathematics and optics, learned in Oriental religions, active in governmental and ecclesiastical affairs. In a crisis between the papacy and Venice, based on old and cherished enmity between them, the pope laid the interdict on Venice. Sarpi emerged as a strong apologist for Venice, and argued that the pope's position in the church was a usurpation. In his history of Trent Sarpi made the papacy a villain and exposed the conniving of the curia to protect the interests of Rome. Sarpi stressed the unpredictable events in history, rather than legality or uniformity, and showed how plans often have results quite different from those intended. Since accidents defeat human designs, chance severely delimits the area in which an individual can maneuver. In answer to Sarpi, the Jesuit historian Pallavicino wrote a history of his own. He had no difficulty in demonstrating that Sarpi had altered documents and manipulated facts to put the Holy See in a bad light. He defended the integrity of the council and warmly approved of its results, which he considered had been achieved through Providential guidance.

In retrospect, it seems quite clear that after the invasions of Italy by the northern powers and the wars on Italian soil, as well as the economic decline of Italy and the loss of vitality and initiative, the Renaissance was dead or dying in Italy even before the Counterreformation gained strength and turned repressive. It lingered on into the sixteenth century in Venice, which produced a version of civic humanism, the Venetian school of art, and intellectuals such as Sarpi. But it was the demise of the Renaissance and the enervation of Christian humanism that allowed the Counterreformation to develop its narrow rigidity and authoritarian character by default. The Spaniards were not alone to blame for the turn things took.

The continuity of the Counterreformation with medieval efforts at reform is very striking. The Council of Trent was reminiscent of the Fourth Lateran Council of 1215, when ecclesiastical reform was tied up with the crusades against the Moslem heretics. The intervention of nascent national interests into the affairs of the church is more fully developed at Trent, but directly related to particularist interests asserted against the universalism of the church during all the last centuries of the Middle Ages. Ideas make for change, institutions make for stability. It may not be too fanciful to see in the systematic response of the world's oldest continuous institution, the Roman Catholic Church, to the prophetic call of the evangelicals to repentance and faith one more grand dramatization of that age-old conflict of prophets and priests which reaches far back into the history of Israel.

To the historian who has some feeling for the great forces of change and continuity in history, the struggle of Reformation and Counterreformation offers a fascinating spectacle. He cannot help viewing with awe and respect the response of the Catholic Church to the most traumatic crisis of her long history, a crisis that, as the Erasmian cardinals observed in 1537, had "well nigh overwhelmed her." Something of this sort of sentiment must have touched the Whiggish English historian Thomas Babington Macaulay when he wrote in his review of Leopold von Ranke's *History of the Popes* (1840):

> There is not and there never was on this earth a work of human policy as deserving of examination as the Roman Catholic Church. . . . She saw the commencement of all the governments and of all the ecclesiastical establishments that now exist in the world; and we feel no assurance that she is not destined to see the end of them all. She was great and respected before the Saxon had set foot on Britain, before the Frank had passed the Rhine, when Grecian eloquence still flourished in

Antioch, when idols were still worshipped in the temple of Mecca. And she may still exist in undiminished vigor when some traveler from New Zealand shall, in the midst of a vast solitude, take his stand on a broken arch of London Bridge to sketch the ruins of St. Paul's.

Bibliography

General:

BRANDI, KARL. *Gegenreformation und Religionskriege,* vol. 2 of *Reformation und Gegenreformation.* Leipzig, 1942.

BURNS, EDWARD M. *The Counter Reformation.* Princeton, 1964.

DANIEL-ROPS, HENRY. *The Catholic Reformation.* London and New York, 1962.

DELUMEAU, J. *La vie économique et sociale de Rome dans la seconde moitié du XVIe siècle.* Paris, 1957.

DICKENS, A. G. *The Counter Reformation.* New York, 1969.

GARSTEIN, OSKAR. *Rome and the Counter-Reformation in Scandinavia (1539–1583).* Bergen, 1963.

HUGHES, PHILIP. *Rome and the Counter-Reformation.* London, 1944.

JANELLE, PIERRE. *The Catholic Reformation.* Milwaukee, 1949.

JEDIN, HUBERT. *Reformation, Katholische Reform, und Gegenreformation,* vol. 3 of *Das Handbuch der Kirchengeschichte.* Freiburg, 1967.

KIDD, B. J. *The Counter-Reformation.* London, 1933.

MOURRET, F. *A History of the Catholic Church,* vol. 5. St. Louis, 1930.

OLIN, JOHN C., ed. *The Catholic Reformation: Savonarola to Ignatius Loyola.* New York, 1969.

TUCHLE, HERMANN; BOUMAN, C. A.; and LEBRUN, JACQUES. *Réforme et Contre-Réforme,* vol. 3 of *La nouvelle histoire de l'Église.* Paris, 1968.

WARD, A. W. *The Counter-Reformation.* London, 1888.

Catholic reform:

BENDISCIOLI, MARIE. *La riforma Cattolica.* Rome, 1958.

BREZZI, PAOLO. *Le riforme Cattoliche dei secoli XV e XVI.* Rome, 1945.

DOUGLAS, RICHARD M. *Jacopo Sadoleto, 1477–1547: Humanist and Reformer.* Cambridge, 1959.

EVENNETT, H. OUTRAM. *The Spirit of the Counter-Reformation,* ed. John Bossy. Cambridge, 1968.

JOURDAN, G. V. *The Movement Towards Catholic Reform in the Early Sixteenth Century.* London, 1914.

MCNALLY, ROBERT E., S.J. *Reform of the Church.* New York, 1963.

——. *The Unreformed Church.* New York, 1965.

MAURENBRECHER, WILHELM. *Geschichte der Katholischen Reformation.* Nordlingen, 1880.

PONELLE, L., and BORDET, L. *St. Philip Neri and the Roman Society of His Times.* London, 1932.

PROSPERI, ADRIANO. *Tra evangelismo e controriforma: G. M. Giberti, 1495–1543*. Rome, 1969.

Jesuits:
BÖHMER, HEINRICH. *The Jesuits.* Philadelphia, 1928.
——. *Ignatius von Loyola.* Stuttgart, 1951.
BRODRICK, JAMES. *The Economic Morals of the Jesuits.* London, 1934.
——. *St. Peter Canisius.* London, 1935.
——. *The Origins of the Jesuits.* London, 1940.
——. *The Progress of the Jesuits.* London, 1947.
——. *St. Francis Xavier.* London, 1952.
——. *St. Ignatius Loyola: The Pilgrim Years.* New York, 1956.
CAMPBELL, T. J. *The Jesuits,* 2 vols. New York, 1921.
DUDON, PAUL. *St. Ignatius of Loyola.* Milwaukee, 1949.
RAHNER, HUGO. *Ignatius von Loyola.* Freiburg, 1956.
SCADUTO, MARIO, S.J. *Storia della Compagnia di Gesù in Italia,* 3 vols. to date. Rome, 1964.
SCHURHAMMER, GEORG. *Franz Xaver, sein Leben und seine Zeit.* Freiburg, 1963.
SEDGWICK, H. D. *St. Ignatius Loyola.* New York, 1923.
TACCHI-VENTURI, PIETRO, S.J. *Storia della Compagnia di Gesù in Italia,* 2 vols., rev. ed. Rome, 1950–1953.
VAN DYKE, PAUL. *Ignatius Loyola, the Founder of the Jesuits.* New York, 1926.

Inquisition and Index:
BETTEN, F. S. *The Roman Index of Forbidden Books.* Chicago, 1935.
COULTON, G. G. *Inquisition and Liberty.* New York, 1938.
HAUBEN, PAUL J., ed. *The Spanish Inquisition.* New York, 1969.
LEA, H. C. *History of the Inquisition in Spain,* 4 vols. New York, 1922.
LECLER, JOSEPH. *Toleration and the Reformation,* 2 vols. London, 1960.
ROTH, C. *The Spanish Inquisition.* New York, 1938.
TUBERVILLE, A. S. *The Spanish Inquisition.* New York, 1932.

Council of Trent:
ALBERIGO, GIUSEPPE. *I vescovi italiani al Concilio di Trento (1545–1547).* Florence, 1959.
CRISTIANI, L. *L'Église à l'époque du Conceil de Trente.* Turin, 1948.
EVENNETT, H. O. *The Cardinal of Lorraine and the Council of Trent.* Cambridge, 1940.
HARNEY, M. P. *The Jesuits in History.* New York, 1941.
JEDIN, HUBERT. *A History of the Council of Trent,* 2 vols. to date. St. Louis, 1957–1961.
SARPI, PAOLO. *History of the Council of Trent.* London, 1676.
SCHNÜRER, GUSTAV. *Katholische Kirche und Kultur in der Barockzeit.* Paderborn, 1937.
SCHROEDER, HENRY J., ed. *Canons and Decrees of the Council of Trent.* St. Louis, 1941.
WILLAERT, LÉOPOLD, S.J. *Après le Conceil de Trente: La restauration catholique, 1563–1648,* vol. 18 of *L'histoire de l'Église.* Tournai, 1960.

CHAPTER 19

Civil War in France
and the
Spanish Preponderance

The sixteenth century was the golden age of Spain. Not only did
Spain weather the storms of the Reformation as the mightiest Catholic power, not
only did it found a new empire throughout the world, but during the second half
of the century it overshadowed its old rival France, torn by a confessional crisis
and civil war that threatened it with total ruin. During the year 1559, one year after
the death of Charles V, a number of crucial events pushed history in the course it
would take. In that year the Treaty of Cateau-Cambrésis marked the end of French
efforts to conquer Italy and provided relief in foreign affairs which allowed the
French to turn their attention to domestic problems. In that year the fanatical King
Henry II died and was succeeded by Francis II, a sickly boy of fifteen who in spite
of his youth was already married to the queen of Scotland. That was the year in
which the Reformed congregations held their first national synod in Paris. Above
all, 1559 marked the beginning of the era in which Spain, under its strange and
devoted monarch Philip II, assumed the leadership of the Catholic world and undertook to establish its hegemony in Europe. The rise of Spain was a concomitant
of the turmoil in France, which was rocked by bloody conflicts between rival political and religious factions.

The Wars of Religion in France

A MOST REMARKABLE WOMAN analyzed with great candor the predicament of France in the second half of the sixteenth century. Queen Catherine de' Medici, the widow of King Henry II and daughter of Lorenzo the Magnificent, to whom Machiavelli had dedicated *The Prince,* once wrote to the pope: "It is impossible to reduce either by arms or law those who are separated from the Roman Church, so large is their number." Calvinism was indeed making tremendous inroads in France. Its adherents grew from half a million to a million and a half by 1562, with possibly some decline after that. The conventional statement that Calvinism attracted the bourgeois and lesser nobility whereas the upper nobility and the peasants and urban masses remained Catholic needs to be considerably revised. A good number of the most powerful aristocrats and governmental leaders joined the Reformed cause, and in a number of urban centers the common citizens supplied converts and support for the new movement. In 1559 there were already some two thousand Reformed congregations in France. From 1564 to 1572 French Calvinists considered two competing forms of church government, the congregational and the presbyterian systems. In spite of the pull in two directions, the Calvinists had remarkable cohesion under the guidance of Geneva. But in spite of their reverence for the religious instruction of Calvin and Beza, they ignored their political advice quite freely.

Catherine de' Medici had been condescended to and pushed aside by the haughty French nobility, who considered her the daughter of a "Florentine shopkeeper." But she was a calculating, crafty woman who loved beautiful art and furniture and was indifferent to matters of religion. She was dedicated to maintaining Valois power so long as she or any of her children remained alive to exercise it. She wrote with complete candor: "I am resolved to seek by all possible means to preserve the authority of the king my son in all things, and at the same time to keep the people in peace, unity, and concord, without giving them occasion to stir or to change anything." Opportunistic and skillful, she played the parties within France against each other and fended off her son-in-law, Philip II of Spain, until at last she died in 1588, the year in which his hopes of ruling all of Europe sank with the Armada.

When Henry II died of his jousting wound, the Calvinists hoped for some relief from royal persecution, but their hopes were to be disappointed. Francis II devoted himself with adolescent fervor to his young bride, Mary Stuart, and allowed her fervent Catholic uncles Francis of Guise and Charles, cardinal of Lorraine, to dominate the government. The powerful nobles whom the Guises excluded from influence in the government secured Huguenot support for the opposition. They held that Antoine de Bourbon should serve as regent for the young king, and Constable Montmorency and the Bourbons maneuvered for positions of power. Catherine de' Medici saw an opportunity to put the crown above both parties and had a mediating moderate, Michel de L'Hôpital (1503–1573), appointed chancellor in 1560. But strong Catholics held both the executive and the judicature, and Catherine's attempt to rise above the battle failed. The Conspiracy of Amboise, in March 1560, to capture the king or at least to free him from domination by the Guises, was foiled. The prince of Condé was arrested for complicity in the plot, but at the very moment when prospects for a total victory for the Guises were most promising, King Francis II died (December 5, 1560) and the situation took a new turn.

The new king, Charles IX (1560–1574), was only ten years old, which gave Catherine her opportunity to step in as regent, with Antoine, king of Navarre, as lieutenant general of the realm. Mary Stuart left for Scotland and the Guises were maneuvered to one side, a development they were not about to accept as final. At Easter in 1561 a triumvirate made up of the duke of Guise, Montmorency, and the sieur de St.-André, marshal of France, succeeded in establishing themselves as the real force in the government. Catherine naturally now looked to the Bourbons and the Huguenots for support. Acts of violence multiplied and radical proposals increased. At a meeting of the estates general at Pontoise a Protestant member of the third estate proposed that all the secular possessions of the church should be sold with the exception of a single residence for each benefice holder, and that the proceeds should be used for the support of the church and clergy and to amortize the public debt. The frightened clergy voted a subvention to the regent to relieve the financial difficulties of the state. Catherine pressed for the reconciliation of the parties by sponsoring a colloquy at Poissy in September 1561. The French government invited Beza rather than Calvin to represent the Reformed cause, but there was no real dialogue, for Beza was not permitted to answer the rebuttal of Charles of Guise. Lainez, the general of the Jesuit order, present at the colloquy, urged the Catholics to drive out these "wolves, foxes, and serpents."

Catherine then made an important move toward religious peace. She summoned to St.-Germain-en-Laye the representatives of all the parlements, the principal courts of justice, to discuss the religious question. Then on January 17, 1562, she pronounced through her moderate chancellor, L'Hôpital, the famous edict that for the first time gave the Huguenots official recognition and an important measure of toleration. L'Hôpital had called her the "kindest woman on earth," but her move was dictated by expediency more than by any humanitarian impulse. The edict demanded that the Huguenots return the churches of which they had taken possession, but they were now given permission to hold services outside of towns; inside the cities they would be permitted to worship only in private houses. The preamble of the edict states expressly that the edict was not intended to sanction permanently two religious confessions in one state, but to preserve peace and concord until God restored true unity. Catherine and L'Hôpital were *politiques*, fostering toleration to promote the interest of the state over all religious factions. Still, recognition of the Huguenots' legal right of existence was a development of tremendous importance. The feudal particularist interests of the nobles and the republican sentiment of the burghers were given freer expression. But the Catholic Guises refused to honor the provisions of the edict, and two months after the edict was announced, France was torn by an outbreak of hostilities that were to last over thirty years and leave the land exhausted.

The massacre of Vassy precipitated the first in the series of bloody wars. The Guises maneuvered to win the support of Philip II of Spain for the Catholic side, and at the same time they met in Zabern with the Lutheran duke Christoph of Württemberg in order to forestall Protestant support for the Calvinists. Returning to France, Duke Francis of Guise encountered a congregation of Huguenots worshiping in Vassy in Champagne. His troops attacked them and killed over three hundred. The Catholics celebrated the duke's return to Paris as a great military victory. The triumvirate now forced Catherine to move to Paris from Fontainebleau and to work more closely with the Catholics.

The Huguenots, led by Admiral Gaspard de Coligny and the prince of Condé, now took up arms to enforce the January edict and to free Catherine and Charles IX from the Guises, and captured Orléans, Lyon, and other cities. Calvinist chaplains accompanied the army into battle, conducted services on the field, and led in the singing of psalms. Queen Elizabeth of England sent troops to occupy Le Havre as a hostage for Calais. Catherine hired Swiss and German mercenaries and appealed to the pope and to Philip II of Savoy for help. Duke Francis captured Condé, and an assassin murdered Duke Francis on the Loire bridge in February 1563. This left Admiral de Coligny as leader of the Huguenots, and he greatly rejoiced at God's judgment upon Duke Francis. But after suffering defeat at Rouen and being held to a stalemate at Dreux, the Huguenots were happy to accept the Peace of Amboise (1563), which allowed Calvinist nobles to hold services in their castles and burghers to maintain one church in each bailliage. Calvin and Coligny, however, were critical of the peace, and the pope, the emperor, and Philip II of Spain were equally dissatisfied. Guerrilla bands continued to ransack towns and destroy crops. Catherine made a goodwill tour to sell the peace, but destroyed the effect she was trying to create by meeting (1565) at Bayonne with the hated duke of Alba and her daughter Elizabeth, who had married Philip II after Bloody Mary's death and was now queen of Spain. Fear of a sinister plot to wipe out Protestants goaded the Huguenots into preparing once again for war.

War came again in 1567, the Huguenots crying out that they would "free the king" from Catherine. They nearly captured the court in Meaux and forced Catherine to take precipitous flight, an indignity she never forgave. Both sides were exhausted and agreed to a new peace on March 23, 1568.

Catherine felt desperate, for conciliation and repression alike had failed. Both sides were now organizing politically, and new Catholic leagues, such as the Brotherhood of the Holy Ghost in Burgundy, were forming to serve as vigilantes against the local Huguenots. The Huguenots fortified La Rochelle on the Atlantic coast and other strong points. Condé led some 30,000 men, but in March 1569 he was captured in battle at Jarnac and killed. Admiral de Coligny carried on alone. Happily for him, Catherine now became suspicious of Charles of Guise's proposal that Philip II of Spain inherit the throne if none of her children had heirs, and she moved closer to the Huguenots. The Edict of St.-Germain (August 8, 1570) granted freedom of conscience to the Calvinists and places to worship, as before the war.

Coligny now very unwisely pressed his advantage too far. With four major strongholds in La Rochelle, Cognac, Montauban, and La Charité, the Huguenots felt new unity and strength. Coligny tried to organize the French for a move against Spain, aimed at dividing up the Spanish Netherlands with Ludwig of Nassau and England. Coligny even dared say to Catherine de' Medici that anyone who opposed war with Spain was not a good Frenchman. He had pushed Catherine too far, and she decided that France must be rid of Admiral de Coligny once and for all. She connived in a plot on his life, but the assassin sent to kill him failed to finish him off. The Huguenots demanded an inquiry, and Catherine and the Guises, fearing exposure, agreed that not only Coligny but all the top Calvinist leadership had to go. The result was the massacre of St. Bartholomew's Night, one of the great horrors in Western history, which has seen so many.

Much mystery still surrounds the actual circumstances of the massacre, including the extent of the knowledge and involvement of young King Charles IX. Catherine seems to have been involved in the plot but did not foresee the extent of the slaughter. On the night of August 23–24, 1572, assassins broke into Coligny's chambers in Paris, stabbed him, and hurled his body from the window. That same night other leading Huguenots were murdered. The conspirators had decided in advance that young Condé and Henry of Navarre, who had married another of Catherine's daughters only the week before, would be given an opportunity to save their lives by converting to Catholicism, and they hastily agreed. While the two princes were being taken into custody, fanatical mobs went on a mad hunt for heretics throughout Paris, killing at least three thousand men. The wholesale slaughter spread to the provinces and lasted into October, resulting in death for thousands of Huguenots, in order, as Catherine put it, "to wipe out those subjects who were rebellious to God and to Charles IX." Pope Gregory XIII celebrated the massacre with a *Te Deum* and had a medal struck to commemorate the event.

It is said that when Philip II learned of the massacre, he laughed for the first time in his life.

The massacre was a bad mistake. The Huguenots rallied, won new sympathizers, and determined upon continued armed resistance. Powerful nobles resolved to restore traditional feudal independence and oppose the "despicable despotism" of King Charles. But moderate Catholics, the *politiques,* joined milder Calvinists to form a middle party to work for stability within the state. Through their spokesman, Marshal Darnville, son of the constable Montmorency, they declared their loyalty to the king but asked for freedom of worship for the Protestants. At this juncture, in 1574, Charles IX died and his brother Henry III rushed back from Poland to ascend the throne.

Henry III was politically stupid. Catherine's spoiled favorite, he grew up a wastrel, a sensuous roué, given to debauches and lascivious living. He kept a bevy of "darlings," pretty boys in women's dress, for his amusement. The Calvinists responded to the leadership of this new monarch with very little enthusiasm. In 1576, to keep the Huguenots in their place, Duke Henry of Guise, son of the murdered Francis, organized the Catholic League, with local chapters to keep the faith and the king supreme in all the provinces. The league favored the ancient freedoms of the nobility and the medieval prerogatives of the third estate and gained a good deal of support for its cause. Henry III decided that if he could not lick them, he would join them, and made himself head of the league. He thereby alienated the *politiques* and the Huguenots and still failed to placate Henry of Guise and the ultra-Catholics. Alarmed, Henry III declared all leagues dissolved and allied himself with Henry of Navarre, who had renounced his enforced Catholicism at the first opportunity and was now leader of the Huguenots. Civil war and riots went right on. To the surprise of a number of people, Henry III and some of his *mignons* proved to be fine military commanders.

In 1584 Henry III's last brother, Francis, duke of Alençon, died and the Valois line was played out. Duke Henry of Guise tried to exclude Henry of Navarre, a Bourbon, from possible succession to the crown on the grounds of his heretical faith. Henry of Navarre attacked and the "war of the three Henrys" was on. Henry III tried to assert his authority at the meeting of the estates general in Blois, but Duke Henry of Guise and the Catholic Leaguers proved that they were in control. Fearing the duke of Guise, Henry III committed his final blunder. He had the popular Duke Henry murdered in the castle of Blois. He is said to have kicked the dead body and callously remarked, "My, but he is tall." The next day Duke Henry's brother Louis was also killed. Henry III thought that he was at last truly king, but the Catholics were now in open rebellion. Queen Catherine saw at once that Henry III had blundered again. "You have cut out, my son," she exclaimed, "but you must sew together!" Thirteen days later, in January 1589, Queen Catherine de' Medici departed from this vale of tears in despair at having to leave her son in such a spot. Terrified when members of the Catholic League assembled in Paris to avenge the murders of the Guises, Henry III fled to the protection of Henry of Navarre. But on August 1, 1589, a fanatical Dominican murdered Henry III, not realizing that he thereby prepared the way to the throne for the Huguenot. With his last breath Henry III acknowledged Henry of Navarre as his heir and successor to the throne of France.

Handsome, generous, eloquent, soldierly, the thirty-five-year-old Henry IV quickly won the affection of the people, though his religion was unacceptable to the Catholic majority. He issued a statement that he would not harm the Catholics but within six months would assemble a council to deliberate on the religious question. The *politiques* and moderate Protestants such as Philippe du Plessis-Mornay favored him. When the milder Catholic Leaguers declared that their only objection to Henry IV was that he was Protestant, Henry allowed the archbishop of Bourges to declare that he was ready to become Catholic (again). On July 25, 1593, he abjured his Reformed faith, early in 1594 he was anointed in Chartres, and on March 22, 1594, he entered Paris. He is reported to have commented, "Paris is worth a mass."

Henry IV now enjoyed such popular support that he felt confident enough to battle in alliance with England against Philip II of Spain. On May 2, 1598, at the urging of Pope Clement VIII, who was dismayed at a war between Catholic powers, Henry agreed to the Peace of Vervins. A few weeks before the end of the Spanish war, Henry IV moved to aid his former coreligionists with the famous Edict of Nantes (April 13, 1598), the edict of toleration for the Huguenots. The Huguenots could hold church services in two locations in every bailiwick except in Paris and within five miles of the capital, and some other large cities. They were to enjoy all political privileges, including the holding of public offices and membership in the parlements. For eight years some two hundred towns were to be places of security under Huguenot governors, and their garrisons were to be maintained at government expense. Pope Clement VIII, the Paris parlement, and the Catholic clergy opposed these concessions, but Henry pushed them through.

Henry IV now labored with energy and intelligence to heal the wounds of three decades of civil war and to build up France internally once again. Maximilien de Béthune, duke of Sully, the gloomy but honest and efficient Calvinist that he appointed to oversee the economic recovery, fought inflation by cutting expenses and reducing corruption in tax collection. He believed that ultimately land was the true source of wealth, and accordingly worked to improve agriculture, build new farm-to-market roads, drain swamps, dig canals, construct bridges, and protect the peasants from marauding bands of robbers. He set up a commission on commerce to promote industry, such as silk manufacturing in Lyon. Sully even originated Henry IV's grand design to make France the head of a *république chrétienne* for the promotion of peace and order in Christendom. Looking beyond Europe, the crown established new colonies in North America and Asia. In 1608 Champlain established French settlements in Port Royal and Quebec.

When all seemed to be going well, fate once again intervened. Henry IV continued his pressure on Spain, especially in the Netherlands, and he allied himself with several German Protestant princes to keep the small state of Jülich-Cleves from falling into the hands of Spain. While preparing to join his forces on the eastern front, Henry was murdered on a street in Paris on May 14, 1610, by a Catholic fanatic who believed that Henry intended to wage war on the pope. Unhappy France fell victim once again to forces that threatened disintegration.

For seven years Henry's widow, Marie de' Medici, served as regent for her young son Louis XIII (1610-1643). With the great Cardinal Richelieu as his minister from 1624 on, Louis XIII was able to continue successfully the Bourbon policy of making the king supreme in France and France supreme in Europe, which came to full fruition with the reign of his son, Louis XIV. No doubt the fear and fatigue generated by the civil war made the French people readier to accept absolutism than they might otherwise have been. France had come a long way since the rosy days of Francis I, when the humanists hailed the advent of the golden age. The Habsburg-Valois wars had bled her and the wars of religion had ravished her. By the seventeenth century the will to resist absolutism was greatly weakened. The struggle of the Huguenot minority with the Valois, however, stimulated new political theories of sovereignty and the right of resistance that were of great significance at the time and in the subsequent age of democratic revolutions.

The Development of French Political Thought

It used to be thought that the French Calvinists went along with the Genevan's teaching on obedience to civil authority until their precarious position was rendered so critical by the St. Bartholomew massacre in 1572 that they then developed full-blown theories of the limitations of the sovereign and the right of resistance to the monarch. The truth is that medieval political theory had in the main reflected the reality of limited monarchy, with sovereignty subject to the good old laws and shared with lesser feudal authorities and with the estates. The canon lawyers who supported papal claims to the *plenitudo potestatis,* or fullness of power, and Renaissance proponents of *The Prince* contributed something to the theoretical basis of absolute monarchy. Such an absolutist theory of monarchy did develop in the France of Francis I, extending the theories of the lawyers from Louis IX onward to enlarge the powers of the crown in every possible direction.

Their conception was that of a monarch ruling as vicegerent for God, independently of popular will and consent. The Roman legists tended to see the very essence of sovereignty as the lawmaking power.

Some theorists, such as the humanist Guillaume Budé, argued that if the king acted contrary to reason and equity or to his own ordinances he was guilty of *lèse majesté,* but the king was ultimately the judge of what constituted right reason. Claude de Seyssel, a bishop who had served as chancellor and as ambassador to England, implied in his *Le grand monarchie de France* (1518) that the whole complex of traditional and actual restraints upon the royal will belonged in a real way to the unwritten constitution of the French monarchy. Monarchy rests on custom and expediency, not on divine right, he argued, and the problem of government is how best to maintain peace, order, and justice. Queen Catherine's chancellor, Michel de L'Hôpital, asserted that the ruler held his authority directly from God. He believed that France's only hope for peace and order lay in the ruler's power to make law and to determine all questions without appeal. The subject was never justified in rebellion, regardless of what the ruler did, and tyrannicide was an abomination. Only the ruler's full sovereignty could maintain unity in the state.

The most powerful political thinker of the sixteenth century was indisputably Jean Bodin (*c.* 1529–1596), author of *The Method for the Easy Comprehension of History* (1566) and of *The Six Books of the Republic* (1576). Bodin taught at the University of Toulouse and then moved to Paris to write on jurisprudence, with all France as his focus. He saw the family, under the natural authority of the father, as the true source and origin of the republic. The state, he argued, is an association of families, over which it has sovereign power, which should be directed toward the realization of all good for mind and body. The government of a well-ordered state will be concerned with justice, defense, and economics. Sovereignty is the recognized and unlimited authority to make law. Bodin considered such sovereignty indispensable to calm the disorders of his times. Nevertheless, he was a proponent of limited monarchy. In a letter to a friend around 1580 he wrote these striking lines:

> What could be more democratic than what I dared to write, that the king was not permitted to exact tribute without the consent of the citizens? Of how great importance is the fact which likewise I stated, that princes are held by divine and natural law, by a sterner bond than are their subjects? That they are held by compacts just like other citizens?[1]

Against the background of such monarchical political theory, the Calvinist theories of resistance to the state stand out as truly revolutionary. In opposition to the ancient French tradition of *un roi, une loi, une foi* (one king, one law, one

---

[1] Bodin to Du Faur, October 3, 1580(?), cited in Beatrice Reynolds, *Proponents of Limited Monarchy in Sixteenth-Century France: Francis Hotman and Jean Bodin* (New York, 1931), pp. 185–86.

faith), dissident nobles challenged the unity of the consolidated state and non-conforming Calvinists pressed the claim for legalized diversity of religion. Calvin had taught a doctrine of nonresistance and had carefully dissociated himself from the Conspiracy of Amboise. But Calvin openly criticized tyrants, and he allowed an important exception to his rule of nonresistance: when the authority of man conflicts with duty to God, one must obey God rather than man. The lesser magistrates, like the Spartan ephors or Roman tribunes, were duty bound to protect the people from tyranny. Later Calvinists went on to develop ideas with truly revolutionary consequences. The shoddy historian Hilaire Belloc was wrong, of course, but not entirely wrong, when he wrote, "No Calvin, no Cromwell."

Some of Calvin's close associates developed theories of resistance even before their situation in France became desperate—new ideas prior to the concrete realities. Theodore Beza (d. 1605) argued as early as 1554 in his treatise *De haereticis* that persons in inferior positions of authority have the right to lead popular uprisings against higher authority in the name of "true religion." This idea he spelled out without any ambiguity in his 1574 treatise *De jure magistratuum*. Beza cited the precedent of the city of Magdeburg, which defended itself—justly, Beza claimed—against the armies of Charles V during the Schmalkald War. Another Swiss reformer, Pierre Viret (1511–1571), followed Calvin in urging obedience to kings, magistrates, and civil laws as a general principle, but criticized tyrants, urged passive resistance, and even declared that he could conceive of instances when the Lord would countenance "righteous disobedience" to tyrannical political edicts that were contrary to God's will.

A prominent Huguenot legist, François Hotman, published in Geneva his *Francogallia,* a passionately rhetorical treatise on French history and constitutional law. Although he published the work in 1573, he actually wrote it during the six months preceding the St. Bartholomew massacre, so it was not merely a *livre de circonstance* prompted by that outrage. His purpose was to prove that from the time of pre-Roman Gaul the sovereignty of the people, expressed through a national representative body, had been traditionally recognized, except for the period of Roman intervention. The right of the representative body, derived from the sovereignty of the people, to make laws, appoint magistrates, and even depose the king, he maintained, had been recognized until the end of the preceding century, and had been usurped by the Valois kings. Hotman's history was bad, but his treatise served as an effective instrument of propaganda.

An even more astonishing tract was the anonymous *Vindiciae contra tyrannos* (1579), which declared that the prince was bound by a contract expressing the immutable will of God, which neither the king nor the people could break with impunity. Although the *Vindiciae* was weak on specifics, the emphasis on contracts suggested the idea of reciprocal obligation, with emphasis on the obligations of the prince. The people in every kingdom were the true lord and sovereign. Rebellion was always justified against a tyrant, since he had broken his contract by his tyrannical behavior and therefore did not have a just title to his throne. When a legitimate prince has become a tyrant, ruling without regard for law, justice, or piety, he is at enmity with God and man. All may judge when the prince has become a tyrant, but a single individual may not act upon his own responsibility. Only the community may act through its representatives, the nobles and magistrates. For all its tentativeness and fuzziness, the *Vindiciae,* in proclaiming the sovereignty of the people, had very revolutionary implications. The evolution of political thought in France, as in John Knox's Scotland and Puritan England, was of great importance for the embryonic development of modern democratic ideas. Though he is often criticized for overstating the case, there is nevertheless much evidence in support of the historian John L. Motley's claim that Calvinist Protestantism inspired and sustained man's most successful effort to break the yoke of unjust authority. "It is certain," he wrote, "that France, England, the Netherlands, and North America owe a large share of such political liberties as they have enjoyed to Calvinism."[2]

The Spanish Preponderance

FOR SPAIN the sixteenth century was a golden age. While its great rival France was torn apart by internecine warfare, Spain rose to a position of preeminence that it had never before enjoyed and which no other power could equal. Spanish armies paraded their triumphs from Sicily to the North Sea. Spanish fleets roamed the waters from the Gulf of Lepanto to Manila Bay. Spanish *conquistadores* crushed great Indian empires. And Spanish authors and artists produced an efflorescence of culture such as the Iberian peninsula had never known before and has not seen again.

Charles V had hoped to see his only legitimate son, Philip II, succeed him on the throne of the Holy Roman Empire, but the plan failed. Instead the Habsburg dominions were divided between Vienna and Madrid, the house of Austria taking the Danubian inheritance and the imperial crown, Philip II inheriting the kingdom of Spain with its possessions in Africa, Italy (Sicily, Naples, Milan), Burgundy, the Netherlands, Asia, and the New World.

KING PHILIP II OF SPAIN

Philip's mother, Isabella of Portugal, was deeply conscious of the great destiny awaiting her child as she lay in labor on May 21, 1527, in Valladolid. She feared

---

[2] John Lothrop Motley, *History of the United Netherlands* (New York, 1900), vol. 4, p. 431.

that any sign of weakness or suffering would diminish the dignity of that auspicious event. When a lady in attendance urged her to cry out to ease the pain and tension, the queen exclaimed, "Silence! Die I may, but wail I will not!" She then commanded that her face be hidden from the light so that no one could see her grimaces. To such a dedicated, devout mother was born the sickly child who became Spain's mightiest ruler. She died when he was only twelve.

Historians have differed wildly in their estimates of Philip II. To Motley he was "the incarnation of evil," to Roger Merriman "the prudent king." To Leopold von Ranke he was a "dilatory hermit of the Escorial," a patient clerk whose heart was in another world and whose mind was lost in myriad administrative details. The "black legend" about Philip as a vicious, monstrous man who betrayed friends, assassinated enemies, burned heretics, murdered his own son Don Carlos, and lurked like a spider in the dark recesses of the Escorial was a product of the calumnies of Antonio Pérez, a secretary who defected to the enemy, and of the Dutchman William the Silent's *Apologia,* a piece of anti-Spanish propaganda. Recent historians see him as a man who was born into a narrowly circumscribed tradition and who never sought to transcend it. He was well intentioned, but was victimized by circumstances. He was a dutiful son, a devoted husband, and a good father.[3]

From the time Philip was sixteen, Charles V left him to rule as regent whenever he himself was out of the country, and he wrote out a number of letters of instruction to guide him. The most characteristic advice he offered his son was to trust no one and to "depend on none but yourself." Philip spent a lifetime fighting to keep his courtiers from dominating him. He was careful to give rival parties equal representation on the governing councils, so that the decisive voice would be his own. Philip had a grave, dignified, and self-possessed bearing, but he tended to be excessively enigmatic, secretive, crafty, and cautious. Though his Germanic inheritance was revealed in his blue eyes, fair hair, and prominent Habsburg jaw, Philip was Spanish to the core. After signing the Peace of Cateau-Cambrésis in 1559, he never left Spain again until the day of his death nearly forty years later, in 1598. The Spaniards loved him as their very own.

Philip's life was personally tragic. Before he was sixty he had already buried seventeen members of his family. His son Don Carlos, by his Portuguese queen Maria, who died soon after giving birth, was physically stunted and mentally retarded, perhaps the hapless victim of too many consanguineous marriages in his lineage. (His own parents were cousins.) To keep him from falling into the hands of his enemies, Philip kept Don Carlos in close custody, and when he died, Philip's enemies accused him of murdering his own son.

After Maria died, Philip married another cousin, Queen Mary of England, hoping desperately to produce an heir who would unite the Spanish and English

---

[3] See John C. Rule and John J. Te Paske, *The Character of Philip II* (Boston, 1963).

empires as Catholic dominions. He landed at Southampton on July 20, 1554, bearing gifts for friends and foes alike. Three days later, in the episcopal palace of Winchester, Mary saw Philip for the first time and fell desperately in love with him. He was wearing a suit of white kid covered with gold embroidery and a gray satin French surcoat. Mary was a washed-out little woman eleven years older than he, with virtually no eyebrows. Philip had come to beget an heir and he did not blanch even in the face of this challenge, but he failed in the mission. Mary was perhaps even more anxious than Philip to produce a child, for she loved the man; so anxious, in fact, that when a year had passed and Philip left for Brussels to take over the rule of the Netherlands from his father, she experienced a false pregnancy that lasted many more than the traditional nine months. But there was no child, and still Philip did not come. When at last he did return, after an absence of a year and a half, he stayed only long enough to gain England's assistance in Spain's war against France. That was the last Mary saw of him. After her death he had thoughts of trying again with her half-sister, Elizabeth I, but nothing came of them, and to seal the peace with France he married instead Elizabeth of Valois, daughter of Henry II and Catherine de' Medici, with the duke of Alba standing in as his proxy in Paris.

A Spanish writer of the sixteenth century, Pedro de Medina, observed, "There is and has always been in Spain so much fervor for the Holy Catholic Faith that it is something which is not to be found elsewhere." The fervor of the crusades against the Moors and the strength of the hierarchy in resisting Protestant encroachments paid rich dividends in the high religious spirit of the sixteenth century. Pious Philip was in a sense the very embodiment of this Spanish spirit. Not long after his return to Spain in 1559 he resolved to build a seat of government outside of hot Madrid. That massive granite pile, the Escorial, which he built northwest of the city in the foothills of the Sierra de Guadarrama, was in Prescott's phrase "a palace, a monastery, and a tomb." As a palace it was the center of elaborate courtly ceremonies, a part of the inherited Burgundian tradition. As a monastery it was the home of the Hieronymite monks, and with them the pious Philip practiced his religion with fervor, observing long vigils and fasts, praying for long periods, and doing penance. He attended mass every day, and the Venetian ambassador reported that he regularly consulted his confessor on the effect of proposed actions upon conscience. It is not to be supposed, however, that Philip's religious devotion made him a papal lackey or instrument of the hierarchy. Quite the contrary; as he conceived it, his role as Catholic king required his personal control over the papacy. And finally, when Philip's long reign came to an end, the Escorial became a tomb for him and his descendants.

Philip gave detailed attention to nearly every domestic and foreign problem, poring conscientiously over dossiers and annotating dispatches with loving care. Like Frederick the Great and Napoleon, he looked after details personally, but unlike them, he could not distinguish the significant from the insignificant. The government ground along laboriously. "If God decreed my death through the Escorial," a Spanish official commented, "I would be immortal." At the head of the government was a council of state, which was entirely dependent upon the king. The direction was toward absolutism, and the French ambassador once wrote to Catherine that the king secretly meant "to cut the claws and dock the privileges" of the members of the Aragonese cortes, which made them so "insolent and almost free." Philip reformed the judicial system, promoted public works projects, and tried to be a benevolent ruler.

Economic difficulties mounted during Philip's reign. Spain's highland terrain was hot, desiccated, and largely empty. Nearly six million of its eight million inhabitants lived in Castile. Although production did increase during Philip's reign, Spain's industrial base was still so meager that most of the gold and silver that poured in from the New World merely passed through the hands of foreign bankers on its way to the Netherlands and other commercial and industrial centers of Europe. That which remained in Spain added to inflationary pressures there. The sea battles in the Mediterranean, the attempt to suppress the revolt of the Netherlands, and the adventurous assault on England cost Philip enormous sums. In 1573 the government had already spent its income for the next five years. In 1577 taxes were tripled in Castile. On seven occasions Philip repudiated his debts, and still two-thirds of the state's income was paid out in interest on debt by the end of his reign.

FOREIGN AFFAIRS

Philip was the great-grandson of that Ferdinand whom Machiavelli had so admired, and he inherited all of his cunning but little of his luck. Philip's record in foreign affairs was basically tragic, for his two triumphs, the acquisition of Portugal and victory over the Turks in the Mediterranean, were more than offset by the long and costly revolt of the Netherlands and the disaster of the Armada sent against England.

Portugal Won. As with a majority of the Habsburgs' most impressive gains, Philip owed to family ties his inheritance of Portugal and its overseas possessions in South America, India, and the Far East. In 1578 King Sebastian of Portugal was killed in the battle of Alcazarquivir near Tangiers while on a crusade against the Moslems in Morocco. Since he died without male heirs, his granduncle Cardinal Prince Henry assumed the rule until his death early in 1580. Philip, who was the grandson of Manuel I of Portugal (his mother was Manuel's daughter), now saw the need to reinforce his claim to the inheritance by armed intervention. By autumn his army under the duke of Alba had crushed the feeble opposition and

Portugal was united with Spain under the personal sovereignty of the king, though it retained a great deal of autonomy.

The Turks Defeated.   Philip continued the crusading tradition of Ferdinand and Isabella and the warfare at sea of Charles V against the Ottomans. He completed the integration or elimination of the Moslems still living in southern Spain, but gaining control of the sea was another matter. In 1559 the Ottoman Turks and their North African vassals still dominated the Mediterranean. Philip commissioned the viceroy of Sicily to attack Tripoli in alliance with the Knights of St. John on Malta. They scored some successes as long as Suleiman I was preoccupied with his war against Persia, but in 1565 the Turks struck back and took Malta itself, except for a single fortification. The Spaniards drove off the Turkish fleet and Suleiman died on a campaign against Hungary. Philip II, urged on by Pope Pius V, dreamed of dealing the Turks a fatal blow, but the Netherlands were giving him trouble and he could not give full attention to the Turks.

Philip was rocked by the revolt of the *Moriscos* in Granada at the end of 1568, aided by North African Moslems. Don Juan of Austria, an illegitimate son of Charles V, assumed command of the royal army, crushed the *Moriscos,* and went on to plan a counterattack against the Turks. With support from the Venetian, papal, and Genoese fleets, Don Juan maneuvered a weaker Turkish fleet into the bay of Lepanto near Corinth in Greece. On October 7, 1571, he directed the allies in an attack on the Turks that has gone down in history as one of the great sea battles of the century. Of some 208 Turkish galleys and 66 smaller ships, the Spanish forces sank 15 and captured 177, and freed from 12,000 to 15,000 Christian galley slaves. The battle was not so decisive as the West jubilantly believed, for the very next year the Turks sent a fleet of some 250 ships to rove through the Mediterranean. But it was nevertheless the first massive defeat of the Ottomans at sea, and it relieved the pressure on western sea lanes.

The Netherlands Revolt.   The revolt of the Netherlands against Spain has long captured the imagination of Western man. It has all the pathos and heroism of David's battle with Goliath or the Greeks' struggle with mighty Persia. It has appealed to all the deepest emotions of liberal, republican, progressivist Protestant historians. John Lathrop Motley, for example, in his three-volume *Rise of the Dutch Republic,* saw Spanish Catholicism and absolutism as the powers of darkness, while Dutch Protestantism was a force for liberty, democracy, and light. The revolt was indeed one of the most moving spectacles in European history, but the issues at stake were far too complex to be depicted in simple black and white.

During Philip's rule most of the seventeen provinces of the Netherlands rebelled, but only the seven northernmost provinces, located above the great rivers that flow into the North Sea, managed to gain independence, and it took them eighty years to secure Spain's official acknowledgment of the freedom they had won. The seven United Netherlands, together with certain territories to the south and east, comprise the present-day kingdom of the Netherlands. The core of the remaining provinces, which continued under Spanish rule, comprises the present-day kingdom of Belgium. The larger part of the Netherlands was inhabited by people who spoke a Low German dialect, whereas in the Walloon area to the south and to the west French was the predominant language; the division can be traced back to the Frankish invasions of the sixth century. Economically some of the medieval centers of trade, such as Ghent and Bruges, were in decline, while Antwerp and other cities were on the rise. The textile industries were suffering from increased competition from England and other areas. In spite of the inflation produced by the influx of bullion from the New World through Spain, which worked a hardship on certain classes, economic life was not so vigorous as it had been, and as it would be again with Dutch imperial expansion.

Unlike his father, who was at home in the Netherlands, Philip II was a Spaniard and a foreigner. Although his policies were the same as his father's, coming from him the measures were *a priori* less acceptable to the people. Philip attempted to win over the nobility, but disaffection actually developed first among the privileged upper classes and gradually spread to the commoners.

Protestantism had made early inroads into the area. In spite of Charles V's harsh repressive measures, first Lutheranism, then Anabaptism, but then most successfully Calvinism won many adherents. Guido de Bray composed the Calvinist creed *Confession de foi des églises des Pays-Bas*. But Calvinism was professed by only a tiny fraction of the population at the time of the revolt. The burnings of heretics and executions of Reformed pastors added fuel to a growing anticlerical feeling. Economic and ideological elements coalesced into a stubborn determination to rid the land of foreigners.

Although the earlier governor of the Netherlands, Charles V's sister Mary, had got by with few incidents, Philip II had hardly taken command before serious opposition began, in the fall of 1555. There was general resentment over the taxes levied to support the war against the French, which they considered to be a Spanish affair. Margaret of Parma, Philip's half-sister, appointed as governor, seemed very much a foreigner to the people. When one of her officials, Cardinal Granvelle, reorganized the church dioceses and established himself at their head, the estates and upper nobility feared that their traditional privileges were in jeopardy. Resistance to the extranational tendencies of Philip's rule, to excessive centralization, to the loss of ancient rights, to religious persecution, to the presence of Spanish troops arose first among the politically privileged classes and centered around William of Nassau and Orange, lord of Breda and governor of Holland, Zeeland, and Utrecht.

William of Orange has most inappropriately come to be called William the

Silent, a sobriquet earned by his great discretion during early years under Catholic surveillance, though he was by nature articulate and loudly assertive. Born in Dillenburg in 1533, William was brought to his family's lowland possessions as a boy. He was not a man of strong religious feeling, but since he was pacific and tolerant, he strove to unite the Calvinists and Lutherans in opposition to Granvelle's measures in 1564. In response to Philip's harsh religious edicts the next year, William of Orange, the count of Egmont, and the count of Hoorne-Montmorency withdrew from the council of state. In April 1565 the nobles who were inclined toward resistance petitioned Margaret in Brussels to mollify the harsh religious edicts and end the Inquisition. The president of the council on finance referred to the petitioners as "beggars" (*gueux*), a name taken up with pride by the resistance movement. Although Margaret promised amelioration, she reserved the final decision for Philip, a half measure that enfuriated everyone. Religious opposition to "papal idolatry" grew, and Calvinism gained new adherents. A few radicals attacked Vlissingen and Antwerp in February 1567. Alarmed, Philip ordered the duke of Alba from Italy to the Netherlands with an army of Germans, Walloons, and Spaniards to suppress the dissidents.

The duke of Alba rode into Brussels on August 22, 1567, and began his reign of terror by having Egmont, Hoorne, and other nobles arrested. Then he set up a "blood council" to punish everyone who had contributed to the disturbances of the preceding year. Believing that the interest of the state demanded the intimidation of all its subjects, he was inhibited by neither law nor equity. Even while the people were spreading rumors of a general pardon in January 1568, Alba was writing to the king:

> A great deal remains to be done first. The towns must be punished for their rebelliousness with the loss of their privileges; a goodly sum must be squeezed out of private persons; a permanent tax obtained from the States of the country. It would therefore be unsuitable to proclaim a pardon at this juncture. Everyone must be made to live in constant fear of the roof breaking down over his head. Thus will the towns comply with what will be ordained for them, private persons will offer high ransoms, and the States will not dare to refuse what is proposed to them in the King's name.[4]

On one day in March 1568 over five hundred new arrests were made. City officials of high position were "pinioned, manacled, and handcuffed like the meanest criminal." On June 1 Alba had eighteen noblemen beheaded in Zavel Square in Brussels and four days later he executed Egmont and Hoorne at the Great Market Square in that city. The "Iron Duke" paralyzed the people with fear.

If the duke of Alba was the villain of the piece, William of Orange was its hero. He made a feeble effort to invade Flanders, but had to take refuge in France. The

---

4 Pieter Geyl, *The Revolt of the Netherlands (1555–1609)*, 2nd ed. (New York, 1958), pp. 102–3.

Dutch took to their ships, and the Sea Beggars, reinforced from England and La Rochelle, whittled away at the Spanish fleet and liberated towns along the coast. William of Orange now became a Calvinist and led the opposition, with Holland and Zeeland as the main base of the resistance.

When Alba was recalled, Luis de Requeséns continued his nonsensical policies without concessions. Following his death in 1576, Don Juan of Austria, the victor of Lepanto, arrived as governor. Don Juan tried to move toward a peaceful settlement and made concessions on the quartering of Spanish troops, but he insisted upon the restoration of Catholicism in all the provinces. In January 1578 the Spanish troops won a telling victory over the soldiers of the estates general. England's Queen Elizabeth supplied subsidies and the Protestant John Casimer, elector of the Palatinate, sent auxiliary troops to the Beggars. William's brother, John of Nassau, organized the Union of Utrecht to resist Alexander Farnese, duke of Parma, who replaced Don Juan upon his death.

Treachery now robbed the resistance forces of their leader. Philip II put a high price on the head of William of Orange, for there was a movement to make William sovereign over the Netherlands. On July 10, 1584, a Catholic fanatic who had posed as a Calvinist shot William in Delft. The man whom Philip II had called the "plague of Christendom" was gone. Although William's son Maurice took over the leadership of the revolt, the Dutch were badly demoralized by their great loss, and Alexander Farnese took many cities. Elizabeth's expeditionary force under the earl of Leicester was ineffective. Shortly before his death, Philip loosened

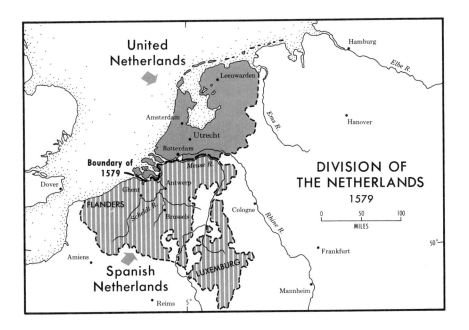

the tie to Spain by making Archduke Albert of Austria, husband of his daughter Isabella, governor of the Netherlands, a rule that extended from 1598 to 1621.

The syndics of the urban centers were men of wealth and independence. A leader representative of this Dutch bourgeois class, Johan van Oldenbarneveldt (1547–1619), promoted the organization of the Dutch East India Company in 1602, a step that led to further commercial and naval rivalry with the Spanish fleets around the world. At last, after four decades of warfare, combat fatigue took its toll. In March 1609 the Spaniards agreed to a twelve-year truce with the northern Netherlands, which became virtually an independent republic. Even though fighting was resumed at the end of the long truce, the statehood of the northern Netherlands was secure, and at the Peace of Westphalia in 1648, which brought an end to the wars of religion in Europe, its independence was finally internationally acknowledged.

The Armada Fails. Philip's most disastrous and desperate venture was dispatching the Spanish Armada against England in 1588. Few episodes have gone down in history as such arrogant acts of aggression, and few events have been so commonly misrepresented. For the truth is that Philip, far from being carried away by "o'erweening pride," was exceedingly apprehensive about the plan, and regarded it as a last resort in a seemingly lost cause. He had been maneuvered into a duel to the death with Elizabeth, the "English Jezebel," through a long series of diplomatic misfortunes. Melanchthon, the fifteenth-century astronomer Regiomontanus, and other seers had found ominous indications in the books of prophecy that the year 1588 would be a year of disaster. It seemed almost as though Philip were being drawn to his rendezvous with destiny by irresistible forces.

In the early years of Elizabeth's reign, Philip had been a source of strength to her, for he shared her fear of Mary Stuart, queen of Scots. As the daughter of James V of Scotland, Elizabeth's first cousin, Mary was next in the line of succession to the English throne and was considered the only legitimate heir by the Catholics, who refused to recognize the marriage of Elizabeth's mother, Anne Boleyn; as the niece of the powerful French duke of Guise, Mary also posed a threat to Philip, for if her English supporters ever succeeded in placing her on the throne, England would then be allied with France, which coveted Flanders and other Habsburg holdings in the Low Countries. As long as Spain feared France, Philip had to allow Elizabeth many liberties. Her privateers engaged in piracy and smuggling, ran cargoes of Negro slaves to Spanish colonies in the New World, seized Spanish treasure ships, and supported the Sea Beggars in their raids on Spanish strongholds. She repeatedly interfered in the revolt of the Netherlands. This situation persisted for some two decades, until at last the political situation within France deteriorated to such an extent that Philip, relieved of his fears in that quarter, felt free to act against his Protestant foe and imperial rival, Elizabeth of England. Elizabeth in turn, fearing Catholic plots to put Mary Stuart on her throne, had her executed on February 18, 1587. The situation had become deadly serious.

Philip spun a web of intrigue from the Escorial, and when none of his plots against Elizabeth succeeded, he resolved on a direct frontal attack, an invasion of the island, which he anticipated would be greeted by an uprising of the Catholics in England and put an end once and for all to the machinations of the illegitimate queen of heretics. Philip, who habitually counseled others "to enjoy the benefits of time," now was impatient to get on with his grand design. "In so great an enterprise as that of England," he had once written, "it is fitting to move with feet of lead." Now he wrote to his captains, "Success depends mostly upon speed. Be quick!"

The assurance of a papal subsidy strengthened Philip in his resolve to undertake the expedition promptly. Pope Sixtus V sent a special observer to Lisbon to note the progress of the enterprise. This observer reported a conversation with one of the highest and most experienced officers of the Spanish fleet which was most revealing in a number of ways:

PAPAL EMISSARY: And if you meet the English Armada in the Channel, do you expect to win the battle?

SPANISH OFFICER: Of course.

PAPAL EMISSARY: How can you be sure?

SPANISH OFFICER: It's very simple. It is well known that we fight in God's cause. So, when we meet the English, God will surely arrange matters so that we can grapple and board them, either by sending some strange freak of weather or, more likely, just by depriving the English of their wits. If we can come to close quarters, Spanish valour and Spanish steel (and the great masses of soldiers we shall have on board) will make our victory certain. But unless God helps us by a miracle, the English, who have faster and handier ships than ours, and many more long-range guns, and who know their advantage just as well as we do, will never close with us at all, but stand aloof and knock us to pieces with their culverins, without our being able to do them any serious hurt. So we are sailing against England in the confident hope of a miracle.[5]

The miracle was denied the Spaniards and the Spanish commander's analysis proved to be remarkably accurate.

One of Philip's most experienced admirals, Santa Cruz, urged that the English sea power should be totally destroyed before a landing operation was undertaken. Although Philip ignored this perfectly sound advice, Santa Cruz literally worked himself to death in preparing the fleet for the risky venture. Instead Philip planned to have the Armada transport the army of Alexander Farnese in the Netherlands to England for a direct assault on the island. In the spring of 1587 Sir Francis Drake made a preventive attack upon Lisbon and Cádiz, wreaking such havoc upon the Spanish ships and supplies that the expedition was delayed a whole year.

---

[5] Garrett Mattingly, *The Defeat of the Spanish Armada* (London, 1959), pp. 191–92.

At last on May 29, 1588, the Armada set sail from Lisbon with 130 ships and more than 30,000 men under the command of the duke of Medina Sidonia. The ships were galleon types with high, vulnerable wooden hulls and banks of oars, useful in the Mediterranean but of far less value than sails on the open sea. Severe storms hit the fleet between Lisbon and La Coruña, and the ships had to put into La Coruña for refitting and could not go to sea again until July 22. When the Armada reached the channel, on July 29, Lord Howard of Effingham set sail from Plymouth with the English fleet—a larger number of low-slung, fast, and maneuverable ships, with longer range guns. Medina Sidonia might have bottled the English up in the harbor and repeated the victorious Spanish tactic of Lepanto, but his orders were to proceed to the Straits of Dover to take aboard the army of Farnese, and he tried to do as he had been told. He realized too late that the English were behind him. On August 6 the Armada lowered anchor off the coast at Calais, but the Dutch blockaded Farnese's fleet of small transport ships at Nieuport and Dunkirk, so that the Spanish army never reached the Armada. The next night the English sent fire ships against the Armada, and in a panic the Spanish captains cut the anchor ropes and put out to sea.

The English and Dutch now had the Armada between them, and attacked from both sides. With water and munitions running low, the Spaniards did not dare risk running the channel again, and fled instead into the North Sea. As the fleet took the long way home, northward around Scotland and Ireland, severe storms drove many ships onto the rocky coasts. Only fifty-three of the larger vessels ever again reached the safety of a Spanish harbor. King Philip received the news of the disaster with calm resignation, as though the defeat of the Armada were what he had expected all along, despite the wild reports of victory that he received from Don Bernardino de Mendoza, his ambassador in Paris. He was gracious and generous toward his defeated commander, for he realized that he had been defeated as much by the forces of nature as by the enemy.

Philip had trained himself to control his emotions with a near iron will. Moreover, his piety and devotion were so deeply rooted that even the disaster that befell the Armada could not shake his faith in Providence. On October 13 of that fateful year he wrote the news of the Armada's fate to the Spanish bishops, reminded them of the uncertainties of warfare on the high seas, and concluded:

> We are bound to give praise to God for all things which He is pleased to do. Now I give thanks to Him for the mercy He has shown. In the storms through which the armada sailed, it might have suffered a worse fate, and that its ill fortune was no greater must be credited to the prayers for its good success, so devoutly and continuously offered.[6]

The next year Elizabeth added insult to injury by sending a punitive expedition of twenty thousand men to raid La Coruña and attack Lisbon. In 1595 the

---

[6] *Ibid.,* p. 327.

Spaniards hit the Cornish coast to aid Irish rebels against the English. In 1596 Howard of Effingham retaliated with an attack by ten thousand troops under the earl of Essex and five thousand Dutch troops under Louis of Nassau. They captured Cádiz and held it for ransom. Philip planned to send another fleet against England, but it was scattered by storms before it was able to set sail. "An admiral, like a doctor, must have fortune on his side," a Spaniard commented at the time.

THE SPANISH EMPIRE

If Philip fared badly in the Old World, the fortunes of Spain still prospered in the New World. The personal union of Iberia under Philip brought together the widespread Portuguese domain with the mighty Spanish empire. While the French, Dutch, and English challenged Spain's power abroad, they were not able to destroy it for many decades.

Tiny Portugal, with its small population of about two million, was able, thanks to the ability and energy of its commanders, to control an empire several hundred times its own size. The explorations of Henry the Navigator, the explorations along the coast of Africa and around the Cape of Good Hope to India, and the discovery of Brazil by Cabral in 1500 established Portugal as a power around the world. By 1503 the Portuguese had already discovered that a few thousand soldiers in garrisons at strategic coastal spots could dominate a large populous hinterland. The great admiral Francisco Almeida worked out a comprehensive plan resting upon sea power and without emphasis upon political domination. The viceroy Albuquerque contemplated a territorial empire fanning out from power centers such as Goa, Calcutta, and Malacca. Lisbon became a great new center of commercial activity, the capital of the profitable spice trade. The king of Portugal received 25 percent of the commercial profits, but the Portuguese largely confined their operations to transporting cargoes and failed to take advantage of the opportunities of selling them in the European markets. The Portuguese were overextended, and during the second half of the century the attrition began to make itself evident.

The rise of Spain's colonial empire is one of the grand sagas of Western history. The iron will, the supreme self-confidence and national pride of the *conquistadores* as they sailed with small ships out into the "ocean sea," explored vast lands never before seen by Europeans, fought native bands, conquered empires, and won vast treasures will forever command the awe and respect of small boys and grown men. The Catholic kings of Spain and many of their captains in all sincerity viewed their enterprise as a mission to extend the blessings of the church and save the souls of the heathen even more than a search for earthly treasure. The stories of Hernán Cortés (1485–1547), who conquered the Aztec civilization with a band of unreliable soldiers, and Francisco Pizarro (c. 1471–1541), who took the mountain redoubts of the Incas and seized their vast treasures, will always remain stirring chapters in the history of Spain.

The Spanish colonial policy differed from the Portuguese in attempting to control an entire area, not just the key ports. Spanish colonial government, administered by viceroys in Mexico and Peru, was superior to that of the Portuguese. Men of established fortunes took posts for honorific reasons (though it is doubtful that they lost any money by their devotion to duty). An advisory council, or *audiencia,* was established in the main city of each of the larger provinces to supervise the operations of the viceroyalty. From time to time the viceroy sent inspectors to gather firsthand information on the local administrations. Finally, there were *residencias* to review the viceroy's record after his term was completed. In Spain the Council of the Indies, drawing on the experience of retired viceroys and administrators, directed the overseas possessions. But the areas controlled by the viceroys were so vast and so diverse that the viceroys could seldom keep abreast of local conditions, and the overdirection and control of the viceroys from the homeland stifled initiative and had an inhibiting effect upon colonial development.

Even though the Spaniards exercised such close political control over their colonies, they did allow private initiative in the development of landed estates (*encomiendas*) and trade. Under the *encomienda* system, the crown made a Spaniard responsible for the education, protection, and religious training of a particular group of Indians, in return for which the Spaniard was entitled to their labor. The system permitted penniless Spaniards who had taken part in the conquest to build up vast landed estates and other economic enterprises, and there was no supervision of the education, protection, or religious training the Indians received. The evils of the system became so notorious that attempts were made to replace it with the *repartimiento,* under which the Indians were still forced to work for the Spaniards, but under contract, on a temporary basis, and for wages. Actually the *encomienda* system lingered on into the eighteenth century, and for a long period the two systems were employed simultaneously.

Twenty percent of all treasure taken from the Indians and of the income of private entrepreneurs went to the king; the "king's fifth," it was called, and it came off the top, before any other allocation was made. Spanish economic policy was aimed at obtaining bullion and raw materials for the homeland; there was to be no colonial competition with such home industries as wine and olive oil production. The influx of silver and to a lesser extent of gold created an inflationary spiral in Andalusia, then in all Spain, and finally in the Spanish Netherlands and other parts of Europe. Spanish prices were 3.4 times higher at the start of the seventeenth century than they had been a hundred years before. In economics even gold does not always glitter.

The Spaniards were not bad maritime organizers at all. In order to protect the ships bearing the silver, gold, and other cargo from pirates, English sea dogs (from 1562 on), and Dutch raiders, they developed the convoy system, which they used down to 1800. Contrary to English legend, there were very few successful raids on Spanish convoys.

Immigration to the Spanish colonies was carefully controlled, and no foreigner, religious irregular, or anyone who was even related to anyone who had been charged by the Inquisition was allowed entry. An exception was made in the case of an English Catholic priest named Thomas Gage, since, like most Englishmen who wished to become priests in those days of militant Protestantism, he had been trained in a Spanish seminary. But Gage only proved the soundness of the rule. After twelve years in Guatemala he became discouraged about his prospects for preferment, returned to England, became a vicar of the Church of England, and wrote a splendidly biased account of conditions in the Spanish colonies, which nevertheless gives revealing insights into the workings of the colonial system. This, for example:

> The miserable conditions of the Indians . . . is such, that though the kings of Spain, have never yielded to what some would have, that they should be slaves, yet their lives are as full of bitterness as is the life of a slave. . . . Thus are the poor Indians sold for threepence a peece for a whole week's slavery, not permitted to goe home at nights unto their wives, though their worke lie not above a mile from the Town where they live; nay some are carried ten or twelve miles from their home who must not returne till Saturday night late, and must that week do whatsoever their Master pleaseth to command them. The wages appointed them will scarce find them meat and drinke. . . . This same order is observed in the city of Guatemala and Townes of Spaniards, where to every family that wants the service of an Indian or Indians, though it be but to fetch water and wood on their backs, or to goe of arrants, is allowed the like service from the neerest Indian townes.[7]

Bishop Bartolomé de Las Casas was a remarkable advocate of the humane treatment of Indians, although he was more influential in Spain than in the colonies. He had a medieval conception of the duty of the ruler toward his subjects, and as a Thomist he employed all the arguments derived from reason and natural law to oppose the colonial *encomiendas* as unjust and tyrannical. Ironically, his concern for the welfare of the Indians led him to recommend the importation of Africans, who could do heavy labor in the heat without the ill effects suffered by the Indians, who, as a Mongoloid people genetically adapted to cool climates, could survive in the tropical lowlands only by adopting a slow rhythm of life—or, as the Europeans liked to say, by being "lazy." It is noteworthy that today the populations of most of the hot coastal regions of Latin America are heavily black, while in the cool mountain regions a black man is a distinct rarity.

The Latin peoples were less loath to cross color lines than were the English and Dutch, and a colorful spectrum of peoples emerged in the Latin colonial areas. The *castillanos* were the Spaniards born in Spain; the *criollos,* or creoles, were people born in America of Spanish parents; the *mestizos* were part Spanish or creole, part Indian; the *mulatos* were part white, part Negro; and the *zambos* were part Indian and part Negro.

---

[7] Thomas Gage, *The English-American His Travail by Sea and Land: Or a New Survey of the West Indies* (London, 1648), pp. 139–40.

PHILIP THE PRUDENT

Philip II was called "the Prudent," which was perhaps the most charitable epithet that could be applied to this dedicated but essentially uninspiring king. He was more fit for the pen and desk than for the sword and saddle. Unlike his father, who traveled incessantly and looked after his empire in person, Philip was bound to the Escorial. Had his capital been Antwerp or Brussels, he would have been able to control his dynastic holdings more effectively, and the revolt in the Netherlands might not have become an albatross around his neck, bringing him endless grief and disaster.

Many circumstances worked against him. The enormous debt of some fifty million ducats bequeathed to him by Charles V gave him an initial financial handicap that he never overcame. New taxes, monopolies, the sale of offices, the "king's fifth" from the New World, all together never came close to meeting the enormous expenditures for government and warfare. At its height the income from America met no more than one-fourth of the government's requirements, which were sent skyrocketing by the wars against the Netherlands and England.

If all these circumstances lay beyond Philip's control, he must nevertheless bear the responsibility for his laborious, meticulous paternalism, for his lack of insight into the financial and economic predicament of Spain, and for his failure to create policy that would slow the forces of debility and disintegration, if it could not halt them.

Bibliography

French political history and the wars of religion:
ARMSTRONG, EDWARD. *The French Wars of Religion,* 2nd ed. Oxford, 1904.
BAIRD, H. M. *History of the Rise of the Huguenots,* 2 vols. New York, 1900.
———. *The Huguenots and Henry of Navarre,* 2 vols. New York, 1909.
BATTIFOL, LOUIS. *The Century of the Renaissance.* London, 1927.
CHARTROU-CHARBONNEL, J. *La réforme et les guerres de religion.* Paris, 1936.
ELLIOTT, J. H. *Europe Divided, 1559–1598.* New York, 1968.
ENGLAND, SYLVIA. *The Massacre of Saint Bartholomew.* London, 1938.
JACKSON, C. *Last of the Valois, and Accession of Henry of Navarre,* 2 vols. London, 1898.
JENSEN, DE LAMAR. *Diplomacy and Dogmatism: Bernardino de Mendoza and the French Catholic League.* Cambridge, Mass., 1964.
LIVET, GEORGES. *Les guerres de religion.* Paris, 1962.
NEALE, J. E. *The Age of Catherine de' Medici.* London, 1943.
PALM, F. C. *Politics and Religion in Sixteenth-Century France.* Boston, 1927.
———. *Calvinism and the Religious Wars.* New York, 1932.
RANKE, LEOPOLD VON. *Französische Geschichte vornehmlich im 16. und 17. Jahrhundert,* 6 vols. Leipzig, 1868–1876.

ROELKER, NANCY L. *The Paris of Henry of Navarre.* Cambridge, Mass., 1958.
———. *Queen of Navarre Jeanne d'Albret, 1528–1572.* Cambridge, Mass., 1968.
SALMON, J. H. M. *The French Religious Wars in English Political Thought.* Oxford, 1959.
———, ed. *The French Wars of Religion: How Important Were Religious Factors?* Boston, 1967.
SEDGWICK, H. D. *Henry of Navarre.* Indianapolis, 1930.
———. *The House of Guise.* Indianapolis, 1938.
STÉPHAN, RAOUL. *L'épopée huguenote.* Paris, 1945.
———. *Histoire du protestantisme française.* Paris, 1961.
SUTHERLAND, N. M. *The French Secretaries of State in the 16th Century.* London, 1962.
———. *Catherine de' Medici and the Ancien Régime.* London, 1966.
THOMPSON, J. W. *The Wars of Religion in France.* Chicago, 1909.
VAN DYKE, PAUL. *Catherine de' Medici,* 2 vols. New York, 1922–1927.
VIENOT, JEAN. *Histoire de la réforme française des origines à l'Édit de Nantes.* Paris, 1926.

French political thought:
ALLEN, J. W. *A History of Political Thought in the Sixteenth Century.* London, 1928.
CHURCH, W. F. *Constitutional Thought in Sixteenth-Century France.* Cambridge, Mass., 1941.
DODGE, G. H. *The Political Theory of the Huguenot Dispersion.* New York, 1947.
FRANKLIN, JULIAN. *Jean Bodin and the Sixteenth-Century Revolution in the Methodology of Law and History.* New York and London, 1963.
———. *Constitutionalism and Resistance in the Sixteenth Century: Three Treatises by Hotman, Beza, and Mornay.* New York, 1969.
GIESEY, RALPH. *The Royal Funeral Ceremony in Renaissance France.* Geneva, 1960.
GÖRING, MARTIN. *Weg und Sieg der modernen Staatsidee in Frankreich.* Tübingen, 1946.
KINGDON, ROBERT M., and LINDER, ROBERT D., eds. *Calvin and Calvinism—Sources of Democracy?* Lexington, Mass., 1970.
LINDER, ROBERT. *The Political Ideas of Pierre Viret.* Geneva, 1964.
REYNOLDS, BEATRICE. *Proponents of Limited Monarchy in Sixteenth-Century France.* New York, 1931.

The Spanish preponderance and Philip II:
ALTIMIRA Y CREVEA, RAFAEL. *A History of Spain from the Beginnings to the Present Day.* New York, 1949.
BERTRAND, LOUIS. *Philippe II à l'Escorial.* Paris, 1928.
——— and PETRIE, CHARLES. *The History of Spain.* London, 1952.
BRATLI, CARL G. *Philippe II, roi d'Espagne: Étude sur sa vie et son caractère.* Paris, 1912.
DAVIES, R. TREVOR. *The Golden Century of Spain, 1501–1621.* London, 1937.
ELLIOTT, J. H. *The Revolt of the Catalans: A Study in the Decline of Spain (1598–1640).* Cambridge, 1964.
FORNESON, H. *L'histoire de Philippe II,* 4 vols. Paris, 1887.
HAUSER, HENRI. *La prépondérance espagnole,* vol. 9 of *Peuples et civilisations.* Paris, 1948.
HUME, MARTIN A. S. *Spain: Its Greatness and Decay, 1479–1788.* Cambridge, 1925.
LIVERMORE, HAROLD. *A History of Spain.* London, 1958.

LYNCH, JOHN. *Spain Under the Hapsburgs,* vol. 1 of *Empire and Absolutism, 1516–1598.* New York, 1964.

MAASS, E. *The Dream of Philip II.* Indianapolis, 1944.

PETRIE, CHARLES. *Philip II of Spain.* New York, 1963.

PRESCOTT, W. H. *History of the Reign of Philip II,* 3 vols. Philadelphia, 1874.

Spain's foreign affairs and the Spanish empire:

BLOK, P. J. *A History of the People of the Netherlands,* 5 vols. New York and London, 1898–1912.

BRAUDEL, FERNAND. *La Méditerranée et le monde méditerranéen à l'époque de Philippe II.* Paris, 1949.

CADOUX, C. J. *Philip of Spain and the Netherlands.* London, 1911.

CHUBODA, BOHDAN. *Spain and the Empire, 1519–1643.* Chicago, 1952.

GEYL, PIETER. *The Revolt of the Netherlands (1555–1609),* 2nd ed. New York, 1958.

HAMILTON, EARL J. *American Treasure and the Price Revolution in Spain, 1501–1650.* Cambridge, Mass., 1934.

HARING, C. H. *Trade and Navigation Between Spain and the Indies in the Time of the Habsburgs.* Cambridge, Mass., 1918.

KOENIGSBERGER, H. G. *The Government of Sicily Under Philip II of Spain.* London, 1959.

LEWIS, MICHAEL. *The Spanish Armada.* London, 1960.

MATTINGLY, GARRETT. *The Defeat of the Spanish Armada.* London, 1959.

MERRIMAN, ROGER B. *The Rise of the Spanish Empire,* 4 vols. New York, 1918–1934.

MOTLEY, J. L. *The Rise of the Dutch Republic,* 3 vols. New York, 1864.

CHAPTER 20

England
Under
Elizabeth

The reign of Queen Elizabeth (1558–1603) may well be described as a forty-five-year love affair between her majesty and the English people. Seldom in history has there been such a happy correspondence of purpose and program between sovereign and subjects as prevailed during that greatest age in English history. Elizabeth's long reign saw England turn thoroughly Protestant and become the leader among Protestant nations. As a national state on the Atlantic, England won a world empire during those decades and experienced a cultural flowering that was its true renaissance. Historians are now inclined to revise downward their estimates of what Elizabeth contributed personally to the government of England. They feel that she improvised and temporized, "muddled through," rather than providing statesmanlike guidance and vision. But when the effusions of her admirers have been recognized as the patriotic pieties they are, and Elizabeth herself has been reduced to human scale, she remains a remarkable woman who presided over England in an exciting era.

By the time Elizabeth ascended the throne at the age of twenty-five, she was an experienced and worldly-wise young woman, moderately tall, with pale red hair, an olive complexion, striking, expressive eyes, graceful hands, and a dignified bearing. Shrewd, calculating, dissembling, capable of playing coquette or the cold administrator, with the self-confidence to make quick decisions and the strength of nerve for Fabian tactics, Elizabeth was far better suited to occupy the throne of her royal father than either Edward or Mary had ever been.

The transfer of power from Mary to Elizabeth took place smoothly, for while Mary lay dying at St. James's the people were already rallying to Elizabeth at Hatfield. Feria, the Spanish ambassador, reported, "She is much attached to the people and is very confident that they are all on her side, which is indeed true." Her coronation took place on January 15, 1559.

A certain antifeminist bias was widespread and people generally expected the queen to marry. There were suitors enough for her royal hand. Her brother-in-law, Philip II, offered to do the honors, but Elizabeth was far too astute to marry the Catholic monarch, especially after Mary's unhappy experience. Her passionate lover Robert Dudley, earl of Leicester, was spoiled, impulsive, and undependable. The uncertainty about the cause of his wife's death, either from an accidental fall or by suicide, created a public scandal. Although Elizabeth was strongly attracted to him, she characteristically allowed her head to rule her heart and put the "weal of the kingdom" above her personal feelings. A "modern woman" who could speak French, Latin, and Italian, Elizabeth was also skilled at double-talk, and kept many ambitious men living in hope and at her service. The Scottish ambassador remarked to her, "Madam, I know your stately stomach: ye think if ye were married, ye would be but queen of England, and now ye are king and queen both; ye may not suffer a commander." To Protestants the "virgin queen" was a heroic Judith; to Catholics she was a Jezebel, a servant of infamy, the refuge of evil men.

The Elizabethan Settlement

ELIZABETH CHOSE as her closest adviser William Cecil, later Lord Burghley, a moderate Protestant who had served under Somerset and Northumberland, and even for a short time under Queen Mary. He served Elizabeth during nearly all of her reign, first as secretary of state and then as lord treasurer, counseling to action with moderation, to decisiveness with discretion. Elizabeth appointed only Protestants to her council—men more devoutly Protestant and more favorable to Puritans than she herself was. Her secretary of state from 1573 to 1590, Sir Francis Walsingham, followed a policy of active support for the beleaguered Protestants on the continent, especially the Dutch Reformed and French Huguenots. He was energetic in exposing Catholic intrigues against Elizabeth, employing an elaborate counterespionage system against the Spaniards and Jesuits.

Elizabeth recognized England's great need for peace and tranquillity and pursued a religious policy of moderation, seeking the *via media* for the church and the realm. She had a certain religious depth (when she was only eleven she had translated Marguerite d'Angoulême's *Mirror of the Sinful Soul*) and an aesthetic and sentimental appreciation for religious rites and ceremonies; but the rapid religious changes of the preceding reigns had taught her to be tentative and tolerant, and secular in her interests. She once observed that she would sooner hear a thousand masses than be guilty of the millions of crimes done by some who suppressed masses. As a matter of personal choice as well as a policy of state, Elizabeth fostered an Anglican settlement in doctrine and discipline, and held both the Catholics and the radical Protestants in check. John Knox once observed that Elizabeth was "neither good Protestant nor yet resolute Papist." As archbishop of Canterbury she appointed Matthew Parker, a moderate who had once served as her mother's chaplain and as her own tutor. Parker had been a disciple of Martin Bucer, was married, and had long friendships with many of the Marian exiles. Elizabeth had to choose most of her bishops from among the returning exiles, most of whom were considerably more radical in their Protestantism than she was.

The success of her policy was assured by action of parliament, where the religious issue was neatly settled, or nearly settled itself. At the beginning of the sixteenth century parliament was basically a legislative and taxing body, meeting only intermittently. During the course of the century it became an increasingly powerful political force as the House of Commons grew in prestige, position, and initiative. Henry VIII had been party to a marriage of convenience with the Commons, increasing its power because it largely shared his aims. Under Elizabeth the will of the crown and the will of parliament, which is another way of saying the will of the gentry of England, were often at odds. But there was still romance in the marriage, and with a bit of cajoling and manipulating the queen could usually have her way.

Parliament assembled on January 25, 1559, to act on the religious question, for Elizabeth realized that parliament would have to initiate the reformation of the clergy; the Convocation of the Clergy, with most of the bishops appointees of Queen Mary, held to the Catholic doctrines of transubstantiation and the sacrifice of the mass. A combination of the Protestants on the council and in the House of Commons forced a more rapid settlement than Elizabeth actually wanted. She and Cecil hoped for an act of supremacy, with an act of uniformity later. But neither she nor Cecil was able to control the first parliament.

In April parliament passed an act of supremacy that recognized the queen as head of the English church. All royal officials, judges, and the clergy were to take a loyalty oath acknowledging the supremacy of the crown over the church, on pain of deprivation of office. To uphold the authority of any foreign prince or prelate was high treason, punishable by death. Mary's Catholic legislation having been rescinded, the Act of Uniformity restored the ecclesiastical statutes of Henry VIII and reintroduced the *Second Prayer Book* of Edward VI, modified somewhat by the addition of a few more traditional passages from the 1549 edition. Members of the clergy who refused to conform were replaced, so that the sees were eventually filled by appointees favored by Elizabeth.

When the second parliament met in 1563, it reaffirmed the Act of Uniformity and passed measures ensuring its strict enforcement. That same year the Convocation of the Clergy at Canterbury worked out the doctrinal platform of the new dispensation. Edward VI's Forty-two Articles were slightly revised to become the Thirty-nine Articles, the basic Anglican confession. The articles were designed to accommodate moderate beliefs, avoiding overly subtle distinctions and extremes. The definition of the real presence of Christ in the Eucharist was carefully phrased to accommodate private main-line evangelical interpretations, expressly denying the Catholic doctrine of transubstantiation on the one hand and the Zwinglian symbolic interpretation on the other. The Scriptures were declared to be the source and norm of faith. Predestination was accepted, but not in an extreme Calvinist form. The bishop of Salisbury, John Jewel, an able defender of the national church, presented the first systematic statement of the Anglican position in his *Apology for the Anglican Church* (1562). The next year a work of even greater importance was published, the first English edition of John Foxe's *Acts and Monuments,* which for many generations was read nearly as faithfully as the Bible and the prayerbook by the clergy and the literate laity of both England and the American colonies. This crimson martyrology helped to create a specifically Protestant, anti-Roman consciousness that blended with the nationalistic sentiment of the Protestant English-speaking world.

CATHOLICS

At the outset of Elizabeth's reign the great mass of the English people were Catholic in their religious views, as were also a great many of the conservative upper nobility. But the most prominent men of the time, the younger men rising to positions of influence and power in business and government, were Protestants. The House of Commons reflected these energetic and progressive elements. Only about two hundred of nine thousand clergymen would not take the oath acknowledging royal supremacy during the first six years after the act was passed. In the course of Elizabeth's rule the Roman Catholics in England dwindled to a tiny minority, until they constituted only a small percentage of the population of some four million. Nevertheless, between the years 1569 and 1588, Catholicism, aided and encouraged by Spain, seemed to the English to be a real menace. The Catholic-feudal northern rising in 1569–1570, instigated by the duke of Norfolk to advance Mary Stuart's cause, failed to involve more than a limited area. The rebels did not even come close to taking York. The papacy was at a loss as to how to proceed against Elizabeth. The queen had refused to send representatives to the third session of the Council of Trent, citing as one of the main reasons the Catholic efforts to stir up sedition against her.

At last Pope Pius V completed the alienation of England by using the bull *Regnans in excelsis,* excommunicating Elizabeth, on February 25, 1570. The bull asserted that since the Roman pontiff had power over all nations and kingdoms, and since Elizabeth, the slave of vice, had usurped the place of the supreme head of the church, had sent her kingdom to perdition, and had celebrated the impious mysteries of Calvin, she was cut off from the body of Christ and deprived of her rule, and all her subjects were absolved of their oaths of allegiance. During the last three decades of Elizabeth's reign the Seminarists and Jesuits redoubled their efforts to win converts for Rome, and in certain areas they had some success. A decade after the bull of excommunication, the Jesuit mission in England claimed 120,000 converts, although it offered no substantiation for the figure. Whatever the number of "converts," most of them were undoubtedly Catholics from the start, rather than newly won followers. There had always been a fringe of people who remained loyal to Rome, but it is impossible to determine their numbers. The priests in this Catholic underground came often from aristocratic families and were trained abroad by the Jesuits or in Cardinal Allen's colleges in Douay and Rome. They lived precarious lives, moving in disguise from one country house to another, ministering to the households of Catholic squires. Recurrent rumors of assassination plots by recusants or foreign agents kept Lord Cecil on the alert and filled the popular imagination with dread and hate. Pope Gregory XII stated that the bull of Pius V justified taking up arms against "that guilty woman of England" in any way whatsoever, and even sanctioned a plot to murder her.

Elizabeth responded to the papal bull with a statesmanlike proclamation that she

> would have all her loving subjects to understand that, as long as they shall openly continue in the observation of her laws, and shall not wilfully and manifestly break them by open actions, her majesty's means is not to have any of them molested by any inquisition or examination of their consciences in causes of religion, but to accept and entreat them as her good and obedient subjects.

In 1571 parliament passed several antipapal laws forbidding bringing the papal bull into England and declaring it treason to say that Elizabeth should not be queen, or that she was a heretic, usurper, or schismatic. In 1585 an act banishing the Jesuits was passed in order to temper public outrage and fanatical attacks upon ordinary Catholics. Throughout Elizabeth's forty-five-year reign, only 221 Catholics suffered death for their faith, compared with 290 Protestants who died during the five years of her sister Mary's rule. Most of these were executed for treason rather than for heresy, a significant shift in emphasis, though the victims were quite as dead.

Elizabeth's firmness in dealing with Catholic dissidents was due in large part to the fact that their disloyalty played into the hands of her enemies at home and abroad. Fear of a general Catholic resurgence was largely responsible for her handling of Mary Stuart. The switch on the part of the most Catholic king of Spain to an aggressive policy culminating in the assault of the Spanish Armada brought the question of treason at home into sharp focus. But if the Anglican solution was plagued with a persistent Catholic minority, it was itself intimately involved in a broad general religious movement known as Puritanism and harassed by a few extremists of a Protestant variety.

PURITANS

That Puritanism was potentially more explosive and dangerous to the Anglican establishment than Catholicism became evident in the civil war of the seventeenth century. Particularly after 1640, separatism and Presbyterianism emerged as rival forms of doctrine ready to struggle for mastery over church policy. When we think of Puritanism during the reign of Elizabeth, we must take care not to read back into the sixteenth century the developments of later decades. Puritanism was a movement, to borrow Milton's phrase, "for the reform of reformation." The term first appeared around 1564, and was applied to those Protestants, all at that time safely within the fold of the national church, who wished to eliminate any trace of "popery" and "Roman superstition" from the Anglican establishment. A broad stream of younger clergy, including many Marian exiles, had been inspired by the theology emanating from Geneva and continued to look to the Reformed churches and theologians on the continent for learning and inspiration. Very few at this time thought of separatism. Calvin, Bucer, and Knox had not specifically denounced the episcopal office, so that one quite "reformed" in outlook could still live within the established church.

Elizabeth's religious posture was really quite conservative. She had no time for Protestant evangelicalism or for its demands for a preaching ministry. Although many of her bishops were willing to tolerate diversity in matters indifferent and were even ready to drop practices offensive to the reformers, Elizabeth forced Archbishop Parker to issue his "advertisements" in support of conformity. She dismissed Grindal, her own archbishop, for his defense of preaching and prophesying, which offered the best chance of incorporating Puritan evangelicalism within the establishment. It was not until she discovered John Whitgift that she found an archbishop anywhere near as conservative as she was, and she even rapped him on the knuckles for promulgating the Lambeth Articles in 1595. Given Elizabeth's stance and at the same time the growing pressure in the direction of evangelical Protestantism, the religious situation during her reign was bound to be one of tension and occasional confrontation.

A series of controversies during Elizabeth's reign led to more serious troubles

later. The vestiarian controversy of 1563 hardly compared with the Arian controversy of the ancient church, and there was more noise than damage. The Puritans
felt that the vestments prescribed for the clergy should not be a matter of compulsion. They scrupled about the clerics' practice of wearing cap and gown during
the week and the surplice on Sunday. Very shortly they added to the list of Roman
practices offensive to conscience such things as making the sign of the cross at
baptism, kneeling at communion, observation of what they felt to be an excessive
number of church holidays, the ring in marriage ceremonies, and (shades of
Zurich!) the use of organs in churches. When a petition was presented to the
Convocation of the Clergy to abolish various Roman practices and all vestments
except the surplice, it lost out by a single vote.

Agitation about a weightier issue developed in 1572, when Thomas Cartwright
and a Puritan group in London pressed for a Presbyterian form of church government to replace the Episcopal system. The "First Admonition," published in that
year, urged that the congregations elect their ministers, who would supplant the
bishops. The "Second Admonition" developed a Presbyterian model for church
government, drawing heavily on Calvin's *Institutes*, urging the organization of
presbyteries to administer church discipline, the congregational calling of ministers,
and a directory of public worship. This threat to order and stability roused Elizabeth and her counselors, who seemed to recognize that bishops and the crown
needed each other. Cartwright fled into exile in 1574, but the Presbyterian movement lingered on. John Field, the devoted organizer of the Presbyterian underground, died in 1589. By 1592 the system had been destroyed, and one might say
that the Presbyterian episode was over. It enjoyed no serious renewal until the
time of the civil wars.

A more radical departure was advocated by Robert Browne of Cambridge, the
first separatist. Browne was a cantankerous character who was hauled up on one
occasion for wife-beating. The account of the episode reveals the intellectual subtle-
ties of which he was capable: "Old father Browne, being reproved for beating his
old wife, distinguished that he did not beat her as his wife but as a curst old
woman." He developed a congregational theory of the church as the body of those
who were "called out" or "gathered" from the great mass of men and voluntarily
associated with each other in a local church. In his *Book Which Showeth the Life
and Manners of All True Christians* he argued that each congregation should be
free of state control and independent also of bishops and presbyteries. The congregation should elect the pastors, teachers, and elders, not necessarily the well educated, and its worship should follow a very plain order of service. Around 1580
Browne actually gathered such a congregation at Norwich. Alarmed, the government set the wheels of repression in motion.

Elizabeth's new archbishop of Canterbury, John Whitgift, undertook the task
of bringing the deviationist Puritans back into line. Although he severely disci-

plined Puritans who opposed the use of surplices, Whitgift was theologically a strong Calvinist who at one point even criticized Cartwright for conceding that the doctrine of free will was not "repugnant to salvation." Archbishop Whitgift, whom Elizabeth referred to as "my little black husband," in his first sermon at St. Paul's Cross, on November 17, 1583, let it be known that the Puritans would have to conform to the established order. The Six Articles that same year made mandatory the assent to royal supremacy in church as well as state and the acceptance of the *Book of Common Prayer* and the Thirty-nine Articles as authority and norm. The Court of High Commission brought offenders to justice and a total of some two hundred parish priests were suspended. In 1586 he established censorship for theological works, hoping to check Puritan extremists, but the shocking "Martin Marprelate" tracts appeared in spite of his efforts, attacking the bishops as "petty antichrists, proud prelates, intolerable withstanders of reformation, enemies of the gospel and covetous wretched priests." In 1593 the Conventicle Act demanded exile or death for all who refused to attend the established church and worshiped in separate groups. Whitgift's Lambeth Articles in 1595, however, still held to a consistent and severe predestinarian doctrine.

Not until Elizabeth's last years was there a shift in the theological views of the top leadership, when Richard Bancroft, bishop of London, began virtually to exercise the power of primate in the interest of more latitudinarian churchmen in 1599. At the Hampton Court Conference in 1604 Bancroft prevented the Puritans from making Whitgift's Lambeth Articles a part of the official credal statement. The most influential and characteristic work to emerge from the Anglican Reformation was the work of a modest cleric who was never prominent as a churchman or academician, Richard Hooker's *Laws of Ecclesiastical Polity,* the first four books of which appeared in 1593. Hooker's *Laws* were directed against a Puritan divine, Walter Travers, who attacked the established church on biblical grounds. Hooker rejected the Puritan arguments and in a masterful literary style worthy of the theme laid down the platform for Anglican polity as a proper structure for the church. He stressed the necessity for humility before God, the need for unity, peace, reason, and good order for attaining to tranquillity on earth and happiness in eternity. He appealed to the laws of God, nature, and the Scriptures to support the soundness of the Anglican establishment.

Mary Stuart, Queen of Scots

WHEN MARY STUART fled to England in 1568, she brought with her an implicit threat to Elizabeth's security that kept the English queen uneasy for nineteen years. One of her bishops remarked that Elizabeth had a "bear by the tail." It was the circumstance of Mary's birth as the only legitimate child of James V of Scotland, her Catholicism, her potential as a pawn in the international political game rather than anything formidable about her person that made her a threat. Mary was in many ways the antithesis of her cousin Elizabeth. She grew up in the gay and brilliant French court, was educated with the dauphin and his sisters, and developed into a woman of the world who preferred chivalric romances and Rabelaisian satires to the classics. She had a passionate temperament given to violent loves and virulent hates. Not strong physically, she nevertheless had remarkable endurance. If not the equal of Elizabeth in regal qualities, she was a worthy rival. The first fateful decision Mary made was to return from France, where the enmity of her mother-in-law, Catherine de' Medici, made her life at court difficult, to Scotland, a poor and backward country, but her own. James V, Mary's father, died on December 14, 1542, just one week after she was born. Six years later she was sent to France. In 1558 she was married to the dauphin, Francis. When Queen Mary of England died that same year, Mary and her husband adopted the royal arms of England. The next year, on the death of King Henry II, she became queen consort of France. Meanwhile the Scottish lords revolted, and the Reformed forces and their English allies forced Mary's French garrison to surrender. Mary's representatives signed the Treaty of Edinburgh, ending the civil war, in 1560; but since one of its provisions acknowledged Elizabeth as queen of England, Mary herself procrastinated and managed never to sign it. On December 5 her husband died and Mary resolved to return to Scotland as queen, to which the reformers reluctantly agreed. Mary arrived in Scotland on August 19, 1561.

For some time Mary ruled but did not really govern, for the clans were powerful and the reformers were persuasive. In 1565 Elizabeth allowed Henry Stuart, Lord Darnley, a great-grandson of Henry VII, to return to Scotland. He was a Catholic and in other ways eligible to be Mary's consort, and from Elizabeth's point of view he was less dangerous than a French or Spanish alliance. Mary, now twenty-three, fell violently in love with him. Protestant nobles rebelled, but Mary defeated them and married young Darnley. As a husband he proved to be mean and murderous. Jealous of Mary's Italian secretary, David Rizzio, a cheerful fellow who entertained Mary with music and handled her foreign correspondence, Darnley plotted his death. On March 9, 1566, a band of assassins burst into the queen's apartment while she was present, dragged Rizzio just outside the door, and stabbed him to death. Mary was imprisoned, but escaped and lived to despise her contemptuous husband. She turned now to James Hepburn, earl of Bothwell, who was willing to go to extraordinary lengths for her.

Darnley lay sick in Mary's lodgings at Kirk o'Field when between two and three o'clock on the morning of February 10, 1567, the place blew up. Darnley and his page were found strangled in the garden. It appeared as though Darnley had discovered he was about to be blown up and managed to get out at the last moment, so that the conspirators were forced to leave telltale evidence of murder at the scene of what was supposed to look like a mysterious accident. Placards with Bothwell's picture appeared on the streets with the legend "Here is the murderer of the king." Bothwell was charged with murder but naturally was acquitted by his peers, who had been glad enough to see Darnley disposed of. He carried Mary off to Dunbar, seemingly by force but probably with her consent, since only a public scandal would force his wife to seek a divorce and the courts to grant it, and without the appearance of innocence betrayed Mary could not hope to win acceptance of their marriage so soon after Darnley's death. As it happened, any such hopes were misplaced. Mary and Bothwell were married on May 15 and a month later the Protestant lords rose against them. They allowed Bothwell to escape but imprisoned the queen in Lochleven Castle.

How guilty was Mary of complicity in Darnley's murder? The "casket letters," said to have been written by Mary to Bothwell during the fatal crisis, are very damaging, but their authenticity is still questioned by some apologists, who also accept Mary's protests that it was only a lucky coincidence that on the night of Darnley's death she had suddenly remembered she had promised to attend a wedding reception, which providentially kept her away from Kirk o'Field until after the explosion had demolished it.

Mary managed to escape and raise an army, but it was defeated at Langside on May 13, 1568, and Mary fled to England, where she threw herself on Elizabeth's mercy. Cecil had her tried and an open verdict was found: "Nothing has been sufficiently proved whereby the Queen of England should conceive an evil opinion of her good sister." Elizabeth was not a fool, but it seemed to her quite possible and infinitely preferable to clip Mary's wings without destroying her. Mary was kept confined in a series of castles and country estates, with a household of thirty of her own servants, full use of her French dowry, and the deference customarily accorded a queen. She had the freedom to receive guests in private and had little difficulty in corresponding with her supporters.

The rising of Catholics in the north in 1569 and the pope's excommunication of Elizabeth in 1570 compromised Mary, but no further measures were taken against her. An Italian banker, Roberto Ridolfi, was caught in a plot to murder Elizabeth and, with papal sanction, to arrange the marriage of Mary with the duke of Norfolk. Cecil's agents broke up the plot and the duke was beheaded on June 2, 1572.

Mary's imprisonment, insupportable to a woman of her temperament and ambition in spite of its luxuries, continued for fourteen more years. Her eventual undoing came when once again she placed too much confidence in a man. This time the man was Thomas Morgan, an agent who passed letters for her but betrayed her secrets to Sir Francis Walsingham, who headed Elizabeth's secret service. Learning of Mary's complicity in another plot against Elizabeth, Walsingham arranged to have some of his own agents infiltrate the circle of conspirators, and they compiled damaging evidence against Mary. In October 1586 she was tried for plotting against the queen. Mary confessed to seeking escape, but denied that she had "procured or encouraged any hurt against her majesty." The evidence against her was more persuasive than her denials, however, and she was condemned to death as "Mary Stuart, commonly called Queen of Scotland."

She was more magnificent in death than she had been in life. "Mr. Dean," she told the dean of Peterborough, who admonished her to repentance, "I shall die as I have lived, in the true and holy Catholic faith. All you can say to me on that score is but vain, and all your prayers, I think, can avail me but little." Although Mary had married Bothwell in a Protestant ceremony, she was determined now that the world should know that she was dying not only in the Catholic faith, but for it. When the ax fell, her blood would wash away all the plots and accusations and would cry out for vengeance. Mary acted out her last scene to perfection. Holding a crucifix high, she prayed her Catholic prayers, asked God's grace for England and mercy for Elizabeth, and forgave her enemies. Her black velvet gown fell to her feet and she stepped forward in silk of brilliant red, the color of martyrs. She knelt over the chopping block and commended her soul to God, and then the executioner's ax struck twice. The axman, his face covered by the customary black mask of the executioner, stooped, picked up the head to show it to the crowd, and shouted, "Long live the queen!" But all he held in his hands was an auburn wig. At the edge of the platform lay the gray-stubbled head of Mary, queen of Scots.

England's Relations with France and Spain

ENGLAND's RELATIONS with Scotland and Ireland and Elizabeth's with Mary fitted into the larger pattern of England's struggle for survival against two larger, wealthier, more powerful Catholic rivals, France and Spain. Elizabeth dubbed her policy "underhanded war," as she sent aid to the Huguenots in France and to the Protestant Netherlands. During the first five years Cecil played the game cautiously while Elizabeth consolidated her position at home; after that England became increasingly independent and aggressive in order to escape from the slough in which Mary had left the land.

Philip II had induced Mary to declare war on France, with the result that England lost Calais in 1558. But Elizabeth was glad to have Philip's support in the peace negotiations at Cateau-Cambrésis in 1559. For the time being Philip was more interested in using England as a counterbalance to France than he was in wiping out Protestantism in the island. The French king was also virtually the ruler of Scotland, through his regent, Mary of Guise. Mary Stuart was then the wife of the French dauphin. England thus lay within the jaws of a French vise, and for a decade Elizabeth had to play Spain's game. But even though Philip was now married to the daughter of the French king, France still posed a threat to Spain, so for a time Philip permitted England to develop unmolested. Elizabeth took advantage of the opportunity and by decisive intervention saw the French thrown out of Scotland bag and baggage. England's back door was barred at last.

Elizabeth's policy toward Ireland was not so wise or so successful. "Ireland for the English" was the aim. English Protestantism was forced upon the Irish at the point of the soldiery's pikes. Irish feeling for the ancient faith grew even more fervent under oppression, and hostility to England was driven deep into the Irish soul. England's policy was shortsighted, impractical, and inconsistent. English statesmen who crossed the channel as viceroys or lord deputies returned beaten down and dispirited, determined never to go there again. In his last years Henry VIII had promoted a plan to convert the Irish land system into English tenures, with the collaboration of the Irish chiefs. Edward's "statesmen" turned to conquest and extermination. Mary followed with a policy of expropriation and the establishment of English military colonies.

The Ireland that Elizabeth inherited in 1558 was a land lacking political cohesion and racial homogeneity, and with religion at low ebb. Elizabeth was less concerned about introducing her Protestant state church to Ireland than she was about civilizing a barbarous people and making them safe for English imperial control. A plan for colonization of the island evolved, sponsored for a time by Sir Walter Raleigh. The Spaniards sought to exploit Irish hostility to England and even planned to use Ireland as a base of attack. But clan feuds kept the Irish disunited and weak, so that while they could damage the English, they could not offer a serious threat to English security. From 1594 on, a crafty leader, Tyrone, proved a wily and stubborn foe who cost the English enormously in money, men, and arms. The final four and a half years of the war with Ireland cost the English treasury £1.25 million. England at last completely subjugated Ireland by cruel measures. Mountjoy crushed Ulster by the deliberate and systematic destruction of all livestock, crops, and dwellings. By the time Tyrone surrendered, the English found many of the Irish who survived this genocidal policy living in caves and eating grass and roots. Elizabeth succeeded in establishing a policy of "pacification," but the emerald isle remained a sullen, unreliable part of the realm, ready to break into rebellion again when it could.

During the early years of Elizabeth's reign Spain was considered a protector against France, the traditional enemy across the channel; but a shift in power soon pitted England against Spain in a desperate struggle for survival and eventual leadership. England was much relieved when Francis II, Mary Stuart's husband, died in 1560, and the effective power passed into the hands of Catherine de' Medici, who had little love for Mary or the Guise family. The wars of religion soon paralyzed France, and Elizabeth felt she had less to fear from France than from Spain. By the Treaty of Blois in 1572 France became an ally of sorts with England. The new-found friendship was severely tested but not destroyed when the massacre of St. Bartholemew enraged English Protestant feelings. A series of artificial marriage negotiations between Elizabeth and the duke of Anjou, who later became Henry III, and then with his brother the duke of Alençon, served the diplomatic purpose of making Anglo-French relations appear to be more cordial than they were in actual fact. The alliance at least served to prevent a Franco-Spanish coalition against Protestant England. While it inhibited the role Elizabeth could play in behalf of the Huguenots, it gave her a freer hand to support the Protestant Netherlands.

England's aid to the Dutch and the raids of English seamen on the Spanish main enraged Philip II and convinced him that he would never end the rebellion in the Netherlands or secure his Spanish-Portuguese empire overseas until England had been conquered. A series of events ignited the final conflagration: the murder of William of Orange in 1584, the expulsion from England of the Spanish ambassador Mendoza for plotting with Elizabeth's foes in 1586, and the death of Mary Stuart in 1587. Mary's execution eliminated Philip's hope for a Catholic rebellion if he were to assault England. But he also came to believe that he could take over England as he had taken over Portugal, for Mary had left to Philip her claims to the English throne. There followed then the attack of the "invincible" Spanish Armada in 1588, the Spanish seizure of Calais in 1596, the "invisible armada" of 1599, England's counterattacks on Portugal, and its establishment of "vantage at sea." Now France under Henry IV rebuilt its internal unity and strength to serve as a barrier to Spain's ambitions. England had stood up to the mightiest power in the world and won; a new surge of confidence and pride lifted the British on a wave of patriotism and ambition.

England Expands

TUDOR ENGLISHMEN were not by nature or tradition world explorers or empire builders. It took the attractions of the Spanish main, the gospel, and gold to draw the seafaring folk of southwest England into the game of global expansion. Giovanni Caboto, a Venetian navigator, had voyaged to the northeast coast of North America under the English flag, first in 1497 and again in 1498. The English called him John Cabot and hailed him as a hero, but their enthusiasm for his explorations was largely focused on his reports of an abundance of fish in the waters off Newfoundland. A new cod fishing station might make them independent of the Icelandic fishermen. But it was a great distance to go for fish, and eventually the excitement died down. Another sixty years passed before England became actively involved again in overseas expansion. During these years England was preoccupied with domestic and religious issues. Moreover, there was little risk capital available for large-scale piracy or colonial development until after the collapse of the cloth trade in 1551. The final closing of Antwerp in the 1570s added to the economic impetus toward geographical exploration and the search for new markets and sources of raw materials abroad. Now Protestant England had a special incentive to contest the papal allocation of the New World to Spain and Portugal. The priva-teers sailed the seas with Elizabeth's blessing, but without official authorization, plundering Spain's ships and raiding its colonies. Hawkins, Drake, Frobisher, Raleigh, and dozens of others were really buccaneers, raiding outside the law, and knowing full well that if they were caught they could expect to be hanged for piracy.

Although during these decades the actual results in permanent colonies were slight, the idea took root and the vision of empire caught the English eye. "Plant-ing of countries," wrote Francis Bacon in his essay "Of Plantations," "is like plant-ing of woods; for you must make account to lose almost twenty years' profit, and expect recompense in the end." The Elizabethans had little patience for this tedious cultivation of colonies. They wanted quick profits, and nothing compared with raids on Spanish ships for procuring sudden wealth easily.

In 1561 Cecil shocked the bishop of Aquila, Álvarez de Quadra, by declaring that the pope had no right to partition the earth and bestow kingdoms on whom he pleased. The very next year John Hawkins of Plymouth tested the validity of the Spanish monopoly by cutting himself into the Negro slave trade. He procured a cargo of Negroes by raiding the coast of Africa south of Cape Verde and by purchase from Portuguese slavers, then crossed the Atlantic to Hispaniola and sold the Negroes as slaves on the Spanish plantations. His profits were enormous in gold, silver, jewels, sugar, hides, and other wealth of the Indies. The queen, Cecil, and other nobles bought shares in Hawkins' second expedition, two years later. The Spanish government had issued orders that its colonies were not to trade with the English, so Hawkins armed his flotilla, expecting the worst. But again the Spanish planters bought his Negroes and again he returned home with a great profit. Now the Spanish colonial administrators were aroused, however, so on his third expedition, in 1567, Hawkins sailed with a convoy of seven battleships, with Captain Francis Drake in command of the *Judith*. On this trip Hawkins blockaded the port of Río de la Hacha and fought a pitched battle on land with the Spaniards. He burned the town, seized its treasure, and forced the settlement to trade. Trapped in the harbor at San Juan de Ulloa in 1568, Hawkins had to shoot his way out, and lost 120 men and several ships, including the *Jesus,* a round-bottomed boat ac-quired from the Hanse.

The most persistent and implacable foe to sail the Spanish seas was Francis

Drake. Drake's ire was aroused by the disastrous humiliation at San Juan de Ulloa. He had returned from that battle a ruined man. From then until he died, in 1595, he lived with two goals in mind: to recoup his personal losses and to strengthen England by weakening Spain. With each act of plunder he tightened the garrote around the throat of the Spanish monarchy. A superb seaman, Drake operated most effectively beyond the line and outside the law. The Spanish treasure ships crossed the Atlantic in well-regulated, heavily protected convoys. Not until 1580 did anyone dare to attack them in European waters. Drake's keen eye spotted the weakest link in the silver chain that stretched from the mines of Peru to Lima, across the spine of the Isthmus of Panama to Nombre de Dios, and from there across the Atlantic to Spain. In 1572 Drake raided Nombre de Dios, ambushed the treasure convoy on the way to the port, and escaped with the loot before the Spanish troops at Panama could act. Not all English seamen had Drake's good fortune. When John Oxenham tried to repeat this exploit a few years later he ran into an armed transport column, was caught, and was hanged in Lima as a pirate. Andrew Barker was killed in a skirmish with the Spaniards while raiding the coast of Central America and his ship sank on the way home.

Francis Drake next moved the theater of operations to the Pacific. He sailed around the tip of South America through the Strait of Magellan into the Pacific (1577–1580). A storm blew him far into the Antarctic Ocean and made it evident that no land bridge ran from South America all the way to the pole. Drake scourged the Spanish, but beyond this mischief he had a tremendous vision of founding a New England in California, an empire for Elizabeth reaching from the beautiful Pacific coast to Florida. He explored the California coast, looking for harbors and bays suitable for ports and colonies. The western end of the legendary Northwest Passage was not to be found, and Drake gave up the search around Vancouver. From there he proceeded westward across the Pacific and Indian oceans, rounded the Cape of Good Hope, and headed home. When his ship nosed into Plymouth in September 1580, it carried aboard a treasure of £1.5 million, or nearly half of the Spanish treasure yielded in a year's exploitation of the mines of the New World. Drake was compensated for the losses he had sustained at San Juan de Ulloa over a decade before and the rest of the enormous treasure was kept in the Tower of London, despite the protests of Ambassador Mendoza, until the accounts between Elizabeth and Philip, including compensation for the Spanish role in the Irish rebellion, could be settled.

Sir Francis Drake—for Elizabeth now knighted him—was to play a further role in settling accounts with Philip. Elizabeth unleashed him again in 1585, when he set sail in his great corsair accompanied by a fleet of thirty ships to raid the Spanish ships and harbors. He sailed first to the Canaries and the Cape Verde Islands, burning Santiago and Praia. Then he struck at Santo Domingo, the jewel city of the Caribbean colonies, extracting a ransom of twenty-five thousand ducats for sparing most of the town, and hit Cartagena on the South American mainland the same way. He took the Spanish fort at St. Augustine, Florida, then rescued the survivors of the faltering colony that Sir Walter Raleigh had founded at Roanoke Island and took them home to England. Not only had Drake cost the Spaniards an enormous toll in booty; he had demonstrated the vulnerability of King Philip and helped to drive him to that measure of desperation, the launching of the Armada, which proved to be his undoing. The English were well informed about Spanish preparations for the invasion. When the fleet in the harbor of Cádiz was nearly ready in the spring of 1587, Drake sailed from Plymouth, took the Spaniards by surprise, destroyed thousands of tons of shipping and supplies, including vital barrel staves, and even gutted the admiral's own galleon. Drake had indeed singed Philip's beard. In the final confrontation with the Armada in 1588, Drake, in charge of a smaller squadron out of Plymouth under the fleet command of Lord Howard, acquitted himself well, although the wind and waves made truly heroic deeds dispensable. A ballad of 1591 about a triumphant duel of an English corsair with a Spanish galleon celebrated Elizabeth as the "Lady of the Sea." The scepter of the seas had passed from Spain to England.

Other adventurers followed Drake's pattern of exploration and plunder. Thomas Cavendish roamed the seas from 1586 to 1588, and sailed back to London with his ships adorned with sails of blue damask and each man sporting a golden chain. But of more lasting value were the geographic and navigational expeditions, which, though less thrilling than the buccaneering, were in the long run more significant. The greatest impetus was the search for trade, especially the search for a northwest passage to Cathay, and eventually also the search for lands suitable for colonizing.

The English initiated the search for a northeast passage, although in later years it was taken over by Dutchmen and Danes. "The company of merchant adventurers for discovery of regions, dominions, islands and places unknown," whose first master was John Cabot's son Sebastian, in 1553 sent out a fleet of three ships under Sir Hugh Willoughby, headed for China. Two of them were frozen in near the North Cape and all aboard perished, but the third, under the senior navigator, Richard Chancellor, reached Archangel. The Russians there treated the Englishmen well but warily until they were able to get word to Moscow of the foreigners' arrival and receive instructions on what to do with them. Tsar Ivan IV, who was a young man then and not yet so Terrible as he was later to become, invited them to Moscow and offered them favorable terms for trade. As a direct result of this exploration, a group of merchants organized the Muscovy Company in 1555 to initiate trade with Russia.[1] The year after its founding the company commissioned Stephen Burrough to discover a passage to China around

---

[1] J. H. Parry, *The Age of Reconnaissance* (New York, 1964), pp. 222–23.

the North Cape, an effort doomed to founder in the ice and fog. Another agent penetrated Asia overland as far as Bokhara in search of markets. The Merchant Adventurers exploited the continental markets in Antwerp and up the Rhine and Elbe. In 1579 the Eastland Company began to compete with the remnants of the Hanse in the Baltic.

Humphrey Gilbert, a scholarly gentleman, was caught up in the idea of finding a northwest passage to Cathay. He gathered every scrap of information he could from ancient chronicles and accounts of voyages, and wrote his famous *Discourse to Prove a Northwest Passage*. Martin Frobisher, an experienced seaman, was so obsessed with the idea that he made three voyages (1576–1578) to look for the passage north of Labrador. Although his efforts were foredoomed to failure, he did discover the strait that still bears his name. The efforts of the Muscovy Company to find a northeast passage (1580) were no more successful. The following year the Levant Company was organized to develop trade in the Near East, with some success. The final and most dramatic efforts to find the Northwest Passage were undertaken by John Davis in three voyages (1585–1587). He reached the Northumberland Inlet, north of Frobisher Strait, at latitude 66° 40′, but once again the ice pack blocked the way. These adventures, for all the excitement they aroused, were not so rewarding commercially as the English had hoped. Gradually the idea took shape that colonies on the American seaboard peopled by Englishmen would provide sources for raw materials and markets for English products. The day of colonization was dawning.

Richard Hakluyt, famous as the author of *Voyages and Discoveries* (1589), was one of the fathers of the colonial idea and one of its principal publicists. Raw materials, new markets, a way station to Cathay, a dumping ground for England's vagabonds and unemployed, the opportunity to Christianize the Indians—none of these motives were overlooked in Hakluyt's argument. In 1578 Sir Humphrey Gilbert procured a royal patent to found a "plantation" in the New World and a few years later he undertook to establish a colony in Newfoundland. He lacked the stability to see the project through, however, and he was himself lost at sea.

In 1584 Queen Elizabeth transferred Gilbert's patent to his half-brother Walter Raleigh, who had become her favorite at court, and the following year she knighted him. As the site of his proposed colony Raleigh chose Roanoke Island in the territory he called Virginia, after the Virgin Queen, where the climate was mild and the natives were reportedly friendly. The island lies off the coast of what is now the state of North Carolina. Under Raleigh's auspices, a hundred colonists were settled on Roanoke by Sir Richard Grenville in the spring of 1585, but when Grenville returned in June of the next year he found the colony thoroughly demoralized, half-starved, and at odds with the Indians. Drake repatriated the remnants on his way back from his famous raids of 1585–1586. In 1587 Raleigh tried again at the same location, but when the governor of the second colony, John White, returned to Roanoke with new supplies in 1590, he could find no one, alive or dead. These pioneers had probably been massacred by the Indians, although they may have attempted to resettle in a new location and been lost to the sea or forest. Raleigh claimed to have spent £40,000 on the undertaking, and in 1589, before the final disaster at Roanoke, he signed over his rights in the colony to a company of merchants, keeping only a small rent and a fifth of any gold that might be discovered in the territory. There was of course no gold, but neither was there any need for Raleigh to provide for his old age, since enemies he had acquired as Elizabeth's favorite contrived his downfall after her death.

When Elizabeth died in 1603 Raleigh had long since ceased to be her favorite. She had even had him thrown into the Tower for a time when she discovered he had secretly married one of her ladies-in-waiting. But her vindictiveness passed, and in 1595 he sailed for the Orinoco River with dreams of finding a way to penetrate the Spanish empire in South America. His *Discoverie of Guiana,* published the following year, described in overenthusiastic terms the empire awaiting England in Guiana.

At Elizabeth's death she was succeeded by James VI of Scotland, Mary Stuart's son, who had his own favorites and his own reasons for washing his hands of Elizabeth's. When Raleigh's enemies brought charges of treason against him, he was stripped of his possessions and once again lodged in the Tower. This time it was thirteen years before he was able to contrive his release in order to lead an expedition up the Orinoco and establish his empire. Raleigh seems to have had a touch of piracy in mind even before he crossed the Atlantic. He was in a desperate situation and desperate measures seemed all that remained to him. But he found no treasure, and his own son was killed in an attack on a Spanish outpost guarding the approach to Guiana—an action specifically forbidden the expedition, since England wanted no trouble with Spain. Raleigh was doubtless correct in believing that if the attack had succeeded, it would have been considered no trouble at all. But it did not succeed, and Raleigh was returned to England and executed in 1618.

Englishmen followed him to the coastal regions around the Orinoco, developing plantations, logging camps, and small trading operations, but the dream of an English empire to rival Spain's in Latin America died with Raleigh.

The Economy

IN INDUSTRY AND COMMERCE the reign of Elizabeth was anything but a golden age. Problems mounted in the crucial textile trade and a severe general inflation created difficulties for nearly everyone. The boom years in textiles, which were England's major export—approximately 75 to 90 percent by value—came in the late 1530s and

1540s. The remainder of England's exports was made up of raw wool, tin and lead from marginal mines, grain, beer, and fish. A severe economic crisis in 1551 cut trade drastically, and although there was a partial recovery, England's exports still remained well below the levels of 1548–1550. Elizabeth's reign was marked by periodic depressions, which became most serious in the 1590s. England gradually lost its old established markets for cheap unfinished cloth, and the new "draperies" did not begin to compensate for this loss until the seventeenth century. Cecil's major motive in pushing the Statute of Apprentices or Artificers in 1563, as his own memoranda reveal, was to freeze labor in the land. He hoped to prevent industrial expansion, since this seemed to be the only solution to the periodic depressions in the textile industry, which tended to expand its output beyond the market's ability to absorb it.

The population was increasing, and so were the prices. The cost of food was a particularly acute problem, for in bad years England did not produce enough food to feed the population. Industrial prices lagged and by the end of the century inflation had seriously reduced real wages. The propertied classes on the whole managed to raise rents enough to keep up with the rising prices, but the peasants and town proletariat suffered severe privations. The depressed state of the economy made it impossible to provide jobs or land for continually greater numbers of people, which led to a great deal of concern about overpopulation. The desirability of shipping excess population abroad provided a negative motive for overseas expansion. The depressed state of the economy persisted through the early Stuart period. There were major depressions in the early 1620s and between 1629 and 1633; a great expansion of commerce was achieved only after 1660.

At the beginning of Elizabeth's reign agriculture was in the final phase of its evolution from a manorial structure to a system of individual enterprise. The gentry continued to fence in lands that had previously been allotted to the common use of the peasantry. The story of the "deserted village" was often repeated as people forced off the land moved into town or drifted about in increasingly hopeless search of work. The lands thus enclosed were given over to the raising of sheep, which brought great profits because of the demand for English wool, acknowledged to be the best in the world. Furthermore, during the last half of the century a gradual growth in acreage given over to grain production became noticeable, another use of land more efficient than subsistence farming by peasant families. Because of the ease of storage and transportation, grain production was important in sustaining the growing urban population.

Social change reflected these gradual alterations in the agrarian economy. Servile labor and villeinage were now virtually nonexistent. The tenancy at will, the copyhold, and the leasehold, all old by Elizabeth's reign, continued to be important forms of landholding. The freeholders were the most enterprising element in the lower agrarian echelons, although many yeomen made a very good living out of leaseholds. They enjoyed the benefit of fixed rents in a period of rising prices. This happy development gave them a profit margin that enabled them to educate their sons, who in turn could climb a few rungs higher on the social ladder.

There is a tempest in the scholarly teapot over the gentry, the landed families who ranked above the yeomen but below the old aristocratic families. Historians have traditionally held that the gentry (like the middle class) was always rising and that the old aristocracy was in decline. More recent opinion holds that the aristocrats, far from playing out their useless days riding to hounds, were actually remarkably adaptable. A good name and a good seat on a horse, after all, never had been enough in themselves to keep power from slipping into the hands of able, ambitious newcomers. Now that economic conditions were facilitating upward social mobility on a larger scale than before, it was the aristocratic families more than the gentry that began to educate their sons at the universities and the "legal university," the Inns of Court, so that they could enter commerce and branches of government service that required practical knowledge for success. The gentry, less secure in their social authority and thus more reluctant to risk their prestige by going into trade, formed a conservative corps that eventually trapped many of them in a social backwater. Meanwhile, middle-class families of means were buying their way into the countryside as gentry. Historical facts always tend toward the more complex rather than the simple solution. When the dust of controversy settles, in all likelihood some truth will still be found in the old hypothesis, but the revisionist view will probably be more generally accepted.

With a population of 120,000, London was already in Elizabeth's day the economic hub of England. Although the London merchants were far less wealthy than the Medicis, Albizzis, Welsers, and Fuggers had been in their day, English merchants exerted themselves to find new markets and sources of wealth. English industry was simply not so well developed technically as that of the Rhineland, northwest France, and Italy. In introducing new industries such as silk, lace, glassware, needles, thread, felt, and so on, the English were often obliged to import skilled craftsmen to do the work and train apprentices. A naïve display by the *nouveaux riches* was almost inevitable. The new town houses, sumptuous dress, exaggerated costuming, and elaborate posturing of Elizabethan gentlemen made a colorful display. They made a grand audience at the Globe for Shakespeare's plays.

Elizabeth's End

The achievements of the English people in the sixteenth century have not without justice been credited to the fortunate circumstance of Elizabeth's long reign. She was a symbol of victory, the idol of the people, the emblem of national unity and purpose. And yet when one examines her acts of state with care, one is amazed to see how little initiative she showed and how few programs of a progressive nature she contributed. Basically conservative, she performed a holding action, presided over developments that she could not prevent or control, reigned rather than ruled. She even failed to develop a creative solution to the problem of her own succession. But perhaps what the nation believed to be true of its chief of state was more important for its history than anything she actually did or left undone. Myth is a powerful force upon history as well as upon historians.

As Elizabeth aged, her face grew thin and seemed longer than ever, her teeth were yellow and uneven, and to top it all off she wore a massive reddish wig. Still she played her love games, making an asset of her greatest liability as sovereign, her femininity. Her affection for one of the young bloods at court, the earl of Essex, led to a final heartbreak for her. Essex was a spendthrift and incompetent as a military commander, but he was her weakness. Exploiting her love for him, believing that if he were persistent enough there was no limit to the heights he might reach, the handsome Essex played a dangerous game. During a luckless siege of Rouen he wrote:

> Most fair, most dear, and most excellent Sovereign. . . . The two windows of your Privy Chamber shall be the poles of my sphere, where, as long as your Majesty will please to have me, I am fixed and unmovable. When your Majesty thinks that Heaven too good for me, I will not fall like a star, but be consumed like a vapor by the sun that drew me up to such a height. While your Majesty gives me leave to say I love you, my fortune is as my affection, unmatchable. If ever you deny me that liberty, you may end my life, but never shake my constancy, for were the sweetness of your nature turned into the greatest bitterness that could be, it is not in your power, as great a Queen as you are, to make me love you less.[2]

Elizabeth gave him the chance to prove his mettle on the battlefield. The Irish revolt was still raging, and Essex, a young hawk, cried for the armed conquest of the island. Elizabeth appointed him lord deputy of Ireland against his will, for he was loath to leave the court. At a meeting of the queen's counselors he once disagreed with the queen, and when she rejected his views he turned his back on her. Furious, she boxed his ear, and Essex put his hand on his sword declaring that he would not have taken such an insult from Henry VIII himself. Essex was indulging in that pride which goes before a fall. With 22,000 men at his command he put down little rebellions in Munster but failed to destroy Tyrone, the Irish rebel. He allowed his men to plunder, made a quick peace with Tyrone, and hurried back to Elizabeth.

Essex had made powerful enemies who undermined his position at court, and he was soon put under house arrest. The privy council received word that he was gathering a military force at his estate and summoned him to appear. Instead he

---

[2] Cited in J. E. Neale, *Queen Elizabeth* (New York, 1934), pp. 322–23.

marched into London, expecting the city to rise in his behalf, a vain hope. He was accused of treason, tried, and found guilty. Then Elizabeth had to sign the death warrant of the foolish young man she had loved. On Ash Wednesday, February 25, 1601, Essex emerged from his room in the Tower dressed in a suit of black velvet and satin and walked to a scaffold in the courtyard. He bowed to all present, made a gracious courtly speech, confessed his sins, removed his hat, and placed his head upon the wooden block. It was severed with three blows of the executioner's ax.

Elizabeth never recovered from the shock of all this, and during her last years she frequently fell into periods of deep depression. In 1601 she summoned her last parliament to provide funds for a final effort in Ireland. Lord Mountjoy succeeded in suppressing the revolt, forced the Spanish forces there to surrender, and negotiated terms with Tyrone. The victory in Ireland was a last gleam of success for her.

Elizabeth's health had been reasonably good most of her life, but now time was taking its toll. On September 7, 1602, she reached her sixty-ninth birthday. Many of her old counselors and friends had already died. Christmas of that year saw a final flickering of that bright gaiety for which her court had been renowned. Then soon after the first of March in 1603 Elizabeth fell ill. "I am not sick," she said, "I feel no pain, and yet I pine away." Weak of body but strong in will, she refused to take the doctors' medicines, which might have prolonged her life. On Wednesday, March 23, the privy counselors made bold to ask her to perform her final duty as sovereign, to name her successor. She named her "nearest kinsman, the king of Scots," James VI, son of Mary Stuart, who was to rule after her as James I of Great Britain.

Shortly after six o'clock that evening she summoned Archbishop Whitgift to her bedside. He spoke to her of her Christian faith and of the final glory she was soon to know when she would appear before the King of Kings. She moved her hand and eyes in agreement, and prayed with him until she fell asleep. Between two and three in the morning she passed away.

Bibliography

Elizabeth I:
BLACK, J. B. *The Reign of Elizabeth.* New York, 1936.
BROWNING, A. *The Age of Elizabeth.* New York, 1935.
CHAMBERLAIN, F. *Elizabeth and Leicester.* New York, 1939.
HURSTFIELD, JOEL. *Elizabeth I and the Unity of England.* London, 1960.
JENKINS, ELIZABETH. *Elizabeth the Great: A Biography.* New York, 1959.
McNALTY, ARTHUR S. *Elizabeth Tudor: The Lonely Queen.* London, 1954.
MAYNARD, THEODORE. *Queen Elizabeth.* Milwaukee, 1940.
NEALE, JOHN E. *Queen Elizabeth.* New York, 1934.

——. *Elizabeth I and Her Parliaments,* 2 vols. London, 1953–1957.

OAKESHOTT, WALTER F. *The Queen and the Poet.* London, 1960.

READ, CONYERS. *Mr. Secretary Walsingham and the Policy of Queen Elizabeth.* Cambridge, Mass., 1925.

——. *Mr. Secretary Cecil and Queen Elizabeth,* 2 vols. New York, 1955–1960.

——. *Lord Burghley and Queen Elizabeth.* New York, 1960.

STRACHEY, LYTTON. *Elizabeth and Essex.* New York, 1928.

WALDMAN, MILTON. *England's Elizabeth.* Boston, 1933.

——. *Elizabeth and Leicester.* London, 1945.

——. *Queen Elizabeth.* London, 1952.

WILLIAMS, NEVILLE. *Elizabeth the First, Queen of England.* New York, 1968.

WILSON, ELKIN. *England's Eliza.* Cambridge, Mass., 1939.

Kingdom and empire:

ANDREWS, K. R. *Elizabethan Privateering During the Spanish War, 1585–1603.* Cambridge, 1967.

BINDOFF, S. T. *Tudor England.* Harmondsworth, 1950.

BOWDEN, PETER J. *The Wool Trade in Tudor and Stuart England.* London, 1962.

BYRNE, M. *Elizabethan Life in Town and Country.* London, 1947.

CAM, HELEN MAUD. *England Before Elizabeth,* 3rd ed. London, 1967.

CAMPBELL, M. *The English Yeoman Under Elizabeth and the Early Stuarts.* New Haven, 1942.

CECIL, ALGERNON. *The Life of Robert Cecil.* London, 1915.

ELTON, GEOFFREY R. *England Under the Tudors.* London, 1955.

HARRISON, DAVID. *Tudor England,* 2 vols. London, 1953.

HEXTER, JACK. *Reappraisals in History.* London, 1961.

LOCKYER, ROGER. *Tudor and Stuart Britain, 1471–1714.* New York, 1964.

MORRIS, CHRISTOPHER. *Political Thought in England: Tyndale to Hooker.* London, 1953.

NEALE, JOHN E. *The Elizabethan House of Commons.* London, 1949.

NEF, JOHN U. *Industry and Government in France and England, 1540–1640.* Philadelphia, 1940.

QUINN, D. B. *Raleigh and the British Empire.* London, 1947.

ROWSE, A. L. *Tudor Cornwall.* London, 1941.

——. *The England of Elizabeth.* London, 1950.

——. *The Elizabethan Age,* 2 vols. London, 1950–1955.

——. *The Expansion of Elizabethan England.* London, 1955.

RUDDICK, A. A. *Italian Merchants and Shipping in Southampton, 1270–1600.* Southampton, 1951.

SHIRLEY, F. J. *Richard Hooker and Contemporary Political Ideas.* London, 1949.

STONE, LAWRENCE. *The Crisis of the Aristocracy, 1558–1641.* Oxford, 1965.

TAWNEY, R. H. *The Agrarian Problem in the Sixteenth Century.* London, 1912.

TAYLOR, EVA. *Tudor Geography, 1485–1583.* London, 1930.

——. *Late Tudor and Early Stuart Geography, 1583–1650.* London, 1934.

TREVOR-ROPER, H. R. *The Gentry, 1540–1640.* Cambridge, 1953.

WILLIAMSON, JAMES A. *Maritime Enterprise, 1485–1558.* Oxford, 1913.

——. *The Life and Growth of the British Empire.* Oxford, 1940.

——. *The Ocean in English History.* Oxford, 1941.

————. *The Age of Drake.* London, 1946.
————. *Hawkins of Plymouth.* London, 1949.

Religion:
BABBAGE, STUART B. *Puritanism and Richard Bancroft.* London, 1962.
BIRT, H. N. *The Elizabethan Religious Settlement.* London, 1907.
BOOTY, JOHN E. *John Jewel as Apologist of the Church of England.* London, 1963.
BROOK, V. J. K. *Whitgift and the English Church.* London, 1957.
————. *A Life of Archbishop Parker.* Oxford, 1962.
CLAYTON, J. *The Historical Basis of Anglicanism.* London, 1925.
COLLINSON, PATRICK. *The Elizabethan Puritan Movement.* Berkeley, 1967.
CREMEANS, CHARLES. *The Reception of Calvinist Thought in England.* Urbana, Ill.,
    1949.
DAVIES, E. T. *The Political Ideas of Richard Hooker.* London, 1946.
————. *Episcopacy and Royal Supremacy in the Church of England in the Sixteenth
    Century.* Oxford, 1950.
DAWLEY, POWEL M. *John Whitgift and the English Reformation.* New York, 1954.
HALLER, WILLIAM. *The Rise of Puritanism.* New York, 1938.
————. *Elizabeth I and the Puritans.* Ithaca, N.Y., 1964.
HAUGAARD, WILLIAM P. *Elizabeth and the English Reformation.* Cambridge, 1968.
JORDAN, WILBUR K. *The Development of Religious Toleration in England,* 4 vols. Cam-
    bridge, Mass., 1932–1940.
KNAPPEN, M. M. *Tudor Puritanism.* Chicago, 1939.
KNOX, S. J. *Walter Travers, Paragon of Elizabethan Puritanism.* London, 1962.
McGINN, DONALD J. *John Penry and the Marprelate Controversy.* New Brunswick, N.J.,
    1966.
McGRATH, PATRICK. *Papists and Puritans Under Elizabeth I.* New York, 1967.
MEYER, CARL S. *Elizabeth I and the Religious Settlement of 1559.* St. Louis, 1960.
NEW, JOHN. *Anglican and Puritan.* Stanford, 1964.
PEARSON, A. F. SCOTT. *Thomas Cartwright and Elizabethan Puritans.* Cambridge, 1925.
POLLARD, ARTHUR. *Richard Hooker.* London, 1966.
POLLEN, J. H. *The English Catholics in the Reign of Queen Elizabeth.* London, 1920.
RUPP, E. GORDON. *The English Protestant Tradition.* Cambridge, 1947.
SEAVER, PAUL S. *The Puritan Lectureships: The Politics of Religious Dissent, 1560–1662.*
    Stanford, 1970.
SOUTHGATE, W. M. *John Jewel and the Problem of Doctrinal Authority.* Cambridge,
    Mass., 1962.
THORNTON, LIONEL S. *Richard Hooker: A Study of His Theology.* London, 1924.
TRIMBLE, WILLIAM. *The Catholic Laity in Elizabethan England, 1558–1603.* Cam-
    bridge, Mass., 1964.
USHER, ROLAND G. *The Reconstruction of the English Church,* 2 vols. New York, 1910.
WALZER, MICHAEL. *The Revolution of the Saints: A Study in the Origins of Radical
    Politics.* Cambridge, 1965.
WOODHOUSE, H. F. *The Doctrine of the Church in Anglican Theology, 1547–1603.* Lon-
    don, 1954.
WOODWARD, G. W. O. *Reformation and Resurgence, 1485–1603.* London, 1963.
WRIGHT, LOUIS B. *Religion and Empire: The Alliance Between Piety and Commerce in
    English Expansion, 1558–1625.* Chapel Hill, N.C., 1943.

CHAPTER 21

The Impact
of the Renaissance
and the Reformation
on Society and Culture

The student of history nearing the end of a subject such as ours, one of the great ages of the past, can appreciate Thomas Carlyle's modest disclaimer: "Listening from the distance of centuries across the death chasms and howling kingdoms of decay, it is not easy to catch everything." Around 40 B.C. the ancient Roman historian Sallust pronounced the writing of history the most difficult of tasks. The collation of facts and description of events, however, seem easier (though the ease is deceptive) than the analysis of their influence on society and culture. The pages that follow must therefore be thought of as suggestive and tentative, open, as history must always remain, to discussion.

The Protestant Whig interpretation of history very naturally saw the Renaissance and Reformation movements as great progressive forces toward modernity. Lord Thomas Babington Macaulay asserted flatly that since the sixteenth century the Protestant nations have made decidedly greater progress than their neighbors. In his *History of England* he pronounced his judgment that under the church of Rome

> the loveliest and most fertile provinces of Europe have . . . been sunk in poverty, in political servitude, and in intellectual torpor, while Protestant countries, once proverbial for sterility and barbarism, have been turned by skill and industry into gardens and can boast a long list of heroes and statesmen, philosophers and poets.

> ... Whoever passes in Germany from a Roman Catholic to a Protestant canton, in Ireland from a Roman Catholic to a Protestant county, finds that he has passed from a lower to a higher grade of civilization.[1]

Such grossly prejudiced and unqualified value judgments are today considered neither acceptable nor respectable. By whose standard is a competitive industrialized country superior to a traditionalist agrarian society? What of Catholic France as a "modernized" land? What role did the difference in religion actually play compared with other factors? Was the Reformation a more powerful solvent of the medieval cultural system than the Renaissance? Questions come crowding in like harpies upon anyone who ventures a dogmatic judgment.

That the era of the Renaissance and Reformation saw revolutionary changes in European culture comparable to those that occurred at the end of the eighteenth century seems obvious to many historians, but is contested by others. The humanists and reformers, looking to the standards of the past for guidance, propelled Western man at an accelerated rate of speed toward the future. The clever comment of Francis Bacon clearly applies to them: "By show of antiquity they introduce novelty."

State, Church, and Political Theory

THE REFORMATION forced men to reconsider the concepts and relationships of church and state in radically new terms. This development meant more than merely another chapter in the old story of the struggle between the spiritual and temporal powers. The political circumstances had altered, for the Renaissance state had burst the bonds of the feudal system. The secular state, freed from any de facto control by the church, provided a sanctuary for the development of Renaissance culture and the possibility of independent churches. The medieval church could not maintain itself against the twofold attack of the secular state from without and increased religious concern from within. With the coming of Calvinism, Protestant piety took on a more polemical cast and provided a religious ideology for the nationalistic struggles during the half century that followed. The so-called confessional wars stemmed from the close ties of political and ecclesiastical-religious commitments. The *raison d'état* of the princely dynasties and, after 1789, of the nations was a natural concomitant of the more sharply delineated particularism of the various secular states as they developed during the fifteenth and sixteenth centuries.

The ecclesiastical-political pattern was nearly stabilized by the end of the sixteenth century and was altered only in border states by the wars of the seven-

---

[1] Thomas Babington Macaulay, *The History of England from the Accession of James the Second,* 7th ed. (London, 1850), vol. 1, pp. 47–48.

teenth century. In Spain the Habsburg monarchy faithfully served the Roman Catholic Church. In France, which was moving toward princely absolutism (though less absolute than historians formerly thought), Catholicism became a national faith, much as in the various states of Italy. England and the Scandinavian countries adopted an episcopal form of Protestantism well suited to the alliance of altar and throne. The Netherlands offers the most interesting spectacle, for its linguistic and confessional base was mixed, Walloon and Flemish, Catholic and Calvinist. The tensions between its high predestinarian Calvinism, enshrined in the confessional statement of the Synod of Dort (1618–1619), and the latitudinarian position further complicated its religious history. The homeland of Erasmus, the Netherlands transmitted a tradition of tolerance to modern liberalism. Hugo Grotius, the founder of an enlightened doctrine of natural law and of a new concept of international law, owed much to this tradition.

Recent research has disclosed that the Reformation did not contribute immediately to an increase in the power of the Protestant princes in their own territories. Many of them were placed in personal jeopardy by declaring for the new faith, and lesser landholders and commoners profited more than they from the expropriation of ecclesiastical property, since 60 to 80 percent of the income from secularized monastic and church lands was subsequently devoted to education, hospitals, and charity. Some territorial estates actually increased their own prerogatives at the expense of princely authority during the sixteenth century. Petty absolutism developed later, under altered circumstances.

In establishing reforms based on the conception of the church as a community of believers rather than an institution under rigid hierarchical control, the reformers gave renewed emphasis to the importance of each individual member of the fellowship and challenged the hierarchy's claims to temporal power. They taught with Paul that Christ alone is the true head of the church and that all believers are members of its body. This invisible church, known only to God, is the true communion of saints. The visible church of Christ on earth is marked by the gospel and the sacraments. Martin Bucer declared at Strasbourg in 1523 that the kingdom of Christ and the true church are surely where the word of Christ is heard with pleasure and observed with diligence. Zwingli added discipline and Calvin ceremonies as aids for distinguishing the true evangelical church.

In urging men to avoid "papal assemblies," Bucer declared in his *Instruction in Love* that the true apostolicity of the church is established when the church's ministers, as well as all its members, have the mind of Christ (Philippians 2:5) and of his apostles; that is, when they enjoy no special status or power, but live in service to the brethren and in deeds of love for their neighbors. The reformers thus effectively removed the church from the juridical area, challenging the religious propriety and legal validity of canon law as well as the political use of the great ban. The history of the preceding period had already made the effectiveness of papal

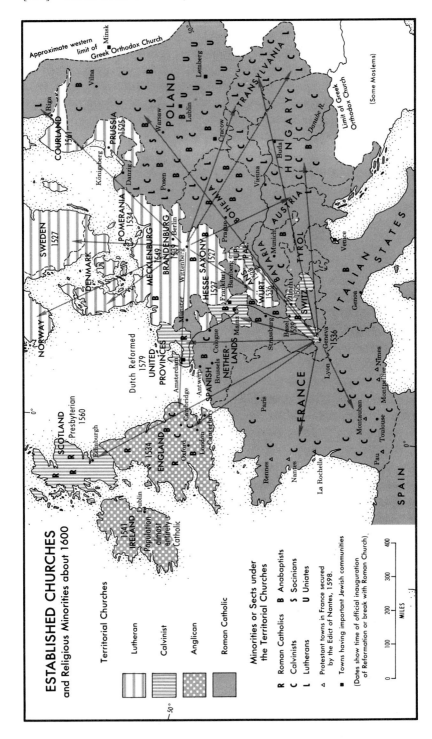

ESTABLISHED CHURCHES
and Religious Minorities about 1600

Territorial Churches

Lutheran

Calvinist

Anglican

Roman Catholic

Minorities or Sects under
the Territorial Churches

R Roman Catholics B Anabaptists
C Calvinists   S Socinians
L Lutherans   U Uniates
△ Protestant towns in France secured
   by the Edict of Nantes, 1598.
■ Towns having important Jewish communities

(Dates show time of official inauguration
of Reformation or break with Roman Church).

MILES
0   100   200   300   400

political actions questionable, and now the reformers further weakened the papacy as a counterpoise to temporal rulers. The Vatican's political maneuvering had the debilitating effect of bringing the church's spiritual mission into question and of producing the kind of hostility toward the church that was all too evident in the sixteenth century.

Luther left the matter of church polity open, suspended midway between a congregational ideal and an organization directed by council or consistory. From the Christian congregation the minister received his call to serve by preaching and administering the sacraments. Goethe once joked that by limiting the office of the ministry to a service, Luther had scraped the butter off his colleagues' bread. In holding that the priest or minister is of the same estate as all other Christians and is distinguished only by his office, Luther did introduce a leveling process into the structure of the church. Holding up Paul himself as his model, Luther insisted that "the man to whom has been committed the office of preaching has committed to him the highest office in the Christian church." In 1520 he wrote, "If they [the clergy] were forced to admit that as many of us as have been baptized are all equally priests, as we truly are, and that only the ministry was committed to them but with our consent, they would soon know that they have no right to rule over us except in so far as we freely agree to it." Calvin, too, held up the ministry as the first office of usefulness in the church, since God employs ministers as instruments in the performance of his work. The *Second Book of Discipline of the Kirk of Scotland* reflects Calvin's position, in which Knox concurred, referring to all officeholders in the church as ministers, since all are ordained for serving. A reverse current in the direction of high clericalism and bureaucracy developed quite early. Melanchthon and Osiander tried to upgrade ordination by suggesting that the minister was called to an especially holy life. The younger "Christians in authority" had fewer compunctions than Luther did about assuming roles of command.

Betrayed by his own patriotism and personal involvement, Zwingli made more concessions to state-churchism than did the other major reformers. A recent study, however, shows that the traditional charge against Zwingli, that he fostered a theocracy or fusion of church and state, is not justified. Calvin tried to achieve a form of church government based on the New Testament pattern and developed an organization that, although closely commingling the church and the Genevan government, in the context of the larger states achieved real independence for the church. The Anabaptists turned in a minority report on questions of ecclesiology. They held—if one may speak of these splinter groups collectively—that the visible church must be a sanctified body and remain separate from civil society, abjuring oaths. The Church of England meant to many of its clergymen the universal church in England, so that in spite of the obvious factor of nationalism involved, the idea of Christendom persisted in England through the sixteenth century.

With their new ethos of Christian vocation the reformers transcended the medieval dualism of sacred and secular callings. The natural order was for them no longer on a lower plane than the spiritual order. God's majesty was revealed in the created world, to which government belonged as a divine ordinance. With their strong sense of God's immanence the reformers saw the state as subject to God's will and judgment, the "kingdom of God's left hand." They knew nothing of a strictly secular state divorced from "natural law" or freed from ethical ties. The reformers, preeminently Calvin, sought to quicken the conscience of rulers. They enlarged the state's area of competence in social welfare and education, extending a trend already under way in the centuries preceding. Rulers should act like Christians, although the basis of their authority was in natural law under God and not in their church membership.

In accordance with Christ's injunction to "render unto Caesar the things that are Caesar's and unto God the things that are God's," the reformers asserted an absolute distinction between the secular and spiritual authorities. Protestant states were caught up in the general tendency toward tight political cohesion on a territorial or national level. Especially after the revolts and wars of religion, men felt the need for centralized control and strong rulers. The step from the distinction of secular and spiritual authorities to the principle of the separation of church and state, advocated most vigorously by the smaller sects and nonconformists, came only in later centuries.

Religious pluralism had a loosening effect on society. Protestant and Catholic minorities responded to the biblical injunction that one must obey God rather than man. When the need to act according to conscience is affirmed, an explosive potential is introduced. Faith in the King of Kings put earthly rulers in a proper perspective. Luther's sharp criticism of the princes found appreciative readers in subsequent centuries. The Calvinist stress upon predestination and the covenantal theology (the idea that at creation God made a compact with man, each agreeing to do his work) served as a leveling device, for believing oneself to be of the elect was not conducive to a submissive mentality. The famous confrontation between Mary Stuart and John Knox is illustrative. Queen Mary, exasperated at having to discuss her marriage with a commoner, exclaimed to Knox, "What have ye to do . . . with my marriage? Or what are ye within this commonwealth?" Knox retorted, "A subject born within the same, madam. And albeit I neither be earl, lord, nor baron within it, yet has God made me (how abject that ever I be in your eyes) a profitable member within the same."

Reformation thought contributed several basic elements essential to the growth of representative government and democratic institutions. The conception of the universal priesthood of all believers was essentially antihierarchical and corrosive of a pyramidal political structure. There is a link between congregationalism and a democratic ethos. As Knox once declared, "Take from us the freedom of assemblies, and take from us the evangel." The covenant idea in Calvinism, along with the stress on natural law as a basis for positive law, contributed to the idea of the social contract. The doctrine of vocation contributed to the development of an industrious and self-reliant citizenry, the kind of men useful to any government but absolutely essential to a democracy. Calvin concluded the final edition of his *Institutes* with these telling words: "And that our hearts may not fail us, Paul stimulates us with another consideration—that Christ has redeemed us at the immense price which our redemption cost him that we may not be submissive to the corrupt desires of men, much less be slaves to their impiety."[2]

Constructing a model of the good Protestant layman who possesses the qualities of which a perfect republic can be created, as we have just done, is easy enough. "Puritanism," burbled James Russell Lowell, "believing itself quick with the seed of religious liberty, laid without knowing it the egg of democracy." But at least three other important considerations need to be developed in order to put the Protestantism-democracy thesis into perspective.

First, socioeconomic factors had to come into play in conjunction with ideas to produce change in the political patterns. "Thoughts dwell closely together," Goethe observed, "but things jostle one another in space." Only as concrete circumstances produced disaffection toward monarchs did popular forces successfully assert themselves. When the truly revolutionary breakthrough came at the end of the eighteenth century, effecting a thorough destruction of the old religious and political authorities in Europe, it came under the auspices of "enlightened" leadership and in France, a nominally Catholic country.

Second, Catholic thinkers, too, contributed in an important way to natural law and social contract theory. St. Robert Francis Bellarmine (d. 1621), known for his unhappy involvement in the Galileo case—he was obliged to inform Galileo that the pope forbade the teaching of his heliocentric theory, although he himself was in sympathy with both Galileo and his teachings—developed a social contract theory that was antiroyalist in nature, reflecting the views of the Italian church. Bellarmine joined the Jesuit order in 1560 and rose to high positions: rector of the Roman College, provincial of Naples, theologian to Clement VIII, cardinal, examiner of bishops, and consultor of the Holy Office. Involved in an acrimonious controversy with antipapal Venice and concerned about the disabilities of the Catholics in England, Bellarmine argued on Thomist premises that as the supreme bearer of the spiritual sword the pope had indirect authority over secular rulers. Moreover, he contended, the authority of secular rulers is derived from the community by a social contract. The king was thus subject to deposition by the pope, who could absolve the allegiance of the people if the ruler defaulted in his duties. Although Bellarmine was considered a controversial figure in his lifetime, he was canonized and proclaimed a doctor of the church in the 1930s.

---

2 John Calvin, *Institutes of the Christian Religion*, trans. John Allen (Philadelphia, 1936), vol. 2, bk. 4, chap. 20, p. 806.

The vehement Spanish Jesuit Juan de Mariana (d. 1624), author of a lengthy history of Spain, defended the deposition and killing of tyrants in *The King and Institution of the King* (1599), which he wrote as a "mirror of princes" for the education of future kings. This book stirred up such a storm in France that the Jesuit general had to forbid members of the order to preach that it is lawful to kill despots.

Francisco Suárez (d. 1617), who joined the Jesuits in 1564, distinguished himself not only as a scholastic philosopher but as a political theorist. In his *Treatise Concerning the Laws and God the Legislator* (1612) Suárez argued that the pope, as the spiritual head of the family of Christian nations, was the proper spokesman of all its members. Thus the pope had indirect power to regulate secular rulers for spiritual ends. The state originates in the voluntary agreement of the heads of families, for the power of society to govern itself rests with the social group. Since political power is inherent in the group, no form of political structure is absolute and unchangeable. Government therefore rests upon natural law and is subject to change if it fails to meet its obligations.

Third, certain natural law doctrines, the conception of an international law, and ideas of toleration developed out of a secularized thought not derived by necessity from a theological basis. The doctrine of natural law as Suárez developed it really set politics apart from theology. In spite of his intention to elevate the papal position, his doctrine was not far removed from the thought of the Dutch Calvinists Johannes Althusius (d. 1638) and Hugo Grotius (d. 1645). Althusius continued the line of the antiroyalist French Calvinists. He identified natural law with the law of Moses, but his political theory depended logically upon the central idea of social contract. Men naturally associate in groups and sovereignty necessarily resides in the people as a corporate body. This corporate body bestows its power upon the administrators for effective management of collective affairs. But should the administrators default in their duties, they forfeit this power, which thereupon reverts to the people.

Grotius, in some ways very traditional, filled his concept of natural law with the heady wine of the ancients: substantial justice, good faith, the sanctity of covenants. The definition of natural law which he offered in his great book *On the Law of War and Peace* (Book 1, Chapter 1) was not really revolutionary:

> The law of nature is a dictate of right reason, which points out that an act, according as it is or is not in conformity with rational nature, has in it a quality of moral baseness or moral necessity; and that, in consequence, such an act is either forbidden or enjoined by the author of nature, God.

It was his methodology that was of greatest importance, for his appeal to reason provided the kind of rational thinking that men of his century could regard as a scientific method for arriving at a body of propositions underlying political arrangements within a state, its positive laws, and the laws that should govern relations between nations. To say that Grotius' system was not dependent upon theological premises is not to say that he was not moved by religious considerations. He was himself a product of the meliorating, tolerant Christian humanist tradition of his homeland. Commenting upon the gains of totalitarianism in the twentieth century, the distinguished Cambridge historian Herbert Butterfield has ventured to say in his *Liberty in the Modern World:*

> Because Christianity cannot forgo the basic principle of freedom—the right to worship the true God even against the requirements of the majority of a given society—it is possible, in view of the way in which the world is developing, that all the props of freedom and individualism will fail except the religious one.[3]

Protestantism and Capitalism

THE GREAT DEBATE continues as to whether the Protestant Reformation, especially Calvinism, had a decisive influence upon the rise and development of modern capitalism. But it is less acrimonious than in previous decades and the outlines of a scholarly resolution have begun to emerge. The controversy began over half a century ago, when the great German sociologist Max Weber published his essay on *The Protestant Ethic and the Spirit of Capitalism* (1904–1905). Weber defined the rational organization of free labor as the essence of capitalism. He argued that the spirit of capitalism was reinforced by the religious ethic of Calvinism. Sobriety, thrift, stewardship, rational and systematic behavior, high ethics, a sense of vocation, earthly rewards as signs of grace, social constraints as well as self-discipline—all of these elements were related to Calvinistic "worldly" asceticism. These values contributed to the development of a well-ordered capitalistic way of economic life. The thrust of Weber's argument was directed against materialistic determinism and stressed the importance of a religious movement to an economic development. R. H. Tawney, in his *Religion and the Rise of Capitalism* (1926), supported Weber's general position, but broadened the argument to include all of Protestantism and the socioeconomic and political circumstances at that critical juncture. While Weber never claimed a unicausal link between Calvinism and capitalism, many of his less sophisticated supporters and critics fought over just this issue. As a result, there has been extensive research and much revisionism, so that a far more complicated picture has emerged.

Capitalism clearly antedated the Reformation by many centuries. Certain instruments of capitalism were preserved in the eastern half of the Roman Empire and were transmitted to the West during the Middle Ages. East-West trade was never totally suspended, and commercial capitalism developed with the towns, very

---

3 Herbert Butterfield, *Liberty in the Modern World* (Toronto, 1952), p. 8.

noticeably from the twelfth century on. The great Italian banking houses of the Renaissance made a highly refined and astonishingly successful use of the financial methods of mercantile and industrial capitalism. Double-entry bookkeeping was of medieval origin. During the Reformation period most of the major banking families were and remained Catholic. The great financial centers, such as Genoa, Venice, Lyon, and Antwerp, were in Catholic countries. In the seventeenth century the Jesuits encouraged the same "economic virtues," thrift and an orderly life, as the Calvinists and Puritans.

The reformers were personally opposed to the practices of unfettered capitalism. Luther drew upon "nature" and the Scriptures for his economic norms. He considered agrarian life more natural and wholesome for man than industry or commerce. As the son of a relatively small but highly successful mining entrepreneur, he was hostile to such big-time operators as the Fuggers, who built up monopolies, squeezed out the little men, and used their money to manipulate politics. Luther espoused a labor theory of value and endorsed just-price theories and a self-sufficient economy for each country. He saw worldly goods as useful and had little sympathy with the radical sects that abolished private property. But he held with the traditional theological opposition to usury or high interest on loans, applying to capitalists the Old Testament injunction against "taking usury or increase" from a brother in need. In his "Little Sermon Against Usury" (1519), his "Large Sermon Against Usury" (1520), and his "Admonition to Pastors to Preach Against Usury" (1540) he reaffirmed his stand, but with little hope that the rising tide of interest-charging finance capitalism could be stemmed. On the basis of Matthew 5 Luther declared that Christ had distinguished three levels in the giving of temporal goods to one's fellow man. The highest was to give more to a man who had already taken from you. The next was to give to a neighbor in need. The lowest was to lend to someone. He would leave it to the law to decide under what circumstances 4, 5, or 6 percent interest could be justified, but he was certain that any higher rate was a sign of greed.

Geneva, at the crossroads of Europe, had long been a lively trading center. Calvin's bourgeois background and legal training made him less medieval and conservative than Luther, and he was in tune with the city's commercial life. In his reply to Claude de Sachins's questions on usury in 1545 he cut through some of the traditional church restrictions on usury, but he still hedged his position so carefully with restrictions of all sorts that it can hardly be said that he "unleashed" finance capitalism. On the contrary, he fought greed and avarice, self-aggrandizement, and exploitation, and he opposed speculative operations such as buying interest without security.

Calvin certainly never pointed to material success as a sign of God's election to salvation. Such a distortion does appear in seventeenth-century Calvinism, but obsessive concern with worldly possessions developed only when genuine religious feeling began to wane. One can, of course, point to extremely wealthy Protestant financiers in the seventeenth century, capitalists such as de Geer, d'Herworth, Rambouillet, and de Witte, who made political loans not only to the Protestant monarchs Christian IV of Denmark and Gustavus Adolphus of Sweden, but to Cardinal Richelieu of France and the Habsburgs of Spain and Austria. But these men were "cool" Calvinists who showed no trace of religious asceticism, wheelers and dealers in the big-time money markets of Antwerp and Liège. Catholicism of the Counterreformation often drove the anticlerical bourgeois of the city-states into exile with their republican notions. Except for a few court favorites who were granted special privileges and monopolies, the Catholic rulers in the southern Netherlands, Spain, and Italy (with the exception of republican Venice) harassed and even drove out their progressive merchants and bankers, forcing able men into difficult situations that by a kind of challenge-and-response mechanism further stimulated their drives toward economic compensation and security.

It would be a mistake to identify seventeenth-century Calvinism mainly with those very wealthy financiers who all too easily attract the eye, for Calvinism's major appeal was to the "little men," the tradesmen and craftsmen. The sense of sobriety, good order, and spiritual strength it conveyed was much more congenial to them than the radical ideas of the sects or the seemly lax and liberal teachings of the Dutch theologian Jacobus Arminius, who opposed the strict predestinarian doctrine and held that salvation was possible for all. H. T. Buckle was more correct than he often was when he wrote, "Calvinism is a doctrine for the poor, Arminianism for the rich. . . . In the republics of Switzerland, North America, and of Holland, Calvinism was always the popular creed. . . ."[4] At least in the Netherlands the regent class opted for the liberal theology of the seventeenth century. In view of all the evidence, the Weber-Tawney hypothesis on the relationship of Protestantism and capitalism scarcely seems to retain any validity as an overall explanation. And yet by instilling into the laboring classes a view of life that raises work from drudgery to a source of self-respect, Protestantism and especially Calvinism helped to build up a group of productive and reliable people, a solid base for a capitalist society.

The Heritage of Humanism

THE POET T. S. ELIOT spoke of culture as "the incarnation of religion" or "lived religion."[5] The theologian Paul Tillich wrote in *The Protestant Era,* "Religion is the substance of culture and culture the form of religion."[6] No cultural creation, he believed, can hide its religious ground. If there is truth in such assertions, one might

---

[4] H. T. Buckle, *History of Civilization in England,* 4th ed. (London, 1864), vol. 1, pp. 775–76.
[5] T. S. Eliot, *Notes Towards the Definition of Culture* (London, 1948), pp. 15, 33, 67–82.
[6] Paul Tillich, *The Protestant Era* (Chicago, 1938), p. 57.

well expect that an age that saw the juxtaposition of the Renaissance and the Reformation would reveal intimate cultural ties connecting the two movements. And although the Reformation was a far more radical movement than the Renaissance, strong cultural ties did bind the two together.

EDUCATION

One such tie was the deep concern of humanists and reformers for education. "Civilization," as H. G. Wells once remarked, "is a race between education and catastrophe." The humanists made important contributions to education through their renewed emphasis on the classics, the introduction of new studies into the curriculum, and new methods of instruction. They were, of course, elitist in their philosophy of education and served the interests of aristocratic and upper bourgeois circles. The reformers owed them a double debt, for their enthusiasm for learning and their appreciation of the classical languages and literature; but they went beyond the humanists in their stress upon popular education and universal literacy as well as in their special emphasis upon teaching as a divine vocation.

Luther urged compulsory universal education for both boys and girls, with special opportunities for children of exceptional ability. No labor or expense should be spared in educating the youth, he wrote. All who had the wit should be taught to read, so that the Scriptures might be widely studied and known. Education was to prepare men for service in the state as well as in the church, for, as Melanchthon put it, "the ultimate end which confronts us is not private virtue alone but the interest of the public weal." In the same vein Calvin wrote in the *Ordinances* of 1541: "Since it is necessary to prepare for the coming generations in order not to leave the church a desert for our children, it is imperative that we establish a college to instruct the children and to prepare them for both the ministry and civil government." In 1536 the citizens of Geneva had taken an oath that they would "maintain a school to which all would be obliged to send their children." In this tradition the great seventeenth-century educator Comenius admonished, "Let none therefore be excluded unless God denied him sense and intelligence." In 1560 John Knox and his co-workers drew up *The First Book of Discipline*, which envisioned a national system of education. It was no accident that universal literacy was first achieved in Scotland and in several German Protestant states.

The reformers were at one in their praise of the teaching vocation as a service of love to man. "If I had to give up preaching and my other duties," Luther wrote in 1530, "there is no office I would rather have than that of schoolteacher. For I know that next to the ministry it is the most useful, greatest, and best; and I am not sure which of the two is to be preferred." Melanchthon admonished teachers "to take up a school vocation in the same spirit that you would take up the service of God in the church." Theodore Beza believed that in working as a professor of Greek he was performing as great a service in promoting religion as he would have done in the pulpit.

Luther, who considered the Renaissance revival of learning the direct fore-runner of the Reformation, urged the cultivation of Latin, Greek, and Hebrew. "Let this be kept in mind," he wrote,

> that we will not preserve the Gospel without the languages. The languages are the scabbard in which the Word of God is sheathed. . . . Therefore it is evident that where the languages are not preserved, there the Gospel will become corrupted. . . . It is our evident duty to cultivate the languages, now that God has restored them to the world through the revival of learning.

He took the initiative in reforming the curriculum of the University of Witten-berg, replacing Aristotle and scholastic philosophy with Augustine, the Scriptures, and the classics. "I am persuaded," he wrote, "that without knowledge of literature pure theology cannot at all endure." The study of poetry and rhetoric fitted people as nothing else could "for grasping sacred truth and for handling it skillfully and happily." Melanchthon was a prime mover in the founding of the new gymnasia or secondary schools with humanist curricula in Nuremberg and elsewhere. He held sound instruction in letters to be a necessary condition for the teaching of religion.

Calvin, who had been a French humanist in his youth, always retained his love of literature. He admired Cicero especially, and his pages sparkle with citations from the classics. He also believed that much could be learned from the classical treatises on science and the practical arts. And he practiced what he preached, for in founding the Geneva Academy he established a curriculum that included the ancient languages and humanist disciplines. The Calvinists founded new universities in Edinburgh, Leiden, Amsterdam, Groningen, Utrecht, Franeker, Nimes, Montauban, Saumur, and Sedan. They reformed others in Calvinist areas, such as Heidelberg, and founded Emmanuel College at Cambridge. For the re-formers higher education was a *negotium cum deo,* an activity carried on together with God. Higher culture, too, was a "sphere of faith's work."

Johannes Sturm, the founder of the evangelical gymnasium in Strassburg, which became a model for all the secondary schools of Europe, adopted as his motto "Wise and eloquent piety," revealing his conviction that faith and literary culture fitted well together. Here and in the other schools of the reformers, Protestant seri-ousness combined with humanist ideals to produce an educational enterprise of which Europe has every right to be proud.

In the new Jesuit schools the students read Cicero's epistles and *Tusculan Disputations,* Terence or Virgil's *Eclogues,* Ovid's *Tristia,* Sallust, and Horace's *Arts poetica.* By 1551 there were Jesuit colleges in Rome, Bologna, Florence, Ferrara, and Venice, and in many parts of northern Europe. But in Catholic and Protestant schools alike, classical studies dwindled in time to a school discipline. What they gained in technical precision they lost in spontaneity. The "safe classics," useful for moral instruction, were taught, but this pedagogical humanism lacked the zest and abandon that had characterized Poggio, Filelfo, and Aretino.

No one would argue that the Reformation ushered in a new Periclean age. The education of a creature so limited and self-centered as man is always a struggle. In the first stormy years of the Reformation, while the reformers attacked scholastic studies and society was in turmoil, enrollments at the universities plummeted downward; Erlangen, for example, which had 311 students in 1520–1521, had only 14 in 1527. Wittenberg, too, dropped briefly, but soon began attracting great numbers. The reformers constantly complained about the lack of talent and wrong motivation of the students. Martin Bucer growled:

> Nobody will learn anything nowadays except what brings in money. All the world is running after those trades and occupations which give least work to do and bring the most gain, without any concern for their neighbor or for honest and good report. The study of the arts and sciences is set aside for the basest kinds of manual work. . . . All the clever heads which have been endowed by God with capacity for the nobler studies are engrossed by commerce.

Nearer the end of the century the minor French humanist Louis Le Roy found the young virtually uneducable: "Students, if they are poor, apply themselves to gainful arts in order to have something to live on, after profiting only moderately from letters. If they are rich, they want pleasure, seeking the easy surface of learning and not its painful depths." By the late seventeenth century the universities had lost their position of leadership and did not rise again in preeminence until the nineteenth century.

THOUGHT AND LETTERS

"Learning, wisdom, and writers should rule the world," Luther pontificated in one of his *Table Talks,* "and should God ever in his wrath take away all learned men from the world, what else would the people who are left be except beasts!" The magisterial reformers took a positive attitude toward letters, a happy circumstance, for if the attitude of certain anti-intellectual sects or the cultural atavism of the practical types had prevailed, the golden ideals of the Renaissance might have sunk forever out of sight.

Italy.   Apollo moved his habitation to the north during the sixteenth century as the homeland of the Renaissance groaned under the weight of Spanish occupation, petty tyrannies, and Counterreformation repression, and Italian letters went into decline. Spain controlled Milan and Naples. In Rome Julius III was the last Renaissance pope, and then the Inquisition moved in to suppress free thought and creativity. Cosimo I, duke of Florence, set up a repressive regime. Eleanor of Toledo introduced Spanish etiquette to the Palazzo Vecchio. The many academies that sprang up in Florence, Ferrara, Bologna, and Rome cultivated an elegant Ciceronian style in speech and fine manners suited to the court life of a decadent period.

By mid-century many of Italy's best intellectuals were dead. Cardinal Sadoleto, the Erasmian humanist, died in 1547. Lazzaro Buonamici and Romolo Amaseo, the leading Ciceronians in Padua and Bologna, died in 1552. Petrarchism was barely perpetuated by very mediocre writers. Erotic poetry withered away under the hot breath of the inquisitors. Rhetoric as a discipline declined to the level of banal posturing. Pietro Bembo (d. 1547) continued in the Platonic tradition of the Florentine Academy, but he and his generation contributed virtually nothing original or noteworthy. After the death of the logician Marco Antonio Zimara in 1532, the University of Padua failed to produce any new Aristotelian philosopher of note. The sixteenth century in Italy has, in fact, been nicknamed the *saeculum victorianum,* after the Florentine Vettori or Victorius, an eminent but dull scholar who edited numerous Greek and Latin texts, wrote commentaries on Aristotle, and published thirty-eight books of *Variae lectiones.* Classical studies had moved from the piazza into the study.

Italian historiography accompanied classical studies into decline. Dominated by foreigners and even more disunited than before, Italians had little confidence that historical analysis could be of any profit to political leaders who seemingly had neither the ability nor the opportunity to apply its lessons. Not a single general history of Italy appeared after Guicciardini's until far into the following century. At the end of the sixteenth century the Florentine historian Scipione Ammirato wrote his official *Florentine Histories,* replete with erudite and antiquarian detail, providing many data but little understanding.

Near the close of the century there was a brief flowering of historiography in Venice, reminiscent of the days when civic humanism and patriotism had flourished in Bruni's Florence. Niccolò Contarini, who later became doge, wrote a substantial history of Venice, which was candid about the deficiencies of the age and offered a broad view of developments. Paolo Paruta, who became the official historian of Venice and ambassador to the Holy See, wrote a series of dialogues in praise of the civic life. Paolo Sarpi, author of a history of the Council of Trent, belonged to this Venetian group of historians. The fact that Venice was able to retain its independence, cultivate civic pride, and enjoy the triumph of Lepanto gave the republic an élan that had withered and died elsewhere in Italy. Its civic humanism, like its renaissance in art, came late and glowed in autumn colors.

The Empire. While Italy suffered the effects of its political ordeal and the repression of the Counterreformation, the states of western Europe moved on toward greater national cohesion and more independent cultural traditions. During the half century following the Peace of Augsburg (1555), much energy went into

theological controversy and confessional writings. During the two decades following the peace, Protestantism continued in the ascendancy in the empire. The evangelical faith came very close to becoming the universal creed of Germany. If it had
succeeded, the religious ideological ground for conflict would have been removed.
But three developments prevented such an easy solution: the expansion of militant
Calvinism, internal dissension within Lutheranism, and the success of the Counterreformation within the empire.

The Peace of Augsburg provided for a mutual toleration of Catholics and
Lutherans, but deliberately excluded concessions to Calvinism. Calvinism, refusing
to be thus ignored, penetrated in depth among the learned doctors of theology at
Heidelberg. It won the heart of Elector Frederick III of the Palatinate, although he
continued to protest his loyalty to the Augsburg Confession. In 1540 Melanchthon
published a revised version of the Augsburg Confession (*Confessio augustana
variata*) in which he rephrased certain passages to make them more acceptable to
other Protestants. In Article 10, for example, he worded the sentences on the Lord's
Supper in such a way as to allow for a Calvinist spiritual interpretation. After
Melanchthon's death Frederick III published the Heidelberg Catechism, which became a basic text in all Calvinist or "Reformed" churches in Europe and America.

During the decades after Luther's death, Lutheranism was torn by internal dissension and dogmatic quarrels that threatened to fragment the movement and
render it impotent. Political rivalries played a part in the development. The Schmalkald War, through which Ernestine Saxony lost to Albertine Saxony the privilege
of taking part in the election of the emperor, sowed seeds of discord in both
Saxonies, and there was constant tension between the Saxonies and Hesse over the
leadership of evangelicals. But beyond politics, the emphasis upon right belief in
the sense of correct dogmatic formulation, the readiness to condemn the views of
others, and a professional tendency to join schools and factions produced intolerance
and an intolerable situation.

The leadership of Lutheranism fell very naturally to Philipp Melanchthon, the
brilliant scholar for whom Luther had always felt the deepest affection. Because of
his broad humanist background, his peaceful persuasion, and his desire to see good
in the ideas of others, Melanchthon came to deviate from a strict Lutheran doctrinal position on a number of central points. He was, for example, willing to
grant the cooperation of the human will in the reception of divine grace (syner-
gism). He and his followers, called the Philippists, were attacked by the Gnesio-
Lutherans (literally, true or genuine Lutherans), led by the very conservative and
polemical Matthias Flacius Illyricus (1520–1575), the watchdog of orthodoxy.

The doctrinal controversies that followed fill shelffuls of pamphlets, dogmatic tomes, reports on conferences and synods, attacks and apologies. The need
for doctrinal unity and peace within Lutheranism became increasingly urgent.
Jakob Andreae, chancellor of Tübingen, supported by moderate Lutheran theolo-

gians and princes, worked toward a doctrinal formula to which all Lutherans might agree. The result was the Formula of Concord (1577), which became the definitive confession of a large majority of the Lutheran principalities and kingdoms. On June 25, 1580, precisely fifty years after the presentation of the Augsburg Confession to the diet of the empire, the *Book of Concord* was published, bringing together the three ecumenical creeds and the specifically Lutheran confessions.

It has been estimated that by 1570 seven-tenths of all the people in the empire were evangelical. The two immediate successors to Emperor Charles V, Ferdinand I (1558-1564) and Maximilian II (1564-1576), were in no position to suppress Protestantism. But as the century moved on, internal strife weakened the evangelical cause and the Catholic Counterreformation picked up momentum.

Even in the 1540s individual Jesuits were at work in the empire. Peter Canisius (1511-1597) wrote a popular catechism as an answer to Luther's and established excellent Jesuit schools. From 1549 on the Jesuits worked in the Habsburg domains, in Bavaria, and in the archepiscopal territories along the Rhine. Their appeal to the common people rested upon their genuine piety, religious ceremonies of great emotional appeal, processions, pilgrimages, and impressive architecture. The Collegium Germanicum in Rome trained German priests in the Jesuit spirit. Pope Gregory XIII (1572-1585) was especially zealous about bringing the Germanies back to the faith. He appointed able nuncios to the empire and in 1573 he established the Congregatio Germanica, a permanent committee of cardinals to handle the "German question."

The results of these efforts were remarkable and to the evangelicals most alarming. By 1600 Bavaria, Baden-Baden, Styria, Carinthia, and Carniola were once again safely Catholic. In the south, Bamberg, Würzburg, and Salzburg, which had large evangelical populations, became overwhelmingly Catholic again. Even in the north several key ecclesiastical territories were recatholicized: Eichsfeld, Fulda, Münster, Paderborn, and Cologne. The battle for Cologne was particularly critical, for it was the key to Westphalia and the lower German Rhineland. As Catholicism gained in power, the possibility of a religious war between fairly evenly matched opponents became a real threat.

The interest and energies absorbed during this period by theological controversy and the ecclesiastical struggle for supremacy limited intellectual creativity and aesthetic accomplishments in the Germanies. A few men of unusual ability appeared in other areas of endeavor—the Silesian poet Martin Opitz, the Augsburg architect Elias Holl, the Tübingen Aristotelian Jakob Schegk, the Saxon musician Heinrich Schütz. In religion itself there was a dearth of creative thought, and a theologian such as Johann Valentin Andreae stands out largely for lack of competitors. Popular religious writing—devotional literature, books of sermons, hymnals—made up an important part of the literature of Protestant Europe.

One literary genre that achieved notable successes was history. During the course of the Leipzig debates Luther had cited historical precedents against Eck and called history "the mother of truth." During his last years he read histories of all kinds and even wrote an introduction to a history by Galeatius Capella, a Sforza historian. Melanchthon wrote an introduction to a chronicle by Carion and rewrote a large part of the chronicle itself. The spiritualistic Sebastian Franck wrote a world history that in originality, independence of viewpoint, and cultural scope may be judged superior to Melanchthon's. But the most impressive work was that of Johannes Philippson, or Sleidanus, as he was called, after the town of Schleiden in the Rhineland. In 1555 Sleidanus published his *Commentaries on the State of Religion and on the Reign of Charles V,* in which he sought to write objectively and impartially, as he explained with care:

> All these things I recite plainly, simply and truly as everything was done: neither use I also any color of rhetoric, nor write anything in the hatred or favor of any man.... I frame my style only and use mine own words, that the speech may be always like and equal, and I bestow each thing in its place, as they follow in order.

The *Bavarian Chronicle* of Johannes Aventinus (d. 1534) was a notable history, going back to the sources in the humanist tradition. Reformation historiography followed the humanist assumption that history, like philosophy, has pragmatic utility, teaching by example. Protestant historians, sharing the humanists' view of the medieval period as a dark age, frequently saw the hand of God in history, rewarding and punishing. The ways of looking at history that had developed during the Renaissance and the Reformation, including its periodization, lived on into modern times, and some still persist today.

France.   French letters continued to prosper during the second half of the sixteenth century, despite the fact that King Henry II and his successors were never as enthusiastic patrons of literature as Francis I had been. The religious wars took their toll, but some remarkable literary figures emerged during those decades. Calvin was himself an accomplished French stylist, and his *Institutes* especially exercised a most constructive influence upon the French language and literature.

The imitation of classical models and the influence of Italian Renaissance thought continued to be very much in evidence in French literature. A group of writers known as the Pleiades cultivated the French language, but at the same time believed that literary perfection was to be achieved by a close study and imitation of classic authors such as Cicero and Virgil. Joachim du Bellay's *Defense and Illustration of the French Language* (1549) developed these theories of the Pleiades. Du Bellay (1522–1560), inspired by both Plato and Christ, adhered to theories of tender and delicate love. Pontus de Tyard, an exquisite poet, was a student of Marsilio Ficino's writings and reflected his Neoplatonic theories of love. Pierre de Ronsard (1524–1585), the best known of the group, met du Bellay in a hostel in Touraine and became his fast friend. Ronsard was voluptuous, sensual, even lewd, not at all in the spirit of Ficino, but his theories of poetic madness were derived from Plato. He spoke of France as the "mother of the arts."

It is fascinating to note the development of rationalism and skepticism side by side with Catholic orthodoxy and Calvinist fideism in sixteenth-century France, in part in reaction to the religious controversies. A real intellectual fluke was the Averroist doctrine of Francesco Vimercati, a Lombard student of the Paduan neo-Aristotelians, who became the physician of Francis I and received a chair of philosophy, protected by the church. Between 1550 and 1556 he published commentaries on Aristotle in which he presented the Averroist doctrine of the one eternal intellect and argued for the eternity of the universe, determinism, and the constancy of natural laws. He was opposed by Gentien Hervet and others, but his most publicized critic was Peter Ramus (Pierre La Ramée), who launched an all-out attack upon Aristotle himself.

Peter Ramus (1515–1572) was a writer of extraordinary brilliance and force. The thesis he defended when he took his M.A. at Paris in 1536 suggests the direction of his thought: "All Aristotle's doctrines are false." He remained throughout his life the fierce opponent of Aristotelianism. Fighting Aristotelianism was a tough assignment indeed, for throughout Europe it remained the predominant philosophy of the universities, including even Wittenberg, where it made a comeback under Melanchthon's aegis. In 1543 Ramus published his two major works, *Aristotelicae animadversiones* and *Dialecticae institutiones,* written in a fine humanist style. The University of Paris condemned his work, and eventually Francis I appointed a committee to judge a disputation between Ramus and his major critic, Anthony of Gorea. The committee condemned Ramus as "rash, arrogant, and impudent," a judgment the king confirmed. Ramus objected to the sterility of Aristotelian logic as it was then being officially taught. He favored enlarging the area of rhetoric in combination with logic and a closer union of the arts of exposition and argumentation. Ramism was opposed in most continental universities, but it had a considerable influence in England and in the American colonies. Thanks to the protection of the cardinal of Lorraine, Ramus secured a "royal lectureship" at the College of Navarre after the accession of Henry II. In 1562 he left the Catholic Church and became a Calvinist. Ten years later he paid the price of his nonconformity and defection by being murdered in the massacre of St. Bartholomew.

The greatest man of French letters in that era, some would say in all times, was that urbane, exquisite intellectual Michel de Montaigne (1533–1592). Montaigne was the scion of a wealthy Bordeaux family and grew up with all the advantages of skilled tutors and schooling. He studied at the College of Guyenne for seven years, then spent two years in logic and dialectics at Bordeaux and studied law before entering public life as a counselor and member of the parliament. At the age of thirty-eight he retired to the Château de Montaigne, where from 1571 to 1580 he wrote his *Essays.* He spent a year and a half traveling through Alsace, Switzerland, Bavaria, Venice, and Rome, recording his experiences in his *Journal.* His life in his rural retreat was reminiscent of the *vita solitaria,* the contemplative life away from the marketplace cultivated by Petrarch, Sadoleto, and other humanists. Embellished by a library of classics and the company of intellectual friends, his urbane style of life anticipated the eighteenth-century salon. Through the wit and charm of his writing shines the evanescent quality that Matthew Arnold must have had in mind when he spoke of a "sad lucidity of soul."

The *Essays* are a long, polished relation of Montaigne's reflections and recollections, his experiences garnered in life and gained vicariously by reading. Although he himself is the subject of the book, it reflects the foibles and strengths of all humanity. Highly rational, Montaigne had a strong sense of the limitations of reason when confronted by the big questions of life. When he considered the variety of customs and ethical and aesthetic standards revealed in the cultures of Asia, Africa, and the New World, he concluded that such matters are relative to the cultural experience of the people concerned. His skepticism has brought down upon him charges of Pyrrhonism. "I generally observe," he commented wryly, "that when a matter is set before them, men are more ready to waste their time in seeking the reason of it than in seeking the truth of it . . . so much uncertainty is there in all things." An unbending elitist as a young man, he learned that the unlettered peasant and fisherman may possess a practical wisdom not to be found in books. Montaigne's humane, witty, pithy, and often wise observations on the human condition place him in the best humanist tradition. Many of his theories on education were very influential in later years. But his acute sense of the limitations of human reason and the frailty of mankind set him apart from the ebullience and naïveté of some Renaissance men. In that sense his work marks the end of an era.

Spain.   During the reign of Philip II Spain experienced its golden age of culture. Thomist theology revived and an Erasmian tradition persisted in letters. Lope de Vega and Pedro Calderón de la Barca flourished. But above all the incomparable Miguel de Cervantes (1547–1616), author of the classic *Don Quixote,* raised Spanish literature to new triumphs. In painting, the names of Velázquez and El Greco became immortal.

The Spanish cultural efflorescence is an intriguing phenomenon, coming as it did in a period of absolutistic tendencies and inquisitorial repression. Perhaps the imperial glory proved inspiring, so that for the first time in their history Spaniards felt themselves culturally superior to other Europeans. In art and literature Spain developed strong traditions of its own and Spanish intellectuals exuded a new confidence, revealing a predilection for ethical, legal, and religious problems rather than for science and philosophy. The decline from greatness was gradual but seemingly inevitable in the century that followed.

England. It can be argued with some plausibility that the real English Renaissance began during the age of Elizabeth. The earlier efflorescence of culture during the reigns of Henry VII and Henry VIII, the days of Latimer, Grocyn, Linacre, Colet, More, and Erasmus, were pale compared with the flowering of native genius during Elizabeth's reign. The first phase was indispensable to the second and the Italian influence was of critical importance to both. Essential carriers were the English who went to Italy, such as the earl of Surrey and Sir Thomas Wyatt. "They," wrote the Elizabethan poet and critic Richard Puttenham, "having traveled into Italy, and there tasted the sweet and stately measures of the Italian poesie, greatly polished our rude and homely manner." Italians who came to England, such as Polydore Vergil, brought with them the finest literary products of the Renaissance, and courtly manners in addition.

The new and improved schools spread learning among increased numbers of Englishmen. In 1531 Sir Thomas Elyot, in *The Boke Named the Gouvenour,* fused the literary aims of Vives and Erasmus with the idea of the "gentleman" promoted by Castiglione. He urged a Renaissance approach to education, Latin as a living language, tutors for the children of "governors" or public servants, and the teaching of music, art, and physical education. The aim of education was to be the cultivation of wisdom learned from the ancients and applied for the good of society. In this humane tradition the greatest English educator of all, Roger Ascham (1515–1568), wrote *The Schoolmaster,* published two years after his death. It was the best treatise in English on classical education, and stressed the need for gentleness in teaching the very young and for cultivating "hard wits" rather than "quick wits." Ascham argued that by education a man learns vicariously and safely in one year what would take twenty to learn by experience. The educational theories and curricula recommended by such distinguished Renaissance humanists as Juan Luis Vives were put into practice in schools even in remote northern provinces. As humanist learning spread out from court circles to a larger segment of the population, the way was prepared for the secular cultural rejuvenation in the age of Elizabeth. There is a unity in the cultural developments that came to a climax in the triumphs at the end of the century and ripened to maturity in the decades after Elizabeth's death.

Although it is difficult to document the correlation between the adventures of the Elizabethans on the sea, the naval triumph over the greatest Catholic power, the growth of a national spirit, and the upward surge of literary and artistic culture, the sense of exhilaration and exuberant energy is evident throughout all aspects of English life, including literature. The writings of greatest genius and most enduring quality were universal in concept rather than merely national. But it was Elizabeth as Gloriana, a symbol of Britain's greatness, and the heroic deeds of Englishmen advancing England's interests that quickened men's minds and set their pens in motion. An age of action leads men to think in epic terms. Just as the Italian

Renaissance produced great chronicles and accounts of Italian affairs by Bruni, Machiavelli, and Guicciardini, so now pride and patriotism led the Tudor historians to relate Britain's greatness to events of the past, now seen as glorious.

A certain sense of destiny that ran deeper than mere chauvinism and self-glorification informed this new historical consciousness. John Lyly's pedagogical moralistic novel *Euphues and His England* (1580), for all the stilted language and affectation that made it the object of much ridicule, provided a key to this new English mystique and helped to develop a Protestant mythology. England, Lyly piously intoned, was the new Israel, the chosen people of God, destined to carry the gospel and to do his will. William Camden, headmaster of Westminster College, published his *Brittania,* an antiquarian geography of every county in England, in order to "restore Britain to antiquity and antiquity to Britain." This Renaissance genre, made famous by Biondo's *Italy Illustrated* and Celtis' *Germany Illustrated,* served the purposes of a people in the process of rediscovering its own heritage. Camden's annals of Elizabeth's reign, written after her death, proved him to be more than a mere antiquarian. Another student of antiquity, John Stow, was so eager a scholar that he "wasted his substance, neglected his business, and spent all his money" in pursuit of his studies, until in old age he had to receive from King James I permission to beg from the churches. His creditors are long forgotten, but Stow is still remembered for his *Survey of London,* on the early history of England's queen city. William Harrison's *Description of Britain* was the most outstanding account of Elizabeth's England. Raphael Holinshed enjoyed the good fortune of having his *Chronicles* exploited by Shakespeare, so that their names are intertwined in luxuriant tangles of Elizabethan scholarship.

History attracted some of the strongest minds of the age. Francis Bacon's *History of Henry VII* had real literary quality and gained considerable renown. But perhaps the most remarkable achievement was Sir Walter Raleigh's outstanding *History of the World,* written to keep his mind occupied during his long years of imprisonment. His preface reveals some of the presuppositions of the age about history. Hearing boys outside his prison window arguing over things that had happened only a short time before, he reflected upon how much more difficult it is to be certain about events of ages gone by. The general notions of a cyclical pattern in history, the pragmatic use of history as philosophy, the assumption that the lessons of history can be applied to daily life and present times—these were typical Renaissance conceptions and were derived immediately from classical theories of history. The fact that Shakespeare's historical plays (*King John, Richard II, Richard III, Henry IV, Henry V*) belong to the years between 1592 and 1600 may suggest that the historical subject matter is related not only to Shakespeare's personal development, but also to the exuberant patriotism and interest in England's national dynastic history in that period.

Classical and Italian models were important to the development of *belles lettres*. Translations became increasingly numerous and some gained lasting fame, such as Chapman's version of Homer's *Iliad*, Harrington's translation of Ariosto's *Orlando furioso*, and Fairfax's rendition of Tasso's *Jerusalem Delivered*. But the classical forms were now filled by native genius. Secular literature came to replace religious poetry as sonnets, lyrics, odes, and popular ballads and madrigals rose to prominence. In a beautiful treatise *In Defence of Poesie* Sir Philip Sidney vindicated the power of the poetic imagination against the dull and prosaic limitations that mere nature imposes upon man. Nature, he wrote, "never set forth the earth in so rich tapestry as divers poets have done, neither with so pleasant rivers, fruitful trees, sweet-smelling flowers, nor whatsoever else may make the too much loved earth more lovely. Her world is brazen; the poets only deliver a golden." Sidney offered a noble argument for the glories of Elizabethan letters. His own masterpiece was his *Arcadia*, which in a somewhat confused mixture of medieval and classical surroundings offered a pastoral story of love and chivalry, setting a high standard for the age. His sonnets reflected his own love experiences and helped to popularize that relatively easy Italianate poetic form. Sidney was important in his own times as the exemplar of the new ideal of Protestant knighthood. In later centuries Raleigh and Essex came to represent the epitome of Elizabethan courtier culture, but their Protestant gentlemen contemporaries saw Sidney as the cultural hero of the age.

Elizabethan men of letters, like the men of affairs, were concerned for the most part with the real world about them. There is very little romantic longing for an imagined golden age of the past. With some justification literary historians have traditionally dated the birth of Elizabethan letters from the *Shepheards Calendar* of 1579, a satire by Edmund Spenser. Spenser was educated at Cambridge, was patronized by the earl of Leicester, and in 1580 went to Ireland as secretary to the viceroy. He lived there, near Cork, for nearly two decades, until the Irish rebels under Tyrone burned his house and forced him to flee to England in 1598. He died in London a year later. A friend of Sir Walter Raleigh, active in Munster, Spenser was close to the Elizabethan scene in spite of his seclusion in Ireland. His *Faerie Queen* was the great epic of the age, revealing the influence of Tasso and Ariosto. Spenser imagined a day when chivalry was more than idle form, peopled his world with such knights and ladies as never were, and carried his readers with him on rhythmic waves of poetry to a land of aesthetic delight. And yet it would be a mistake to interpret his poetry as merely romantic in its use of old forms, for his legends and chivalric symbols carry the spirit of a new age in politics and religion. The *Faerie Queen* is quite simply a masterpiece, and in his devotion to the Protestant ethic as well as his literary concerns, Spenser was a spokesman for his age.

Few men of the time so incorporated in their own persons the Renaissance gentleman, the Elizabethan politician and man of affairs, the genial man of letters, and the serious philosopher as did Francis Bacon. This courtier was only forty-two when Elizabeth died. His career as rival of the formidable legist Sir Edward Coke, his disgrace, and his trial for bribery came during the reign of James I, but he was formed as an Elizabethan, published his famed *Essays* during her reign (1597), and was in many ways typical of the brash, aggressive, profane circle of Elizabethan statesmen. His thoughts on society and science have had enduring influence. His moral essays reflect practical political wisdom derived from an unsentimental observation of Elizabethan politics. His thoughts were weighty but of a practical kind, expressed in short, pithy sayings easily transformed into clichés. Like Erasmus' *Adages,* Bacon's essays grew in number from ten in the first edition to fifty-eight in the edition of 1625. In later life he displayed his pride in the English past by writing a *History of Henry VII,* a lively narrative with a skillful characterization of the monarch.

The fame of Francis Bacon will always rest on his philosophical treatises, which contributed so much, though deviously, to the rise of the modern scientific method. While still a student at Cambridge he came to the conclusion that the methods employed in various sciences were erroneous and sterile. Although he retained a certain respect for Aristotle as a thinker, he reacted strongly against the prevailing Aristotelian philosophy. "The knowledge whereof the world is now possessed," he wrote, "especially that of nature, extendeth not to magnitude and certainty of works." All his life Bacon poured out a stream of treatises, some, such as *On the Advancement of Learning,* of enduring value. His major work on natural philosophy, *Novum organum* (1620), was written in Latin, the language of scholars.

Bacon's basic criticism of philosophy was that men had been too much concerned with "the satisfaction which men call Truth" and too little concerned with operation. In a famous section he analyzed the "idols," the kinds of fallacies or general classes of error into which the mind is apt to fall. There are four false ways of looking at nature, he wrote. The first kind of error he called the idols of the tribe, common to all mankind, such as the tendency to suppose greater order in nature than actually exists, the inclination to support a preconceived opinion, the readiness to generalize on a few instances, and the proneness to give concreteness to the abstract constructs of the mind. The second class, idols of the cave, is a product of the individual's mental and physical peculiarities, the inclination, for example, to prefer the ancient to the modern or vice versa, the tendency to exaggerate similarities or differences, and the like. The third class, idols of the marketplace, arises from the tyranny exercised over the mind by mere words. The fourth class, idols of the theater, is the mistaken modes of thought resulting from traditional philosophical systems and from fallacious methods of demonstration. Against these systems Bacon opposed his new method.

Science was for Bacon really natural philosophy, which is concerned with God, nature, and man, of which the most significant to the scientist is nature. He had a firm grasp of the physical character of natural principles; the "forms" that the natural philosopher studies are not abstract ideas but highly general physical properties. The *prima philosophia,* or first philosophy, undertakes to demonstrate the unity of nature by organizing into one system the general principles of the various individual sciences. The three levels in this philosophy are experience or natural history, physics, and metaphysics. The new method is *induction,* the thread that leads the mind through the great labyrinth of nature. Through natural history— that is, experience—the scientist collects the facts by observation. Man as interpreter of nature must follow a natural and experimental history, moving by induction from particular observations, properly excluding, rejecting, and eliminating data, to the general principle. Bacon made no application of the method to achieve scientific discoveries of his own, nor did he really lay down the basic experimental method of modern science. But as an index to the growing concern with nature and as an inspiration for scientific thought his intellectual contribution has had lasting value.

The true genius of that dramatic age was given its most perfect expression in Elizabethan drama. Christopher Marlowe began to write in the turbulent years just before the Armada. Marlowe lived a wild, dissolute life, and was stabbed to death in a tavern brawl in 1592, when he was only twenty-eight. His dramas, too, displayed the lack of restraint and the *terribilità* of the Italian Renaissance, giving vent to the most extravagant passions and fearful deeds. In his *Tamburlaine the Great* (1586) he portrays the Tatar emperor caught up in *hybris,* false pride that tempts fate, as he rages against God and man. In *The Rich Jew of Malta* (1589) he has Machiavelli recite a prologue, mocking religion as "a childish toy" and holding that "there is no sin but ignorance." His most famous play was *Dr. Faustus* (1588), based on the medieval legend of the Rhenish doctor who sold his soul to the devil in exchange for knowledge and the power it gives. Marlowe's characters, like the Elizabethan adventurers, all seemed larger than life-size.

There were others in Marlowe's day much like him, though less skillful. Notable among them was Robert Greene (1560?–1592), a pamphleteer, novelist, and dramatist who managed to live a little longer than Marlowe but no less extravagantly. After leaving Cambridge he wandered through Italy and Spain, and was impressed by Italian literary models. A restless soul, he did as he pleased, abandoned his wife, and followed the precept that "what is profitable ceases to be bad." His own dramas were hurriedly written and did not approach the excellence of Marlowe's. Yet he ventured to call young William Shakespeare an "upstart crow beautified with our feathers," a mere actor who dared to invade the profession of the playwright.

Shakespeare came to London when Marlowe's earliest play was first appearing. The son of a Stratford tradesman down on his luck, Shakespeare was only nineteen when he married Anne Hathaway, who was eight years older. Poverty and a charge of poaching on a noble's land led him to abandon Stratford to try his fortunes in London, where he became an actor at twenty-two. His invasion of the dramatists' guild was a most happy event. He began with comedies. His earliest play, *Love's Labor Lost,* was a spoof on pedantry and contrived style and verbiage. His *Comedy of Errors* was an adaptation of a Latin play, amusing but lacking in depth of ideas and characterization. In his *Midsummer Night's Dream* he conjured up a fairyland of elves and clumsy clowns. As his fame grew, Queen Elizabeth herself listened with delight, and it is said that he wrote *The Merry Wives of Windsor* to amuse the queen, who had expressed a wish to see Falstaff in love.

After the premature death of so many leading playwrights, Shakespeare virtually had the stage to himself from 1592 to the end of the century, years in which his historical plays responded to the patriotic fervor of the English. From 1601 to 1608 a pessimistic strain crept into his "gloomy comedies," such as *Measure for Measure* and *All's Well That Ends Well,* and into his tragedies, *Hamlet, Othello, King Lear, Macbeth,* and *Timon of Athens.* During the last eight years he softened some, toning down the harsh, tragic element and adding a note of tolerance and romance to leaven the disillusionment and futility in his last plays, as in *The Winter's Tale* and *The Tempest.*

Shakespeare was the universal genius, surpassing all others in depth of insight, in inventiveness, in power of characterization, in versatility and charm. He was a culmination and summation not only of the Elizabethan awakening, but of the entire Renaissance. The major themes of Renaissance humanism found unexcelled expression in the lines of Shakespeare. Consider, for example, how the whole Renaissance discussion of the dignity and misery of man is given its ultimate poetic expression in Hamlet's soliloquy (Act II, Scene 2):

> What a piece of work is a man! How noble in reason! how infinite in faculty! in form, in moving, how express and admirable! in action how like an angel! in apprehension how like a god! the beauty of the world! the paragon of animals! And, yet, to me, what is this quintessence of dust? man delights not me; no, nor woman neither, though, by your smiling, you seem to say so.

Shakespeare was a genius, but his genius was always controlled. He could drink with the cleverest wits of London at the Mermaid Tavern, but he bought land near Stratford and lived out his last years in ease and comfort. He died there in 1616 at the age of fifty-two. Not even Ben Jonson, whose plays *Volpone, or the Fool* (1605), *Epicene, or the Silent Woman* (1609), *The Alchemist* (1610), and

Bartholemew Fair (1614) were of high order, equaled Shakespeare's sympathetic bond with all mankind.

THE FINE ARTS

The Reformation and Counterreformation made a visible impression upon the fine arts, which were more easily correlated than literature with the religious thrust. The Protestant areas in the north suffered a decline of quality and creativity in the visual arts, although music continued to flourish. The Catholic areas suffered at first from the puritanism of the Counterreformation, but in due course developed from mannerism to high baroque, a style expressive of the new religious ardor of the Catholic resurgence.

Architecture and Art in Protestant Europe. Luther was capable of returning from a visit to Cologne and commenting later on nothing more than the poor acoustics in that grand cathedral. His trip to Italy was hurried and of far shorter duration than Erasmus'. But like Erasmus he could return to the north without reacting in the least to Italy's artistic wonders. Luther did admire the skill of artists and craftsmen, and he had no objection to ecclesiastical art in churches so long as it was recognized as adornment and not put to idolatrous use. In fact, when Luther learned of the radicals' destruction of religious statuary and stained-glass windows in Wittenberg while he was in hiding at the Wartburg Castle, he rushed back to stop them. But that very incident shows the danger to religious art inherent in the Puritan component of Protestantism. That tendency was full-blown in Zwingli, who was convinced that artistic representation of Christ and the saints was inherently idolatrous and prepared the people of Zurich for the iconoclastic "cleansing of the temple," when the Great Minster was stripped of its artwork and whitewashed. Calvin had a more positive attitude toward ecclesiastical art, though he favored simplicity. The Anabaptists had little positive to say and nothing constructive to offer in the arts.

The Reformation as a whole affected architecture and art in three major ways. First, the attitude of the reformers toward art, especially ecclesiastical art, affected its fortunes. Second, their religious teachings were reflected in art. Third, the social, political, and military events in which religious issues were involved affected the prosperity of the artists and art itself. The Protestants had no real need to develop a distinctive architecture, for they inherited many more churches and chapels in the overchurched cities and towns than they had need for. Because of the rejection of the veneration of saints and, especially in Calvinist areas, the warning against graven images, sculpture fell into a precipitous decline. It persisted only in Catholic Bavaria and in Austria, thanks to the Italian influence imported by the Jesuits.

Artists still flourished in the early years of the Reformation, but no second generation equal to those masters emerged. Albrecht Dürer (1471–1528), the Nuremberg genius, became Luther's faithful follower. Luther's teachings had helped him "out of great anxieties," and he lived thereafter and died a "good Lutheran." His art reflected his conversion both in subject matter and in style. While he was still a Catholic, Dürer had done more than any other artist to show the north the Renaissance spirit of pagan antiquity. After his conversion to Lutheranism he practically abandoned the depiction of secular subjects except in scientific illustrations, travelers' records, and portraits (of Melanchthon and others), gave up the "decorative style" almost entirely, and concentrated increasingly on religious subjects. The lyrical and visionary element gave way to a scriptural virility that ultimately tolerated only the apostles, the evangelists, and the passion of Christ. His style changed from scintillating splendor and freedom to a forbidding yet strangely impassioned austerity.[7]

Hans Baldung Grien died in 1545. Hans Holbein the Younger, famous for his portraits of Erasmus, reformers, and English royalty, died in London in 1543. Lucas Cranach, the Wittenberg apothecary who produced a host of portraits, group pictures, and altarpieces for evangelical churches, died in 1553, leaving no successors equal to him.

Architecture and Art in Catholic Europe.   Dilettantes of universal history have offered grandiose explanations for the cultural differences between north and south. Thus northern Europe, cold and rugged, is said to represent the male principle. There philosophy and scientific theology, the products of hardheaded thinking, flourished. Southern Europe, warm and soft, represents the female principle. There the fine arts and music, the offspring of sensuous, sensitive living, flourished. Such theories, so simple yet apparently so profound, have always had their followers, but unfortunately they fail to take into account the flourishing of philosophy in Athens, Florence, and Rome and the glories of Flemish painting from van Eyck to Rembrandt. The causal factors involved—church patronage, theology, the social cohesion of the city-state, foreign domination, inquisitional repression, personal decision and dedication, traditions, economic base—all offer a better chance of understanding the reasons for the differences between Catholic and Protestant Europe. In the case of the arts such differences are very real and very striking.

Italy's political and military catastrophes had a depressing effect upon Renaissance art. Artists were now subjects of despots, domestic or foreign, rather than citizens of free states. The contrast is not absolute, for in better days Leonardo had served the Sforzas, and Titian, Veronese, and Tintoretto now prospered in republican Venice. But Italy's political humiliation and the Counterreformation produced a most important change in art and architecture. The immediate effect

---

[7] Erwin Panofsky, *The Life and Art of Albrecht Dürer* (Princeton, 1955), p. 199.

ALBRECHT DÜRER. *Perspective.*

of the puritanical rigor and prudery of the Counterreformation was a reaction against some of the finest work of the Renaissance. The nudes in the Borgian apartments of the Vatican were dressed. The papal court hired a "breeches painter" to clothe some of the nudes in Michelangelo's *Last Judgment* on the wall of the Sistine Chapel. Ammanati, the sculptor who had done the exquisite nudes on the fountain of Neptune in Florence, repented publicly for his indiscretion.

The high Renaissance in art, which one may date from about 1500 to the death of Raphael in 1520, was followed by a disturbed and unsettled period in which art took on new characteristics that reveal the frustration and uncertainty of the times. The transition from classical measure and balance, characteristic of Renaissance painting, to the new phase is to be seen in the later work of three great masters of the sixteenth century, Michelangelo, Titian, and Tintoretto. All three lost the decorum of their more confident period and gave way in some of their work to less controlled emotion. The younger generation followed their lead in giving violent and unmasked expression to deep and sometimes unpleasant emotions. Their style has in recent years been called mannerism.

The term "mannerism" is awkward, but so was the situation, for the sixteenth-century artists were in a transitional period between two major styles, Renaissance and baroque. In some ways they retained elements of the old and in others pointed toward the new. Mannerism as a term may suggest the eclecticism of the new art, for the younger artists are said to have painted *in the manner* of the late Michelangelo or of Titian. The message of that greatest of all art historians, Giorgio Vasari, seemed to be a commendation of eclecticism. In his indispensable *Lives of the Most Eminent Painters, Sculptors, and Architects* (1550) he lauded extravagantly such a variety of artists as to suggest that the *belle manière* meant many different things. But mannerism has another, less flattering connotation, the quality of excessive singularity; these artistic creations were artificial, affected. The giants of the era—Michelangelo (1475–1564), the architect Andrea Palladio (1518–1580), Titian (*c.* 1477–1576), and Tintoretto (1518–1594)—carried on the best traditions of the Renaissance, modified by their own individual styles. But the artists of lesser stature were more extravagant in their eclecticism and lack of emotional restraint.

Abandoning the effort to achieve verisimilitude in the portrayal of nature, Parmigianino (1503–1540) attempted to express an inner aesthetic vision of the beauty that he seemed to remember from an earlier age when men were still united with the deity. The result was a self-conscious and highly affected style. In his *Madonna del Collo Longo,* done around 1535, for example, the Madonna has a swanlike neck and a curving, serpentine body. The child Jesus is long-limbed, lying lightly and precariously on Mary's lap. The abstract figures are posed against a sensuously draped background. This is a total departure from the natural, classical, decorous idealism of Raphael and Leonardo. The *Deposition* and *Joseph in Egypt* of Pontormo (1494–1557), the *Moses Defending the Daughters of Jethro* of

Il Rosso Fiorentino (1494–1540), the *Portrait of a Young Man* of Bronzino (1503–1572), all exhibit the extravagance, uncertainty, affectation, and strange personal vision that collectively are called mannerism.

The artistic style that gave the most characteristic expression to the religious revival of the Catholic Church was the baroque. Rome itself gave birth to baroque. After the first repressive years of the Counterreformation, it became increasingly clear that Catholicism would not be able to regain the half of Europe lost to Protestantism, and the papacy then undertook to celebrate the glories of Catholicism in those areas where the people had remained steadfast. Pope Sixtus V (1585–1590) was singularly successful in bringing the Papal States under effective control, implementing the decrees of the Council of Trent, and beautifying Rome as a proud capital of a resurgent Catholicism. He enlarged the Vatican, built the Vatican Library, and saw the dome of St. Peter's finished at last. Designed by Bramante, the great church had been begun in 1506. Michelangelo took charge in 1547, redesigned it, and by the time of his death had completed the drum beneath the dome. Now under Sixtus V Giacomo della Porta completed the dome. Significantly, the great colonnades around the magnificent piazza, the baldacchino, and much of the church's interior were the creations of Giovanni Bernini (1590–1680), the greatest artist of the baroque.

A plausible argument can be made that the universal genius Michelangelo created the baroque style, for nearly all its elements are to be found somewhere in his works, including the tendency toward heroic proportions. Baroque artists and architects executed grand designs, and baroque buildings and piazzas are as large as the funds available allowed. If classical forms produced a sensation of solidity, stability, symmetry, and completion, the baroque set things in motion. A Greek column is complete in itself; the baroque architect held that no part of a structure should be self-sufficient, but that each must depend on another. Columns became serpentine and curved into vaulting arches. The forces pulling away from each other were constrained by a rigorous overall balance. Order was superimposed upon turbulence. All surfaces were ornamented with bright colors, curving lines, and a wide variety of shapes. The baroque painter had a predilection for biblical scenes and classical allegories filled with large crowds of people. Apotheosis scenes, showing the bodily elevation of Christ or the Virgin into heaven, were ideal for the high ceilings and domes of baroque buildings. The themes were often derived from the special emphases of Counterreformation theology: the assumption of Mary, Mary as queen of heaven, Corpus Christi processions, regnant pontiffs holding the keys of Peter.

The prototype of baroque churches was the Gesù, the central church of the Jesuits of Rome. Michelangelo offered to design the church and it is possible that the architects who actually constructed it after his death followed his advice or even his plans. Giacomo Vignola (1507–1573) supervised its construction, which features a wide tunnel-vaulted nave, a modest-sized dome over the crossing, and a series of small side chapels instead of the aisles that normally run along each side. Light streams down from the dome, and the use of light through oval apertures became a marked characteristic of the baroque style. Giacomo della Porta (1541–1604) designed the façade, which became a model for churches throughout Catholic Europe in the centuries that followed. The great monastery-palace of Philip II of Spain, the Escorial, and the Louvre in Paris are only two of the architectural monuments erected during the baroque age.

Two of the many artistic creations of the most prominent baroque artist in Europe, Giovanni Bernini, illustrate the impact of the Catholic Reformation upon art. The first is Bernini's sculpture *The Ecstasy of St. Teresa.* The Spanish mystic is portrayed as a young woman swooning at the moment when the arrow of divine love pierces her breast. Only El Greco (*c.* 1548–1614), with his elongated figures and high color, had a comparable feeling for the religious fervor of Spanish piety. The second is Bernini's shrine for the chair of St. Peter in the cathedral. The mighty throne encloses a wooden stool, which allegedly had once been St. Peter's own. It is held aloft by the four great doctors of the church who supposedly had supported papal supremacy in their times. Christ's presentation of the keys of the kingdom to St. Peter ornaments the back of the chair. Above, *putti* carry aloft the papal triple tiara and the keys to the kingdom. At the very top the Holy Spirit hovers in the form of a dove. This whole creation gives powerful expression to that sense of triumph which characterized the resurgent Catholicism of the Counterreformation.[8]

Music.   The sixteenth century has been called the golden age of music. Masters of the Flemish school, such as Jean d'Okeghem (d. 1495) and Jacob Obrecht (d. 1505), had developed polyphony by introducing the technique of imitation, by which the individual voices begin not simultaneously, but one after the other. This repetitive device made for elasticity and intricate polyphonic patterns. A pupil of Okeghem, Josquin Des Prez (d. 1521), was a master composer, combining pleasing symmetries and contrasts so that his music heightened the expressiveness of the text it accompanied.

The two greatest centers of music in Italy during the sixteenth century were Rome and Venice. Giovanni da Palestrina (*c.* 1525–1594) was perhaps the most famous composer of the century. He employed all the advances made by Flemish composers and his style was the exemplar of Flemish contrapuntal technique. His music embodied the loftiest impulses of the Catholic Reformation. For over forty years he served various churches in Rome and became the composer for the papal choir. The Council of Trent sanctioned his work as the official model for all composers in the service of the church. In Venice a Flemish musician, Adrian Willaert (*c.* 1480–1562), became the choir director in St. Mark's Cathedral. The greatest

---

[8] See John Ives Sewall, *A History of Western Art,* rev. ed. (New York, 1961), pp. 665–77, on sixteenth-century mannerism; pp. 678–87 on the origins of baroque art.

Venetian composer, Giovanni Gabrieli (1557–1612), developed a unique concert style, using two choirs, and in compositions for vocalists and instruments he assigned independent parts to the instruments. He influenced several prominent German composers, such as Jacob Handl (1550–1591) and Heinrich Schütz (1585–1612).

The grandest musical invention of the sixteenth century was opera. All the techniques of polyphonic music needed to interpret musically the visual scenes of a drama on stage—the fusing of solo voices, choral groups, and instruments, the expression of personal emotions vocally and instrumentally, and orchestration—had been developed during the course of the century. The Italians' feel for the visual fused with their love of music in the development of opera. A group of Florentines met between the years 1580 and 1589 at the house of Count Giovanni dei Bardi, a wealthy gentleman scholar. This group included Vincenzo Galilei, a lutist and the father of the famous astronomer Galileo; Ottavio Rinuccini, a poet; and Jacopo Peri and Giulio Caccini, musicians. They recognized from their study of Greek drama that the ancient texts had been delivered in a declamatory manner, and they believed the effects of dramatic poetry would be intensified by the addition of music. In that group opera was born. Peri's *Dafne* (1597) was the earliest opera. His setting of Rinuccini's dramatic poem *Euridice* was actually performed in 1600 for the wedding festival of Marie de' Medici and Henry IV of France. The great operatic composer Claudio Monteverdi (1567–1643) composed *Orfeo,* produced at Mantua in 1607, just a decade after *Dafne.* It is still presented in opera houses today.

The Catholic parts of the empire, the courts of Bavaria and Austria, tended to follow the musical lead of Rome. At the Bavarian court Orlandus de Lassus (*c.* 1532–1594), from Flanders, was perhaps the most versatile composer of the time. His two thousand compositions covered secular and sacred music in nearly every form, madrigals, *chansons,* motets, masses, and magnificats. Very cosmopolitan, he used for his texts everything from Petrarchan sonnets to the verses of Hans Sachs. Music is an interfaith as well as an international language. Luther greatly admired the compositions of the Catholic Swiss musician Ludwig Senfl (*c.* 1492–1555) at the Wittelsbach court in Munich, and even wrote him a fan letter. Luther considered music the noblest of the arts. He once wrote:

> I am not satisfied with him who despises music, as all fanatics do; for music is an endowment and a gift of God, not a gift of men. It also drives away the devil and makes people cheerful; one forgets all anger, unchasteness, pride, and other vices. I place music next to theology and give it the highest praise. And we see how David and all saints put their pious thoughts into verse, rhyme, and songs, because music reigns in times of peace.[9]

Luther was himself a talented musician and composed at least eight original hymns, the most famous of which is, of course, "A Mighty Fortress Is Our God."

---

[9] Ewald Plass, *What Luther Says* (St. Louis, 1959), vol. 2, p. 980. See also Helmut Huchzermeyer, "Luther und die Musik," *Zeitschrift der Luthergesellschaft,* 39 (1968):14–25.

He also composed the first part of the German mass. In addition, he provided sacred texts for familiar German folk tunes. Congregational singing became an important part of the evangelical church service. The Lutheran chorale, or congregational hymn, gave expression to the faith and prayers of all the members of the church. Music in worship was no longer the exclusive province of the chanting priest or choir, while the congregation stood mutely by. The first Lutheran hymnbook was published in 1524. It is impossible to conceive of the great hymns of Paul Gerhard (1607–1676) or the glorious creations of Johann Sebastian Bach (1685–1750)—the *St. John Passion,* the *St. Matthew Passion,* the *Mass in B Minor*—outside the tradition of evangelical music initiated by Luther.

Zwingli too, as we have seen, had a personal love for music and was quite accomplished in it. In regard to music he owed a somewhat ambivalent debt to humanism. He presumably learned from humanists such as Conrad Celtis a new appreciation for Renaissance music, but at the same time he also learned from the humanists a profound dissatisfaction with musical practices in the churches. Zwingli's radical formal principle that only those liturgical practices that were derived from the Scriptures were acceptable gave to his Reformed Church its peculiar stamp. The whitewashing of the church walls in Zurich was accompanied by the removal of organs as well. But years after Zwingli's death there was a resurgence of music even in the Great Minster; congregational singing was introduced and an organ was even installed. Music continued to prosper in Zurich, as did the visual arts, at least in secular settings.

Calvin favored the singing of the Psalms, and in 1562 the first completed edition of the French Psalter was published with Calvin's approval. The French poet Marot composed the majority of the 150 or so versified renditions of the Psalms and Theodore Beza completed the edition. This popular songbook adapted popular French *chansons* to the versified Psalm texts and was such a success that it was translated into twenty languages. Claude Goudimel (1505–1572), one of the best Calvinist composers, published several editions of musical settings for the Psalms.

The Reformation and Science

THE AMERICAN INTELLECTUAL HISTORIAN Carl Becker once commented that we moderns necessarily think of everything in terms of history or of science. The scientific revolution, which made its first giant strides in the seventeenth century, has won such a total victory through its apparent domination of nature that the Western mind has virtually capitulated to its criteria of truth. The relation of the Reformation and science, therefore, presents a fascinating historical problem. Why did modern science and technology develop as a socially significant force in the

West rather than in other cultures? Why in Christian countries rather than, say, Moslem? And why did it follow so closely upon the heels of the Reformation?

The role of Protestantism in the rise of modern science is still one of the most controversial issues among contemporary historians. A nineteenth-century French Protestant historian, Alphonse de Candolle, pointed out that of the ninety-two foreign members elected to the Academy of Sciences in Paris from its founding in 1666 to 1866, some seventy-one were Protestant, sixteen Catholic, and the remaining five either Jews or of indeterminate religious position. Correlating these statistics with the number of European Catholics (107 million) and Protestants (68 million) outside of France, Candolle concluded that there were six times as many Protestants as Catholics sufficiently eminent to rate election to the academy. Checking the statistics of the Royal Society of London (founded 1662) at two points in the nineteenth century confirmed his conclusion that Protestants tended to predominate over Catholics among the great scientists of Europe. Other studies brought to light the connections between Puritanism and science in seventeenth-century England. No one can deny the preponderance of Protestants among scientists after the 1640s. Lutherans, Anglicans, and preeminently Calvinists made more scientific discoveries than Catholics and appeared to be more flexible in putting them to use. Moreover, the most rigorous Calvinists contributed proportionately more scientists than did Anglicans, and after the astronomer Johannes Kepler, who died in 1630, the Lutherans produced no scientist of major stature until the nineteenth century.

These circumstances, about which there is a considerable amount of agreement among historians, have released a great flow of speculation as to the relation of religion to the rise of modern science. Were the fragmented Protestants merely less able than the Catholics to prevent the rise of science? Was the sociologist Max Weber right when in 1905 he suggested that ascetic Calvinism had a propensity toward empiricism, which was an essential element in scientific method? Were forces operative that had nothing whatsoever to do with religion, or which had at most only a tenuous connection to it? Is the situation after 1640 actually relevant to the problem of the *origins* of modern science, since by 1640 the work of Galileo, Harvey, and Descartes was virtually complete and science had thus already risen? It is, of course, impossible to rehearse all the arguments or marshal even a respectable fraction of the facts here. But these big questions may profitably be kept in mind while we scan scientific developments after the Reformation.

Among the causes alleged by some historians for the disproportionate number of Protestant scientists, at least after 1640, are (1) a certain concordance between the early Protestant ethos and the scientific attitude in the questioning of authority and spiritual individualism; (2) a certain congruity between the more abstract elements of the Protestant theologies and the theories of modern science, such as the antihierarchical implications of the concept of the priesthood of all believers and the idea that man is a microcosm of the great macrocosm; and (3) the use of science by the later Calvinists, especially the English Puritans, for the attainment of their religious aims, for they considered the study of nature a duty, included scientific research among the good works beneficial to humanity, and even considered scientific success, like material prosperity, to be a reassuring indication that a man had been elected for salvation.

Luther has frequently been referred to as the Copernicus of theology and Copernicus as the Luther of astronomy. The identification of the reformation in religion with the revolution in science is very old. Thomas Sprat, an Anglican clergyman and an early fellow of the Royal Society, commented on the

> agreement that is between the present design of the Royal Society, and that of our church in its beginning. They both may lay equal claim to the word Reformation; the one having compassed it in Religion, the other purposing it in Philosophy. . . . They both have taken a like course to bring this about; each of them passing by the corrupt copies, and referring themselves to the perfect originals for their instruction, the one to the Scripture, the other to the huge volume of creatures. They are both accused unjustly by their enemies of the same crimes, of having forsaken the Ancient Traditions, and ventured on Novelties. They both suppose alike that their ancestors might err; and yet retain sufficient reverence for them. They both follow the great Precept of the Apostle of trying all things. Such is the harmony between their interests and tempers.[10]

Luther himself believed that the world was seeing a new sunrise that would bring not only a reform of religion but a new appreciation of nature. He objected to scholastic philosophy, to Neoplatonic cosmology (although in his commentary on Genesis he used the concept of man as a microcosm), and to the humanists' bookishness. They all failed to take nature seriously and to appreciate it as fully as the doctrines of creation and the incarnation warranted. In one of his *Table Talks* he expressed this feeling and took a sideswipe at Erasmus in passing:

> We are at the dawn of a new era, for we are beginning to recover the knowledge of the external world that we had lost through the fall of Adam. We now observe creatures properly, and not as formerly under the papacy. Erasmus is indifferent, and does not care to know how fruit is developed from the germ. But by the grace of God we already recognize in the most delicate flower the wonders of divine goodness and omnipotence. We see in His creatures the power of His word. He commanded and things stood fast. See that force display itself in the stone of a peach. It is very hard, and the germ it encloses is very tender; but when the moment has come, the stone must open to let out the young plant that God calls into life. Erasmus passes by all that and takes no account of it, and looks upon external objects as cows look at a new gate.

This biblical naturalism of Luther's is of the same genre as the "Gothic" naturalism of St. Francis, which is said to have been an important ideological factor in the rise of Franciscan physics during the thirteenth and fourteenth centuries.

---

[10] Thomas Sprat, *The History of the Royal Society of London, for the Improving of Natural Knowledge* (London, 1667), p. 371 (misprinted as 363). Pt. 3, secs. 14–23 are particularly significant for the science-religion problem.

As an intensification of certain main-line attitudes toward nature unique to the Judeo-Christian (and "heretical" Moslem) West, Reformation theology contributed to certain essential presuppositions important to natural science in its incipient stages. The dogma that God created the universe by fiat out of nothing (*creatio ex nihilo,* an interpretation dating from the rabbinical commentators at the time of the Maccabees) underlined the qualitative gap between Creator and creation. Creatures are not extensions or emanations of God's being, and therefore do not share in his divinity. They are thus subject to examination without taboos. God's commission to Adam to "subdue" all creatures established man's sovereignty over nature. The idea that a "reasonable God" is the author of natural laws as well as of human reason was reassuring to the inquirer. The Western mind, trained in legal concepts by Roman and canon law and by exegetic and hermeneutic rules, was easily directed into concepts of law in natural philosophy. When the use of experiment was combined with rational interpretation, preferably expressed in the language of mathematics—and here the Hellenic inheritance was of crucial importance—the ingredients for the rise of science were brought together. The scientific mentality, described by the philosopher Alfred North Whitehead as the passionate interest "in the application of reason to stubborn facts," owed much to this cultural inheritance, which was revitalized by the Reformation in the religious sphere.

Luther and Calvin meant by "philosophy" the sum total of human sciences. They believed that the world of nature was subject to reason and open to its probing power. The Scriptures were the carriers of the word of God to man, not a textbook of natural science. The major reformers were not biblical literalists, and where there was an apparent conflict between the word of God and natural philosophy, they usually resolved the difficulty not on the basis of a "double theory of truth," but by a concept of multiple discourse, two separate levels of knowledge, divine and natural. They did, nevertheless, consider it legitimate to refute scientific theories by citing Scriptures.

Luther was quite open to the authentic scientific advances of the age and expressed wonder at the mechanical inventions of the day. The Germanies were hospitable to the sciences. Georg Agricola studied mining techniques and metallurgy up to 1555. The mathematician and geographer Sebastian Münster offered his *Cosmographie* (1544) in German. Gerard Kremer (Mercator), from Ruppelmonde in Flanders, famous for his great map of the world published in 1539, entered the service of Jülich-Cleves and made Duisburg an active center of geographic studies. Luther referred at least once to the new overseas discoveries when in 1522 he commented that "recently many islands and lands have been discovered, to which this grace [of God] has not appeared for fifteen hundred years." Luther attacked the superstition of the astrologers, but he was quite ready to accept the conclusion of astronomers that the moon was the smallest and lowest of the stars. He suggested that when the Scriptures called the sun and moon "great lights," they were merely accommodating themselves to man's everyday way of looking at things. If the same principle of accommodation had been developed further by Calvin, the conflict about Copernicus' heliocentric theory would have been unnecessary. But a conflict did develop during the second half of the sixteenth century and became a *cause célèbre* in the case of Galileo.

The year 1543 saw the publication of two of the most important books of modern times, *The Structure of the Human Body* by the Flemish anatomist Vesalius and *On the Revolutions of the Heavenly Bodies* by the Polish astronomer Nicolaus Copernicus. On the basis of his own dissections of cadavers Vesalius demonstrated the errors of Galen, who had been accepted since the second century A.D. as the greatest authority on anatomy. This brave beginning was followed up in the seventeenth century by important advances in physiology based upon further observation and laboratory experiment. In 1628 William Harvey's *On the Movement of the Heart and Blood,* based upon laboratory work that included the vivisection of animals, established the continuous circulation of blood through the arteries and veins. An Italian scientist, Marcello Malpighi, who had the advantage of using the newly discovered microscope, confirmed Harvey's theory in 1661 by finding the networks of capillaries that connected arteries and veins. The Dutchman Anton van Leeuwenhoek used the microscope to discover bacteria, blood corpuscles, and spermatozoa. Science was truly an international enterprise. While some scientists were exploring the infinitely small through the microscope, others pondered the great universe above, eventually with the telescope.

Copernicus' heliocentric theory was the most sensational hypothesis to be advanced, for it clearly upset the time-honored order of the cosmos. Ever since Copernicus, Nietzsche once observed, man has been falling away from the center of the universe. The implications of the Copernican theory were contrary to the cherished assumptions of reformers and humanists alike. Beyond that, the Copernican theory defied the authority of the second-century Alexandrian astronomer Ptolemy, who had described the cosmos as geocentric. At the center of the universe, Ptolemy held, was the earth, which was surrounded by a series of transparent crystalline spheres, each carrying a luminous heavenly body that revolved around the earth. Nearest to the earth was the moon; then came Mercury, Venus, the sun, outer planets, and finally the outer sphere containing the fixed stars, which circled the earth majestically like a jeweled curtain. Aristotle's cosmos was even simpler than Ptolemy's, for he made no real effort to explain mathematically the difference in the planets' brightness and size at their nearest and farthest points from the earth as they revolved about it, as he assumed they did. Aristotle's prestige and authority were so enormous, especially in the universities, that any theory that challenged his cosmology inevitably produced fierce opposition.

Copernicus, born in Poland of Polish and German background, came from

FLÖTNER. *Light Reflections.* Optics becomes a science.

a family of merchants, but he had an uncle who was a high churchman and a learned man. Copernicus studied in Italian universities, where he encountered Novara, a Platonist, and others who questioned the Greeks' measurements of the earth's latitude and the mathematical precision of Ptolemy's observations. When he returned to the north, Copernicus made further observations of the skies and realized that if the planets were assumed to revolve around the sun rather than around the earth, the mathematical calculations necessary to accommodate their observed movements would be greatly simplified. His interest was theoretical, and he even credits certain ancient Pythagoreans with inspiring him to develop his hypothesis that the sun was the center around which revolved the fixed stars and the planets, of which the earth was one. This heliocentric theory enabled him to eliminate some of the cycles and epicycles that had been introduced to make the Ptolemaic system seem workable.

Among the "most eminent and learned men" who were interested in his work, Copernicus wrote in his dedicatory preface to Pope Paul III, were certain Lutherans. Copernicus may have had the manuscript of his major work completed as early as 1530. The *Commentariolus,* a brief account of his ideas, which Copernicus had written during the first decade of the century, had been circulated in manuscript among his friends. In the spring of 1539 one of Melanchthon's protégés, Georg Rheticus, a mathematics professor at Wittenberg, journeyed to Frauenburg in Ermland, where Copernicus was a canon in the cathedral chapter, to consult the great astronomer himself. He became convinced that Copernicus was right, and published a report on the theory of the astronomer who, as Melanchthon said, "has caused the sun to stand still and the earth to move." Rheticus was commissioned to publish the great work. The Lutheran theologian Osiander wrote a favorable, if tentative, preface, and the theologian Caspar Cruciger and the mathematician Erasmus Reinhold, colleagues of Luther's, openly advocated his theory. Reinhold even published astronomical tables based upon it.

Luther himself made one disparaging remark in one of his rambling *Table Talks*. Someone had mentioned some new "astrologer," he reported, who was trying to prove that the earth moves and not the sun and moon; that to believe otherwise was to be like a man in a moving boat who thought that he himself was standing still while the earth and trees were moving. That's the way it is nowadays, Luther commented; anyone who wants to be clever can't be satisfied with the opinions of others, but has to produce something of his own, "as this man does, who wants to turn the whole of astrology upside down. But even though astrology has been thrown into confusion, I, for my part, believe the sacred Scripture; for Joshua commanded the sun to stand still, not the earth." Luther made no further mention of the matter and certainly no attempt at repression. Melanchthon, of course, defended Aristotle's position and used scriptural arguments against Copernicus. Calvin actually seemed to be unaware of the Copernican theory, for the one negative comment often ascribed to him turns out to be spurious.

During the first fifty years after 1543 opposition to the theory was quite defensible. But after Kepler and Galileo, no informed man could continue to support the "common-sense" observation of the rising sun, and it took a dedicated obscurantist to carry on opposition to the new theory. Yet acceptance of the theory required such a radical readjustment of ideas that the gradualness of its reception is understandable. Tycho Brahe (1546–1601), the leading expert on the positions and movements of the heavenly bodies in the decades after Copernicus, did not accept the Copernican system in its entirety. Johannes Kepler (1571–1630), his assistant and successor, did accept it, and refined it by demonstrating that the orbits of the planets were ellipses. He was ecstatic about the mysterious harmonies of mathematical forms, and the correspondence he found between mathematics and observed astronomical phenomena was not only personally exciting to him, but very useful in his careful preparation of horoscopes for the emperor.

Galileo Galilei (1564–1642) constructed a telescope in 1609 and observed that the moon, far from being a perfect orb, had pocks, valleys, and mountains, that the sun had spots, that the planets had breadth, and that Jupiter had satellites. He believed the fixed stars to be an incalculable distance from the earth. In developing the concept of inertia, according to which matter remains at rest or in uniform motion unless acted upon by some external force, he continued the line of inquiry developed by the fourteenth-century Franciscans. Galileo's difficulties with the Inquisition and his subsequent retraction and house arrest were due as much to academic conservatism and personal hostilities as to the opposition of Catholic theologians to his views.

The indispensable language for science, especially for astronomy and physics, which long overshadowed the other disciplines, was mathematics. The sixteenth and early seventeenth centuries witnessed important advances in this field. Niccolò Tartaglia (1500–1537) first solved the cubic equation and developed the use of coefficients, thus going far beyond the achievements of the Hindus and Moslems. Another Italian mathematician, Girolamo Cardano (1501–1576), developed a theory of numbers and an algebraic synthesis. Simon Stevin (1548–1620) of Bruges helped develop the decimal system. The Scotsman John Napier (1550–1617) unveiled logarithms in 1614. The noted French philosopher René Descartes (1546–1650) helped to prepare the way for coordinate geometry. These steps forward were followed by Pascal with his theory of probabilities and by the simultaneous development of calculus by Newton in England and Leibniz in Germany. The precision and the complexity of quantitative measurements made possible by these advances were indispensable to modern scientific developments.

Other major discoveries in physics and chemistry were made during this period. William Gilbert (1540–1603), Queen Elizabeth's physician, in his book *On the Magnet, on Magnetic Bodies, and on the Earth as a Great Magnet,* developed theories on magnetism and electricity based on his own laboratory experiments. He attributed the rotation of the earth to its magnetic character. The erratic Swiss doctor Paracelsus (1493–1541) was proud of his originality. "For even as Avicenna was the best physician of the Arabs," he boasted, "Galen of the men of Pergamon, and Marsilius of the Italians, so also most fortunate Germany has chosen me as her indispensable physician!" He experimented with victims of mining disasters and tried cures with new drugs, the "science" of iatrochemistry. His greatest contribution may have been his bombastic attacks upon old authorities, as when he dared to burn the books of Galen in the courtyard of Basel University. The Flemish doctor Jean Baptiste van Helmont (1577–1644), although a superstitious pedant, was a better medical chemist than Paracelsus. He invented the term "gas," discovered carbon dioxide, and made basic observations on the qualities and behavior of gases. The Swiss biologist Conrad Gesner (1515–1565) contributed to the systematic observation and cataloging of plants and animals. The German botanist Leonard Fuchs (1501–1566) wrote a glossary of botanical terms and produced a fascinating collection of woodcuts of plants. As the seventeenth century wore on and the body of knowledge structured about the new scientific theories grew in substance, geniuses such as Evangelista Torricelli, Christian Huygens, Otto von Guericke, and the incomparable Sir Isaac Newton (1642–1727) entered the scene. Confidence in man's ability to conquer nature mounted. One can well appreciate Alexander Pope's ecstatic outburst in the eighteenth century, as he reflected on the beauties of the Newtonian system:

> Nature and nature's laws lay hid in night;
> God said, "Let Newton be," and all was light.

Was the Reformation important for the rise of modern science? It is quite clear that a conflict of theology and science leading to the repression of science is scarcely in evidence, and that the opposition to science was hardly effective. Possibly academic conservatism was as great a hindrance as religious fanaticism. The introduction of religious pluralism and theological novelty eventually made for greater toleration of new and nonconforming scientific views as well. Much of the driving force behind these early scientists' explorations of nature was the zeal of religious men to discover and admire God's handiwork. They were "thinking God's thoughts after him," as Kepler put it. Even considerably later the Prussian Academy of Sciences announced as its purpose "the propagation of the gospel through the sciences." The English pneumatician Robert Boyle (1627–1691), who experimented with the weight of air and devised the law that the pressure exerted by a given quantity of gas is directly proportional to its density, stated in his will that he wished the fellows of the Royal Society a most happy success in their laudable attempts to discover the true nature of the works of God, and [prayed] that they and all other searchers into physical truths may cordially refer their attainments to the glory of the Author of Nature and the benefit of mankind.[11]

It is quite obvious that before 1640 many of the greatest scientists were Catholic, others Lutheran and Anglican, and only some Calvinist. No particular confession had anything essential to contribute to the origins of science. There was no distinctively "Protestant ethic" yet at work. That the Puritan ascetic ethic may have reinforced the empirical approach to science later in the seventeenth century can still be asserted, but there were certainly other factors operative by then. For the interest in invention and practical discoveries was in large part a response to economic need, the exigencies of a lively maritime enterprise in the Netherlands and England, of mining in the empire, of war and disease everywhere. As southern Europe regressed economically and politically in comparison with northern and western Europe and Great Britain, its contributions to science fell behind as well.

The Reformation had one effect upon the rise of science which has been little noticed: By stimulating controversy in religious matters, it made the study of nature seem safe and uncontroversial in comparison, a neutral ground where men could forget their theological differences. Science provided an escape from dogmatism on the one hand and skepticism on the other, for it provided knowledge that was intellectually and emotionally satisfying, and apparently certain, safe, and incontrovertible. Men of the seventeenth century can hardly be blamed for their failure to foresee the controversies that Darwin's evolutionary theory would precipitate two centuries later; and what eighteenth- or nineteenth-century scientist, transfixed by the glory of Newtonian physics, could have anticipated Einstein? Descartes tells in his *Discourse on Method* that he preferred mathematics to the humanities because the humanities never came to any conclusions. Pascal had a similar experience, and as a result built up a great enthusiasm for Archimedes. Thomas Sprat wrote in his fascinating *History of the Royal Society of London* of the satisfaction to be found in scientific studies, in which "philosophical heads unite with mechanical hands." Natural philosophy, he wrote, was the best subject for study if one wished to breathe free air. Politics and theology were excluded from debate for nature alone could entertain pleasantly, without controversy. "If only more Englishmen would turn to science," wrote Sprat, "they would be less violent and dogmatical and more certain." So perhaps the Puritans did, after all, make a distinctive, though negative, contribution to the progress of science. Science seems to have been the child of the new religious thinking rather than its sire. That sci-

---

[11] He even published a volume entitled *The Excellency of Theology, Compared with Natural Philosophy* (London, 1674).

ence has shown itself to be less incontrovertible than was once supposed and in the long run has proved to be only a very inadequate substitute for religious faith constitutes one of the problems of contemporary humanity.

Bibliography

Religion and culture:

BOYER, MERLE. *Luther in Protestantism Today.* New York, 1958.

✓BREEN, QUIRINUS. *Christianity and Humanism.* Grand Rapids, 1967.

BROWN, ROBERT MCAFEE. *The Spirit of Protestantism.* New York, 1961.

———. *The Ecumenical Revolution: An Interpretation of the Catholic-Protestant Dialogue.* Garden City, N.Y., 1967.

BRUNNER, PETER, and HOLM, BERNARD. *Luther in the Twentieth Century.* Decorah, Ia., 1961.

✓CUSHMAN, ROBERT E., and GRISLIS, EGIL, eds. *The Heritage of Christian Thought.* New York, 1965.

FORELL, GEORGE W., et al. *Luther and Culture.* Decorah, Ia., 1960.

✓ FRAME, DONALD M. *Montaigne's Discovery of Man.* New York, 1955.

FRIEDLAENDER, WALTER F. *Mannerism and Anti-Mannerism in Italian Painting.* New York, 1957.

GARRISON, WINFRED E. *A Protestant Manifesto.* New York, 1952.

✓GELDER, ENNO VAN. *The Two Reformations in the Sixteenth Century.* The Hague, 1961.

✓HARBISON, E. HARRIS. *The Christian Scholar in the Age of the Reformation.* New York, 1956.

———. *Christianity and History.* Princeton, 1964.

HOLL, KARL. *The Cultural Significance of the Reformation.* New York, 1959.

HOOGSTRA, JACOB T. *John Calvin, Contemporary Prophet.* Grand Rapids, 1959.

LECLER, J. *Toleration and the Reformation,* 2 vols. New York, 1960.

✓ PAUCK, WILHELM. *The Heritage of the Reformation.* Boston and Glencoe, Ill., 1950.

PELIKAN, JAROSLAV. *From Luther to Kierkegaard.* St. Louis, 1950.

———. *Obedient Rebels: Catholic Substance and Protestant Principle in Luther's Reformation.* New York, 1964.

———, ed. *Interpreters of Luther.* Philadelphia, 1968.

PREUSS, ROBERT D. *The Theology of Post-Reformation Lutheranism.* St. Louis, 1970.

RABB, THEODORE, and SEIGEL, JERROLD E., eds. *Action and Conviction in Early Modern Europe.* Princeton, 1969.

RUPP, E. GORDON. *The Old Reformation and the New.* Philadelphia, 1967.

✓SCHOWOEBEL, ROBERT, ed. *Renaissance Men and Ideas.* New York, 1970.

TROELTSCH, ERNST. *Protestantism and Progress.* New York, 1912.

Church and state:

BAINTON, ROLAND H. *Christian Attitudes Toward War and Peace.* New York, 1960.

BATES, MINER SEARLE. *Religious Liberty: An Inquiry.* New York, 1945.

MUELLER, WILLIAM A. *Church and State in Luther and Calvin*, 2nd ed. Garden City, N.Y., 1965.

SPITZ, LEWIS W. "The Impact of the Reformation on Church-State Issues," in *Church and State Under God*, ed. Albert Huegli. St. Louis, 1964.

TROELTSCH, ERNST. *The Social Teaching of the Christian Churches*, 3 vols. New York, 1931.

Protestantism and capitalism:

BARGE, HERMANN. *Luther und der Frühkapitalismus*. Gütersloh, 1951.

BENDIX, REINHARD. *Max Weber*. New York, 1959.

GREEN, ROBERT W., ed. *Protestantism and Capitalism: The Weber Thesis and Its Critics*. Boston, 1959.

HILL, JOHN E. CHRISTOPHER. *Reformation to Industrial Revolution: The Making of Modern English Society, 1530–1780*. New York, 1968.

KITCH, M. J. *Capitalism and the Reformation*. London, 1967.

NELSON, JOHN O., ed. *Work and Vocation*. New York, 1954.

SAMUELSON, KURT. *Religion and the Rise of Capitalism*. London, 1926.

WEBER, MAX. *The Protestant Ethic and the Spirit of Capitalism*. London, 1930.

Elizabethan Renaissance:

BRADNER, LEISTER, ed. *The Poems of Queen Elizabeth I*. Providence, 1964.

CHAMBERS, SIR E. *A Short Life of William Shakespeare*. Oxford, 1935.

CRAIG, HARDIN. *The Enchanted Glass: The Elizabethan Mind in Literature*. New York, 1936.

———. *An Interpretation of Shakespeare*. New York, 1948.

———. *A New Look at Shakespeare's Quartos*. Stanford, 1961.

———. *A History of English Literature*, rev. ed. New York, 1962.

GOTCH, JOHN A. *Early Renaissance Architecture in England*. London, 1901.

HOOPES, ROBERT. *Right Reason in the English Renaissance*. Cambridge, Mass., 1962.

LEVY, FRED J. *Tudor Historical Thought*. San Marino, Cal., 1967.

NUGENT, ELIZABETH M., ed. *Thought and Culture of the English Renaissance*. Cambridge, 1954.

RYAN, LAWRENCE. *Roger Ascham*. Stanford, 1963.

SPENCER, THEODORE. *Shakespeare and the Nature of Man*. New York, 1942.

SPINGARN, JOEL. *Literary Criticism in the Renaissance*. New York, 1963.

TALBERT, ERNEST W. *The Problem of Order: Elizabethan Political Commonplaces and an Example of Shakespeare's Art*. Chapel Hill, N.C., 1962.

TILLYARD, E. M. W. *The Elizabethan World Picture*. London, 1943.

——— *The English Renaissance: Fact or Fiction?* London, 1952.

WATSON, C. B. *Shakespeare and the Renaissance Concept of Honor*. Princeton, 1961.

Protestantism and science:

BOAS, MARIE. *The Scientific Renaissance, 1450–1630*. New York, 1962.

CALLOT, E. *La renaissance des sciences de la vie au XVIᵉ siècle*. Paris, 1949.

CROMBIE, ALISTAIR C. *Medieval and Early Modern Science*, 2nd ed. Garden City, N.Y., 1959.

DILLENBERGER, JOHN. *Protestant Thought and Natural Science*. New York, 1960.

HILL, CHRISTOPHER; KEARNEY, H. F.; and RABB, T. K. "Science, Religion, and Society in the Sixteenth and Seventeenth Centuries." *Past and Present,* July 1965, pp. 97–126.

HOOYKAAS, R. *Humanisme, science, et réforme.* Leyden, 1958.

KEARNEY, HUGH F. *Origins of the Scientific Revolution.* London, 1964.

KOCHER, PAUL. *Science and Religion in Elizabethan England.* San Marino, Calif., 1953.

KUHN, THOMAS S. *The Copernican Revolution.* Cambridge, 1957.

———. *The Structure of Scientific Revolutions.* Chicago, 1962.

MERTON, ROBERT K. *Social Theory and Social Structure,* rev. ed. New York, 1967.

O'MALLEY, DONALD. *Andreas Vesalius.* Berkeley, 1964.

PAGEL, KARL. *Paracelsus.* New York, 1958.

PAULI, WILHELM. *The Interpretation of Nature and Psyche.* New York, 1955.

PRICE, DEREK J. DE SOLA. *Science Since Babylon.* New Haven, 1961.

SANTILLANA, GIORGIO DE. *The Crime of Galileo.* Chicago, 1959.

WIGHTMAN, WILLIAM. *Science and the Renaissance,* 2 vols. New York, 1963.

WOLF, ABRAHAM. *A History of Science, Technology, and Philosophy in the Sixteenth and Seventeenth Centuries,* 2nd ed. London, 1950.

Index

Abano, Pietro d', 186
Abelard, Peter, 146
Acciaiuoli, Agnolo, 108
Acciaiuoli, Donato, 180
Acontius, Giacomo, 436, 437
Acton, Lord, 92, 329, 332
Adelmann, Bernhard, 304
Adelmannsfelden, Adelmann von, 134
Adolf of Nassau, Holy Roman emperor, 65
Adrian VI, pope, 59, 295, 317–18, 358, 367, 470
Adriani, Marcello Virgilio, 242
Aegidius of Viterbo. *See* Egidio da Viterbo
Affair of the Placards, 415
Africans, enslavement of, 259, 519, 536
Agincourt, Battle of, 73–74
Agricola, Georg, 135, 583
Agricola, Michael, 373
Agricola, Rudolf, 277–78, 315
Agriculture:
    in Elizabethan England, 541–42
    in Middle Ages, 7–9
Ailly, Pierre d', 29, 32, 35, 255
Alba, duke of, 499, 508, 509, 512–13
Albert, archduke of Austria, 514
Albert, duke of Prussia, 371, 372
Albert of Brandenburg, archbishop of Magdeburg
    and Mainz, 315, 335, 360, 375
Albert of Saxony, 185–86
Alberti, Leon Battista, 149, 197–99, 229
    as architect, 158, 198–99, 210
    as art theoretician, 199
    as social thinker, 119, 163, 199
Albizzi, Maso degli, 105–6
Albizzi, Piero degli, 105
Albizzi, Rinaldo degli, 106
Albornoz, Gil de, 95

Albrecht, Holy Roman emperors:
    Albrecht I, 65
    Albrecht II, 68
Albret, Charlotte d', 241
Albret, Henry d'. *See* Henry, kings of Navarre:
    Henry II
Albuquerque, Affonso de, 517
Alciati, Andrea, 414
Alcuin, 3
Aldine Press, 176, 189. *See also* Manutius, Aldus
Aleander (Italian humanist), 275
Aleander, Girolamo, 329–30, 338, 350, 471, 484
Alençon, Duke Charles of, 286
Alençon, Duke Francis of, 501, 535
Alexander, popes:
    Alexander V, 31
    Alexander VI, 50–52, 54, 57, 235–36, 240
        division of Spanish and Portuguese possessions
            by, 54, 270
        and Pico della Mirandola, 54, 178
        and Savonarola, 239
Alexander II, tsar of Russia, 15
Alexander of Aphrodisias, 180–81
Alfonso I, king of Sicily and Naples (Alfonso V of
    Aragon), 96, 100, 163, 166, 235–36
Alfonso V, king of Portugal, 258
Allen, William, 482, 527
Almeida, Francisco, 263, 517
Althusius, Johannes, 554
Álvarez Cabral, Pedro, 263
Amadeo, counts of Savoy:
    Amadeo VI, 99
    Amadeo VII, 99
    Amadeo VIII, duke of Savoy, 99. *See also* Felix V,
        pope
Amaseo, Romolo, 561

Ambassadors, 112–13
Amboise, Conspiracy of, 498, 505
Amboise, Georges d', 240
Amboise, Peace of, 499
Ambrosian Republic, 97–98
Ambrosius, St., 49
Ameaux, Pierre, 427
Amerbach, Johannes, 306, 393
America:
    Catholic missions in, 259–60, 482
    discovery and exploration of, 263–71
    English colonies in, 539–40
    English voyages to, 535–39
    Spanish colonies in, 517–19
Ammanati, Bartolommeo, 577
Ammirato, Scipione, 561
Amsdorf, Nicholas von, 371
Anabaptists, 396–405, 408, 434, 461, 551
    and Calvin, 399, 422–23
    excesses of, 399–403
    and fine arts, 573
    and Schleitheim Confession, 398–99
    and Zwingli, 397–99
Anastasius I, Byzantine emperor, 21
Anchieta, José de, 482
Andersson, Lars, 373
Andreae, Jakob, 562–63
Andreae, Johann Valentin, 563
Andrew, prince of Hungary, 95
Angelico, Fra, 200
Angelus, Jacobus, 254
Anghiera, Pietro Martire d', 271–72
Anglican settlement, 524–30
Annates, 24, 313
Anne of Bohemia (daughter of Emperor Charles IV), 82
Anne of Bohemia (daughter of King Wenceslas), 34
Anne of Brittany, 76, 240
Anne of Cleves, 458–59
Anne of Hungary and Bohemia (sister of King Louis II), 360
Anthony of Gorea, 565
Anticlericalism, 551
    in England, 446–47
    in Holy Roman Empire, 323
    in Scotland, 465
Anti-Trinitarians, 374, 396, 405, 437–38
Antoine de Bourbon, king of Navarre, 429, 498
Aquinas, St. Thomas:
    and Aristotle, 44, 180, 292, 348
    and mysticism, 39
    and predestination, 420
    and Reformation, 308, 309
    and usury, 123
Aquino, Maria d', 147
Archeology, 165
Architecture:
    baroque, 577–78

French Renaissance, 283–84
    Gothic, 148–49
    Italian Renaissance, 198–99, 209–12, 223
    post-Renaissance, in Catholic Europe, 574–78
    post-Renaissance, in Protestant Europe, 573–74
Argyropoulos, John, 150, 155, 180, 187
Aristotle, 123, 156
    and Aquinas, 44, 180, 292, 348
    cosmology of, 254, 584
    physics of, 185
    political theory of, 91–92
    See also Neo-Aristotelianism
Armagnacs, 73, 74
Arminius, Jacobus, 557
Arnold, Matthew, 566
Arnold of Brescia, 95
Arras, Treaty of, 76
Arthur (son of Henry VII of England), 84, 86, 442
Arts:
    and Counterreformation, 574–79
    effects of Black Death on, 11–12
    German, 325, 573–74, 579–80
    Renaissance revival of, 4–5
    See also Architecture; Music; Painting; Sculpture
Ascham, Roger, 459, 567
Asia:
    Catholic missions in, 482–83
    exploration of, 250–53, 262–63, 271
    trade with, 133, 251–52, 258, 262–63, 514
Aske, Robert, 457
Assafar, Aben, 256
Astrology, 49, 177
Astronomy, 582–87
Atumano, Simon, 153
Augsburg, Peace of, 369, 378, 431, 490, 562
Augsburg Confession, 354, 373, 488, 540
Augsburg Interim, 377, 490
Augustine, St., 22, 146, 173, 254
    and mysticism, 38–39
    theology of, 418, 420
Augustinian order, 42, 316–17
Aurispa, Giovanni, 155
Aussa, Melchior von, 323
Austria, 367–68, 375
Aventinus, 279–80, 564
Averroës, 40, 180, 181
Avicenna, 40
Avignon papacy, 16, 20, 23–24
Azarquiel, 256

"Babylonian Captivity," 16, 20, 23–24
Bach, Johann Sebastian, 580
Bacon, Francis, 44, 62, 84, 189, 245, 536
    philosophical works of, 570–71
    on study of antiquity, 304–5, 548
Bacon, Roger, 255
Baddi, Taddeo, 193
Bainton, Roland, 406
Balance of power, 111

Balboa, Vasco Núñez de, 271
Balduin, Urban, 348
Bale, John, 305, 451–53
Ball, John, 14
Baltic states, Lutheranism in, 373
Bancroft, Richard, 530
Banking, 103, 124–28
Barbaro, Ermolao, 285
Barbo, Pietro, 50
Barcelona, Peace of, 365
Bardi, Count Giovanni dei, 579
Bardi bank, 103, 124–25
Barker, Andrew, 537
Barlowe, Jerome, 449
Barnabite order, 474
Barnes, Robert, 449, 451, 453
Baroque style, 228, 577–78
Barzizza, Gasparino da, 149
Bascio, Matteo de, 474
Basel, Council of, 32, 33, 37, 174, 393
Basil, St., 173
Bayazid II, sultan of Ottoman Turks, 53, 112, 253
Beaton, David, 465
Beaufort, Margaret, 448
Bebel, Heinrich, 277
Beccario, Battista, 266
Becker, Carl, 580
Becon, Thomas, 449
Bede, Venerable, 254
Beghards, 49, 397
Beguines, 49, 397
Behaim, Lorenz, 113
Behaim, Martin, 250, 266
Bellarmine, St. Robert, 168, 482, 492, 553
Bellay, Jean du, 285, 287, 471
Bellay, Joachim du, 564–65
Bellini, Gentile, 225
Bellini, Giovanni, 213, 225–27
Bellini, Jacopo, 225
Belloc, Hilaire, 505
Belon, Pierre, 5
Bembo, Pietro, 58, 145, 436, 471, 561
Benedict XIII, antipope, 26, 30–32
Benedictine order, 316, 474
Benivieni, Girolamo, 183
Bentivoglio, Giovanni, 236
Berlichingen, Goetz von, 321, 343
Bernard, St., 25
Bernard of Clairvaux, 39, 40
Bernini, Giovanni, 577, 578
Bessarion, John, 33, 155, 172, 180, 189
Bethancourt, Jean de, 259
Beza, Theodore, 2, 408, 421, 498, 505, 580
  on Calvin, 416, 428
  and education, 429, 558–59
  on Genevans, 422, 425
Biel, Gabriel, 46, 308, 315, 331
Bilney, Thomas, 449, 451
Biondo, Flavio, 5, 165

Biondo, Giovanni del, 12
Biró, Matthias, 375, 433
Bisticci, Vespasiano da, 149, 158, 283
Black Death. *See* Plague
Blaurock, Georg, 397, 398
Blois, Treaty of, 535
Blount, Charles, Baron Mountjoy, 535, 544
Blount, William, Baron Mountjoy, 296, 448
Bobadilla, Francisco de, 270
Boccaccio, Giovanni, 4, 12, 145–48, 153, 193, 290
Bockelson, Jan. *See* John of Leiden
Bodin, Jean, 504
Boeckh, August, 1
Bohemia, 66, 67, 374
  humanism in, 282–83
  Hussite revolt in, 33–37
Bohemian Brethren, 37, 374
Böhme, Jakob, 40
Boleyn, Anne, 294, 441, 445, 455, 458–59
Bologne, Concordat of, 322
Bolsec, Jerome Hermes, 427–28
Bonaventure, St., 39
Boniface, popes:
  Boniface VIII, 16, 23, 58, 66, 317
  Boniface IX, 30
Bonner, Edmund, 463
Bono, Pietro, 229
Bora, Katherine von. *See* Luther, Katherine
Borgia, Alfonso. *See* Calixtus III, pope
Borgia, Cesare, 54, 113, 187, 216, 236, 240–41, 243
Borgia, Giovanni, 54
Borgia, Lucretia, 54
Borgia, Rodrigo. *See* Alexander, popes: Alexander VI
Borromeo, St. Charles, 491–92
Boscoli, Piero Paolo, 243
Bossuet, Jacques, 484
Bosworth, Battle of, 83, 442
Bothwell, earl of (James Hepburn), 531–32
Botticelli, Sandro, 53, 109, 202–4
Botzheim, Johann von, 304
Bourbon, Antoine de, king of Navarre, 429, 498
Bourbon, Constable Charles of, 224, 362, 364
Boyle, Robert, 588–89
Brahe, Tycho, 587
Bramante, 54, 55, 58, 212, 217–20, 577
Brant, Sebastian, 133–34, 277, 315
Bray, Guido de, 511
Brentano, Luigi, 119
Brenz, Johannes, 372, 391, 392
Brès, Guy de, 431
Brethren of the Common Life, 41–43, 276, 295, 317, 472
Brethren of the Free Spirit, 49, 397
Brethren of St. Ursula, 312
Bretigny, Treaty of, 72
Briconnet, Guillaume, 286, 287, 478
Bronzino, 577
Brooks, bishop, 463

Brotherhood of the Holy Crusade, 58
Brotherhood of the Holy Ghost, 500
Browne, Robert, 529
Browning, Elizabeth Barrett, 102
Browning, Robert, 102
Bruce, Robert, 80
Brunelleschi, Filippo, 197, 206, 207, 210–12
Bruno, Giordano, 175, 181–83
Bruno, Leonardo, 5, 161–64, 172, 179, 210
    on humanist studies, 140, 154, 158–59
Brussels, Treaty of, 360
Bryce, Lord, 65, 66
Bucer, Martin, 370–71, 376, 424, 461, 473, 549, 560
    and Calvinism, 424, 528
    and sacramentarian controversy, 389, 391–92
Buckle, H. T., 557
Budé, Guillaume, 5, 284–85, 504
Bugenhagen, Johannes, 372, 373, 450
Bullinger, Heinrich, 383, 395, 412
Bundschuh, 321, 344
Bunzli, Gregor, 382
Buonacorsi, Philip (Callimachus), 283
Buonamici, Lazzaro, 561
Buonarroti, Michelangelo. *See* Michelangelo
Burckhardt, Jacob, 1, 5–6, 102, 110, 113, 197, 303
Bure, Idelette de, 424
Burgundy, 12, 16–17, 66, 73–78
Buridan, Jean, 185
Burns, Robert, 421
Burrough, Stephen, 538–39
Bussi, Giovanni Andrea di, 158
Butterfield, Herbert, 555

Cabot, John, 535
Cabot, Sebastian, 538
Caccini, Giulio, 579
Cajetan, Dominican master general and cardinal, 282, 316, 337, 471
Cajetan, St. *See* Gaetano da Thiene
Calderón de la Barca, Pedro, 566
Calixtines. *See* Utraquists
Calixtus III, pope, 51–52, 335
Callimachus. *See* Buonacorsi, Philip
Caltabellotta, Treaty of, 91
Calvin, John, 286, 371, 399, 411–31, 473, 549
    and art, 573
    and Castellio, 407–8
    and church polity, 551, 553
    and education, 558–59
    and exiled reformers, 436, 438
    as French stylist, 564
    in Geneva, 411, 421–28
    and Huguenots, 497, 499
    and Luther, 411–12
    and music, 424, 580
    and Servetus, 406–7, 427
    theology of, 416–21, 552–53
    youth and early career of, 411–16

Calvinism:
    appeal of, to workingman, 557
    and capitalism, 119, 555–57
    compared with Jesuitism, 481, 556
    in eastern Europe, 432–33
    in England, 460, 461, 528–30, 573, 581–82, 589
    in France, 428–30, 497–503
    in Germany, 431–32, 562
    in Netherlands, 431, 511–12
    and political theory, 503–6, 548–55
    and science, 581–83
    in Scotland, 465–66
    in Spain, 433–34
    and theories of resistance, 503–6
Cambrai, League of, 241
Cambrai, Treaty of, 365
Camden, William, 568
Campanella, Tommaso, 183–84
Campeggio, Lorenzo, 445, 471
Camus, Albert, 230
Canary Islands, colonization of, 259
Candolle, Alphonse de, 581
Canisius, St. Peter, 482, 491, 563
Cão, Diago, 262
Capella, Galeatius, 564
Capella, Martianus, 254
Capitalism, 118–36, 555–57
    and Counterreformation, 557
    finance vs. enterprise, 122
    in France, 130–31
    in Germany, 131–34
    and industrial growth, 120–21, 134–36
    in Italy, 122–28
    Marxist theory of, 119–20
    merchant enterprise view of, 120–22
    in northern Europe, 128–30
    and Protestantism, 119, 555–57
    qualitative theory of, 119
Capito, Wolfgang, 370, 371, 391–93, 454
Cappel, First Peace of, 394
Cappel, Second Peace of, 394
Capuano, Raimondo, 20
Capuchin order, 474
Caraffa, Giampietro, 434–36, 471, 474, 475, 477–78. *See also* Paul, popes: Paul IV
Cardano, Girolamo, 587
Cardinals, Renaissance, 50–51, 94
Carion (chronicler), 564
Carlos, Don (son of Philip II of Spain), 507
Carlotta of Naples, 240–41
Carlstadt, Andreas, 341, 390–91, 397, 401
Carlyle, Thomas, 547
Carmelite order, 475–76
Carnesecchi, Pietro, 435, 436, 438
Caroli, Pierre, 423
Carpaccio, Vittore, 227
Carrara, Francesco di, 144
Carrara, Ubertino, 156
Carthusian order, 150–51, 316, 456

Cartwright, Thomas, 529
Casel, Gregory, 391
Casenove-Coullon, Guillaume de, 266
Cassell, Battle of, 14
Cassirer, Ernst, 174, 187–88
Castellio, Sebastian, 407–8
Castiglione, Balthasar, 57
Cateau-Cambrésis, Treaty of, 366, 430, 490, 496, 507, 533
Catherine of Aragon, 84, 86, 294, 364, 442–45, 453, 458–59
Catherine of Siena, St., 20, 41
Catholic Church. *See* Roman Catholic Church
Catholic League, 501, 502
Cauvin, Gerard, 413
Cavalieri, Tommaso dei, 223
Cavendish, Thomas, 538
Caxton, William, 291
Cecil, William, Lord Burghley, 524–25, 527, 532, 533, 536, 541
Cellarius, 2
Cellini, Benvenuto, 223–24, 229, 284
Celtis, Conrad, 272, 278–79, 282, 321, 382, 580
Cennini, Cennino, 195–96
Cervantes, Miguel de, 288, 566
Cervini, Cardinal, 489
Chalcondylas, Demetrius, 155
Champlain, Samuel de, 503
Chancellor, Richard, 538
Chapels, private, 48, 123
Chapman, George, 569
Charlemagne, 3
Charles, Holy Roman emperors:
  Charles IV, 67, 91, 95
  Charles V (Charles I of Spain), 357–68, 507
    and Calvinism, 430–31
    and Council of Trent, 485, 489, 490
    and Fuggers, 132, 319
    and Habsburg-Valois wars, 77, 361–66, 444, 445
    lands ruled by, 69, 358–61
    and Luther, 328–29, 338, 340, 353
    and Lutheranism, 369, 376
    and Spain, 86, 359–61, 378, 477
    and Turkish invasions, 365–68
Charles, kings of France:
  Charles IV, 66, 73
  Charles V (the Wise), 72–73
  Charles VI (the Mad), 73
  Charles VII, 74–75, 131, 322
  Charles VIII, 76, 86, 87, 96, 110, 233–37, 485
  Charles IX, 498–501
Charles I, king of Spain. *See* Charles, Holy Roman emperors: Charles V
Charles III, king of Naples (Charles of Durazzo), 96
Charles VIII, king of Sweden, 64
Charles the Bold, duke of Burgundy, 76–78, 127, 358

Chateaubriand, Edict of, 430
Chemistry, 587–88
Chieregati (papal legate), 318, 323
Chivalry, 9
Christendom, concept of, 21–22
Christian, kings of Denmark:
  Christian II, 361, 372
  Christian III, 372–73
  Christian IV, 557
Christian Brethren, 452
Christina of Ducal Saxony, 376
Christoph, duke of Württemberg, 378, 407, 437, 499
Chrysoloras, John, 151
Chrysoloras, Manuel, 148, 154
Church councils:
  Basel, 32, 33, 37, 174, 393
  Constance, 29, 31–33, 35, 68, 150, 156, 162, 447
  Ferrara-Florence, 32, 153–54, 252, 260
  Fifth Lateran, 55, 57–58, 317–18, 484, 485
  Fourth Lateran, 23, 313, 493
  Nicea, 31, 312–13
  Pisa (1409), 29, 31
  Pisa (1511), 55
  Trent, 472, 473, 483–91, 527, 578
  Vienne, 153
Church of England, 454, 457–59, 551. *See also* Anglican settlement
Cicero:
  on eloquence, 140
  on fatherland, 295
  on history, 164
  on men as heavenly spectators, 171
  on oligarchy, 100
Cimabue, Giovanni, 192
Cinthio, Giraldi, 145
Ciompi revolt, 93, 105, 160
Cities:
  cultural vs. political success of, 91–92
  gifts of merchant princes to, 123
  growth of, 121
  Hanseatic, 128–30
  of Holy Roman Empire, 319–23
  See also Italy, city-states of; Towns
Clemanges, Nicholas de, 25, 283
Clement, popes:
  Clement IV, 23
  Clement V, 24
  Clement VII, 59, 221, 245–47, 368
    and Council of Trent, 485
    and Counterreformation, 469–71, 473, 477
    and Habsburg-Valois wars, 364–65
    and Henry VIII, 376, 445, 453
  Clement VII (antipope), 25–27, 98
  Clement VIII, 492, 502
Clement of Alexandria, 173
Clouet, François, 284
Clouet, Jean, 284
Cluniac monks, 151

Coeur, Jacques, 118, 130–31
Cognac, League of, 364, 473
Coke, Edward, 570
Colet, Henry, 291
Colet, John, 291–93, 296, 449
Coligny, Gaspard de, 429, 430, 499–500
Colle, Bonifacio da, 475
Collegium Germanicum, 563
Colleoni, Bartolommeo, 209
Colombo, Domenico, 266
Colón, Bartolomé, 267
Colón, Diego (brother of Columbus), 270
Colón, Diego (son of Columbus), 267
Colón, Ferdinand, 267
Colón, Luis de, 267
Colonna, Oddo. *See* Martin V, pope
Colonna, Vittoria, 223, 435
Colt, Jane, 293
Columbus, Christopher, 86, 257, 263–70
Commerce. *See* Trade
Communes, 9, 92–93, 96
Commynes, Philippe de, 76, 127
Conciliarism, 26–30, 175, 484. *See also* Church
    councils
Condé, princes of. *See* Henry I, prince of Condé;
    Louis I, prince of Condé
Confessio tetrapolitana, 371
Conrad of Gelnhausen, 28–29
Consiglieri, Paolo, 475
Constance, Council of, 29, 31–33, 35, 68, 150, 156,
    162, 447
Constantine, Roman emperor, 31
    donation of, 167–68
Constantinople:
    attack on, by Fourth Crusade, 10, 101, 153
    fall of, 2–3, 33, 111–12, 153, 253
Contarini, Gasparo, 323, 424, 436, 471–74, 488
Contarini, Niccolò, 561
Conversini, Giovanni, 149
Cop, Michel, 413
Cop, Nicholas, 413–15
Copernicus, Nicolaus, 175, 182, 584–87
Cordatus, Conrad, 374–75
Cordier, Mathurin, 413
"Corporate persons," 92
Corsini, Marietta, 243
Cortés, Hernán, 271, 517
Cosimo I, duke of Florence. *See* Medici, Duke
    Cosimo I de'
Cosmology, 253–55, 584–87
Counterreformation, 469–94
    and arts, 573–80
    and capitalism, 557
    and Council of Trent, 472, 473, 483–91
    in Holy Roman Empire, 482, 562–63
    and post-Tridentine reform, 491–94
    and repression, 476–78
    and spiritual renewal, 472–76
Coverdale, Miles, 458, 463

Cranach, Lucas, 574
Cranmer, Thomas, 437
    and Cromwell, 454, 457
    and divorce of Henry VIII, 453, 455
    and religious reform, 458, 460, 461
    trial and death of, 463–64
Crécy, Battle of, 72
Crema, Battista da, 474
Crépy, Peace of, 485
Croce, Benedetto, 245
Cromwell, Thomas, 453–55, 457–59
Cruciger, Caspar, 391, 586
Cusanus, Nicholas, 30, 40, 51, 166, 168, 186
    philosophy of, 174–75, 182

Dalberg, Johannes von, 277
Dante Alighieri, 4, 21, 48, 96–97, 101, 102, 168,
    254
    compared with Petrarch, 145
    and Emperor Henry VII, 66, 87
    Florentine cultists of, 183
    on Giotto, 192
Darnley, Lord (Henry Stuart), 531–32
Darnville, Marshal, 501
Darwin, Charles, 589
Datini, Francesco di Marco, 133
Davis, John, 539
Day, John, 452
Defoe, Daniel, 119
Del Monte, Gianmaria, 486. *See also* Julius, popes:
    Julius III
Del Valle Lersundi, Fernando, 266
Denck, Hans, 399, 404–5
Denmark:
    and Hanse, 130
    Lutheranism in, 371–73
    union of, with Sweden and Norway, 64
Descartes, René, 185, 581, 587, 589
Des Prez, Josquin, 578
Dessau, League of, 375
Dévay, Matthias Biró. *See* Biró, Matthias
Devereux, Robert, earl of Essex, 517, 543–44, 569
Devotio moderna. See Brethren of the Common
    Life
Dias, Bartolomeu, 262, 263
Dietrich of Niem, 30
Dimitri, pretender to Russian throne, 481–82
Dionysius the Areopagite, 175, 176, 291
Diplomacy, development of, 17, 110–16
Djem (son of Mohammed II), 53, 54, 236
Dobb, Maurice, 120
Dolet, Étienne, 284
Dominican order, 39, 316, 337, 474
    and Reuchlin controversy, 281, 316
Donatello, 204, 207–8
Doria, Andrea, 100, 364–65, 368
Dort, Synod of, 549
Drake, Francis, 515, 536–38
Drama, Elizabethan, 571–73

Droysen, Gustav, 1
Dudley, John, duke of Northumberland, 460–62
Dudley, Robert, earl of Leicester, 513, 524, 569
Duns Scotus, 44, 175, 185, 292, 297
Duprat, Antoine, 314–15, 363
Durant, William, 112
Dürer, Albrecht, 277, 279
    death in art of, 47, 325
    and Reformation, 326, 574
    Renaissance style of, 5, 213, 214
Dutch East India Company, 514

Eanes, Gil, 261
Eastland Company, 539
Ebreo, Leone, 183
Eck, Johannes, 134, 308, 337, 338, 348
Eckhart, Johannes (Meister), 39–40, 42, 43, 175
Edinburgh, Treaty of, 531
Edrisi, 254
Education:
    of clergy, 314
    in Elizabethan England, 567
    humanist, 155–59, 558
    Jesuit, 481–82, 559, 563
    Reformation, 347–48, 371, 429–30
Edward, kings of England:
    Edward I, 71, 79–81
    Edward II, 73, 80
    Edward III, 28, 71–73, 80–82, 103, 125
    Edward IV, 83
    Edward VI, 436, 448, 459–62
Edward the Black Prince, 72, 73
Effingham, baron of. *See* Howard, Charles
Egidio (Aegidius) da Viterbo, 57, 172, 174, 317,
    470
Egmont, count of, 512
Egnatius, Baptista, 435
Einstein, Albert, 589
Eleanor (daughter of Emperor Charles V), 363–64
Eleanor of Toledo, 560–61
Eliot, T. S., 557
Elizabeth I, queen of England, 448, 455, 464, 499,
    523–44
    and Essex, 543–44
    and Mary Stuart, 514–15, 526, 528, 530–33
    and Netherlands revolt, 513, 514, 533, 535
    and Philip II of Spain, 508, 514–16, 524, 533–38
    religious settlement of, 524–30
    and Shakespeare, 572
Elizabeth of Valois, 499, 508
Elizabeth of York, 83, 442
Elyot, Thomas, 567
Emanuel of Constantinople, 291
Encomienda system, 518
Engelhard (Swiss reformer), 386
Engels, Friedrich, 119–20
England:
    Catholic restoration in, 462–64

England—*cont.*
    Church of, 454, 457–59, 551. *See also* Anglican
        settlement
    development of centralized monarchy in, 63–64,
        78–84
    development of parliament in, 79–82, 525
    development of royal government in, 81–82
    Elizabethan, 523–44
        Catholics in, 526–28
        economy of, 540–42
        education in, 567
        and Ireland, 534, 543–44
        literature in, 567–73
        overseas expansion of, 535–40
        and privateers, 536–38
        Puritans in, 528–30
        relations of, with France and Spain, 533–35
        religious settlement in, 524–26
        and Spanish Armada, 514–17
        and trade with Russia, 538
    fiefs of, in France, 12, 71
    humanism in, 290–94
    and Hundred Years' War, 12–13, 71–75, 82–83,
        124–25
    peasant revolt in, 14, 82
    Reformation in, 441–64
    and Wars of the Roses, 83–84
Enríquez de Arana, Beatriz, 267
Erasmus, Desiderius, 5, 285, 291, 293–98, 323, 413
    on Agricola, 277
    and Henry VIII, 442–43
    on Julius II, 56
    and Reformation, 303, 343, 348–50, 383, 392,
        393, 448–50
    reform program of, 296–98
    on Renaissance cardinals, 50
    on schoolmen, 44, 46
Erastus, 432
Eratosthenes, 254
Ercole II, duke of Ferrara, 438
Eric, king of Denmark, Norway, and Sweden, 64
Eric the Red, 266
Erich of Brunswick, 375
Ericson, Leif, 266
Ericson, Thorwald, 266
Erigena, John Scotus, 38, 175
Escorial, El, 508, 578
Essex, earl of. *See* Devereux, Robert
Este, Alfonso d', 214
Este, Beatrice d', 214
Este, Hercules d', 478
Este, Ippolito d', 315
Estouteville, William d', 51
Eugenius IV, pope, 32, 33, 106, 167
Evangelical rationalists, 396, 404–8
Exploration, 250–72
    and ancient cosmology, 253–55
    by England, 535–40
    of Far East, 250–53, 258, 262–63

Exploration—*cont.*
  by Portugal, 257–63, 270–71
  ships and instruments used in, 255–58
  societal forces toward, 258–61
  by Spain, 263–71

Faber, Felix, 314
Faber, John, 385
Faber, Peter, 482
Fabriano, Gentile da, 195, 225
Fairfax, Edward, 569
False Dimitri I, 481–82
Famine, 10–11
Farel, Guillaume, 286, 411, 416, 422–24, 428
Farnese, Alexander. *See* Paul, popes: Paul III
Farnese, Alexander, cardinal (grandson of Paul III), 471
Farnese, Alexander, duke of Parma, 513, 515–16
Fazio degli Uberti, 179
Federigo, king of Naples, 240–41
Felix V, pope, 33, 51. *See also* Amadeo, dukes of Savoy: Amadeo VIII
Feltria, Giovanna Felicia, 216
Ferdinand I, Holy Roman emperor (earlier duke and regent of Austria), 360–61, 367–69, 375, 376, 378, 394, 563
Ferdinand of Aragon, king of Spain:
  and Holy League, 112, 443–44
  and Inquisition, 477
  and League of Cambrai, 241
  and League of Venice, 236
  and overseas expansion, 257, 259, 268–70
  statecraft of, 85–86, 113
  and unification of Spain, 64
Feria (Spanish ambassador), 524
Ferrante, kings of Naples:
  Ferrante I, 96, 111, 235
  Ferrante II (Ferrantino), 96, 236–37
Ferrara-Florence, Council of, 32–33, 153–54, 252, 260
Feudalism:
  bastard, 84
  decline of, 8–9, 13, 62–63, 321
  Marxist view of, 120
Ficino, Marsilio, 109, 175–78, 182, 291, 472
Field, John, 529
Fifth Lateran Council, 55, 57–58, 317–18, 484, 485
Filelfo, Francesco, 149, 151–53
Finland, Reformation in, 373
Fish, Simon, 447
Fisher, John, 448–51, 455
Fitz-James, Richard, 446
Flanders:
  art in, 213
  and Burgundy, 77–78
  in Hundred Years' War, 71
  peasant revolt in, 13–14
Florence, 15, 93, 102–10
  art in, 197–200, 202–24

Florence—*cont.*
  banking houses of, 103, 124–28
  and Black Death, 12, 104
  and Black and White Guelph conflict, 66, 102
  under Bruni, 61–63
  and Ciompi revolt, 93, 105, 160
  and conflicts with Milan, 105–6, 160–62
  cult of Dante in, 183
  government of, 103, 107–8
  and Guelph-Ghibelline conflict, 66, 95, 102
  guilds of, 102–3, 108
  humanism in, 150, 151, 154, 159–63, 171–72
  and invasion of Charles VIII, 236
  and Machiavelli, 242–43, 245
  and Medici family, 106–10, 125–28, 242, 246–47
  and *monte communale,* 104–5
  Neoplatonism in, 175–78
  and Peace of Lodi, 111
  Quattrocento economic conditions in, 134
  as republic, 239, 242
  under Salutati, 159–61
  under Savonarola, 237–40
  See also Ferrara-Florence, Council of
Forli, Jacopo da, 186
Formula of Concord, 563
Foscari, Francesco, 101
Fourth Lateran Council, 23, 313, 493
Foxe, John, 306, 451, 463, 526
Foxe, Richard, 443, 448, 449, 451
France:
  capitalism in, 130–31
  and Catholic Reformation, 476
  development of political thought in, 503–6
  growth of centralized monarchy in, 63, 70–71, 75–77
  and Habsburg-Valois wars, 86, 361–66
  humanism in, 283–88
  and Hundred Years' War, 12–13, 71–75
  Inquisition in, 478
  peasant revolt in, 14
  post-Renaissance literature in, 564–66
  Protestants in, 415–16, 428–30, 478, 497–503
  Renaissance architecture in, 283–84
Francesca, Piero della, 196, 199, 202
Francis, duke of Guise, 497–99
Francis, kings of France:
  Francis I, 98, 135, 187, 322
    as art patron, 216, 224–25, 284
    and Charles V, 77, 359–66, 444
    and humanists, 284–85, 295, 565
    and Protestants, 415–16, 430, 431, 478
  Francis II, 466, 496–98, 531
Francis II, Holy Roman emperor, 65
Franciscan order:
  Conventual and Observantine branches of, 316
  influence of, on Giotto, 193
  and mysticism, 39
  and physics, 185–86, 582
Franck, Sebastian, 405, 564

Franklin, Benjamin, 119
Frederick, electors of the Palatinate:
　　Frederick II, 368
　　Frederick III, 431–32, 562
Frederick, Holy Roman emperors:
　　Frederick II, 65, 102, 319
　　Frederick III, 32, 33, 68, 91, 278, 485
Frederick I, king of Denmark, 372, 401
Frederick III (the Wise), elector of Saxony, 312,
　　323, 329, 337, 340, 346, 360
Friends of God, 41
Frith, John, 449, 451
Fritz, Joss, 344
Froben, Johannes, 296, 306, 337–38, 393
Frobisher, Martin, 536, 539
Froissart, Jean, 12
Froment, Antoine, 422
Froschauer, Christopher, 385, 386
Froude, Hurrell, 463
Froude, James, 303, 441
Frundsberg, Georg von, 362, 364
Fuchs, Leonard, 588
Fugger family, 132–34, 319, 335

Gabrieli, Giovanni, 579
Gaetano da Thiene, 186, 474, 475
Gage, Thomas, 519
Gaguin, Robert, 296
Galen, 584, 588
Galerius, Roman emperor, 22
Galilei, Galileo, 185–88, 553, 581, 584
Galilei, Vincenzo, 579
Gama, Vasco da, 262–63
Gansfort, Wessel, 41
Gardiner, Stephen, 448, 451, 457–59
Garin, Eugenio, 179
Garret, Thomas, 449
Gascony, 12
Gattamelata, Erasmo, 208
Geiler von Kaisersberg, Johann, 133–34, 277, 312,
　　315, 316, 370
Gelasius I, pope, 21
Genazzano, Mariano da, 237
Geneva, under Calvin, 421–28
Geneva Academy, 429–30, 559
Genghis Khan, 251
Genoa, trading activities of, 10, 99–100, 122
Gentillet (Huguenot publisher), 245
Georg, duke of Saxony, 322, 344, 372, 375
George of Podiebrad, king of Bohemia, 53, 96
George of Trebizond, 180
Gerard of Cremona, 254
Gerbellius, Nicholas, 276
Gerhard, Paul, 580
Germany. *See* Holy Roman Empire
Gerson, Jean, 29
Gesner, Conrad, 588
Ghiberti, Lorenzo, 155, 206–7
Ghirlandaio, Domenico, 53, 109, 195, 202, 219

Gibbon, Edward, 305
Giberti, Gian Matteo, 471–74
Gide, André, 188
Gilbert, Humphrey, 539
Gilbert, William, 588
Giorgione, 227
Giotto, 48, 192–95
Giovio, Paolo, 5
Glareanus, Heinrich, 382
Godric of Finchale, St., 121
Godunov, Boris, 481
Goethe, 38, 304, 319, 321, 438, 551, 553
Golden Bull, 67
Golden Rose, 337
Goldi, Heinrich, 383
Gonzaga, Francesco, 237
Gonzaga, Gian Francesco I, marquis of Mantua,
　　157
Gonzaga, Giulia, 435
Gonzaga, Ludovico, marquis of Mantua, 158
Gotha, League of, 375–76
Goudimel, Claude, 580
Granada, Treaty of, 241
Granvelle, Cardinal, 511–12
Great Ordinance of 1439, 71
Great Schism. *See* Papal schism
Grebel, Conrad, 397–98
Greco, El, 566, 578
Greek Orthodox–Roman Catholic reunion, 32–33
Greek revival, 153–55
Greene, Robert, 571–72
Gregory, popes:
　　Gregory VII, 22, 23, 319
　　Gregory XI, 20, 25, 28, 73, 160
　　Gregory XII, 30–32, 527
　　Gregory XIII, 492, 500, 563
Grenville, Richard, 539
Grey, Jane, 461–62
Grey, William, 290
Grien, Hans Baldung, 574
Grindal, Edmund, 528
Grocyn, William, 291
Groote, Gerard, 41–42, 276, 317
Grotius, Hugo, 113, 549, 554–55
Grünewald, Matthias, 325
Guarino, Battista da, 158
Guarino da Verona, 149, 157, 158
Guelph-Ghibelline conflict, 66, 95, 102
Guericke, Otto von, 588
Guesclin, Bertrand du, 72–73
Guicciardini, Francesco, 50, 165, 233, 244, 246–48
　　on ambassadors, 112
　　on Julius II, 55
　　on Lorenzo the Magnificent, 109
Guild system, 9–10, 102–3, 108
Guise, Charles of, cardinal of Lorraine, 497, 498,
　　500, 565
Guise, dukes of. *See* Francis, duke of Guise; Henry,
　　duke of Guise

Guise, Mary of, 465, 533
Guizot, François, 303
Gustavus Adolphus, king of Sweden, 557
Gustavus Vasa, king of Sweden, 373
Gutenberg, Johannes, 134–35

Habsburg emperors, 65, 68–69
Habsburg-Valois wars, 17, 86, 361–66
Hakluyt, Richard, 539
Haller, Berchthold, 392
Hamilton, Patrick, 464
Handl, Jacob, 579
Hanse, 69, 93, 128–30, 361
Hardcastell, James, 446–47
Harrison, William, 568, 569
Harvey, William, 581, 584
Hasištein, Bohuslav, 283
Hathaway, Anne, 572
Hätzer, Ludwig, 386, 405
Hauser, Henri, 248
Hawkins, John, 536
Hawkwood, John, 105, 205
Hegel, G. W. F., 323–25, 394
Hegius, Alexander, 276, 277
Heidelberg Catechism, 432, 562
Heine, Heinrich, 303
Henneberg, Berthold von, 318–19
Henry, duke of Guise, 421, 501
Henry, duke of Saxony, 372
Henry, Holy Roman emperors:
    Henry IV, 23
    Henry VII, 65–67, 87, 91, 94
Henry, king of Portugal, 509
Henry, kings of England:
    Henry IV, 34, 82–83
    Henry V, 73–74, 83
    Henry VI, 74, 83
    Henry VII, 83–84, 293, 442
    Henry VIII, 55, 84, 86, 290, 295, 376, 525
        and Charles V, 362–64, 366
        and Ireland, 534
        and More, 293–94, 444, 448, 450, 453–56
        and Reformation, 441–45, 448–50, 453–59
Henry, kings of France:
    Henry II, 362, 365, 366, 377, 490, 496, 564
        and Protestants, 430, 478, 490
    Henry III, 501–2, 535
    Henry IV, 502–3. *See also* Henry, kings of Na-
        varre: Henry III
Henry, kings of Navarre:
    Henry II, 286
    Henry III, 500–2. *See also* Henry, kings of
        France: Henry IV
Henry I, prince of Condé, 500
Henry II, duke of Brunswick, 375
Henry of Langenstein, 28–29
Henry the Navigator, 261, 517
Herjulfson, Bjarni, 266
Hermes Tresmegistus, 176, 181–82

Hertford, earl of. *See* Seymour, Edward, duke of
    Somerset
Hervet, Gentien, 565
Hessus, Eobanus, 349
Hipparchus, 255
Historiography, 164–65, 561, 563–64, 567–68
Hochstetter, Ambrosius, 133
Hoen, Cornelius, 390, 392
Hofmann, Melchior, 400–2
Hofmann, Rudolf, 386
Hohenstaufen emperors, 10, 91
Holbein, Hans, the Younger, 459, 574
Holcot, Robert, 308
Holinshed, Raphael, 568
Holl, Elias, 563
Holy League, 55, 112, 242, 443
Holy Roman Empire, 65–70, 357–78
    administration of, 319
    Calvinism in, 431–32, 562
    cities of, 319–23
    Counterreformation in, 482, 562–63
    decentralizing tendencies in, 63, 65, 69–70, 319–
        21
    electoral college of, 67
    Habsburg rulers of, 65, 68–69. *See also* Charles,
        Holy Roman emperors: Charles V; Ferdi-
        nand I, Holy Roman emperor; Maximilian,
        Holy Roman emperors
    Hohenstaufen rulers of, 10, 91
    humanism in, 276–82
    Lutheranism in, 369–72, 375–78, 431, 562–63
    Luxemburg rulers of, 65–68
    peasant unrest in, 14, 321, 343–47
    post-Renaissance thought and letters in, 561–64
    Renaissance decline of, 16
    Roman Catholic Church in, 321–26
    as setting of Reformation, 318–25
    territorial principalities of, 69–70, 319, 322
    trade and banking in, 131–34
Holywood of Halifax, John, 254
Hooker, Richard, 530
Hooker, Thomas, 21
Hooper, John, 461, 463
Hoorne-Montmorency, count of, 512
Horace, 50, 153
Hotman, François, 428, 505
Howard, Catherine, 459
Howard, Charles, baron of Effingham, 516, 517,
    538
Howard, Henry, earl of Surrey, 567
Howard, Thomas, duke of Norfolk, 457–59, 526,
    532
Hubmaier, Balthasar, 343, 398, 400, 405
Hübner, Johann, 34
Hugo, Victor, 230
Hugo of Siena, 186
Huguenots. *See* France, Protestants in
Huizinga, Johan, 148, 297
Humanism, 139–68, 274–98

Humanism—*cont.*
  civic, 159–64
  concerns of, 139–41
  contributions of, to Catholic reform, 472–74
  contributions of, to Reformation, 304–5, 333, 388–89, 397, 448–49, 557–80
  in eastern Europe, 282–83
  and education, 155–59, 558, 567
  as elitist phenomenon, 149
  in England, 290–94, 448–49
  and Erasmus, 294–98
  and exploration, disinterest in, 271–72
  in France, 283–88
  in Germany, 276–82
  and Greek revival, 153–55
  and history, 164–68
  in Italy, 141–68
  in northern Europe, 274–76
  and recovery of ancient manuscripts, 147, 149–51, 155
  in Shakespeare, 572
  in Spain, 288–89
  spread of, 149–50
Humboldt, Wilhelm von, 139
Hume, David, 17–18, 441
Humiliati, 49
Humphrey, duke of Gloucester, 290
Hundred Years' War, 12–13, 71–75, 82–83, 87, 124–25
Hungary:
  Calvinism in, 432–33
  Reformation in, 375
  Turkish invasions of, 52, 68, 365–68
Hunne, Richard, 446
Hunyadi, János, 52
Hus, Jan, 33–35, 37, 68, 374
Hussite revolt, 36–37, 282
Hut, Hans, 400
Hutten, Ulrich von, 5, 7, 281–82, 321, 342–43, 484
Hutter, Jakob, 400
Huygens, Christian, 588

Illyricus, Matthias Flacius, 435, 562
"Incorporation of the church," 313
Index librorum prohibitorum, 476, 478
Index of Trent, 478
Indians, American, 259, 268, 269, 517–19
Indulgences, sale of, 34, 47, 312, 335–36, 471
Industry:
  decline of, in Elizabethan England, 540–42
  development of, 120–21, 134–36
    and banking, 125–28
Inge, Dean, 312
Innocent, popes:
  Innocent III, 23, 24, 179, 313, 319
  Innocent VII, 30, 156, 162
  Innocent VIII, 49, 53, 54
Inquisition, 53, 182, 434–36, 472, 476
  in France, 478

Inquisition—*cont.*
  in Italy, 477–78, 560
  in Netherlands, 511-12
  in Spain, 85–86, 476, 477
Interest, charging of. *See* Usury
Ireland, 534, 543–44
Irenicus (humanist), 347
Isabella (daughter of Philip II of Spain), 514
Isabella of Castile, queen of Spain, 64, 85–86, 112, 259, 268–70, 289, 477
Isabella of Portugal, 360, 506–7
Isabelle of France, 80
Isidore of Seville, 254
Italy:
  capitalism in, 122–28
  city-states of, 17, 91–116, 127
  decentralization in, 87, 91–93
  diplomacy in, 110–16
  historiography in, 164–65, 561
  humanism in, 141–68
  Inquisition in, 477–78, 560
  invaded by Charles VIII, 76, 86, 87, 96, 110, 233–37
  invaded by Louis XII, 240–42
  post-Renaissance art and architecture in, 574–78
  post-Renaissance thought and letters in, 560–61
  Protestantism in, 434–38
  religious contradictions of, 16
  Renaissance architecture in, 198–99, 209–12, 223
  Renaissance painting in, 192–205, 213–23, 225–28
  Renaissance sculpture in, 205–9, 220–23
  as theater of Habsburg-Valois wars, 362–66
Ivan IV (the Terrible), tsar of Russia, 374

Jacquerie, 14, 72
Jagiello, king of Poland, 68
James, kings of Scotland:
  James IV, 84, 442, 444
  James V, 531
  James VI. *See* James I, king of Great Britain
James I, king of Great Britain, 540, 568, 570
James, William, 146
Jane, Cecil, 267
Jedin, Hubert, 483
Jerome, bishop of Brandenburg, 335
Jerome, St., 173
Jerome of Prague, 33, 34
Jesuit order. *See* Society of Jesus
Jewel, John, 526
Jews:
  and development of capitalism, 119
  expelled from Spain, 86
Joachim, electors of Brandenburg:
  Joachim I, 360, 375
  Joachim II, 372
Joachim of Flora, 401
Joachimsen, Paul, 140
Joan of Arc, 41, 74–75

Joanna, queens of Naples:
  Joanna I, 95–96
  Joanna II, 96
Joanna the Mad, queen of Spain, 68–69, 86
John, elector of Saxony, 352, 375
John, kings of Portugal:
  John II, 262, 268
  John III, 483
John, popes:
  John XXII, 27, 67
  John XXIII, 31–32, 35, 150, 162
John II, king of France, 72, 77
John VIII Palaeologus, Byzantine emperor, 154
John Casimer, elector of the Palatinate, 513
John Frederick, elector of Saxony, 353, 376–77
John of Alexandria. *See* Philopon
John of Capistrano, 51, 312
John of Leiden, 402–3
John of Monte Corvino, 252
John of Nassau, 513
John of Plano Carpini, 251
John of Salisbury, 4, 140
John of the Cross, St., 40, 41, 475, 476
John the Fearless, duke of Burgundy, 73, 74, 77
Johnson, Samuel, 275
Jonas, Justus, 352, 391
Jonson, Ben, 571–73
Joris, David, 400, 401
Joye, George, 451
Juan of Austria, Don, 368, 510, 513
Jud, Leo, 384–86
Julius, popes:
  Julius II, 54–57, 241–43, 282, 332, 335
    as art patron, 217, 220–21
    and Fifth Lateran Council, 55, 57, 485
    and Henry VIII, 443, 445
  Julius III, 472, 489–90. *See also* Del Monte,
    Gianmaria
Jung, Carl, 309
Justin Martyr, 173

Kalmar, Union of, 64
Kant, Immanuel, 40
Kepler, Johannes, 581, 587, 588
Knights of St. John, 53, 510
Knights' War, 341–43
Knipperdollinck, Bernt, 402, 403
Knox, John, 461, 465–66, 525, 528, 551, 552, 558
Knutsson, Karl. *See* Charles VIII, king of Sweden
Kollauer, Johann, 272
Krämer, Heinrich, 49
Kremer, Gerard (Mercator), 583
Kublai Khan, 251

Lactantius, 179
Ladislas, king of Naples, 34, 96, 106, 161
Laetus, Pomponius, 53, 283
Lainez, Diego, 480, 488, 490, 498
La Marche, Olivier de, 78

Lambeth Articles, 528, 530
Landino, Cristoforo, 154, 183
Lando, Michele di, 105
Langen, Rudolf von, 277
La Ramée, Pierre. *See* Ramus, Peter
La Roche, Alain de, 309
Lascaris, Constantine, 155
Lascaris, John, 155
Las Casas, Bartolomé de, 267, 268, 519
Lasco, John à, 432, 461
Lassus, Orlandus de, 579
Latimer, Hugh, 451, 463
Latimer, William, 291
Latini, Brunetto, 140
League of Cambrai, 241
League of Cognac, 364, 473
League of Dessau, 375
League of Gotha, 375–76
League of the Elect, 397
League of Torgau, 375–76
League of Venice, 236–37
Lee, Edward, 450
Lefèvre d'Étaples, Jacques, 285–87, 291, 415, 478
Leibniz, 166, 185, 484, 587
Leicester, earl of. *See* Dudley, Robert
Leipzig Interim, 377, 435
Leo X, pope, 57–59, 247, 295, 443, 470
  as art patron, 58, 216, 221
  and Charles V, 360, 362
  and church appointments, 50, 313
  financial dealings of, 317, 322, 335
  and Luther, 337, 338, 340
  See also Medici, Giovanni de' (son of Lorenzo the
    Magnificent)
León, Luis de, 476
Lepanto, Battle of, 368, 510
Levant Company, 539
L'Hôpital, Michel de, 498–99, 504
Libraries, 189
Light metaphysic, 177
Lilly, William, 292
Linacre, Thomas, 291, 293, 314
Linck, Wenceslas, 350, 370
Lipan, Battle of, 37
Lippi, Filippino, 202
Lippi, Fra Filippo, 202
Literature:
  patristic, 172–73
  post-Renaissance, 560–73
    in England, 567–73
    in France, 564–66
    in Holy Roman Empire, 561–64
    in Italy, 560–61
    in Spain, 566
  sixteenth-century popular, 183
Lithuanian Unitarians, 396
Lodi, Peace of, 111–12
Lollards, 15, 28, 33–34, 83, 447–48
Lorenzo the Magnificent. *See* Medici, Lorenzo de'

Lorraine, 16–17
Lorraine, cardinal of. *See* Guise, Charles of
Lotzer, Sebastian, 343
Louis, duke of Orléans, 73
Louis, kings of France:
    Louis VI, 12
    Louis IX, 251
    Louis XI, 70, 75–76, 131, 235, 485
    Louis XII, 55, 76–77, 84, 98, 240–42, 442, 485
    Louis XIII, 503
    Louis XIV, 24, 503
Louis, kings of Hungary:
    Louis I, 67, 95–96
    Louis II, 360, 367
Louis I, prince of Condé, 429, 498–500
Louis of Anjou, 96
Louis of Nassau, 517
Louis of Taranto, 96
Louise of Savoy, 286, 361, 363, 365
Lowell, James Russell, 553
Loyola, St. Ignatius, 413–14, 464, 479–81, 488
Lüber, Thomas. *See* Erastus
Luchino, Benedetto, 434–35
Luder, Peter, 276–77
Ludovico il Moro, 98, 112, 187, 214, 235, 236, 241
Ludwig of Bavaria, Holy Roman emperor, 44, 67, 91
Lull, Raymond, 285, 476
Lupus of Ferrières, 3
Luther, Hans, 330, 331
Luther, Heinrich, 330
Luther, Katherine, 350–52, 354, 372
Luther, Martin, 328–55
    Bible translation of, 340, 371
    and Calvin, 412–13
    and Catholic Reformation, 471, 474, 481, 491
    and church polity, 551
    and Diet of Augsburg, 353–54
    at Diet of Worms, 328–29
    economic theories of, 556
    and education, 317, 558–59
    and fine arts, 573, 579–80
    and humanists, 168, 280, 281, 286, 298, 348–50
    influence of, in England, 449–53
    influence of, in Scotland, 464–65
    last years of, 354–55
    marriage of, 350–52
    and medieval reformers, 168, 374
    ninety-five theses of, 335–37
    position of, on armed rebellion, 344–46, 375
    position of, on divorce of Henry VIII, 453
    and predestination, 420
    as professor, 347–48
    as publicist, 337–38
    and radical Protestants, 389–92, 400, 401
    and reformatory forces of sixteenth century, 301–8, 315–17, 325–26, 375
    and science, 582–86
    and second marriage of Philipp of Hesse, 376

Luther, Martin—*cont.*
    as student of history, 564
    theology of, 332–35, 349–50
    youth of, 330–31
Lutheranism:
    in Baltic states, 373
    doctrinal controversies within, 561–63
    in eastern Europe, 374–75, 432–33
    in Germany, 369–72, 375–78, 431, 562–63
    in Netherlands, 431, 511–12
    in Scandinavia, 372–73
    in Spain, 434
Luxemburg emperors, 65–68
Lyly, John, 568

Macaulay, Thomas Babington, 248, 457, 493–94, 547–48
Machiavelli, Bernardo, 242
Machiavelli, Girolamo, 107
Machiavelli, Niccolò, 100, 242–48
    admiration of, for Ferdinand of Aragon, 86, 113
    on arming of peasantry, 14–15
    career of, 242–44
    and Cesare Borgia, 54, 98, 243
    as historian, 165, 244, 245
    and Lorenzo de' Medici, 90, 245
    as political analyst, 93, 98, 184, 244–46
Macrobius, 177
Madrid, Treaty of, 363–64
Madruzzo, cardinal, 486
Magellan, Ferdinand, 271
Maimonides, Moses, 40, 180
Majid, Ahmed ibn, 262
Major, John, 485
Malatesta, Sigismondo, 198
Malocello, Lancelot, 259
Malpighi, Marcello, 584
Malta, 510
Mandeville, Jehan de, 252
Manetti, Giannozzo, 163–64, 179
Mannerism, 228, 576–77
Manorial system, 7–9, 15
Mantegna, Andrea, 158, 204–5, 225–27
Mantua, humanism in, 157–58
Mantuanus, Baptista, 172, 183, 474
Manuel I, king of Portugal, 57, 258, 263, 509
Manuel II Palaeologus, Byzantine emperor, 31, 154
Manutius, Aldus, 188–89, 198, 296, 306
Manz, Felix, 397, 398
Marcel, Étienne, 72
Marcellus II, pope, 472
Margaret (daughter of Henry VII of England), 84, 442
Margaret, queen of Denmark, Norway, and Sweden, 64
Margaret of Austria, 76, 358, 365
Margaret of Flanders and Artois, 77
Margaret of Parma, 511–12
Margaret of York, 358

Marguerite d'Angoulême, 286–87, 415
Maria of Portugal, 507
Mariana, Juan de, 554
Mark, Robert von der, 362
Markolf, 484
Marlowe, Christopher, 571
Marot, Clément, 287, 426, 580
Marsigli, Luigi, 150
Marsiglio of Padua, 27, 67
Marsilius of Inghen, 46
Martin V, pope, 32, 36
Martini, Simone, 193
Martins de Roriz, Fernâs, 267
Martyrs' Synod, 399, 405
Marx, Karl, 119–20
Mary (daughter of Henry VII of England), 84, 442
Mary, queen of England, 436, 437, 445, 458, 461–64, 524, 534
  and Philip II, 462–63, 507–8, 535
  and suppression of Protestantism, 162–64
Mary, queen of Scots, 465–66, 496–98, 535, 552
  and Bothwell, 531–33
  and Elizabeth, 514–15, 526, 528, 530–33
  and Darnley, 531–32
Mary of Burgundy, 68, 76, 279
Mary of Guise, 465, 533
Mary of Hungary, 360, 511
Masaccio, 200
Massala, 256
Mathematics, 186, 587
Mattei, Rodolfo de, 244
Matthew Corvinus, king of Hungary, 68, 282
Matthew of Janov, 34
Matthew's Bible, 458
Matthys, Jan, 402–3
Maurice, duke of Saxony, 376–77, 490
Maurice of Nassau, 513
Maximilian, Holy Roman emperors:
  Maximilian I, 68, 98, 235, 243, 362, 485
    and Fugger bank, 132
    and Holy League, 112, 236–37
    and humanists, 279
    and League of Cambrai, 241
    and Luther, 337
    and Swiss War, 381
    and Treaty of Arras, 76
  Maximilian II, 563
Mechthild of Magdeburg, 39
Medals, commemorative, 195
Medici, Catherine de', 362, 365, 497–502, 534
Medici, Cosimo de':
  banking operations of, 125–27
  and control of Florence, 106–8, 111
  and humanists, 151–52, 154, 175–76
Medici, Duke Cosimo I de', 242, 247, 436, 477–78, 560
Medici, Giovanni de' (father of Cosimo), 53, 106, 107, 125

Medici, Giovanni de' (son of Lorenzo the Magnificent), 110. *See also* Leo X, pope
Medici, Giuliano de' (cardinal), 217
Medici, Giuliano de' (son of Piero the Gouty), 108–9, 470
Medici, Giulio de'. *See* Clement, popes: Clement VII
Medici, Isabella de', 438
Medici, Lorenzo de' (the Magnificent):
  as art patron, 214, 219
  attack on, in Florence Cathedral, 53, 109
  and Ferrante of Naples, 96, 109
  and humanists, 152, 198
  and neglect of banking operations, 110, 127
  as poet, 182–83
  as ruler of Florence, 108–11, 236
  and Savonarola, 110, 238
Medici, Lorenzo de' (grandson of Lorenzo the Magnificent), 90, 245
Medici, Marie de', 503
Medici, Piero de' (the Gouty) (son of Cosimo), 108, 127
Medici, Piero de' (son of Lorenzo the Magnificent), 110, 235–36, 238
Medici, Salvestro de', 106
Medici family:
  banking activities of, 125–28
  and Guicciardini, 246–47
  sponsorship of artists by, 202–4, 214, 219, 220–21
  sponsorship of humanists by, 237
Medina, Pedro de, 508
Medina Sidonia, Alonso, duke of, 516
Melanchthon, Philipp, 376, 461, 514, 551
  and Augsburg Confession, 354, 540
  and Calvin, 412, 417, 424
  and Catholic Reformation, 473–74, 490
  and Copernicus, 586–87
  doctrinal deviations of, 562
  and education, 317, 558–59
  as historiographer, 564
  and humanism, 182, 305, 348
  and Leipzig Interim, 377, 435
  and Luther, 337, 352–54, 371, 391–92, 412
  and spiritualists, 341
Melville, James, 466
Melzi, Francesco, 216
Memling, Hans, 284
Mendoza, Bernardino de, 516, 535, 537
Mennonites, 404
Mercator, 583
Merchant Adventurers, 538–39
Merle d'Aubigné, Jean Henri, 325, 425
Merriman, Roger, 507
Merswin, Ruleman, 41
Metaphysics, Renaissance, 182–84
Metsys, Quentin, 213
Mettringham, Thomas, 446–47
Meuting family, 133

Meyer, Anna Reinhard, 387
Michelangelo, 200, 207, 219–23, 238
  as architect, 58, 212, 221, 223, 577
  paintings of, 54, 216
    fresco, in Sistine Chapel, 55, 220–23, 469, 576
    later, 576
  as poet, 183
  sculptures of, 55–56, 220–23
  training of, 195, 219
Michelet, Jules, 76
Michelozzi, Michelozzo, 176, 212
Middle Ages:
  communes in, 92–93, 96
  institutional church crisis in, 20–37
  politicoeconomic development in, 62–63
  religious trends in, 38–49
  as seen by humanists, 3
  socioeconomic conditions in, 7–15
Milan, 96–99, 105–6, 111, 152
Miltitz (papal chamberlain), 337
Mining, 135
Minturno, Antonio, 146
Mocenigo, Tommaso, 101
Model Parliament, 79–80
Mohammed II, sultan of Ottoman Turks, 52, 253
Molière, 44
Monarchy, centralized. *See* Nationalism, rise of
Monasteries, dissolution of, 456–57
Monasticism, 316–17, 474–75, 481
Monmouth, Humphrey, 452
Montaigne, Michel de, 408, 565–66
Montefeltro, Federico da, duke of Urbino, 158
Montesquieu, 303
Monteverdi, Claudio, 579
Montmorency, Duke Anne de, 498
Montreuil, Jean de, 283
More, Margaret, 293
More, Thomas, 21, 291–94, 296, 446, 453–56
  on human pride, 116
  martyrdom of, 455–56
  political rise of, 294, 444, 453
  and religious controversy, 448, 450, 451, 453–54
  on schoolmen, 44
  Utopia, 116, 292–94
Morgan, Thomas, 532
Morison, Richard, 448, 458
Morley, Lord John, 411
Motley, John L., 506, 507, 510
Mountjoy, barons. *See* Blount, Charles; Blount, William
Müller, Johannes. *See* Regiomontanus
Müller von Bulgenbach, Hans, 343
Münster, Kingdom of, 401–4
Münster, Sebastian, 583
Müntzer, Thomas, 341, 344, 395, 397
Murmellius, Johannes, 277
Muscovy Company, 538–39
Music, 228–29, 578–80

Mysticism, 38–40, 475–76
  evangelical, 39

Nantes, Edict of, 502
Napier, John, 587
Naples:
  invaded by Charles VIII, 236–37
  Protestantism in, 435
  and Sicily, 95–96
Napoleon Bonaparte, 94, 98, 319
Nationalism, rise of, 62–64, 70–87
  in England, 63, 78–84, 87
  in France, 63–64, 70–78, 87
  and overseas expansion, 260–61
  in Spain, 63–64, 84–87
Navigation instruments, 255–57
Nazianzen, Gregory, 173
Neckam, Alexander, 256
Nemesius of Emessa, 179
Neo-Aristotelianism, 144, 179–82, 565
Neoplatonism, 173–79, 182–84
Neri, St. Philip, 474
Nesi, Giovanni, 183
Netherlands, 16, 549
  music in, 228–29
  Protestantism in, 431, 511–12, 557
  revolt of, 510–14, 520, 533, 535
Neville, George, 290–91
Newton, Isaac, 587, 588
Niccoli, Niccolò, 150, 154, 162
Nicea, Council of, 31, 312–13
Nicholas V, pope, 33, 51, 112, 166, 168, 189
Niethammer, F. J., 139
Nietzsche, Friedrich, 6, 54, 584
Nizolius, Marius, 282
Nogaret, Guillaume de, 23
Nominalism, 39, 45
Norfolk, duke of. *See* Howard, Thomas
Northeast Passage, search for, 538–39
Northumberland, duke of. *See* Dudley, John
Northwest Passage, search for, 537–39
Norway:
  Lutheranism in, 373
  union of, with Denmark and Sweden, 64
Novara (Platonist), 586
Nuremberg, Peace of, 369

Obrecht, Jacob, 578
Occam, William of, 27, 44–46, 67, 185, 292, 297, 308
Ochino, Bernardino, 435–37, 461, 474
Odoric of Pordenone, 252
Oecolampadius, Johannes, 295, 371, 391–93, 412
Okeghem, Jean d', 578
Olivetan, 413, 414, 422
Opera, development of, 579
Opitz, Martin, 563
Oratory of Divine Love, 472, 474–75
Order of the Golden Fleece, 78

Oresme, Nicolas, 185–86
Orléans, Duke Charles of, 73, 74
Osiander, Andreas, 391, 405, 551, 586
Otto, Holy Roman emperors:
  Otto I (the Great), 3
  Otto III, 3–4
Otto of Freising, 260
Ottoman Turks. *See* Turks, European invasions by
Ovid, 65
Oxenham, John, 537

Pace, Richard, 450
Pack, Otto von, 376
Padua:
  art in, 204, 208
  physicists in, 186
Painting:
  apprenticeship in, 195
  baroque, 577
  Flemish, 213
  fresco, 196
  German, 325, 573–74. *See also* Dürer, Albrecht
  Italian Renaissance, 192–205, 213–23, 225–28
  mannerist, 576–77
  perspective in, 197
  post-Renaissance, 573–77
  Renaissance themes in, 48
  techniques of, 195–97
Palestrina, Giovanni da, 578
Palladio, Andrea, 576
Pallavicino, Pietro Sforza, 472, 493
Palmieri, Matteo, 163, 183, 193, 209, 210
Pannonius, Janus, 282
Papacy:
  in Avignon, 16, 20, 23–24
  claims to power of, 21–24
  mining enterprises of, 135
  political position of, in Rome, 94
  Reformation, 470–72
  Renaissance, 49–59
Papal bulls:
  Benedictus Deus (Pius IV), 491
  Bull of Convocation (Paul III), 485–86
  Decet romanum pontificem (Leo X), 340
  Execrabilis (Pius II), 33, 50, 484
  Exsurge domine (Leo X), 338
  Iniunctum nobis (Pius IV), 491
  Pastor aeternus (Leo X), 58
  Regimen militantis ecclesiae (Paul III), 480
  Regnans in excelsis (Pius V), 527
  Salvator noster (Sixtus IV), 335
  Summis desiderantes affectibus (Innocent VIII), 49
  Unam sanctam (Boniface VIII), 23, 58, 317
Papal schism, 16, 20, 25–26, 30–33
Papal States, 17, 21, 25, 30, 50, 55, 94
Paracelsus, Philippus Aureolus, 588
Parker, Matthew, 525, 528
Parker, T. H. L., 418–19

Parliament, English, development of, 79–82, 525
Parmigianino, 576
Parr, Catherine, 459
Paruta, Paolo, 561
Pascal, Blaise, 587, 589
Passau, Peace of, 377
Passavanti, Jacopo, 11
Pastor, Adam, 405
Pastor, Ludwig, 59
Patristic literature, 172–73
Patrizzi, Francesco, 181–82
Paul, popes:
  Paul II, 53, 283
  Paul III, 59, 323, 365
    as art patron, 223, 224
    and Council of Trent, 484–86, 489
    and Counterreformation, 416, 434, 471–73, 477
    and Jesuits, 480, 483
    and Reformation, 376, 455
  Paul IV, 434, 436, 472, 478. *See also* Caraffa, Giampietro
Paul of Venice, 186
Paumgartner family, 133
Pavia, Battle of, 363
Peasant revolts, 13–15
  in England, 14, 82
  in Holy Roman Empire, 343–47
Pegolotti (Bardi agent), 124–25, 252
Pérez, Antonio, 507
Peri, Jacopo, 579
Perrin, Ami, 424, 427
Perugino, Pietro, 53, 55, 202, 216–17
Peruzzi bank, 103, 124
Peterson, Christian, 372
Petrarch, Francesca, 142
Petrarch, Francesco, 2, 141–46, 153, 155–56, 184
  and church fathers, 172
  compared with Dante, 145
  influence of, 5, 149
  on Plato vs. Aristotle, 174
  religious thought of, 143–44
  and Rienzo, 94
  and sense of history, 4, 142–43
Petri, Olaf and Lars, 373
Peuerbach, Georg, 186
Peutinger, Conrad, 133, 279, 313
Pflug, bishop of Naumburg, 377
Philibert, prince of Orange, 224
Philip, duke of Savoy, 499
Philip, dukes of Burgundy:
  Philip the Bold, 77
  Philip the Good, 74, 77, 78
Philip, kings of France:
  Philip II Augustus, 70
  Philip IV (the Fair), 23, 69, 70, 71
  Philip VI, 71–73
Philip, kings of Spain:
  Philip I, 68–69, 86

Philip, kings of Spain—*cont.*
  Philip II, 378, 431, 463, 496, 506–17
    and Armada, 514–17
    and Elizabeth, 508, 514–16, 524, 533–38
    and French religious wars, 497, 499–501
    and Mary, 462–63, 507–8, 535
    and Netherlands revolt, 510–14, 520
Philipp, count of Eisenach, 344
Philipp, landgrave of Hesse, 371, 375–76, 389, 391, 392, 394
Philippe, Jean, 423, 425
Philippson, Johannes. *See* Sleidanus
Phillips, Henry, 452
Philopon, 181, 185
Philosophy, Renaissance. *See* Humanism; Metaphysics; Neo-Aristotelianism; Neoplatonism
Physics:
  Aristotelian, 185
  Franciscan, 185–86, 582
  Paduan, 186
  post-Renaissance, 587–88
Piccolomini, Aeneas Silvius, 279. *See also* Pius, popes: Pius II
Pico, Francesco, count of Mirandola and Concordia, 178
Pico della Mirandola, Giovanni, 178–80, 182, 183, 238, 472
Pighius, Albert, 427
Pilatus, Leontius, 153
Pilgrimage of Grace, 457
Pilgrimages, 47–48, 312
Pinturicchio, Bernardino, 54, 202
Pinzón brothers, 268–69
Pirckheimer, Willibald, 280, 391
Pirenne, Henri, 14, 121
Pisa:
  conquered by Florence, 106, 243
  Council of (1409), 29, 31
  Council of (1511), 55
  and maritime trade, 10, 99
  sculpture in, 205–6
Pisanello, 195
Pisano, Giovanni, 206
Pisano, Nicola, 205–6
Pitti, Luca, 108, 210
Pius, popes:
  Pius II, 33, 37, 50, 52, 158, 484. *See also* Piccolomini, Aeneas Silvius
  Pius III, 54
  Pius IV, 490–91
  Pius V, 436, 492, 510, 527
  Pius X, 492
  Pius XI, 492
Pizarro, Francisco, 271, 517
Pizzicolli, Cyriaco de', 155
Pizzinghe, Jacopo, 148
Plague, 11–12, 47, 72, 384
Plato, 9, 91, 174, 181, 254. *See also* Neoplatonism
Platonic Academy (Diacceto's), 182

Platonic Academy (Ficino's), 176
Platter, Thomas, 384, 416
Pleiades, 564
Plessis-Mornay, Philippe du, 502
Pletho, Gemistos, 154–55
Plotinus, 176–77
Poggio Bracciolini, Giovanni Francesco, 51, 149–53, 161, 167, 179, 290
Poitiers, Battle of, 72
Poland:
  humanism in, 283
  Reformation in, 374, 432–33
Pole, Reginald, 448, 454, 456, 458, 464, 471, 474
Polish Brethren, 396
Politian, 109, 183, 204
Political thought, impact of Reformation on, 503–6, 548–55
Pollaiuolo, Antonio, 209
Polo, Marco, 99, 251–52
Polo, Matteo, 251
Polo, Niccolò, 251
Polybius, 255
Pomponazzi, Pietro, 180–81
Ponce de León, Juan, 271
Pontano, Giovanni, 183
Pontormo, Jacopo da, 576–77
Pope, Alexander, 588
Popular religion:
  in England, 446–48
  on eve of Reformation, 309–12, 323–25
  late medieval, 47–49
Population:
  fourteenth-century decline in, 11, 13, 104
  in major cities in early fourteenth century, 9
  sixteenth-century rise in, in England, 541
Porphyry, 176
Porta, Giacomo della, 577, 578
Portugal:
  overseas expansion of, 257–63, 270–71, 517–18
  and unification with Spain, 64, 509–10
Postel, William, 476
Poussin, Nicolas, 188
Pragmatic Sanction of Bourges, 322, 485
Predestination:
  Anglican, 526
  Calvinist, 419–21
  Valla's theory of, 166–67
  views of Aquinas, Augustine, and Luther on, 420
  Zwinglian, 388–89, 420
Presbyterianism, 466, 528–29. *See also* Calvinism
Prescott, William H., 508
Prester John, 260
Prierias, 337
Priests, poverty of, 313–14
Primaticcio, Francesco, 284
Printing and publishing, 48, 134–35, 176, 188–89, 291, 306, 393
Privateers, 536–38
Proclus, 175, 176, 181

Proles, Andreas, 316
Proprietary church, 22–24, 322–23
"Protestant," origin of, 353
Protestantism. *See* Reformation
Provision, principle of, 23
Ptolemy, 254–55, 584, 586
Pufendorf, Samuel, 318
Pulci, Luigi, 109, 183
Puritanism, 528–30, 573, 581–82, 589
Puttenham, Richard, 567

Quadra, Álvarez de, 536
Quercia, Jacopo della, 207

Rabelais, François, 5, 274, 287–88, 413
Radewyns, Florentius, 41–42
Radziwill, Nicholas, 432
Raleigh, Walter, 534, 536, 538–40, 568, 569
Ramus, Peter, 565
Ranke, Leopold von, 1, 245, 306, 318, 493, 507
Raphael, 54–55, 58, 199, 216–19
Reformation:
    and art and architecture, 573–74
    in Baltic states, 373
    Calvinist, 411–38
    and capitalism, 119, 555–57
    Catholic. *See* Counterreformation
    and conditions in Holy Roman Empire, 318–25
    in eastern Europe, 374–75, 432–33
    and education, 347–48, 371, 429–30, 558–60
    in England, 441–64
    in France, 415–16, 428–30, 497–503
    in Holy Roman Empire, 369–72, 375–78, 430–
        32, 562–63
    in Italy, 434–38
    links of, with Renaissance, 301–6, 333, 397,
        557–80
    Lutheran, 325–26, 328–55, 369–78
    and music, 578–80
    in Netherlands, 431, 511–12, 557
    and political thought, 503–6, 548–55
    popes of, 470–72
    radical, 341, 395–408
    reasons for, 308–18
    in Scandinavia, 372–73
    and science, 580–90
    in Scotland, 464–66
    and social unrest, 341–47
    in Spain, 433–34, 437
    Zwinglian, 381–95
Reformation Parliament, 453–56
Reformed Church. *See* Calvinism
Regiomontanus, 186, 256, 514
Reinhold, Erasmus, 586
Reliquaries, 312
Renaissance:
    architecture of, 198–99, 209–12, 223, 283–84
    cardinals of, 50–51, 94
    concept of, 2–6

    in eastern Europe, 282–83
    English, 290–94
    French, 283–88
    German, 276–82
    Italian, 90–116, 171–89, 192–230, 233–48
    metaphysics and literature in, 182–84
    music in, 228–29
    Neo-Aristotelianism in, 179–82
    Neoplatonism in, 173–79, 182
    and overseas expansion, 250–72
    painting and sculpture in, 192–209, 213–28
    patristic revival in, 172–73
    political aspects of, 16–17, 62–87, 171–72, 233–
        48
    popes of, 49–59
    science in, 184–88
    socioeconomic aspects of, 7–16, 62–64, 148–49,
        171–72, 274–76. *See also* Capitalism
    Spanish, 288–89
    spread of learning in, 188–89
    See also Holy Roman Empire; Humanism; Na-
        tionalism, rise of; Roman Catholic Church
Renan, Ernst, 146, 428
Renée, duchess of Ferrara, 416, 438, 478
Repartimiento system, 518
Requeséns, Luis de, 513
Reservation, principle of, 23, 24, 313
Reuchlin, Johannes, 280–81, 316, 348
Rhenanus, Beatus, 295, 304, 306
Rheticus, Georg, 586
Rhodes, Turkish capture of, 367
Riario, Girolamo, 53
Ricci, Matthew, 483
Richard, archbishop of Trier, 360
Richard, duke of York, 83
Richard, kings of England:
    Richard II, 33–34, 82, 83
    Richard III, 83, 442
Richelieu, cardinal, 557
Ridley, Nicholas, 451, 461, 463
Ridolfi, Roberto, 532
Rienzo, Cola di, 94–95
Rinuccini, Alamanno, 160
Rinuccini, Ottavio, 579
Ritschl, Albrecht, 396
Rizzio, David, 531
Roanoke Island, English attempts to colonize, 538–
    40
Robbia, Luca della, 208
Robert, king of Naples, 67, 95, 142
Robert, Pierre. *See* Olivetan
Robertson, H. M., 121–22
Roger II, king of Sicily, 254
Rogers, John, 463
Roman Academy, 53, 283
Roman Catholic Church:
    administration of, 22–25, 313
    and anticlericalism, 323, 446–47, 465, 551
    and concept of Christendom, 21–22

Roman Catholic Church—*cont.*
doctrinal deviations in, 308–9
feudalization of, 22
in Holy Roman Empire, 321–26
medieval reform movements in, 20–21, 26–28,
33–37
medieval spiritual trends in, 37–49
Renaissance decline of, 16, 309–18
restoration of, in Marian England, 462–64
reunion of, with Greek Orthodox Church, 32–33,
252
See also Church councils; Conciliarism; Counterreformation; Inquisition; Papacy; Papal
bulls; Papal schism
Romano, Ezzelino da, 102
Romanus, Egidius, 23
Rome:
as city-state, 93–95
corruption in, 313, 315
sack of, 364
as world capital, 3, 93
Ronsard, Pierre de, 564–65
Rossellino, Antonio, 209
Rossi, Roberto de', 162
Rosso, Il, 284, 577
Roswitha, 278
Rothmann, Bernard, 402, 403
Roussel, Gerard, 286
Rovere, Francesco della. *See* Sixtus, popes: Six-
tus IV
Rovere, Giuliano della. *See* Julius, popes: Julius II
Rubeanus, Crotus, 281, 329
Rudolf I, Holy Roman emperor, 65
Rudolf IV, duke of Austria, 69
Rupert of the Palatinate, Holy Roman emperor, 67,
106
Russell, Bertrand, 304
Russia:
and False Dimitri, 481–82
freeing of serfs in, 15
and trade with England, 538
Ruysbroeck, Johannes van, 41

Saal, Margaret von der, 376
Sabellicus, 279
Sachins, Claude de, 556
Sachs, Hans, 326
Sacramentarian controversy, 389–92
Sacrobosco. *See* Holywood of Halifax, John
Sadoleto, Jacopo, 58, 425, 471–74, 561
"Safe classics," 42, 276
St.-André, marshal of France, 498
St. Bartholomew massacre, 500–1, 535
St. Denis, cardinal, 220
St.-Germain, Edict of, 500
St. Peter's Cathedral (Rome), 55, 58, 335, 577, 578
Sallust, 547
Salmerón, Alfonso, 480, 488, 490
Salutati, Coluccio, 154, 156, 159–62, 165, 179

Samson, Bernardin, 383
San Gallo, Giuliano da, 55
Sannazzaro, Jacopo, 183
Santa Cruz, Álvaro, marquis of, 515
Sarpi, Paolo, 492–93, 561
Sarto, Andrea del, 284
Sattler, Michael, 398–99
Saum, Conrad, 391
Savonarola, Girolamo, 54, 87, 110, 204, 237–40
Savoy, 16–17, 99
Scandinavia:
Reformation in, 372–73
unification of, 64
Schegk, Jakob, 563
Schinner, Matthias, 242
Schleitheim Confession of Faith, 398–99
Schmalkald League, 354, 376, 377, 489, 490
Schmalkald War, 132, 133, 369, 562
Scholasticism, 43–47, 308
and science, 185–87
School of St. George, 475
School of St. Rochos, 475
Schütz, Heinrich, 563, 579
Schweitzer, Albert, 6
Schwenkfeld, Caspar, 370, 401, 405
Science:
Bacon's contributions to, 571
Renaissance, 184–88
role of Reformation in development of, 580–90
Scotland:
under Mary Stuart, 465–66, 531–32
Reformation in, 464–66
victory of, at Bannockburn, 80
Scriptoris, Paul, 277
Scrovegni, Enrico, 48
Sculpture:
Italian Renaissance, 48, 205–9, 220–23
post-Renaissance, 573, 578
Sea Beggars, 513, 514
Sebastian, king of Portugal, 509
Sects:
evangelical, 396–97
heretical, 308–9, 397
medieval mystical, 41
Selim I, sultan of Ottoman Turks, 253
Seneca, 254
Senfl, Ludwig, 579
Senlis, Treaty of, 235
Separatism, 528, 529
Seripando, Jacopo, 488
Servetus, Michael, 406–7, 427
Settignano, Desiderio da, 208
Seymour, Edward, duke of Somerset, 459–60
Seymour, Jane, 459
Seyssel, Claude de, 504
Sforza, Anna, 214
Sforza, Ascanio, 471
Sforza, Bianca, 98
Sforza, Francesco, 98, 107, 108, 111, 152, 214

Sforza, Francesco Maria, 364
Sforza, Gian Galleazo, 235
Sforza, Ludovico. *See* Ludovico il Moro
Sforza, Massimiliano, 98, 242
Shakespeare, William, 445, 568, 571–73
Shaw, Bernard, 408
Shirwood, John, 291
Sicilian Vespers, 91
Sicily, 95–96
Sickingen, Franz von, 341–42, 362
Sidney, Philip, 569
Siena:
    art in, 193–95, 206
    and Black Death, 12
Sigismund, Holy Roman emperor, 31–33, 35–36,
        67–68, 156
Sigismund, kings of Poland:
    Sigismund II Augustus, 374, 432
    Sigismund III, 481
Simons, Menno, 404, 405
Sixtus, popes:
    Sixtus IV, 50, 53, 85, 96, 106, 152
    Sixtus V, 492, 515, 577
Skelton, John, 442
Slavery, 122–23, 259, 519, 536
Sleidanus, 564
Smith, Adam, 262
Social contract theory, 505–6, 553
Society of Jesus, 475, 476, 478–83, 492
    compared with Calvinism, 481, 556
    and Council of Trent, 488, 490
    in Holy Roman Empire, 563
    missions of, 482–83, 527
    schools of, 481–82, 559, 563
Socinians, 374, 396
Socinus, Laelius. *See* Sozzini, Lelio
Socioeconomic conditions:
    in Elizabethan England, 540–42
    on eve of Reformation, 309
    in Middle Ages, 7–15, 21
    in *Quattrocento*, 15–16, 148–49, 171–72
    and rise of nationalism, 62–64
    in western and northern Europe, 62–64
Soderini, Piero, 216, 220, 242, 243
Sodoma, 55
Solera, Temistocles, 90
Somatian order, 475
Sombart, Werner, 119
Somerset, duke of. *See* Seymour, Edward
Sorel, Agnes, 131
Soto, Dominique, 186
Sozzini, Fausto, 374, 437–38
Sozzini, Lelio, 374, 437–38
Spain:
    and Armada, 514–17, 538
    and Charles I, 359–61, 378, 477
    and defeat of Turks, 510
    development of political unity in, 64, 84–86
    economic problems of, 509, 518, 520

Spain—*cont.*
    expulsion of Jews from, 86
    hegemony of, 496, 506–20
    humanism in, 288–89
    Inquisition in, 85–86, 476, 477
    Moorish occupation of, 64, 86, 510
    mysticism in, 475–76
    and Netherlands revolt, 510–14
    overseas expansion of, 86, 259–60, 263–71, 517–
        19
    post-Renaissance cultural flowering of, 566
    Protestantism in, 433–34, 437
    and unification with Portugal, 64, 509–10
Spalatin, Georg, 326, 329, 348–49
Spengler, Lazarus, 370
Spengler, Oswald, 171, 306
Spenser, Edmund, 569
Spiera, Francesco, 435, 436
Spinoza, Baruch, 245
Spiritualists, 341, 392, 396, 404–5, 408
Sprat, Thomas, 582, 589
Sprenger, Jakob, 49
Stadion, Christoph von, 315
Stafileo, bishop, 470
Stagel, Elsbeth, 41
Stanley, Thomas, Lord, 442
Starkey, Thomas, 448, 457–58
Statute of Laborers, 82
Staupitz, Johannes, 316, 331, 370
Steinli, Martin, 386
Steno, Michele, 101
Stevin, Simon, 587
Storch, Nicholas, 341
Stow, John, 568
Strabo, 254
Stralsund, Peace of, 130
Strozzi, Niccolò, 140
Strozzi, Palla, 150, 154
Stuart, Alexander, 296
Stubbs, William, 443
Stübner, Mark, 341
Sturm, Jacob, 370, 371
Sturm, Johannes, 371, 391, 424, 559
Sturm, Kaspar, 329
Suárez, Francisco, 554
Suleiman I (the Magnificent), sultan of Ottoman
        Turks, 253, 365–69, 510
Sully, duke of, 502–3
Summenhart, Conrad, 277
Surrey, earl of. *See* Howard, Henry
Suso, Henry, 41
Sweden:
    Lutheranism in, 373
    union of, with Denmark and Norway, 64
Swiss Brethren, 397–98, 405
Swiss (Swabian) War, 381
Switzerland, 16
    Calvinism in, 411–12, 416, 421–28

Switzerland—*cont.*
civil war in, 392–95
Zwinglian Reformation in, 381–95
Sylvester, pope, 167–68

Taborites, 36–37
Taisan de l'Étoile, Pierre, 414
Tamerlaine, 252
Tartaglia, Niccolò, 186, 587
Tauler, Johann, 40–41
Tausen, Hans, 372
Tawney, R. H., 119, 555, 557
Telesio, Bernardino, 181–82
Tempier, Étienne, 185
Teresa of Ávila, St., 41, 475–76
Tertullian, 173
Tetzel, John, 335–37
Theatine order, 475
Theodore of Gaza, 180
Theodosius I, Roman emperor, 22
Thomas, William, 275
Thomas a Kempis, 42
Thomas of Gloucester, 82
Tieck, Johann Ludwig, 145
Tillet, Louis du, 415, 416
Tillich, Paul, 557
Tinctoris, Johannes, 228
Tintoretto, 227–28, 475, 574, 576
Tiptoft, John, 290
Titian, 227, 574, 576
Tito, Santi di, 243
Tordesillas, Treaty of, 270
Torgau, League of, 375–76
Tornabuoni, Lucrezia, 108
Torricelli, Evangelista, 185, 588
Torrigiani, Torrigiano, 219, 290
Toscanelli, Paolo, 187, 267–68
Towns:
fourteenth-century population decline in, 11, 15
growth of, 8–10, 63, 121, 128–30
Toynbee, Arnold J., 7, 110–11
Trade, 8–10, 62–63, 120–33
in England, 536, 538–42
with Far East, 133, 251–52, 258, 262–63, 514
in France, 130–31
by Hanse, 128–30
in Holy Roman Empire, 131–33
in Italy, 99–100, 122–28
with Russia, 538–39
in slaves, 122–23, 259, 536
Tranini, Francesco, 12
Transylvanian Unitarians, 396, 438
Travers, Walter, 530
Traversari, Ambrogio, 155, 172, 206–7
Trebonius, 330
Treitschke, Heinrich, 304
Trent, Council of, 472, 473, 483–91, 527, 578
Triana, Rodrigo de, 269
Trithemius, abbot of Sponheim, 113, 316

Troeltsch, Ernst, 396
Troyes, Treaty of, 74
Truchsesz von Waldburg, Georg, 342, 343
Tschudi, Valentin, 393
Tucher, Anton, 119
Tunstall, Cuthbert, 448, 452
Turks, European invasions by, 47, 52, 68, 111–12, 252–53, 365–68, 510
Turmair, Johann. *See* Aventinus
Tyard, Pontus de, 564
Tyler, Wat, 14
Tyndale, William, 449, 451–53, 458
Tyrone, earl of, 534, 543, 544, 569

Uberti, Fazio degli. *See* Fazio degli Uberti
Uccello, Paolo, 197, 205
Ulrich, duke of Württemberg, 371–72
Unitarians. *See* Anti-Trinitarians
Urban VI, pope, 25, 96
Usury, 123, 133–34, 556
Utraquists, 36–37, 374
Utrecht, Union of, 513

Vadian, 346, 393
Valdés, Alfonso, 326
Valdés, Juan de, 435–36
Valeri, Nino, 116
Valla, Lorenzo, 165–68, 172, 184
Van Braght, Tilman J., 399
Van der Weyden, Roger, 213
Van Eyck, Hubert, 213
Van Eyck, Jan, 213, 284
Van Helmont, Jean Baptiste, 588
Van Leeuwenhoek, Anton, 584
Van Leyden, Lucas, 213
Van Oldenbarneveldt, Johan, 514
Van Orley, Bernaert, 213
Vasari, Giorgio, 5, 188, 193, 198, 200, 205, 213, 576
Vega, Lope de, 566
Velázquez, Diego, 566
Venice, 93, 99–102, 561
art in, 209, 225–28
civic humanism in, 434, 561
government of, 100–2
League of, 236–37
Protestantism in, 434–35
rivalry of, with Genoa, 10, 99–102
Verdi, Giuseppi, 90
Vergerio, Pietro Paolo, 156–57, 162, 436–37, 477
Vergil, Polydore, 290, 567
Vermigli, Peter Martyr, 435, 436, 461
Veronese, Paolo, 227–28, 574
Verrocchio, Andrea del, 195, 209, 213
Vervins, Peace of, 502
Vesalius, Andreas, 584
Vespasiano, 189
Vespucci, Amerigo, 257, 270
Vettori, Francesco, 244

Vettori, Piero, 561
Victorine mystics, 39
Vienna, Turkish attack on, 367–68
Vienne, Council of, 153
Vignola, Giacomo, 577
Villani, Filippo, 4, 195
Villani, Giovanni, 4, 102, 104, 164
Villani, Matteo, 4, 104, 164
Vimercati, Francesco, 565
Vinci, Leonardo da, 4, 213–16, 284, 574
    artistic training of, 195–96, 214
    as engineer, 214, 216
    paintings of, 47, 214–16
    and perspective, 197, 200
    as scientist, 186–88
    sculpture of, 214
Vinci, Piero da, 213–14
Viret, Pierre, 411, 422, 429, 505
Visconti, Bernabò, 97
Visconti, Bianca, 98
Visconti, Filippo Maria, 97, 106, 149, 152, 161–62
Visconti, Galeazzo, 97
Visconti, Gian Galeazzo, 30, 97, 105–6, 160
Visconti, Giovanni, 97
Visconti, Giovanni Maria, 97
Visconti, Matteo (nephew of Giovanni), 97
Visconti, Matteo (nephew of Ottone), 97
Visconti, Ottone, 97
Vitez, John, 282
Vitruvius, 198
Vittorino da Feltre, 149, 157–58, 166
Vives, Alfonso, 434
Vives, Juan Luis, 434, 567
Voltaire, 1, 303, 441–42

Waldensians, 53, 430
Waldseemüller, Martin, 270
Walker, Myles, 447
Walsingham, Francis, 524, 532–33
Walter of Brienne, duke of Athens, 104
Warham, William, 443, 448–50
War of Chioggia, 99–100
War of the Three Henrys, 501
Wars of the Roses, 83–84
Warwick, earl of. *See* Dudley, John, duke of
    Northumberland
Watt, Joachim von. *See* Vadian
Weber, Max, 119, 555, 557, 581
Wells, H. G., 558
Welser family, 133
Wenceslas, Holy Roman emperor, 67, 97
Wenceslas, king of Bohemia, 35, 36
Westminster Shorter Catechism, 418
Westphalia, Treaty of, 16, 381, 514

White, John, 539–40
Whitehead, Alfred North, 39, 187, 308, 408, 583
Whitgift, John, 528–30, 544
Wied, Hermann von, 372
Willaert, Adrian, 578
William, duke of Bavaria, 376
William, duke of Cleves, 366, 372
William of Durand, 313
William of Moerbeke, 180
William (the Silent) of Orange, 507, 511–13, 535
William of Rubruck, 251
Willoughby, Hugh, 538
Wimpfeling, Jacob, 277, 370
Wishart, George, 465
Witchcraft, 49
Wittenberg Concord, 371, 392
Wölflin, Heinrich, 382
Wolmar, Melchior, 414
Wolsey, Thomas, 443–46, 450–51, 453–54
    as chancellor, 443–44
    as churchman, 314, 444–45
    fall of, 294, 445
    and More, 293, 453
Wordsworth, William, 100
Worms, Edict of, 329, 353
Wotten, Henry, 113
Württemberg Concord, 392
Wyatt, Thomas, 567
Wyatt, Thomas, the Younger, 462
Wycliffe, John, 27–28, 33–34, 168, 447
Wyttenbach, Thomas, 382, 393

Xavier, St. Francis, 480, 482–83
Ximénez de Cisneros, Francisco, 86, 288–89, 433,
    477

Zabarella, Francesco, 29, 156, 186
Zacuto of Salamanca, 256
Zapolya, John, 367, 375
Zbynek, archbishop of Prague, 34
Zell, Catherine, 370
Zell, Matthew, 370
Zimara, Marco Antonio, 561
Zizka, John, 36
Zurara, Gomes Eanes de, 261
Zwick, Johannes von, 370
Zwilling, Gabriel, 341
Zwingli, Ulrich, 343, 349, 381–95, 412, 549
    and art, 386–87, 573
    and church government, 551
    and music, 382, 384, 387, 580
    and radical sects, 397–99
    and sacramentarian controversy, 389–92

PRINTED IN U.S.A.